# Crises and Integration in European Banking Union

# Crises and Integration in European Banking Union

*To Build or To Burn*

Christopher Mitchell

Great Clarendon Street, Oxford, OX2 6DP,
United Kingdom

Oxford University Press is a department of the University of Oxford.
It furthers the University's objective of excellence in research, scholarship,
and education by publishing worldwide. Oxford is a registered trade mark of
Oxford University Press in the UK and in certain other countries

© Christopher Mitchell 2023

The moral rights of the author have been asserted

All rights reserved. No part of this publication may be reproduced, stored in
a retrieval system, or transmitted, in any form or by any means, without the
prior permission in writing of Oxford University Press, or as expressly permitted
by law, by licence or under terms agreed with the appropriate reprographics
rights organization. Enquiries concerning reproduction outside the scope of the
above should be sent to the Rights Department, Oxford University Press, at the
address above

You must not circulate this work in any other form
and you must impose this same condition on any acquirer

Published in the United States of America by Oxford University Press
198 Madison Avenue, New York, NY 10016, United States of America

British Library Cataloguing in Publication Data

Data available

Library of Congress Control Number: 2023939253

ISBN 9780198889069

DOI: 10.1093/oso/9780198889069.001.0001

Printed and bound by
CPI Group (UK) Ltd, Croydon, CR0 4YY

Links to third party websites are provided by Oxford in good faith and
for information only. Oxford disclaims any responsibility for the materials
contained in any third party website referenced in this work.

*For Thomas, the best son anyone could possibly ask for*

*For my mother; thanks for everything!*

# Acknowledgments

Any project of this scale is of course only possible with the support of a wide range of people and institutions. Please understand that any oversights here on my part in no way reflect a lack of gratitude for your assistance. I would very much like to thank Mount Holyoke College for both indirect and direct support of this project, and the University of Massachusetts, the George Washington University, Smith College, and Amherst College for access to their resources. Thanks to Andy Reiter, Cora Fernandez-Anderson, Robert Darrow, Ali Aslam, Adam Hilton, and Sergi Kapanadze for invaluable feedback throughout the writing and research process. Thanks to Fred Baumgartner, Laura Bundesen, and Julie Russell for help with the grants and funding process. Thank you to Harvey Feigenbaum, Susan Sell, Emmanuel Teitelbaum, and all my instructors and mentors.

Above all, thanks to my wonderful family for your love and support, and in particular my wife Elizabeth Mitchell.

# Contents

| | |
|---|---|
| *List of Figures* | xi |
| *List of Abbreviations* | xii |

| | |
|---|---|
| **1. Crises in European Integration** | **1** |
| Introduction | 1 |
| Crises and Narratives of European Integration | 4 |
| Crises and European Integration in History | 4 |
| Crises, Integration, and the Grand Theories | 6 |
| The Theory in Brief | 9 |
| Plan of the Book | 11 |
| | |
| **2. Building a Theory of Crises and European Integration** | **17** |
| Introduction | 17 |
| Theorizing Crises Generally | 17 |
| Crises and the Window of Opportunity in a Destabilized Status Quo | 18 |
| Identifying and Defining Crises | 20 |
| Who Defines Them? | 21 |
| The Role of Master Narratives | 25 |
| Master Narratives Deployed in Crises | 27 |
| The Usefulness of the Grand Theories | 31 |
| Intergovernmentalism | 32 |
| Neofunctionalism | 32 |
| Postfunctionalism | 33 |
| The Theory and the Grand Theories | 33 |
| The Essential Dimensions for Disruption of the Status Quo in a Crisis | 34 |
| Origin | 35 |
| Severity | 36 |
| Methodology and Case Selection | 41 |
| The Advantages of Focusing on Financial Sector Integration | 41 |
| Explaining Case Selection | 43 |
| Methodology | 44 |
| Crises and the Development of European Financial Integration in the Twenty-First Century | 46 |
| Theoretical and Political Issues in European Financial Integration | 46 |
| Staggered Integration in Practice | 49 |
| Alternative Explanations | 52 |
| Idiosyncrasies of Individual Cases | 52 |

# viii Contents

| | |
|---|---|
| Structural Changes on the Private Side | 53 |
| Changes to the Regulatory Architecture | 54 |
| Growing Euroskepticism | 55 |

## 3. The 2007–09 Banking Crisis: Patch-Up Reform and Creation of the European System of Financial Supervision — 63

| | |
|---|---|
| Introduction | 63 |
| Classification of the Crisis | 64 |
| An Endogenous Crisis | 64 |
| A Moderate Crisis | 68 |
| Implications of a Moderate Endogenous Crisis | 71 |
| Initial Responses from the European Commission and the European Central Bank | 72 |
| The Proposed Common European Bailout Fund | 73 |
| Creation of the European Banking Authority | 76 |
| Weaknesses in the Existing Regulatory Regime | 77 |
| The de Larosière Report | 80 |
| Responses to the de Larosière Report | 81 |
| Debates over Implementation | 84 |
| The End of the Crisis Period | 93 |
| Conclusion | 93 |

## 4. The 2010–14 European Debt Crisis: Monnet Crisis and Banking Union — 104

| | |
|---|---|
| Introduction | 104 |
| Outlining the Crisis | 105 |
| The Banking Crisis in the Debt Crisis | 108 |
| Legacy Issues of the Banking Crisis | 109 |
| Unresolved Regulatory Gaps | 111 |
| The Doom Loop | 112 |
| Classification of the Crisis | 113 |
| Endogenous | 113 |
| Severe | 114 |
| A Monnet Crisis | 117 |
| The European Stability Mechanism | 117 |
| Resistance to the ESM | 118 |
| Contrasting Resistance to the ESM | 121 |
| Evaluation of the ESM | 122 |
| The Terms of Debate and Coalitions on Banking Union | 123 |
| The Functional Argument for Banking Union | 123 |
| The Divisions within Banking | 126 |
| The National Divisions | 129 |
| Crises as Key to Breaking the Status Quo Equilibrium | 132 |
| Creation of the Single Supervisory Mechanism | 133 |
| The EBA Stress Tests | 134 |
| The Cajas Crisis | 135 |

| | |
|---|---|
| Changing Positions in the Big Banks and France | 137 |
| Germany's Shifting Position | 139 |
| Evaluating the Single Supervisory Mechanism | 141 |

The Bank Recovery and Resolution Directive   142
Creation of the Single Resolution Mechanism   144

| | |
|---|---|
| Coalitions on the SRM | 146 |
| The Persistence of the Doom Loop and the Undesirability of the Status Quo | 148 |
| Evaluating the Single Resolution Mechanism | 150 |

The Failure to Create a European Deposit Insurance Scheme   153
Other Potential Elements of Banking Union   160
Limitations of the Partial Banking Union   162
Conclusion   163

## 5. Brexit and the Failure to Reform   178

Introduction   178
Classification   179

| | |
|---|---|
| Exogenous | 179 |
| Moderate | 183 |
| The Window of Opportunity in an Exogenous Moderate Crisis | 195 |

Minor Enacted Changes Out of Brexit   196

| | |
|---|---|
| The Relocation of the European Banking Authority | 196 |
| The Relocation of Euro Clearing | 198 |

The Big Attempted Reform: Capital Markets Union   201

| | |
|---|---|
| Capital Markets Union before Brexit | 201 |
| Reshaping the Case for Capital Markets Union as Crisis Response | 202 |
| The Politics of Capital Markets Union | 205 |
| Proposals and Outcomes | 208 |
| Explaining the Failure of CMU Reforms | 210 |

Conclusion   212

## 6. The 2020–21 COVID Pandemic: Weatherproofing Integration and the Single Resolution Fund Backstop   225

Introduction   225
A Brief Summary of the Crisis   226

| | |
|---|---|
| The Pre-Pandemic Situation | 226 |
| Phases of the Pandemic | 228 |

Classification of the Crisis   229

| | |
|---|---|
| Severe | 229 |
| Exogenous | 235 |

The Perceived Window for Action   235
Major Crisis Response Proposals   238
Temporary Emergency Measures   239

| | |
|---|---|
| Emergency Regulatory Relief | 239 |
| NextGenerationEU | 245 |
| Common Themes | 248 |

x    Contents

Ambitious but Unsuccessful Proposals to Confront
Nonperforming Loans: The European Bad Bank and the
Solvency Support Instrument                                              249
    Discussion                                                            251
Completing Banking Union: The European Deposit Insurance
Scheme and Capital Markets Union                                        252
    The Coalition for Action                                             254
    Arguments for Action Now                                             256
    The Failure to Link Regulatory Architecture Reforms to
      Crisis Recovery                                                    259
Backstopping the Single Resolution Fund                                 261
    Why Was a Backstop Needed?                                           262
    The Backstop and the Pandemic                                        264
    Why Does the Backstop Pass Where EDIS Failed?                        265
Conclusion                                                              266

**7. Conclusion**                                                       **283**

Introduction                                                            283
Comparing the Crises                                                    283
    The Impact of Severity                                               283
    The Impact of Origin                                                 287
    Comparing the Most-Different Cases                                   291
    Overall Lessons from Comparing the Crises                            292
Implications for the Future of EU Finance                               294
    Crises and the Future of European Financial Integration              295
    The Disintegrative Alternative                                       297
Other Crises and the Model                                              298
    Immigration Policy                                                   298
    Energy Policy                                                        301
    Foreign and Security Policy                                          303
Implications Outside of Europe                                          305
    Crises in Federal States                                             306
    Crises in Strong Regional Associations                               307
Concluding Remarks                                                      307

*Bibliography*                                                          310
*Index*                                                                 349

# List of Figures

| | | |
|---|---|---|
| 1.1. | A Typology of Crises | 10 |
| 2.1. | Schoenmaker's Trilemma | 47 |
| 2.2. | Crises and European Financial Integration | 52 |
| 3.1. | State Bank Aid in Select States as a Percentage of GDP, 2007–09 | 69 |
| 4.1. | Nonperforming Loans as a Percentage of Gross Loans, Eurozone States 2009 | 110 |
| 4.2. | Deposit Money Banks' Assets to GDP (%) for the Eurozone, UK, and US, 2009 | 113 |
| 5.1. | Bank Nonperforming Loans to Gross Loans (%) for Select European Union States, 2016 | 185 |
| 5.2. | Global Financial Centres Index Top European Financial Centres, March 2016 | 188 |
| 5.3. | Eurozone–UK Import and Export Composition, Percentage of Total, 2015 | 191 |
| 6.1. | Cases and Deaths of COVID-19 in Selected EU Member States, March–April 2020 | 231 |
| 6.2. | Bank Nonperforming Loans as a Percentage of Gross Loans, Selected Eurozone States, 2019 | 233 |
| 6.3. | Deposit Money Banks' Assets to GDP (%), Select Eurozone States, 2009 and 2019 | 233 |

# List of Abbreviations

| | |
|---|---|
| ABI | Association of British Insurers |
| AFME | Association for Financial Markets in Europe |
| BdB | Bundesverband deutscher Banken |
| BIS | Bank of International Settlements |
| BRRD | Bank Recovery and Resolution Mechanism |
| CCPs | Central Counterparty Clearing Houses |
| CEBS | Committee of European Banking Supervisors |
| CEIOPS | Committee of European Insurance and Occupational Pensions Supervisors |
| CESR | Committee of European Securities Regulators |
| CMU | Capital Markets Union |
| CSFI | Centre for the Study of Financial Innovation |
| DG Comp | Directorate-General for Competition |
| DGS | Deposit Guarantee Scheme |
| EBA | European Banking Authority |
| EBF | European Banking Federation |
| ECB | European Central Bank |
| ECOFIN | Economic and Financial Affairs Council |
| EDIS | European Deposit Insurance Scheme |
| EEA | European Economic Area |
| EEC | European Economic Community |
| EFSF | European Financial Stability Facility |
| EFSM | European Financial Stabilization Mechanism |
| EIOPA | European Insurance and Occupational Pensions Authority |
| EMA | European Medicines Agency |
| EMIR | European Market Infrastructure Regulation |
| ESFS | European System of Financial Supervision |
| ESMA | European Securities and Markets Authority |
| ESRC | European Systemic Risk Council |
| FDIC | Federal Deposit Insurance Corporation |
| IMF | International Monetary Fund |
| LTRO | Long Term Refinancing Operation |
| MPS | Banca Monte dei Paschi di Siena |
| NATO | North Atlantic Treaty Organization |
| NGEU | NextGenerationEU |
| NordLB | Norddeutsche Landesbank |
| NPLs | Nonperforming Loan |
| OCC | Office of the Comptroller of the Currency |
| OECD | Organisation for Economic Co-operation and Development |

| | |
|---|---|
| OMT | Outright Monetary Transaction |
| OTS | Office of Thrift Supervision |
| PEPP | Pandemic Emergency Purchase Program |
| RBS | Royal Bank of Scotland |
| SFEF | Société de Financement de l'Economie Française |
| SPPE | Société de Prise de Participation de l'Etat |
| SRB | Single Resolution Board |
| SRF | Single Resolution Fund |
| SRM | Single Resolution Mechanism |
| SSI | Solvency Support Instrument |
| SSM | Single Supervisory Mechanism |
| TARP | Troubled Asset Relief Program |
| TLTRO | Targeted Longer-Term Refinancing Operation |

# 1
# Crises in European Integration

## Introduction

Jean Monnet, the first President of the High Authority of the European Coal and Steel Community and a founding father of European integration, argued that "Europe will be forged in crises and will be the sum of the solutions adopted for those crises."[1]

Monnet's understanding of European integration as driven by the need to respond to crises has become conventional wisdom among both policy-makers and scholars of European integration, and for good reason. There are many examples of crises spurring movement toward "ever closer union," from the founding of the European Coal and Steel Community through to the twenty-first century. As a result, advocates of "ever-closer union" cite Monnet and predict deeper integration with every crisis that strikes Europe. However, while many crises have indeed spurred integration, there is also no shortage of crises that have battered Europe without driving deeper integration. Some have even increased division and resistance to integration. Despite this, the literature's treatment of the role of crises has been largely undertheorized, especially in forming ex ante expectations of what separates integration-spurring "Monnet Crises" from other challenges. This book fills that crucial gap by explaining how the origins and severity of the crisis shape the ability of the pro-integration narrative to crowd out alternatives, and in doing so use crises to spur integration. It does so by examining the relative impact of a series of crises on the centralization of European banking regulation in the twenty-first century, and thus also makes an important contribution to the literature on European financial regulation and the construction of a European banking and capital markets union. It not only addresses a significant theoretical gap, but also provides a foundation for policymaking in response to future crises by building a framework to identify which challenges are most likely to provide an opportunity for deeper integration.

It should come as no surprise that Monnet's dictum has found widespread acceptance, given the plethora of examples of crises which have driven a deepening of integration.[2] Pro-integration forces have good reason to see

*Crises and Integration in European Banking Union.* Christopher Mitchell, Oxford University Press.
© Christopher Mitchell (2023). DOI: 10.1093/oso/9780198889069.003.0001

## 2  Crises and Integration in European Banking Union

crises as opportunities for deeper integration.[3] However, this emphasis on the integrating consequences of crises rests on a selective examination of the crisis–integration link. There are a similar number of events described as crises either in their time or after which failed to produce substantial deeper integration. Because of this mixed record, it becomes possible to separate crises in Europe based on their impact on integration. What I will term Monnet Crises produced substantial deepening of integration, but not all events identified would have that impact. Some produced only modest deepening of integration. Other crises produced no significant change in levels of integration, and a final, to-date relatively rare, group of crises produced disintegration and retreat from "ever closer union."

This book addresses a substantial gap in the literature on European integration by building a theory of an ex ante set of characteristics that make reform more likely. European policymakers and scholars across a wide range of approaches use crises to explain the punctuated equilibrium of European integration, where long periods of stability are separated by brief windows of substantial change. However, this literature almost exclusively focuses on *ex post* analysis of *how* crises drive integration rather than theorizing which *ex ante* characteristics of crises make integration more or less likely. This weakness is shared by neofunctionalists, who emphasize the role of European institutional actors such as the European Commission and European Central Bank (ECB), by intergovernmentalists who focus on the centrality of member state governments, and postfunctionalists who focus on rising euroskepticism in the European public.

I examine the broader social science literature of crises, including how it complements the existing Grand Theories of European integration, building to a focus on the importance of narrative frames as to the sustainability of the status quo. Specifically, I focus on how two dimensions, the severity of the crisis and its origins within or outside of the sector of interest, shape the ability of pro-reform actors to make a compelling case that the status quo is unsustainable and the crisis must be met with deeper integration. Together, these two factors determine not only the vulnerability of the status quo, but also the capacity of sectoral reform to address the underlying issues. Threat severity is an obvious but insufficient dimension, as some severe threats have produced only modest integration. Crisis origin within or outside of the sector of interest provides a crucial second dimension. A crisis originating in the sector itself suggests fundamental flaws demanding reform, while external origins allow status quo players to resist reform by arguing that it would not prevent a recurrence of the crisis. These two dimensions allow for a four-part typology of crises: exogenous moderate crises where no substantial reform is expected, exogenous severe crises where modest "weatherproofing" reform is likely, endogenous moderate crises where similarly modest "patch-up" reform is likely, and finally endogenous severe crises, which are most likely to produce substantial reforms in line with the expectations of Monnet.

I demonstrate this approach through an examination of four successive crises hitting European finance: the 2007–09 Banking Crisis, the 2010–14 European Debt Crisis, the 2016 Brexit Crisis, and the 2020–21 COVID Pandemic. Through this period, the European financial regulatory architecture has suffered from a fundamental instability due to the mismatch of transnational banking and national supervision and resolution. Despite this flaw being well known since the 1990s, efforts to address it have been halting and incomplete. Pro-reform actors called for substantially deeper integration in response to all of these crises, but with varied success. Only the 2010–14 Debt Crisis produced truly substantial reform of the European financial regulatory architecture, though even here reforms failed to fully resolve the underlying issues. The 2007–09 Banking Crisis and 2020–21 COVID Pandemic each produced more modest reforms, while the EU response to Brexit produced no substantive financial regulatory reforms. I trace how this variance in crisis response can be traced to the variance in the severity and origin of the crises themselves.

Focusing on banking integration provides two benefits. The first is that it allows me to compare four crises with common underlying dynamics, with the same core institutional actors involved and the same underlying structural tensions between transnational bank operations and national bank regulation. The second is the importance of efforts to centralize regulation of European banking and finance in the twenty-first century is of clear relevance to integration debates more broadly. The steps already taken toward European banking union have been widely agreed to have been the most significant steps toward integration since the 1992 Maastricht Treaty created the euro, making this a topic of substantive interest to both scholars of European integration and those focused on global finance.

The rest of this chapter will outline the role of crises in the major Grand Theories of European integration, identifying how these approaches all assign crises a pivotal role as a driver of change, but undertheorize why some crises have greater effect than others. It then briefly summarizes the theory laid out in the remaining chapters, and concludes with an outline of the rest of the book.

## Crises and Narratives of European Integration

Broadly speaking, there have been two dominant narratives of what drives European integration, the first focusing on integration as a Pareto-improving move, and the second focusing on integration as a reaction to crises confronting the member states. Both of these narratives find a role in intergovernmentalist accounts emphasizing the primacy of national governments and domestic forces and in neofunctionalist accounts emphasizing spillover effects and supranational actors.

Both intergovernmental and neofunctionalist accounts consider that European integration may be Pareto-improving, leaving member states and Europe as a whole in a net superior position than without integration, though they differ on the specific mechanisms. Intergovernmentalists focus more on the gains to individual states, and to actors within those states. Such improvements may focus on domestic metrics, in particular integration as improving the economic position of various key sectors or actors. They may also focus on international position, focused potentially on the relative position of member states to each other or to the broader international community. Here, for instance, can be found the cliché that the purpose of European integration is to hide French weakness and German strength. Neofunctionalist accounts are more likely to focus on improvements to the position of the European Union as a whole, and improvements to transnational groups rather than specifically domestic coalitions. Neofunctionalist accounts also focus on the potential for integration to create its own momentum, as gains created by integration create an appetite for deeper integration.

However, both the intergovernmental and neofunctional stories here encounter a similar issue. If deeper integration is Pareto-improving, why does integration progress in fits and starts, rather than steadily moving toward the Pareto-optimal point where the net benefit is maximized? Here the second major narrative of European integration comes into play, focusing on integration as a response to various crises hitting the European states.

## Crises and European Integration in History

It has become conventional wisdom that crises provide one of the most effective methods of breaking logjams that block Pareto-improving deeper European integration. That European integration frequently follows from crises is well borne out by the historical record. In a very real sense, the entire European project itself is a response to the successive crises of the

Second World War and the Cold War. The Second World War, the third major Franco-German conflict in 70 years, highlighted the need to build an enduring peace between France and Germany, and among the Western Europeans generally. That security need was further highlighted by the external threat of the Soviet Union, which necessitated not only Franco-German peace, but also a rapid reconstruction and maximization of European growth to be able to resist the threat from the east.

Since the creation of the European project, there has been no shortage of crises which have been associated with some manner of integration. Many major steps toward deeper integration have been associated with crises either external or internal, such as the Saar Crisis helping drive the creation of the European Economic Community (EEC); the stagflation of the 1970s leading to the restarting of European integration with the Single European Act; and the Yugoslav Wars of the 1990s deepening the Common Foreign and Security Policy.

Just within the financial sector, there are numerous examples of crises leading to deeper integration. The collapse of West German bank Herstatt in 1974 exposed the inadequacies of the existing bank resolution regimes to handle cross-border bank failures, and therefore led to the creation of new European Settlement Risk Rules. The collapse of the first major attempt to harmonize European currency exchange rates, the "Snake," led to the creation of the European Monetary System, deepening monetary coordination. The struggles of the Bank of France and Bank of Italy to manage the franc and lira in the 1980s similarly created momentum toward the signing of the Maastricht Treaty and the creation of European Monetary Union.

This dynamic is not surprising to students of crises, as moments of extreme strain often change the dynamics of a system. Most immediately, the need to respond rapidly to changing circumstance can prompt a shift out of "normal" politics into an "emergency" mode, with fewer actors and a more streamlined decision-making process, which in turn can produce different outcomes than the slower process with broader input that can characterize normal politics.[4] Even absent a shift to emergency policymaking, crises can change the circumstances in which actors operate in a way that alters their preferences. They may become receptive to arguments they had previously dismissed, either through a revised cost–benefit calculus or a process of policy learning.

Given this pattern and these factors, it is no surprise that it has become conventional wisdom among policymakers, commentators, academics, and other observers that crises are one of the prime drivers of European integration. Perhaps the most famous quote on the topic comes from Jean Monnet, the "Father of Europe" and first President of the European Coal and Steel

**6  Crises and Integration in European Banking Union**

Community, who argued in his memoirs that "Europe will be forged in crises and will be the sum of the solutions adopted for those crises." Another of Europe's Founding Fathers, Robert Schuman, the first President of the European Parliamentary Assembly, echoed this view of European integration through fits and starts when he argued that "Europe will not be made all at once, or according to a single plan. It will be built through concrete achievements which first create a de facto solidarity." As a result, virtually every time Europe hits an event that can plausibly be described as a "crisis," advocates of deeper integration cite historical precedent and Monnet's epigram, arguing for and expecting this new crisis to produce deeper integration. In the words of one Bundesbank representative, "the key phrase is 'never waste a good crisis.'"[5]

However, while there are no shortage of examples of crises leading to integration, many other crises produced little or no impact on integration. While the external threat of the Soviet Union spurred the creation of the European project, other foreign policy crises, such as the Suez Crisis, did little to impact integration. Although the outbreak of Mad Cow (variant Creuzfeld-Jakobsen vCJD) disease in the 1990s led to new phylosanitary rules, other disease-related shocks, such as MERS and SARS, failed to lead to significant integration.[6] Specifically within finance, several major crises did little to shift integration. The East Asian Financial Crisis and the Dot Com Crisis had relatively minor impact on European finance generally, so this may be relatively unsurprising. However, the Latin American Debt Crisis of the 1980s directly involved multiple major European financial institutions without producing a significant change in the European regulatory architecture. Instead, the crisis and its impacts were chiefly managed by the non-EU London Club of creditor banks and Paris Club of creditor states. Closer to home, the United Kingdom's "Black Wednesday" crash of 1992 involved a major European member state, but did little to shape the trajectory of integration, apart from arguably increasing euroskeptic sentiments within Britain.

## Crises, Integration, and the Grand Theories

All three of the Grand Theories of European integration see crises as playing a key role in the development of European integration. Both the intergovernmentalists and neofunctionalists see them as ways to drive integration deeper, with neofunctionalists further emphasizing crises as a product of incomplete integration. The postfunctionalists, meanwhile, emphasize crises as both a product of incomplete integration, and as a potential path toward European disintegration rather than integration. However, while all of these theories assign a key role to crises, all of them also undertheorize why some crises produce deeper integration, and others do not.

## Intergovernmentalism

Intergovernmental approaches focus on the tendency of the EU toward stable equilibria. A crisis for the intergovernmentalists is something that disrupts that equilibrium, which is almost inevitably external to integration itself. A well-functioning system should be able to identify and eliminate endogenous problems before they rise to the level of crises. As such, intergovernmental approaches generally assume crises producing integration are exogenous in nature, something that disrupts that equilibrium and the balance of power between status quo forces.

The exogenous shock of a crisis is likely to produce deeper integration if it causes pro-integration forces to become ascendant in the domestic politics of crucial states, such that the interstate negotiation shifts to a new, more deeply integrated, equilibrium. The intergovernmentalist focus on integration through a shift in the balance of power of states and subnational actors puts the intergovernmentalists in a very good position to explain the terms and outcomes of international negotiations around crisis. However, they are left with a rather bare bones and contingent theory as to which crises are likely to force the system out of equilibrium. It is bare bones in that the only real qualifier is that it must affect states' cost–benefit calculus on integration, and contingent in that each individual crisis will have its own particular impact on the cost–benefit calculus of domestic interests who themselves will vary case by case in their influence. As such, it offers an essentially ad hoc understanding of which crises are likely to matter.

## Neofunctionalism

The neofunctionalists put crises closer to the heart of their understanding of integration, by focusing on how incomplete integration creates spillover driving a constituency to desire deeper integration to maximize the benefits and eliminate the flaws of extant integration.[7] This spillover may occur in the course of noncrisis normal politics. Crises play a central role, however, as the neofunctionalist approach also offers an understanding of crises as endogenous to the integration process. Crises, in this account, are mostly the inevitable product of failing to "complete" integration. They thus play a role in highlighting the flaws of an incomplete integration and demonstrating the value of deeper integration. Monnet's own understanding of crises largely reflects this approach. Although the neofunctionalist approach focuses largely on endogenous crises, numerous scholars have also used this approach to examine exogenous crises.[8]

However, this approach suffers from weaknesses of its own. Perhaps most prominently, the neofunctionalist approach overpredicts the integrative impact of crises, as it is not clear when a crisis will indicate a functional need for deeper integration to a sufficient degree as to produce a constituency for integration. Therefore, it also is left without a coherent explanation as to why only some crises lead to integration, nor the degree of integration a crisis will produce. It thus also lacks an explanation of why "spillover" crises fail to generate sufficient will to fully address the core flaws. Moreover, the neofunctionalists' focus on spillover and crises limits their ability to evaluate the impact of exogenous shocks on integration as opposed to crises originating within the existing system.

### Postfunctionalism

The newest of the Grand Theories of integration, postfunctionalism, emphasizes how a growing discontent with the processes of European integration is leading to a politicization of previously technocratic questions of integration and the shift from a "permissive consensus" to a "constraining dissensus" of euroskeptics challenging the narratives around "ever closer union" and deeper integration.[9] Postfunctional accounts sit somewhere between intergovernmental and neofunctional accounts in regards to crises and the status quo. Like neofunctionalists, they see crises as endogenous to integration, but emphasize the costs of integration in terms of diminished legitimacy. In these accounts, continued integration creates a growing or increasingly mobilized movement hostile to the status quo, making it unsustainable. Like intergovernmentalists, on the other hand, they emphasize the role of shifting domestic coalitions changing member state preferences on integration. Although the forces postfunctionalists identify as generating the populist backlash are supranational, the nationalist nature of euroskeptic movements means that their impact, at least to date, has been primarily felt through intergovernmental factors.[10] Therefore, postfunctionalist accounts of change through crises emphasize both how the status quo has become undesirable to a critical mass of the population and how this intensifying movement renders the status quo unsustainable. The great importance of the postfunctionalist narrative in European crises going forward may be in undermining the pro-integration discourse, both by questioning whether the costs of disintegration really outweigh the benefits and by relegitimizing questions about the normative good of integration which had been taken off the table in earlier periods of normative construction.

Postfunctionalism also focuses not just on the specific crises of integration, but also on what might be dubbed the "metacrisis" of integration, the increasing tension as integration becomes politicized. In this sense, it offers valuable insights in explaining the increased frequency of crises and challenges in managing them, and provides a valuable focus on how it can increasingly not be taken for granted that pro-integration forces will triumph and that disintegration is increasingly a viable potential outcome. However, at the same time, the postfunctionalists have, in a mirror image of the neofunctionalists, overpredicted the disintegrative impact of crises.[11] Outside of the decision of the United Kingdom to exit the European Union, there have been no substantial moves toward disintegration in the twenty-first century. Instead, the European Union has persisted, with a series of small-to-substantial steps toward deeper integration.

## The Theory in Brief

The Grand Theories of European Integration make crises central to their narrative, but largely undertheorize why crises only sometimes provide a spur for changes to European integration. The argument made in this book is that it is possible to move beyond an ad hoc approach to identifying which crises are most likely to produce substantial reform to European integration by examining two dimensions of crises: origin and severity. Severity is the more obvious dimension; the larger the threat to European integration, the more urgent the arguments in favor of reforms to manage that threat become. Although severity obviously exists on a spectrum, one can broadly conceive of three tiers of severity. Minor threats are extremely unlikely to endanger integration or to impose significant costs without further integration. Moderate threats may not endanger integration, but will have much greater costs if managed independently by member states rather than addressed in a collective integrative fashion. Finally, severe threats, if left unaddressed, may lead to a chaotic disintegration of the current European status quo.

That a larger threat would increase the likelihood and degree of integration is obvious; however, an examination of European history reveals that severity of threat alone provides only a limited guide. Threats of comparable severity may produce widely different reform outcomes. In some cases severe threats produce less integration than moderate threats, and some moderate threats

## 10  Crises and Integration in European Banking Union

produce no significant reform. This therefore points to the need to consider a second dimension, the origin of the crisis. All else being equal, an endogenous crisis, one which originates with a flaw in the European institutions themselves, is more likely to generate reform than an exogenous crisis, which originates outside of the European institutions. Endogenous crises, because their origins lie at least in part with flaws of European integration, will therefore keep recurring unless and until those flaws are addressed. This, in turn, creates a compelling argument for action to prevent a repetition of the current crisis. Exogenous crises, on the other hand, originate outside of any flaws in European integration. Deeper integration may help the EU withstand the impact of those crises, but no amount of reform will prevent a new crisis of that type from arising, dampening the arguments for more ambitious reform.

Taken together, these two dimensions produce four kinds of crises, with four expected outcomes, as depicted in Figure 1.1. Moderate exogenous crises are the least likely to produce change, as the crisis can be passed off as merely a passing thing to be endured. A severe exogenous crisis will likely produce modest "weatherproofing" reforms to ensure the system can endure similar external challenges, but will not fundamentally alter the status quo. A crisis originating within the sector, however, highlights clear flaws in existing arrangements, making reform of some degree likely. A moderate endogenous crisis will likely produce modest "patch-up" reforms, as pro–status quo forces will take the minimum necessary action but resist more substantial change. Truly transformative reforms, such as those envisioned by Monnet, are thus only likely in the face of a crisis which is both severe and endogenous to the sector.

|  | Origin | |
|---|---|---|
|  | **Endogenous** | **Exogenous** |
| **Threat — Moderate** | Moderate "Patch-Up" Reform | No Reform |
| **Threat — Severe** | Substantial Reform & "Monnet Crisis" | Moderate "Weatherproofing" Reform |

**Figure 1.1**  A Typology of Crises

## Plan of the Book

Chapter 2 lays out the theoretical model of crisis response in greater detail. It begins with an analysis of the existing literature on the politics of crises and crisis response, both in the broader literature and in the literature on European integration. Having established the existing theoretical underpinnings, the chapter outlines in detail the theoretical expectations of how the EU will likely respond to different kinds of crises. It then lays out both the process-tracing methodology that will be used to examine a variety of crises and the logic of the case selection. All of the cases examined will be cases that hit the European financial sector in the twenty-first century. This focus allows for two key advantages. The first is that the core problem and core reform agendas remained constant in that period. European finance has a fundamental instability because of the mismatch between deep transnational financial integration and a reliance chiefly on national regulators to supervise banks and resolve them when they fail. This problem has been well documented since the late 1990s, and the solution, a move toward European-level bank regulation, has been equally clear. What has been lacking, therefore, has been the political will to move away from national regulation. By examining a series of crises all rooted in the same core structural limits, the analysis focuses on the same essential proposals and constellations of actors from case to case. The second advantage of examining European finance in the twenty-first century is that the sector has been hit by a wide and diverse range of crises in that period, covering the four major types of crisis identified by the typology. Each of the four most significant crises will be examined in its own chapter, but in brief, the 2007–09 Transatlantic Banking Crisis provides an example of a moderate endogenous crisis producing a modest patch-up reform, the creation of the European System of Financial Supervision (ESFS); the 2010–14 European Debt Crisis offers a severe endogenous crisis producing significant reform in form of the creation of the Single Supervisory Mechanism (SSM) and Single Resolution Mechanism (SRM); the shock of the 2016 decision of the UK to leave the EU provides a moderate exogenous crisis producing no significant reform; and finally the 2020–21 COVID-19 Pandemic presented a severe exogenous crisis, producing a modest weatherproofing reform, chiefly through the creation of a backstop for the Single Resolution Fund (SRF).

Chapter 3 examines the 2007–09 Transatlantic Banking Crisis in detail. This was the first major financial crisis to hit Europe since the introduction of the euro, as earlier crises such as the Dot Com Crash of 2001–2002 failed to spur significant panic. It provides an example of an endogenous moderate crisis. It was clearly endogenous to the financial system, a classic bursting of a speculative bubble in the mortgage-backed securities market. It also was a crisis significantly exacerbated by weaknesses in the European financial regulatory architecture. The patchwork system of national regulators managing increasingly transnational banking operations meant that banks were able to engage in regulatory arbitrage, seeking out the most permissive regulators, and in some cases effectively escaping oversight altogether. At the same time, however, it posed only a moderate threat to European integration. The national financial systems hardest hit by the crisis were generally among the wealthiest European states, including Germany, the Netherlands, and the United Kingdom. They therefore proved capable of managing the crisis with their own resources, without risk of an integration-endangering sovereign default or need for bailouts from their fellow member states. Even the weakest economy heavily hit by the crisis, Ireland, substantially increased its sovereign debt, but without serious discussion of default risk or the need for a European exit or bailout.

This combination of endogeneity and moderate threat would produce a modest reform. The threat posed was insufficient to convince key actors of the need to move to banking union or other increased solidarity, but did indicate weaknesses in the European financial regulatory architecture that needed a "patch-up" reform. Chapter 3 thus traces how the Banking Crisis led to the creation of the European System of Financial Supervision, as series of new institutions which enhanced coordination and standardization of rules between national regulators, but created neither a supranational authority above them nor a mechanism for transfer of funds or mutualization of resolution.

Chapter 4 examines the 2010–14 Debt Crisis, an endogenous severe crisis, and the one that best fits the classic "Monnet Crisis" narrative of crises driving deeper integration. Like the Banking Crisis, the Debt Crisis was clearly endogenous to the financial system, driven by a series of weaknesses in the European financial regulatory architecture, including legacy issues from the Banking Crisis, remaining unaddressed regulatory gaps, and perhaps most significantly the "Doom Loop" or sovereign-bank nexus where banks became too large and too exposed to home-country sovereign debt to be effectively managed in failure, weakening both banks and sovereigns. Unlike the Banking Crisis, however, the Debt Crisis posed a very clear threat to European integration. At various points, observers speculated on the ability of states ranging from Greece to Italy to even France to remain in the eurozone, and the survival of the single currency itself came into question. The choice very soon became between deeper integration via enhanced joint supervision and resolution mechanisms, a managed disintegration via the exit of one or more members from the eurozone or even the EU, or an unmanaged collapse. Given the imminent collapse of the status quo, it is no surprise that this crisis produced the most substantial integration of any of the crises under examination, and arguably the most significant integration since the introduction of the euro itself. The Single Supervisory Mechanism established the European Central Bank as the direct regulator of the most significant eurozone banks, and gave it oversight over national regulators in charge of the remaining smaller eurozone banks. The Single Resolution Mechanism created a common authority to manage the resolution of those SSM-regulated banks, as well as a transnational fund to share the costs of those resolutions across the eurozone member states. This thus presented a significant move toward integration, even if questions remained as to the reach and operation of the SSM and SRM, the size of the SRM's resolution fund, and the need for a European Deposit Insurance Scheme (EDIS) and Capital Markets Union (CMU).

Chapters 5 and 6 examine how the subsequent crises failed to produce the necessary pressures to address these remaining holes in integration. Chapter 5 focuses on Brexit, an exogenous moderate crisis. Brexit posed a threat to European financial integration, not just from the direct loss of the EU's main financial hub, but also for fear that the shock would trigger a new banking crisis. As such, advocates of deeper integration attempted to use the crisis to spur the completion of banking union and Capital Markets Union. However, these efforts were undermined by two factors. The threat from Brexit was ultimately only a moderate one, which could be managed by negotiating favorable terms for the post-Brexit terms of access between the UK and the EU. Additionally, the crisis was clearly exogenous to the financial system in origin. The forces pushing for Britain's departure were almost entirely outside of finance, and in fact the UK financial sector strongly advocated for remaining in the European Union. As such, Britain's departure did not suggest a flaw in the financial regulatory architecture that needed to be addressed. Therefore, Brexit produced only essentially cosmetic reform: the relocation of the headquarters of the European Banking Authority (EBA) from London to Paris and a to-date indefinitely postponed proposal to relocate euro clearing out of London. Reformers attempted to link the crisis to a need for more ambitious proposals, including a completion of European Capital Markets Union, but failed to gain traction.

The COVID-19 Pandemic, discussed in Chapter 6, posed a substantially greater threat to European integration. The rapid contraction of economic

**14   Crises and Integration in European Banking Union**

activity from both mandatory quarantines and a general spread of social distancing among the general population threatened to create a massive surge in loan defaults, while the need for government support to manage both the public health and economic shocks threatened to balloon government deficits. Compounding these threats, the first member states to be hit hard by the Pandemic, Italy and Spain, had among the most fragile banking systems and sovereign financial positions, having been also among the hardest hit in the Debt Crisis. Therefore, the Pandemic posed a very real risk of reigniting the dangers of that earlier crisis, and thus of again threatening disintegration of the currency union. As such, advocates of deeper integration argued that this crisis also called for substantial integration, including introduction of a European Deposit Insurance Scheme and Capital Markets Union and greater transnational mutualization of risk, especially in form of a European "bad bank" for nonperforming loans (NPLs). However, unlike the Debt Crisis, the Pandemic was unambiguously exogenous in origin. It posed a significant threat, but not one that suggested a fundamental flaw in the European financial architecture. As such, advocates of deeper reform in the financial sector won few supporters, and the EU's financial reforms focused instead on "weatherproofing" reforms that made little in way of fundamental changes but aimed to increase the resilience of the financial sector to future shocks. The most significant of these changes was an acceleration of the backstopping of the Single Resolution Fund with the European Stability Mechanism, ensuring that the bank resolution fund would have automatic access to the ESM's additional resources if its own resources were to be exhausted. This was more than a cosmetic reform, but not a fundamental shift in the financial architecture, and thus provided the sort of modest reform to be expected from an exogenous severe crisis.

The final chapter summarizes the argument in light of the cases presented and examines those cases in comparison with each other. It in particular focuses on the differences and similarities in the political dynamics across the cases, and how they can be traced to the origin and severity of the different crises. Having examined the previous crises in financial integration, it includes a discussion of the likely prospects for future integration. This discussion includes what kinds of crises are most likely to produce breakthroughs on European financial integration, and the potential impact of the inflationary pressures of 2022–23. The chapter will also briefly outline how the theory here presented may be applied to other sectors, including immigration policy, energy policy, and foreign and security policy. It also engages with the potential applicability of this theory to the impact of crises on other polities with unsettled center–region tensions, including federal states such as the United States and Canada, and other international organizations such as the African Union.

## Notes

1. Jean Monnet, *Memoirs*, First edition (Garden City, NY: Doubleday, 1978).
2. Desmond Dinan, Neill Nugent, and William E. Paterson, *The European Union in Crisis* (Macmillan International Higher Education, 2017); Sam-Sang Jo, *European Myths: Resolving the Crises in the European Community/European Union* (University Press of America, 2007).
3. Jeffrey J. Anderson, "A Series of Unfortunate Events: Crisis Response and the European Union After 2008," in *The Palgrave Handbook of EU Crises*, ed. Marianne Riddervold, Jarle Trondal, and Akasemi Newsome, Palgrave Studies in European Union Politics (Cham: Springer International Publishing, 2021), 765–789, doi:10.1007/978-3-030-51791-5_45; Nathalie Brack and Seda Gürkan, "Introduction: European Integration (Theories) in Crisis?," in *Theorising the Crises of the European Union* (Routledge, 2020); Markus Konrad Brunnermeier, Harold James, and Jean-Pierre Landau, *The Euro and the Battle of Ideas* (Princeton: Princeton University Press, 2016).
4. Jonathan White, *Politics of Last Resort: Governing by Emergency in the European Union*, First edition (Oxford: Oxford University Press, 2020).
5. Bundesbank Official, Interview by author, 2022.
6. Per Larsson, Eva Hagström Frisell, and Stefan Olsson, "Understanding the Crisis Management System of the European Union," in *Crisis Management in the European Union: Cooperation in the Face of Emergencies*, ed. Stefan Olsson (New York: Springer Berlin Heidelberg, 2009), 1–16.
7. Demosthenes Ioannou, Patrick Leblond, and Arne Niemann, "European Integration and the Crisis: Practice and Theory," *Journal of European Public Policy* 22, no. 2 (2015): 155–176; Arne Niemann, *Explaining Decisions in the European Union* (New York: Cambridge University Press, 2006).
8. Eleanor Brooks et al., "EU Health Policy in the Aftermath of COVID-19: Neofunctionalism and Crisis-Driven Integration," *Journal of European Public Policy* 30, no. 4 (April 2023): 721–739, doi:10.1080/13501763.2022.2141301.
9. Liesbet Hooghe and Gary Marks, "Grand Theories of European Integration in the Twenty-First Century," *Journal of European Public Policy* 26, no. 8 (August 2019): 1113–1133, doi:10.1080/13501763.2019.1569711;Liesbet Hooghe and Gary Marks, "A Postfunctionalist Theory of European Integration: From Permissive Consensus to Constraining Dissensus," *British Journal of Political Science* 39, no. 1 (January 2009): 1–23, doi:10.1017/S0007123408000409; Liesbet Hooghe, Brigid Laffan, and Gary Marks, "Introduction to Theory Meets Crisis Collection," *Journal of European Public Policy* 25, no. 1 (January 2018): 1–6, doi:10.1080/13501763.2017.1310282; Douglas Webber, "Trends in European Political (Dis)Integration. An Analysis of Postfunctionalist and Other Explanations," *Journal of European Public Policy* 26, no. 8 (August 2019): 1134–1152, doi:10.1080/13501763.2019.1576760; Dermot Hodson and Uwe Puetter, "The European Union in Disequilibrium: New Intergovernmentalism, Postfunctionalism and Integration Theory in the Post-Maastricht Period," *Journal of European Public Policy* 26, no. 8 (August 2019): 1153–1171, doi:10.1080/13501763.2019.1569712.

10. Samuel Salzborn, "Extreme Right-Wing Parties in and Against Europe. A Systematizing Comparison," in *The State of the European Union: Fault Lines in European Integration*, ed. Stefanie Wöhl et al., Staat—Souveränität—Nation (Wiesbaden: Springer Fachmedien, 2020), 103–130, doi:10.1007/978-3-658-25419-3_5.

11. Pieter de Wilde, "Rebound? The Short- and Long-Term Effects of Crises on Public Support and Trust in European Governance," in *The Palgrave Handbook of EU Crises*, ed. Marianne Riddervold, Jarle Trondal, and Akasemi Newsome, Palgrave Studies in European Union Politics (Cham: Springer International Publishing, 2021), 667–683, doi:10.1007/978-3-030-51791-5_39; Pieter de Wilde, "Media Logic and Grand Theories of European Integration," *Journal of European Public Policy* 26, no. 8 (August 2019): 1193–1212, doi:10.1080/13501763.2019.1622590.

# 2

# Building a Theory of Crises and European Integration

## Introduction

As discussed in Chapter 1, crises have consistently been assigned a key role in the development of European integration, but have largely themselves been undertheorized. This chapter will lay out a theory of what characteristics make a crisis most likely to generate minimal, moderate, or substantial integration in the European Union. It begins with a discussion of the broader literature on crises in the political science, sociology, and media studies literatures, focusing on identifying in general terms how to define crises and why they provide "critical junctures" where more radical change becomes possible. It then turns to the most valuable insights on the role of crises from the Grand Theories of European integration before laying out a novel theory of crises and integration focused on two dimensions, the origin of a crisis and the severity of the threat it poses to integration, and the four-part typology of crises that focus produces. A discussion of methodology and case selection follows, explaining why financial integration in the twenty-first century provides a valuable set of cases to explore the validity of the theory. Finally, the chapter concludes with a discussion of potential alternative explanations.

## Theorizing Crises Generally

Given their prominence, frequency, and impact, it is no surprise that the social science literature has a robust discussion of crises, providing a useful framework to discuss how to identify and define them, and to build a baseline understanding to theorize their impact. At its core, this literature understands crises as a threat to the status quo. Rosenthal et al. provide what is among the most widely cited baseline definitions, describing a crisis as "a serious threat to the basic structures or the fundamental values and norms

*Crises and Integration in European Banking Union.* Christopher Mitchell, Oxford University Press.
© Christopher Mitchell (2023). DOI: 10.1093/oso/9780198889069.003.0002

18 Crises and Integration in European Banking Union

of a system, which under time pressure and highly uncertain circumstances necessitates making vital decisions."[1] Ikenberry offers a similar take, focusing on a crisis as a moment when change becomes somewhere between possible and necessary.[2]

In the institutionalist literature, crises are conceptualized as "critical junctures," a point where the historically stable equilibrium of the system is disturbed, creating the possibility of arriving at a new equilibrium.[3] This understanding of crisis as critical junctures captures why crises are an important topic to examine: they offer a moment where substantial change becomes possible.[4] Even in the absence of dramatic structural changes, crisis management strategies are often built in response to previous crises, laying the groundwork for management of the next crisis.[5] However, it should not be taken for granted that such critical junctures necessarily produce change. Maintenance of the status quo at the end of the crisis remains a plausible outcome.[6] It may even be the most likely, given the advantages that defenders of the status quo have in any debate over institutional change. These advantages may be institutional, as Schimmelfennig highlights.[7] They may also be discursive, as it can be hard to displace a dominant narrative.[8] Both Hay and Cross highlight how crises may even serve to reinforce the status quo. For Hay, crises drive the state to reconsolidate itself to resolve limitations and maintain equilibrium going forward.[9] For Cross, crises offer a moment of "catharsis," when tensions are acknowledged and confronted in a way that ultimately reinforces the pre-crisis equilibrium.[10] Additionally, Stark cautions that a single crisis-shock may open multiple critical junctures in different elements of the policy space.[11] Therefore, a single crisis may have a range of impacts across policy areas, with a substantial impact in one area and a minimal impact in another.

## Crises and the Window of Opportunity in a Destabilized Status Quo

### Normal vs. Emergency Policymaking

Key to understanding how crises produce moments of significant change is the shift in the mode of politics from "normal" to "emergency" policymaking.[12] Normal politics typically involves a large number of stakeholders with widely divergent interests operating in a relatively stable status quo. The stability of the status quo is key to the dynamics of normal politics, as it produces a relatively relaxed timeline. The status quo may be undesirable for some parties, but not unsustainable, meaning that they will be willing to engage in strategies of delay or blockage in order to get as close as possible to their preferred outcome. This slower policymaking process in turn helps bring in a wider cast of stakeholders, as it gives actors more time to mobilize and potentially draw in mass support.

By contrast, the need for rapid action in a crisis leads to a shift to emergency politics. Emergency politics operates in a more streamlined fashion, paring decision-making down to the most essential stakeholders and a rapid decision-making process that cuts out lengthy debate and amendment in favor of producing policy in time to respond to a quickly changing crisis context. Moreover, the danger of rapid deterioration of the status quo makes strategies of blocking reform to win concessions less viable, as they risk making the perfect the enemy of the good to a much greater degree than in normal politics. Crises become focusing events, where actors narrow their attention to an immediate and essential challenge.[13] Emergency politics out of crisis therefore creates the opportunity for reforms not possible in normal politics, where veto-wielding stakeholders might block or delay action to maximize their preferences.

Hay casts this as a significant change in the operation of a state.[14] He casts normal politics as the "conjunctural mode" of politics where minor tinkering is possible and the state does not act as a unitary actor with a unifying vision but rather as a series of disparate elements pursuing their own agendas. However, a crisis provides a focusing event and shifts politics into a "structural" mode where a unifying vision permits unitary state action and substantial restructuring of the state becomes possible. Oberndofer notes that if the state remains in this "exceptional" mode long enough, democratic constraints will be effectively removed and a semi-permanent shift to "authoritarian statism" will result, where perceived technocratic functional needs will consistently trump democratic legitimacy and mass input.[15]

The specific degree of shift from normal to emergency policymaking will of course vary from system to system, as systems with fewer veto points in normal politics retain greater capacity for substantial reform than systems that incorporate more veto players. Nevertheless, the shift may be seen in virtually all political systems. Even the famously sclerotic US policymaking process has proved capable of rapid action. In 2008, for instance, at the height of the Transatlantic Banking Crisis, the President, Secretary of the Treasury, and Congressional leadership proved capable of passing massive emergency spending provisions dramatically expanding the authority of the Treasury to involve itself in financial markets despite partisan division between the bodies and an ongoing presidential campaign.

## Kingdon's Multiple Streams

The policy changes that are advanced in the emergency policy moment frequently are not bespoke to the challenge at hand, but rather the product of policy entrepreneurs taking advantage of a window of opportunity. Per Kingdon's "multiple streams" conception, policy change comes through the intersection of three independent elements: problems, policies, and politics.[16] Problems, or threats to the status quo, provide an opportunity for change, but do not themselves dictate the options or the choice between them. Policies, the suite of alternatives that may address problems, frequently exist independently of and prior to problems. In other words, policy advocates have an agenda they wish to advance before a problem arises, and they use the problem to cast their favored policies as the ideal solution, rather than developing new solutions to confront the new problems.[17] Finally, politics captures those factors determining the choice between policies to confront problems, including not just the functional utility of the proposed policies, but also the feasibility of their passage in the face of actors opposed to the changes.[18]

The key point out of this approach for examining crises in a European context is the idea that the reform proposals in response to crises reflect not just the exigent needs of the current moment, but also policymakers taking advantage of a window of opportunity that the crisis shift to emergency politics creates to advance long-sought policy aims. The European Commission often operates explicitly in this mode, identifying potential solutions to anticipated problems, then waiting until a crisis prompts a shift to emergency politics and creates the political will to act. In the words of one European Commission representative, such a dynamic occurred with Eurobonds. "Things are not done until they are responses to things that are happening. Eurobonds were impossible, though we were saying that we need Eurobonds as they will allow us to lower the costs of borrowing in a crisis. Then when needed to fund European initiatives, then they were accepted (with conditions). We rush to put the solutions on the table . . . This is the reality of politics not just in finance but generally."[19]

# Identifying and Defining Crises

Understanding crises as critical junctures which create windows of opportunity identifies why crises matter, but not which crises matter and to what degree. Wunderlich and Gänzle stylize four possible outcomes out of a critical juncture, rooted in a historical institutionalist path dependency framework.[20] The first is that the system may continue moving forward along the current path. This is the expected outcome of a Monnet Crisis, where the critical juncture drives ever closer union. The second is that the system may be diverted onto a new path. The 1966 Empty Chair crisis would fit here, when Charles de Gaulle acted on his concern that the increasing centralization of power in European institutions inappropriately infringed on national prerogatives by simply refusing to show up at crucial European Economic Community (EEC) meetings, and in doing so ground EEC business to a halt. The resulting Luxembourg Compromise, which allowed for national vetoes on certain issues, diverted European integration toward a more intergovernmental direction. Similarly, the stagflation of the 1970s lead to a reinvigoration of European integration and the 1986 Single European Act put the European integration back onto a path toward deeper integration. Wunderlich and Gänzle's third outcome is a muddling through, where the status quo is maintained with at best minor changes. Numerous crises producing little to no change would fit here. If negative results from popular referenda rise to the level of crisis, the various defeats of European integration in referenda since the 1990s would fit here. Finally, a critical juncture may lead to a full or partial institutional dissolution. With the exception of the British exit from the European Union, such events have essentially been avoided to date in European integration, though as the postfunctionalists highlight, an increasingly mobilized populist and euroskeptic population means that this pattern may shift in the future.

However, outlining the range of outcomes is only one step in identifying the expected outcome. Each of the four outcomes can and has happened in European crises. The Grand Theories of European integration here offer expectations of what the likely key players and forces shaping outcomes will be, as do the various strands of institutionalism.[21] Prior to identifying the range of outcomes from a crisis and their likelihood, however, is a crucial second question about critical junctures, which is how to identify what constitutes a critical juncture. Claiming that a critical juncture is one that produces change is tautological, and moreover misses those critical junctures which lead to a persisting or even strengthening of the status quo. Therefore, a standard to identify critical junctures and crisis independent of their outcomes becomes necessary.

## Who Defines Them?

### The Objective/Subjective Nature of Crises

Within the literature on crises, there are broadly three approaches to identifying crises. One strand sees them as objective events, occurring independent of

## 22 Crises and Integration in European Banking Union

whether actors recognize that they are within a crisis moment or critical juncture. A second sees crises as almost entirely subjective in nature, determined by whether or not actors believe themselves to be in a crisis with objective events all but irrelevant. Finally, the third approach, and the one that forms the basis of my approach, focuses on crises as interpretive events, where both an objective event and a subjective interpretation are necessary components in understanding a critical juncture.

### Objective Approaches

Objective approaches proceed from the position that crises are the product of functional or mechanical breakdowns in existing systems, breakdowns that exist independent of actors interpreting or even in some cases observing them.[22] Such breakdowns may be due to exogenous shocks, as in the classic rational institutionalist framework.[23] They may alternatively be due to the internal contradictions or flaws in the system itself, whether due to erosion of efficacy or inherent flaws or limitations in institutional design. This latter approach captures both classical Marxist accounts of crises of capitalism and the neofunctionalist account of spillover from incomplete integration.[24]

Objective approaches, however, undervalue the role of interpretation in constructing responses. While a functional breakdown of a system may preclude the continued operation of the status quo, this on its own says very little about the next steps. The important element of a critical juncture is the shift from normal politics to emergency policymaking. This means that social action is therefore inseparable from socially constructed ideas about what defines a crisis and whether the objective circumstances fit that definition.[25] The functional linkages between action and outcome are similarly a matter of perception, such that not only identifying whether a crisis moment exists, but also what the most effective action to take in response to it are socially determined.[26]

At the extreme, an objective approach may lead to problems of "false negatives," where material changes threaten the status quo but fail to be recognized as crises, and thus do not trigger rapid action and a shift to emergency policymaking. Hay terms such scenarios "catastrophic equilibria."[27] In a European context, the existence of such catastrophic equilibria lies at the heart of neofunctionalist analysis, that flaws from incomplete integration will generate periodic instability that requires integration in response. Since integration is almost inevitably incomplete, this leaves Europe perpetually "primed" for a catastrophic equilibrium to become recognized as a problem, producing a shift to emergency politics. As such, it becomes hard to identify *why* a given development should cause actors to *now* decide to address the flaws of integration, rather than at some earlier or later point. If the flaws are not recognized in advance, this becomes a relatively straightforward story of social learning and updating of preferences. However, the more common scenario in European integration is that the flaws are known in advance but without actors willing to take action to address them. For example, as will be discussed in depth in the Crises and the Development of European Financial Integration in the twenty-first century section, the flaws in European financial regulation have been well known since the late 1990s, but no serious action was taken to address the problems until the introduction of the European Banking Authority (EBA) in 2009 and more substantially the introduction of partial banking union in the early 2010s. Even with these reforms, the flaws remain to a large degree unaddressed. Similar stories can be told about flaws in many other areas, including, immigration, energy, and defense policy.

### Subjective Approaches

The inverse of an objective approach, subjective approaches understand crises as purely discursive events. While objective approaches focus on crises as material events and discount interpretation, subjective approaches maintain that a crisis is determined by actors thinking that they are in a crisis, independent of or even driving objective facts on the ground.[28] In financial politics, the classic example of a subjective crisis would be the self-fulfilling prophecy of financial panics, where market actors respond to other market actors' panic, creating a spiral of destruction that ultimately may only be caused by baseless fears.[29] More broadly, subjective crisis narratives focus on how nonemergency situations may be pushed to be interpreted as "crises" in a wider range of circumstances.

While the financial panic example offers an example of a subjective crisis triggered by mass movements, most of the work in this approach focuses on crises as constructs of elites and media actors. Elites in these accounts create or promote a crisis so that they may advance their ideology or policy agenda and delegitimize other options that would be otherwise attractive in a normal politics mode.[30] Klein, for instance, argues that the Bush administration argued that the potential presence of weapons of mass destruction in Iraq constituted a crisis, in order to achieve their favored goal of regime change.[31] Media actors also can play a crucial role in shaping even elites' perceptions of whether a crisis exists or not through how they present and frame events.[32] Per Ross, "in a media-drenched age, the term crisis is often invoked to dramatize what are in fact relatively small emergencies."[33] However, unlike political elites, media actors are usually not looking to advance an agenda

**24  Crises and Integration in European Banking Union**

beyond attracting viewers or readers, in line with the hoary dictum that "if it bleeds, it leads."

However, if objective approaches suffer from a "false negatives" problem, subjective approaches face a "false positives" issue, of actors attempting to promote a crisis narrative but failing to effect real change out of it. While social construction may play a crucial role, it must still rest upon a real physical universe.[34] Attempts to build a narrative or understanding without such a concrete grounding are unlikely to provide a credible basis for mobilization or to survive for long, and thus less likely to serve as an effective basis for substantial and sustained political action.[35] The status quo or gradualism bias in most systems is very strong, and except in the very unlikely event of an elite consensus to generate a crisis without an objective basis, any elite attempt to generate a crisis would face an elite attempt to refute it in defense of the status quo.[36] A truly substantial reform would offer substantial costs alongside any benefits, and almost inevitably produce an interrogation of the underlying need increasing with the greater potential costs. Therefore, most truly subjective panics may attract a great deal of media and public attention, but also flame out relatively quickly. Something like the "Satanic panic" in the United States of the 1980s is here emblematic, as a wave of media stories and parental groups focused on the putative dangers of heavy metal music and role-playing games only to fade into a historical footnote by the 1990s. Elites or media actors may promote an interpretation of crises that exaggerates the severity, but absent a genuine underlying objective reality are unlikely to be able to produce real substantial reform out of the crisis moment. The case for weapons of mass destruction in Iraq was overstated, but given the historical record of Iraq both developing and deploying such weapons, not baseless. Panics in financial markets may be triggered by trivial events, but that is only possible because most actors in those financial markets understand that markets exist in a state of perpetual fragility due to structural information asymmetries. If anything, the status quo and cost-aversion biases in most systems are such that "false negatives" are far more prevalent than "false positives." Prior to the emergence of COVID-19, the threat of a global pandemic was consistently dismissed despite the warnings of experts and "near misses" including MERS, SARS, and the Avian Flu.

This dynamic also applies in a European context. Europe would reasonably be expected to be fertile ground for subjective crises. A preexisting understanding that integration is incomplete already dominates, and the Monnet logic that crises will lead to deeper integration creates a clear incentive for pro-integration actors to generate crises or promote existing disturbances as crises requiring deeper integration. However, as has been discussed, virtually every disturbance the EU hits has been dubbed a crisis by at least some actors, and only some produce genuine policy shifts. Instead, a critical mass of key actors waits to see the scale of the crisis, and resists action even in cases where the functional logic of the need for action seems relatively straightforward.

### Interpretive Crises

The two understandings of crises can be synthesized in a way that captures much of the strengths and addresses the weaknesses of both by focusing on crises as objective events *interpreted* through a subjective framing. Crises do not become so automatically. Riddervold et al. distinguish between "turbulence," where the system is threatened, and "crises," the moment when the necessity of decisive action is recognized.[37] Hay builds a four-part typology, based on whether states recognize they confront a systemic threat, and whether they take action to confront such a threat.[38] He terms recognized problems without decisive action "failures," becoming "crises" only when they are accompanied by decisive action. If the problem goes unrecognized, but nevertheless is resolved by action where actors did not realize the importance of the moment, this constitutes a "tipping point." Finally, a problem both unrecognized and unaddressed produces a "catastrophic equilibrium."

Crises therefore require a narrative attached to them to guide action. A crisis cannot generally be manufactured out of whole cloth, but at the same time a critical juncture acquires specific understandings as a guide for social action only through the narrative frame attached to it. To that end, an understanding of crises and their potential for structural change requires both an understanding of the objective structural issues and also the narrative frame through which those issues are examined.[39] This, therefore, requires attention to the role of master narratives in shaping systems and how they respond to crises.

## The Role of Master Narratives

A key component of how a crisis is evaluated and the solutions considered will be the challenge to the narrative framework of the system hit by a crisis. Narrative frameworks are essential to both define the policy community and provide a framework for understanding challenges and evaluating potential alternatives.[40] They may be divided between master narratives, which provide an overarching sense of community and logic of action, and derivative narratives which apply the framework of the narrative to individual policy

**26** Crises and Integration in European Banking Union

choices. Both are essential to understanding decision-making in times of crisis.

Master narratives are essential in specifying the overarching goals of the system and a broad ranking of priorities. The member states of the European Union and the social actors within them are divided, at times bitterly, over a wide range of issues. Just on economics, the member states split between a neoliberal framework embraced by the UK, a Keynesian framework promoted by France, and a German-led Ordoliberal tradition. Similar divides exist on immigration, the role of the state in society, and a host of other issues. What holds the European project together is a master narrative about the essential need for a European Union to avoid far worse alternatives.[41] Fundamental to this narrative is the concept of Europe as the "land of dark tragedy," of centuries of bloodshed and strife culminating in the First and Second World Wars, and integration as the only way to escape that tragic path.[42] Beyond that, the specific shape of European integration is shaped by a series of related myths. White emphasizes the importance of Christian Democratic values together with Ordoliberal principles in shaping early integration.[43] Jones identifies six key myths underlining European economic policy, broadly focused around the idea that integration was inevitably the surest and best path to prosperity and away from conflict for Europe.[44] The master narrative's core idea that integration must be preserved at all costs also drives perhaps the most central derivative narrative around Europe in crisis, that crises will drive integration. Crises provide a moment where the Europeans must choose between integration and disintegration, and since the master narrative precludes disintegration, crises must produce integration if the master narrative is to hold.

Understanding the master narrative is important to understanding crises in the European Union. The master narrative plays a key role in setting the agenda of what issues are considered, and which problems are considered to be "crises."[45] As such, they also shape the derivative narratives in every element of Kingdon's framework. At the problem stream, narratives define the scope of the challenge. Broadly, narratives create perceptions of functional linkages by creating an understanding of causal relationships.[46] The narrative frame adopted crystalizes a story about the key drivers of the problem and the nature of the problem. In part this can be about defining what constitutes a crisis. In the case of the European debt crisis, a number of different narratives could all have explained the events of late 2009 and early 2010. At its core, the problem could have been framed either as a crisis of banks or sovereign states, with blame falling on northern lenders for lending irresponsibly, or on southern borrowers for taking on unsustainable loans.[47] Casting the crisis as a "morality tale" blaming Greece and other Mediterranean countries' unsustainable borrowing carries a different set of policy implications than focusing on a "sudden stop" story based on banks triggering a crisis by refusing to lend.[48] Moreover, a narrative that cast Greece as emblematic of bigger problems both within the other southern states and within the institutional design of the EMU itself created a wider understanding of the problem than a narrative that would cast Greece as a unique case without clear connection to the issues in Spain, Portugal, or elsewhere.

The frame also clearly shapes how available solutions are evaluated both in terms of likely efficacy and legitimacy. McNamara traces how a neoliberal frame defined how actors evaluated alternatives in not just the design and management of the EMU, but the desirability of a common currency itself.[49] Brunnermeier, James, and Landau similarly link general principles of French and German economic ideology to a preference for different policy solutions in response to financial crises.[50] Above all of this, the master narrative shapes what solutions are considered not just viable, but legitimate. So long as a widespread belief as to the importance of European integration remains, disintegrative solutions are not considered legitimate. Thus, in the Greek sovereign debt crisis, it was widely discussed that a "Grexit" where Greece abandoned the euro would enable Greece to default and devalue its new currency, a classic formula for countries in sovereign debt crises. This option was rejected in part because cost–benefit analysis suggested that Greece remaining in the eurozone was ultimately better for both Greece and the rest of the eurozone. However, a crucial part of the rejection was also due to a sense that a retreat from integration would be a body blow to the European project. Moreover, the master narrative itself arguably helped shape the cost–benefit analysis itself by highlighting the risks of disintegration and advantages of remaining in the eurozone and EU. The role of the narrative also captures in part why the UK's decision to exit the European Union was cast as a potentially catastrophic event. Beyond the expected economic costs of disentangling a major economy from the single market, Brexit raised the possibility of further unraveling of the European project.

## Master Narratives Deployed in Crises

Understanding the role of master narratives is crucial because they play a key role in determining the scale and direction of reform out of a crisis. The degree to which the problem identified can be credibly linked to a threat to the master narrative, and the degree to which deeper integration can be

**28** Crises and Integration in European Banking Union

credibly framed as essential to preserving that master narrative, will profoundly shape the coalitions around policy responses to a crisis.

Broadly speaking, one can conceive of three coalitions of actors in response to a crisis, centered in a European context around the question of integration as a crisis response. Status quo players who want minimal change, reformers who want ambitious change in the form of deepening integration, and skeptics who want to retreat from integration as a crisis response. All three groups are present in both normal times and crises, though the shift to emergency politics in a crisis shifts both their power and ability to peel off members of other coalitions.

The first two groups, the status quo coalition and the reformers, share an embrace of the master narrative, though they differ on their satisfaction with the current level of integration. Status quo actors, dominant in normal politics, want little to no change in noncrisis moments by definition, as wanting change would push them into the reformer camp. Reformers want more ambitious changes, but generally lack the political strength to achieve their aims in normal politics. The third group, skeptics, differ from the first two in that they reject the master narrative. In European terms, these are euroskeptics who want to roll back European integration. However, like the reformers, they lack sufficient political strength to advance their agenda in normal politics.

When a crisis hits, the master narrative provides a crucial frame through which both the scale of the threat and the range of alternatives are evaluated. Scale of threat is determined not just by the direct change in material conditions, but also by the degree to which that change in conditions plausibly threatens the continuance of the master narrative and the core goals of the system. Similarly, the range of legitimate responses to that threat must be congruent not just with the direct material challenge, but also the long-term preservation of those core goals. The master narrative thus casts disintegrative solutions in the EU as broadly illegitimate, and inappropriate except perhaps as a last resort after efforts at deeper integration have collapsed.

This in turn shapes the power dynamics between these three groups. The master narrative holds the reform coalition together, flattening their differences and rallying them around their common goal of protecting and deepening integration. It also plays a role in delegitimizing the skeptic coalition, by identifying their aims as hostile to the master narrative. Finally, and most crucially, it helps push the status quo coalition in the direction of reform. Because the status quo actors broadly accept the master narrative, their preference order can be conceived of as first for the status quo, then for deeper integration, and finally last for disintegrative solutions. Therefore, as the status quo becomes less viable, or just less desirable, as conditions deteriorate, this acceptance of the master narrative drives those status quo actors to the reformer camp rather than the skeptics, tilting the balance of power toward reform. This also gives the skeptics a harder task to use a crisis to advance their agenda, as they must not only convince the status quo actors that reform is essential, but also that the integrationist master narrative should be rejected in favor of a new disintegrative narrative.

This creates a powerful incentive for pro-reform actors to promote an understanding of a crisis which promotes their agenda, though it does not on its own determine either the potential or degree of reform out of the crisis. Actors may play an active role in deploying frames for strategic advantage, promoting an understanding of both problems and solutions in a way that promotes their own favored outcomes. What Jabko terms "strategic constructivism" does not guarantee success at the decision stage, but can tilt the debate to their advantage, especially in the early stages.[51] A common framework can unite relatively disparate actors into a common position, even if their own internal divisions remain substantial. Moreover, it can delegitimize policy alternatives and narrow the acceptable range of outcomes. This framing may help bind coalitions even when they are uncertain as to the ultimate outcomes.[52] This is especially crucial in crisis policymaking, when rigorous cost–benefit analysis may not be possible due to both time constraints and incomplete information preventing detailed and extensive analysis. In such circumstances, actors are more likely to fall back on principled action if rational analysis is impossible, and the dominant frame will determine the contents of what is meant by "principled action."[53]

Such strategic constructivist strategies, however, cannot operate in a vacuum. Whether in a crisis nor not, substantial barriers to change typically exist. Those barriers will be axiomatically stronger in periods of normal politics, as by definitional a critical juncture is a period where the barriers to change are weaker. As the barriers weaken, the status quo equilibrium may be vulnerable to disruption. However, a weakening of status quo forces should not be mistaken for an elimination of those forces. Even in a crisis, people are likely to prefer the known benefits of the status quo over the uncertain outcome of a move to an alternative state.[54] Here, therefore, a central question will be whether the framing successfully casts the status quo as undesirable, unsustainable, or both.

The first path would be to cast maintaining the status quo as no longer desirable, at least among a key segment of actors who would come join the reform coalition or, or because key actors' resources to combat the reform are eroded. This essentially fits with the intergovernmental understanding of change, which attributes change in crises or otherwise to a shift in the domestic coalition of EU member states. Implicit in the intergovernmental crisis accounts is that the desire for change is independent of the crisis itself, and a product of external shocks changing the power balance such that the reform coalition may become ascendant in a critical mass of member states. This will likely be the harder path toward change in a crisis, however. While status quo players may be weakened, they are not eliminated. Moreover, the general trend toward risk aversion may actually intensify in times of crisis, as an environment of uncertainty causes people to retreat back to the known and a desire to return to the old normal politics status quo. As White argues, the desire for a return to normal politics and a rapid exit from emergency politics can be substantial, and the quickest route out of a crisis will be a return to pre-crisis status quo ante.[55]

The stronger case for change out of a crisis may be a narrative which casts the status quo as no longer sustainable. This is the course emphasized by both neofunctional and postfunctional accounts. Neofunctional accounts trace crises as endogenously emerging from incomplete integration, meaning that they are a product of flaws in the status quo which can only be addressed by changing it. In neofunctional accounts, the assumption is that the superior course of reform will be a deepening of integration that will maintain the benefits of existing integration while patching up flaws to allow the system to persevere. Postfunctional accounts are in essence the mirror image of neofunctional arguments. Like the neofunctionalists, they see crises as endogenously emerging from incomplete integration, but focus on the possibility of disintegration rather than deeper integration as the most viable solution.

An argument for the unsustainability of the status quo is likely to be the stronger case for change. The most powerful discursive tool here will be the "There Is No Alternative" (TINA) discourse, arguing that what matters is not so much the desirability of change so much as the necessity of change. By casting reform as a matter of technocratic "functional imperatives" rather than a matter for discursive argument, a TINA discourse depoliticizes crises responses and shuts out a host of actors who might otherwise challenge the favored course of action.[56] Instead, the target reforms are cast as the only rational way forward in the fact of an unsustainable status quo and a set of undesirable alternatives. Such alternatives may be cast as undesirable for practical reasons, such as that they are politically nonviable or that they will not solve the underlying problems causing the crisis. They may also be cast as normatively undesirable and illegitimate, and therefore beyond the pale of acceptable policy responses.[57] Alternatives may also be cast as both; disintegration in response to European crises is simultaneously cast as impractical and normatively undesirable. It is cast as impractical because the benefits lost from losing integration will so dramatically outweigh the benefits of disintegration as to render the cure worse than the illness, and it is cast as normatively undesirable by linking European integration to broader narratives of the importance of unity and integration as a way to prevent intra-European warfare. In sum, the real power of the TINA discourse lies in casting dissatisfaction with the reforms as essentially irrelevant; if there are no viable alternatives, then dissatisfaction is regrettable but cannot be a barrier to action.

Of course, a discourse on the necessity of reform will not become the dominant frame automatically. It also may not remain in place once established. Boin and Rhinard highlight that the "meaning making" of actors early in a crisis often has only a short "honeymoon" before other actors deploy counter-narratives.[58] Moreover, not all crises provide a suitable set of circumstances to successfully promote a discourse on the necessity of reforming the status quo, especially in its strongest TINA form. In a European context, pro-reform actors will attempt to do so in virtually every crisis, attempting to take advantage of a Kingdon-style window of opportunity. However, the mixed track record of success shows that this is only sometimes successful. This success rate is not accidental, but can be ascribed to a general set of conditions of the crisis at hand.

## The Usefulness of the Grand Theories

The study of European integration has long been dominated by three "Grand Theories," each emphasizing different key causal forces and different expected outcomes. All of these approaches make crises central to their accounts of European integration, albeit with an emphasis on different causal mechanisms and expectations of the most likely impacts. Despite the prominence assigned to the role of crises in advancing integration in all three approaches, it is surprising that the major Grand Theories of European integration lack a compelling theory to identify a priori which crises are likely to drive integration, especially given the mixed historical record of the impact of crises. Instead, all three focus more on *post hoc* explanations of *how* those crises which *did* drive integration did so. Despite this, all three Grand Theories do offer important insights toward building an a priori theory of crisis impacts.

## Intergovernmentalism

Intergovernmentalism's chief contribution lies in its emphasis on the status quo bias in the EU. In times of normal politics, the system is at an approximate equilibrium, and as such change in normal times should come only gradually. Interest groups should be expected to keep their preferences in normal times, so change only comes from shifts in the balance of power between them. Crises are important therefore for two reasons. The first is that they can cause rapid shifts in the balance of power between groups. The second is the potential for social learning as actors are forced to adjust their preferences faced with new information. This is most likely to occur when the crisis threat causes the status quo to become unsustainable, forcing actors to set new goals. However, the utility of a learning approach is limited by the fact that frequently the flaws of European integration are well known in advance, and simply go unaddressed. Moreover, intergovernmental approaches themselves are neutral as to which direction those new preferences are likely to run, a gap filled by the neofunctionalists and postfunctionalists.

## Neofunctionalism

Neofunctionalism provides two key insights toward building a theory of crises. The first is its emphasis on the endogenous instability of the EU due to incomplete integration, in contrast to the intergovernmental focus on exogenous crises. This divergence between the two approaches allows for the possibility that different mechanisms of crisis response may exist depending on the nature of the crisis origin, a distinction that will be explored in greater depth in the following section. As such, neofunctionalism captures that the EU may exist in a state akin to Hay's catastrophic equilibrium, with instability left unaddressed. Jones et al. argue that these spillover effects will produce a "failing forward" to a lowest common denominator solution that will do the least possible to address the problem at hand.[59] This could be framed to capture a set of expectations of when a state will fail forward. Brooks et al, for instance, argue that such failing forward is most likely when a crisis is encompassing, unfamiliar, and existential.[60] However, Jones himself, writing with Anghel, argues that such efforts to model failing forward are unlikely to yield success, as crises are frequently too sui generis to make broader predictions.[61]

The second major contribution of neofunctionalism is its detailed exploration of what has historically been the central master narrative of the EU in response to crises, the focus on "ever closer union" and the Monnet logic of integration through crises. While groups favoring the status quo may dominate normal politics, as captured by the intergovernmentalist emphasis on stable equilibria, even those groups will prefer integration over disintegration. For the neofunctionalists, a central role of crises is to make the status quo unsustainable, forcing actors to choose between integration and disintegration. When forced to choose, then, the master narrative of ever closer union pushes actors toward integration as the preferable alternative in the absence of a status quo option.

## Postfunctionalism

The postfunctionalist approach, perhaps the most of any of the three Grand Theories, highlights the importance of an interpretive understanding of crises and of frames of understanding. The postfunctionalist emphasis on the shift to a "constraining dissensus" highlights the contingent nature of the integration master narrative. The postfunctionalist counter-narrative conceives of the possibility of a group favoring disintegration over either the status quo or deeper integration. This preference order was obviously ascendant in the "Leave" vote in the United Kingdom, though since Brexit, euroskepticism has generally declined elsewhere in the EU. Potentially more important, especially to the study of crises, is the persistence and perhaps increase in number of actors essentially satisfied with the European status quo, but who would sooner accept disintegration rather than agree to deeper integration. This may be essentially salient in times of crisis when the status quo becomes unsustainable. While the neofunctionalists assume that such crises that remove the status quo option cause the majority of actors to default to a second preference of integration, the postfunctionalists highlight the increasing possibility that a critical mass of status quo actors may favor disintegration over integration if forced to choose.

## The Theory and the Grand Theories

The theory discussed here can be mapped onto the Grand Theories essentially as follows:

1) It starts from the intergovernmental focus on the tendency of the EU to maintain the status quo with only slight modifications in normal politics. A crisis becomes salient if it causes the status quo to become less desirable in the eyes of key actors, and in particular, if the status quo comes to be seen as unsustainable.

2) At this point, the neofunctionalist master narrative of integration over disintegration pushes previously status quo actors to push for integration as necessary. This does not happen automatically, but as a result of pro-integration actors, both domestic and supranational, activating that narrative framework.

3) This contingent nature is important, as it acknowledges the possibility highlighted by the post-functionalists that a disintegrationist narrative may at some point challenge the integration narrative, arguing that in the absence of a stable status quo, disintegration is preferable to deeper integration. This has happened only rarely, though the possibility of disintegration as a response is arguably growing, not shrinking, over time. When that contest over narratives truly emerges in response to a crisis, Europe will have truly reached the "metacrisis" of legitimacy the postfunctionalists highlight.

## The Essential Dimensions for Disruption of the Status Quo in a Crisis

As established in the Usefulness of Grand Theories section, the degree to which the terms of the crisis connect to a threat to the master narrative plays a key role in determining the politics around a crisis, and ultimately the likely degree of reform to emerge from the policy response. The success of a pro-integration narrative around a crisis, and thus whether a crisis will become an integration-spurring Monnet Crisis, a disintegrating crisis, a crisis producing moderating reform in either direction, or a crisis that ultimately leaves the status quo intact will hinge on a key question: whether the crisis's fundamental characteristics can credibly support a narrative that the status quo is unsustainable, undesirable, or both. Doing so, especially if a TINA discourse can be crafted, will produce a robust case for change, making a Monnet Crisis, or conversely a disintegration crisis, much more likely. Because the narrative is built upon a crisis outside of the control of the policy entrepreneurs, it becomes possible to identify the key characteristics which make a radical change narrative more viable. While the severity of the threat to the current status quo plays a key role, this provides an insufficient guide, given the imperfect relationship between degree of threat and intensity of response. The origin of the crisis, either within or outside of the sector, therefore also plays a key role.

## Origin

The first key element to consider is the origin of the crisis as identified by the dominant crisis narrative. Whether the crisis originated in the sector of interest or whether the sector was merely affected by a crisis originating in a different sector will play a key role in determining the efficacy of reforms for the longer-term stability of the system.

A crisis originating within the sector itself, regardless of scale, is caused by some flaw in the architecture of the crisis, as identified by the neofunctionalist logic of spillover. In an endogenous crisis, reform can plausibly prevent future crises by remedying the flaw. Conversely, and potentially more important in motivating action, failure to reform essentially guarantees that the problem will continue to generate future crises until it is addressed. Therefore, the status quo itself an unstable equilibrium, and the question becomes how to address that flaw. However, the degree of will to address that flaw will vary depending on the scale of the crisis, determining whether actors will favor a fundamental overhaul of the architecture or a more modest "patch-up" reform that fixes some of the problems while preserving more of the status quo.

Alternately, a crisis may affect the sector but have its origins outside of the sector itself. In such a case, no amount of reform of the sector itself will prevent crises of this kind from reoccurring. The threat will always return because the permanent fix lies elsewhere, if indeed such a fix is even possible. Therefore, the goal of crisis policymaking is not to fix the flaw, which cannot be accomplished through reform of the affected sector, but rather to ensure that the system survives the current crisis and potential future exogenous shocks. The status quo here is generally sustainable, with the potential need to provide some manner of insulation against shocks, depending on the degree of the threat.

The differing capacity to permanently fix the problems depending on the origins will shape the likelihood of actors changing their preferences during the course of the crisis. In an exogenous-origin crisis, the goal will be to reach a post-crisis point of stability with minimal changes to the status quo. On the other hand, an endogenous crisis may change preferences, as if the current architecture of the sector itself is causing the crisis, this suggests that the status quo cannot be sustained and must be changed in some form, if the master narrative and its goals are to be protected. In the words of a representative of the Association of German Banks (BdB), "if you have an internal crisis, the changes are much bigger."[62] In this sense, this metric links with the

## Severity

The second dimension on which to conceptualize the likelihood of a crisis triggering integration is the intensity of the crisis, which directly impacts the sustainability of the status quo. Without some degree of a threat to the system, politics will not shift from normal to emergency mode, and the normal barriers to reform will remain extant. The greater the scale of the crisis, at least as portrayed in crisis narratives, the more that maintaining the status quo becomes manifestly impossible.

One important caveat must be stated in discussion of scope: the focus here is on crises of integration, meaning survival of the integrated polity itself, not the general welfare of the society as a whole. A robust federation faces many threats to the general welfare of its population, but few crises where the very terms of integration themselves are questioned. The United States, for instance, has really only encountered a handful of crises where the terms of the union were seriously contested. In the post–Civil War era, the most prominent of these moments came in the mid-twentieth-century civil rights struggle, when the federal government asserted a role in forcing desegregation over the objection of recalcitrant state governments. Other threats that the United States has faced, including the Great Depression, the Second World War, and more recently the attempted Trump Coup, threatened the general welfare of the United States but not the unity of the federation. However, European integration is a much more fragile thing, to the point where whether to describe the EU as a federation, confederation, or simply an international organization remains a matter of debate.[63]

Threats to the general welfare are unlikely to produce either greater integration or disintegration unless they are linked to the terms of integration. A decline in welfare of the citizens in one member state likely will not motivate other member states to provide substantial assistance purely out of altruism unless the union is already so strong as to cause citizens to think of themselves as members of a single community. A robust federation such as the United States may have such a strong common identity, but Europe clearly has yet to reach that level of solidarity. As Schimmelfennig identifies, member states are most likely to concern themselves with the general welfare of their neighbors only to the degree that interdependence means that the member's own welfare may be tied up with the neighbor's.[64] When such interdependence exists, however, it becomes easier to argue that deeper integration is welfare-enhancing for all parties.

Even within the subset of crises that directly impact integration, important distinctions must be made between minor, moderate and severe threats. Origin can generally be more precisely pinpointed, though some debate may still occur. Severity, however, inevitably manifests on a spectrum, rather than a binary. This model simplifies that to moderate and severe crises, and to minor events which fail to spark even notable failed reform efforts, but boundary cases will nevertheless occur. However, in principle, the distinction between a moderate and severe threat may be established as follows: a moderate threat is one where deeper integration can substantially reduce the potential costs and long-term danger to the Union, but where the risk of disintegration from inaction is low. A severe threat is one where inaction will very likely produce disintegration in the near future. Obviously, drawing the specific boundaries may be imprecise, and will heavily depend on the narrative framework used by key actors. The key distinction however may be reduced to whether disintegration seems like a plausible proximate outcome of inaction.

Neither origin nor severity of threat on its own provides sufficient context to evaluate the likely outcome. A severe crisis does not in itself preclude maintenance of the status quo, especially if the problem's origins cannot be traced to flaws in integration. If the crisis cannot be linked discursively to the solution, it becomes easier to argue that the better solution is not substantial structural reform, but rather to endure the current crisis until it passes, and return to the *ex ante* status quo. This is especially likely if the vested interests which favor the status quo are in a position to maintain or regain their prominence rather than be permanently diminished by the effects of the crisis. By the same token, an endogenous crisis may be more likely to produce a reform of some form than an exogenous one, but the historical record demonstrates a wide range of responses to both kinds of crisis, such that origin alone also provides an incomplete guide.

The focus on these two factors produces a four-part typology of responses to crises, as illustrated in Figure 1.1. This in turn points to crises producing what may be stylized as four outcomes: maintenance of the status quo, modest "weatherproofing" reform, modest "patch-up" reform, or substantial reform. These outcomes correspond to Hall's three orders of change.[65] Maintenance of the status quo, Hall's first-order change, sees no consequential change in policy goals and instruments, but only minor policy adaptation. Modest reform, whether weatherproofing or patch-up, corresponds to Hall's second-order change, where the policy goals remain stable but with substantial revision of the instruments involved. Finally, substantial reform sees a change in the hierarchy of goals themselves, the point where a substantial revision of the system is possible, as in the classic Monnet Crisis.

To date, the majority of crisis reforms have been integrative, but the framework allows for the possibility that they could go in the other direction, as was for instance the case in the Empty Chair Crisis. What matters most is the degree and nature of the perceived threat to the status quo; whether it's large enough to make the status quo unsustainable, and whether it's a threat that demands a large or small overhaul of the sector itself or an insulation without fundamental changes. However, the importance of the master narrative of "ever closer union" does make integrative solutions more likely than disintegrative ones, at least so long as that master narrative continues to hold sway over a majority of the status quo actors.

The first dimension is the origin of the crisis. A crisis where the origins can be traced to endogenous flaws in the system itself more readily lends itself to a TINA narrative, where reform becomes an imperative because the status quo has become untenable. On the other hand, a crisis with origin exogenous to the sector itself may cause a threat to sectoral integration, but since the flaws do not truly lie within the sector, reform is not necessarily essential, and endurance may instead become an option. Note that while others in the literature use endogenous and exogenous to refer to geographic origin within or outside of Europe, in this context, it refers to sectoral integration. In a globally integrated sector such as finance, the geographic point of origin may matter much less than the sectoral origin, especially when sector-wide trends create global weaknesses. In the 2007–09 Banking Crisis, for instance, the widespread use of credit derivatives and mortgage-backed securities in both the US and Europe, and the exposure of European banks to American markets and vice versa, meant that whether the crisis originated in American or European finance is not only not particularly relevant, but unclear. While much of the literature points to the American bubble in subprime mortgages, among the first banks to run into substantial problems which triggered a global panic were the British Northern Rock and French BNP Paribas.

The second dimension is the scale of threat to integration. The greater the threat to integration and the less sustainable the status quo, the greater the likelihood of reforms, and of deep reforms. Since an event that produces no threat to integration cannot be plausibly referred to as a crisis, such events drop out of the analysis, leaving crises to fall on a spectrum somewhere between moderate and severe. The crucial breaking point between the two is whether the status quo can plausibly endure absent some degree of change, even if the endurance of the status quo is suboptimal. A severe threat requires at least a modest level of reform to avoid a system collapse, though it may be argued that more substantial reform would be optimal. On the other hand, a moderate threat could create a negative impact, making reforms desirable, but even an unaddressed threat would not be likely to threaten the overall integration of the sector.

Note that this theory focuses on the dynamics of crisis and integration in a single sector. As noted by Stark, a single crisis can produce multiple critical junctures in different sectors. This may then effectively lead to multiple different stories about integration in various sectors, especially as the crisis may be endogenous to one sector and exogenous to another, or a severe threat to integration in one sector but only a moderate threat in another.[66] A single crisis could produce substantial integration in one sector and modest or no integration in another, or even plausibly disintegration in one sector and integration in another. This analysis takes the dynamics in each individual sector as essentially independent as a necessary simplification. While much of the current dynamics in Europe have they dynamics of a "wicked" crisis, where action in one sector may have negative implications for another, this analysis focuses on providing a foundational theory for likely impacts of crises. As such, the potential interaction effects between sectors are left to future research projects.

This two-dimensional typology provides four classifications of crises, with four expectations as to the outcome for integration.

## Exogenous Moderate: No Reform

In an exogenous moderate crisis, the point of origin lies outside the sector of interest and the threat is only moderate. Deeper integration (or potentially greater disintegration) could potentially reduce the threat by providing greater capacity for a coordinated response, but will not prevent the crisis from reoccurring, as its origins are external. Moreover, the threat is not so great as to make disintegration a likely consequence of inaction. This will not stop pro-integration or pro-disintegration actors from attempting to use the crisis as evidence of the need for reforms, but are unlikely to sway the dominant pro–status quo actors. Therefore, the expectation here is that pro-integration actors will argue that the crisis demands integrative (or disintegrative) reform, but are unlikely to convince a critical mass of actors that the status quo cannot be preserved. As such, these kinds of crises are expected to produce a conversation about reform, but no reforms of more than cosmetic significance.

## Endogenous Moderate: Modest "Patch-Up" Reforms

Similarly to an exogenous moderate crises, an endogenous moderate crisis will not in itself disrupt integration of the sector. Therefore, it may be plausible to make an argument that the crisis should simply be endured without modification to the status quo. At the same time, however, the origin of the crisis within the sector does highlight flaws in the current architecture of the sector. Therefore, absent some manner of reform, the crisis will very likely reoccur, and over time recurring crises linked to flaws in integration may undermine the support for and legitimacy of integration. For this reason, the status quo becomes less desirable. Some pro-integration actors may propose more fundamental changes, but since the scale of the crisis doesn't match the scale of the reforms, this more radical reform is unlikely to succeed. However, more modest "patch-up" reforms that will prevent the problems that emerged out of the last crisis without truly transforming the system are a likely outcome. Such reforms will attempt to address flaws in the system that contributed to the crisis, but without dramatic change. In Hall's framework, this will entail a change in policy instruments, but not a dramatic shift in the power or goals of the system.[67]

## Exogenous Substantial: "Weatherproofing" Reforms

In an exogenous substantial crisis, the threat to integration of the sector is substantial, meaning that a strategy of endurance to maintain the status quo will not be viable. There is a real risk that integration will unravel if action is not taken. On the other hand, no amount of reform will make the problems go away, as the origins of the crisis are outside of the sector. Here the underlying architecture of the sector is not really the problem, and as such it will be hard to convince pro-status quo actors that a fundamental reform is essential. As with exogenous moderate crises, the real solution must lie elsewhere. Unlike with exogenous moderate crises, however, this does not mean the threat can be ignored. The substantial threat means that reforms to increase the robustness of the system's capacity to absorb external shocks, "weatherproofing" against future crises, may be essential. Such reforms will not fundamentally alter the architecture of the system, but will be more than the cosmetic reforms expected in an exogenous moderate crisis. "Weatherproofing" reforms will be comparable in scale to "patch-up" reforms, insofar as they will change the instruments available to policymakers but not the fundamental goals of the system. However, while patch-up reforms will focus on modifying the operation of the system itself to prevent the generation of problems, weatherproofing reforms will instead focus on the capacity of the system to absorb shocks. Both would be second-order changes in Hall's typology.[68]

### Endogenous Substantial: "Monnet" Crises

The final category of crises is where Monnet Crises producing substantial integration are likely to be found. As with endogenous moderate crises, the origin of the crisis can be traced to a fundamental flaw in the architecture of the system itself. Crucially, however, the negative consequences of that flaw are substantially greater. As with exogenous substantial crises, the most likely outcome of inaction will be a chaotic disintegration, not merely the suboptimal performance of an endogenous moderate crisis. As such, the underlying architecture *must* be fixed, and with a remedy commensurate with the scale of the threat. Even if modest reform would get the system through the current crisis, it would likely not prevent the next one, and since the sector itself produced a substantial threat, reform becomes necessary. The only plausible alternatives become deeper integration, a managed disintegration, or catastrophic disintegration and collapse of integration. Given the general bias toward integration over disintegration, this is where we are most likely to encounter the policy response identified by Monnet and Schuman of substantial change out of crises.

## Methodology and Case Selection

### The Advantages of Focusing on Financial Sector Integration

This theory will be explored through an exploration of four crises hitting European finance in the twenty-first century. While the specifics of European finance will be discussed in greater detail later in this chapter, broadly speaking a focus on finance is valuable because it controls for the fundamental nature of the crisis and broadly speaking the actors in play. The core problem confronting European financial regulation since the lowering of barriers to the movement of money and services, and especially since the introduction of the euro, has been the tension between transnational banking activity and regulation, including supervision and resolution, rooted in national authorities. Although reforms out of some of these crises have somewhat reduced that tension, the core problem endures. This, therefore, enables comparison between cases with common core issues, whereas comparing, for instance, a crisis in immigration policy and one in financial policy would

**42** Crises and Integration in European Banking Union

introduce additional variance due to the differing underlying issues. Additionally, focusing on a single sector means that the key institutional actors, and in some cases even the key individuals, remain unchanged, as do their broadly defined interests and the distribution of power between them. The dynamic between the member states, for instance, remains broadly consistent through this period. The wealthier northern member states led by Germany generally resist measures that might produce intra-European fiscal transfers while the relatively poorer southern members including Spain and Italy favor them. France generally straddles this gap, sometimes aligning with the northern group and sometimes the southern, while Britain, until its exit, acted primarily to protect the City of London from European oversight and maintained an arms-length distance from the debates centered in the eurozone. Similarly, among private actors the division across cases remains a split between the massive transnational banks and the smaller regional banks, with the former favoring deeper integration to facilitate cross-border banking and the latter generally looking to preserve national discretion and protection from foreign competition. Because the actors and the balance of power between them remains relatively stable across cases in finance, arguments rooted in different inter-actor relations in different sectors cannot explain variation in outcomes.

One other similarity across twenty-first century crises in European finance was in the range of solutions proposed by various policy entrepreneurs. From the first crisis examined to the last, the most ambitious demands of reformers were essentially the same: the creation of a full European banking union, including the creation of a European supervisor to replace national authorities for all EU banks, the creation of a commonly funded and centrally administered European resolution authority, including both the authority and funding to resolve failed banks and a common European Deposit Insurance Scheme (EDIS), and the implementation of a true European Capital Markets Union (CMU). In the face of opposition, the same essential compromises were proposed to varying degrees of success, including restricting European supervision to eurozone-only banks and/or only to banks above a certain threshold, compromises on the hierarchy of authority in any resolution authority, and co-insurance of national deposit guarantee schemes (DGS) in lieu of a central EDIS. The maximal demands of reformers and the broad terms of debate did not vary, but the degree to which they were able to achieve their aims changed significantly. As will be demonstrated in the subsequent chapters, this variance can be traced to the differences in the origins and severity of the individual crises.

## Explaining Case Selection

The second advantage of exploring European finance in the twenty-first century is that it has been hit by four successive crises which span the four types of crises identified by the origin and severity typology. Two of these crises, the 2007–09 Transatlantic Banking Crisis and the 2010–14 European Debt Crisis, are fairly unambiguously endogenous crises. Both are crises that clearly originated in whole in or in large part from flaws in the European financial regulatory architecture. As discussed in Chapter 3, while many of the factors that drove the 2007–09 Banking Crisis originated in the United States, others are unambiguously products of the regulatory limits, gaps, and confusion of the European financial regulatory architecture. Similarly, the 2010–14 Debt Crisis can be traced to a combination of the Doom Loop of massive banks that overwhelm their sovereigns' capacity to resolve them and the pressure on member state finances from monetary union without fiscal union.

The other two crises considered, the fallout of the UK's 2016 decision to leave the European Union and the 2020–21 COVID Pandemic, provide examples of exogenous crises for European finance. The origins of both crises lie outside of European finance and its regulatory architecture, but both crises nevertheless posed threats to the stability of the European financial system due to spillover effects. The 2016 Brexit vote was clearly driven by forces other than finance, as the City of London and UK financial actors had been almost unanimously among the strongest advocates of remaining in the European Union. Nevertheless, the UK's decision to leave threatened European financial stability due to the shock of losing unrestricted access to the City of London, Europe's chief hub for financial activity, and the risk that either a continental or British bank should fail and trigger a broader panic. The COVID-19 Pandemic even more clearly originated outside of the financial system, but again threatened the stability of the financial system. The sudden cessation of economic activity out of emergency lockdowns threatened to bring a surge of nonperforming loans (NPLs) from individuals and firms no longer able to pay their debts, which combined with the legacy issues out of the earlier crises could bring down already less-than-robust European banks. Moreover, the capacity of individual states to manage such bank failures was constrained by the need to expand public spending in other areas to manage both the surging health care costs and the direct impact of the attendant economic crisis on individuals and other firms. That the hardest-hit states early in the Pandemic were Spain and Italy, among the weakest states out of the Debt Crisis, only exacerbated the threat to European finance from the Pandemic.

Just as these four crises provide examples of both endogenous and exogenous crises, they also provide examples of both moderate and severe crises. The Banking Crisis and Brexit provide examples of moderate crises. The Banking Crisis imposed substantial costs on the affected member states, but never really threatened European integration. Because the most-affected states were almost entirely the wealthier states, this was a crisis that member states could manage with their own resources. Failure to act would risk another banking crisis emerging out of the same root problems, but would not lead to immediate pressure on European integration. Similarly, Brexit posed real risks to European financial stability, but the controlled nature of the UK's departure from the EU gave European and member state officials room to manage and anticipate problems, meaning that the risk of spillover from Brexit remained real but moderate.

The other two crises, the Debt Crisis and the Pandemic, both posed more severe challenges. Both, in essence, presented a real risk of dissolution of the union through the sovereign default of one or more member states. In the Debt Crisis, this was directly connected to flaws in the financial system, as banks in key southern member states such as Spain and Italy had grown beyond the capacity of those states to manage bank failures. This Doom Loop between bank failure risk and sovereign default risk created a real and proximate risk of one or more member states engaging in a sovereign default. Such a default would almost certainly have required them to leave the monetary union, and potentially leave the EU altogether. The Pandemic created similar risks, largely in the same member states. Although the Pandemic obviously did not originate in the financial system, the economic contraction out of the emergency responses dramatically strained banks. Both Spain and Italy still faced Doom Loop pressures, and the failure of large banks or a wave of smaller banks in either state could rapidly return the European Union to the same sovereign default pressures it had faced at the peak of the Debt Crisis. The Pandemic differed in origins from the Debt Crisis, but the risk it raised, the sovereign default of one or more member states, especially in southern Europe, was thus essentially the same as the Debt Crisis. As such, both crises should be classified as severe threats to European integration.

## Methodology

The cases are explored through a process-tracing methodology. Relying on a combination of interview research and analysis of public statements by participants, I will focus on reconstructing the terms of debate out of the crisis.

In particular, I will focus on four phases of the crisis, and how actors attempted to use the parameters of the crisis to link the crisis to calls for reform or to refute those linkages.

Any successful attempt to promote reform out of a crisis must be linked to an objective challenge which can credibly be described as a crisis. Given the substantial barriers to challenging the status quo, it is not credible to conceive that elites or media actors could manufacture a crisis perceived to be serious enough to drive a substantial deepening of integration. This is especially likely to be the case given that many elite actors will be among the defenders of that status quo. However, a challenge only becomes a crisis through a social process of recognition of it as a crisis. The first major element to focus on will therefore be the discourse around the crisis, and the degree to which key actors identify it as a crisis in order to justify the shift to emergency politics. These actors must be powerful and/or numerous enough to achieve widespread acceptance of this narrative, though there will also be actors promoting a counter-narrative that the turbulence does not rise to the level of crisis, and therefore that the shift to emergency politics is unjustified. The specific crisis narrative adopted will carry great consequences for the policy debate to follow on how to respond to the crisis, as the reasonable solutions will inevitably be linked to the understanding of the underlying problem to be addressed.

This leads into the second element, which is that once an event occurs and is framed as a crisis, a course of action, or potentially choices of course of action out of the crisis must be put forth. The menu of solutions must be compatible with both the understanding of the crisis and the broader master narrative of the society as a whole. It should also be noted that the people promoting the narrative of the crisis may or may not be the same as those promoting a solution. Frequently the understanding of the crisis and the optimal solutions are promoted simultaneously, but this is not necessary. It is also conceivable the crisis narrative and the solution narrative may be promoted by different actors with different goals. Regardless, a key part of the analysis will be a discursive analysis of the various policy proposals put forward, and how the advocates of those proposals attempt to link their favored path forward to the specifics of the crisis, its origins, and the likelihood of confronting similar crises in the future.

This will lead then into an analysis of the third phase, the politics around the optimal path forward. Again, the focus will be on an analysis of public statements and interviews demonstrating the degree to which arguments about the appropriateness of various responses links to the structural challenges presented by the specific crisis. Finally, this analysis focuses on the dynamics of reform efforts under emergency politics, but the crisis will eventually pass and normal politics will return. Therefore, a final element will be to analyze how the key actors settled on a consensus as to when the crisis moment ended and normalcy returned to EU policymaking.

## Crises and the Development of European Financial Integration in the Twenty-First Century

These dynamics can be seen perhaps most clearly in the efforts to reform regulation of banking and finance in the European Union from 1999 to present. Financial reform provides an ideal subject for comparative analysis because the fundamental problems undergirding the financial system have been well known through the entire period under examination, and the financial sector has been buffeted by a variety of crises which produced a range of reforms of varying degrees of substance to address those flaws. As such, finance provides an opportunity to engage in comparative analysis of crisis and crisis response while controlling for the underlying institutional architecture to a degree which is not possible in sectors such as migration, where the institutional context has changed dramatically, or security threats, where the range of threats is not broad enough to capture the full range of possibilities.

### Theoretical and Political Issues in European Financial Integration

The essential weakness of European finance is that a transnational financial system is overseen by a patchwork of national regulators. Transnational financial activity expanded substantially in the 1990s, following the removal of capital controls in the 1980s, and accelerated in the 2000s with both the introduction of the common currency and the increase in communications technology through the spread of the internet. However, for most of that period, regulation of banks and other financial institutions has remained chiefly the province of national financial regulators. The introduction of a European-level supervisor under the Single Supervisory Mechanism (SSM) came only in 2014 and covered only the largest eurozone banks, excluding both smaller eurozone banks and all non-eurozone European Union banks from direct centralized regulation. As such, European finance has been in the grips of Schoenmaker's Trilemma, as depicted in Figure 2.1.[69] In essence, the Europeans have to choose between three options. The status quo option through most of the twenty-first century has been to attempt to supervise transnational banks with national regulation, a formula for regulatory arbitrage as banks pick and choose their regulators, negative regulatory competition as regulators compete in a race to the bottom in regulatory standards, and regulatory gaps as a complicated assignment of responsibilities means even systemically significant firms may escape meaningful oversight. As such, this is a recipe for perpetual instability, or in Hay's terms, a "catastrophic equilibrium."[70] However, two paths exist to escape that instability. The first would be a "Balkanization" of European finance, re-raising the barriers to cross-border finance such that national regulators can once again effectively supervise their national banks. However, this would both limit consumer choice among Europeans enjoying the ability to access foreign banks and diminish the ability of European banks to reach a scale to compete with the massive American banks with a continental customer base. The last alternative, per Schoenmaker's Trilemma, therefore, is to match transnational finance with transnational regulation, and transfer regulatory and supervisory authority from national governments to a supranational body.

This challenge has been well known to both policymakers and academics since the 1990s, and has grown in importance with the growth of the largest European financial firms in that time.[71] The 2001 European Union Report on the Regulation of European Securities Markets, commonly known as the Lamfalussy Report after its chair, Alexandre Lamfalussy, identified the problems of harmonizing national regulation of transnational banking from the

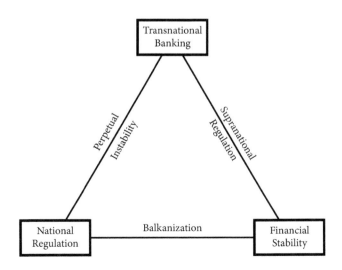

**Figure 2.1** Schoenmaker's Trilemma

early years of the euro's existence.[72] Therefore, when crises hit European finance, it was not a case of policymakers learning that a functional flaw existed in the regulatory architecture and a fix was needed. The flaws and solutions were well known, even if the scale of the problem and its implications for the integrity of the European Monetary Union (EMU) itself were underappreciated. The vulnerability existed because of a lack of political will to alter the regulatory status quo rather than an incomplete theoretical understanding or a lack of available policy alternatives. A certain degree of instability is inherent in any financial system, given the fundamental asymmetry of banks relying on on-demand deposits and other short-term borrowing to fund long-term liabilities such as mortgages. However, systems such as Canada's have shown much greater stability, demonstrating that the problem is not unmanageable.[73] Moreover, the policy solution, a transfer of regulation to a supranational body, has been clear throughout this period as well.

The barriers to stabilizing European finance, in short, have been due to political resistance rather than a theoretical weakness or lack of known solutions. The large transnational banks, such as France's BNP Paribas or Germany's Deutsche Bank, have been able to grow to global competitiveness because of their ability to access a customer base across Europe, and therefore strongly oppose any move to retreat to national banking.[74] They would, however, be generally willing to accept a shift to supranational regulation. While they benefited from national protection in their earlier growth stages, they are now large enough to appreciate the benefits of supranational regulation in removing the friction of adapting to different national regulatory systems in different markets and in removing the remaining regulatory protectionism of their smaller, nationally focused rivals. This leaves them in a position of ordering their preferences first for supranational regulation, then the underregulated status quo, and last Balkanization of finance. The smaller nationally focused banks, on the other hand, would welcome a Balkanization of European finance, which would diminish the impact of foreign competition. However, if they cannot get that, they would prefer the maintenance of national regulators, as those national regulators could continue to provide some limited protectionism in the face of competition from transnational banks. Therefore, their preference order would be split between two groups. Some, especially the more vulnerable, would first favor Balkanization, then the unstable status quo, and last supranational regulation. Others, typically those in a more stable position, may be reconciled to the status quo but favor disintegrating Balkanization over deeper integration if the status quo is no longer sustainable. This combination of preferences in the financial world creates a situation where the stable political compromise became a combination of supranational banking and national regulation, even at the cost of perpetual economic vulnerability to crises. It also means that crises become an opportunity to make substantial overhauls, not because crises change the positions of either the large or small banks, but because they create opportunities for those banks to sway other actors either previously indifferent to the problems or reluctant to support either integration or disintegration over maintenance of the status quo to take a side, and thus assemble a winning coalition in favor of reform.

An added political barrier to action emphasized in particular by intergovernmental accounts comes from the fear of the transfer union implications of a joint resolution mechanism for banks in the mostly northern creditor countries. This fear became increasingly acute as the twenty-first century progressed. Banks across the eurozone had significant amounts of bad debt coming out of both the subprime mortgage bubble of the early 2000s and the expansion of credit in the southern states with the introduction of the euro. However, the southern states stricken by sovereign debt crises in the 2010s lacked the resources to clean up their banks in distress, while the northern states still could afford to underwrite legacy bad debts in their banks. This meant that a common system of bank resolution would likely result in northern creditor states contributing to bank resolution in the southern debtor states more than the other way around. Therefore, while actors in the northern states may have supported a banking union without these legacy issues, fear of this underwriting led them to resist common resolution and deposit insurance unless these legacy bad debts could be resolved without a contribution from them.

## Staggered Integration in Practice

This political dynamic means that, despite an understanding of the problem and its possible solutions, very little changed in European financial regulatory integration until a series of crises hit starting in 2007. The 2001 Lamfalussy Report highlighted the vulnerabilities, but the Lamfalussy Process created out of that report focused only on a modest and voluntary harmonizing national of regulatory standards rather than creating a common European regulator.[75] In some ways, this outcome exacerbated the problem by increasing cross-national banking and allowing banks to grow even larger. Without the creation of a true supranational regulator, the overall effect intensified rather than mitigated the issues identified by Schoenmaker.

**50** Crises and Integration in European Banking Union

Starting with the response to the 2007–09 Transatlantic Banking Crisis, a series of reforms were introduced that offered an increasing, but still partial, attempt to address these vulnerabilities. The European System of Financial Supervision (ESFS), including the European Banking Authority, was introduced in 2011, and increased harmonization of national regulators through the introduction of a common rulebook for financial regulation, though actual regulation remained in the hands of national regulators. The introduction of the Single Supervisory Mechanism in 2014 made the European Central Bank (ECB) the direct regulator of systemically important banks in the eurozone, introducing a common supranational regulator for the first time. However, the SSM gave the ECB only indirect supervision of nonsystemically important institutions, with direct supervision still in the hands of national regulators, and did not cover non-eurozone EU banks at all.[76] The Single Resolution Mechanism (SRM), also introduced in 2014 and fully operational by 2016, centralized resolution of failing banks out of a common funding source, the Single Resolution Fund (SRF). However, the SRF remained only partially funded and arguably insufficient for the scale of potential challenges, and critics argued that the SRM's complicated decision-making process, with a large role for national governments, would be too cumbersome and slow-moving in a large-scale banking crisis.[77] Finally, as of 2022, efforts to introduce a common European Deposit Insurance Scheme and European Capital Markets Union remain stalled, despite the former being described as the essential "third pillar" of a complete and robust banking union alongside the SSM and SRM, and the latter offering a way to diminish the threat of banking crises to the broader economy by encouraging the development of nonbank channels of finance to diminish the central role of banks.

This pattern of development is not obvious, and its stalling out cannot be easily explained through a purely functional interpretation. The refusal to introduce EDIS even after the introduction of the SRM is particularly curious. If anything, the SRM offers a greater potential possibility of burden-sharing among the member states. A well-functioning deposit guarantee scheme is a deposit guarantee scheme that is likely never to be used. The purpose of deposit insurance is nominally to ensure that depositors are made whole in the event of a bank failure, but the greatest impact of such a scheme is likely to be felt in its role in preventing bank failures through panics. In a classic bank run, even a healthy bank can be brought down due to the self-fulfilling prophecy nature of a run.[78] In the absence of deposit insurance, savers know that the bank cannot afford to pay out all deposits at once. Therefore, if a critical mass of depositors start to withdraw their savings, the rational thing for an individual to do is to withdraw their own savings, even if the cumulative effect is to cause a bank to fail. Deposit insurance short circuits that process, by ensuring that individuals' assets are protected and thus that there is no need to participate in a run. Therefore, a well-funded deposit insurance scheme will not only be unlikely to actually need to pay out, but will also help ensure that the more general resolution fund will never be needed. A resolution fund, on the other hand, does not prevent bank failure in the same way, but merely serves to limit the damage when a bank fails. Therefore, if anything, fear of interstate transfers should be more of a barrier to the SRM than to EDIS, but that was not the case.

This pattern of development also cannot be easily explained through structural changes or changing preferences. Structurally, there have been no substantial changes to the broad architecture of finance in the European Union since the introduction of EMU. The one exception to this lack of structural change, Brexit removing the City of London, previously the Union's largest financial center, from the integrated single market, produced a crisis that *didn't* prompt significant reform. Bank preferences did change in the 1990s and the 2000s, as transnational banks outgrew the need for national protection and came to value the advantages of supranational regulation, but that change mostly happened before the wave of crises starting in 2007, and so cannot really explain the changes in the subsequent decade and a half.[79]

What did change in that period was the sustainability of the status quo, as it was battered by a series of crises. Since these crises had an uneven impact on a persisting problems, this makes European financial integration a prime subject for an examination of the origins of crises and how they relate to potential change in regulation. The crises that struck European finance varied in both origin and intensity, and they in turn produced reforms of varying degrees of intensity, as summarized in Figure 2.2. Two crises, the 2007–09 Transatlantic Banking Crisis and the 2010–14 European Debt Crisis, originated in the financial system itself, while the other two, the 2016 vote for Britain to exit the European Union and the 2020–21 COVID-19 Pandemic, created threats to the financial system and its integration but originated elsewhere. They also varied in intensity. The Debt Crisis and the Pandemic threatened potentially catastrophic dangers to European financial integration, while the threats from the Banking Crisis and Brexit were more modest. As will be explored in later chapters, these differences would have substantial consequences for the reform outcomes of the different crises.

## 52 Crises and Integration in European Banking Union

|  | | **Origin** | |
|---|---|---|---|
|  | | Endogenous | Exogenous |
| **Threat** | **Moderate** | *2007–09 Banking Crisis*<br><br>Moderate<br>"Patch-Up" Reform<br><br>Creation of ESFS | *Brexit*<br><br>No Reform<br><br>– |
|  | **Severe** | *2010–14 Debt Crisis*<br><br>Substantial Reform &<br>"Monnet Crisis"<br><br>*Creation of SSM, SRM* | *2020–21 COVID Pandemic*<br><br>Moderate<br>"Weatherproofing" Reform<br><br>*SRF linked to ESM* |

**Figure 2.2** Crises and European Financial Integration

# Alternative Explanations

It is of course worth considering alternative explanations for the pattern of responses to crises, both within finance and more broadly in European integration. A survey of the literature suggests four major alternative explanations. Each, however, are more limited in their explanatory power than the theory outlined in the previous section, both within finance and more generally.

## Idiosyncrasies of Individual Cases

The first alternative explanation is simply that every crisis is essentially sui generis, with the outcomes dictated by the specific constellation of details of the crisis at hand and which individuals and groups are politically ascendant when the crisis hits. This is essentially the default position assumed by much of the existing literature on European crises, which engages with individual crises but without a comparative examination of why different crises produce different outcomes. At best, much of this literature takes an extremely high-level focus on whether supranational actors such as the European Commission and European Central Bank or national or subnational actors consistently play the most pivotal role. Anghel and Jones make this case explicitly, arguing that cases with broad similarities have often produced differing outcomes.[80] They, however, focus on the overall direction of European integration, rather than changes within specific sectors.

While many of these ad hoc explanations offer compelling accounts for individual crises, it is theoretically unsatisfying to dismiss the possibility of systematic accounts of why some crises produce deeper integration than others. It is also unnecessary. As will be demonstrated in the subsequent chapters, it is possible to build a credible framework to systematically explain the variation in response to crises, especially if the focus is on a specific sector rather than the overall direction of European integration.

## Structural Changes on the Private Side

One alternative explanation would be to look at how the constellation of private interests has systematically changed to favor or oppose deeper integration from one crisis to the next. This explanation fits most closely with the Intergovernmentalists' focus on the shifting power of pro- and anti-integration interest groups and coalitions within the member states, with a change in the balance of power for whatever reason the key determinant as to whether integration proceeds, stalls out, or reverses.

Within European finance, the most prominent of these explanations is a focus on the shifting interests of "national champions," large financial conglomerates promoted by member states to ensure that they would be the home country of Europe's largest banks. Such national champions favored national regulation in the early stages of their development, when the benefits of regulatory favoritism by their home country outweighed the friction created by dealing with different regulatory environments in their foreign operations.[81] However, once those large banks reached a certain scale, that calculus flipped, and the national champions came to see national regulation as more hindrance than help. In their view, national regulatory favoritism now benefited smaller banks in both home and host countries, and the national champions now saw a common European regulator as more advantageous.

This account is compelling in itself, but suffers from two problems as an explanation for the pattern of response to the crises hitting European finance in the twenty-first century. The first problem is that the strongest moves toward European integration, the creation of the Single Supervisory Mechanism and of the Single Resolution Mechanism, came at a moment when the national champions were in fact retreating from transnational operations to focus on their home markets.[82] Therefore, it would be an odd moment for them to push for transnational regulation. Additionally, it would mean that the most significant advancement of transnational regulation came at a moment of weakness, as the retreat to home markets was a defensive strategy for banks battered by both the 2007–09 Banking Crisis and the 2010–14 Debt Crisis.

The second problem is that it is not clear why reform has stalled since the Debt Crisis. The large French, Italian, and Spanish banks still have cause to want a European Deposit Insurance Scheme. The large German banks have largely opposed the specific EDIS proposals put forward to date, but have conceded that *some* form of European deposit insurance would be advantageous.[83] This means the disagreement is not over the broad concept of EDIS, but a seemingly bridgeable one over details of implementation. Moreover, Deutsche Bank in particular, with its substantial investment bank operations, would have clear reason to push for Capital Markets Union, giving it a goal in common with the non-German European banks with large investment arms.[84] All of these large transnational banks should want an expansion of the Single Supervisory Mechanism, so that the ECB, and not national regulators, directly regulates their smaller rivals. Advocates of these reforms attempted to use both Brexit and the COVID-19 Pandemic to create momentum for completion of banking union, but to no avail. Since the large banks were both stronger and more transnational at that time than they were at the time of the creation of the SSM and SRM, this explanation is incomplete.

More broadly such a focus on structural changes may be viable within an individual sector but does not translate well across sectors. Therefore, it provides at best a limited basis on which to build a general theory of which crises are most likely to drive deeper integration.

## Changes to the Regulatory Architecture

Another alternative explanation is that the existing reforms have "satisficed" the need for change, and that subsequent crises have simply not been large enough to drive deeper integration.[85] Within finance, the argument would be that the Single Supervisory Mechanism and Single Resolution Mechanism, were good enough to shore up the weaknesses in the European financial regulatory architecture. Their creation sapped the momentum for further reform, which may be regarded as "nice to have" but not necessary. As will be discussed in Chapter 4, this explanation carries some power specifically within the Debt Crisis, when initial reforms diminished the immediate threat and debates shifted out of emergency politics and back to normal politics before EDIS could be enacted.

On a longer scale, this satisficing explanation becomes less compelling. Very few observers on either the private or public side think that the flaws in European financial architecture are fixed in a stable and long-term way.[86] Virtually all major players see the need for further reform. Rather, the debate has stalled out as to the form of that reform. Broadly speaking, the debate splits into three camps. The first camp, those favoring an immediate EDIS that would also cover legacy debts of the previous crises, including France and most of the southern economies, prioritize immediate stability gains. The second camp, including Germany and most of the northern economies, want an EDIS that excludes those legacy debts, especially sovereign debts, for fear of introducing moral hazard and a subsidization of the southern economies by the northerners. Finally, a third, smaller, camp, dominated by smaller banks, argues that the solution should be a retreat from the integration that already exists and a Balkanization of European finance. What unites all of these groups, regardless of their specific preferences, is the sense that the current status quo is not sustainable, and is vulnerable to a future crisis of sufficient scale. The question that remains, therefore, is why the crises since the Debt Crisis were insufficient to drive a compromise on the solutions, especially given the general agreement on the problems broadly speaking.

More broadly, this explanation falls short because it cannot account for why severe crises have failed to produce substantial integration in multiple cases. The second dimension of crisis origin therefore provides a crucial supplement to explain why crisis severity alone cannot account for why some severe crises fail to produce significant reform and some moderate crises produce reform and others do not.

## Growing Euroskepticism

A final alternative explanation, drawing on the insights of the postfunctionalists, argues that deeper integration has simply become more difficult over time, as euroskeptic attitudes have spread and the appetite for integration has weakened. Although this account cannot explain why the Debt Crisis produced deeper integration than the earlier Banking Crisis, it offers a potential explanation for why deeper integration has not followed since by arguing that increasingly potent anti-integration forces have blocked any further reforms.

However, this explanation has its own set of problems. The first is that euroskepticism has not manifested as a chief barrier toward further

**56** Crises and Integration in European Banking Union

movement on EDIS and CMU. Rather, debates have frozen over *how* to achieve deeper integration through EDIS, not *whether* to do so or not. More broadly, euroskeptic attitudes appeared to peak shortly after Brexit. After a brief surge when anti-EU actors sought to follow the British path out of the Union, the practical consequences of Brexit seem to have dampened the appeal of such arguments. If anything, the COVID-19 Pandemic and more recently European solidarity in the face of the Russian invasion of Ukraine have deepened European solidarity and dampened euroskepticism's appeal. However, this shift has not been accompanied by deeper moves toward financial regulatory integration.

As will be demonstrated in the subsequent chapters, each of these alternative explanations fall short in explaining the impact of crises on European integration. Although obviously some factors will vary from crisis to crisis, and sector to sector, a focus on origin and severity of crisis provides a sturdy guideline for identifying a clear pattern of which crises cause deep, moderate, or minimal integration beyond ad hoc explanations and in the absence of structural changes in either private or public systems.

## Notes

1. Uriel Rosenthal, Arjen Boin, and Louise K. Comfort, *Managing Crises: Threats, Dilemmas, Opportunities* (Springfield, IL: Charles C Thomas Publisher, 2001), 10. Cited in Marianne Riddervold, Jarle Trondal, and Akasemi Newsome, "Theoretical Approaches to Crisis: An Introduction," in *The Palgrave Handbook of EU Crises*, ed. Marianne Riddervold, Jarle Trondal, and Akasemi Newsome, Palgrave Studies in European Union Politics (Cham: Springer International Publishing, 2021), 51–60, doi:10.1007/978-3-030-51791-5_2; Maïa K. Davis Cross, *The Politics of Crisis in Europe* (Cambridge, United Kingdom; New York, NY: Cambridge University Press, 2017); Arjen Boin et al., *The European Union as Crisis Manager: Patterns and Prospects*, electronic resource (Cambridge, England; New York: Cambridge University Press, 2013), https://ebookcentral.proquest.com/lib/uma/detail.action?docID=1303716.
2. G. John Ikenberry, "The Rise of China and the Future of the West-Can the Liberal System Survive," *Foreign Affairs* 87 (2008): 23.
3. Giovanni Capoccia and R. Daniel Kelemen, "The Study of Critical Junctures: Theory, Narrative, and Counterfactuals in Historical Institutionalism," *World Politics* 59, no. 3 (2007): 341–369; Nathalie Brack and Seda Gürkan, eds., *Theorising the Crises of the European Union* (London: Routledge, 2020), doi:10.4324/9781003001423; Colin Hay, "Crisis and the Structural Transformation of the State: Interrogating the Process of Change," *The British Journal of Politics and International Relations* 1, no. 3 (1999): 317–344; Leonardo Morlino and Cecilia Emma Sottilotta, eds., *The Politics of the Eurozone Crisis in Southern Europe: A Comparative Reappraisal*, 1st ed. 2020 edition (Cham, Switzerland: Palgrave Macmillan, 2020); Benjamin Braun, "Preparedness, Crisis Management

# Building a Theory of Crises and European Integration    57

and Policy Change: The Euro Area at the Critical Juncture of 2008–2013," *The British Journal of Politics and International Relations* 17, no. 3 (2015): 419–441; Mathis Heinrich and Amelie Kutter, "A Critical Juncture in EU Integration? The Eurozone Crisis and Its Management 2010–2012," in *Moments of Truth: The Politics of Financial Crises in Comparative Perspective*, ed. Francisco Panizza and George Philip (New York: Routledge, 2014); Alastair Stark, "New Institutionalism, Critical Junctures and Post-Crisis Policy Reform," *Australian Journal of Political Science* 53, no. 1 (2018): 24–39.

4. Jo, *European Myths*; Naomi Klein, *The Shock Doctrine: The Rise of Disaster Capitalism* (Macmillan, 2007); Uwe Wunderlich and Stefan Gänzle, "Asean and the EU in Times of Crises: Critical Junctures from the Perspective of Comparative Regionalism," in *Theorising the Crises of the European Union* (New York: Routledge, 2020); Stefanie Wöhl et al., eds., "The State of the European Union: Fault Lines in European Integration," *Springer EBooks*, (New York: Springer, 2020); White, *Politics of Last Resort*; Juergen Habermas, *Legitimation Crisis*, trans. Thomas McCarthy, 1st edition (Boston, Mass: Beacon Press, 1975).

5. Stefan Olsson, *Crisis Management in the European Union. [Electronic Resource]: Cooperation in the Face of Emergencies*, Springer EBooks (Springer Berlin Heidelberg, 2009), http://proxy.mtholyoke.edu:2048/login?url=https://search.ebscohost.com/login.aspx?direct=true&db=cat06626a&AN=mhc.015053998&site=eds-live&scope=site.

6. Wunderlich and Gänzle, "Asean and the EU in Times of Crises."

7. Frank Schimmelfennig, "Brexit: Differentiated Disintegration in the European Union," *Journal of European Public Policy* 25, no. 8 (August 2018): 1154–1173, doi:10.1080/13501763.2018.1467954.

8. Hans-Jürgen Bieling, "Shattered Expectations: The Defeat of European Ambitions of Global Financial Reform," in *Europe's Place in Global Financial Governance after the Crisis* (New York: Routledge, 2014), 31–51.

9. Hay, "Crisis and the Structural Transformation of the State."

10. Cross, *The Politics of Crisis in Europe*; Maïa K. Davis Cross and Xinru Ma, "A Media Perspective on European Crises," in *Europe's Prolonged Crisis: The Making or the Unmaking of a Political Union*, ed. Hans-Jörg Trenz, Carlo Ruzza, and Virginie Guiraudon, Palgrave Studies in European Political Sociology (London: Palgrave Macmillan UK, 2015), 210–231, doi:10.1057/9781137493675_11; Maïa K. Davis Cross, "Social Constructivism," in *The Palgrave Handbook of EU Crises*, ed. Marianne Riddervold, Jarle Trondal, and Akasemi Newsome, Palgrave Studies in European Union Politics (Cham: Springer International Publishing, 2021), 195–211, doi:10.1007/978-3-030-51791-5_10.

11. Stark, "New Institutionalism, Critical Junctures and Post-Crisis Policy Reform."

12. White, *Politics of Last Resort*.

13. Charlotte Burns, Judith Clifton, and Lucia Quaglia, "Explaining Policy Change in the EU: Financial Reform after the Crisis," *Journal of European Public Policy* 25, no. 5 (2018): 728–746.

14. Hay, "Crisis and the Structural Transformation of the State."

15. Lukas Oberndorfer, "Between the Normal State and an Exceptional State Form: Authoritarian Competitive Statism and the Crisis of Democracy in Europe," in *The State of the European Union: Fault Lines in European Integration*, ed. Stefanie Wöhl et al., Staat—Souveränität—Nation (Wiesbaden: Springer Fachmedien, 2020), 23–44, doi:10.1007/978-3-658-25419-3_2.

## 58  Crises and Integration in European Banking Union

16. John W. Kingdon, *Agendas, Alternatives, and Public Policies*, Updated second edition, Longman Classics in Political Science (Boston: Longman, 2011).

17. Christof Roos and Natascha Zaun, "The Global Economic Crisis as a Critical Juncture? The Crisis's Impact on Migration Movements and Policies in Europe and the US," *Journal of Ethnic and Migration Studies* 42, no. 10 (2016): 1579–1589.

18. Mark Copelovitch and David A. Singer, "Tipping the (Im)Balance: Capital Inflows, Financial Market Structure, and Banking Crises," *Economics & Politics* 29, no. 3 (2017): 179–208, doi:https://doi.org/10.1111/ecpo.12097.

19. European Commission official, Interview by author, 2022.

20. Wunderlich and Gänzle, "Asean and the EU in Times of Crises."

21. Hodson and Puetter, "The European Union in Disequilibrium"; Hooghe and Marks, "Grand Theories of European Integration in the Twenty-First Century"; Theresa Kuhn, "Grand Theories of European Integration Revisited: Does Identity Politics Shape the Course of European Integration?," *Journal of European Public Policy* 26, no. 8 (August 2019): 1213–1230, doi:10.1080/13501763.2019.1622588; Riddervold, Trondal, and Newsome, "Theoretical Approaches to Crisis"; Frank Schimmelfennig and Thomas Winzen, "Grand Theories, Differentiated Integration," *Journal of European Public Policy* 26, no. 8 (August 2019): 1172–1192, doi:10.1080/13501763.2019.1576761.

22. Paul Pierson, *The Path to European Integration: A Historical Institutionalist Analysis* (London: Palgrave Macmillan, 1998).

23. Arne Niemann, "Neofunctionalism," in *The Palgrave Handbook of EU Crises*, ed. Marianne Riddervold, Jarle Trondal, and Akasemi Newsome, Palgrave Studies in European Union Politics (Cham: Springer International Publishing, 2021), 115–133, doi:10.1007/978-3-030-51791-5_6; Frank Schimmelfennig, "Liberal Intergovernmentalism," in *The Palgrave Handbook of EU Crises*, ed. Marianne Riddervold, Jarle Trondal, and Akasemi Newsome, Palgrave Studies in European Union Politics (Cham: Springer International Publishing, 2021), 61–78, doi:10.1007/978-3-030-51791-5_3; Vivien Ann Schmidt, *Europe's Crisis of Legitimacy: Governing by Rules and Ruling by Numbers in the Eurozone*, First edition (Oxford, UK: Oxford University Press, 2020), http://proxy.mtholyoke.edu:2048/login?url=https://search.ebscohost.com/login. aspx?direct=true&db=cat06626a&AN=mhc.017482341&site=eds-live&scope=site; Henry Farrell, "The Shared Challenges of Institutional Theories: Rational Choice, Historical Institutionalism, and Sociological Institutionalism," in *Knowledge and Institutions*, ed. Johannes Glückler, Roy Suddaby, and Regina Lenz, Knowledge and Space (Cham: Springer International Publishing, 2018), 23–44, doi:10.1007/978-3-319-75328-7_2.

24. Erik Jones, R. Daniel Kelemen, and Sophie Meunier, "Failing Forward? The Euro Crisis and the Incomplete Nature of European Integration," *Comparative Political Studies* 49, no. 7 (June 2016): 1010–1034, doi:10.1177/0010414015617966; Ioannou, Leblond, and Niemann, "European Integration and the Crisis"; Niemann, "Neofunctionalism"; Dennis Smith, "Not Just Singing the Blues: Dynamics of the EU Crisis," in *Europe's Prolonged Crisis: The Making or the Unmaking of a Political Union*, ed. Hans-Jörg Trenz, Carlo Ruzza, and Virginie Guiraudon, Palgrave Studies in European Political Sociology (London: Palgrave Macmillan UK, 2015), 23–43, doi:10.1057/9781137493675_2.

25. Carroll L. Estes, "Social Security: The Social Construction of a Crisis," *The Milbank Memorial Fund Quarterly. Health and Society* (1983): 445–461; Cross, *The Politics of Crisis in Europe*.

Building a Theory of Crises and European Integration   59

26. Niemann, Explaining Decisions in the European Union; Hans Vollaard, *European Disintegration: A Search for Explanations* (New York: Springer, 2018).
27. Hay, "Crisis and the Structural Transformation of the State."
28. Benjamin Farrand and Marco Rizzi, "There Is No (Legal) Alternative: Codifying Economic Ideology into Law," in *The Crisis behind the Eurocrisis: The Eurocrisis as a Multidimensional Systemic Crisis of the EU*, ed. Eva Nanopoulos and Fotis Vergis (Cambridge: Cambridge University Press, 2019), 23–48, doi:10.1017/9781108598859.002.
29. Douglas W. Diamond and Philip H. Dybvig, "Bank Runs, Deposit Insurance, and Liquidity," *Journal of Political Economy* 91, no. 3 (1983): 401–419.
30. Farrand and Rizzi, "There Is No (Legal) Alternative."
31. Klein, *The Shock Doctrine*.
32. Cross, "Social Constructivism"; Marianna Patrona and Joanna Thornborrow, "Mediated Constructions of Crisis," in *The Mediated Politics of Europe* (New York: Springer, 2017), 59–88.
33. George Ross, *The European Union and Its Crises: Through the Eyes of the Brussels' Elite* (New York: Palgrave Macmillan, 2011), 1, http://proxy.mtholyoke.edu:2048/login?url=https://search.ebscohost.com/login.aspx?direct=true&db=cat06626a&AN=mhc.012139324&site=eds-live&scope=site.
34. John R. Searle, *The Construction of Social Reality* (New York: Simon and Schuster, 1995); Erik Jones, "The Economic Mythology of European Integration," *JCMS: Journal of Common Market Studies* 48, no. 1 (2010): 89–109, doi:10.1111/j.1468-5965.2009.02043.x; Hay, "Crisis and the Structural Transformation of the State."
35. David Archard, "Myths, Lies and Historical Truth: A Defence of Nationalism," *Political Studies* 43, no. 3 (1995): 472–481; Vincent Della Sala, "Political Myth, Mythology and the European Union," *JCMS: Journal of Common Market Studies* 48, no. 1 (2010): 1–19, doi:10.1111/j.1468-5965.2009.02039.x.
36. Bieling, "Shattered Expectations"; Schimmelfennig, "Brexit."
37. Riddervold, Trondal, and Newsome, "Theoretical Approaches to Crisis."
38. Hay, "Crisis and the Structural Transformation of the State."
39. This of course raises questions as to whether the objective crisis can be understood at all, or if social construction so permeates as to make objective reality unobservable. This analysis assumes a constructivist rather than critical theoretical epistemology.
40. Della Sala, "Political Myth, Mythology and the European Union"; Jo, *European Myths*; Hay, "Crisis and the Structural Transformation of the State"; Hans Blumenberg, *The Legitimacy of the Modern Age* (Cambridge, MA: MIT Press, 1985); John W. Meyer and Brian Rowan, "Institutionalized Organizations: Formal Structure as Myth and Ceremony," *American Journal of Sociology* 83, no. 2 (1977): 340–363.
41. Pinar Akman and Hussein Kassim, "Myths and Myth-Making in the European Union: The Institutionalization and Interpretation of EU Competition Policy," *JCMS: Journal of Common Market Studies* 48, no. 1 (2010): 111–132, doi:10.1111/j.1468-5965.2009.02044.x.
42. Jo, *European Myths*.
43. White, *Politics of Last Resort*.
44. Jones, "The Economic Mythology of European Integration."
45. Sebastiaan Princen, *Agenda-Setting in the European Union*, Palgrave Studies in European Union Politics (New York: Palgrave Macmillan, 2009), http://proxy.mtholyoke.

60 Crises and Integration in European Banking Union

edu:2048/login?url=https://search.ebscohost.com/login.aspx?direct=true&db=cat066 26a&AN=mhc.010916262&site=eds-live&scope=site.

46. Niemann, *Explaining Decisions in the European Union*; Vollaard, *European Disintegration*.

47. Kenneth Dyson, "Playing for High Stakes: The Eurozone Crisis," *The European Union in Crisis*, 2017, 54–76.

48. Morlino and Sottilotta, *The Politics of the Eurozone Crisis in Southern Europe*.

49. Kathleen R. McNamara, *The Currency of Ideas: Monetary Politics in the European Union*, Cornell Studies in Political Economy (Ithaca, NY: Cornell University Press, 2019).

50. Brunnermeier, James, and Landau, *The Euro and the Battle of Ideas*.

51. Nicolas Jabko, *Playing the Market: A Political Strategy for Uniting Europe, 1985–2005* (Ithaca, NY: Cornell University Press, 2012), http://ebookcentral.proquest.com/lib/mtholyoke/detail.action?docID=3138289; Nicolas Jabko, "The Hidden Face of the Euro," *Journal of European Public Policy* 17, no. 3 (2010): 318–334; Craig Parsons, *A Certain Idea of Europe* (Ithaca, NY: Cornell University Press, 2003).

52. Jabko, *Playing the Market*.

53. Jabko.

54. Catherine E. de Vries, *Euroscepticism and the Future of European Integration* (Oxford; New York, NY: Oxford University Press, 2018).

55. White, *Politics of Last Resort*.

56. Asimina Michailidou and Hans-Jörg Trenz, "The European Crisis and the Media: Media Autonomy, Public Perceptions and New Forms of Political Engagement," in *Europe's Prolonged Crisis: The Making or the Unmaking of a Political Union*, ed. Hans-Jörg Trenz, Carlo Ruzza, and Virginie Guiraudon, Palgrave Studies in European Political Sociology (London: Palgrave Macmillan UK, 2015), 232–250, doi:10.1057/9781137493675_12.

57. Parsons, *A Certain Idea of Europe*.

58. Arjen Boin and Mark Rhinard, "Crisis Management Performance and the European Union: The Case of COVID-19," *Journal of European Public Policy* 30, no. 4 (April 2023): 655–675, doi:10.1080/13501763.2022.2141304.

59. Jones, Kelemen, and Meunier, "Failing Forward?"; Erik Jones, R. Daniel Kelemen, and Sophie Meunier, "Failing Forward? Crises and Patterns of European Integration," *Journal of European Public Policy* (Taylor & Francis, 2021).

60. Brooks et al., "EU Health Policy in the Aftermath of COVID-19."

61. Veronica Anghel and Erik Jones, "Is Europe Really Forged through Crisis? Pandemic EU and the Russia—Ukraine War," *Journal of European Public Policy* 30, no. 4 (April 2023): 766–786, doi:10.1080/13501763.2022.2140820.

62. Bundesverband deutscher Banken official, Interview by author, 2022.

63. Vollaard, *European Disintegration*.

64. Schimmelfennig, "Liberal Intergovernmentalism."

65. Peter A. Hall, "Policy Paradigms, Social Learning, and the State: The Case of Economic Policymaking in Britain," *Comparative Politics* (1993): 275–296.

66. Stark, "New Institutionalism, Critical Junctures and Post-Crisis Policy Reform."

67. Hall, "Policy Paradigms, Social Learning, and the State."

68. Hall.

69. Dirk Schoenmaker, "The Financial Trilemma," *Economics Letters* 111, no. 1 (2011): 57–59; Dirk Schoenmaker, *Governance of International Banking: The Financial Trilemma* (Oxford: Oxford University Press, 2013).

70. Hay, "Crisis and the Structural Transformation of the State."
71. Eirik Tegle Stenstad and Bent Sofus Tranøy, "Failing Forward in Financial Stability Regulation," in *The Palgrave Handbook of EU Crises*, ed. Marianne Riddervold, Jarle Trondal, and Akasemi Newsome, Palgrave Studies in European Union Politics (Cham: Springer International Publishing, 2021), 401–419, doi:10.1007/978-3-030-51791-5_22.
72. Alexandre Lamfalussy et al., "Final Report of The Committee of Wise Men on The Regulation of European Securities Markets," ESMA document (Brussels: European Council, February 2001).
73. Charles W. Calomiris and Stephen H. Haber, *Fragile by Design* (Princeton, NJ: Princeton University Press, 2014). The United States of course has also had its own issues with fragility, but that can itself be attributed to policy choices in the US to favor profitability over stability rather than a fundamental instability in the sector.
74. David Howarth and Lucia Quaglia, *The Political Economy of European Banking Union* (New York: Oxford University Press, 2016).
75. Michelle Everson and Ellen Vos, "European Union Agencies," in *The Palgrave Handbook of EU Crises*, ed. Marianne Riddervold, Jarle Trondal, and Akasemi Newsome, Palgrave Studies in European Union Politics (Cham: Springer International Publishing, 2021), 315–337, doi:10.1007/978-3-030-51791-5_17.
76. Non-eurozone EU members are able to join the SSM and SRM voluntarily. However, to date, no state has chosen to do so. Katalin Méró and Dora Piroska, "Banking Union and Banking Nationalism—Explaining Opt-out Choices of Hungary, Poland and the Czech Republic," *Policy and Society* 35, no. 3 (2016): 215–226.
77. Karen Braun-Munzinger et al., "From Deadlocks to Breakthroughs: How We Can Complete the Banking Union and Why It Matters to All of Us," in *New Challenges for the Eurozone Governance: Joint Solutions for Common Threats?*, ed. José Caetano, Isabel Vieira, and António Caleiro (Cham: Springer International Publishing, 2021), 69–90, doi:10.1007/978-3-030-62372-2_4; Anna Gelpern and Nicolas Veron, "Europe's Banking Union Should Learn the Right Lessons from the US," *Bruegel-Blogs*, October 2020, http://proxy.mtholyoke.edu:2048/login?url=https://search.ebscohost.com/login.aspx?direct=true&db=edsgao&AN=edsgcl.640581704&site=eds-live&scope=site; David G. Mayes, "Banking Union: The Problem of Untried Systems," *Journal of Economic Policy Reform* 21, no. 3 (September 2018): 178–189, doi:10.1080/17487870.2017.1396901; Giuseppe Pennisi, "The Impervious Road to the Single Resolution Mechanism (Srm) of the European Banking Union (Ebu)," *Rivista Di Studi Politici Internazionali* 82, no. 2 (326) (April 2015): 229–238.
78. Diamond and Dybvig, "Bank Runs, Deposit Insurance, and Liquidity."
79. Lucia Quaglia and Aneta Spendzharova, "The Conundrum of Solving 'Too Big to Fail' in the European Union: Supranationalization at Different Speeds," *JCMS: Journal of Common Market Studies* 55, no. 5 (2017): 1110–1126; Lucia Quaglia, David Howarth, and Moritz Liebe, "The Political Economy of European Capital Markets Union," *JCMS: Journal of Common Market Studies* 54 (2016): 185; Jakub Gren, David Howarth, and Lucia Quaglia, "Supranational Banking Supervision in Europe: The Construction of a Credible Watchdog," *JCMS: Journal of Common Market Studies* 53 (2015): 181.
80. Anghel and Jones, "Is Europe Really Forged through Crisis?"
81. Rachel A. Epstein and Martin Rhodes, "International in Life, National in Death? Banking Nationalism on the Road to Banking Union," 2016a.

82. Christian de Boissieu, "The Banking Union Revisited," in *Financial Regulation in the EU* (New York: Springer, 2017), 85–103.
83. Bundesverband deutscher Banken official, Interview by author.
84. Tony Boyd, "Brexit Suits Germany's Merkel," *Australian Financial Review*, June 2016.
85. Jones, Kelemen, and Meunier, "Failing Forward?"; Stenstad and Tranøy, "Failing Forward in Financial Stability Regulation."
86. Bundesbank Official, Interview by author; Bundesverband deutscher Banken official, Interview by author; European Commission official, Interview by author.

# 3
# The 2007–09 Banking Crisis

Patch-Up Reform and Creation of the European
System of Financial Supervision

## Introduction

The first major shock to the European financial system of the twenty-first
century was the Transatlantic Banking Crisis of 2007–09. The wave of bank
failures starting in 2007 and peaking in the fall of 2008 drew in many European states, as well as the US. While the European Central Bank (ECB)
provided liquidity support for affected eurozone member states, this wave
of bank failures would primarily be managed by the affected member states
themselves, which spent hundreds of billions of euros or pounds to contain the crisis. Unlike the subsequent European Debt Crisis, which also was
largely driven by bank failures and weaknesses, this action did not strain
the budgets of the affected states to the point of risking a sovereign debt
crisis, and as such did not pose a threat to European integration of the
magnitude of the subsequent crisis. Nevertheless, the wave of bank failures
across Europe revealed significant flaws in the regulation of cross-border
banking in the European Union, especially in determining the responsible
national regulator for cross-national banking operations. These flaws exacerbated the crisis in Europe, especially in the cases of the Benelux bank
Fortis and the German lender HypoRE and its Irish arm Depfa. As such,
reformers used the crisis to push for an overhaul of the European system
of overseeing national regulators, replacing the Lamfalussy Committees with
the new European System of Financial Supervision (ESFS), including the creation of the European Banking Authority (EBA) and European Securities and
Markets Authority (ESMA). These reforms increased coordination and communication between national regulators, without displacing those national
regulators as the central authorities in charge of financial supervision. However, more ambitious proposals, effectively amounting to the introduction
of a full European banking union including European supervision, resolution, and deposit insurance, failed to gain traction. The Banking Crisis, being

---

*Crises and Integration in European Banking Union.* Christopher Mitchell, Oxford University Press.
© Christopher Mitchell (2023). DOI: 10.1093/oso/9780198889069.003.0003

essentially manageable by the member states themselves, failed to generate a severe enough threat to drive such substantial reforms. It would take the following Debt Crisis, with a much greater threat to European integration, to motivate more substantial reforms, though even there those efforts met with only partial success.

# Classification of the Crisis

The 2007–09 Banking Crisis provides an example of an endogenous moderate crisis. While there may be some debate as to whether the crisis began in the United States or in Europe, there can be little doubt that this was a crisis which began in the financial system, and which could to a large degree be attributed to flaws in the regulatory architecture of that system. Classifying it as moderate may on the surface appear more questionable, but key to this understanding is that it was a crisis chiefly managed by the resources of the member states, with the EU providing only secondary support beyond the liquidity support of the European Central Bank, and that it was a crisis where virtually no one questioned whether the Union could survive without radical emergency action.

## An Endogenous Crisis

That the Banking Crisis originated in the financial system can hardly be debated. While later crises such as Brexit and the COVID-19 Pandemic produced strain on the banking system due to exogenous shocks, no similar external cause exists for the panic which began in 2007. The problems clearly originated in the banking sector, and as such pointed to flaws in the regulation of that sector. The key point of debate would be over which regulators bore the greatest blame for the crisis, with arguments to be made that the root causes lay in the United States, the various member states, or in the EU itself. This debate would carry implications for management of the crisis more broadly, as a crisis primarily laid at the feet of US regulators would imply that European regulators were largely blameless, and produce a very different conversation over the necessity of reform than one originating closer to home. To be sure, all of these explanations carry some validity, and all of them should probably be more broadly grouped as symptoms of a transatlantic epistemic shift away from strict regulation and towards a more laissez-faire approach to banks and risk. They nevertheless are worth considering individually.

The case for a crisis originating in the United States focused primarily on two policy choices. The first was the "Greenspan Put," the decision of the Federal Reserve to respond to the strains of the Dot.Com Crash in 2000 with expansionary monetary policy. This cushioned the blow of the attendant recession, but, combined with a "flight to safety" from emerging markets to American and European markets after the 1997–98 East Asian Financial Crisis, created a wash of liquidity in the United States, and to a somewhat lesser degree Europe. This would in turn fuel the rise of a bubble in subprime mortgages, and the bursting of that bubble would be at the heart of the 2007–09 Crisis. The second was the decision by US regulators to allow Lehman Brothers, the United States' fourth largest investment bank, to collapse into bankruptcy on September 15, 2008. US regulators would argue that they lacked the legal authority to prevent the failure, and that Lehman's failure was a symptom of the broader crisis, not a cause.[1] Many European regulators, however, would focus on the subsequent panic to argue that the Lehman collapse itself triggered the broader crisis.

Both of the explanations carry a seed of truth, but neither carry enough causal force to allow the Europeans to escape culpability. The subprime mortgage boom can largely be traced to US monetary policy, but no attempt was made by European regulators to deter European banks from heavy investment in those assets. Moreover, while much of the subprime lending concentrated in the United States, a significant portion of it involved European banks supporting subprime lending to European borrowers, especially in Iberia and Central and Eastern Europe. On the question of the impact of Lehman Brothers' failure, Vince Cable, the Shadow Chancellor of the UK Liberal Democratic Party, probably best captured its significance in describing it as the "Franz Ferdinand" moment of the crisis.[2] It triggered a broader panic, but only because markets were primed to panic after thirteen months of growing anxiety. From August 2007, when UK lender Northern Rock experienced a bank run, German bank IKB received a bailout, and French lender BNP Paribas froze €1.6 billion in funds, through the March 2008 failure of Bear Stearns, the US's fifth largest investment bank, and steadily through the following summer, tensions had been growing steadily, and the Lehman failure is better understood as the moment the building tension broke rather than causal in its own right.

The second cluster of explanations focuses on failures and missteps of individual European regulators. Here the specific stories vary from country to country, but generally have a common theme of excessive regulatory

**66** Crises and Integration in European Banking Union

forbearance in an effort to either protect domestically focused banks from transnational competition or to promote a country's transnational banks as "national champions" to dominate European finance. The first category includes regulatory protection of the German Landesbanken and Spanish cajas, small to midsized regional lenders which would fall into crisis in the 2007–09 and 2010–14 Crises respectively. The second includes Ireland promoting the development of banks with assets many times the size of the country's GDP, as well as efforts of the UK to promote London as a low-regulation center for European financial activity. All of these explanations, as with the American factors, carry some validity, but are insufficient on their own, given how the same patterns occurred across Europe. This, therefore, points to a common European cause, and thus to flaws in the Europe-wide financial regulatory architecture.

The core argument for the crisis as a product of a weakness in the Europe-wide financial regulatory architecture is that the growth and cross-border expansion of Europe's banks exceeded the ability of national regulators to effectively manage them. Schoenmaker captures this as a trilemma of international financial activity, where a financial system can have only two of the three of transnational financial integration, national regulation, and financial stability.[3] The Europeans, having deep financial integration paired with almost exclusively national financial regulation, left themselves vulnerable to financial instability, due chiefly to two problems: regulatory competition and regulatory confusion.

The removal of barriers to movement of capital and financial services made transnational banking possible on a scale previously not viable, and the introduction of the common currency only accelerated these trends. The years prior to the crisis saw both a wave of cross-border mergers and acquisitions and an expansion of foreign activity by national banks, all of which strained the capacity of nationally focused regulation. The most iconic cross-border merger, and likely the most consequential in the crisis, was the acquisition of and division ABN AMRO, the second largest bank in the Netherlands by a consortium of three other massive banks: the Benelux bank Fortis, British bank Royal Bank of Scotland (RBS), and Spanish bank Santander. Even without mergers, both midsized and large alike banks were expanding their foreign operations. The German Landesbanken expanded beyond their traditional focus on the German *Mittelstand* (small and medium-sized industries) to compete with the larger German commercial banks over larger German firms and even moved into international markets.[4] Both Ireland and Iceland (the latter outside the EU but inside the European Economic Area) developed massive banks that dwarfed their national populations and GDP by reliance on foreign customers, to ultimately devastating results. Ireland's efforts to save its three largest banks would increase the country's national debt by almost 400 percent. The failure of Iceland's Landsbanki would trigger deep tensions between Iceland and the UK and the Netherlands, after Iceland's deposit insurance scheme refused to pay out to the bank's British and Dutch customers due to lack of resources. To a large degree, all of this international growth was actively promoted by the member states themselves, having adopted a "national champions" strategy predicated on the idea that European integration meant that Europe would be dominated by a handful of massive banks, and that each member wanted at least some of those to be theirs.[5]

The problems of the massive size of European banks relative to their sovereigns would come to the fore in the subsequent European Debt Crisis, as discussed in Chapter 4. The more immediate issues in the 2007–09 Banking Crisis came from the rapid growth of transnational activity and the underregulation that followed. In principle, assigning responsibility for cross-national bank operations was straightforward. Branches, which shared a common capital pool with the mother bank, were the responsibility of the home country of the mother bank. Subsidiaries, on the other hand, were legally distinct entities with their own separate capital requirements, and the responsibility of the host country regulator. In practice, however, this branch–subsidiary division of responsibilities created both problem of regulatory arbitrage and regulatory confusion.

The branch–subsidiary distinction produced regulatory arbitrage because a bank could essentially choose between whether they wanted their foreign operations to be overseen by the home or host country regulator. Home and host regulators each had incentive to want these operations under their remit to retain control over "their" banks, meaning all the operations of their bank in the case of the home country or all the banking operations taking place in their country for the host regulator. Such control would both enable them to best safeguard their broader economy and use regulation to direct bank activity in their favored direction. This, in turn, created competition between home and host regulators to offer the most favorable regulations in order to gain regulatory oversight over those operations, a competition that created a downward pressure on regulatory scrutiny and severity, and encouraged bank-favoring "light touch" regulation.

The second problem of the branch–subsidiary system was the capacity for regulatory confusion. In part this reflected the complexity of modern financial conglomerates. A subsidiary might be legally distinct with its own capital reserves, but in practice the collapse of a subsidiary would almost certainly

## 68    Crises and Integration in European Banking Union

prompt the mother bank to dip into its own capital reserves to save the operation. On the other hand, a branch may be legally part of the mother bank but still retain enough independence to get both itself and the mother bank into trouble. Moreover, the complexity of internal operations of financial conglomerates may obscure whether an entity is in fact a branch or subsidiary. The paradigmatic case here may be Depfa, the Irish operation of German bank Hypo Real Estate. The German regulators regarded Depfa as the responsibility of the Irish regulators, while the Irish considered it to be the Germans' task.[6] As a result, Depfa effectively operated without oversight, and managed to accrue enough losses to bring down Hypo itself, which became the first bank nationalized by a German government since 1931.

All of these factors point inexorably to a crisis clearly endogenous to the financial system, and to a significant degree to the European financial system specifically. While the US certainly bears a significant share of the blame for its origins, the EU and its member states also played major roles in co-creating the problem. EU investment helped fuel a bubble in both the US and Europe and the crisis itself began in Europe in late 2007 and spread *to* the United States in 2008. Moreover, the underlying instability of national regulation of cross-national banking in Europe left the European financial system underregulated and massively vulnerable to shocks, whether originating in the European Union or elsewhere.

## A Moderate Crisis

If the Banking Crisis is unambiguously an endogenous crisis, on the surface describing it as a moderate one may seem curious, given the scale of losses and its substantial long-term economic impact. Certainly, it was a substantial crisis for national economies, and Eurogroup Chair Jean-Claude Juncker warned that the Europeans would "have to deal with the consequences [of the crisis] for a while."[7] However, it ultimately functioned more as a series of national crises in Europe, rather than a *European* crisis. The losses to European banks and the money states spent to resolve the crisis were immense in absolute terms, of course. However, in almost every case, these costs were within the capacity of the affected countries to pay. Unlike the subsequent European Debt Crisis, the Banking Crisis generally most heavily affected the wealthiest European states. As Figure 3.1 illustrates, the systemic bailouts of the main states affected all introduced only a manageable increase in fiscal burdens to the state. Even the Netherlands, which took on extensive costs largely related to the collapse of ING, only saw a modest increase in its

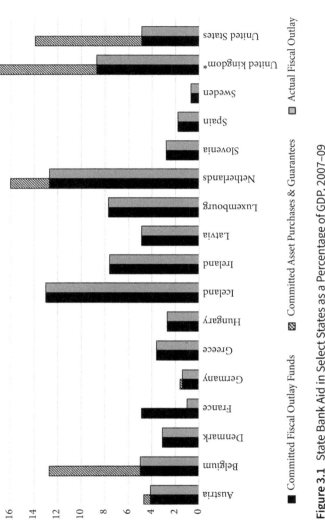

**Figure 3.1** State Bank Aid in Select States as a Percentage of GDP, 2007–09

*UK Committed Asset Purchases & Guarantees were 27.9 percent of GDP.
*Source:* Laeven and Valencia, 2010

## 70   Crises and Integration in European Banking Union

debt-to-GDP ratio, from 41.97 percent in 2007 to 55.83 percent in 2009.[8] A chief driver of the Debt Crisis would be the sovereign–bank Doom Loop, wherein the inability of states to bail out their banks weakened both bank and state. This simply was not an issue for the majority of countries hit by the Banking Crisis, meaning that a coordinated European response, while arguably advantageous, was not necessary to prevent catastrophe in 2007–09.

The most significant exception to this pattern was Ireland. The Irish state's rescue of its three largest banks caused a massive increase in the country's government debt-to-GDP ratio, from 26.5 percent to 123.7 percent, a substantially greater increase in public debt than even the increases from the comparably large Dutch and British bailouts.[9] Even here, however, the rescue relied solely on Irish resources, and not on contributions from fellow member states. This was possible because the state offered guarantees to be paid only as necessary rather than direct support. As such, while Ireland could potentially be on the hook for truly massive costs, its direct expenditure was within its capacity to absorb.[10]

The most important reason to classify the Banking Crisis as a moderate crisis was simply that very few people cast it as a threat to the European project. It did not threaten either a risk of a sovereign default of an affected country, nor a threat of disintegration of the eurozone or European integration more broadly. Juncker, when asked about the danger of either of those possibilities, bluntly stated that "it is a risk that does not exist."[11] To the contrary, existing European integration was broadly referenced as a vital tool to help states manage the crisis. The European Central Bank provided extensive liquidity support to member states, and market actors generally regarded membership in in the Single Market and the eurozone as a stabilizing factor.[12] Christine Lagarde, the French Finance Minister, would declare "thank goodness we have the euro," arguing that it protected Members from major shifts and devaluations more than national currencies would have done. In sharp contrast to the later Debt Crisis, when remaining outside of the eurozone helped insulate the UK from problems, British politicians would lament this time that the UK had not adopted the euro. Prime Minister Gordon Brown's change of tone and enthusiasm at Economic and Financial Affairs Council (ECOFIN) meetings led him to be described as a "repenting sinner," while MEP Andrew Duff would call for a "rigorous examination" of the UK's continued opt-out from the euro.[13]

The risk that *was* seen as coming out of the Crisis lay not in the immediate impact, but in the longer-term implications for continued integration and exposed vulnerabilities of the European financial architecture. The Crisis laid bare the risks of Schoenmaker's trilemma, that states could only have two of the three of cross-national banking, national regulation, and financial stability. However, this formula suggested two longer-term paths to stability: deeper integration through a deepening of transnational regulation at the expense of national regulatory discretion or a retreat from cross-national banking back to national banks overseen by national regulators. This latter choice, which came to be known as "Balkanization," was seen as the more serious long-term threat to European integration from the crisis.[14] This concern prompted Bundesbank President Axel Weber to say that his true fear out of the crisis was "refocusing banks on their national credit and lending operations rather than fostering their pan-European endeavors."[15]

## Implications of a Moderate Endogenous Crisis

A moderate endogenous crisis of this type created a need for action, but not necessarily for dramatic action. Because the crisis originated out of flaws in the financial regulatory architecture, a failure to address those flaws would mean a recurring cycle of crises. Given that the damage to the financial system and the broader economy was substantial, the sooner those flaws could be addressed, the better.[16] Jacques de Larosière, before he chaired the panel which would provide the blueprint for the post-crisis reforms, captured this sense in an interview with Institutional Investor, warning that "we need to act with speed and determination to restore confidence."[17] The crisis's proximate origin in the United States, and in Anglo-American financial models more generally, also helped fuel general unhappiness with a European regulatory approach largely following Anglo-American regulatory models.[18]

However, while the damage from the crisis was substantial, it was not unsustainable. The danger was that another crisis would produce substantial costs, not that it would break the European project. This in turn reduced the need for dramatic action, and opened up space for more modest reforms. The speed with which the main crisis period concluded further contributed to this dynamic. While it was preceded by approximately a year of gradually growing apprehension and tension, and followed by a long period of "mopping up" and recession, the main "crisis" period lasted only a few months in late 2008. Most of the peak panic was in fact concentrated in September and early October 2008, from the failure of Lehman Brothers through the introduction of systemic rescue plans in most of the crisis-hit states. Once those systemic rescue plans were deployed, states had the tools to manage any subsequent bank failures, and while costs would continue to mount, the sense of panic receded. This, in turn, meant that the emergency politics moment of the crisis, when the need for rapid action led to a streamlining of the decision-making process, lasted only a relatively short period of time. Although there was widespread dissatisfaction with the Anglo-American model of financial regulation in that time, there also was not an existing clear alternative model that had widespread support, and none emerged before the crisis period ended.[19] By early 2009, normal politics and policymaking began to again become the dominant mode as the need for immediate action diminished. This meant a return to a wide range of stakeholders taking part in a relatively slow policymaking process, against a backdrop of a status quo which was sustainable at least for the medium term.

This combination of factors pointed toward "patch-up" reforms out of the Banking Crisis. The Crisis demonstrated real weaknesses that needed to be addressed to prevent a repeat crisis, but also failed to provide enough of a threat to overcome opposition to a truly fundamental transformation. As with other European crises, advocates of deeper integration would attempt to use the Banking Crisis to push a maximal agenda, including a Europe-wide bailout mechanism and a transformation of European regulation that would have amounted to a complete European banking union beyond even what emerged from the Debt Crisis. However, such reforms exceeded what was necessary to fix the problems at the root of the Banking Crisis, and as such immediately ran into opposition. The reforms that did pass, most significantly the creation of the European Banking Authority, fit the origins and scale of the crisis as endogenous and moderate.

## Initial Responses from the European Commission and the European Central Bank

As noted, states played the primary role in managing the initial emergency responses to the wave of bank failures. Both the European Commission and the European Central Bank played important, albeit minor, roles in supplementing those state responses. For the Commission, this consisted primarily of a review of state aid to banks to evaluate their compliance with existing state aid rules by the Directorate-General for Competition (DG Comp). While in some cases, such as the United Kingdom, bank rescues generally cleared state aid rules with minimal issues, others ran afoul even of the looser standards adopted in recognition of the extraordinary nature of the crisis. The DG Comp in particular directed Germany on multiple occasions to temper the generosity of its rescue plans, in particular the assistance to

Commerzbank and WestLB. In both cases, the DG Comp ordered the rescued bank to be broken up to bring the assistance back into compliance with state aid rules.[20] The Commission's role at this stage in the crisis, moderate loosening of standards notwithstanding, essentially was to provide a brake to state generosity, and an enforcement of existing rules rather than a reshaping of them.

The European Central Bank played a more direct role in supporting the banks, especially in the eurozone, through an expansive provision of liquidity. Although the ECB initially reacted cautiously in the early period of the crisis, by September 2008 it pivoted to increasing liquidity access through several mechanisms. The first, the fixed rate full allotment shift, removed any restriction on provision of liquidity other than that they provide good collateral. Moreover, the ECB expanded the definition of good collateral for bank refinancing operations, to further expand liquidity access. It also launched Long Term Refinancing Operations (LTROs) with a six-month maturity for loans collateralized with sovereign debt, later expanded to twelve months, an expansion on the typical pre-crisis three-month maturity. Finally, it partnered with the US Federal Reserve to ensure liquidity access to US dollars as well as euros.[21] All of these actions, while enacted as temporary responses to the crisis moment, operated well within the normal operations of the ECB and attracted little controversy. In essence, it simply served its role as a central bank in time of crisis, lending freely on good collateral to minimize the risks that banks would fail simply due to liquidity concerns rather than solvency issues. As such, these actions carried far fewer implications for the broader reform of the European financial regulatory architecture than the ECB's more controversial and expansive actions in the subsequent Debt Crisis and COVID-19 Pandemic.

## The Proposed Common European Bailout Fund

The first major attempted European response, a floated proposal to create a common pool to fund bank resolutions, emerged at the very peak of the financial crisis in early fall 2008. The initial proposal, to create a common European bailout mechanism, would have been a significant step toward European fiscal solidarity. This, however, never advanced beyond vague speculation before being shot down by member states hostile to the idea, especially Germany and Britain. A second revision, to create a co-insurance scheme, similarly gained no traction, and ultimately all that emerged was a

**74** Crises and Integration in European Banking Union

synchronized announcement of national bailout commitments. It neverthe-less remains important to discuss, as it demonstrates both how some actors in Europe accurately identified problems that would manifest in the com-ing years, but lacked the political will to overcome those forces opposed to more radical action out of the only moderately severe Banking Crisis. More-over, while later discussions of revising the European financial regulatory architecture would come after the peak crisis moment, this proposal was both floated and rejected in the very heart of the crisis.

Debate on the need for a common bailout fund began in the last week of September 2008. On September 21, US Treasury Secretary Henry Paul-son announced the first version of the US systemic rescue plan, the Troubled Asset Relief Program (TARP). This prompted immediate discussion over the potential need for an EU equivalent, although the Commission was quick to dismiss those ideas. Most prominently, EU Monetary Affairs Commissioner Joaquin Almunia told a conference in Slovakia that national governments would have to decide how to proceed on their own the day after Paulson's announcement.[22] However, as the crisis continued to escalate, the idea gained more traction in the following days. By October 1, French Finance Minister Christine Lagarde, in an interview with German newspaper Handelsblatt, argued that "We are in agreement within the EU that we need to support the financial sector," and thus "the question arises: Do we need a European rescue fund to save banks?"[23]

Lagarde's interview prompted a flurry of activity. Reporting immediately following the interview suggested a price tag of approximately €300 billion for a potential common pool.[24] Jean-Claude Juncker, the Commission Pres-ident, in a shift from the Commission's position a week earlier, now argued that "I think we need to systematize the European response."[25] Belgium, the Netherlands, and Luxembourg, themselves in the midst of a joint bailout of Benelux bank Fortis, signaled support for the idea.[26] The European Bank-ing Federation (EBF) also stressed the need for a common response, with Secretary-general Giodo Ravoet arguing that "No one can solve this prob-lem on their own because the banking sector is so interconnected across Europe."[27]

At the same time, opponents of the proposal gathered quickly. Although the Commission had signaled some interest, the European Central Bank took a much more skeptical line. ECB President Jean-Claude Trichet argued that such an idea was simply infeasible in Europe, maintaining that "We are in Europe in a framework which is not a political federation. We do not have a federal budget, so the idea that we could do the same as what is done on the other side of the Atlantic doesn't fit with the political structure of Europe."[28]

The 2007–09 Banking Crisis **75**

While Trichet argued that the proposal was infeasible, resistance from Britain and Germany would go further, arguing that it was not just infeasible but strongly undesirable. Gordon Brown, the UK Prime Minister, argued that what was needed was action by national governments, and that it was not the time for "grand European solutions."[29] The German response was similarly hostile. Chancellor Angela Merkel said Germany "cannot and will not issue a blank cheque for all banks, regardless of whether they behave in a responsible manner or not."[30] Finance Minister Peer Steinbrück agreed, warning that "to put it mildly, Germany is highly cautious about such grand designs for Europe. Other countries are free to think about it. I just don't see any German interest in it."[31] A Finance Ministry spokeswoman would further rebuke the idea, arguing that "We are not convinced that an umbrella fund to cover everything would be a good solution."[32]

In the face of this opposition, the French government disowned the proposal. French President Nicolas Sarkozy announced that "I deny the sum and the principle" of the plan, and instead suggested the more modest idea that each state should set up its own bailout fund.[33] Shortly thereafter, a spokesman for Lagarde walked back her support, saying that "it was an idea worth debating, not a proposal."[34] Officials further suggested that reporters had mistakenly attributed the proposal to the French, and that it actually originated with the Netherlands. Even as it walked back support for a common European bailout, the French government noted the possibility that some states may not be able to afford the necessary bailouts, acknowledging the potential risk from relying on purely national responses.[35]

The Dutch also distanced themselves from initial proposals for a common pool, instead calling for only a requirement for each member state to set up their own bailout fund worth 3 percent of GDP. Wouter Bos, Dutch Finance Minister, argued that "if all European countries simultaneously show that they are prepared, that would send a terrific signal of confidence to European citizens."[36] Italian President Silvio Berlusconi attempted to revive the idea after the French and Dutch walk-back, but the Germans were again quick to reject the proposal.[37]

Ultimately, as Belgian Finance Minister Didier Reynders acknowledged, "there [was] no question of setting up a European fund."[38] Instead, the chief outcome of this initial attempt at deeper integration out of the crisis was simply a joint announcement of national systemic response plans. This was intended to accomplish Bos's goal of a stronger signal through coordinated action, but lacked either the collective European funding of more substantial proposals or even a more modest commitment to common funding targets.

The rise and fall of the common funding proposal is noteworthy because it demonstrates that European actors already understood the potential threat of states being unable to afford to bail out their banks. This sovereign–bank nexus, or Doom Loop, would become an acute problem in the subsequent European Debt Crisis, when multiple member states would risk sovereign default out of their struggles to contain a new wave of bank failures. The Doom Loop was a nonissue in the Banking Crisis only because the most affected states, Ireland excepted, were also among the wealthiest in the EU. Despite this, however, insufficient will existed to tackle the problem with deeper integration so long as national solutions would suffice in the immediate moment. It is therefore no coincidence that support for common funding was strongest in the Benelux countries, which themselves already faced the challenge of a joint resolution of a cross-border bank in Fortis, and in Italy, one of the countries which would prove to be most vulnerable to the Doom Loop in the subsequent Debt Crisis. French initial interest can also be traced to Doom Loop concerns. The top five French banks' total assets were equivalent to 74 percent of French GDP, making France acutely vulnerable to Doom Loop concerns.[39] However, as one of the EU's largest economies, France could also afford a massive state bailout of those banks early on to shore them up before the costs spiraled out of control. This bailout consisted of two components, the Société de Financement de l'Economie Française (SFEF), a state-backed capital raise for banks authorized to raise up €320 billion, and the Société de Prise de Participation de l'Etat (SPPE), a €40 billion direct capital injection from the French state to the banks. This two-part plan committed the French state to up to €360 billion of assistance, one of the largest potential fiscal commitments of any national plan. However, since only €77 billion of the SFEF would be used, the actual cost to the French government was in line with comparable bailouts from Britain and Germany. On the other hand, Germany and Britain both could afford the costs of their bank bailouts, and in the absence of an immediate threat from a sovereign–bank nexus in another member state, had little interest in contributing to bailouts elsewhere. This crisis simply was not big enough to spark deeper integration.

## Creation of the European Banking Authority

While there would ultimately be no movement on a common European bailout mechanism until the creation of the European Stability Mechanism in the throes of the next crisis, there would still be a real, if more modest, transformation of the European financial regulatory architecture. The creation of the European System of Financial Supervision, and in particular the creation of the European Banking Authority, was a real concrete step toward deeper integration of financial regulation. At the same time, however, it did not go as far toward establishing a common European regulator as many reformers wanted, as it retained the primacy of national regulators and national discretion.

## Weaknesses in the Existing Regulatory Regime

At the outbreak of the Crisis, the principal mechanism for coordination of financial regulation was via three advisory groups: the Committee of European Banking Supervisors (CEBS), the Committee of European Securities Regulators (CESR) and the Committee of European Insurance and Occupational Pensions Supervisors (CEIOPS). These three were collectively referred to as the "Lamfalussy Committees," having been the chief policy recommendation of the 2001 Lamfalussy Committee for how to manage the challenge of transnational banking and national regulation as European integration deepened, especially with the introduction of the euro.[40] Each committee consisted of the heads of the relevant national regulatory agencies (and in the case of CEBS national central banks and ECB) and served primarily as a "talk shop," where those regulators could exchange "best practices" and make recommendations. They had no obligation to share data across supervisors, and no ability to set and enforce common standards. The vulnerability of such a system was apparent at the time of its creation, given the possibilities for regulatory arbitrage and confusion. However, in part because cross-national banking remained more limited than it would be in the subsequent decade, there was little political will to push for a change.

That would change with the outbreak of the Banking Crisis, which highlighted the vulnerability of the existing system. By 2008, Europe's forty-four cross-border banks held two-thirds of European deposits, and national regulators strained to regulate these entities.[41] A wide range of actors, including representatives of European agencies and international organizations, member state governments, and private actors, would soon coalesce around a common framing. They broadly agreed that the crisis had been at least partially caused and certainly exacerbated by weaknesses in the European-level regulatory architecture, and that the clearest solution to this problem going forward was to transfer significant regulatory authority to a European body. At the peak of the Crisis in 2008, EU Economic and Monetary Commissioner Joaquin Almunia warned that "we are now seeing the consequences

**78** Crises and Integration in European Banking Union

of their inadequate supervision and regulation," and Eurogroup President, Jean-Claude Juncker argued that the most important task would be "to fix common rules to be applied by all the national supervisory authorities."[42] In the following months, they would be joined by Internal Market and Services Commissioner Charlie McCreevy, who held that "the financial crisis has demonstrated the need to further strengthen EU supervisory arrangements," and CESR Chairman Eddy Wymeersch, who cautioned that the current system created instability because "harmonised rules were subject to different interpretations by regulators."[43]

Actors outside of the European bodies also adopted this understanding. Polish Finance Minister Jacek Rostowski argued that the current model was "bad for Europe because it is scattered. And it [was] bad for Poland, because it [was] dominated by supervision in countries in which parent companies that have subsidiaries in Poland are located."[44] At the international level, an Organisation for Economic Co-operation and Development (OECD) report cautioned that the existing framework "[increased] the likelihood of severe financial market problems," especially in the eurozone where member states had fewer tools to address the weaknesses.[45]

These critics soon began to coalesce around the idea of a "hub and spoke" reform, wherein national regulators would be increasingly coordinated by a central harmonizing body, though they split between casting the ECB or a revamped form of the Lamfalussy Committees as best suited for the role.[46] Perhaps unsurprisingly, members of the European Central Bank cast their institution as ideally placed to harmonize regulation and facilitate communication between the national regulators.[47] Trichet maintained that such a move "would be a natural extension of the mandate already assigned to us by the [EU] Treaty, namely to contribute to financial stability."[48] The potential value of an expanded ECB role was also embraced by representatives of the OECD and the French Finance Ministry, as well as investment bank Goldman Sachs.[49] The think tank Centre for European Policy Studies cast an expanded ECB role as all but inevitable in the absence of other action, arguing that "if no initiative is taken at a policy level, there will be a feeling that the ECB has to step in."[50]

Significantly, even at this early stage, some reformers issued calls for an even more ambitious transformation of the European regulatory architecture in form of the creation of a single supervisor for the entire EU, or at least the entire eurozone. The Association of British Insurers (ABI), for instance argued that the "failure of trust" between national regulators demonstrated that a pan-European "super-regulator" should be "actively pursued."[51] Sir Howard Davies, a former chair of the chief British regulatory body, the Financial Services Authority, and at the time the Director of the London School of Economics, argued that the crisis demonstrated the need to move to either a single European supervisory authority or a retreat from cross-national banking. He castigated "hub and spoke" solutions as a "third way" "ramshackle structure [that] seems unlikely to solve the Iceland problem and will create many others."[52] At this point, however, most of these calls cast such a transformation as ideal but unlikely. Pervenche Berès, Chairwoman of the European Parliament's Economic and Monetary Affairs Committee, noted that she had called for a common rulebook and common supervisor well before the crisis, but could not rally sufficient support in the European Parliament.[53] Juncker allowed that he "not exclude that one day we would have a centralised supervision," while Christine Lagarde, the French Finance Minister specifically cited the idea of a centralized supervisory role for the ECB as worth exploring.[54] However, both would immediately temper these calls. Juncker argued that "it's more important to fix common rules to be applied by all the national supervisory authorities," while Lagarde cautioned that any solution "has to be politically acceptable and efficient." Lagarde further foresaw problems with a central role for the ECB because "the ECB doesn't have the authority on the whole of the EU," and specifically cited the UK as potentially problematic in this regard.[55]

At the same time, by as early as January 2009, barely weeks removed from the peak of the Crisis, British actors in particular began marshaling opposition to more ambitious reform proposals. Although Lord Myners, the UK Minister for the City of London urged the City to "be open-minded about all options," both other politicians and private actors began active pushback against regulatory centralization.[56] Lady Cohen of the British House of Lords questioned if "there is a need for an EU-wide supervisory body," while John Tattersall at PricewaterhouseCoopers cautioned that "the UK has a lot to lose if it were decided to centralise more regulation in Europe."[57] The British Bankers' Association warned that a single European banking regulator would result in "too much centralisation and bureaucracy [and] also risks a one-size-fits-all stance that is unlikely to benefit UK banking or London as a financial centre."[58] Therefore, even before the development of formal responses and while the Crisis remained an active concern, centralization opponents in London had already begun efforts to reject a narrative that cast deeper integration as essential.

## The de Larosière Report

The first major step toward an overhaul of the European financial architecture came in October 2008, at the height of the crisis. Commission President José Manuel Barroso commissioned the High Level Group on Financial Supervision, more commonly called the de Larosière Group after its chair, Jacques de Larosière, a former Managing Director of the International Monetary Fund (IMF), Governor of the Bank of France, and President of the European Bank for Reconstruction and Development. Barroso tasked the Group with developing "comprehensive rethinking" of the "mismatch between a continental-scale market and national systems of supervision."[59] Even from the beginning, however, he acted to temper ambitions, cautioning in the same statement where he announced the Group's formation that "this is not the time nor the place for political posturing and grandstanding, for announcing grand initiatives that have no chance of being followed through."[60]

The findings of that Group, the de Larosière Report, came out in late February 2009, and called for two major institutional innovations in response to the weaknesses highlighted by the Banking Crisis. The first would be to replace the Lamfalussy Committees with a new European System of Financial Supervision. Under this proposal, each of the individual Committees would be replaced with a new Authority, with CEBS replaced by a European Banking Authority, CESR replaced by a European Securities and Markets Authority, and CEIOPS replaced by a European Insurance and Occupational Pensions Authority (EIOPA). These new Authorities would retain the membership and tasks of their precursor Committees, but also gain the ability to impose binding supervisory standards and technical decisions, mediate disputes between national supervisors, and directly supervise the credit rating agencies. If the new ESFS worked as intended, it would find a way to preserve national regulatory independence but limit the possibilities of regulatory arbitrage and confusion. The Authorities' common standards would help establish a regulatory floor, diminishing the incentive to race to the bottom in standards. Their ability to mediate disputes would also help clarify which national authorities bore responsibilities for which arms of a cross-national bank, preventing operations from escaping regulation through confusion.

The second major reform would be the establishment of a European Systemic Risk Council (ESRC), to consist of the General Council of the ECB and the Chairs of the Lamfalussy Committees or their successor Authorities. This body would provide a channel for information-sharing both between the ECB and the ESFS Authorities and between national authorities.

In interviews around the rollout of the Report, de Larosière would empha-size his understanding that the core problem in European crisis management lay in the lack of information-sharing. He argued that with these reforms in place, "I think you would largely have avoided the problems of Fortis ... You would have had the obligations between supervisors to communicate the information."[61]

These were substantial changes to the European regulatory architecture, but did not go nearly as far as some reformers had called for. De Larosière for his part acknowledged the appeal of a pan-EU "super-regulator," but argued that if they had called for such a thing, "we might have been accused of being unrealistic." If such a pan-European regulator was politically unfeasible, he continued, Europe faced a choice between "chacun pour soi [each for him-self] solutions or ... an enhanced, pragmatic sensible European co-operation for the benefit of all."[62]

## Responses to the de Larosière Report

Many actors warmly greeted the de Larosière recommendations, both for addressing the problems highlighted by the crisis and for its relative lack of ambition, opting for a patch-up solution in form of tighter harmonization of regulation rather than a transfer of regulation to a supranational body. Commission President José Manuel Barroso praised its emphasis on a col-lective European response over "every-man-for-himself solutions," while EU Monetary Affairs Commissioner Joaquín Almunia commended the Report for "wisely ... not putting forward ideas that would require treaty reforms."[63] Several member state governments also embraced the recommendations, with French President Nicolas Sarkozy describing it as "excellent" and argued that "speedy action should be taken at the EU's next summit."[64] Multiple business organizations also indicated their support. The French Banking Federation called it "an essential contribution," a judgment seconded by the European Insurance Federation.[65] Significantly, given the opposition from other actors in the UK, the Association of British Insurers also wel-comed the recommendations. Stephen Haddrill, the ABI's Director-General, argued that "the crisis has shown that international markets must be effec-tively supervised by regulators that understand cross-border risks," and that "De Larosière's group is therefore right to propose strengthening the co-ordination of supervision across Europe's boundaries."

Initial critiques of the Report can be broadly divided into two groups: those arguing that the recommendations offered an inadequate response to

**82** Crises and Integration in European Banking Union

the scale of the problem and those arguing that the proposals amounted to EU or continental member state institutions attempting a power grab beyond what was necessary to resolve the crisis. The former arguments came from voices across the EU, while the latter chiefly came from British interests concerned about the impact of the reforms on London's continued preeminence in European finance.

Critiques that the reforms offered an inadequate remedy generally argued that attempts to preserve a central role for national regulators preserved or potentially even worsened problems of complexity and would slow the ability of authorities to respond quickly. Karel Lannoo at the Brussels-based think tank the Centre for European Policy Studies argued that including such a plethora of voices raised questions of "who pulls the trigger [and] who will finally be in charge and says when a bank is in trouble."[66] Financial journalists Jeremy Warner and Hugo Dixon would describe the structure with sixty-two representatives at the table as, respectively, "a dog's dinner" and "a nightmare."[67] Both would also question the viability of a system which would increase European supervision while still leaving resolution as a national responsibility. Chris Giles of the *Financial Times* would reinforce this concern, arguing that disagreement between regulators and central bankers had kept them from deploying macro-prudential tools before the Crisis, and that this system appeared to perpetuate that instability.[68] As such, observers argued that neither of the most prominent failures of cross-border regulation in the Crisis—the collapse of Benelux bank Fortis and the failure of Ireland-based lender Depfa and its German mother-bank HypoRE—would have been prevented by the new framework.[69] Because of this, Pierre Jouyet, a former French State Secretary for EU Affairs, argued that "the EU (June) summit should propose a more ambitious architecture."[70] The IMF would echo this call, with representatives in a *Financial Times* opinion piece seeing the need for a "dedicated European Union-level resolution framework that can credibly discipline Europe's large cross-border banks while offering depositors protection equivalent to national deposit guarantee schemes (DGS)."[71] What all of these critiques share is a common sense that the crisis presented a larger threat to the stability of European finance than the authors of the de Larosière Report acknowledged, and thus that a larger solution was necessary.

At the same time, however, another school of criticism cast the Report as overly ambitious, and ultimately about pursuing a centralizing agenda beyond the need presented by the Crisis. These critics generally had two related concerns: that greater centralization would mean a loss of control, and that it would be economically harmful. In the UK, euroskeptic Member of Parliament Bill Cash warned that "regulation at European level will be subject to majority voting. This will inevitably mean that the United Kingdom financial services and banking arrangements . . . would be run on lines dictated by the interests of other countries rather than our own national interests and must be resisted."[72] Vladimir Tomsik of the Czech National Bank similarly warned that the combination of multinational regulation and national responsibility for resolution created a circumstance "with which we cannot entirely identify ourselves."[73] In addition to the potential direct costs to states, critics also feared the new system would cause economic harm to their jurisdictions. *The Daily Telegraph* cautioned that "global agreement and coordination are essential, but the nitty-gritty of what each bank is up to must be tackled at a local level."[74] Others, especially in the UK, saw not just a risk from mis-regulation, but a deliberate plot to tear down the City of London's central role in European finance. A partner at law firm CMS Cameron McKenna similarly worried that "the French and German demands have as much to do with a desire to topple London from its pre-eminence as Europe's financial centre as with the improvement of regulation."[75] Simon Walker of the British Venture Capital Association argued that "private equity is significantly regulated already" and that the real goal of the reforms was "to destroy private equity completely."[76] All of these critics shared an understanding of the crisis as essentially unrelated to problems in the European regulatory architecture, and therefore exogenous to that system, a framing rejected by advocates for deeper reform.

The de Larosière Group themselves countered that their recommendations would have precisely the opposite effect, that "far from weakening the City this model [would] put it at the heart of the system" and that "it's not in the interests of the City, which must be submitted to greater regulation, that we repeat the mistakes of the past."[77] Despite that, implicit in the critiques of these actors was the sense that the de Larosière recommendations offered a cure that was worse than the illness. For the UK in particular, this reflected a different cost–benefit structure than for the Continental Europeans. The City of London's status as the financial services hub of Europe reflected in part the depth of London's capital markets and the long experience of both public and private actors there, but it was also a product of a regulatory approach seen by many as more favorable to financial services, and especially to capital markets, than continental alternatives. As such, the UK was keen to preserves its advantages, especially given the importance of financial services to the overall British economy.

## Debates over Implementation

Negotiations on the creation and implementation of the European System of Financial Supervision would begin in earnest in April of 2009 and stretch through August of 2010. To a large degree, the initial responses to the de Larosière Report set the template for the subsequent discussion, with some actors, especially in the European Commission, France, and Germany, casting the reforms as both essential and appropriate, while opponents split between two camps. The first group, led by the United Kingdom and including some of the smaller member states, argued that the reforms were an excessive and unwarranted infringement on national regulatory discretion, and advocated for a significantly smaller reform agenda. The second group, most prominently represented by the European Parliament, and coming more to the fore later in the process, cast the reforms as insufficient to the need revealed by the crisis. This group would instead press for a complete European banking union. Both the advocates of a more modest reform agenda and those pushing for a more expansive one would argue that the changes were necessary to preserve the European financial system against a repeat of the Banking Crisis. However, the relatively rapid resolution of the main period of crisis, without a serious strain on continued European integration, meant that the forces favoring a less ambitious reform agenda could credibly wield a blocking veto over movement, at least until the next wave of crisis with the European Debt Crisis.

### Initial Conflicts over the Commission's Proposals

The initial proposals unveiled by the European Commission in May 2009 hewed closely to the recommendations of the de Larosière Report, replacing the Lamfalussy Committees with a series of new authorities, and creating a European Systemic Risk Council. Debates in response to these proposals, across most of 2009, largely centered around three broad sets of issues concerning the hierarchy of regulators, the role of the ECB in the ESRC, and the breadth of the regulatory agenda.

The first main point of contention focused on how much more authority the new ESFS bodies should have relative to the Lamfalussy Committees they would replace. The de Larosière report, and the Commission's initial proposals, gave the new Authorities both binding mediation power over national regulators and direct supervisory responsibility over cross-border entities. While the Crisis had demonstrated how conflicts and gaps between national regulators could create problems, this solution created the possibility of a scenario where national regulators could be ordered to engage in bank resolutions or other activities which would impose a direct cost on member state budgets.[78] Without this binding authority, however, the Authorities could only rely on moral suasion, and would be only slightly more capable of resolving conflicts and confusion than the Lamfalussy Committees.[79]

The second main point of contention concerned who would chair the new European Systemic Risk Council. Initial proposals called for this position to be filled automatically by the President of the European Central Bank, on the logic that this new task already overlapped with the President's own mandate to oversee the financial stability of the entire European Union financial system.[80] Member states outside of the eurozone, however, immediately objected to this as leaving them in a second-tier position, given that the ECB obviously primarily concerned itself with the eurozone.

Finally, the third point of contention focused on the breadth of regulation, especially over whether to extend European-level regulation over hedge funds. Proponents saw underregulation of hedge funds both in Europe and globally as a major source of instability, while opponents argued that hedge funds had not actually been an issue in the Crisis, and that this was a target of opportunity for European regulators, not an essential component of a crisis response. While division on the previous two points of contention broadly followed national lines, debates on breadth of regulation prompted more internal national debates. This proved especially the case in the UK, where hedge funds both played the largest role and became the target of great public concern.

## Initial Positions

The European Commission cast these proposals as an essential reform for preventing another banking crisis and, in the words of Internal Market Commissioner Charlie McCreevy, "safeguarding financial stability."[81] Commission President Barroso argued the reform not only provided an essential patch-up, but also must be done in the current crisis moment, arguing that "It's now or never that we build a consensus on financial supervision. I think we will do it."[82] If the EU could not come together to address the flaws in the financial regulatory architecture in the immediate aftermath of those flaws' dramatic consequences, it would be hard to see what would build such a consensus. The ECB, for its part, embraced the proposals as well. ECB Vice President Lucas Papoademos argued that the ESRC in particular would help to prevent future crises, and that the reforms required not only increased information-sharing, but also "adequate institutional mechanisms" if ESRC warnings were to be actually translated into action and not just be cheap talk.[83]

The proposals were rapidly embraced by both France and Germany. French President Nicolas Sarkozy and German Chancellor Angela Merkel issued a joint statement arguing that the EU "must move resolutely towards a European regulatory framework."[84] Sarkozy went further, echoing Papoademos and arguing that in order to be effective, the new reforms must have binding consequences, when he stressed that "for years we have been unable to escape from soft supervision" and that Europe suffered "not from a lack of rules but from a lack of sanctions."[85] He would further argue that rapid US reforms in response to the crisis only increased the need for EU action, lest the European Union gain a reputation as unstable and incapable of reform. In his words, "if we did not take these initiatives, people would have said 'oh la la, they aren't doing the same as the United States.'"[86] France and Germany were joined in their support for the reforms by most of the other large European member states, including Italy and Spain.[87] Perhaps even more significant was the support of Poland, as the second largest non-eurozone EU economy, after the UK. While the UK was far more skeptical, Polish Finance Minister Jacek Rostwoski argued that the reform proposals offered "the only way to create a safe and consistent system for the whole EU."[88]

Opposition to the reforms came most prominently from the United Kingdom, which staunchly resisted new Authorities capable of direct regulation and of making binding decisions for national regulators, as well as opposing establishing the ECB President as the chair of the European Systemic Risk Council. At the core of the UK government's position was its own subtly different diagnosis of the fundamental flaws in the European financial regulatory architecture, as laid out in the UK Financial Services Authority's equivalent to the de Larosière Report, the Turner Review.[89] To a large degree, the Turner Review's conclusions mirrored those of the EU's report, to the point where critics described it as a "cut-and-paste," and "European ideas wrapped in a British flag."[90] It certainly echoed much of the content of the de Larosière Report, but differed crucially but subtly in its proposed remedies. While both reports called for a deepening of European-level financial regulatory cooperation, they differed in how they balanced national regulatory autonomy and European-level oversight. While the de Larosière proposals called for Authorities capable of issuing binding decisions on member state regulators, the Turner Review proposals explicitly limited the envisioned bodies to nonbinding decisions, calling for them to have "no powers over national supervisors to change individual regulatory decisions, nor to prescribe detailed supervisory practice."[91]

These conclusions were widely embraced by representatives of the UK government, and became the core of their negotiating position. Prime Minister

Gordon Brown in the immediate aftermath of the Turner Review's publication declared that "our policy is that regulatory rules should be set at an international level but that direct supervision is a matter for our national authorities."[92] He further asserted that "it is only logical that where a supervisory decision would have an impact on the taxpayer, that decision should be for the relevant national authority," and not for the new Authorities.[93]

Alistair Darling, the Chancellor of the Exchequer, similarly accepted the need for greater harmonization and even more common rules, but made it clear once negotiations got underway that binding decisions by the new Authorities, especially those which could have financial consequences for member states, constituted a "very, very important" red line for the UK. In his words,

> the thing that concerned us, which we could not live with, was a proposal whereby there might be an agreement reached by regulators at a European level that would have had domestic fiscal consequences for domestic governments. In other words, they might have been able to say to a government "you've got to do something about a bank", therefore that government would have had to ask its taxpayers to contribute.[94]

In his vision, it would be sufficient for the new Authorities to be limited to "name and shame" rule-breaking member states but not to have power over national supervisors.[95]

The Brown–Darling position thus proposed an update to European-level financial supervision that increased the detail of the common rules promulgated by would-be Lamfalussy successors, but without a meaningful increase in their ability to enforce those rules. Even this, however, was seen as a bridge too far for some elements in the UK. City Minister Paul Myners warned that the proposed European oversight "[cut] across the basic principle of vesting supervision in national authorities."[96] He further argued that it was unacceptable that there could never be a British chair of the ESRC if that position was reserved for the President of the ECB.[97] One particular concern of Myners was the creation of a binding European institution headed by a non-Briton focused on regulation of hedge funds. In his words, "it is perhaps easy for other European countries to make political capital out of demanding intrusive regulation of an industry of which they have little or no direct experience," and that the proposed rules were "woefully short-sighted" and "bordering on a weak form of protectionism."[98] In this he was joined by then Mayor of London Boris Johnson, who cautioned that overregulation of hedge funds threatened to "cut off a vital supply of investment funding

**88** Crises and Integration in European Banking Union

at a time when the economy needs it most."[99] Of particular note is the critique of John McFall, Chairman of the Commons Treasury Committee, who argued that the process was unduly rushed and that "we remain convinced of the need for more effective financial regulation and supervision; we simply believe it's much more important to get it right than rush it through."[100] McFall's rejection of urgency, despite the still simmering crisis, demonstrated that significant elements within British politics were willing to accept no forward motion, at least for some time, unless their concerns were addressed. This demonstrates that at least some British actors already had rejected the crisis framing and emergency politics in favor of a return to normal policymaking.

British hostility to binding authority was thus not only clear, but backed up by the presence of domestic critics who argued that even the Brown–Darling position of enhanced but nonbinding supervision and rule-making represented too extreme a stance. German Finance Minister Peer Steinbrück would lament that "there is clearly a lobby in London that wants to defend its competitive advantage tooth and nail."[101] Only Romania, Slovakia, and Slovenia publicly joined the UK in opposing the degree of authority to be invested in the new bodies. However, Finland, Ireland, and Luxembourg were all rumored to be unhappy with the proposals.[102] Even in Germany, which broadly supported the reforms, some raised concerns that, in the words of one German official, "Binding powers for EU regulators would undermine the prerogatives of national oversight bodies."[103] British intransigence and some softness in support for the full proposed suite of powers to the new Authorities made it difficult for the Commission and reform advocates to push the full de Larosière recommendations. There was no discussion at that time of a eurozone-only integration, the course which would be pursued on banking union in the next crisis. Instead, the dominant view was that a European System of Financial Supervision which failed to include the UK would fail to achieve a sufficient increase in stability. The £45 billion UK bailout of RBS, one of the largest in the Crisis, only highlighted this problem, as RBS's collapse came largely because of its involvement in Fortis, one of the most complex and largest cross-border bank failures.[104]

Given that no satisfactory movement forward was possible without the UK, and that the UK would not shift on its main red lines, negotiations instead focused on how much of a compromise the UK would accept on other areas. One readily agreed compromise was that the ECB President would not automatically be chair of the ESRC, but rather "a Governor elected by the ESRC members," meaning the chair could plausibly be the Governor of the Bank of England.[105] This removed one British objection in principle, while amounting to little change in practice, as it was widely expected that the ECB President would win at least the initial election and that memories of the Bank of England's early stumbles in the Crisis, especially around the failure of Northern Rock, would keep the UK from the position for some years to come.[106] A more consequential bargain was struck over the reach of the new Authorities ability to dictate terms to national regulators. The new Authorities would gain the ability to make a binding decision in the case of a conflict over jurisdiction in cases of cross-border banking operations, and thus could designate which national regulator would bear responsibility for the resolution of a financial firm failure. However, they could not dictate how national regulators dealt with that failing firm, leaving it to national discretion whether to bail out the failing firm or let it fail.[107] This compromise therefore offered a solution to the problems of regulatory complexity and ambiguity that caused significant problems in the crisis. It did leave open the possibility that a national regulator deemed responsible could refuse to act to bail out its failing institutions, either because it chose not to or lacked the means to do so. This, however, had not been a problem in the 2007–09 Crisis for any EU member state, as even Ireland had managed to assume the burden of bailing out its banks. The only instance where a national regulator failed to assume its responsibilities, Iceland's refusal to honor its obligations to Landsbanki depositors in the UK and the Netherlands, involved a non-EU state's obligations to EU citizens, and thus would be beyond the capacity of any internal EU reform to address.

This compromise attracted some ire among the more strident opponents of the reform in the UK, who saw the binding assignment of responsibility as a significant increase in the EU's supervisory power that would lead to even greater authority in time.[108] Shadow Financial Secretary Mark Hoban argued that "the Government has caved in on its red line that there should be no fiscal impact from the activities of the European supervisory authorities," implicitly accepting that, were the UK to be designated the responsible authority, it would step up to assume those responsibilities, even if not explicitly commanded to pay by EU authorities.[109] Other critics warned that the increase in common European regulation would lead to a long-run pressure on UK regulatory autonomy, with think tank Open Europe warning that "the UK can be outvoted at any time."[110] In response, Charlie McCreevy, the European Internal Market Commissioner countered that "there would be little good in having an authority if in areas of dispute there was no binding recommendation. If there was not, it would be no different than the present situation."[111] In other words, addressing the regulatory gaps exposed by the crisis required binding recommendations as a minimum response.

At the same time, the compromise was celebrated by reform advocates as a significant breakthrough and an appropriate response to the flaws exposed by the crisis. Irish Finance Minister Brian Lenihan asserted that "one of the clear lessons of the Irish banking crisis is that we needed intensive financial supervision," while Swedish Finance Minister Anders Borg concluded that the reform demonstrated that Europe had "drawn the necessary conclusions from the crisis."[112] French President Nicolas Sarkozy was fulsome in his praise for the British decision to accept the deal, arguing that agreeing to a "European system of supervision with binding powers" represented "a sea change in Anglo-Saxon strategy" and that "Mr. Brown has assumed his responsibilities."[113] Part of the reason for Sarkozy's celebration lay in his belief that the remit of these new bodies would grow over time. This was a belief held by many actors who supported deeper reforms. Manfred Weber, the chief executive of the Bundesverband deutscher Banken (BdB), the association of the German commercial banks, argued that the compromise proposals were "an important step," but that "it should not stop there. A next step is that powers to regulate cross-border banks should be brought together at a European level to ensure effective oversight."[114]

## Struggles with the European Parliament

While disputes with a British government wanting to rein in the scope of reforms were largely resolved by September of 2009, the winter of 2009–2010 would be dominated by disputes with a significant block of Members of the European Parliament advocating for a considerably broader post-Crisis reform agenda. This group, led by members of the European Peoples Party, spanned a wide ideological swath, including members of the European Conservatives and Reformists, the Greens, and the Socialists & Democrats.[115] What united them was a broad sense that that the Commission's proposals were insufficient to the challenges revealed by the Banking Crisis. Instead, the European Parliament's Economic and Monetary Affairs Committee unveiled a much more substantial set of reform proposals.[116] The Parliament's proposals, calling for a unified Frankfurt-based European "super-regulator" with authority over national regulators and the establishment of a European bailout fund, essentially amounted to a call for the creation of a European banking union half a decade before the enactment of the Single Supervisory Mechanism (SSM) and Single Resolution Mechanism (SRM) out of the European Debt Crisis. Moreover, the proposals also called for a European deposit guarantee fund, a goal that continues to elude European reformers.

In making the case for the more expansive reforms, the Parliament Committee explicitly argued that the more modest alternatives were insufficient to the scale of problems revealed by the Crisis. The Parliament's statement said that "EU supervision must be much stronger than what the Commission and Council are proposing, in order to prevent the kind of slow and fragmented supervisory responses seen in the 2007–08 crisis."[117] Representatives called before the Economic and Monetary Affairs Committee argued that the Commission's proposals went "in the right direction but they could go even further," and that they would leave the system as "overall fragmented and really costly." The statement further asserted that "insurance, banking and investment are now so highly integrated that their standard-setting bodies must be equally integrated."[118] Committee Chair José Manuel García-Margallo argued that mere harmonization would be insufficient, and that the only stable solution would be for the EBA to directly supervise at least cross-border financial institutions "of a European dimension."[119] He also called for the creation of a European Financial Protection Fund to bail out large banks in times of crisis to be funded by a levy on the banks and to amount to 2.5 percent of EU GDP.[120] He maintained that to do otherwise would be to create substantial risk of a Doom Loop from states unable to afford bank bailouts. In his words, "What will happen when things do go wrong? Would we not need some form of fund?"[121] Indeed, this would prove to be the case three years later, when the EU would be forced to hurriedly construct bailout mechanisms to prevent bank failures from triggering sovereign debt crises in Spain and Italy. The Parliament reformers thus attempted to promote an understanding of the crisis as reflecting broader flaws and risking a more severe crisis, but in the absence of more direct manifestations of those flaws failed to win support for a framing of the crisis as a severe endogenous one sufficient to justify more expansive reforms.

Advocates argued that these positions had the support of a substantial majority of the European Parliament.[122] Moreover, polling indicated that at least in some member states, companies and financial institutions broadly supported them as well. A poll by Greenwich Market Pulse found that approximately two-thirds of French firms, 55 percent of German firms, and nearly three-quarters of Belgian firms supported giving the ESAs direct regulatory authority. Even the proposed bank levy enjoyed some support, with approximately 20–25 percent of firms in France, Germany, and Italy willing to accept a financial transactions tax.[123]

Despite this, the Parliament's proposals ultimately met with little success. The UK in particular, which was already only reluctantly supportive of the modified Commission proposals, took a hard line. Chancellor George

Osborne, in his own words, "made [it] clear that we did not support proposals for a European resolution fund. There was no agreement on that issue."[124] While the British, French, and Germans all broadly agreed to require member states to raise bailout levies, both the British and French insisted that the distribution of that money must remain the sole province of the member states. Stuart Frasier, the policy director of the City of London, pushed back against greater regulatory centralization, holding that "we want [national regulators] to be given maximum discretion on supervision. We can't have one size fits all in Europe."[125] These views were widespread among British firms as well. The same Greenwich Market Pulse survey that found a majority in support of centralized regulation in France, Germany, and Belgium reported that 90 percent of British firms rejected such centralization.[126]

Even actors broadly supportive of the reform agenda worried that the Parliament's proposals were overly ambitious, and risked precipitating a total collapse of even the more modest reforms proposed by the Commission. In the words of the Investment Management Association's head of European affairs, "the Parliament has taken a very extreme position going much further than the Commission. We are quite in favour of this single rulebook approach. But this goes much further—supervision should still be with national regulators this goes too far, too fast."[127] Eddy Wymeersch, the outgoing Chairman of Committee of European Securities Regulators, dismissed calls for greater centralization as "a nice political beauty contest, but in the urgency of the crisis cannot be a priority."[128]

The European Council ultimately aligned itself with the forces in opposition to the Parliament, and took a hard line against both direct supervision and common funding.[129] This produced a standoff with the European Parliament that lasted into September of 2010, though ultimately resolved broadly in favor of the Commission's proposals. The UK's lobbying early on had secured an agreement for the EBA to be located in London, not Frankfurt, as the Parliament had supported. Moreover, the UK's intransigence meant that the new European Supervisory Authorities (ESAs) had little ability to overrule national authorities and no ability to impose fiscal costs on any member state or national regulator. The ESAs did gain greater ability to codify a common rulebook, though in the absence of legal authority would need to rely on "moral pressure" to compel national authorities to comply.[130] Nevertheless, given that advocates of deeper reform had already conceded that the more modest proposals from the Commission still reflected a substantial step forward, and given the refusal of the UK to move from its "red lines" despite at this point well over a year of pressure, the Parliament agreed to the revision.

While the UK was willing to scuttle the entire proposal if it failed to meet the UK's demands, the European Parliament was unwilling to make the perfect the enemy of the good.

## The End of the Crisis Period

The final agreement on the creation of the ESFS was broadly seen as the end of the crisis period out of the Banking Crisis. Commission President José Manuel Barroso argued as much in September 2010, that "the economic outlook in the EU is now better than when I last addressed you, not least because of our joint action [and] the recovery is gathering pace." He attributed this in large part due to confidence "that the institutional architecture of Europe will be substantially stronger as we exit the crisis."[131] Olli Rehn, the European Commissioner for Economic and Monetary Affairs similarly argued that same week that "Europe's economic recovery has gained momentum and we are exiting from the financial crisis," which he also attributed to the ESFS.[132] Critics would continue to note substantial flaws in the European financial regulatory architecture. Nicholas Véron, for instance, argued that "What is needed remains unchanged: a triage process that credibly identifies capital gaps among Europe's most important financial institutions, and leads to adequate recapitalization and restructuring." However, he acknowledged that "the good news is that the creation of a European Banking Authority, due in January 2011, in principle provides a possible basis for a centralized European Union-wide assessment process."[133] Even Barroso would concede that "we are now solid on substance but still fluid in terms of process and communication."[134] Regardless of these continued gaps, two years removed from the peak of the Crisis it now became clear that the momentum for substantial post-crisis reforms had abated. Absent immediate pressure for action, the arguments for reform could no longer be presented as urgently essential. While reformers would continue to push for more changes, they could no longer be framed in terms of necessary crisis response, and as such had shifted out of emergency politics, and back into normal politics.

## Conclusion

The reform process out of the Banking Crisis is more complex than a simple story of policy learning. The flaws in the European financial regulatory architecture were well known in advance, from at least the Lamfalussy Report in

**94** Crises and Integration in European Banking Union

2001.[135] It was not a question of learning that the flaws existed, but rather of gathering the political will to address them. The debate thus focused on what level of response constituted a *necessary* response, given the lack of political will, not just what reforms would be most desirable. Virtually all key actors agreed that the 2007–09 Banking Crisis was endogenous in its origins, but the gap between their preferred solutions hinged on their understanding of the scale of the crisis.

The literature on European economic policymaking has generally divided countries into two blocs, a liberal "market-making" bloc led by the UK and including many northern member states, and a "market-shaping" bloc favoring tighter regulation led by France and including many southern member states, with Germany vacillating between the two groups from issue to issues.[136] The debate over post-Banking Crisis reforms saw the market-making bloc hold together, while the market-shaping bloc split between those favoring minimal reforms and those advocating a more ambitious agenda.

The market-making bloc, most prominently represented by the UK, saw a minimal crisis and thus minimal need for reform. In this view, while the Banking Crisis undeniably produced substantial costs to states, it did not pose a fundamental threat to either European integration or the solvency of any member state. As such, there was little risk of an escalation of problems out of the crisis. That these views were most prominent in the UK can be to a degree attributed to the greater tolerance for crises in states with a more liberal orientation, but in any case, members of this camp saw little need for substantial reform out of the crisis. Instead, the greatest fear of many in this camp was rather that the Crisis would provide the pretext for regulatory overreach. UK financial columnist Allister Heath is here broadly representative, arguing that "It is true UK monetary, regulatory and fiscal policies were a disgrace; the Labour government paid the price for its incompetence. But that doesn't justify handing power to unaccountable bureaucracies. European countries and Brussels itself failed even more miserably on every count." For Heath, and for many who saw a minimal crisis, "the real answer is to decentralise power, and make governing structures as local and accountable as possible."[137]

While the market-making bloc had a unified position on crisis reforms, the market-shaping bloc split into two camps.[138] One camp saw both a substantial danger exposed by the crisis and a need for substantial reform. In debates over creation of the EBA, the European Parliament was the key advocate of this position, advocating for both a pan-European bailout and a move toward banking union well before its actual enactment out of the Debt Crisis. For this camp, perhaps the most important lesson out of the crisis was that it was a "near miss." Although the Banking Crisis had been one largely manageable using only national resources, to a degree this was only fortunate chance as the hardest-hit states were also the wealthiest. In subsequent crises, a heavier cost to states less able to pay might well spark much greater escalation. In that sense, these cautions were prophetic, as the next crisis, the Debt Crisis, would essentially be driven by the fact that the next wave of bank failures hit the southern Europeans, states less capable of managing a crisis with their own resources. For this camp, the main problems at the heart of this crisis related to the still-unresolved problems of Schoenmaker's Trilemma, that international finance without international regulation is a recipe for instability due to inevitable gaps in regulation, the scope for regulatory arbitrage, and "race to the bottom" competition between regulators. This camp's greatest fear out of the crisis reform process, therefore, was the inverse of that of the previous camp: if the minimal-crisis camp feared overregulation, this camp feared that the reform agenda would prove insufficient, and that Europe would be left scrambling to cobble together an improvised solution in face of a cascading and escalating crisis.

Finally, the third group, the other half of the market-shaping bloc, saw a moderate crisis requiring moderate reform. This was ultimately the position endorsed in the de Larosière Report and adopted by France, Germany, and the European Commission. Their account of the crisis saw one that was caused by relatively fixable flaws in information-sharing and regulatory confusion, which could be addressed with a relatively modest reform agenda. Truly sweeping reforms, such as a pan-European bailout mechanism or a single European regulator, may be desirable but ultimately unnecessary. Moreover, the great fear of this camp was that such ambitious reform attempts might backfire, meaning that even the more moderate and essential reforms would fail. This was seen as particularly a risk if the United Kingdom could not be brought on board.

Key to the negotiating dynamics was the passage of time. While in the later, more severe, Debt Crisis and Pandemic Crisis, reforms were necessary at the peak of the crisis moment, the Banking Crisis's most intense period, the five months between late August 2008 and early January 2009, passed before substantial European-level reform efforts got underway. Substantial work remained to clean up the longer-term economic fallout from the wave of bank failures, but the longer time passed from the core crisis moment, the less essential the case for reform became and the stronger the opponents of reform would become. Given that the greatest fear of the moderates was that no reform would occur, this created a strong incentive to act quickly. Since the advocates of more expansive reforms also conceded that moderate reforms were superior to no reforms, this left the advocates of minimal reform in a strong position. The longer that the UK held to its red lines, the most likely it became that no reform would be forthcoming. As such, the debate quickly turned to what the UK was willing to accept.

The final outcome was touted by moderates as successfully addressing the core problems that the EU faced out of the Banking Crisis. Michel Barnier at the European Commission celebrated the agreement on the EBA, arguing that "the fact is that we did not see the crisis coming. We did not have the monitoring tools to detect the risk which was accumulating across the system. And when the crisis hit, we did not have effective tools to act." The reforms, in Barnier's view, would give Europe "the control tower and the radar screens needed to identify risks, the tools to better control financial players and the means to act quickly, in a coordinated way, in a timely fashion."[139] Despite Barnier's optimism, the literature has generally regarded these reforms as an incremental deepening of the existing structures, rather than a truly pathbreaking overhaul of European financial regulation.[140]

The European response to the Banking Crisis is important in its own right, but also provides an important prelude to the dynamics surrounding the Debt Crisis. Reformers in both cases identified the same dangers from the Doom Loop and the risk of a banking crisis pushing into a sovereign debt crisis, and even proposed essentially the same policy responses. However, only in the latter case did they win sufficient support to advance truly fundamental changes in supervision and resolution. The Banking Crisis, while coming from the same endogenous flaws as the Debt Crisis, simply failed to manifest a sufficiently large threat to the integration status quo to drive a more fundamental reform. As such, it produced only a real but modest patch-up reform, sufficient to the immediate issues but leaving fundamental vulnerabilities acknowledged and unaddressed.

## Notes

1. Christopher Mitchell, *Saving the Market from Itself: The Politics of Financial Intervention* (Cambridge: Cambridge University Press, 2016).
2. Nathalie Thomas and Rosemary Gallagher, "The Lehman's Legacy: Has Banking's Dragon Finally Been Tamed?," *Scotland on Sunday*, September 2009.
3. Schoenmaker, "The Financial Trilemma"; Schoenmaker, *Governance of International Banking*.
4. Mark K. Cassell, "A Tale of Two Crises: Germany's Landesbanken and the United States' Savings and Loans," *Journal of Banking Regulation* 17, no. 1 (2016): 73–89.

The 2007–09 Banking Crisis  **97**

5. Howarth and Quaglia, *The Political Economy of European Banking Union*; Lucia Quaglia and David Howarth, "The Policy Narratives of European Capital Markets Union," *Journal of European Public Policy* 25, no. 7 (2018): 990–1009.

6. David Crawford and Marcus Walker, "Germany Ignored Regulator's Hypo Warning; Documents Show Market Watchdog Bafin Raised Alarm Bells Six Months before Massive Government Bailout," *The Globe and Mail (Canada)*, May 2009, sec. REPORT ON BUSINESS: INTERNATIONAL; CREDIT CRISIS; William Tinning and Torquil Crichton, "Pressure on Darling as Germany Guarantees All Savings," *Herald-Scotland*, October 2008, https://www.heraldscotland.com/default_content/12368486. pressure-darling-germany-guarantees-savings/.

7. Jean-Claude Juncker and Jean-Claude Trichet, "Trichet en Juncker voorzichtig optimistisch over economish herstel in 2010 (en)" (Reparks to the European Parliament, March 2009), https://www.parlement.com/id/vi3tivff3lwt/nieuws/trichet_en_juncker_voorzichtig.

8. Marialuz Moreno Badia, Samba Mbaye, and Kyungla Chae, "Global Debt Database: Methodology and Sources" (International Monetary Fund, 2018).

9. Moreno Badia, Mbaye, and Chae, "Global Debt Database."

10. Iceland also faced substantial costs from its banking crisis, forcing the Icelandic state to default on its Deposit Guarantee Scheme's obligations to British and Dutch customers. However, because Iceland was only a European Economic Area member and not an EU member state, its default did not directly threaten the EU's stability and integration the way the subsequent sovereign debt crises of Member States would in 2010–14.

11. Juncker and Trichet, "Trichet en Juncker voorzichtig optimistisch over economish herstel in 2010 (en)."

12. Geoff Meade, "'Early Warning System' Plan For Banks," *Press Association Mediapoint*, February 2009, sec. Home News.

13. David Gow, "Britain Is Favour of Europe Again—at Least for a While," *The Guardian*, March 2009, sec. World news, https://www.theguardian.com/business/2009/mar/26/britain-in-favour-of-europe; Andrew Duff, "Why Britain Needs the Euro," *Financial Times*, March 2009, https://www.ft.com/content/aa181ad4-19e1-11de-9f91-0000779fd2ac.

14. Philip Andrews, "Is the EU Breaking Up?," *Business & Finance Magazine*, n.d.

15. Ralph Atkins and James Wilson, "Transcript of FT Interview with Axel Weber, President of the Bundesbank," *Financial Times*, April 2009, https://www.ft.com/content/085d83b4-2e9f-11de-b7d3-00144feabdc0.

16. Lucia Quaglia, "The 'Old' and 'New' Politics of Financial Services Regulation in the European Union," *New Political Economy* 17, no. 4 (2012): 515–535.

17. "Jacques de Larosière, the Reformer," *Institutional Investor*, April 2009, https://www.institutionalinvestor.com/article/b150qb2kyg5t0x/jacques-de-larosire-the-reformer.

18. Bieling, "Shattered Expectations"; Stefano Pagliari, "A Wall around Europe? The European Regulatory Response to the Global Financial Crisis and the Turn in Transatlantic Relations," *Journal of European Integration* 35, no. 4 (2013): 391–408; Manolis Kalaitzake, "Brexit for Finance? Structural Interdependence as a Source of Financial Political Power within UK-EU Withdrawal Negotiations," *Review of International Political Economy* 28, no. 3 (2021): 479–504.

## 98  Crises and Integration in European Banking Union

19. Bieling, "Shattered Expectations"; Burns, Clifton, and Quaglia, "Explaining Policy Change in the EU"; Elliot Posner and Nicolas Véron, "The EU and Financial Regulation: Power without Purpose?," *Journal of European Public Policy* 17, no. 3 (2010): 400–415.

20. Mitchell, *Saving the Market from Itself.*

21. European Central Bank, "The ECB's Response to the Financial Crisis," *ECB Monthy Bulletin*, October 2010, https://www.ecb.europa.eu/pub/pdf/other/art1_mb201010en_pp59-74en.pdf.

22. Glenn Somerville and David Milliken, "G7 Partners Cool to U.S.-Style Bailout Plans; Guarded Promises to Co-Operate. European Union Makes It Clear It Will Not Join Any Sort of Rescue Package," *The Gazette*, September 2008, sec. Business.

23. Stephen Castle and Katrin Bennhold, "European Officials Debate Need for a Bailout Package," *The New York Times*, October 2008, sec. Business, https://www.nytimes.com/2008/10/02/business/worldbusiness/02regulate.html.

24. "Sarkozy Floats Idea of EU-Wide Plan," *Irish Times*, October 2008.

25. Marcus Walker, Joellen Perry, and David Gauthier-Villars, "Germany, France Disagree on Bailout Strategy," *The Globe and Mail*, October 2008, sec. Report on Business: International.

26. Edward Cody and Kevin Sullivan-Washington Post Foreign Service, "European Leaders Split on Rescue Strategy," *The Washington Post*, October 2008, sec. A SECTION.

27. Jamie Smyth, "German Finance Minister Dismisses Proposed Pan-European Rescue Fund," *Irish Times*, October 2008.

28. Smyth, "German Finance Minister Dismisses Proposed Pan-European Rescue Fund."

29. Tony Barber et al., "Sarkozy Recoils from EU-Wide EUR300bn Bail-Out," *Financial Times*, October 2008, sec. GLOBAL FINANCIAL CRISIS.

30. Huw Jones and Paul Taylor, "France, Germany Clash on Financial Rescue; Paris Floating Plan for EU Bailout Fund for Banks," *The Ottawa Citizen*, October 2008, sec. Business & Technology.

31. Walker, Perry, and Gauthier-Villars, "Germany, France Disagree on Bailout Strategy."

32. Cody and Service, "European Leaders Split on Rescue Strategy."

33. Barber et al., "Sarkozy Recoils from EU-Wide EUR300bn Bail-Out"; "Sarkozy Floats Idea of EU-Wide Plan."

34. Walker, Perry, and Gauthier-Villars, "Germany, France Disagree on Bailout Strategy."

35. Barber et al., "Sarkozy Floats Idea of EU-Wide Plan."

36. Barber et al., "Sarkozy Recoils from EU-Wide EUR300bn Bail-Out."

37. Gernot Heller and Kevin Krolicki, "Key German Bank Rescued; Italy Presses for EU-Wide Bailout Fund," *The Windsor Star*, October 2008, sec. Business.

38. Katrin Bennhold et al., "European Leaders Agree to Inject Cash Into Banks," *New York Times (Online)*, October 2008, sec. business, https://www.proquest.com/news/docview/2221377680/abstract/20483DF84EFC44AFPQ/376.

39. Davide S. Mare, Ata Can Bertay, and Nan Zhou, *Global Financial Development Database* (The World Bank), accessed January 23, 2023, https://www.worldbank.org/en/publication/gfdr/data/global-financial-development-database.

40. Lamfalussy et al., "Final Report of the Committee of Wise Men on the Regulation of European Securities Markets."

41. Ian Traynor, "European Commission Keen for More Market Co-Operation," *The Guardian*, October 2008, sec. Business, https://www.theguardian.com/business/2008/oct/09/europe.eu.

The 2007–09 Banking Crisis **99**

42. Traynor, "European Commission Keen for More Market Co-Operation."
43. Nikki Tait and Jennifer Hughes, "Trichet Urges More Oversight," *Irish Times*, February 2009; "EU to Fund Supervisory Bodies for Accounting, Auditing," *Xinhua General News Service*, January 2009, https://www.theglobaltreasurer.com/2009/01/27/commission-looks-to-strengthen-standard-setting-bodies-for-accounting-and-auditing/.
44. "Polish Finance Minister Comments on Banking Sector, Euro Adoption Plan," *BBC Worldwide Monitoring*, November 2008, sec. BBC Monitoring Europe—Political.
45. Ralph Atkins, "EU Warned on Risk of Financial Market Problems," *Financial Times*, January 2009, sec. WORLD NEWS.
46. Tait and Hughes, "Trichet Urges More Oversight."
47. Lorenzo Bini Smaghi, "Regulation and Supervisory Architecture: Is the EU on the Right Path?" (Speech, February 2009), https://www.ecb.europa.eu/press/key/date/2009/html/sp090212.en.html; Tait and Hughes, "Trichet Urges More Oversight."
48. Jean-Claude Trichet, "Remarks on the Future of European Financial Regulation and Supervision" (Speech, February 2009), https://www.ecb.europa.eu/press/key/date/2009/html/sp090223.en.html.
49. Atkins, "EU Warned on Risk of Financial Market Problems"; Ben Hall, "Transcript: Christine Lagarde," *Financial Times*, February 2009; Ralph Atkins and Nikki Tait, "Crisis Mismanagement Casts ECB as Saviour," *Financial Times*, January 2009, sec. WORLD IN RECESSION.
50. Atkins and Tait, "Crisis Mismanagement Casts ECB as Saviour."
51. Nikki Tait, "UK Insurers Back Idea of EU Regulator," *Financial Times*, February 2009, https://www.ft.com/content/860fa482-f84d-11dd-aae8-000077b07658.
52. Howard Davies, "Europe's Banks Need a Federal Fix," *Financial Times*, January 2009, sec. COMMENT.
53. David Gow, "Berès Leads the Charge for Tougher European Regulation," *The Guardian*, October 2008, sec. Business, https://www.theguardian.com/business/2008/oct/21/europe-regulators.
54. Huw Jones, "EU Sets up Crisis Unit to Boost Financial Oversight," *Reuters*, October 2008, sec. Banks, https://www.reuters.com/article/eu-financial-supervision-idUSLG70246420081016; Hall, "Transcript."
55. Huw Jones, "ECB and France Spar over Future Bank Supervision," *Reuters*, February 2009, sec. Financial Services and Real Estate, https://www.reuters.com/article/eu-financial-supervision-idUKLK24496720090220.
56. House of Lords—European Union Committee, "The Future of EU Financial Regulation and Supervision," Minutes of Evidence (London: House of Lords, January 2009), https://publications.parliament.uk/pa/ld200809/ldselect/ldeucom/106/9012702.htm.
57. House of Lords—European Union Committee; Marcus Killick, "Time for an EU Banking Regulator?," *Gibralter Magazine*, March 2009, https://issuu.com/thegibraltarmagazine/docs/march2009.
58. Jennifer Hughes, "UK Makes Its Presence Felt on Financial Reform," *Financial Times*, January 2009, sec. WORLD NEWS.
59. Traynor, "European Commission Keen for More Market Co-Operation."
60. Tony Barber et al., "European States Seek Financial Fraternity," *Financial Times*, October 2008, sec. GLOBAL FINANCIAL CRISIS.
61. Nikki Tait, "Brussels Left to Finish 'Mission Impossible,'" *Financial Times*, February 2009, sec. FINANCIAL REGULATION.

## 100    Crises and Integration in European Banking Union

62. Nikki Tait, "Taskforce Calls for New Risk Bodies," *Financial Times*, February 2009, sec. FINANCIAL REGULATION.

63. José Manuel Barroso, "Financial Reform Is Necessary and Urgent" (Speech, February 2009), http://www.efmlg.org/Docs/Meeting%2030/Item%208%20-%20JMD%20 Barroso%20speech.pdf; Tony Barber and Ralph Atkins, "Extracts from FT Interview with Joaquín Almunia," *Financial Times*, February 2009, https://www.ft.com/content/ 0f8fe744-0357-11de-b405-000077b07658.

64. "Reams of Reform," *Financial Times*, March 2009, sec. Financial Advisor.

65. Tait, "Taskforce Calls for New Risk Bodies"; Huw Jones, "Report Urges Phased Reform of EU Financial Oversight," *Reuters*, February 2009, sec. Business News, https://www. reuters.com/article/uk-financial-eu-sb-idUKTRE51O3TT20090225.

66. Jones, "Report Urges Phased Reform of EU Financial Oversight."

67. Jeremy Warner, "Clamour Grows for More Regulation," *The Independent*, February 2009, sec. Business; Hugo Dixon, "Diplomacy Dilutes Europe's Crisis-Prevention Plan," *Breakingviews.Com*, May 2009, https://www.breakingviews.com/considered-view/diplomacy- dilutes-europes-crisis-prevention-plan/.

68. Chris Giles, "Grand Ideas Fail to Mop up the Mess," *Financial Times*, February 2009, sec. FINANCIAL REGULATION.

69. Simon Carswell, "A Failure to Tackle Cross-Border Banking," *Irish Times*, February 2009; Peter Thal Larsen, "Bank Regulation Needs Straightening Out," *Financial Times*, March 2009, https://www.ft.com/content/723612ce-1d42-11de-9eb3-00144feabdc0.

70. "Brussels Pushes for Pan-European Financial Regulators," *Deutsche Presse-Agentur*, May 2009, sec. Finance.

71. Marek Belka and Wim Fonteyne, "A Banking Framework to Secure Single Market," *Financial Times*, June 2009, https://www.ft.com/content/01193d96-5082-11de-9530- 00144feabdc0.

72. Bill Cash, "EU Supervisory Scheme That Will Be against UK's Interests," *Financial Times*, February 2009, sec. LETTERS TO THE EDITOR.

73. "Plan for EU Financial Sector Supervision Has Faults-CNB's Tomsik," *CTK Business News Wire*, March 2009, sec. Business News.

74. Tracy Corrigan, "The Most Sensible Solution Is to Police the Banks from the Bottom Up," *The Daily Telegraph*, February 2009, sec. City.

75. Jennifer Hughes, "London's Nervous Wait for Tougher Regulation," *Financial Times*, March 2009, https://www.ft.com/content/2b16a9b8-1e1d-11de-830b-00144feabdc0.

76. "City Resists European Reform 'Straitjacket,'" *Investment Adviser*, March 2009.

77. David Gow, "Brussels Looks at Europe-Wide Bank Regulation," *The Guardian*, February 2009, sec. Business, https://www.theguardian.com/business/2009/feb/26/brussels- europe-bank-regulation.

78. Nikki Tait, "European Plan for Financial Regulation Faces UK Obstacles," *Financial Times*, May 2009, sec. WORLD NEWS.

79. Adam Cohen and Charles Forelle, "Leading the News: EU Proposes New Bloc-Wide Regulators—They Would Monitor Risk and Companies; U.K. Likely to Object," *Wall Street Journal*, September 2009, Europe edition.

80. Leigh Thomas, "Britain Fights EU Pressure on Financial Supervision," *Agence France Presse*, June 2009.

The 2007–09 Banking Crisis    **101**

81. "Financial Services: Commission Proposes Stronger Financial Supervision in Europe," Press Release (Brussels: European Commission, May 2009), https://ec.europa.eu/commission/presscorner/detail/en/IP_09_836.

82. Jamie Smyth, "Barroso Calls for Consensus on Financial Supervision," *Irish Times*, May 2009.

83. Lucas Papademos, "Presentation of the ECB's Annual Report 2008 to the European Parliament" (Introductory Statement, April 2009), https://www.bis.org/review/r090423e.pdf.

84. Ben Hall, George Parker, and Nikki Tait, "Britain Heads for EU Rift over Regulation," *Financial Times*, March 2009, sec. NATIONAL NEWS.

85. Ian Traynor and David Gow, "Brown Backs New Franco-German Plan to Curb City Excesses," *The Guardian*, March 2009, sec. World news, https://www.theguardian.com/world/2009/mar/21/gordon-brown-european-central-bank.

86. "EU Pushes Ahead with Finance Oversight Shake-Up," *Agence France Presse*, June 2009.

87. Hall, Parker, and Tait, "Britain Heads for EU Rift over Regulation."

88. "Financial Supervision for EU," *Polish News Bulletin*, April 2009, sec. Law News.

89. Turner Jonathan Adair, "The Turner Review: A Regulatory Response to the Global Banking Crisis" (London (UK), United Kingdom: Financial Servcies Authority, n.d.).

90. Gow, "Britain Is Favour of Europe Again—at Least for a While"; Press Association, "Brown Blueprint Rejected as 'European Ideas Wrapped in a British Flag,'" *The Guardian*, March 2009, sec. Politics, https://www.theguardian.com/politics/2009/mar/19/gordon-brown-economic-blueprint-brussels.

91. Jonathan Adair, "The Turner Review: A Regulatory Response to the Global Banking Crisis," 103.

92. Gordon Brown, "Spring European Council—Hansard—UK Parliament" (Speech, March 2009), https://hansard.parliament.uk//Commons/2009-03-23/debates/0903235000002/details.

93. Ian Traynor, "Brown Wins Independence from European Banking Regulator," *The Guardian*, June 2009, sec. Business, https://www.theguardian.com/business/2009/jun/18/brown-independence-europe-banking-watchdog.

94. Heather Stewart, "Darling Wins Brussels Battle over Financial Super-Regulator," *The Guardian*, June 2009, sec. Business, https://www.theguardian.com/business/2009/jun/10/alistair-darling-european-finance-regulator.

95. Alex Barker and Nikki Tait, "EU Set for Regulatory Reform," *Financial Times*, March 2009, sec. FRONT PAGE—COMPANIES & MARKETS.

96. David Miliband (Chair) and Paul Myners, "'European Affairs' on Tuesday 16 June 2009." (Debate, June 2009), https://hansard.parliament.uk//Commons/2009-06-16/debates/09061634000001/EuropeanAffairs.

97. Sean O'Grady, "Sarkozy's Plan to Muscle in on the City?," *The Independent*, June 2009, sec. Business.

98. Sam Jones, "UK Slams EU Hedge Fund Rules," *Financial Times*, July 2009, https://www.proquest.com/news/docview/229220082/citation/F002DE44158A4712PQ/1.

99. Tony Barber, "London Mayor Back to Do Battle with Brussels," *Financial Times*, September 2009, https://www.proquest.com/news/docview/229291127/citation/16F6F87D8AA84B5BPQ/1; Hélène Mulholland, "Boris Johnson Warns of Threat

## 102 Crises and Integration in European Banking Union

from EU Regulation Plans," *The Guardian*, September 2009, sec. Politics, https://www.theguardian.com/politics/2009/sep/02/boris-johnson-eu-regulation.

100. Brooke Masters and George Parker, "Darling Pressed to Hold Back on EU Regulation," *Financial Times*, November 2009, sec. NATIONAL NEWS.

101. Allan Hall, "Germany Hits out at Britain over 'blocks' on Strict Rules," *London Evening Standard*, September 2009, West End final ed. edition, sec. News.

102. Hall, Parker, and Tait, "Britain Heads for EU Rift over Regulation"; Thomas, "Britain Fights EU Pressure on Financial Supervision"; "Brown to Defend City of London against EU Financial Supervision," *Irish Examiner*, June 2009, sec. IE-Business/BUSINESS.

103. Ambrose Evans-Pritchard, "Germany Wants to Rein in EU Plans," *The Daily Telegraph*, September 2009, sec. City.

104. Mitchell, *Saving the Market from Itself*.

105. Aoife White, "EU: Central Banks to Pick New Regulator Chief," *Associated Press Internatioanl*, June 2009, sec. Business News.

106. O'Grady, "Sarkozy's Plan to Muscle in on the City?"

107. Jonathan Braude, "U.K. Wins Only Limited EC Concessions," *Daily Deal/The Deal*, June 2009.

108. Bill Jamieson, "The Future of Regulation Is up in the Air," *Scotland on Sunday*, June 2009.

109. Tim Shipman, "Hands off the City Chancellor Warns Sarkozy's EU Man [Edition 3]," *Daily Mail*, December 2009, sec. News.

110. Shipman, "Hands off the City Chancellor."

111. David Charter, "Brussels Regulators Could Order Britain to Bail out Banks under New Rules," *The Times (London)*, September 2009, sec. News.

112. Aoife White, "Amid Divisions, EU Agrees New Financial Regulation," *Associated Press Internatioanl*, December 2009, sec. Business News.

113. David Charter, "Jubilant Sarkozy Sees EU Take Powers over the City," *The Times* (London), June 2009, https://www.thetimes.co.uk/article/jubilant-sarkozy-sees-eu-take-powers-over-the-city-nrrkcfdm87h.

114. Brooke Masters, Nikki Tait, and James Wilson, "Common Rules Likely to Be Enforced," *Financial Times*, September 2009, sec. WORLD NEWS.

115. "ECON Hearing on Financial Supervisory Package—de Larosière Stresses Progress Has Been Satisfactory," Press Release (Brussels: European Parliament Economic and Monetary Affairs Committee, January 2010); Jim Brunsden, "Showdown over Supervision," *Politico*, March 2010, https://www.politico.eu/article/showdown-over-supervision/; John Schranz, "The European Parliament and Financial Supervision Reform," Press Release (Brussels: European Parliament, September 2010), https://www.europarl.europa.eu/news/en/press-room/20100506BKG74226/the-european-parliament-and-financial-supervision-reform.

116. John Schranz, "MEPs Vote to Beef up Financial Supervisory Package," Press Release (Brussels: European Parliament Economic and Monetary Affairs Committee, May 2010), https://www.europarl.europa.eu/pdfs/news/expert/infopress/20100510IPR74360/20100510IPR74360_en.pdf.

117. Schranz, "MEPs Vote to Beef up Financial Supervisory Package."

118. Schranz, "MEPs Vote to Beef up Financial Supervisory Package."

119. Brunsden, "Showdown over Supervision."

120. Brunsden, "Showdown over Supervision."

121. "ECON Hearing on Financial Supervisory Package—de Larosière Stresses Progress Has Been Satisfactory."
122. Schranz, "The European Parliament and Financial Supervision Reform."
123. "EU Regulators' Role Sparks Debate," *Global Investor*, September 2010.
124. Ian Traynor, "George Osborne Rules out Taking Part in European Bank Bailout Fund," *The Guardian*, September 2010, sec. Business, https://www.theguardian.com/business/2010/sep/07/osborne-rules-out-euro-bailout-fund.
125. Nikki Tait, "EU Oversight Reform given Backing," *Financial Times*, July 2010, https://www.proquest.com/news/docview/594872539/citation/8098126AFCA34809PQ/1.
126. "EU Regulators' Role Sparks Debate."
127. "European Parliament Plans Super-Regulator," *Investment Adviser*, May 2010.
128. Eddy Wymeersch, "Giving Europe a Single Voice," *Professional Wealth Management*, sec. Market Monitor, accessed January 20, 2023, https://www.pwmnet.com/Archive/Giving-Europe-a-single-voice.
129. Schranz, "The European Parliament and Financial Supervision Reform."
130. Cohen and Forelle, "Leading the News."
131. José Manuel Barroso, "Fostering Economic Recovery: The EU Moves from Crisis Management to Reform" (Speech, September 2010), https://www.cfr.org/event/fostering-economic-recovery-eu-moves-crisis-management-reform-0; Daniel Bases, "EU's Barroso Urges Shift to Reforms from Crisis," *Reuters*, September 2010, sec. Business News, https://www.reuters.com/article/uk-eu-recovery-barroso-idUKTRE68N07Y20100924.
132. Olli Rehn, "The Euro Is Back, But There Is No Room For Complacency" (Introductory Statement, September 2010), https://www.parlement.com/id/viiulz17dkyj/nieuws/toespraak_eurcommissaris_olli_rehn_over.
133. Nicolas Véron, "The European Union Has Not Yet Solved Its Banking Problem | PIIE" (Peterson Institute for International Economics, October 2010), https://www.piie.com/blogs/realtime-economic-issues-watch/european-union-has-not-yet-solved-its-banking-problem.
134. José Manuel Barroso, "Opening Remarks by President Barroso at the Friends of Europe Working Dinner" (Opening Remarks, October 2010).
135. Lamfalussy et al., "Final Report of the Committee of Wise Men on the Regulation of European Securities Markets."
136. Pagliari, "A Wall around Europe?"; Quaglia, "The 'Old' and 'New' Politics of Financial Services Regulation in the European Union"; Ulrich Krotz and Joachim Schild, "Back to the Future? Franco-German Bilateralism in Europe's Post-Brexit Union," *Journal of European Public Policy* 25, no. 8 (August 2018): 1174–1193, doi:10.1080/13,501,763.2018.1467951.
137. Allister Heath, "EU Not City Dictates Capital's Future," *CityAM*, November 2010, https://www.cityam.com/eu-not-city-dictates-capitals-future/.
138. Quaglia, "The 'Old' and 'New' Politics of Financial Services Regulation in the European Union."
139. "Europe Agrees New Agencies to Supervise Financial Firms," *BBC News*, September 2010, sec. Business, https://www.bbc.com/news/business–11171800.
140. Quaglia, "The 'Old' and 'New' Politics of Financial Services Regulation in the European Union"; Burns, Clifton, and Quaglia, "Explaining Policy Change in the EU"; Bieling, "Shattered Expectations."

# 4
# The 2010–14 European Debt Crisis

Monnet Crisis and Banking Union

## Introduction

The 2010–14 European Debt Crisis presented a challenge that both posed a severe endogenous threat to European financial integration and which produced substantial reform. As such, it provides the clearest example in the twenty-first century of a "Monnet Crisis," a crisis which provided a clear spur toward a fundamental deepening of European integration. It both clearly originated in the European financial system and presented a substantial threat to continued integration of the financial system, the eurozone, and potentially the European Union itself. While the Banking Crisis hit the wealthiest member states the hardest, the Debt Crisis hit states much less capable of managing the crisis with their own resources, making default and exit from the eurozone a very real possibility. Moreover, the substantial exposure of northern banks to southern markets created a direct threat to virtually all member states. The scale and transnational nature of the crisis thus presented a stark choice of either unravelling the currency union to allow for national defaults or a move toward deeper integration by moving supervision and resolution to the European level to sever an overly cozy bank–national regulator relationship and draw on Continental fiscal resources. As a substantial endogenous threat, the Debt Crisis produced the most substantial move toward integration, resulting in both the centralization of eurozone bank regulation in the Single Supervisory Mechanism (SSM) and the centralization and mutualization of bank resolution in the Single Resolution Mechanism (SRM). Both of these reforms constitute substantial overhauls of the financial regulatory architecture of the eurozone, making substantial changes to deal with a substantial internal problem. However, the crisis ended before the third "pillar" of banking union, the proposed European Deposit Insurance Scheme (EDIS), could be completed. The Debt Crisis thus demonstrates both how a severe endogenous crisis can spur reform and how the closing of the crisis period

*Crises and Integration in European Banking Union.* Christopher Mitchell, Oxford University Press.
© Christopher Mitchell (2023). DOI: 10.1093/oso/9780198889069.003.0004

can also bring a close to the window of opportunity to advance further changes.

## Outlining the Crisis

As with any crisis driven by complex underlying dynamics, dating the beginning and end of the European Debt Crisis is somewhat fraught. Some observers group the 2007–09 Banking Crisis and 2010–14 Debt Crisis into a single crisis, and as will be discussed, the two crises do share some underlying causes.[1] However, especially for the purposes of this analysis, it makes sense to separate them into two events, for two key reasons. The first is that they were largely framed at the time as separate events. As discussed in Chapter 3, the Banking Crisis was generally understood as resolved by early 2010, and the Debt Crisis seen as a new challenge. The understanding of the Debt Crisis as animated by the same underlying weaknesses in the European financial system only came later. The second is that the nature and scale of the threat was substantially greater. The Banking Crisis represented only a moderate threat to European finance as a whole, as the crisis-stricken states had the resources to deal with the crisis nationally and thus there was relatively little threat to integration. The Debt Crisis, however, both because of the scale and nature of the problem, and because of the weaker fiscal position of the affected states, posed a real threat to integration and could only be managed either with transnational action or some degree of dissolution of the eurozone and potentially the EU.

The Debt Crisis can be itself divided into three phases, governed by different understandings of the nature and scale of the crisis, and thus different strategies in response. In the first phase, the crisis was understood as chiefly a problem of Greek sovereign debt, and one that should be dealt with without EU assistance, in line with the "no bailouts"' clause in the Maastricht Treaty.[2] A second phase began in May 2010, as the crisis spread to other southern states and the no-bailouts standard became untenable. At this point, the EU began offering assistance to states, but not to banks, as the crisis was still chiefly framed as a sovereign debt crisis. Finally, by summer 2012, the crisis came to be understood as a banking crisis driving sovereign debt pressure, and European responses shifted to direct support of banks and construction of a European banking union.

Phase one began on October 4, 2009, when the newly elected Prime Minister of Greece, George Papandreou, revealed that the previous Greek government had dramatically understated the scale of the Greek budget deficit. Bond traders responded with a massive sell-off of Greek government debt, beginning a climb in yields that would ultimately produce an almost 650 percent rise on ten-year bonds from September 2009 levels.[3] Given the relatively small size of the Greek economy, this was a big problem for Greece, but did not in itself seem to be a great challenge to the eurozone as a whole. However, two developments caused this relatively small crisis to grow dramatically. The first is that key eurozone actors, in particular Bundesbank Chair and European Central Bank (ECB) Governing Council Member Axel Weber, indicated that they would continue to honor the "no bailouts" clause of the Maastricht Treaty, and that Greece could not expect support from the rest of the eurozone to manage its growing crisis.[4] This was contrary to the expectations of many market investors, who had assumed that this pledge would be too costly to enforce, and thus that the sovereign debt of all eurozone states could be treated as essentially equivalent in risk. The credible suggestion that the no bailouts pledge would be enforced substantially increased markets actors' perception of the risk of Greek debt, causing a further rise in bond yields and risk of default.

The second key development was the spread of the crisis to other southern eurozone states. This was a function both of an increasing sense that the no bailouts clause may be honored and of the self-fulfilling nature of runs. Just as in the East Asian Financial Crisis a decade earlier, bond traders began reducing their exposures not just to the country in crisis, but also to countries regarded as similar in profile. Regardless of the fundamentals of neighboring countries, bond traders anticipated that their peers would sell their sovereign debt holdings, so they themselves sold while the price was relatively good, and in doing so created the very run they anticipated. In the European case, this meant dramatically increasing pressure on Portugal, followed by pressure on Spain and Italy. Drawing the third and fourth largest economies in the eurozone into a sovereign debt crisis dramatically increased the stakes of the crisis, raising serious questions as to the sustainability of the "no bailouts" position.

By May of 2010, it had become clear that the no bailouts position was unsustainable, and the second phase began, marked by temporary emergency provisions. The European Financial Stabilization Mechanism (EFSM) was introduced in May, and followed in June by the European Financial Stability Facility (EFSF), temporary facilities designed to provide emergency support and haircuts on sovereign debt in exchange for austerity measures and economic restructuring in the crisis-afflicted countries. However, these measures, in particular the severe austerity provisions, proved to be tremendously unpopular, sparking a rise of anti-bailout movements on both the left and right in the affected countries. They also proved to be ineffectual. Growth in the crisis-affected countries continued to decline and bond yields continued to rise amid a growing sense that the temporary emergency provisions were ineffectual.

The European commitment to resolving the crisis reached a key inflection point on July 26, 2012, when the President of the European Central Bank Mario Draghi delivered his "whatever it takes" speech, vowing to take whatever extreme measures were necessary to contain the crisis and preserve the common currency. This was followed by the introduction of a series of permanent institutions that would replace the temporary measures. In particular, the European Stability Mechanism (ESM), ratified on September 27, 2012, provided a permanent replacement for the EFSF and EFSM, at last replacing the ineffectual "no bailouts" provision with a sustainable mechanism to manage eurozone members in sovereign debt crises. This was complemented by a series of updates to the Stability and Growth Pact designed to tighten fiscal discipline among member states, the "six pack" implemented in December 2011 and the "two pack" implemented in May 2013.

These measures helped contain the sovereign debt crisis and bring down the bond yields in the affected countries, but failed to address the banking crisis driving the sovereign debt crisis. A series of banking crises across southern Europe soon demonstrated the continued danger from instability in the financial sector. Most prominently, the collapse of the midsized regional caja banks in Spain in June 2012 necessitated the Spanish government tapping the EU's emergency funding mechanisms to contain the crisis. The Cypriot banking sector would follow Spain into crisis later that summer. By November of that year, Banca Monte dei Paschi di Siena (MPS), the fourth largest bank in Italy and by some measures the oldest bank in the world, would also fall into distress. This proliferation of banking crises across the eurozone would help drive the introduction of a partial banking union which would be introduced in 2013 and 2014. The first key measure, the Single Supervisory Mechanism, made the European Central Bank the direct supervisor for the most significant banks in the eurozone, and the indirect supervisor, over the national supervisors, for the remaining institutions. It would be ratified on October 15, 2013, and come into force the following November 3. It would be followed by the introduction of the Bank Recovery and Resolution Mechanism (BRRD) on May 15, 2014, which established common rules for bank resolution across the European Union. The most significant of these would be the "bail-in" mechanism, establishing conditions by which creditors would be converted to equity-holders, in principle dramatically reducing the need for taxpayer-funded bailouts by pushing costs onto creditors. Finally, the Single Resolution Mechanism created a Single Resolution Board (SRB) to manage bank resolution and a Single Resolution Fund (SRF), a common pool of money to pay for the costs of those resolutions. Created on July 15, 2014, and in force a month later, it would be the last major institutional response to the European Debt Crisis.

By late 2014, the crisis moment had passed, as problems persisted but no longer triggered the same panic and shift to emergency politics. Bond yields for all the major affected countries except Greece fell below their levels at the start of the crisis in October 2009. Greek levels were similarly falling until a snap election in late 2014 brought the far-left Syriza party to power on an anti-austerity platform. However, while Syriza's election and the following stand-off with the Troika of the ECB, European Commission, and International Monetary Fund (IMF) caused Greek yields to rise again, they failed to rise as high as the early crisis peak. More crucially for the stability of the currency union as a whole, the spike in Greek yields failed to trigger a new wave of financial contagion to neighboring states. Similarly, a series of banking failures in Italy and Spain would test the new bank supervision and resolution framework. The debates around the Italian Banca Popolare di Vicenza and Veneto Banca and Spanish Banco Popular would be divisive, and raise substantial questions about the future operation of the new banking union.[5] However, these debates were back in the realm of normal bargaining and interest group maneuvering, and whatever questions they raised about the need for long-term reform, they no longer rose to the level of a crisis for the eurozone.

## The Banking Crisis in the Debt Crisis

Much of the discussion around the crisis, especially early on, focused on the sovereign debt aspects, as indeed is captured in the widely used term *Debt* Crisis. Implicit in this understanding is that the crisis was fundamentally about excessive public debt reaching a point of unsustainability. This framework carries some explanatory power in some cases, especially Greece and to a lesser degree Portugal. However, this explanation was a poorer fit for Italy and especially Spain.[6] As the crisis progressed, it became clear that the public debt crisis was fueled largely by factors beyond reckless public expenditure. The entanglement of countries with relatively manageable levels of sovereign debts before the crisis indicated that the fundamental problem lay with banks requiring heroic volumes of state support rather than unsustainable state spending patterns. Spain in particular was drawn into crisis by a spreading panic in the southern European banking sector rather than weak fundamentals. The instability of European banking proved to be both a catalyst and an accelerator for the crisis.[7] Bank failure was a catalyst insofar as the continued weakness and collapse of multiple European banks drove a sovereign debt crisis as states took private debt onto public balance sheets in an effort to bail out failing banks.[8] Bank failure was moreover an accelerator as the relative importance of banking to financing the European real economy meant that a contraction in bank lending would have much greater consequences for overall growth, and for thus for government revenue, than in the Anglo-American states with larger capital markets to provide an alternative. The weaknesses in European banking at the start of the crisis can be roughly grouped into three key groups: legacy issues of the Banking Crisis, unresolved regulatory gaps in European banking, and the "Doom Loop" of weak banks and sovereigns undermining each other.

## Legacy Issues of the Banking Crisis

The issues that gave rise to the 2007–09 Banking Crisis and the 2010–14 Debt Crisis were often deeply intertwined. To a large degree, European banks in both the north and south were in weak shape in 2009 because of unresolved legacy issues of the banking crisis. In particular, many banks held significant stores of bad or toxic assets which hurt their profitability and left them vulnerable, as reflected in Figure 4.1. A large volume of nonperforming loans (NPLs), especially linked to subprime assets, remained on balance sheets, requiring a substantial capital buffer and not producing profitable returns.[9] In addition, the rise of complex derivatives and L3 assets in the 2000s left banks with large portions of their balance sheets held by assets of uncertain value. Such assets were not simply worthless, but rather "toxic," meaning that the complexity of the assets and the difficulty in finding buyers for them made them both illiquid and of uncertain long-term value. This made it impossible to gauge the actual long-term health of a bank with significant L3 holdings and extremely difficult for the bank to sell them or use them as collateral for loans to gain liquidity.[10]

These legacy issues meant that southern banks were extremely vulnerable to disruption, in particular the regional banks in Spain and Italy, as well as the large Irish banks still struggling after the 2007–09 Crisis. Especially given their economies heavy reliance on bank financing, this compelled the states

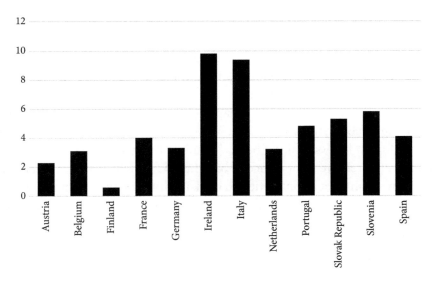

**Figure 4.1** Nonperforming Loans as a Percentage of Gross Loans, Eurozone States 2009

*Source:* Mare, Bertay, and Zhou, *World Bank Global Financial Development Database*

in crisis-hit countries to mount extensive bailouts to contain the damage. As will be discussed, these bailouts would in turn strain the sovereign resources of the affected states.

The lingering weakness of banks after 2007–09 would also shape the crisis response in both France and Germany. Although neither state faced a substantial threat to their public coffers, they also had little appetite to engage in another round of costly bailouts of their banks. Ironically, the rapid action by the French state that spared its banks the worst of the 2007–09 crisis left them more vulnerable in 2010–14, as they had not been forced to go through the painful restructuring and balance sheet cleanup of the British or large German institutions. Like the smaller German savings banks and the southern banks, they continued to have significant drags on their profitability from both NPLs and L3 assets. Neither Germany nor France were willing to contemplate a default by either the state or banks in Greece or the other southern states, as that default would rebound on the balance sheets of German and French banks, requiring a new round of extensive bailouts to contain the damage to the northern economies. The legacy issues of the Banking Crisis, therefore, meant that for France and Germany the choice was either to bail out the southern states or their own banks, and bailing out the southern states at least helped push more of the costs onto the southerners and away from their own populations.

## Unresolved Regulatory Gaps

As discussed in Chapter 3, the Banking Crisis led to a series of "patch-up" reforms aiming to fix the regulatory gaps in European finance, in particular the creation of the European System of Financial Supervision (ESFS) including the European Banking Authority (EBA). However, this fix remained incomplete, and several key regulatory gaps remained.

Perhaps the most significant of these is that the EBA aimed to harmonize the policies of national regulators but did not centralize regulation. Therefore, the incentive structure of national regulators remained largely unchanged.[11] National regulators continued to have close relationships with the banks they regulated, giving the bankers a channel to press for favorable treatment. Moreover, national regulators still had an incentive to maintain or advance the position of their banks relative to foreign competitors, promoting national champions to compete in foreign markets and protecting smaller domestically focused firms against cross-border competition. This therefore meant that the incentive for national regulators to adopt "soft touch" regulation in the interest of promoting their domestic sectors remained.

The EBA also addressed but did not eliminate issues surrounding the supervision of cross-border banking activities.[12] Although the EBA clarified the legal obligations of both host and home countries for branches and subsidiaries, it could not eliminate the implicit moral hazard issues. A home country may not have legal obligation to help a failing subsidiary of one of its banks, and a host country may have no legal obligation to help a failing branch of a foreign bank. However, both host and home country may do so anyway because of the harm the failure of the branch or subsidiary may do to the broader economy in both the host and home countries. Therefore, the incentive to contribute to bailouts remained, and thus the incentive for both host and home country to pressure the other to contribute beyond its legal obligations.[13] In addition, because the branch/subsidiary division remained relevant, and because both host and home regulators had incentives to keep banks under their jurisdiction, the space for regulatory arbitrage remained. Countries looking to keep a bank's operations under their regulatory remit retained capacity to alter their regulatory architecture to be more favorable to the bank business they aimed to attract or keep. This therefore meant that incentive still remained for "soft touch" regulation here as well.

These gaps were well known, as was the preferred solution of the European institutions. The need to close regulatory gaps had been well documented since at least the 2001 Lamfalussy Report, and proposals for a European banking union had circulated for years prior to the crisis.[14] However, prior

**112  Crises and Integration in European Banking Union**

to the crisis, as a European Commission representative put it, "the political momentum was not there."[15] The standoff between those institutions favoring deeper integration and those favoring Balkanization, a retreat from cross-border banking, in response to these tensions blocked movement in either direction, but at least for the time being, both sides were willing to maintain an unstable status quo rather than back down.

## The Doom Loop

Finally, while the ESFS and EBA did take some steps toward addressing those issues, they did nothing on resolution, which remained wholly a national operation outside of the limits on State Aid imposed by the European Commission. This would point toward the final major issue remaining from the Banking Crisis, the Doom Loop. The Doom Loop, or the sovereign-bank nexus, is a product of the mismatch between the size of European banks and European states. As seen in Figure 4.2, European bank assets dwarf their sovereigns in size, especially compared to the United States. In particular, while the largest European banks are comparable in size to their US counterparts, they are supported by states that are much smaller than the United States. Even the largest EU economies, Germany and France, had a GDP of only 21.2 percent and 15.5 percent of US levels respectively in 2010.[16] This means that the US can afford to rescue even its largest banks if they were to collapse, however politically unpalatable it may be to do so. However, even the largest European states would struggle to rescue their large banks, and the attempt would likely be so costly as to trigger a sovereign debt crisis. This problem is compounded by the high concentration of banking activity into a few massive banking groups in many countries. Figure 4.2 also captures how in many countries, the five largest banks contained almost all of the banking assets in the country at the dawn of the Debt Crisis. The problem is even more severe in smaller countries home to large banking groups, such as the Netherlands. This leaves the banks more vulnerable, because market actors know that they do not have a reliable safety net, and it makes states more vulnerable because market actors similarly know that a major banking crisis could dramatically increase the sovereign debt of European states. This problem is compounded by the high exposure of European banks to their home countries' sovereign debt, as a sovereign debt crisis would trigger a banking crisis as banks were forced to write down their sovereign debt assets. Therefore, this combination of size mismatch and exposure creates a situation where banks are made vulnerable by their home states'

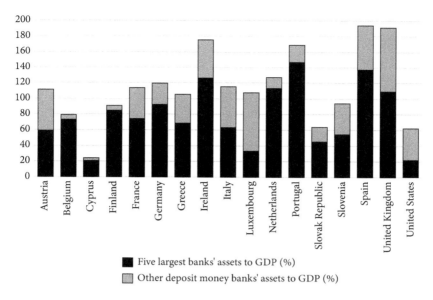

**Figure 4.2** Deposit Money Banks' Assets to GDP (%) for the Eurozone, UK, and US, 2009

*Source:* Mare, Bertay, and Zhou, *World Bank Global Financial Development Database*

weakness, and states are made vulnerable by their banks' weakness. Prior to 2010, bond traders largely discounted these risks, and treated the sovereign debt of essentially all member states as risk-free. So long as that assumption held, states retained the ability to borrow significant amounts, ensuring they had the resources to manage even substantial bank failures, and bank sovereign exposure was considered essentially risk-free. Once that assumption broke down, however, the mutual exposure of states and their banks to each other became a much more prominent issue.

## Classification of the Crisis

### Endogenous

The case that the Debt Crisis is endogenous to European finance is if anything even more clear-cut than that of the Banking Crisis. The Debt Crisis was the culmination of a number of problems that can be linked to the fundamental weaknesses in the design of the euro and the European financial regulatory architecture. As Bénassy-Quéré argues, the single currency itself was not the cause, but the failure to recognize that the introduction of the euro and the dramatic lowering of barriers to cross-border financial activity required a comparably dramatic rethink of the regulatory architecture which failed to materialize.[17] European banking had become extremely integrated, and the ability of banks to expand their customer bases across the eurozone allowed them to grow to a size that their sovereigns could no longer effectively manage their resolution, making the Doom Loop more acute than it otherwise would have been. Moreover, the combination of transnational banking and national regulation created a strong incentive for national regulators to promote growth of their home banks even at the expense of stability. Thus, the problems were not just within the large cross-national banks, but also among the smaller domestically focused ones, which relied on regulatory favoritism to protect them from foreign competition. This problem was especially acute where the smaller domestic banks were tightly integrated, as in the German savings banks and Spanish cajas. This interdependence meant that failures were generally not only correlated among those banks given their similar structures and exposures, but also that a failure in one could drag down its peers easily. This dynamic would bring down the Spanish caja sector in 2012, and although they avoided that fate, similar fears surrounded the German Sparkassen. Finally, the interconnectedness of banks across borders meant that a bank failure or sovereign default in one state would redound heavily on banks in another which were exposed, and the lingering weakness out of the 2007–09 crisis meant that even banks in states with strong public resources were too fragile to easily endure such a blow.

## Severe

The classification of the Debt Crisis as severe is also obvious. It was arguably the greatest threat to European integration at least since the creation of the Single Market, and possibly in the entire history of the European project. The interconnectedness of the European financial system meant that virtually every state in the eurozone was drawn into the crisis. While the southern states were directly affected by the sovereign and banking crises, the exposure of the northern banks meant that they were highly exposed to the risk of default. Moreover, the legacy effects of the Banking Crisis meant that those banks were still too weak to slough off that vulnerability lightly. Outside of the eurozone, the non-eurozone creditor states, especially the United Kingdom, similarly faced a threat from southern default, though as Schimmelfennig outlines, they were less exposed than eurozone states, and therefore had leverage to push the costs elsewhere.[18] Only the Central and Eastern

European non-eurozone states were really in a position to avoid substantial costs out of the Debt Crisis, as their banking sectors were largely dominated by foreign banks, their own banks were small and domestically focused, and the panic in bond traders focused on eurozone states and passed over the Central and Eastern European states.

The severity of the crisis extended beyond just the number of states involved, as the Banking Crisis had also brought in a large number of states without posing a severe threat to integration. The crucial difference here is that while the Banking Crisis could be managed with national responses, the realities of the Doom Loop meant that the only national solutions available entailed at least some degree of dissolution of European integration. The affected southern states could not afford a "fiscal" bailout of their failing banks, as the expenditure would push them into a sovereign debt crisis. Similarly, in those states where the sovereign debt crisis preceded the banking crisis, the inability of the state to manage any additional expenditures left its banks exposed without a safety net and prone to failure. Moreover, the common currency meant that a "monetary" bailout, printing new money to bail out the banks, was also off the table. Such a solution would have been highly inflationary, but would have at least kept the banks solvent at least for national currency-denominated obligations. This, however, was not available to individual states in the eurozone. It was also a step that the ECB was not at this time willing to contemplate, fearing that such a step would both violate the "no bailouts" clause and result in monetary policy becoming subsidiary to fiscal policy.[19]

Since containment of the crisis with national resources was not possible, crisis-affected states faced two unappealing options in the absence of external support. The first would be some manner of default, either private or public. A private default, sending a wave of banks into bankruptcy procedures, threatened turmoil for the country, the eurozone, and the globe. At a national level, the heavy reliance on bank-based financing meant that a wave of bank failures would bring with it a collapse in the real economy of the country. This, in turn, would both slash the tax revenue of the state and require both automatic spending and probably emergency fiscal support, meaning that this option would likely push the state toward a public default anyway. Moreover, bank defaults would bring severe losses to northern creditor banks, likely triggering a financial crisis in those states as well. Finally, as demonstrated by the global fallout from the US government's decision to let Lehman Brothers go into bankruptcy, there were real fears that letting systemically important institutions go bankrupt would trigger a global collapse in confidence in banks and thus a new global banking crisis.[20]

While private defaults would almost certainly be catastrophic, the actual impact of a public default was less clear but potentially even worse in its impact. While some observers believed that it would be possible for a member state to default and remain in the eurozone and the European Union, most agreed that it would mean a rapid exit from the currency union and possibly the EU itself.[21] Beyond that, the actual impact on the defaulting country and its neighbors would be unclear, beyond that it would be extremely damaging with high likelihood of contagion to its neighbors.

The other alterative mooted was an exit from the euro and a return to a national currency, either permanently or on an emergency basis. This would allow for the affected states to adopt the inflationary solutions conventionally used by states in sovereign debt crises with their own currencies, and potentially would also allow for a managed default. However, it presented its own set of challenges. Obviously, replacing a currency rapidly presents logistical challenges and the rumor of it happening may itself exacerbate the panic, as people rush to ensure that their savings are held in euros and not the new, soon-to-be-devalued, local currency. This is precisely what triggered a run on Greek banks in 2015, as depositors rushed to clear out their accounts lest their euro savings be converted to neo-drachma by government fiat.[22] Even if the exit from the euro could be easily managed, inflationary responses are an imperfect solution at best. Argentina's ongoing cycle of inflation, debt, and default illustrates the potential pitfalls of this approach. Moreover, what such an exit would mean for the eurozone and the country itself was also unclear. While some actors talked about a temporary suspension of eurozone membership and readmittance, no such provision existed in the Treaties as written, and such a change would only be possible with the support of both the country itself and the rest of the eurozone.

Ultimately, in addition to the potential harm to the country under pressure, both a default and an exit posed a great, potentially mortal, threat to the European project. A main safeguard for countries in the crisis was that market actors did not think that exit or full default was actually likely, as the cost to the EU would be too high, both in direct fiscal terms and because it would potentially fatally undermine the master narrative of ever deeper integration. The assumption among many market actors was that the question was "when" and "how" the EU would contain the crisis, not "if." The more default or exit appeared likely, the greater the pressure on the crisis-stricken countries. A key reason why Grexit or a Greek default was seen as too costly to the EU was not the damage from Greece itself, but the contagion effects. If Greece went, market actors would immediately assume a Portuguese exit was also likely, and the pressure on Portugal would increase dramatically.

If Portugal were to follow Greece out, pressure would immediately turn to Spain, and then to Italy. The loss of the third and fourth largest members of the eurozone would be a body blow to the project, potentially unravelling the common currency entirely. A Greek exit or default would only be tolerated if some provision could be created to safeguard Portugal. Such a provision would face two challenges. The first would be to somehow convince market actors that the EU's commitment to Portugal was more credible than its commitment to Greece. The second, exacerbated by the likely market skepticism from the first, is that any provision to safeguard Portugal would almost inevitably be more expensive than just saving Greece. Only a fundamentalist commitment to avoiding moral hazard regardless of the costs and a willful dismissal of the importance of preserving integration as an end in itself could therefore justify such a fiscally costly approach.

## A Monnet Crisis

The Debt Crisis is an example of a crisis that is both endogenous to the financial system and a severe threat to European integration. It therefore is the kind of crisis where we would most expect to see substantial reforms as a result. The pre-crisis status quo had become absolutely unsustainable, and the eurozone countries faced a stark choice between either disintegration of the currency union or substantial reforms to preserve it. As will be outlined, it was this fear of a collapsing status quo, not just the functional arguments in favor of deeper integration, which drove the creation of the SSM and SRM. Once that fear faded, functionalist arguments lost their persuasive power, as can be seen in the failure to complete the banking union through the creation of a common deposit insurance scheme and other elements. In the absence of an immediate threat of disintegration, the pro-reform coalition lost the support of its more reluctant members, who now preferred muddling through with the new status quo to reforms that would impose substantial new costs or restrictions.

## The European Stability Mechanism

The first major response from the European Union to the Debt Crisis was the introduction of the European Financial Stabilization Mechanism (EFSM) in May 2010. An explicitly temporary program endowed with the capacity to lend up to €60 billion to crisis-hit member states, it soon proved insufficient, and was supplemented the following month by the European

Financial Stability Facility, which was similarly temporary, but endowed with the ability to lend up to €250 billion to crisis-hit states in the eurozone.[23] The two facilities shared a great deal in common, most prominently that both treated the Crisis as a sovereign liquidity crisis, and thus offered chiefly support in form of loans to states conditional on the acceptance of structural adjustments and reforms.[24]

By 2012, however, the crisis continued to rage, and a consensus grew that the earlier programs should be replaced by a more permanent one, which would ultimately emerge as the European Stability Mechanism (ESM). In addition to seeing the need for a larger fund, advocates of a more permanent program argued that the case-by-case and temporary nature of the existing programs created too much uncertainty to stabilize markets.[25] The only other long-term alternatives to a permanent program were argued to be the disintegration of the eurozone or the move to a full fiscal integration, neither of which were regarded as acceptable.[26] However, multiple key actors remained concerned that the ESM should include more conditions than its temporary emergency precursors, especially on rigorous analysis of debt sustainability and preferential creditor status for ESM debt, to safeguard the fund and member states from losses.

## Resistance to the ESM

Resistance to the ESM came chiefly from two states, the United Kingdom and Germany, and the differences their respective approaches and the reaction of other interested actors both can be linked to the degree to which the two states were exposed to the crisis and the severity of the shock it presented to them. The United Kingdom, although not a eurozone member, nevertheless retained considerable influence over the process, since it had the potential to block any new EU treaty to create the new mechanism. Prime Minister David Cameron therefore used that leverage to advance several British goals. The most prominent of these was to ensure that the UK not be obligated to contribute to any future eurozone rescue efforts. Cameron wanted the crisis resolved, especially as a crisis in the eurozone would inevitably produce spillover effects onto other EU members, with the UK no exception. At the same time, Cameron wanted the eurozone members to solve the issue without British assistance. As he put it early in the debates, "We do need a new mechanism to help the eurozone sort out its problems and its issues. That's important for Britain, but we do need to make sure that Britain is not liable to spend money under that mechanism and I think we need to secure that for the future."[27] More controversially, Cameron also attempted to leverage the need for a British assent to secure a renegotiation of the UK rebate from the EU budget. Although this had no direct connection to the crisis at hand, Cameron attempted to argue that he would need such a concession to overcome domestic euroskeptic resistance. This resistance was most prominent among Conservative backbenchers, with one asserting that "We have had enough of reading of British prime ministers that 'they will stand up for the British national interest' then coming back with a kind of Chamberlain-esque piece of paper."[28] These concerns were echoed in the press as well, with the Telegraph asserting that the EU was planning "an intrusive European body with the power to take over the economies of struggling nations."[29]

The European leaders reacted to these British demands with great anger. French President Nicolas Sarkozy told Cameron that "You missed a good opportunity to keep your mouth shut. We are sick of you criticizing us and telling us what to do. You say you hate the euro and now you want to interfere in our meetings."[30] One French diplomat described Britain's attempt to use a crisis it was insulated from for leverage as "like a man who wants to go to a wife-swapping party without taking his own wife."[31] MEP Guy Verhofstadt of the Liberal group refused to speak English in protest, and in his native Flemish proclaimed that "this selfish British strategy of protecting the City is one we cannot tolerate any longer."[32] Joseph Daul, the leader of the European People's Party, suggested that rather than giving in to Cameron's demands, the UK should instead be stripped of its rebate, arguing that "our taxpayers' money should be used for things other than rewarding selfish and nationalistic attitudes."[33] The strength of the backlash led Nick Clegg, leader of the UK Liberal Democratic Party and Deputy Prime Minister, to conclude that the effort was "bad for Britain" and risked leaving the country "isolated and marginalized."[34] As such, the UK soon backed down from attempts to use the crisis to renegotiate its terms of membership, though Cameron would again attempt such a renegotiation in the run-up to the 2016 Brexit referendum, after the Debt Crisis had passed.

Britain was not alone in raising concerns over the ESM. Germany also raised significant issues with the proposals. German objections can be roughly grouped into two categories: limits on the direct costs to Germany and barriers against the ESM expanding its mission over time. In line with the first goal, the German government drew a hard line against "Eurobonds," or any form of common debt for the member states. It also sought to slow the filling of the ESM fund, to diminish the immediate fiscal burden on Germany, which would be the most significant contributor to the fund, providing €190

**120   Crises and Integration in European Banking Union**

billion of the €500 billion total. On the second goal, Germany insisted that the ESM provide "last resort" funding only, to be tapped only after a member state had exhausted all other resources, to preserve it as a tool for emergency use only.[35] Germany also moved to block granting the ESM a banking license, which would have allowed it to leverage its funding by tapping ECB resources, but also would have allowed it to directly inject money into banks, without a member state as an intermediary.[36] In addition to these goals, Germany was among the most prominent parties insisting that ESM funding be accompanied by regulatory architecture reforms to make the crisis a one-time affair, and insulate against the possibility of future crises.

German domestic support for these positions as both broad and deep, spanning the political spectrum. Multiple major newspapers inveighed against the ESM, with the Bild proclaiming "this time it has to be enough" and the Frankfurter Allgemeine Zeitung arguing that there must be "no carte blanche for a rescue orgy."[37] Within Chancellor Merkel's own governing coalition, the Free Democrats were deeply internally divided. An internal party referendum on whether to block Bundestag approval of the ESM produced only a 54 percent backing for the proposal, well short of the two-thirds majority expected by party leadership.[38] In opposition, the Social Democrats and the Greens also expressed reluctance, though in their case they broadly supported the ESM and wanted to use a moment of German leverage to impose a financial transactions tax over the objections of the Dutch in particular.[39] The most extreme opposition came from the far-left Linke Party, which joined a suit brought in the German Constitutional Court at Karlsruhe alleging that the ESM presented an illegal intrusion into German sovereignty. Linke parliamentary leader Gregor Gysi asserted that the ESM crossed "the line in the sand that is the constitution."[40] That court case would ultimately be resolved in favor of the ESM, with the court ruling that the proposal was constitutional so long as Germany's financial liability remained capped at €190 billion and German parliamentarians retained access to "comprehensive information" about ESM operations, conditions that the German government had already secured.[41]

As with the UK, German recalcitrance attracted widespread pressure. Within the EU, the Austrians, French, and Italians all leaned on Germany to shoulder more of the burden, while outside of the EU, the US, World Bank, and International Monetary Fund all urged approval.[42] However, the tone was notably softer than the scorn directed toward the British, and more focused on the functional need for a large fund to solve the crisis and the essential role Germany must pay in constructing it. This was not without exception, as George Soros would accuse Germany of insisting on terms that would relegate its neighbors to "the status of third world countries," but noticeably lacking the harshness from government representatives that greeted the British.[43]

A final significant source of opposition to the ESM came from France, where the French left wanted to strip the ESM of the regulatory architecture reforms and austerity elements that the German insisted upon. This became caught up in the presidential race between incumbent Nicolas Sarkozy, who had negotiated the ESM and supported the current proposal, and challenger and ultimate victor François Hollande, who sought to loosen the restrictions. In that context, the Socialist Party withheld their support in the French parliament. As party leader Martine Aubry put it, "by this abstention we state our refusal of austerity."[44] This maneuver was criticized by the center-left Liberation newspaper, which described the Socialists as acting like "ostriches."[45] However, even with the Socialist abstentions, the bill still passed with the support of Sarkozy's Republicans.

## Contrasting Resistance to the ESM

The differing sources of resistance to the ESM across these three core states, and the reactions to that resistance, reveals much about the dynamics of crisis response. While both the German and French domestic politicking and maneuvers around the ESM drew considerable international pressure for a rapid passage, they attracted nothing close to the anger directed at the British. This reflects at least in part the nature of the politics around the crisis for the three countries. The Germans and the French, directly exposed to the potential collapse of the eurozone as they were, operated clearly within the realm of emergency politics. As such, there was debate over the scope and size of the ESM, with some wanting a smaller or larger, more restrictive or less restrictive form, but within the political mainstream there was little question about the overall direction of the reform. The French Socialists voted against the ESM, but only with the knowledge that the bill would pass without them, making their action a form of messaging that did not risk the ESM itself. Similarly, the German center-left parties wanted an additional financial services tax, and the center-right had concerns about costs, but neither jeopardized the overall reform. All of these actors were operating in an emergency politics mode, where rapid action took clear priority over maximizing specific policy preferences. Of the German parties, only the far-left Linke actively threatened the creation of the ESM, via a legal challenge to its constitutionality, and they stood well outside of the German political mainstream.

The situation in the UK was different. Although a collapse of the eurozone would inevitably have negative impacts on the British economy, the UK was considerably more insulated than the others, and the UK could continue to frame the crisis as only moderate in threat. As such, UK politics operated much more in the world of normal politics, where strategies of delay and of linking unrelated issues in order to secure a maximal outcome remained more viable. This difference in understanding of the severity of the crisis accounted for much of the anger over the UK's tactics. It also demonstrates in miniature the impact of crisis severity on politics and reforms. For the eurozone countries, this was a severe endogenous crisis that required substantial reform in response. However, for the UK, both the severity and the endogeneity were substantially reduced, meaning that the appetite in Britain for rapid emergency response was substantially lower.

## Evaluation of the ESM

The ESM itself presented a notable step toward integration of the European Union and in particular the eurozone, though its direct impact on financial integration was minimal, given that the ESM could only fund member states, and not directly recapitalize banks. In this it reflects the dominant early understanding of the Debt Crisis as sovereign debt crisis, and one that could be largely addressed with liquidity support. However, as the crisis progressed, it became increasingly clear that the fundamental problem was bank debt, and the need to recapitalize the banks. This in turn led to calls to use the ESM to recapitalize the banks directly. In the words of the ECB's Benoît Cœuré, this move would break "the adverse feedback loop between banks and sovereigns."[46] Although the French government rapidly embraced the proposal, it ran into substantial German opposition. The Bundesbank argued that the ESM lacked both the capacity and expertise for the task.[47] The Social Democrats and Greens both signaled that they would not vote for such a reform, meaning that Merkel would need to pass the measure relying only on her own governing coalition.[48] This became much less likely when Horst Seehofer, the governor of Bavaria and the head of the Christian Social Union, the largely independent Christian Democratic party of Bavaria, signaled his limited willingness to continue expanding the role of the ESM.[49] Given this opposition, Merkel opted instead to insist on the creation of separate institutions to regulate the European banks in form of the Single Supervisory Mechanism and later the Single Resolution Mechanism as a condition of an emergency recapitalization out of the ESM.[50] The ESM thus in itself provided only a minor increase in European financial integration, though it provided a crucial step from the pre-crisis status quo toward the creation of banking union, as discussed in the subsequent section.

## The Terms of Debate and Coalitions on Banking Union

### The Functional Argument for Banking Union

The functional argument for banking union is at its core simply that having a currency union and unrestricted cross-border banking without centralized supervision and resolution creates inefficiencies and instability. As Schoenmaker laid out in his trilemma, states must choose two of the three of financial integration, national regulation, and financial stability. Several specific flaws have been identified in the literature.[51] National regional of transnational banking introduces multiple inefficiencies, as banks can engage in regulatory arbitrage or rely on national protectionism, while customers lose out with the lack of a level playing field. Such national fragmentation will also exacerbate economic downturns and can impede effective transmission of monetary policy from the ECB. Moreover, such fragmentation makes crises more likely and more damaging. The combination of transnational banks and national regulation creates a Doom Loop where banks are too big to be effectively supported by their home country, increasing their vulnerability. Without a resolution mechanism, banks must be bailed out by home countries, which potentially imposes great costs on taxpayers and risks sovereign debt crises. Moreover, a crisis in one country can lead to contagion and even the involuntary exit of a country from the union. Completion of banking union was thus presented not just as necessary for financial stability in itself, but also to preserve the euro.[52]

Banking union offers a solution to these problems. As has been frequently cited by proponents of banking union, the unified regulatory structure in the United States offers much more stability for a comparably sized financial system.[53] While the eurozone in 2010 had a network of national supervisors relatively loosely harmonized under the Committee of European Banking Supervisors (CEBS) and later the European Banking Authority, the US has had national supervision of interstate banking since the mid-nineteenth century.[54] Such a system prevents the regulatory arbitrage and branch/subsidiary confusion found in the European experience.

Moreover, a single resolution and deposit insurance authority, the Federal Deposit Insurance Corporation (FDIC), means that the United States can absorb the failure of even massive banks in a way that even France or Germany would struggle to manage. In the 2007–09 Banking Crisis, for instance, the FDIC managed the failure of both Washington Mutual and Wachovia without recourse to emergency funding. The US only needed to turn to emergency bailouts or other ad hoc actions to manage the collapse of systemically important investment banks including Bear Stearns, Lehman Brothers, and Merrill Lynch.[55] These institutions required ad hoc resolution not because of interstate competition, but because US regulators decided that these institutions had grown so long that the historical approach of letting investment banks fail on the assumption that their clients were "sophisticated investors" would now cause unacceptable levels of damage to the broader economy. The FDIC approach of unified federal resolution and deposit insurance offered two key advantages. The first is that the large standing deposit insurance fund and existing legal recourse to draw on US Treasury funding as a backstop should it be depleted meant that there was virtually no doubt that all covered deposits were safe. This made it no longer necessary for individuals to participate in bank runs, diminishing the likelihood of bank failure. The second is that the FDIC's clearly defined resolution procedures and eight-decade history meant that there was very little uncertainty as to what would happen if a bank did require resolution. While losses may be imposed, they would be assigned in clear way known in advance, diminishing the cause for panic.

A final advantage of the US system is the presence of a unified system of capital markets for the entire US economy. These deep capital markets mean that stocks and bonds provide an alternative source of capital. Such capital markets mean that in principle bank failures are less catastrophic in their broader impact on the real economy, giving regulators more space to act without fear of the broader consequences.[56]

The proposed European banking union would create a US-style financial regulatory architecture for the eurozone and whatever other non-eurozone EU members chose to participate. The Single Supervisory Mechanism would provide an equivalent to the unified US regulation under the Federal Reserve and Office of the Comptroller of the Currency (OCC). The Single Resolution Mechanism would break the Doom Loop and provide a single resolution authority with a single common pool of funding to manage European bank failures in a consistent and well-funded manner. A European Deposit Insurance Scheme would similarly ensure that European depositors had consistent and reliable deposit insurance protection. Finally, completing a Capital Markets Union (CMU) would build a Continental capital market, enabling a US-style move away from the heavy reliance on bank-based provision of capital.

These components were presented in the functional argument as not just necessary individually, but as mutually reinforcing, making all of them necessary for a fully functioning banking union.[57] The SSM, for instance, was necessary to eliminate regulatory favoritism, but would be toothless without a single resolution authority to ensure that failing banks could not just turn to favoritism at the hands of national resolution authorities.[58] Similarly, it would be dangerous to have a Single Resolution Mechanism without unified supervision, as the costs of regulatory mistakes and laxity by national authorities could be dumped on a European resolution authority. Such a scenario would encourage continued lax regulation, so that member states reaped the benefits of underregulation, while the costs were spread to the European Union as a whole.

The last two components, a European Deposit Insurance Scheme and Capital Markets Union, were also presented as essential. Without EDIS, even a fully funded SRM would be sub-optimal, as fears that national deposit guarantee schemes (DGS) would be exhausted would drive depositors to still participate in bank runs. Therefore, an SRM without EDIS would create a scenario where bank panics may happen but be managed effectively, while an SRM with EDIS would ensure that panics do not happen at all, or at least happen with far lower frequency, as in the US case. Finally, CMU would also help diminish the costs of dealing with panics, as deep capital markets would both diminish the costs of bank failure to the real economy and impose greater market discipline on banks which no longer enjoyed a monopoly on provision of capital to European customers.

The European Commission, European Central Bank, and the European Parliament promoted such arguments from early in the crisis.[59] Mario Draghi, president of the ECB, in particular argued that the functional advantages of a banking union were such that that there was no viable alternative to implementation. However, such functional arguments were insufficient on their own. This in part can be demonstrated by the fact that these functional arguments were as valid in the abstract in the 1980s and 1990s, the run-up to the introduction of the euro, as they were in the Debt Crisis itself, but failed to gain traction at that time.[60] Another attempt to move toward banking union in the Banking Crisis also fell short, as discussed in Chapter 3. More important than those functional counterarguments, however, are the political arguments against banking union.

### Functional Counterarguments

In part the failure of the functional arguments reflected the presence of functional arguments against banking union promoted as a counterframe of how to interpret the crisis. The most prominent of these was concern over moral hazard from the introduction of common resolution. In the words of Hans Tietmeyer, then president of the Bundesbank, "supervision by the central bank would implicitly signal a bailout guarantee and hence lead to moral hazard problems."[61] The fear articulated in such functional counter arguments was that if creditors and depositors were sheltered from the costs of failure, they would be more careless in their evaluation of the stability of banks, and remove a crucial source of market discipline. Such arguments are especially common in criticisms of deposit insurance programs, both within and outside of the European context.[62] They also proved especially relevant in a European context, as the shift from national to European regulation would mean that arrangements set up and liabilities incurred under national regulators would now be the responsibility of the new European regulators. Given the legacy of NPLs and toxic assets from the Banking Crisis in particular, this was by no means an insignificant concern. However, set against this is the US experience, where bank failures are not noticeably more prominent than in the EU context, and certainly are not more costly.

A second functional argument focused on the danger of a regulatory "monoculture" discouraging innovation in regulatory approaches and encouraging banks to adopt common risk profiles.[63] This would increase the correlation of risk, making crises perhaps rarer but more catastrophic when they did hit. A variety of regulatory approaches may mean that some approaches would prove inadequate and bank failure would follow, banks regulated by superior approaches would not fail. Thus, bank failures would produce learning as to the superior approach. Moreover, diverse regulatory approaches would diminish the correlation of risk, where all banks were very vulnerable to a particular kind of shock. Such logic has been used in the US context to justify both the persistence of state banking regulators, albeit only of banks barred from interstate transactions, and the historical split between two national bank regulators, the Office of the Comptroller of the Currency and the Office of Thrift Supervision (OTS). Here the historical record indicates that this danger may be overstated, as a diversity of national regulators did not prevent a harmonization of approaches among both banks and regulators in the run-up to the 2007–09 Banking Crisis with catastrophic results. Moreover, the US itself dissolved the OTS and centralized regulation in the OCC in 2010, having concluded that the regulatory competition caused more problems in terms of complexity and arbitrage than it solved by promoting best practices and policy learning in regulation.

## The Divisions within Banking

### Division on the SSM and SRM

Bank positions on the SSM and SRM generally were determined by size and international operations. Large transnational banks initially opposed centralization of both supervision and regulation only to eventually come to favor the SSM and SRM, while smaller domestically focused banks opposed consistently opposed both reforms.

Transnational banks spent the 1990s and 2000s generally opposed to centralization of regulation, as they benefited from national regulation. In particular, in the earlier decades of financial integration, states pursued "national champion" strategies where regulators aimed to facilitate the growth of their own large banks. This would ensure that their own banks would be competitive with foreign national champions, expanding their presence in foreign markets, and minimizing the dominance of the home financial market by foreign banks. However, as the transnational banks grew, they reached a point where the functional advantages of centralized regulation and reduction of cross-border transaction costs exceeded the gains from preserving national protection. This point generally came relatively early in the Debt Crisis, as it became clear that centralization would offer transnational banks two key advantages.[64]

The first of these advantages is that the Single Supervisory Mechanism would create a single regulatory standard for all banks. This in part was an advantage simply by reducing the expense and complexity of having to ensure compliance with unique regulatory requirements in every jurisdiction in which they operated. It also would eliminate regulatory favoritism and allow the advantages of economies of scale from the larger banks to be more fully deployed. While the transnational banks had benefited from regulatory favoritism early on, so had their competitors. Such competitors included both competitors in foreign markets and smaller home-country competitors in the alternative bank sectors, such as the German savings banks and cooperatives and the Spanish cajas. By creating a single common regulator, not only would transaction costs be reduced, but the elimination or reduction of favoritism would ensure that the large banks' advantages from economies of scale were not undercut by regulations designed to diminish those advantages.

The Single Resolution Mechanism would also help the large banks by reducing the risks of the Doom Loop, ensuring that they were supported by an authority capable of credibly supporting them. As Acharya and Yorulmazer outline, banks want to become as big as they can be *within their regulator's jurisdiction* to ensure that they can still secure bailouts or other support as necessary.[65] By the early 2010s, the largest European banks had outgrown their regulators' jurisdiction. Already by the 2007–09 Banking Crisis, the large German banks were just barely small enough to be rescued by the German state, and the French response had been as rapid and large as it was because the French banks had already outgrown the capacity of the

French state to manage a more serious crisis. This outgrowing of their regulators was not just a problem in the event of a failure, but a danger that was priced into the banks' capital and loan raises. The large European banks faced potentially higher funding costs than their American peers because creditors and shareholders could be less certain of state support in the event of trouble.[66] The SRM, by replacing the national jurisdiction with a continental one, solved this problem by expanding the size of the regulator, not reducing the size of the banks.

The domestic banks held the inverse positions for the inverse reasons. They opposed the Single Supervisory Mechanism because the loss of regulatory protectionism would leave them facing the larger banks with fewer resources to offset the advantages of scale of the large banks. They opposed the Single Resolution Mechanism because the Doom Loop was more of a problem for the large banks than the small ones, and they did not want to be in the position of subsidizing the resolution of their larger rivals. This lack of exposure was muted somewhat by the structure of national financial systems, as in some cases, such as the German savings banks and Spanish cajas, interconnectedness among the small banks raised the risks of Doom Loop concerns as well. However, even here, the relative decentralization of the linked banking sectors, as opposed to the more concentrated banking groups of the large transnational operations, meant that this was a less acute concern. These banks generally did not favor disintegration as a first-order preference, but would have preferred a Balkanization of European banking and a return to barriers to freedom of movement over deeper integration, making them euroskeptics insofar as they were reconciled to the status quo but would favor disintegration over deeper integration.

### A Different Division over EDIS

While banks generally took positions on the SRM and SSM based on their size, debates over EDIS prompted a different split, shaped more by the nature of existing national deposit guarantee schemes.[67] National DGS differed on many dimensions, though the most prominent were whether they were funded *ex ante* or *ex post*, the degree of coverage they offered, and whether they were publicly or privately run. The proposed EDIS would have been a publicly managed *ex ante*-funded system with a standardized level of coverage, and banks' support or opposition was to a large degree shaped by the degree to which it would alter their existing arrangements. Layered on top of that was also the question of whether the banks envisioned themselves more likely to pay out to or benefit from the new scheme. This reflects not just whether the country as a whole was a creditor or debtor, but also the health of individual banking groups. Here very few actually wanted rollback on DGS, but the banks did spilt between those favoring deeper integration, generally in those states with more vulnerable national DGS, and those willing to accept an EU DGS if necessary to avoid disintegration, but otherwise focusing on preservation of the status quo.

## The National Divisions

Divisions over banking union among member states generally broke down on three dimensions. The first, and most straightforward, is whether the member state was also a eurozone member. Although the northern non-euro states in particular were also affected by the Debt Crisis, their exposure was relatively low compared to both creditor and debtor states. As such, the non-eurozone states were mostly voluntarily sidelined in the debates, not actively participating in shaping the form of the banking union outside of ensuring that they would not be compelled to participate and could also avoid the costs of any potential bailouts or long-term arrangements. The most important implication of this dimension is that the United Kingdom, otherwise a major player in European Union reforms, voluntarily removed itself from banking union debates, leaving France and Germany as indisputably the two most pivotal states.

The second major division was over the shape of national financial systems, and in particular whether the state was dominated by large banks or had a large number of smaller alternative banks. In general, states dominated by large banks shared the interests of their banks, and supported a centralized SSM and SRM.[68] On the other hand, states with a large presence of alternative banks, which were less likely to benefit from banking union, were more likely to reflect the interests of those alternative banks and resist banking union.[69] While alternative banks had once been more common across Europe, by the outbreak of the crisis, this remained the case only in some states. In particular, alternative banks continued to play a major role in Spain and Germany, especially in the provision of financial services to small and medium-sized enterprises.[70] Conversely, both France and Italy had moved away from that model, France via increasing consolidation into a handful of massive banking groups and Italy by turning its savings banks into joint-stock companies and abolishing the regional principle.[71]

The third major division was whether states were creditors or debtors in the crisis. Regardless of the structure of their national financial systems, direct exposure to the crisis made the southern debtor states acutely aware

## 130 Crises and Integration in European Banking Union

of the dangers of the Doom Loop in particular, and in general their vulnerability to financial crises without external support. As such, they were unsurprisingly strongly in favor of a mutualization of the costs of banking supervision and resolution. Conversely, the creditor states, which would at least in the short term experience a likely net cost from banking union, were more skeptical of the need. At the start of 2010, France, Germany, and the United Kingdom were all opposed to the reform, though the calculus of each state would change as the crisis unfolded and the status quo became unsustainable.[72] However, as the crisis unfolded, the mutual dependence between the creditors and debtors, especially within the eurozone, would put increasing focus on their need to contain the crisis in the south to prevent it from encompassing their own banks.

### France and Germany

The two states which would play the most crucial active role in shaping banking union were France and Germany, both of which faced substantial exposure to southern private and public debt, but with that pressure filtered through very different financial systems. French banking is very homogenous, with 79.9 percent of bank assets held by five massive banking groups in 2010.[73] Moreover, the recent history of these banks was very similar. They avoided the worst of the 2007–09 crisis in part due to large and early state support, which meant that they had not undergone the painful but stabilizing restructuring that their British and German peers had. Instead, the real test for French banks would come in 2010 and after, as they all had substantial exposure to southern debt, especially in Spain.[74] French banks were generally opposed to banking union until the cajas crisis highlighted their vulnerability, whereupon they changed course and enthusiastically embraced the SSM and SRM. The French state followed the preferences of its banks, initially opposing the banking union and then coming around to a full-throated support after the cajas crisis.

Germany's position is more complex, and Germany has often been identified as the crucial state in debates on banking union.[75] It has more specifically been characterized as "the reluctant hegemon," generally only taking up a leadership role in rare moments, most often when its own direct interests are threatened.[76] Other scholars have cast Germany as playing the leadership role in the anti-banking union coalition including Finland, Denmark, the Benelux countries, and Austria, in a role roughly analogous to France's leadership of the pro-banking union group. These framings, however, overstate the power of Germany and underestimate the complexity of German internal debates. While Germany did indeed play a leadership role in the anti-banking union coalition, its role was primarily as a veto player rather than a policy entrepreneur, responding to others' proposals but rarely introducing its own significant innovations. Additionally, while the other anti-banking union states remained more or less firmly opposed to banking union during the Debt Crisis and France swung from opposition to strong support, Germany's position was equivocal and changeable at all stages. In this sense, it is more accurate to cast Germany as the "tipping point" state, rather than a leader, whose assent ensured that a majority existed for a given reform but without great capacity to shape the terms of debate in a nonreactive fashion.

The complexity of the German position reflected both dueling ideological commitments and a fragmented and heterogenous banking sector. Ideologically, Germany's firm commitments to European integration on the one hand and Ordoliberalism on the other were in conflict with each other. The former commitment would call for Germany to do whatever was necessary to preserve European and eurozone unity, potentially including a substantial centralization of authority and mutualization of costs, and downplay the introduction of moral hazard as regrettable but necessary. The latter commitment would emphasize the importance of avoiding moral hazard and limiting support without insistence on strict adherence to commitments to fiscal and monetary discipline. This debate, generally involving the Chancellery and Foreign Ministry against the Bundesbank and Finance Ministry, is a longstanding one in German politics.[77] In the initial phase of the crisis, it could be sidestepped by pushing adjustment costs onto the crisis states, but as enforcing the "no bailouts" clause became more and more impractical, the internal division came more and more to the fore. In part, it would moreover be exploited by supranational actors in efforts to rhetorically trap or persuade Germany to take a position in favor of banking union.[78]

The second source of complexity and internal division in Germany was down to the complexity of its banking system. Unlike the homogenous French banking system, German banking is marked by a division into three distinct pillars. The commercial banks, mostly large transnational banks including Deutsche Bank and Commerzbank, were large enough to have similar interests to the French banks. They were large enough to be concerned about the Doom Loop, being large enough that even Germany might struggle to resolve them. They also saw distinct regulatory advantages in standardized regulation and a severing of a cozy bank-regulator relationship among their competitors. These competitors included not just foreign competition, but also the Landesbanken, the largest banks of the second pillar, the regionally and municipally focused savings banks. The Landesbanken had long taken advantage of their close relationships with the German Länder and the Federal state to gain an advantage in competition with the commercial banks, and were loath to take any steps that would restrict their protections against the commercial banks and foreign banks. The smaller savings banks (the Sparkassen) and the mutual banks of the third pillar were also firmly against the banking union. They, like the Landesbanken, benefited from the regulatory friction and protectionism of a patchwork of national regulators and were reluctant to give it up. The Sparkassen in particular were rumored to have benefited substantially from favorable regulators, and it was widely suspected that a neutral regulator would reveal them to be as vulnerable as the Spanish cajas. They were also less concerned about the Doom Loop, given both their relatively small size and the relative fiscal capacity of the German state.

This internal division meant that, unlike in France, the banking sector did not speak with a single voice on supervision and resolution. As will be discussed in more detail in the section on EDIS, this was not the case with deposit insurance, where all three pillars were keen to preserve their privately funded and privately run systems, to avoid both the additional cost and additional scrutiny that a public system, especially a European system, would require.

## Crises as Key to Breaking the Status Quo Equilibrium

The balance of arguments and interests strongly resisted implementation of banking union from the negotiation of the Maastricht Treaty through the start of the Debt Crisis despite the strength of the functionalist arguments. So long as the large transnational banks and key member states, especially France, remained opposed to banking union, centralized banking regulation remained theoretically advantageous but a political nonstarter.[79] As outlined in Chapter 3, even the 2007–09 Banking Crisis was insufficient to disrupt the anti-centralization status quo. However, the Debt Crisis would change this dynamic not through the introduction of new arguments about banking union, but by vividly demonstrating how flaws in the European financial architecture had rendered the status quo unsustainable. The threat of the Doom Loop in particular to the health of banks in both southern and northern states and even to the survival of the eurozone vividly illustrated how the choice now was between disintegration and integration, and so long as the crisis raged, the key question soon became how, not if, to centralize supervision and resolution in response to the crisis. However, once the crisis moment passed and the initial reforms created a new status quo of at least temporary stability, actors lukewarm on integration pulled back from supporting further reform, opponents of centralization regrouped, and further progress was blocked despite the continuing functional need.

## Creation of the Single Supervisory Mechanism

The first major institutional component of the proposed banking union was the Single Supervisory Mechanism, creating direct European-level supervision of at least the most important European banks. Some form of central supervision had been cast as desirable from a functional standpoint as far back as the Lamfalussy Report in 2001, though that Report itself expressed concern about the political will for even the more moderate harmonization process it endorsed.[80] This assessment certainly proved accurate for the first decade of the euro's existence. Despite support for the idea from the European Commission and European Central Bank, as well as a push by the European Parliament to advance centralized supervision out of the Banking Crisis, little progress had been made by the start of the Debt Crisis.[81] National regulators jealously guarded their prerogatives, especially hoping to protect their national banks, and both large and small banks generally wanted to preserve their existing relationships with those regulators.

This dynamic began to change in the early stages of the crisis. The European Commission and the European Central Bank, both of which had already taken pro-centralization positions, rhetorically linked their long-term goal of creating a Single Supervisory Mechanism to the short-term needs of crisis management.[82] Mario Draghi in particular explicitly adopted a "there is no alternative" framing, arguing that the only reliable way out of the current crisis, and future similar crises, was through a centralization of regulation.[83]

However, these arguments only proved successful in winning the support of the southern states in crisis, where the status quo had already become unsustainable. Once sovereign defaults became not just possible but likely without external support, neither banks nor policymakers in the southern states could argue for the sustainability of current system of financial regulation. In Schoenmaker's terms, the choice was now starkly between surrendering national regulation in favor of supranational regulation or abandoning deep integration, a move that would likely involve not just an exit from the eurozone, but potentially from the European Union itself.

In the early months of the crisis, however, the northern states, including both France and Germany, remained unmoved. French Finance Minister Christine Lagarde expressed fears as to the efficacy of the proposals, noting that "the problem is that the ECB doesn't have the authority on the whole of the EU."[84] German Finance Minister Wolfgang Schäuble, for instance, argued that "it would be very difficult to get approval by the German parliament if [the deal] would leave the supervision for all the German banks to European banking supervision. Nobody believes that it would work."[85] In doing so, he pushed back against functionalist narratives with one of his own, arguing that the proposals were not only unnecessary, but not viable. These states remained relatively insulated from the banking crisis, as their own banks were for the time being spared from the panic. The banks themselves, while exposed to Greek default risk in particular, remained convinced that their governments would be successful in protecting them by pushing the adjustment costs onto the southern states.[86]

## The EBA Stress Tests

Two key developments would disrupt this northern confidence in the status quo, creating an opportunity for advocates of centralized supervision to advance their agenda. The first of these was the demonstrated inadequacy of the main institutional fix coming out of the last crisis, the European Banking Authority. In particular, many market observers considered the stress tests of European banks in 2010 and 2011 to be wholly inadequate.[87] The simultaneous stress tests conducted by US regulators were seen as a key marker in the restoration of American financial stability. Generally regarded as rigorous and unbiased, the tests helped create confidence in market actors that American banks were finally on firm footing after the 2007–09 crisis.[88] The EBA's stress tests, however, had the opposite effect. Multiple banks that "passed" the 2010 tests would fall into distress soon thereafter, including Allied Irish Bank, MPS in Italy, and Caja de Ahorros Mediterráneo and Caja Sur in Spain. The follow-up 2011 tests fared little better, being widely seen as flawed.[89] Jochen Sanio, head of BaFin, Germany's chief banking regulator, went so far as to question the legal basis and legitimacy of the EBA's tests.[90] Another observer captured the overall sense by arguing that "the European tests have always been seen as a poor relation of the US exercise in 2009."[91]

To some degree, these stumbles for the new EBA could be explained as part of the learning process of a new institution. However, given the importance of establishing an early reputation for competence to building long-term credibility, even this narrative weakened the EBA's position. More damaging, however, was the sense that the problem was not just a learning process, but a fundamental flaw in an approach that so heavily relied on national regulators. While the US Federal Reserve collected its own data on the banks, the EBA relied on reporting from the national supervisory authorities, which had incentive to protect their banks and soft-pedal their problems.[92] This diagnosis of the EBA's problems suggested that more time and more practiced staff could not effectively overcome the challenges. A "patch-up" reform which harmonized but did not centralize national supervisory authorities, while perhaps sufficient for the last crisis, was inadequate to the scale of the challenge of the current moment.

## The Cajas Crisis

The demonstrated inadequacy of the EBA alone was insufficient to create movement on banking union. The bank stumbles in the north which the EBA's stress tests had failed to anticipate were still small enough that they could be managed by the home states of the affected banks. The status quo had become less desirable, as the US stress tests were clearly superior to the EBA's, but it was not yet unsustainable. The key turning point would come in the early summer of 2012, when the Spanish caja banking sector fell into a panic.

The collapse of the Spanish cajas was instrumental in shifting the coalitions around the single supervisory mechanism as they vividly demonstrated several reasons why the status quo of national regulation was no longer sustainable. Firstly, the collapse of the cajas illustrated how the incentives of national regulators in a transnational banking environment point toward instability. In such an environment, regulators' interest in stability becomes balanced by an interest in promoting the banks under their jurisdiction from competition by outside institutions. Both banks and regulators want to preserve a close relationship that benefits both the banks, via regulatory protection, and the regulators, by helping promote regional development. Regional banks such as the cajas have a track record of promoting regional development more than larger banking groups which focus on the most profitable markets.[93] They also have a track record of supporting regional politicians' pet projects, creating both economic and political incentives to keep banking local.[94] In Spain, this meant that cajas were allowed to conceal their losses until they became unsustainable, both to protect the banks themselves and increasingly to protect the supervisors from needing to reveal their

**136  Crises and Integration in European Banking Union**

earlier laxity.[95] This, however, was by no means a problem unique to Spain, as small "alternative banks" with close ties to local regulators are common across much of the eurozone. The vulnerabilities of the cozy and mutually advantageous relationship between the German Landesbanken and their Land governments became apparent in the 2007–09 Banking Crisis. Many feared that the Sparkassen, the smaller German savings banks, hid similar problems.[96] The similar dynamics in Germany in 2008 and Spain in 2012 strongly suggested that such collapses could well be a recurring feature of national regulation of regional banks. Moreover, that the cajas ran into trouble after the enactment of the EBA strongly suggested once again that the earlier patch-up reform was no longer sufficient. As Nicholas Véron put it, "at this point I see nothing that reassures me that what has not worked the previous two times will work this time."[97]

The cajas crisis illustrated that such national and subnational crises had transnational implications and could no longer be managed by national governments alone without substantial costs. French banks in particular had substantial exposure to the Spanish cajas, and to the southern banks generally.[98] As such, they faced substantial losses if the cajas were allowed to collapse, costs that could potentially also push French banking into a crisis. Although the French banks were most exposed in the Spanish case, other northern banks had similar exposure across the eurozone, and the next crisis could easily take in the large German or Benelux banks. Together, the European banks held $3 trillion in exposure to southern debt, with the majority of that held by French and German banks.[99]

This was not a new problem, as both French and German banks were acutely aware of their exposure to Greek defaults. This danger had been a key factor in pushing the eurozone states out of the no-bailouts position and into the second phase of the crisis, where support was provided to prevent defaults in exchange for austerity conditions which insulate the northern banks from costs by pushing adjustment onto the southern states. The cajas crisis was crucial here in demonstrating the limits of that strategy because of the continued vulnerability of both northern and southern states to the Doom Loop. Spain was forced to turn to the ESM for funding to afford the actions necessary to prevent an uncontrolled collapse of the cajas. That the second largest of the crisis-stricken countries, and the one in the best fiscal shape prior to the crisis, was still struck by bank panics it could not afford to contain on its own two years into emergency support provisions indicated that the strategy of pushing adjustment costs onto the debtor countries was unsustainable. The danger of a similar Doom Loop feedback cycle triggering elsewhere was palpable, and would either need to be dealt with on an ad hoc basis through the ESM or with more systematic changes. Moreover, the increasing awareness of the inability of the crisis-stricken states to support their banks made such banking crises more likely, as investors would be quicker to pull out and slower to invest in banks that could not be reliably supported by their sovereigns.

The Doom Loop was not just a problem for southern banks, due to the substantial cross-border exposure of the northern banks. The problem was acute in France, given both the average size of the major French banks relative to the state and their exposure to Spain. However, France was hardly the only state with banks facing substantial exposure to crises in other states' banking sector, nor was it unique in its mismatch between size of banks and size of state resources, as captured in Figure 4.2. The Netherlands in particular faced a greater challenge, and most eurozone states had a ratio of bank assets to GDP of well over 100 percent.[100] Therefore, it was necessary to contain the crises in Spain and other debtor states not just for the sake of the southern states, and not even just to preserve their membership in the eurozone, but also as a protective measure for the northern transnational banks.

Finally, the cajas crisis was important because it came over two years into the Debt Crisis, and over five years after the beginning of the previous Banking Crisis. The fixes after the Banking Crisis were demonstrably inadequate to preserve the solvency of banking in eurozone states, with vividly demonstrated spillover effects between states. Moreover, despite two years of emergency support, the crisis in banking in particular was getting worse, not better. Given the credible reasons to think that cajas-style disintegrations were plausible in many other states across the eurozone, it became increasingly clear that emergency provisions and waiting out the crisis was no longer sufficient. The arguments for more radical reform became more compelling because the sustainability of the status quo became increasingly implausible.[101]

## Changing Positions in the Big Banks and France

The major political change out of the cajas crisis was that the large transnational banks shifted from their earlier position opposing a common supervisor to enthusiastically embracing the creation of one. By 2012, the European Banking Federation (EBF) and most of the large European banks launched public campaigns in support of the creation of both a common supervisor and a common resolution authority. The EBF in particular argued that the SSM was "of paramount importance to ensure financial stability and safeguard a level playing field between banks under the mechanism."[102] This shift was a long time coming, as while the large banks had benefited from soft-touch treatment by national supervisors promoting them as "national champions," their increasingly transnational operations meant that they also increasingly suffered from the friction of operating in multiple regulatory environments and national supervisors in host countries protecting their own banks against the operations of the large banks. The cajas crisis crystalized how this system of national supervision not only encouraged the protection of inefficient regional banks, but also created instability with the capacity to threaten the larger banks. This protection of regional banks helped them against not only large foreign banks but also large domestic competitors. It therefore comes as little surprise that Santander, the largest Spanish bank, came to support a reform that would not only smooth its international operations, but also ease its domestic operations. In the words of Emilio Botin, the chairman of Santander, "Santander has met innumerable barriers in its attempts to expand in Europe ... Banking union is an ambitious, complex, and difficult process, both operationally and politically, but we cannot afford to postpone it."[103] The German commercial banks, which had long inveighed against the regulatory protections enjoyed by the domestic Landesbank rivals, also swung to support for a single supervisory mechanism, especially one that would be expansive enough to cover not only the largest European institutions, but also the midsized banks which competed with them for the business of the largest midsized firms. The German commercial bank association, the Association for German Banks (BdB), argued that "the same supervisory rules must apply to the same business, the same risks and to all market participants and these rules must, moreover, be applied in the same way."[104] Deutsche Bank co-chairman Anshu Jain similarly agreed that "it is essential that the banking union does not undermine the EU-wide single market or result in two-tier regulation."[105] In short, the German commercial banks were willing to accept European supervision so long as it also covered their chief domestic rivals, the Landesbanken.

The most immediately significant shift would be among the French banks, the foreign banks most exposed to the cajas crisis. Their exposure to the cajas meant that rapid action to ensure that crisis did not spread to France was essential to their health. The French state quickly shifted position soon thereafter, especially as the danger to the state's credit rating became clear. France had long been mooted as the potential next link in the "daisy chain" of sovereign debt contagion after the spread from Greece to Portugal to Spain to Italy, leaving it in a relatively precarious position versus the other creditor states. Moreover, the massive size of the major French banking groups, coupled with their exposure to the cajas, meant that Doom Loop concerns were much more acute than in Germany, where only Deutsche Bank, Commerzbank, or a sector-wide failure in the savings banks truly threatened the state's solvency. By June of 2012, France's previous joint position with Germany on the Debt Crisis was abandoned. By June of 2012, France had come to support not only direct bank recapitalization by the ESM, but also the creation of a nearly universal single supervisory authority and a mutually funded common banking resolution authority.

## Germany's Shifting Position

France's shift dramatically altered the conversation around banking union. No longer was it a case of southern states attempting to persuade a French–German-led bloc with a clear majority in the key European forums. France's shift meant that debates on the SSM and SRM were now a case of two roughly evenly matched coalitions. The first, now led by France, the European Commission, and European Central Bank, included most of the debtor eurozone states. The second included most of the northern creditor states and was nominally led by Germany. However, Germany's internal debates and ideological commitments would make it the state most likely to change its positions on supervision and resolution of that coalition, and its shift on supervision would prove decisive for the creation of the SSM. Key to this shift would be framing the unsustainability of the status quo in such a way that it appealed to the ideological commitments of German elites toward both European integration and Ordoliberalism.

Making the case that action on supervision was essential to preserving European integration was the more straightforward one. The current status quo in late 2012 was clearly unsustainable, and serious debate only centered on how, not if, to address it.[106] Advocates of European integration, especially in the Commission and European Central Bank, made a strong case for common supervision of as wide a range of European banks as possible. At the December 2012 Economic and Financial Affairs Council (ECOFIN) summit, Draghi would describe it as "crucial" that the SSM cover all eurozone banks.[107] Such arguments found receptive audiences in Germany. Peer Steinbrück, the head of the Social Democratic Party, argued that EU supervision would help minimize taxpayer losses.[108] Wolfgang Schäuble, the Finance Minister argued that the euro was approaching a *Vertrauensrkise*, or crisis of confidence, with dramatic action necessary to preserve it.[109] Finance Minister Wolfgang Schäuble similarly called for a more expansive SSM, arguing that "self-regulation and light-touch supervision just [does] not work in the financial sector."[110]

European supervision was also presented as in line with German elites' commitments to Ordoliberalism. Germany had since the beginning of the Debt Crisis promoted a framing of it as grounded in insufficient fiscal prudence.[111] This framing made austerity in exchange for national bailouts a logical approach in the second, emergency, phase of the Debt Crisis. However, by 2012 the limits of the austerity-for-bailouts approach was clear. Spanish austerity had not prevented the collapse of the cajas, and the structural reasons why caja-style collapses were plausible in a wide range of contexts made it clear that bailouts to rescue banks, not just sovereigns in crisis, seemed to be a likely recurring feature of the eurozone as currently constituted. In this context, in which allowing countries and banks to default was not a viable alternative, the question then became how to make such bailouts both tolerable and as rare as possible. An argument that focused on the weakness or inadequacy of national supervision fit well with Ordoliberalism, as it cast the problem as not of fundamental market instability, as a Keynesian framework might, but instead as a product of inadequate regulation. Replacing inadequate national supervision with more efficient European supervision would therefore be a solution congruent with both the desire to preserve to the euro and the logic of Ordoliberalism. The SSM, in this understanding, became the essential element to make the bailouts tolerable to at least a key element of German elites. It was this understanding that Schäuble embraced when he insisted on the Single Supervisory Mechanism in exchange for the release of ESM funds to Spain.[112] If bailouts were to be a recurring feature of the eurozone, Schäuble would insist that they also were accompanied by a mechanism to enforce rules designed to mitigate their frequency.

The debate within Germany was not just about principles of European integration and Ordoliberalism. While France's relatively homogenous banking sector meant that there were few internal divisions on regulatory architecture reforms, Germany's much more differentiated three-pillar banking sector saw much greater division. The commercial banks, with extensive foreign operations and large enough to have real Doom Loop concerns, like their French peers saw real advantages in the Single Supervisory Mechanism, and became prominent advocates for it. They saw advantages not just in streamlining their international operations, but also in a European supervisor which covered the Landesbanken. These largest of the German savings banks had long been the chief domestic rivals of the commercial banks, and enjoyed the protection of closely allied politicians, especially at the Land level. Therefore, the commercial banks wanted not just a single supervisory mechanism, but one that extended as widely as possible, at a minimum to include the Landes-banken and level the regulatory playing field between the large and midsized banks. For the inverse reasons, the savings banks, including both the Landesbanken and the Sparkassen, as well as the third pillar of mutual banks all strongly opposed the SSM. The introduction of a common supervisor meant the loss of the protections they enjoyed as a result of their close relationship with local regulators and politicians. The Sparkassen and mutuals would be spared direct European supervision for any but the most expansive threshold for which banks were large enough to be covered, so strongly argued for the preservation of local regulation of smaller banks. The Landesbanken were the noncommercial banks most likely to be covered by the SSM, and so fought to keep the threshold high enough to spare them.

This combination of internal political divisions in the banking sector and opportunities for rhetorical framing linking banking union with Ordoliberal commitments gave ways in for proponents of banking union to build a pro-SSM coalition within Germany. Germany became central to debates over the SSM less because of its size as such than because of its role as the crucial "tipping point" state, which could either win support for the SSM by siding with the reform coalition or block it by siding with the anti-reform bloc. If Germany sided with France, their "dual hegemony" could overcome resistance from other states, especially if the other large economies, such as Spain and Italy, were on board.[113] However, if France and Germany split, it would be difficult for any reform to pass.

## Evaluating the Single Supervisory Mechanism

The Single Supervision Mechanism which was ratified by the Council of the European Union on October 15, 2013 was close to the vision of the most ambitious advocates. It made the European Central Bank the direct supervisor of the largest banks in Europe, replacing national supervisory authorities for 120 banks and 85 percent of European banking assets.[114] This threshold could be expanded to include other banks designated as systemically important, and was also broad enough to include the larger midsized banks, including all of the German Landesbanken. It left national supervision in place for the remaining approximately 6000 smaller European banks, but set up the ECB in an oversight role over those national supervisors, with the ability to audit national regulators and in certain circumstances take over direct regulation. It also did not cover non-eurozone banks at all, though non-eurozone member states could opt in to the banking union if they chose to do so.

This was a dramatic increase in centralization of supervision from the pre-crisis institutional arrangements, and a much more substantial reform than the introduction of the EBA after the Banking Crisis. Such a dramatic leap forward was possible because the reform could be cast as the necessary alternative to a messy collapse or a status quo of perpetual crisis and a mix of bailouts and austerity loathed by both creditors and debtors. This, in turn, reflects the crisis in supervision's status as both endogenous to the financial architecture and severe enough to require substantial reform to fix. The endogeneity could be clearly linked to the misalignment of the economic and political incentives of national supervisors in an integrated transnational financial system, as clearly illustrated by inadequacy of the EBA and outbreak of the cajas crisis. The severity was also clear, as the collapse of the cajas threatened not just Spanish finance, but the solvency of the Spanish state, the solvency of French banks, and even the solvency of the French state. In such a context, radical reform became much more viable, as failure to reform would mean perpetually recurring devastating crises. It is reasonable to argue that the SSM reflected an even more radical step toward centralization than the SRM, as while the latter did increase fiscal transfers, it retained strong elements of intergovernmentalism. In practice, the SSM's regulatory harmonization remained incomplete, as some national divergence endured.[115] However, the replacing of national supervisors by the ECB, on the other hand, was a clear and unambiguous move toward supranational governance of European finance.

## The Bank Recovery and Resolution Directive

The next reform to the European financial architecture, the Bank Recovery and Resolution Directive (BRRD), was not nearly as significant a step toward centralization as the Single Supervisory Mechanism or the Single Resolution Mechanism, and is most important here as a prelude of sorts to the debates over the SRM. In substance, it was more a patch-up reform akin to the introduction of the European Banking Authority than the more radical SSM and SRM. However, like the EBA, it covered all European banks, not just eurozone institutions, and it is fruitful to examine both as a precursor to the Single Resolution Mechanism debates to follow and as another example of how a deteriorating status quo in an endogenous crisis can produce reforms. In this case, as in the EBA, a moderate need to fix an endogenous problem produced a modest reform.

In a sense, the BRRD and the SRM both existed to solve the problem of the costs of bank bailouts falling on states, and thus ultimately on taxpayers. Both therefore were intended to signal a transition from a permissive state aid environment, where bailouts would be generous and readily available to Too Big to Fail firms, to a restrictive one. The BRRD's chief innovation was to create standardized rules for "bail in" across the EU. Under the new rules of the BRRD, when a bank fell into distress, creditors would be converted into equity holders. This would create an automatic recapitalization mechanism while also lowering the liabilities of the institution. It would also automatically create burden-sharing for creditors, who in many cases managed to escape the pain of bank failure in the 2007–09 crisis, only taking losses after stockholders were wiped out. In theory, by allowing the bank to recapitalize through conversion of loans into equity, the threshold of bank failure without state support would rise dramatically. Ideally, the remaining liabilities of the banks after bail-in, chiefly retail deposits, would be small enough and protected by deposit guarantee schemes such that even bailouts of large banks could be avoided. The BRRD not only introduced bail-in, in line with the guidelines of the Basel III Accords, but also standardized it across the European Union. In doing so, it reduced the opportunity for regulatory arbitrage by banks, which might otherwise choose to set up operations in the venue with the greatest expectation of favorable treatment in the event of bank distress.

Much like with the components of banking union, the functional case for the BRRD was strong and straightforward, but itself insufficient until the unfolding of the European Debt Crisis. Prior to the crisis, multiple states, including Germany, Austria, the Netherlands, and Finland, all expressed opposition to such a reform, seeing limited benefits and potentially high costs from the reform.[116] As one German government official put it, "an ERA [European Resolution Authority] would impinge upon the autonomy of the member states and there is the danger that the measures taken would affect the national budget."[117] This coalition meant that reform was blocked until the unfolding of the banking crisis.

The return to costly bailouts reduced creditor political power to a low point while at the same time increasing public anti-bailout ire. Again, the cajas crisis played a crucial role. In order to contain the broader fallout from the failure of the cajas, Germany was forced to accept a €39.5 billion bailout of four nationalized Spanish banks out of the EFSF and ESM. This highly visible transfer ensured that the public was well aware of the continuing costs of bailouts in Europe. Moreover, the fact that the BRRD not only did not involve a transfer of funds between member states and in fact would potentially reduce the

**144    Crises and Integration in European Banking Union**

need for such transfers only increased the appeal among northern publics. Germany in fact insisted on the BRRD as a precondition for any Single Resolution Mechanism for precisely this reason, as a first recourse to bail-in would reduce the size of any last-resort bailouts that did end up as the SRM's responsibility.[118] Southerners, who would otherwise be expected to welcome such transfers, generally were also supportive, especially given widespread belief that there were ways around the BRRD's preferences for resolution.[119]

## Creation of the Single Resolution Mechanism

The second major component of the banking union to be implemented, the Single Resolution Mechanism aimed to sever the Doom Loop by creating a European-level resolution authority and fund, taking the task and funding burden away from states. In this way, the banking union could approximate the resolution dynamics of the United States by eliminating the mismatch between the size of the largest banks and the authority in charge of managing their potential failure. Although the largest European banks are comparable in size to the largest American banks, the much larger size (in fiscal terms) of the US compared even to Germany and France both helps reinforce banks and ward off dangers of a Doom Loop by removing doubt that the state could afford to manage the resolution of even the largest institutions. This reinforces the banks, because depositors and creditors can be certain that at worst the collapse of the bank will be managed and orderly, and at best, especially in a crisis where the bank's only fault is contagion from others' faults, the state can afford the fiscal support necessary to prevent failure. In the absence of such support, market actors will be quicker to rush for the exits, as any potential state support may either be insufficient, late in coming, or nonexistent. It also reinforces state solvency, as the threat of a large bank failure is not a threat to the state's creditworthiness. Even the assets of the largest bank in the United States, JP Morgan-Chase, were in 2010 only 7 percent of US GDP.[120] Although it would be politically unpopular to do so, the US could afford to fully guarantee those liabilities without blowing up its debt-to-GDP ratio. By contrast, 90 percent of French bank lending was provided by five institutions, each with assets over €600 billion.[121] The attempt to arrest the collapse of any one of them would plunge the French state into a sovereign debt crisis. This was essentially what happened to Ireland in the aftermath of its 2008 decision to guarantee its three largest banks, a move which overnight increased Ireland's potential liabilities by €400 billion.[122] The Single Resolution Mechanism would eliminate, or at least minimize, this instability through the creation of the Single Resolution Fund, a standing fund to pay for the costs of resolution of any bank in the banking union, paid for by contributions by all banking union member states.

The SRM also would address a second issue of national resolution, the incentive for national resolution authorities to prioritize preserving the competitive position of the national banking system and national champion banks over minimizing the danger of a transnational banking crisis or reducing the costs to taxpayers, especially taxpayers in other political jurisdictions. A generous bailout that keeps national banks operating can ensure that foreign banks cannot gain market share at the expense of national banks, and the national authorities have little incentive to consider the costs that a bailout that risks instability in other jurisdictions imposes on other states and their taxpayers. For that matter, part of the reason that bailouts are unpopular domestically is the sense that taxpayer money is being used to rescue banks from the consequences of their own actions. This dynamic can certainly be seen not only in the states directly affected by the Debt Crisis, but also in the creditor northern states. For all of the German emphasis on minimizing moral hazard in the Debt Crisis, the German bank rescues in the 2007–09 Crisis were among the most generous to the ailing banks. The Directorate-General for Competition of the European Commission (DG Comp) repeatedly demanded revision of German support to its banks on the grounds that it was so generous as to violate State Aid rules.[123] The BRRD in principle solved the problem of national competition to provide more generous state aid by establishing common standards for bank resolution procedures, though subsequent debates over bank resolutions in practice would reveal the limits of the BRRD to produce such a standardized response.[124] However, even beyond such standardization, the decision of whether and when to put a bank into a resolution procedure remained in the hands of national authorities. Such authorities would potentially have an incentive to do so at the last possible minute, especially since many of the costs of waiting would be borne by foreigners. The SRM would address this issue by creating a Single Resolution Board, a European authority to determine when and how to put banks into resolution. The actual operation of this would prove to be complex, but the core idea was simple: relying on a European authority to determine resolution would ensure that the resolution authority considered the costs and benefits of any course of action to the eurozone as a whole, not just the individual member state.

The final functional argument for the SRM was that it would be incoherent and detrimental to have centralized supervision but national resolution.[125] Benoît Cœuré, a French member of the EBC's Executive Board, described

## 146   Crises and Integration in European Banking Union

the SSM without a resolution authority as wading across a river and stopping halfway.[126] Economist Thorsten Beck argued that centralized supervision without resolution was worse than nothing at all.[127] The problem in splitting the levels at which supervision and resolution occurred lay primarily in the mismatch of incentive. Transnational supervisors would favor rapid resolution of failing banks paid for by national resolution authorities, while those national resolution authorities would favor delay in hopes of avoiding the costs of those resolutions.

## Coalitions on the SRM

As with the SSM, the functional logic of the need for an SRM was insufficient. As with the SSM, the major supranational institutions of the EU, especially the Commission and the ECB had long supported a centralization of resolution, but until the Debt Crisis lacked the broader political support to make it happen. The crisis-stricken states also supported it, as they felt the pinch of the Doom Loop most acutely. Ireland's bailout of its massive banks in 2008 had moved it from being one of the eurozone's best states in terms of sovereign debt to one of its worst. Spain had already been forced to seek ESM support to manage the resolution of its caja banks, a maneuver which stretched the purpose of a fund that was more properly designed to rescue states, not banks. Italy, under pressure from the distress of Monti dei Paschi, was in a position to soon need similar support. All of these states had strong incentive to want an SRM, and to want it soon, as they would almost certainly at least in the short run be net beneficiaries rather than net contributors.

France again emerged as the most powerful member state to embrace an SRM early on. The mismatch between the size of the French banks and the French state meant that France saw clear benefits to the SRM. Unlike the southern states, which would potentially make direct recourse to the SRM in the coming years, France was unlikely to tap it immediately. The value to France would be more in confidence-building for both the private funding costs of its banks and France's public debt. The presence of the SRM, even without being tapped directly, would reassure investors in banks that a resolution authority of sufficient capacity existed, and reassure holders of French sovereign debt that a bank stumble would not plunge France into a sovereign debt crisis. For these reasons, French Foreign Minister Pierre Moscovici described a single resolution fund as "a necessity."[128]

The groups in opposition to the SRM also closely resembled the coalition against the SSM, consisting of most of the northern European states, with

Germany in a leadership role alongside Austria, Finland, and the Netherlands. Their formal arguments largely rested on the argument that the SRM represented an expansion of the authority of European institutions beyond the scope of what was possible without Treaty changes. One German government spokesman argued that "the proposal gives the European Commission a competence it cannot have based on the current treaties."[129] German Finance Minister Wolfgang Schäuble proposed that the only alternative possible under existing treaties would be the establishment of a network of national resolution authorities with voluntary capacity to support each other, but nothing that could compel either resolution or funding.[130]

Undergirding these legal concerns was the stark fact that the creation of the SRM would not just create a transfer of legal authority, as with the SSM, but also have substantial redistributive consequences.[131] Unlike the southern states, the coalition of states opposing the SRM would likely be net contributors to the Single Resolution Fund, at least for the foreseeable future.[132] As of 2012–13, the banks in these states were regarded as generally in good health, especially outside of Germany. In some states there was a mismatch between the size of banks and the size of the state, as was the case in the Netherlands. However, two key factors meant that this did not compel them to move toward the SRM the way that France did. The first was that their banks were perceived as being in better health than France's, especially given how the cajas crisis had highlighted French exposure to Spanish debt more than other northern banks. The second was that the sovereign debt position of these states was also generally stronger. This reflected not only France's generally greater tendency to adopt Keynesian fiscal stimulus, but also France's position at the end of the "daisy chain" of financial contagion in the eyes of bond traders. Just as the crisis in Greece prompted a run on Portuguese debt, which in turn lead to runs on Spanish and then Italian debt, France was seen as "next" after Italy. Absent these specifically French concerns, northern states could focus more on the direct and immediate costs to themselves and their banks.

Germany again emerged as the crucial tipping point state, though here the pro-SRM faction was less emphatic than in the SSM. The largest banks in Germany, Deutsche Bank and Commerzbank, were both big enough that their failure would tax the German state, though not to the degree of the largest French banks. The two private banks, together with DZ Bank, the clearing bank of the savings bank pillar, together constituted 76 percent of German bank assets in 2014.[133] Neither of the large commercial banks were seen as in good health, with Commerzbank having required capital support from the German government in 2008 and Deutsche, although not needing

**148** Crises and Integration in European Banking Union

a bailout, nevertheless struggling to return to robust profitability.[134] They therefore saw some advantages from an SRM, but did not see it to be as essential as their French peers found it. They also feared that the funding scheme of the SRM would disadvantage them because Germany's position as the eurozone's largest economy would mean an expected substantial role in funding the Single Resolution Fund.

The other German banks saw little to like in the proposal. The smaller banks, the Sparkassen and the cooperatives, would not have been covered by the SRM except in the most extreme cases, so saw it primarily as a drain on their funding with little benefit. The Landesbanken, which would be covered by the SRM, strongly preferred to keep their national or Land resolution authorities. German bailouts in the 2007–09 crisis were especially favorable to their banks. The bailouts of the Landesbanken in particular were generous in part because the Landesbanken successfully played the federal government and the Länder off each other, with each bidding to be the one to bail out the banks in exchange for either reforming them or maintaining their traditional role respectively.[135]

As a result of this bank opposition, German policymakers were generally skeptical of the SRM early on. Only the Greens, of the major political parties, strongly endorsed the SRM, with Green leader Jürgen Trittin arguing that "we want to give the commission power to close failing banks because we don't trust France to close BNP Paribas or Germany to close Deutsche Bank if necessary."[136] The Bundesbank also endorsed the SRM. Executive board member Andreas Dombret echoed neo-functional arguments insisting that the SSM made the SRM a necessity, as "banks supervised at the European level will have to be resolved at the European level, too."[137]

## The Persistence of the Doom Loop and the Undesirability of the Status Quo

As with the SSM, what moved the debate on the SRM was not the functional argument as to need in the abstract, as that had been clear for years. Rather, as the Debt Crisis persisted, it became clearer and clearer that the cost of failing to address flaws in the current arrangement significantly exceeded those of resisting reform. The case was not as dire as with the SSM, where the status quo was collapsing entirely, reducing the options to disintegration or deeper integration. However, the continued difficulties of Spanish banks, combined with renewed pressure on Italian banks, especially Monti dei Paschi, and Greek banks made it clear that the current status quo meant

The 2010–14 European Debt Crisis    **149**

frequently recurring bank failures. The BRRD would make the allocation of costs more favorable than without it, but because it had no mechanism for interstate funding, would not itself eliminate the Doom Loop.

These dynamics meant that the status quo in the eurozone was already one of mutualization of bank resolution, just one on an ad hoc basis rather than rules-based and governed by a coherent institutional structure. The Spanish and Italian banking crisis had highlighted the vulnerabilities to both banks and states from the bank–state nexus.[138] Once banking crises hit these states, the logic of the Doom Loop meant that the affected states would either need external support or fall into renewed sovereign debt crises. This made the choice for the rest of the eurozone states either to let major member states crash out of the eurozone or accede to ESM support to fund their bank bailouts. Given these options, Germany had agreed to let Spain tap the ESM to fund bank recapitalizations in 2012.

The creation of the ESM meant that a mechanism did exist to provide such funding, and the precedent of providing aid to Spain and Italy meant that similar support could be expected in future cases. This therefore diminished the danger of the Doom Loop but highlighted how undesirable the status quo was for all parties involved. Crisis-stricken states could have funding recourse, but only once their crisis reached such a high threshold that emergency authorization to tap the ESM could be granted. This both increased the damage to the broader real economy in both crisis-afflicted and neighboring states and made the costs to the ESM greater than if it had acted earlier in the crisis. Moreover, the ad hoc and emergency basis for tapping the ESM meant that the rules were more flexible and unpredictable than they would be under a standing Single Resolution Mechanism, even with the presence of the BRRD.

This therefore presented the eurozone member state with, in essence, three options as to how to proceed. The first is that they could attempt to undo the precedent of letting Spain and Italy tap the ESM to fund their bank bailouts. This was clearly the least desirable for all parties involved. It would restore the framework of the 2010–11 early stages of the panic, raising substantial dangers of the disintegration of the eurozone. It was also unclear to what degree it would be possible to make such a move, given that the precedent had already been established and reversing the precedent would be so clearly undesirable to so many parties that market investors would not likely regard such efforts as credible in any event. The second alternative would be to retain the current status quo of ad hoc tapping of the ESM to fund national bailouts, an approach which both imposed greater costs on all member states than early action and gave national governments greater discretion in how to allocate

**150    Crises and Integration in European Banking Union**

European funds than an SRM approach would. The final alternative would be a move toward an SRM.

In negotiations over the SRM, advocates stressed three key arguments to persuade the German government. The first was the danger of spillover from the Doom Loop, which remained in the current status quo of emergency ESM funding and would only be greater if such funding were removed. The ECB in particular made this case to Germany.[139] Secondly, having already agreed to a supranational solution for Spain on an emergency basis, it would be hard for Germany to now argue that only intergovernmental approaches such as voluntary lending between national authorities was a legitimate approach.[140] Germany's own precedent undercut those arguments. Finally, if a return to a pre-ESM status quo was off the table, it was far more congruent with Germany's Ordoliberal commitments to support an institutionalized Single Resolution Authority with established rules and procedures than to continue to accede to a continued series of ad hoc mutualized resolution actions.[141]

German negotiators agreed to an SRM in principle relatively early, and focused much of their attention on debates over how large to make the Single Resolution Fund and how to fund it. On the question of funding, Germany won a minor victory by securing a funding formula based on the size of individual banks, rather than the overall size of the financial sector. Thus, France, with a handful of large banks, would ultimately be a larger net contributor to the SRF than Germany, with a larger overall financial sector but one with a greater role for smaller institutions.[142] Germany would also win a somewhat larger victory over the decision-making process of bank resolution by insisting that the European Council, and thus the member states, retained a role in the process rather than leaving it a purely supranational operation.

## Evaluating the Single Resolution Mechanism

The Single Resolution Mechanism was undoubtedly one of the most significant reforms introduced in Europe since the Maastricht Treaty, as it created a real mechanism for mutualization of bank resolution and a permanent transfer mechanism under the control of an institution, the Single Resolution Board, with very prominent supranational elements. Although the actual size of the Single Resolution Fund was not massive relative to the GDP of the eurozone, its creation and functional purpose pointed toward a path-dependent trajectory of increasing size. Moreover, the construction of the Single Resolution Board gave prominent roles to the European Commission and the European Central Bank, meaning that supranational agents now had a clear role in determining whether member state banks remained open, and how they would be resolved if a resolution were required. These changes are substantial, and well beyond the "patch-up" reforms of the EBA and BRRD, which harmonized financial supervision and resolution decisions but kept the actual authority and funding firmly in national hands.

However, the SRM was not as dramatic a shift toward supranational governance as the SSM, nor was it as complete a victory for advocates of banking union as that earlier reform. The SRM contained much more significant intergovernmental elements and compromises than the SSM. This was most notable in the complicated decision-making structure of the Single Resolution Board, with both the European Commission and the European Council having roles to play before funding could be tapped. Under the terms of the SRM, the SRB's decision on resolution is only the first step in the process. Once the SRB makes its decision, the European Commission has twenty-four hours to either endorse that decision or raise an objection. If the Commission overrules the SRB and rules that the case at hand does not fulfill the public interest requirement to tap the SRF, the decision then goes to the European Council, after which the SRB has an additional eight hours to respond with modifications.[143] This system builds in both supranational and intergovernmental safeguards, ensuring both that the Commission can have oversight of the SRB and that the Council ultimately has veto authority over any decision to tap the SRF. This convoluted procedure was necessary to gain the support of member states which conceded the need for such a resolution authority and fund but remained deeply uncomfortable with the full transfer of such emergency spending authority to supranational institutions. It also created a process of potentially dangerous complexity and delay in decision-making. Rapid action and quiet deliberation in bank resolution can play a key role in minimizing costs to the resolution authority. Public discussion of potential resolution provides a signal for investors to flee the bank before the resolution action, raising the costs of resolution by increasing the distress of the bank. Decision-making under the SRM involves up to thirty-six hours of deliberation in multiple fora even after the SRB makes its decision, a long time in which investors can flee the troubled bank. In contrast, in the United States, the FDIC and the relevant supervisory authorities deliberate behind closed doors, presenting their decision as a fait accompli, typically on a Friday afternoon so market actors must wait until the following Monday when tempers have cooled to respond to the FDIC intervention. Such a compromise potentially weakens the efficacy of the SRM, but was necessary to get assent to such a permanent transfer facility.

## 152 Crises and Integration in European Banking Union

The SRM was also marked by compromises on both the size of the funding mechanism and the calculation of individual member state contributions. The announced size of the Single Resolution Fund was to be €55 billion, to be fully reached only by 2024.[144] This amounts to 0.8 percent of covered deposits in the banking union, short of the €72 billion many experts saw as necessary, and well short of the €100 billion Spain needed to bail out its banks in the cajas crisis.[145] However, creating the fund at all represented a significant change, and once created, the arguments for expanding the size of the fund would likely be easier than those for creating it and establishing the precedent. Therefore, the expectation was largely that path dependence would lead to the growth of the fund to a sufficient size.

The other main issue with the SRF was not just its size, but its lack of a defined backstop if its funds were to be exhausted. The logical candidate for such a role would be the preexisting ESM, but that issue proved too contentious in 2013, and the issue was tabled for the time being.[146] Here the key problem was a break between the French, who were happy to use the ESM as a backstop, and the Germans, who resisted any automatic provision to tap to ESM without first having the authorization of the member states. In the words of Wolfgang Schäuble, the German position was that "the only way to the ESM is through the nation state."[147] The combination of a SRF seen by many as too small for its purpose and the lack of a standing backstop should that expectation prove to be correct created a second major weakness in the new Single Resolution Mechanism.

Concerns over the size of the fund and the complexity of the decision-making process highlights that this was not as complete a triumph for banking union advocates as the SSM, but should not obscure that it nevertheless is a remarkable triumph for deeper integration out of the European Debt Crisis. As with the SSM, key to movement on the SRM was a combination of a problem clearly rooted in the weaknesses of the European financial regulatory architecture and a threat that meant that continuing to address those flaws created a deeply undesirable status quo. However, crucial to explaining the differences between the two outcomes is the difference between an undesirable status quo and an unsustainable one. The Single Supervisory Mechanism and the European Stability Mechanism together had created a circumstance where the most disastrous outcome, a banking crisis that forced a member state out of the eurozone, was extremely unlikely and could only come about if member states made a conscious decision to not allow troubled states to tap the ESM. This was a deeply undesirable outcome, as ad hoc bailouts both were inefficient and more prone to moral hazard problems, but not a fundamentally unsustainable status quo.[148] Moreover, this was an outcome that no party in the eurozone actually wanted, even if some parties, such as smaller northern banks, could be more nonplussed about it than other actors due to a lower threat exposure. Since the only other alternative to some form of unified resolution authority was a return to the "bad old days" of 2010–11's sovereign debt crisis, a far less desirable outcome, negotiations over the SRM were essentially a coordination game, with the question being *what form* the SRM would take, and not *whether* it would exist at all. In that context, the asymmetric exposure of Germany and the northern states, which could afford to wait longer than France and the southern states, gave them space to insist on a resolution mechanism that was closer to their own preferences. It did not, however, give them scope to refuse to create a resolution mechanism at all, as that would mean the persistence of a status quo no one wanted. The result, therefore, was either the most- or second most significant reform of the European financial regulatory architecture of the twenty-first century. It would also prove to be the last reform of comparable scale to date.

## The Failure to Create a European Deposit Insurance Scheme

The third pillar of the proposed banking union was the creation of a European Deposit Insurance Scheme to replace national deposit insurance schemes. This need was presented as essential to finally breaking the Doom Loop between banks and sovereigns. The SSM could reduce the chance of bank failure by enforcing a single common and high regulatory standard and eliminate regulatory favoritism, and the SRM could reduce the risk of bank failure from creditor flight by ensuring a large enough fund to ensure that even the largest banks could be resolved in an orderly and predictable fashion. However, neither could remove the risk of a depositor run, of savers rushing to remove their funds from the bank because they lack faith not just in the bank, but in the national deposit guarantee scheme that should ensure their savings are safe even if the bank collapses. Such a run could cause even the healthiest bank to fail, and is in fact the classic story of the failure of even healthy banks, as depicted in such iconic films as *Mary Poppins* and *It's a Wonderful Life*. Moreover, the 2007–09 Banking Crisis and the Debt Crisis both revealed that such depositor runs remain a danger even in mature financial systems. The first bank to fail in the 2007–09 Crisis, British lender Northern Rock, was ultimately brought down by just such a run despite the presence of a British DGS. Depositors lost faith not only in the bank itself, but also in the ability of the British deposit guarantee scheme to fully reimburse

Northern Rock customers in a timely fashion. The collapse of the Icelandic bank Landsbanki demonstrated the danger even more explicitly, as Landsbanki's obligations to its depositors substantially outstripped the ability of the Icelandic DGS to compensate them. This drove Iceland to make the controversial decision to break its obligations to Landsbanki customers outside of Iceland, especially in the United Kingdom and the Netherlands. In response, the UK would use antiterrorism statutes to seize Icelandic assets in Britain, beginning a long and contentious conflict between the two states.[149] More germane to the debate over EDIS, the Landsbanki case demonstrated how an insufficient DGS makes it wholly rational for depositors to continue to engage in the sort of activity that makes bank runs self-fulfilling prophecies.[150]

In a eurozone context, the reliance on national deposit guarantee schemes meant that even with the SRM, depositor runs in states where the national DGS could be overtaxed would be rational and thus a real danger to bank stability. Even if the SRF were to be large enough to overcome fears that it could not manage a large-scale banking crisis, an orderly resolution would still not be sufficient to dissuade a depositor run. The Northern Rock case demonstrated this amply. Northern Rock was small, and there was no doubt that the UK Treasury could and would eventually honor its DGS obligations, but the fear of not having access to one's savings for weeks or months while the resolution was sorted was enough to cause a run on the bank. In other cases, there may be real doubt as to whether the state could ever afford to fully honor its commitments even with the SRM, in which case the pressure for a bank run would be even greater. Therefore, the creation of a European Deposit Insurance Scheme of some form was seen as absolutely essential to forming a fully functional banking union.[151] Commission representatives portrayed EDIS as the third leg of the three-legged stool of banking union, without which the SSM and SRM could not property function.[152] However, they also acknowledged that "we would have wanted to do everything at the same time, but it was determined a little bit by the reality" that a step-by-step process was more politically viable.[153]

The actual form of the EDIS, as with the SSM and SRM, was a subject of some debate. The aspirational goal of banking union advocates was clear: a single European DGS administered by a single authority covering all European banks and funded by *ex ante* contributions from those banks.[154] Some advocates called for combining DGS and resolution functions into a single institution, as is the case in the US FDIC, though in practice the urgent need to get the SRM up and running as soon as possible meant that it was set up before negotiations on EDIS began in earnest.[155] More modest proposals called for the retention of national DGS, but with an automatic facility for lending between national DGS. This would leave the actual operation and funding of DGS in member states essentially unchanged, but would create a backstop to ensure that no national DGS would be forced to default as Iceland's had. Most actually debated proposals called for a gradual phase-in, with a mutualized network of national DGS to operate for some years while the EDIS deposit insurance fund was gradually built up, leading to EDIS taking over and replacing the national schemes at some point in the future. Much of the particular detail of the debates, therefore, focused on three questions: how long would the phase-in take, how big would the EDIS fund need to be, and what mechanism should be used to determine contributions to the fund.

In theory, EDIS should arguably have been the easiest case to make in functional terms. Creating an SSM meant a significant transfer of authority and influence away from states, compelling them to abandon strategies of promoting national champions, regulatory protectionism, and using regulation to promote favored projects. Creating an SRM entailed another transfer of authority and also a significant transfer of funds not just into a standing facility, but almost immediately to other member states and with the potential for contributions to grow considerably. EDIS presented a smaller risk on both counts. The operation of a deposit insurance scheme typically attracts less public attention than supervision and resolution, diminishing the salience of these debates to the broader national electorates. Additionally, while EDIS also involves contributions to a standing fund, the dynamics of deposit insurance means that it is less likely to be used. The larger a deposit insurance fund, the more it reassures depositors that there is no need to engage in bank runs, meaning the larger the fund, the less likely it is to be used. Therefore, while the SRM would almost inevitably be used to manage bank resolutions, a properly designed and well-funded EDIS would prevent bank failures more than it would pay to manage them.[156] Per one European Commission official, "in Europe the solidarity mechanisms created are there designed in a way in which they should not be used."[157] Moreover, the larger scale of a European DGS means that it should be more effective at discouraging runs than national DGS, making EDIS ultimately more likely to be revenue-neutral than the national schemes it would replace.[158]

Despite the strong functional case, and despite the theoretical arguments that EDIS should be easier than the SSM and SRM, the functional logic proved once again to be unpersuasive.[159] Instead, the self-interest of states and their national banking systems once again prevailed, though the specific logic determining national self-interest changed, especially in the case of Germany. More importantly in determining the ultimately unsuccessful outcome on EDIS, the evolution of the Debt Crisis meant that the status quo had become more viable. In a sense, the earlier reforms did their job too well, and the eurozone had reached an equilibrium not dissimilar to its pre-crisis status quo: significant flaws remained, but absent an immediate crisis, those flaws could be ignored for the time being.

In principle, a key determinant of national positions on EDIS should be the structure of states' existing schemes, and the degree of change a shift to a publicly run, *ex ante* funded EDIS would entail. Banks with privately run deposit insurance systems would be loath to give them up, generally for two key reasons. The first is that a shift to a publicly funded scheme would increase public regulatory oversight, and historically the banks that ran such schemes had preferred to keep a bit more autonomy even if it meant less ability to draw on public funding to manage deposit guarantees. The second, related, reason is that such private schemes meant private oversight of partner banks in the scheme. The move to a public scheme would mean that banks were still funding deposit guarantees in other banks, but would need to rely on public authorities to provide the necessary oversight instead.

In addition to the public–private division, the second key split was between *ex ante* and *ex post* funding schemes. Most academic observers favored *ex ante* schemes, as they ensured that failing banks contributed in advance to the costs their failure imposed on the system, while *ex post* funding pushed the costs onto those banks which did not need such support. Moreover, *ex ante* funding ensured that a large standing fund already existed, while *ex post* systems created pro-cyclical pressure, pushing costs onto other banks at a time of crisis. However, in states with *ex post* funding, a move to an *ex ante* European system would mean a dramatic shift in the upfront costs to banks, which would now need to contribute to a standing fund even in good times.

Even states with *ex ante* systems might be reluctant to move to a European system, however, as it would entail one of two undesirable outcomes. The first outcome would be replacing national deposit schemes and their funds with a European scheme, with national authorities, either public or private, losing control over the fund's distribution. The second would be to create a European system in addition to national systems, which would preserve the national fund, but increase the costs and still raise control issues as the new European authority gained control of the new standing fund. The latter was generally seen as more acceptable to states with *ex ante* and private funds, such as Germany and Austria, which feared those existing funds being drawn down to fund states with *ex post*–funded DGS.[160]

In practice, these structural factors were secondary to the more pressing question of whether states saw themselves as more likely to be net contributors or recipients in the coming years. In structural terms, Italy and France both should have been opposed to EDIS, as both funded their deposit guarantee schemes *ex post*.[161] However, both saw gains in increased stability as more important than the specific costs of the shift to a European Deposit Insurance Scheme, and the two countries would be the key state actors at the head of a coalition of mostly southern, mostly debtor states pushing for rapid creation of EDIS.[162]

Structural factors would play a more important role in Germany, where the three pillars of German banking were far more united than in the debates over the SSM and SRM. Each pillar had long run its own private deposit insurance scheme, and they had all long resisted efforts to replace them with a public scheme run by the German federal state. This in part reflected their desire to avoid the increased regulatory burden such a move would bring.[163] They also feared that a move to EDIS would be a net fiscal loss for them, as they feared they would be called upon to fund deposit guarantees elsewhere in Europe more than they themselves would benefit.[164] Unlike in the earlier debates, the commercial banks broadly shared these views with the smaller and medium-sized savings banks and cooperative banks. All three German banking pillars agreed that it would be "very problematic" to implement EDIS before cleaning up legacy problems.[165] Jürgen Fitschen, the president of the BdB and co-CEO of Deutsche Bank further argued that "we are not prepared to use the funds accumulated in our deposit guarantee scheme over a period of many years in other countries and thus recklessly put citizens 'trust at risk."[166] The three pillars did disagree on whether a long-run solution may be viable, as the BdB allowed that a European mechanism might be helpful if the problems could be solved, but the other pillars were firmly opposed to any EDIS.[167] However, even the BdB opposed the current form, viewing it as "highly political," and inferior to a step-by-step introduction.[168] In large part due to this unified position among the banks, the mainstream political parties apart from the Greens all opposed banking union.[169] Opposition would in fact be enshrined in the coalition document of the Christian Democrat–Social Democrat government that would lead Germany starting in 2013.[170]

A second major concern for German banks and politicians was the presence of substantial legacy debt in many member state banks, including not just NPLs and toxic assets, but also the large sovereign debt holdings such banks held from their states. This would be cited as a major barrier to participation in EDIS among both the Germans and other northern opponents of EDIS.[171] However, the importance of structural and legacy factors as barriers to EDIS need not have been insurmountable barriers. Instead, the key determining factor was that the crisis no longer presented as pressing a challenge to

**158  Crises and Integration in European Banking Union**

the opponents of EDIS. This can most clearly be seen in the case of structural factors. Several of the states strongly supporting EDIS had structural reasons not to want to do so. France's banks funded their DGS through an *ex post* system and moreover were of a size where they would be substantial contributors to an *ex ante* EDIS deposit insurance fund. Similarly, Italy's DGS very closely resembled Germany's, consisting of a network of private DGS with public control, and thus public oversight, long resisted. In both of these cases, such structural reasons to oppose EDIS were overcome because of more pressing concerns over the Doom Loop, which could be activated by a depositor run just as it could be activated by a creditor run. Germany's banks were less exposed to such fears. The German banks enjoyed greater market confidence both because of their better track record since the Banking Crisis and because of the greater fiscal resources of the German state to backstop the private DGS and enhance their credibility than their Italian equivalents.

The second factor, the moral hazard concern over legacy assets, should also not be overstated. Firstly, this was hardly a problem unique to the southern states, as NPLs and toxic assets remained a substantial problem for both northern and southern banks. Secondly, these were not insurmountable problems in the face of political will. This was arguably a greater problem for the SRM, which would directly absorb the costs of those legacy debts causing bank collapse, than the EDIS, which was largely a confidence-boosting measure to ensure that the SRM need not be tapped. Those barriers were not insurmountable for the SRM, in large part because that earlier reform was seen as necessary to preserve the eurozone. Indeed, in late 2014, Germany itself had largely committed itself to finding such workarounds, only to backtrack later.[172]

A crucial difference between the SSM and SRM on the one hand and EDIS on the other was that the perceived sustainability of the status quo shifted. The pivotal moment came with ECB President Mario Draghi's "Whatever It Takes" speech, which essentially did its job too well.[173] In early 2014, the SRM, like the SSM before it, was widely seen not just as a theoretical need for long-term stability, but also as an immediate need to restore market confidence, eliminate ad hoc bailouts, and move out of a crisis moment that had real potential to unravel the European project. The status quo at the time of enactment of the SSM was unsustainable and unravelling quickly. The status quo at the time of the SRM had become deeply undesirable for both southerners, forced to turn to ad hoc bailouts from the ESM, and northerners, forced to offer terms of support that by virtue of being ad hoc were less rigorous and structured than would be possible under the SRM. In these contexts, with the potential survival of the eurozone on the table, all states were willing to move to reforms that would move to a more desirable new status quo, even if it were not the optimal outcome. This was not the case on EDIS. After Draghi's speech, market actors gained increased confidence in the survival of the eurozone and its member states. This did not remove the structural barriers to action, but did increase the timeframe on which practical action must be taken from days or weeks to potentially years. The lack of a European DGS shifted from being an immediate crisis problem requiring rapid resolution to a theoretical one that might be a problem in the future but was not an imminent one. Even the European Commission, a staunch advocate of EDIS, conceded that EDIS was less urgent than the SSM and SRM.[174] Given that the European financial system has subsequently endured for almost a decade without EDIS, this assessment has been now borne out by the historical record.

In this context, all players, but especially the northern creditors, were in a better position to resist an immediate compromise and hold out instead for their favored arrangement. In particular, Germany and the northern states could dig in on the issue of legacy debts on EDIS in a way they could not afford to on the SRM. Manfred Zöllmer, a Social Democrat on the Bundestag finance committee, for instance, argued that "[European] deposit insurance can only occur when the existing risks in the banks have been reduced."[175] The issue was arguably less salient on EDIS than on the SRM, but so was the urgency. However, at the same time, the southern states also felt the pressure less, and therefore were less willing to accede to the northerners' terms on the logic that some form of EDIS was better than nothing. Italian Prime Minister Mario Renzi maintained that Italy would "veto any attempt to put a ceiling on the amount of government debt in banks' portfolios, and we will show exemplary strength and consistency on this, without fail," focusing on preserving Italian fiscal flexibility over immediate action.[176] European Commission and ECB officials continued to press for the need for urgent action, but even ECB Vice President Valdis Dombrovskis conceded that "some may ask, 'why do we need this now?'"[177]

Both sides remained at least officially committed to establishing EDIS, but conflicts had returned to the less-urgent dynamics of normal politics. Both were now in a position where they were willing to wait until the other came around to their position. The northerners, with less need than the southerners due to their asymmetric exposure to shocks in the crisis, could adopt a strategy of waiting longer than the southerners if nothing else changed. The southerners, meanwhile, could rely on three factors in the hopes of a more advantageous deal. The first was that the formal commitments to some form of EDIS among the northerners could eventually be used to rhetorically trap and push them into binding commitments. The second was that, as time progressed, the legacy debt issues would become less salient. If the moral hazard argument against EDIS diminished while the functional argument remained strong, the potential for a mutually acceptable agreement would grow, and the moral suasion to address the functional need became in theory more potent. The final reason for the southerners to wait was to rely on the Monnet logic of integration, that crises would spur integrative action more effectively than negotiation in a time of a reasonably acceptable status quo. As will be seen in Chapters 5 and 6, the advocates of EDIS would attempt to use the logic of integration as a response to crisis in multiple subsequent crises. Although they met with little success in the next two major crises, the southerners could remain hopeful that eventually a new crisis would pose such a clear existential threat to integration that the northerners would finally move toward compromise.

In this context, it is unsurprising that no real movement toward EDIS happened in the end-phase of the Debt Crisis. The only notable change was the April 2014 Directive on Deposit Guarantee Schemes. This Directive standardized terms of repayment, with states to guarantee savers regained access to their funds within fifteen days by 2019 and within seven days by 2024. It also required a standardized floor on coverage of at least €100,000. This helped establish a floor for national DGS to ensure relatively standardized terms, while still allowing states and private DGS to offer "gold-plated" DGS with more favorable terms. In doing so, it potentially smoothed the way toward a European DGS by ensuring that national plans offered comparable coverage already. However, while standardizing terms of repayment, it made no changes to funding of DGS, which remained purely national and at state discretion as to whether to rely on *ex ante* or *ex post* funding. As such, the state–bank ties and Doom Loop danger remained in effect. In that sense, the change was not unlike that of the EBA out of the Banking Crisis, standardizing operations but still leaving a key financial policy task ultimately in the hands of national authorities. As will be seen in Chapters 5 and 6, advocates of EDIS would attempt to use the shift to emergency politics future crisis to spur completion of the banking union as well, but to date without success.

## Other Potential Elements of Banking Union

The same dynamics at work in the failure to secure EDIS played out with the other remaining elements of banking union. Rapid and deep change came while the eurozone states confronted an existential threat from fundamental flaws in the European financial regulatory architecture, producing the SSM and SRM. However, by late 2014, the context had shifted substantially. Fundamental flaws were diminished by the partial banking union, though virtually all actors agreed that the existing reforms were incomplete and vulnerabilities remained. More importantly, the existential threat had subsided. In a context where immediate action was not necessary, normal policymaking returned, and parties became more willing to accept gridlock rather than disfavored reforms. Therefore, in addition to the stalling of EDIS, other key elements of banking union remained absent or incomplete.

The first of these was the expansion of the SSM, which covered only systemically important banks within the eurozone. This meant that it excluded both smaller eurozone banks and all banks, regardless of size, in the non-eurozone member states. The ECB had some authority over the smaller eurozone banks, as it oversaw national regulators and could in some cases take over direct regulation. However, as the cajas crisis demonstrated, a crisis in the smaller banks, if it involved enough banks or enough interbank interdependence, could produce a significant threat just as the failure of a designated systemically important institution could. "Too many to fail" could be as big a problem as "too big to fail."[178] Similarly, unless member states elected to join the banking union, non-eurozone EU banks remained wholly outside of the SSM's jurisdiction, despite the 2007–09 crisis demonstrating how the failure of extrajurisdictional banks could present a substantia threat to financial stability. Two regions in particular suggested substantial problems. The first was the UK, at the time the home to as much as 50 percent of EU financial services by some estimates, and therefore a case where a British banking crisis could easily impact the rest of the EU. The second was the Baltic basin, where banking groups tended toward deep transnational operation among both eurozone states (Finland and the Baltics), non-eurozone member states (Denmark), and even non-EU states (Norway). Such an overlapping set of jurisdictions raised the specter of substantial confusion in the event of bank troubles. Concern was especially raised over Nordea, a systemically important institution with substantial operations both within and outside of the eurozone.[179]

The second major gap concerned the Single Resolution Mechanism. The compromises of its creation produced a mechanism that was arguably too complex to act in a decisive and rapid fashion and a Single Resolution Fund that, even when it reached its target size, was widely feared to be too small to handle anything above a midsized banking crisis.[180] This small size of the fund in itself would not be as problematic if it had a clearly defined backstop

## 162 Crises and Integration in European Banking Union

to which it could turn once the Fund itself was exhausted.[181] However, by the end of the Debt Crisis such a backstop remained absent.[182] The logical candidate for such a backstop was the ESM, an option favored by the Italians and French. Motion toward such a backstop, however, was blocked by Germany, which insisted that any tapping of the ESM could not be automatic and must require the affirmative consent of the member states.[183]

Finally, the Capital Market Union had been presented as a vital counterpart to banking union. The CMU, once operational, would increase the efficiency and viability of European capital markets, and in doing so reduce the dependence of European states on bank-based funding. That, in turn, would mean that bank failures would be less catastrophic for the real economy, as non-bank firms could turn to stock and bond markets as an alternative source of funding. The presence of such deep capital markets had long been seen as an explanation for why bank failure in the US and UK were less problematic than in Continental Europe.

All of these measures had strong functional arguments in their favor, and few functional arguments against them. In the cases of backstopping the SRF and creating the CMU, as with EDIS, a majority of member states in fact made strong commitments to enacting the necessary reforms at some point in the future. However, by the end of the Debt Crisis, all of these commitments remained Augustine promises. Just as St. Augustine famously declared "oh Master, make me chaste and celibate—but not yet!," so too were member states willing to commit to these reforms in the future, but not at the present.[184] With the passing of the crisis moment, and the restoration of a broadly acceptable status quo, actors were in a position to refuse sub-optimal reforms, and deadlock replaced the perceived need for immediate action.

## Limitations of the Partial Banking Union

By the end of the crisis period, work on the banking union had created tremendous steps toward deeper integration, yet substantial gaps remained. Especially compared to the more modest reforms out of the Banking Crisis, the creation of the SSM and SRM presented major steps toward a Europeanization of the financial regulatory architecture. However, EDIS remained out of reach, and competing views on fundamental questions of role of EDIS for legacy problems meant that little progress would follow in the coming years. CMU similarly remained a reform that enjoyed broad support in principle, but the failure to resolve some fundamental issues would leave progress gridlocked. Finally, even the SSM and SRM had limitations

The 2010–14 European Debt Crisis **163**

of their own, even if they worked exactly as intended. Most obviously, both only covered banks in the eurozone, and the SSM only directly regulated the largest banks within those countries. Beyond the obvious issue that London, Europe's main financial hub, lay outside of the reach of the partial banking union, this raised questions of how well the system could handle the failure of a transnational bank with substantial operations both within and outside of the eurozone, such as the Baltic bank Nordea, with significant operations split between eurozone members Estonia, Finland, Latvia, and Lithuania, non-eurozone EU member Denmark, and non-EU state Norway.[185] Moreover, as the failure of the Spanish cajas demonstrated, a crisis consuming a host of smaller banks could be as devastating as that of a single large institutions.

All of these problems would be issues even if the SSM and SRM worked perfectly. However, significant questions lingered as to the efficacy of their operation. Although the SSM appeared to be a purely supranational institution, Fromage argued that significant national elements still factored into its decision-making, raising questions as to the unbiased nature of its decision-making.[186] The SRM, with a much more complicated decision-making structure balancing both supranational and intergovernmental elements, could both struggle to make rapid decisions in a crisis moment and have difficulty imposing a common standard across bank resolutions due to national influence.[187] The latter would prove to be the case in contrasting bank resolutions in the coming years, with the resolution of the Spanish Banco Popular being seen as broadly conforming to the stated goals of the SRM and that of Italian banks Banca Veneto and Banca Popolare di Vicenza as much more generous.[188] Additionally, although these initial bank failures were relatively small, significant doubts remained that the size of the SRF was sufficient to absorb the failure of one or more major European banks. As such, the partial banking union should be considered very much incomplete, with significant gaps remaining, even as it nevertheless presented a substantial step toward deeper European integration.

## Conclusion

The fact that significant components of banking and capital market union remained unaddressed should not distract from the fact that the creation of the Single Supervisory Mechanism and Single Resolution Mechanism were major, fundamental shifts in the European financial regulatory architecture. Multiple scholars have seen the partial banking union as the biggest move toward integration since the signing of the Maastricht Treaty.[189] It presented not just a quantitative shift in the volume of tasks handled by supranational institutions, but a qualitative, paradigm shift in the operation of European bank supervision and resolution.[190] The immediate change was substantial on its own, creating a new supervisory authority and a substantial new channel of transnational risk-sharing for bank resolution. The long-term change may ultimately be more significant. The creation of a European supervisory authority to even partially displace national authorities creates the possibility of that European supervisory scope growing. This seems in fact likely, as while a mechanism exists for the SSM to increase its coverage to individual banks, no such mechanism exists for a claw-back of authority by national supervisors. Moreover, a strong functional argument exists for the SSM to gradually increase its scope. Similarly, while questions remain around the decision-making process and size of the fund for the SRM, having created the SRB and SRF, the easiest way to address those problems going forward will likely be to streamline the SRB's decision-making process and increase the SRF's resources, both by increasing size of the fund itself and by adding an effective backstop. In this light, the remaining gaps, including the lack of a European Deposit Insurance Scheme and Capital Markets Union, should not overshadow a fundamental change in European financial regulation. The SSM and SRM go far beyond a "patch-up" reform such as the EBA, and mark a real break in European regulation, even if they remain incomplete.

The Debt Crisis therefore presents an example of a classic Monnet Crisis, with a crisis producing a unified response of deeper integration, which in itself is likely to lead to even further integration in the future. This outcome occurred because the Debt Crisis presented a threat that was both severe and endogenous to the financial sector. The stakes in the Debt Crisis were high; the partial or complete disintegration of the eurozone appeared not only plausible but potentially imminent for much of the crisis period. Even once the initial panic subsided, the eurozone states were left in a new status quo of perpetual emergency bailouts, an arrangement not beneficial for any parties involved. In contrast to the Banking Crisis, the Debt Crisis presented challenges that could only be dealt with in an acceptable fashion through deeper integration. While member states could afford their bank bailouts in 2007–09, the threat of the Doom Loop meant that the affected states would either need to default and leave the eurozone or receive external support. This therefore demanded some form of substantial action to escape an unsustainable and undesirable status quo. A European Commission representative that such progress only happened because of the crisis, which was "a basic trigger to create common European institutions. This was when we created the banking union. If we hadn't had the sovereign debt crisis, it would never have happened. Probably the member states would be comfortable only with the harmonization."[191]

The second key component was that the crisis was endogenous, a product of fundamental flaws in the European financial regulatory architecture. A combination of transnational banking and national regulation created multiple problems that directly caused the crisis. National regulators' protectionism and promotion of national champions created incentives toward underregulation and over permissiveness toward bank transgressions. The EBA, while helping to simplify the regulatory confusion of the pre-2009 period, could do nothing to fundamentally change these incentives. Moreover, the growth of European banks made possible by the ability to operate on a continental scale meant that they grew beyond the capacity of their home states to resolve them, and in doing so weakened not only their own solvency but that of their sovereign states. Here again the EBA could do nothing to address the problems.

The overall dynamic created by the combination of severity and endogeneity meant that substantial reform became essential. Inaction would clearly be insufficient, as the most likely outcome of such inaction, the disintegration of the eurozone, was too costly to be contemplated. A "weatherproofing" reform would also be insufficient, as the origins of the crisis within the financial sector meant that even if the weatherproofing reforms put the lid on the crisis for the time being, a substantial threat would almost certainly reoccur in relatively short order. This especially became clear as the crisis progressed, and more banks fell into distress due to the same unaddressed fundamental flaws, most clearly in the cases of the Spanish cajas and the Italian Monti dei Paschi. Finally, a "patch-up" modest reform of the European financial regulator architecture was also clearly insufficient. The previous such reform, the EBA, proved unable to handle the severity of the Debt Crisis, and its limitations only highlighted how the core of the crisis lay in the reliance on national authorities. Only a fundamental reform of the financial sector itself, in the form of the introduction of centralized supervision and resolution authorities, could address both the severity and endogeneity of the crisis. As such, the Debt Crisis offers perhaps the clearest example of an integration-producing "Monnet Crisis" in action in decades, not only in European financial regulation, but in the European Union generally.

## Notes

1. Bundesbank Official, Interview by author.
2. The drafters of the Maastricht Treaty anticipated that the interdependence created by a common currency could create a circumstance where one state accrued unsustainable debts, but where the costs of allowing that state to default would be so high to the other states that they would find it better to bail out the debtor state. The "no bailouts" clause explicitly prohibited such actions, and was intended to convince bond traders to therefore price in the risk of default on sovereign bond markets. However, bond traders generally disregarded it, regarding the cost of a default to be too high for the clause to be enforced. The Debt Crisis indicates that they were broadly correct in this assumption.
3. Organisation for Economic Co-operation and Development, "Long-Term Government Bond Yields: 10-Year: Main (Including Benchmark) for Greece," FRED, Federal Reserve Bank of St. Louis (FRED, Federal Reserve Bank of St. Louis, June 1997), https://fred.stlouisfed.org/series/IRLTLT01GRM156N.
4. Reuters Staff, "HIGHLIGHTS-ECB's Weber Says Bailout Talk Not Productive," *Reuters*, March 2010, sec. Hot Stocks, https://www.reuters.com/article/ecb-weber-idUSLDE6280WB20100309.
5. Pepper D. Culpepper and Tobias Tesche, "Death in Veneto? European Banking Union and the Structural Power of Large Banks," *Journal of Economic Policy Reform* 24, no. 2 (June 2021): 134–150, doi:10.1080/17487870.2020.1722125; Ioannis Asimakopoulos and David Howarth, "Stillborn Banking Union: Explaining Ineffective European Union Bank Resolution Rules," *JCMS: Journal of Common Market Studies* 60, no. 2 (2022): 264–282, doi:10.1111/jcms.13212; Mayes, "Banking Union."
6. Howarth and Quaglia, *The Political Economy of European Banking Union*.
7. Richard E. Baldwin and Francesco Giavazzi, *The Eurozone Crisis: A Consensus View of the Causes and a Few Possible Remedies* (CEPR Press Londres, 2015); Jeffrey Frankel, "The Euro Crisis: Where to from Here," *Journal of Policy Modeling* 37, no. 3 (2015): 428–444; Daniel Gros, "Completing the Banking Union: Deposit Insurance," *CEPS Policy Brief*, 2015.
8. Gros, "Completing the Banking Union."
9. Francesca Arnaboldi, *Risk and Regulation in Euro Area Banks: Completing the Banking Union*, Palgrave Macmillan Studies in Banking and Financial Institutions (New York: Palgrave Macmillan, 2019), doi:10.1007/978-3-030-23429-4; Eero Tolo and Matti Viren, "How Much Do Non-Performing Loans Hinder Loan Growth in Europe?," *European Economic Review* 136 (July 2021), http://proxy.mtholyoke.edu:2048/login?url=https://search.ebscohost.com/login.aspx?direct=true&db=ecn&AN=1911048&site=eds-live&scope=site.
10. Arnaboldi, *Risk and Regulation in Euro Area Banks*.
11. Jens Dammann, "The Banking Union: Flawed by Design," *Geo. J. Int'l L.* 45 (2013): 1057.
12. Dammann; Rishi Goyal et al., "A Banking Union for the Euro Area," *Staff Discussion Notes* 2013, no. 001 (February 2013), doi:10.5089/9781475521160.006.A001; Vasso Ioannidou, "A First Step towards a Banking Union," in *Banking Union for Europe*, ed. Thorsten Beck (London, United Kingdom: VoxEU, 2012).
13. Zdenek Kudrna, "Governing the Ins and Outs of the EU's Banking Union," *Journal of Banking Regulation* 17, no. 1 (2016): 119–132; Mayes, "Banking Union."

14. Lamfalussy et al., "Final Report of the Committee of Wise Men on the Regulation of European Securities Markets."
15. European Commission official, Interview by author.
16. OECD, "GDP and Spending—Gross Domestic Product (GDP)—OECD Data," theOECD, accessed July 11, 2022, http://data.oecd.org/gdp/gross-domestic-product-gdp.htm. These figures have remained broadly stable in the following decade. While the UK has at times passed France in GDP, both have consistently had a GDP approximately 15–15.7 percent the size of the US.
17. Agnès Bénassy-Quéré, "Maastricht Flaws and Remedies," *The Eurozone Crisis*, 2016, 71; Agnès Bénassy-Quéré, "The Euro as an International Currency," in *Routledge Handbook of the Economics of European Integration* ed. Richard Baldwin and Francesco Giavazzi (New York: Routledge, 2015), 82–99.
18. Schimmelfennig and Winzen, "Grand Theories, Differentiated Integration"; Frank Schimmelfennig, "European Integration (Theory) in Times of Crisis. A Comparison of the Euro and Schengen Crises," *Journal of European Public Policy* 25, no. 7 (2018): 969–989.
19. Bundesbank Official, Interview by author.
20. The actual impact of the Lehman bankruptcy is subject to some debate. Some observers argued that, while the decision to let Lehman go into bankruptcy did trigger an expansion of panic in markets, the fundamental fragility of the global banking system and confidence in it meant that even if the US government had bailed out Lehman, some other trigger would have driven the panic to the next level, analogous to how the assassination of Franz Ferdinand, while the proximate trigger for the First World War, was ultimately only a minor factor in the outbreak of that conflict. Regardless of actual significance of the Lehman bankruptcy, however, market actors and policymakers widely believed that a similar large-scale bankruptcy in 2010 would trigger a similar global panic.
21. Wolfgang Munchau, "Default Now or Default Later, That Is the Question," *Financial Times*, May 2012, sec. COMMENT; Wolfgang Munchau, "Plan D Stands for Default . . . and the Death of the Euro," *Financial Times*, July 2011, sec. COMMENT.
22. Ferdinando Giugliano, "Athens Faces Uphill Struggle despite Eurozone Deal," *FT.com*, March 2015, https://www.proquest.com/news/docview/2461177393/citation/BDD06560B64C4502PQ/2; Raf Casert and Geir Moulson, "Greece Readies for Bailout Talks as Plan B Details Revealed," *University Wire*, July 2015, sec. From Ap, https://www.proquest.com/news/docview/1699089233/abstract/BDD06560B64C4502PQ/35.
23. Cinzia Alcidi et al., "The Instruments Providing Macro-Financial Support to EU Member States," *CEPS Research Reports* 6 (2017).
24. Charlie Fell, "Only Resolution of Solvency Crisis Can Repair Euro Zone," *Irish Times*, December 2010.
25. Jean Pisani-Ferry, "A Growing Crisis Puts the Euro in Danger," *Financial Times*, December 2010, sec. COMMENT.
26. Jan Straatman, "Eurozone Needs Clarity from Its Policymakers," *Financial Times*, December 2010, sec. INSIGHT—JAN STRAATMAN.
27. Ian Traynor, "Europe in Crisis: A Show of Unity, but Euro Wrangling Continues: Germans May Soften Stance on Bailout Fund: Cameron 'isolated' as He Tries to Get Loophole Closed," *The Guardian*, December 2010, sec. Guardian Financial Pages.

28. James Kirkup and Bruno Waterfield, "Tories Could Wreck EU Talks, Says PM: France 'trying to Poison EU Summit' [Scot Region]," *The Daily Telegraph*, December 2011, sec. News; Front Page.

29. Bruno Waterfield, "German Memo Shows Secret Slide towards a Super-State," *The Daily Telegraph*, November 2011, sec. News.

30. "German Website Sees EU Summit Paving Way for 'Split Continent,'" *BBC Monitoring European*, November 2011, https://www.proquest.com/news/docview/901176193/abstract/71934BF811CA4ABFPQ/15.

31. Kirkup and Waterfield, "Tories Could Wreck EU Talks, Says PM."

32. James Chapman and Hugo Duncan, "Euro in a Tailspin [Edition 3]," *Daily Mail*, December 2011, sec. News.

33. Chapman and Duncan.

34. Steven Erlanger and Liz Alderman, "Euro Saved, for Now, but Danger Is Far from Over: E.U. Deal Doesn't Resolve Several Major Issues and Still Needs to Be Ratified," *International Herald Tribune*, December 2011.

35. Simon Nixon, "Much Euro Ado About Nothing," *Wall Street Journal (Online)*, May 2012, sec. Markets.

36. Arthur Beesley, "Currency Crisis Cannot Be Solved by Institutional Debates," *Irish Times*, December 2011.

37. Paul Taylor, "Sarkozy and Merkel Diverge Over Euro Strategy," New York Times (Online) (New York, United States: New York Times Company, October 2011), https://www.proquest.com/news/docview/2216513006/abstract/71934BF811CA4ABFPQ/14.

38. Quentin Peel, "Merkel Coalition Partner Survives Rebellion," *FT.com*, December 2011, https://www.proquest.com/news/docview/911717253/citation/71934BF811CA4ABFPQ/27.

39. Quentin Peel, "German Opposition Makes Fiscal Treaty Demands," *FT.com*, March 2012, https://www.proquest.com/news/docview/959788101/citation/71934BF811CA4ABFPQ/98.

40. Quentin Peel and Gerrit Wiesmann, "Berlin Denies Pressing Court on Euro Fund," *FT.com*, July 2012, https://www.proquest.com/news/docview/1024371178/citation/71934BF811CA4ABFPQ/100.

41. Quentin Peel, "Constitutional Court Refuses to Block Creation of Rescue Fund," *Financial Times*, September 2012, sec. EUROZONE WOES; Quentin Peel, "German Court Backs ESM Bailout Fund," *FT.com*, September 2012, https://www.proquest.com/news/docview/1039230077/citation/71934BF811CA4ABFPQ/94.

42. "Germany's Possibilities to Rescue Eurozone 'Not Endless'—Chancellor," *BBC Monitoring European*, January 2012, https://www.proquest.com/news/docview/917917025/abstract/71934BF811CA4ABFPQ/61; Ian Traynor, "Eurozone Crisis: Brussels Summit: 24-Hour Strike Expected to Paralyse City as EU Leaders Arrive for Talks," *The Guardian*, January 2012, sec. Guardian Home Pages; Quentin Peel, "Backlash Threat Grows as German Patience Wears Thin," *Financial Times*, January 2012, sec. WORLD NEWS.

43. "Germany's Possibilities to Rescue Eurozone 'Not Endless'—Chancellor."

44. Catherine Bremer, "French Socialists Dig in Heels on EU Austerity," *Cyprus Mail*, February 2012, https://www.proquest.com/news/docview/922568811/citation/71934BF811CA4ABFPQ/63.

45. Bremer, "French Socialists Dig in Heels."

The 2010–14 European Debt Crisis   **169**

46. CITY AM REPORTER, "ECB's Coeure Demands Power to Inject Capital into Banks," *City A.M.*, June 2012, sec. News.
47. David Jolly and James Kanter, "Germany Once More on Defensive in Euro Zone," *International Herald Tribune*, June 2012.
48. "Germany's Merkel Facing Increasing Domestic Opposition to Euro Policy," *BBC Monitoring European*, July 2012, https://www.proquest.com/news/docview/1023319884/abstract/71934BF811CA4ABFPQ/40.
49. "Germany's Merkel Facing Increasing Domestic Opposition to Euro Policy."
50. William Boston, Susann Kreutzmann, and Gabriele Parussini, "Summit Reveals Wider Franco-German Discord," *Wall Street Journal (Online)*, October 2012, sec. Europe.
51. Ansgar Belke et al., "(When) Should a Non-Euro Country Join the Banking Union?," *The Journal of Economic Asymmetries* 14 (2016): 4–19; Rachel Epstein and Martin Rhodes, "From Governance to Government: Banking Union, Capital Markets Union and the New EU," *Competition & Change* 22, no. 2 (2018): 205–224.
52. David Howarth and Lucia Quaglia, "The Steep Road to European Banking Union: Constructing the Single Resolution Mechanism," *Journal of Common Market Studies* 52 (2014): 125.
53. Ansgar Belke and Daniel Gros, "On the Shock-Absorbing Properties of a Banking Union: Europe Compared with the United States," *Comparative Economic Studies* 58, no. 3 (2016): 359–386.
54. There has been some division of regulation of banks by function, most recently in split between the Office of Comptroller of the Currency and the Office of Thrift Supervision, the latter of which supervised savings and loan banks. However, even in that case, both regulators were clearly subsidiary to the Federal Reserve, and as of the 2010 passage of the Dodd–Frank Act, the division no longer exists.
55. Citigroup was at first glance an exception to this pattern. However, it occupied a unique position among American banks as the only true universal bank, with comparably large investment and commercial banking arms. Only its commercial banking operations were covered by the FDIC, and the losses in its investment bank arm threatened to bring down the entire banking group.
56. John Zysman, *Governments, Markets, and Growth: Financial Systems and the Politics of Industrial Change* (Ithaca, NY: Cornell University Press, 1983).
57. Franklin Allen, Elena Carletti, and Andrew Gimber, "The Financial Implications of a Banking Union," 2012 in *Banking Union for Europe: Risks and Challenges* ed. Thorsten Beck. (London: Centre for Economic Policy Research, 2012): 113–118.
58. Thorsten Beck, *Banking Union for Europe: Risks and Challenges*, vol. 16 (Centre for Economic Policy Research London, 2012); Thorsten Beck and Daniel Gros, "Monetary Policy and Banking Supervision: Coordination Instead of Separation. CEPS Policy Brief No. 286, 12 December 2012," 2012.
59. Shawn Donnelly, "Expert Advice and Political Choice in Constructing European Banking Union," *Journal of Banking Regulation* 17, no. 1 (2016): 104–118; Rachel A. Epstein and Martin Rhodes, "The Political Dynamics behind Europe's New Banking Union," *West European Politics* 39, no. 3 (2016c): 415–437; Epstein and Rhodes, "From Governance to Government."
60. David KH Begg, *The ECB: Safe at Any Speed?*, vol. 1 (London: Centre for Economic Policy Research, 1998).

61. Dóra Győrffy, *Trust and Crisis Management in the European Union. [Electronic Resource]: An Institutionalist Account of Success and Failure in Program Countries*, Springer EBooks (Springer International Publishing, 2018), http://proxy.mtholyoke.edu:2048/login?url=https://search.ebscohost.com/login.aspx?direct=true&db=cat066 26a&AN=mhc.016289225&site=eds-live&scope=site.

62. Thorsten Beck, Radomir Todorov, and Wolf Wagner, "Supervising Cross-Border Banks: Theory, Evidence and Policy," *Economic Policy* 28, no. 73 (2013): 5–44; Rosaria Cerrone, "Deposit Guarantee Reform in Europe: Does European Deposit Insurance Scheme Increase Banking Stability?," *Journal of Economic Policy Reform* 21, no. 3 (September 2018): 224–239, doi:10.1080/17487870.2017.1400434; Armen Hovakimian and Edward J. Kane, "Effectiveness of Capital Regulation at US Commercial Banks, 1985 to 1994," *The Journal of Finance* 55, no. 1 (2000): 451–468; Asli Demirgüç-Kunt and Enrica Detragiache, "Does Deposit Insurance Increase Banking System Stability? An Empirical Investigation," *Journal of Monetary Economics* 49, no. 7 (2002): 1373–1406.

63. Richard Bronk and Wade Jacoby, "Avoiding Monocultures in the European Union: The Case for the Mutual Recognition of Difference in Conditions of Uncertainty," *LEQS Paper*, no. 67 (2013).

64. Rachel A. Epstein and Martin Rhodes, "States Ceding Control: Explaining the Shift to Centralized Bank Supervision in the Eurozone," *Journal of Banking Regulation* 17, no. 1 (2016b): 90–103.

65. Viral V. Acharya and Tanju Yorulmazer, "Too Many to Fail—An Analysis of Time-Inconsistency in Bank Closure Policies," *Journal of Financial Intermediation* 16, no. 1 (2007): 1–31.

66. Zdenek Kudrna, "Financial Market Regulation: Crisis-Induced Supranationalization," *Journal of European Integration* 38, no. 3 (2016): 251–264.

67. Asimakopoulos and Howarth, "Stillborn Banking Union"; David Howarth and Lucia Quaglia, "The Difficult Construction of a European Deposit Insurance Scheme: A Step Too Far in Banking Union?," *Journal of Economic Policy Reform* 21, no. 3 (September 2018): 190–209, doi:10.1080/17487870.2017.1402682.

68. Arnaboldi, *Risk and Regulation in Euro Area Banks*; Howarth and Quaglia, *The Political Economy of European Banking Union*.

69. Hendrik Hakenes and Isabel Schnabel, "Banks without Parachutes: Competitive Effects of Government Bail-out Policies," *Journal of Financial Stability* 6, no. 3 (2010): 156–168; Hendrik Hakenes and Isabel Schnabel, "Bank Size and Risk-Taking under Basel II," *Journal of Banking & Finance* 35, no. 6 (2011): 1436–1449.

70. Howarth and Quaglia, *The Political Economy of European Banking Union*.

71. Elena Carletti, Hendrik Hakenes, and Isabel Schnabel, "The Privatization of Italian Savings Banks: A Role Model for Germany?," *Vierteljahrshefte Zur Wirtschaftsforschung* 74, no. 4 (2005): 32–50.

72. Epstein and Rhodes, "The Political Dynamics behind Europe's New Banking Union."

73. World Bank. and World Bank Group., "Financial Structure Database," 2000, https://www.worldbank.org/en/publication/gfdr/data/financial-structure-database. That amount has only increased over time, reaching 85.4 percent by 2020.

74. Iain Hardie and Huw Macartney, "EU Ring-Fencing and the Defence of Too-Big-to-Fail Banks," *West European Politics* 39, no. 3 (2016): 503–525; Epstein and Rhodes, "States

Ceding Control"; Epstein and Rhodes, "The Political Dynamics behind Europe's New Banking Union."

75. Tanja A. Börzel and Thomas Risse, "From the Euro to the Schengen Crises: European Integration Theories, Politicization, and Identity Politics," *Journal of European Public Policy* 25, no. 1 (January 2018): 83–108, doi:10.1080/13501763.2017.1310281; Brunnermeier, James, and Landau, *The Euro and the Battle of Ideas*; Douglas Webber, *New Europe, New Germany, Old Foreign Policy?: German Foreign Policy since Unification* (New York: Routledge, 2014); Dinan, Nugent, and Paterson, *The European Union in Crisis*; Christian Schweiger, "The 'Reluctant Hegemon': Germany in the EU's Post-Crisis Constellation," in *The European Union in Crisis: Explorations in Representation and Democratic Legitimacy*, ed. Kyriakos N. Demetriou (Cham: Springer International Publishing, 2015), 15–32, doi:10.1007/978-3-319-08774-0_2; Christian Schweiger, "The Legitimacy Challenge," in *The European Union in Crisis* (New York: Macmillan International Higher Education, 2017), 188–211; Webber, "Trends in European Political (Dis)Integration. An Analysis of Postfunctionalist and Other Explanations."

76. Simon Bulmer and William E. Paterson, "Germany as the EU's Reluctant Hegemon? Of Economic Strength and Political Constraints," *Journal of European Public Policy* 20, no. 10 (2013): 1387–1405; William E. Paterson, "The Reluctant Hegemon: Germany Moves Centre Stage in the European Union," *JCMS: Journal of Common Market Studies* 49 (2011): 57; Martin Wolf, "Europe's Lonely and Reluctant Hegemon," *Financial Times* 9 (2014); Dirk Schoenmaker, "Banking Union: Where We're Going Wrong," *Banking Union for Europe*, 2012, 97.

77. Karl Kaltenthaler, "German Interests in European Monetary Integration," *JCMS: Journal of Common Market Studies* 40, no. 1 (2002): 69–87.

78. David Schäfer, "A Banking Union of Ideas? The Impact of Ordoliberalism and the Vicious Circle on the EU Banking Union," *JCMS: Journal of Common Market Studies* 54, no. 4 (2016): 961–980.

79. Epstein and Rhodes, "States Ceding Control."

80. Lamfalussy et al., "Final Report of the Committee of Wise Men on the Regulation of European Securities Markets."

81. Stefaan De Rynck, "Banking on a Union: The Politics of Changing Eurozone Banking Supervision," *Journal of European Public Policy* 23, no. 1 (2016): 119–135.

82. De Rynck; Gabriel Glöckler, Johannes Lindner, and Marion Salines, "Explaining the Sudden Creation of a Banking Supervisor for the Euro Area," *Journal of European Public Policy* 24, no. 8 (2017): 1135–1153.

83. Epstein and Rhodes, "From Governance to Government."

84. Nathalie Boschat and Gabriele Parussini, "Lagarde Isn't Sure the ECB Can Easily Oversee EU Banks," *Wall Street Journal, Europe*, February 2009, sec. Economy & Politics.

85. Epstein and Rhodes, "International in Life, National in Death?"; Benjamin Fox, "Franco-German Rift Derails Banking Union Deal," *EUobserver*, December 2012, https://euobserver.com/green-economy/118415.

86. Office of the Bundespräsident, Germany, 2011.

87. Epstein and Rhodes, "States Ceding Control"; Alexandre Violle, "Banking Supervision and the Politics of Verification: The 2014 Stress Test in the European Banking Union," *ECONOMY AND SOCIETY* 46, no. 3–4 (January 2017): 432–451, doi:10.1080/03085147.2017.1408216.

172 Crises and Integration in European Banking Union

88. Violle, "Banking Supervision and the Politics of Verification."
89. Lex, "EU Bank Stress Tests," *Financial Times*, July 2011, https://www.ft.com/content/dc85d1fc-b131-11e0-a43e-00144feab49a.
90. Tracy Alloway, "Bafin Bashes the EBA over Stress Tests," *Financial Times*, June 2011.
91. Epstein and Rhodes, "States Ceding Control."
92. Epstein and Rhodes, "States Ceding Control."
93. Hendrik Hakenes and Isabel Schnabel, "The Threat of Capital Drain: A Rationale for Regional Public Banks?," *Journal of Institutional and Theoretical Economics (JITE)/Zeitschrift Für Die Gesamte Staatswissenschaft*, 2010, 662–689.
94. Office of the Bundespräsident, Germany, interview.
95. Luis Garicano, *Five Lessons from the Spanish Cajas Debacle for a New Euro-Wide Supervisor*, 2012.
96. Derek Scally, "German Banks Resist EU Plan for Regulator," *The Irish Times*, September 2012, https://www.irishtimes.com/news/german-banks-resist-eu-plan-for-regulator-1.540712; Anthony Pepe, "Banking Union: Long March Towards Unity," *Europolitics*, September 2013, No. 4711 edition; James Sillavan, "No End of Trouble," *The Economist*, November 2008, https://www.economist.com/news/2008/11/19/no-end-of-trouble.
97. Gabriele Steinhauser, "Tougher EU Bank Tests Could Ease Crisis," The Globe and Mail (Online) (Toronto, Canada: The Globe and Mail, December 2010), https://www.proquest.com/news/docview/2385154779/citation/438E37CE41144168PQ/6.
98. Douglas Webber, *European Disintegration?: The Politics of Crisis in the European Union* (New York: Macmillan International Higher Education, 2018); Epstein and Rhodes, "The Political Dynamics behind Europe's New Banking Union"; Sara Schaefer Muñoz and Neil Shah, "Europe Reels Amid Investor Fears; Bank Stocks and the Euro Take the Hit; Vulnerability Seen in Exposure to Sovereign Debt of Greece, Portugal, Others," *Wall Street Journal (Online)*, February 2010, sec. Markets.
99. Sarah Gordon et al., "Leaning Lenders," *Financial Times*, June 2010, sec. ANALYSIS.
100. World Bank. and World Bank Group., "Financial Structure Database."
101. Glöckler, Lindner, and Salines, "Explaining the Sudden Creation of a Banking Supervisor for the Euro Area"; Arie Krampf, "From the Maastricht Treaty to Post-Crisis EMU: The ECB and Germany as Drivers of Change," *Journal of Contemporary European Studies* 22, no. 3 (2014): 303–317; Frank Schimmelfennig, "Liberal Intergovernmentalism and the Euro Area Crisis," *Journal of European Public Policy* 22, no. 2 (2015): 177–195; Garicano, *Five Lessons from the Spanish Cajas Debacle for a New Euro-Wide Supervisor*.
102. Tim Wallace, "Euro Leaders Reach Late Night Bank Union Deal," *City A.M.*, December 2012, sec. News.
103. Emilio Botin, "Europe Needs Banking Union to Avert Irrelevance," *Financial Times*, November 2012, sec. COMMENT.
104. "German Commercial Banks Call for Single Supervisor," *GlobalCapital*, August 2012, sec. FIG, https://www.globalcapital.com/article/28mv7umx0dglp46zrwmbl/fig/german-commercial-banks-call-for-single-supervisor.
105. MC Govardhana Rangan and BODHISATVA GANGULI, "I Think Most Would Rather Have India's Problems than the West's: Anshu Jain, Co-CEO, Deutsche Bank [Interviews]," *The Economic Times*, January 2013, https://www.proquest.com/news/docview/1272354088/citation/5CE02F3B15854BF9PQ/1.

The 2010–14 European Debt Crisis    **173**

106. Kudrna, "Governing the Ins and Outs of the EU's Banking Union."
107. Epstein and Rhodes, "The Political Dynamics behind Europe's New Banking Union."
108. Mark K. Cassell and Anna Hutcheson, "Explaining Germany's Position on European Banking Union," *German Politics* 28, no. 4 (2019): 562–582.
109. Cassell and Hutcheson.
110. Wolfgang Schäuble, "How to Protect EU Taxpayers against Bank Failures," *Financial Times*, August 2012, sec. COMMENT.
111. Ben Clift and Magnus Ryner, "Joined at the Hip, but Pulling Apart? Franco-German Relations, the Eurozone Crisis and the Politics of Austerity," *French Politics* 12, no. 2 (2014): 136–163.
112. Howarth and Quaglia, "The Steep Road to European Banking Union."
113. Thomas Pedersen, "Cooperative Hegemony: Power, Ideas and Institutions in Regional Integration," *Review of International Studies* 28, no. 4 (October 2002): 677–696, doi:10.1017/S0260210502006770.
114. Andreas Dombret, "Six Months of European Banking Supervision—What Does This Mean for 'Less Significant Institutions'?" (May 2015).
115. Diane Fromage, "La protection des citoyens de l'Union face aux risques dans le domaine bancaire," *Revue de l'Union Européenne*, no. 654 (January 2022): 17.
116. Quaglia and Spendzharova, "The Conundrum of Solving 'Too Big to Fail' in the European Union."
117. Quaglia and Spendzharova, "The Conundrum of Solving 'Too Big to Fail' in the European Union."
118. Epstein and Rhodes, "The Political Dynamics behind Europe's New Banking Union."
119. Shawn Donnelly, "Advocacy Coalitions and the Lack of Deposit Insurance in Banking Union," *Journal of Economic Policy Reform* 21, no. 3 (September 2018): 210–223, doi:10.1080/17487870.2017.1400437.
120. Federal Reserve Board, "FRB: Large Commercial Banks—March 23, 2010," accessed July 11, 2022, https://www.federalreserve.gov/releases/lbr/20091231/default.htm; Federal Reserve Board, "FRB: Large Commercial Banks—December 31, 2021," accessed July 11, 2022, https://www.federalreserve.gov/releases/lbr/20211231/default.htm. By 2022, that ratio had grown to 11 percent, larger but not enough to change the underlying dynamic.
121. Howarth and Quaglia, *The Political Economy of European Banking Union*.
122. Andreas Gergely and Kevin Smith, "Ireland Guarantees All Bank Deposits," *Reuters*, September 2008, sec. Business News, https://www.reuters.com/article/uk-ireland-banks-guarantee-idUKTRE48T2EA20080930.
123. Mitchell, *Saving the Market from Itself*.
124. Culpepper and Tesche, "Death in Veneto?"
125. Viral V. Acharya, "Is the International Convergence of Capital Adequacy Regulation Desirable?," *The Journal of Finance* 58, no. 6 (2003): 2745–2782; Angelo Baglioni, *The European Banking Union: A Critical Assessment*, Palgrave Macmillan Studies in Banking and Financial Institutions (London: Palgrave Macmillan UK, 2016), doi:10.1057/978-1-137-56314-9; Dammann, "The Banking Union."
126. Epstein and Rhodes, "International in Life, National in Death?"
127. Beck, *Banking Union for Europe*.

## 174    Crises and Integration in European Banking Union

128. Marius Skuodis, "Playing the Creation of the European Banking Union: What Union for Which Member States?," *Journal of European Integration* 40, no. 1 (January 2018): 99–114, doi:10.1080/07036337.2017.1404056.
129. James A. Caporaso and Martin Rhodes, *Political and Economic Dynamics of the Eurozone Crisis* (Oxford University Press, 2016).
130. Epstein and Rhodes, "International in Life, National in Death?"
131. Epstein and Rhodes, "From Governance to Government."
132. Howarth and Quaglia, *The Political Economy of European Banking Union.*
133. Bankscope, "Germany Banking System Concentration—Data, Chart," TheGlobalEconomy.com, accessed July 13, 2022, https://www.theglobaleconomy.com/Germany/banking_system_concentration/.
134. "A Weary Lender; Deutsche Bank," *The Economist* 413, no. 8911 (November 2014): 68.
135. Mitchell, *Saving the Market from Itself.*
136. Derek Scally, "German Greens on Campaign Trail Criticise Irish Corporate Tax Regime: Coalition Option with Merkel Not Ruled out after Shift on Nuclear Issue," *Irish Times*, August 2013.
137. Andreas Dombret, "What Is 'Good' Regulation?," (November 2013).
138. Epstein and Rhodes, "International in Life, National in Death?"
139. Schäfer, "A Banking Union of Ideas?"
140. Epstein and Rhodes, "States Ceding Control."
141. Schäfer, "A Banking Union of Ideas?"
142. Alex Barker, Alice Ross, and Peter Spiegel, "France to Pay Most for Bank Rescue Fund: Brussels Proposal," *Financial Times*, October 2014, sec. WORLD NEWS.
143. Baglioni, *The European Banking Union.*
144. Ioannis G. Asimakopoulos, "International Law as a Negotiation Tool in Banking Union; the Case of the Single Resolution Fund," *Journal of Economic Policy Reform* 21, no. 2 (June 2018): 118–131, doi:10.1080/17487870.2018.1424631.
145. Dammann, "The Banking Union."
146. Skuodis, "Playing the Creation of the European Banking Union."
147. Skuodis, "Playing the Creation of the European Banking Union."
148. Nicolas Jabko, "The Elusive Economic Government and the Forgotten Fiscal Union," in *The Future of the Euro* (New York: Oxford University Press, 2015), doi:10.1093/acprof:oso/9780190233235.003.0004.
149. Tim Wallace, "UK Left out of Pocket as Iceland Draws a Line under Bank Collapse," *Telegraph.Co.Uk*, September 2015, sec. Finance, https://www.proquest.com/news/docview/1713697090/abstract/D81532257B704339PQ/1; Harriet Alexander, "Britain Treated Us like Al-Qaeda, Says Iceland's Former PM as He Avoids Jail," *The Sunday Telegraph*, April 2012, sec. News.
150. Diamond and Dybvig, "Bank Runs, Deposit Insurance, and Liquidity."
151. Donnelly, "Expert Advice and Political Choice in Constructing European Banking Union"; Dirk Schoenmaker and Daniel Gros, "A European Deposit Insurance and Resolution Fund-An Update," *CEPS Policy Brief*, no. 283 (2012); Daniel Gros and Dirk Schoenmaker, "E Uropean Deposit Insurance and Resolution in the Banking Union," *JCMS: Journal of Common Market Studies* 52, no. 3 (2014): 529–546; Gros, "Completing the Banking Union."
152. European Commission official, Interview by author.

The 2010–14 European Debt Crisis **175**

153. European Commission official.
154. European Commission, "Communication from the Commission to the European Parliament, the Council, the European Central Bank, the European Economic and Social Committee and the Committee of the Regions 'Towards the Completion of the Banking Union'" (2015), https://eur-lex.europa.eu/legal-content/EN/TXT/?uri=CELEX:52015DC0587.
155. European Commission official, Interview by author.
156. Arnaboldi, *Risk and Regulation in Euro Area Banks*.
157. European Commission official, Interview by author.
158. Baglioni, *The European Banking Union*.
159. Epstein and Rhodes, "From Governance to Government"; Donnelly, "Expert Advice and Political Choice in Constructing European Banking Union"; Schoenmaker and Gros, "A European Deposit Insurance and Resolution Fund-An Update"; Gros, "Completing the Banking Union."
160. Howarth and Quaglia, *The Political Economy of European Banking Union*; Joachim Schild, "Germany and France at Cross Purposes: The Case of Banking Union," *Journal of Economic Policy Reform* 21, no. 2 (June 2018): 102–117, doi:10.1080/17487870.2017.1396900; Skuodis, "Playing the Creation of the European Banking Union."
161. Howarth and Quaglia, *The Political Economy of European Banking Union*.
162. Skuodis, "Playing the Creation of the European Banking Union."
163. Bundesverband deutscher Banken official, Interview by author; Bundesbank Official, Interview by author.
164. Howarth and Quaglia, "The Difficult Construction of a European Deposit Insurance Scheme."
165. Vanya Daynamora, "German Bank Warns of 'irrational Exuberance' around Eurozone Deposit Insurance," *SNL European Financials Daily*, March 2018, https://www.spglobal.com/marketintelligence/en/news-insights/trending/qohre4uRaJSAkOwhJvzomw2; Tom Keene and Francine Lacqua, "Paul De Grauwe and Hans-Guenter Redeker Are on BB TV.," *CEO Wire*, May 2018, https://www.proquest.com/news/docview/2036784500/citation/6CEBCBE6AD274D6DPQ/2.
166. Jim Brunsden and James Shotter, "Brussels' Plan for Deposits Likely to Set up Berlin Clash: Mutualised System," *Financial Times*, November 2015, sec. WORLD NEWS.
167. Bundesverband deutscher Banken official, Interview by author.
168. Bundesverband deutscher Banken official.
169. Juliet Samuel, "German Election Leaves Macron's Big Idea in Tatters," *The Telegraph*, September 2017, https://www.telegraph.co.uk/business/2017/09/26/german-election-leaves-macrons-big-idea-tatters/; Eric Maurice, "Berlin Risks Being 'culprit' for Stalling EU, Warns Green MEP," *EUobserver*, November 2017, https://euobserver.com/eu-political/140001.
170. Epstein and Rhodes, "From Governance to Government"; Skuodis, "Playing the Creation of the European Banking Union."
171. Horst Tomann, "The Banking Union and Financial Stability," in *Monetary Integration in Europe* (Springer, 2017), 167–179.
172. Schimmelfennig, "Liberal Intergovernmentalism and the Euro Area Crisis."
173. Schimmelfennig, "Liberal Intergovernmentalism and the Euro Area Crisis."

174. David Howarth and Lucia Quaglia, "Banking on Stability: The Political Economy of New Capital Requirements in the European Union," *Journal of European Integration* 35, no. 3 (2013): 333–346.

175. Cassell and Hutcheson, "Explaining Germany's Position on European Banking Union."

176. Jim Brunsden and James Politi, "Italy Pledges to Block Limit on Sovereign Debt Holdings: Eurozone," *Financial Times*, February 2016, sec. WORLD NEWS.

177. Valdis Dombrovskis, "European Union: College Orientation Debate: Vice-President Dombrovskis Remarks on Steps towards Completing Banking Union," *Asia News Monitor*, November 2015, sec. General News, https://www.proquest.com/news/docview/1732351364/abstract/759EBB74A9D64639PQ/4.

178. Acharya and Yorulmazer, "Too Many to Fail—An Analysis of Time-Inconsistency in Bank Closure Policies."

179. Svend E Hougaard Jensen and Dirk Schoenmaker, "Should Denmark and Sweden Join the Banking Union?," *Journal of Financial Regulation* 6, no. 2 (September 2020): 317–326, doi:10.1093/jfr/fjaa005; Dirk Schoenmaker and Arjen Siegmann, "Efficiency Gains of a European Banking Union," SSRN Scholarly Paper (Rochester, NY, February 2013), doi:10.2139/ssrn.2214919.

180. Baglioni, *The European Banking Union*; Giuseppe Pennisi, "The Impervious Road to the Single Resolution Mechanism (SRM) of the European Banking Union (EBU)."

181. Maurice Obstfeld, "Crises and the International System," *International Economic Journal* 27, no. 2 (June 2013): 143–155, doi:10.1080/10168737.2013.793901.

182. Arnaboldi, *Risk and Regulation in Euro Area Banks*; Bénassy-Quéré, "Maastricht Flaws and Remedies"; Florian Brandt and Matthias Wohlfahrt, "A Common Backstop to the Single Resolution Fund," *Journal of Economic Policy Reform* 22, no. 3 (September 2019): 291–306, doi:10.1080/17487870.2018.1482745; Guido Tabellini, "The Main Lessons to Be Drawn from the European Financial Crisis," in *The Eurozone Crisis: A Consensus View of the Causes and a Few Possible Solutions*, ed. Richard Baldwin and Francesco Giavazzi (London: CEPR Press, 2015), https://voxeu.org/article/main-lessons-be-drawn-european-financial-crisis; Charles Wyplosz, "The Eurozone Crisis: Too Few Lessons Learned," in *The Eurozone Crisis: A Consensus View of the Causes and a Few Possible Solutions*, ed. Richard Baldwin and Francesco Giavazzi (London: CEPR Press, 2015), https://voxeu.org/article/eurozone-crisis-too-few-lessons-learned.

183. Howarth and Quaglia, "The Steep Road to European Banking Union."

184. Nuno Cunha Rodrigues and José Renato Gonçalves, "The European Banking Union and the Economic and Monetary Union: The Puzzle Is Yet to Be Completed," in *The Euro and the Crisis: Perspectives for the Eurozone as a Monetary and Budgetary Union*, ed. Nazaré da Costa Cabral, José Renato Gonçalves, and Nuno Cunha Rodrigues, Financial and Monetary Policy Studies (Cham: Springer International Publishing, 2017), 271–288, doi:10.1007/978-3-319-45710-9_16.

185. Hougaard Jensen and Schoenmaker, "Should Denmark and Sweden Join the Banking Union?"

186. Fromage, "La protection des citoyens de l'Union face aux risques dans le domaine bancaire."

187. Moritz Rehm, "Tug of War over Financial Assistance: Which Way Forward for Eurozone Stability Mechanisms?," *Politics and Governance* 9, no. 2 (2021): 173–184.

188. Shawn Donnelly and Gaia Pometto, "Banking Nationalism and Resolution in Italy and Spain," *Government and Opposition*, August 2022, doi:10.1017/gov.2022.27; Culpepper and Tesche, "Death in Veneto?"

189. Epstein and Rhodes, "States Ceding Control"; David Howarth and Joachim Schild, "Reinforcing Supranational Bank Regulation, Supervision, Support and Resolution in Europe: Introduction," *Journal of Economic Policy Reform* 22, no. 3 (September 2019): 203–207, doi:10.1080/17487870.2018.1424519.

190. De Rynck, "Banking on a Union"; Kudrna, "Financial Market Regulation"; Kudrna, "Governing the Ins and Outs of the EU's Banking Union"; Glöckler, Lindner, and Salines, "Explaining the Sudden Creation of a Banking Supervisor for the Euro Area."

191. European Commission official, Interview by author.

# 5
# Brexit and the Failure to Reform

## Introduction

The decision of the United Kingdom to exit the European Union provided the third major shock to EU finance in the twenty-first century. The City of London had for decades been the center of the EU's capital markets and financial services activity. The departure of the UK meant sharply restricted terms of access between London and the EU-27, the remaining twenty-seven EU member states. The shock of this severing risked destabilizing a financial system still fragile from the Banking and Debt Crises only a few years earlier. It also therefore prompted a new push to create a European Capital Markets Union (CMU), with advocates casting it as an essential reform to deal with the short- and long-term strains of the loss of Europe's existing capital markets hub. However, these efforts to link a long-desired reform to the functional need to respond to the crisis would fall short. Of the four crises examined here, Brexit would produce by far the least significant reforms, limited to a geographic relocation of the European Banking Authority (EBA) and a repeatedly delayed proposal to bring euro clearing activity out of London and within the EU-27.

The failure of Brexit to trigger even minor integration can be traced to a combination of the crisis's origin and severity. Brexit, like the COVID-19 Pandemic, presented a crisis with origins clearly outside of the financial system, with British financial actors among the most pro-Remain of any constituency. Because of this, no amount of reform of finance would prevent the emergence of a new "exit" crisis. At the same time, Brexit presented only a moderate threat to the rest of the EU, as a combination of control over the process of exit, a clear and long timeline for implementation, and the presence of opportunities as well as challenges together meant that Brexit did not present a threat on par with the Debt Crisis or the Pandemic. Being neither endogenous enough to justify a patch-up reform, nor severe enough to merit weatherproofing reform, Brexit failed to substantially move the conversation on CMU, which remained stalemated between a French vision for a highly regulated capital markets union and a liberal vision of a

---

*Crises and Integration in European Banking Union.* Christopher Mitchell, Oxford University Press.
© Christopher Mitchell (2023). DOI: 10.1093/oso/9780198889069.003.0005

more decentralized one promoted by a coalition of small northern European member states.

## Classification

### Exogenous

Brexit presented an exogenous shock to the financial system of the European Union. The main causes that animated pro-Brexit actors, and that formed the core of the Leave campaign, including concerns over immigration, national sovereignty, and the ability to escape the oversight of the EU bureaucracy, were almost entirely focused on concerns outside of the financial sector. Arguments about the need to escape burdensome European financial regulation, which cast Brexit as an endogenous product of deepening financial regulatory integration, were made, but as will be discussed gained very little traction among private financial actors and virtually none among regulators. Although the vote to leave the EU would prompt a crisis in European finance, the tensions which led to a Brexit campaign and the issues that motivated Leave voters both came from outside of the financial sector, making Brexit an exogenous shock to European finance.

The clearest evidence that finance did not drive Brexit may be the attitudes of financial actors in the run-up to the vote and in the debates over the post-Brexit EU–UK relationship. Per a Centre for the Study of Financial Innovation (CSFI) survey in the run-up to the vote, an overwhelming 73 percent of financial services sector actors definitely or probably planned to vote Remain, and many of them, along with several prominent actors on the regulatory side, would actively campaign for Remain.[1] Those percentages mirror the ultimate vote totals for London, the heart of the UK financial industry. Greater London, at 59.9 percent Remain was second only to Scotland (62.0 percent Remain) among the nations and regions in voting to stay in the EU. Moreover, nine of the ten most pro-Remain voting districts in the UK were all in London, including the financial district, the City of London, which was the sixth most pro-Remain district at 75.3 percent.[2]

That this should be the case is no surprise, as the vast majority of British financial actors agree that being in the EU has been very good for the British financial sector. Although London had been a global financial center for centuries before joining the European Union, EU membership solidified its place as the financial market hub for the entire continent. In particular,

## 180 Crises and Integration in European Banking Union

"passporting," which allowed for the free movement of money and financial services activities for all EU member states, provided a clear benefit to the British financial industry. Only Britain among the large EU economies had large and deep capital markets, as banks instead dominated the provision of finance in major players such as France, Germany, Italy, and Spain. This first-mover advantage, combined with the freedom of movement of capital within the Union helped London attract investment both from within the rest of the EU and from the rest of the world. European investors would generally prefer to take their business to London rather than smaller Continental capital markets, which both increased the centrality of London and discouraged efforts to develop domestic capital markets in other member states. This, in turn, made London the go-to destination for non-EU financial actors looking to do business in the EU. London's combination of deep capital markets, a long-established and investor-favoring regulatory system, and, crucially, access to the rest of the EU, made it the default site for foreign, especially American, banks to set up their European headquarters.

The seemingly imminent introduction of Capital Markets Union, intended to further reduce frictions on intra-European capital movement, looked likely to further cement the dominance of London as a financial hub. Many of the respondents to the CSFI survey would cite CMU as one of the main reasons to remain in the EU, arguing that the City would be the chief beneficiary of the new proposal.[3] A report from HSBC, Britain's largest bank, argued that "plans to create a single market in services and a capital markets union [would] both play to Britain's strengths."[4] Prime Minister David Cameron would give prominent placement to the CMU in the Chatham House Speech, his centerpiece argument making the case for Remain, arguing that CMU "will help get finance into the hands of entrepreneurs and growing businesses."[5]

Brexit, however, threatened more than just Britain's exclusion from a potential Capital Markets Union. It also risked substantially greater restrictions on the access to European markets which had so benefited British finance to that point. The potential loss of passporting access to the Single Market was described by Sir Gerry Grimstone, the chairman of pensions company Standard Life and of lobbying group TheCityUK as "disastrous for London and the UK."[6] This sentiment was reflected widely across the British financial sector, with warnings before the vote coming from actors including large banks, hedge funds, and insurance companies, with all fearing that Brexit would mean a relocation of business across the English Channel.[7] The head of public policy at find management group Fidelity Worldwide feared

Brexit and the Failure to Reform **181**

the creation of "incentive to move within the boundaries of the EU," concluding that "the sector which will be hardest hit is financial services."[8] Comments by American banks based in London intensified those fears. Jamie Dimon, the CEO of JP Morgan-Chase warned that "if we can't passport out of London, we'll have to set up different operations in Europe."[9] Representatives of Morgan Stanley echoed those concerns, while also warning of the danger of job losses beyond just London as American financial firms shifted to the Continent.[10] These concerns were shared by regulators. Bank of England Governor Mark Carney described Brexit as "the biggest domestic risk to financial stability" as the loss of access would pressure British financial firms.[11]

Bankers and regulators argued that the risks would go beyond concerns over loss of passporting, and focused on the impact of future changes to EU financial regulation. As seen in the debates over creation of the European Banking Authority, as discussed in Chapter 3, the UK had generally had a great deal of ability to block EU changes it saw as adversely affecting its own financial industry, as well as to promote agenda items such as the Capital Markets Union which aimed to serve that industry. Remain advocates, including Lord Jonathan Hill, a member of the House of Lords and the EU Commissioner for Financial Services in the run-up to the Brexit vote, were quick to highlight that this ability would be lost in a post-EU Britain.[12] Once no longer a member, the UK would no longer be party to EU debates over EU financial regulation. Given the importance of European markets to the UK financial sector, and that even a best-case continuation of that access would rely on the EU designating UK regulation as "equivalent" to European regulation, this would force the UK into one of two ways forward. Either Britain could substantially diverge on financial regulation at the cost of access to European markets, or Britain could find itself in the role of "rule-taker," essentially adopting EU regulation it had no hand in shaping in order to maintain that access, and even then only so long as the EU continued to allow that access. Lord Hill made this dilemma the centerpiece of his argument against Brexit, maintaining that he didn't "believe there is a respectable argument which says you can have all your independence and sovereignty [and keep] your single market on the same terms as now," and that claims to the contrary from pro-Brexit forces were "misleading" and "very weird."[13] Moreover, Lord Hill warned that France and German had in the past attempted to move euro clearing and other financial activity out of Britain, and would likely be more successful in future efforts without the UK's ability to block those efforts.[14]

## 182   Crises and Integration in European Banking Union

### Arguments for the Endogeneity of Brexit

While support for Remain was broad among British financial sector actors, it was not universal. Contrary to the predictions of lobbying group TheCityUK of "unanimous rejection," there were some British financial actors who saw Brexit as an opportunity to escape burdensome European regulation.[15] Even among the broadly pro-Europe majority of financial actors, the general sense was, in the words of CSFI director Andrew Hilton that "support for the EU is based on resignation rather than enthusiasm. Yes, the City wants to remain in the EU, but it doesn't like Brussels, it fears European regulation and it is worried about the political drift of the EU."[16] The advantages of being in the European Union, in their eyes, outweighed the costs, but there were nevertheless significant downsides in their eyes. Therefore, it is not surprising that some actors, especially among smaller hedge funds and firms focused primarily on the domestic British market, favored Leave. In the words of one hedge fund manager, "Europe turns us into a colony and we are used to an empire. We are not used to obeying rules we haven't set."[17] This undercurrent of apprehension over greater European control grew after the 2007–09 Banking Crisis prompted increased Continental criticism of "Anglo-Saxon" capitalism and attempts to tighten financial regulations in the European Union.[18] As discussed in Chapter 2, the UK successfully blocked much of this effort, though that failed to quell the fears of some British financial actors.

These arguments, however, do not account for the primary drivers of Brexit. The chief advocates of the Brexit project almost exclusively focused on concerns over immigration, national sovereignty, and regulation in non-financial sectors.[19] The defining conflict, reflected in both the public debate before the referendum and the UK–EU negotiations after, lay in the tensions between a British public increasingly in favor of restrictions on intra-EU immigration and an EU that would not infringe on Freedom of Movement as a core principle of European integration.[20] This framing was reflected not only in the polling data, but also the substance of pro-Leave rhetoric. Both the official Vote Leave and the unofficial Leave.UK made immigration, not financial regulation, the centerpiece of their argument.[21] The vast majority of British financial actors favored Remain, and those financial actors who did favor Leave were not prime movers in the advancement of Brexit. Therefore, while an argument for Brexit as an endogenous response to tightening EU financial regulation existed, it failed to win enough advocates or drive the debate. The vast majority of British financial actors favored Remain, and Continental financial actors had no vote at all; thus, it is safe to say that Brexit's causes were exogenous to the European financial sector.

## Moderate

Brexit ultimately posed what should be considered a moderate threat to the EU financial system. Even the closest potential post-Brexit EU–UK relationship meant an actual partial disintegration of the Union, including the departure of one of the largest, wealthiest, and most financially integrated member states. The worst-case scenarios, that the loss of the EU's main financial hub would trigger a panic either in Europe directly or originating in Britain and spreading to the Continent, or that Brexit would prove to be the first in a wave of countries leaving the EU, were realistic enough to attract serious concern. However, these dangers were mitigated by three key factors: the slow unfolding of the process rather than an unpredictable random shock, the degree of control the EU had over the process, and the ways in which Brexit presented opportunities as well as dangers to the remaining EU member states.

Especially in the early days of the crisis, observers saw the threat from Brexit as potentially very great. Eurasia Group President Ian Bremmer called Brexit "the most significant political risk the world has experienced since the Cuban Missile Crisis," both for its potential threat to the EU itself and to global stability more broadly.[22] Jean-Claude Juncker, the President of the European Commission, described Britain's decision to leave as "an existential crisis" for the EU in his 2016 State of the Union address.[23] Valdis Dombrovskis, the European Commissioner for Financial Services, specifically warned of the danger to finance, arguing that the scale of the threat was comparable to "New York leaving the US and taking Wall Street with it."[24]

### The Political Threat

The threats to European finance can be broadly grouped into two groups: political threats to stall or reverse integration and economic threats that severing London from the rest of Europe would trigger a new financial crisis. Politically, Brexit both fit within a broader wave of euroskepticism in response to the "polycrisis" of European integration and threatened to exacerbate that crisis and reinforce other national euroskeptic movements.[25]

The most severe political threat for advocates of integration, and the greatest hope of its opponents, was that Brexit would inspire similar "Exiteer" movements elsewhere. Both advocates and opponents of integration saw the rise of a "Nationalist International" coming to power and rejecting the European project across the member states as a very real possibility, especially since by the end of 2016, euroskeptic parties were part of the government of nine of the twenty-seven remaining EU member states.[26] It was for this reason that the Bank of International Settlements (BIS) cautioned that, of all the challenges facing the EU at the time, "Brexit represents the biggest medium-to-long-term challenge of all." The BIS report warned that "referendums may mushroom across Europe in a tug-of-war between populist forces and the political establishment and elites. Brexit has the potential to unleash centrifugal forces, leading perhaps to a breakup of the euro."[27] Isabel Schnabel, at the time a member of the German Council of Economic Experts and later a member of the European Central Bank (ECB) Executive Board, feared that these dynamics meant that "a complete break-up of the union would not be an impossible outcome."[28] Especially threatening was the possibility of a "Frexit," of a core founding member of the European project and Europe's second largest economy leaving the Union. Marine Le Pen, the leader of the euroskeptic National Front and widely expected to be one of the two final candidates in the 2017 French Presidential election, explicitly used the Brexit referendum results to call for a similar referendum for her country.[29]

Even if, as proved to be the case, Britain's vote did not set off an immediate wave of similar exits, Brexit still posed a threat to European integration by discouraging efforts to deepen centralization. Juncker lamented in his 2016 State of the Union that "never before have I seen such little common ground between our member states."[30] Even if the euroskeptics failed to win support for exit, observers widely expected a "freeze" in deeper integration as Brexit discouraged pro-integration forces and animated their opponents.[31] A former Italian Treasury official warned that "it seems difficult to imagine that the rest of the [EU] will close ranks and move in the direction of greater integration quickly. Simply, there is no political will. Indeed, the risk is exactly the opposite."[32] Bundesbank Board Member Joachim Wuermeling lamented that Brexit was a "wake-up call" to "all of us who believe that supranational cooperation creates added value for policy, the economy and society."[33] Former Greek Finance Minister Yanis Varoufakis meanwhile cautioned that attempts to respond to the political realignment of Brexit with "federation-lite" would be an ineffective "fallacy."[34]

## The Economic Threat

Brexit also posed a direct threat to European finance by raising the specter of a new financial crisis. European banks in 2016 remained in fragile state following the 2007–09 Banking Crisis and 2010–14 Debt Crisis, meaning that it would take only a relatively minor shock to push them back into a panic. The ECB's Annual Report for 2016 specifically cited the persistence of high volumes of nonperforming loans (NPLs) on bank balance sheets, with only slow progress in reducing those loan stocks, while both sovereign and private default risks remained worryingly high.[35] A report from think tank VoxEU further cautioned that progress on banking union to insulate the EU from a new crisis remained too limited. In particular, the Single Resolution Fund (SRF) was seen as too small to resolve all but the smallest of panics, especially in the absence of a European Deposit Insurance Scheme (EDIS) or a clear backstop to the SRF from the European Stability Mechanism (ESM) or other funding pool. For that reason, they explicitly warned that that "the after-shocks of Brexit could well provide [a] trigger" for a "new bad shock... similar to that of 2010–11."[36] One British financial services lawyer would thus describe the state of the European financial system and its regulatory system as "a nuclear reactor with a crack in the core."[37] As demonstrated in Figure 5.1, nonperforming loans remained an enduring problem across the European Union, especially in those countries hardest hit by the Debt Crisis.

Banks in three of Europe's largest economies, Italy, Spain, and Germany, were seen as especially vulnerable. In Italy and Spain, both countries which had been among the hardest hit by the Debt Crisis, and thus among the most at risk for a new sovereign debt crisis, a series of bank failures would provide the first major tests of the new Single Resolution Authority to mixed results. In Italy, Banca Monte dei Paschi di Siena (MPS), accounted by some measures

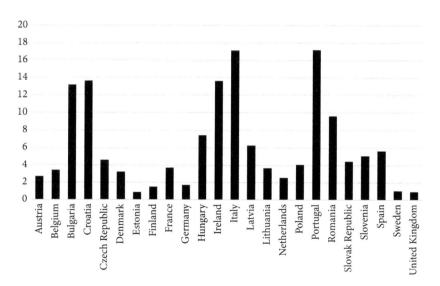

**Figure 5.1** Bank Nonperforming Loans to Gross Loans (%) for Select European Union States, 2016

*Source:* World Bank Global Financial Development Database
*Note:* Cyprus and Greece are excluded because, at 36.7 percent and 36.3 percent respectively, their NPL levels were dramatically higher than others.

the world's oldest bank, and a pair of Venetian lenders, Banca Popolare di Vicenza (BPVI) and Veneto Banca, all petitioned the state for emergency relief. The ultimate terms Italy provided out of its Atlante rescue fund were criticized by many observers as overly generous and stretching the limits of the bail-in procedure and opt-outs to it.[38] The resolution of Banco Popular in Spain was generally considered to be more in line with the spirit of the bail-in rules, and avoided a direct cost to the Spanish government, but still cost Spain €4 billion in deferred tax assets.[39] Germany had escaped direct problems in the Debt Crisis, but its own banking system also remained in a fragile state. Norddeutsche Landesbank (NordLB), one of the regional Landesbanken, required state assistance after putting up a €1.96 billion loss in 2016, fueled by €2.94 billion in losses from shipping loans.[40] Germany's two largest banks, Commerzbank and Deutsche Bank, also were in weak shape. Commerzbank, Germany's second largest bank and the EU's fourteenth largest, had struggled with profitability since the Banking Crisis, producing an annualized return on equity of only 0.6 percent in the previous decade, despite a substantial capital injection from the German state and a retreat from international activity.[41] Deutsche Bank, Germany's largest bank and the EU's second largest, had similar struggles, forced to lay off significant numbers of workers and attempt repeated restructurings.[42] The strain to the European financial sector from a collapse of any of these institutions would both test a new and underfunded banking union and potentially reignite sovereign debt fears. Moreover, Europe's capacity to manage such a crisis would be diminished by the loss of London's capital markets as an alternative channel of financing outside of the banking system.

If European banking seemingly needed only a slight push to fall into a wider panic, Brexit offered two distinct ways to offer that push. The first would be a crisis originating in the British financial system and spreading to the Continent, while the second would be a crisis originating in the EU sparked by the shock of losing access to the UK. The complexity of the European supply chains and uncertainty as to the ultimate form of Brexit made it extremely difficult to model the specific impacts.[43] However, experts predicted recessions in both the UK and the EU out of the Brexit fallout and the risk of a crisis in either the UK or the EU-27 was considered to be quite viable.[44] This can be seen not only in the rhetoric of policymakers, but also in the concrete steps they took toward contingency plans in the event of a maximally impactful "hard Brexit."[45]

Most observers agreed that Brexit posed a greater direct threat to UK finance than to the rest of Europe, given the reliance of British firms on access to the EU. However, that deep integration carried implications for the rest of the EU as well, especially given the size and centrality of the British financial sector. The March 2016 ranking of European financial centers by London think tank Z/Yen presented in Figure 5.2 captures the centrality of London. This ranking, done biennially by combining quantitative measures and survey research, demonstrates that on the eve of Brexit, London dominated the rankings by a healthy margin, and that only two of the top five positions were held by other European Union cities. As ECB President Draghi warned, "certain countries are especially exposed to the UK economy, and of course they will have consequences and the consequences may be serious. And their serious consequences are bound to reverberate on the rest of the continent."[46] Felix Hufled, the president of BaFin, the German banking regulator similarly warned of the risks to German lenders with heavy exposure to the UK.[47] The capacity of such entanglements to bring down banks across national borders had already been acutely demonstrated in the Banking Crisis, where losses from the purchase of Dutch lender ABN AMRO drove Royal Bank of Scotland (RBS), then the world's largest bank by assets, into a collapse only averted by the British government taking an 83 percent ownership stake in it.[48]

A second risk was that Brexit could spark a new crisis on the Continent even if London stayed stable. The International Monetary Fund (IMF) warned that the "Brexit vote implies a substantial increase in economic, political, and institutional uncertainty," especially as "the Brexit shock occurs amid unresolved legacy issues in the European banking system, in particular in Italian and Portuguese banks."[49] Although Italy's problem banks were already struggling before the vote, some observers saw Brexit as potentially triggering an escalation of that crisis.[50] Other countries with greater direct economic exposure to the UK faced a contraction of economic and financial activity from the raising of barriers. Such concerns focused in particular on Germany and Ireland.[51] More broadly, the loss of Europe's main financial hub would cause nonbank financial activity repatriating to Europe to scatter across different countries with different regulatory standards.[52] This, in turn, would create the possibility of regulatory arbitrage of nonbank financial activity comparable to the problems in banking exposed in the 2007–09 Crisis. Europe had previously avoided such a circumstance because of the centrality of London. The concentration of nonbank financial activity in a single city left most of such activity under the regulatory authority of a single state, the United Kingdom. In the absence of a rapidly introduced Capital Markets Union, however, this would no longer be the case and financial activity would likely scatter across the remaining member states. Because of this, Colm Kelleher, formerly the President of Morgan Stanley International,

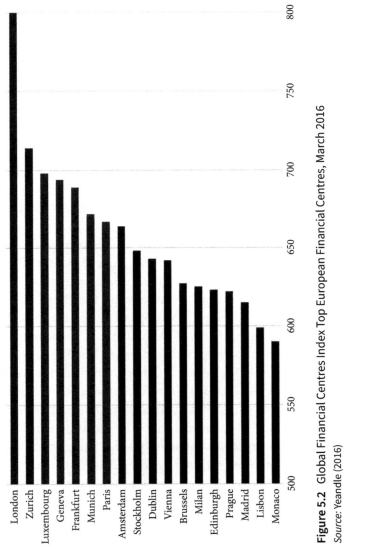

**Figure 5.2** Global Financial Centres Index Top European Financial Centres, March 2016
*Source:* Yeandle (2016)

warned that "European capital markets are still not fit for purpose. They are neither large nor deep enough to support economic growth or to buffer it in hard times." Brexit would only "amplify" these problems.[53] Valdis Dombrovskis therefore warned that, in the absence of an expansion of their authority, Brexit would create legal uncertainty that could threaten "the stability and resilience of our financial markets."[54]

Kalaitzake highlights how European regulators focused specifically on three potential problem areas, and devoted considerable effort to developing contingency planning to minimize the risks.[55] The first of these, settlement risk, focused on the fact that much of the "plumbing" activity, services vital to the day-to-day operation of European firms, took place in London, including the clearing of 70 percent of euro-denominated trades. Secondly, many European investors relied heavily on UK-based funds and fund managers, and would be forced to scramble to find alternatives in the event of a hard Brexit. Finally, Brexit risked a breakdown in regulatory cooperation, opening the potential for regulatory gaps to emerge and firms to engage in regulatory arbitrage, both between the UK and the EU-27, and among EU-27 financial centers as they scrambled to compete for repatriated financial business.

### Factors Mitigating the Threat

Because of the factors outlined in the previous sections, Brexit presented a very real threat to the European Union, and specifically to the stability of European financial markets. However, despite the doomsday rhetoric of some actors, it was seen as only a moderate threat by most actors. Three key factors served to mitigate the danger: the slow motion of the process, the EU's degree of control over the terms of exit, and the offsetting opportunities to fill the gap left behind by the United Kingdom.

The first advantage in managing the impact of Brexit was in timing. The specific outcomes of events could not necessarily be predicted, as can be seen in the degree to which observers were surprised by the victory of Leave in the Brexit vote and concern over what the ultimate shape of the UK–EU relationship would take out of the negotiations. However, the major turning points were all well known months or years in advance, including the Brexit referendum itself in June 2016, the two-year countdown to actual exit once British Prime Minister triggered Article 50 in March 2017, and the British Parliamentary elections of December 2019 that were taken as key to shaping the future of UK–EU negotiations. This stands in sharp contrast to the normal unfolding of crises, which is marked by the unpredictability of when major escalations will occur. The greater predictability of timing, if not of outcomes, gave financial actors increased ability to plan and build up capacity to deal with whatever shocks may occur. European regulators in particular emphasized the importance of preparation in advance of key deadlines. Bundesbank President Jens Weidmann thus could conclude immediately after the Brexit vote that "the vast majority of banks and supervisory bodies had treated the Brexit scenario with the seriousness it deserved and had been prepared for that outcome."[56] ECB President Mario Draghi would similarly conclude as the end of the Article 50 period approached that "it would really take an extraordinary amount of lack of preparation to materialise the financial stability risks that might come from a hard Brexit," given how well documented the process had been to that point.[57] The European Commission similarly had ample time to work on regulations to cover such complications as revised clearing and payment processing.[58]

The second advantage to the EU was the degree of control it had over the terms of the UK's exit. The EU of course could not control the UK's decision to leave. It also could not prevent the UK from rejecting any negotiated agreement and instead defaulting to a "hard" Brexit which would downgrade the UK relationship with the EU to the baseline status of fellow World Trade Organization members. Such a hard Brexit would impose substantial costs on the EU, and Leave campaigners were quick to argue that this gave the UK leverage over the EU. As Daily Telegraph editor Ambrose Evans-Pritchard put it, "the economic fates of the UK and the eurozone are entwined, that if we go over a cliff, so do they."[59]

By the same token, just as the EU could not compel the UK to accept terms, nor could the UK compel the EU to do so. Either side could force a hard Brexit by refusing the other's terms. The impact, however, would not be even between the two parties. In terms of both institutional position and framing, the EU enjoyed the advantage of being the defender of the status quo.[60] Institutionally, the European treaty rules governing a country leaving gave the advantage to the EU. Any agreement would have to first be negotiated by the European Commission, then cleared by the European Parliament, and finally, in the case of any agreement beyond a basic free trade agreement, ratified by the individual member states. These multiple veto points made it hard to forge an exit agreement that diverged much from the pre-Brexit status quo other than European Economic Area (EEA) membership or a basic free trade agreement. EEA membership would minimize disruption but compel the UK to retain EU policies on a host of issues, including free movement, while a basic free trade agreement, covering goods but not services, risked substantial disruption to the EU–UK relationship. In terms of framing, the EU also enjoyed an advantage, as EU negotiators could cast themselves as preserving a broadly acceptable status quo, while the British were the ones advocating for change, and thus the ones required to make an argument that the EU-27 would accept that such change was desirable.

Economically, the EU-27 also enjoyed an advantage. Brexit, and especially a hard Brexit, threatened both economies, but asymmetrically, with a far greater risk to the UK. The EU-27, with an economy five times larger than the UK's, was far more important as a trading partner to the UK than the reverse. As illustrated in Figure 5.3, the $480 billion annual trade (exports plus imports) between the UK and the other twenty-seven EU member states in 2015 constituted 47 percent of the UK's total imports and 39 percent of its total exports, but only 4 percent of the EU's total imports and 6 percent of the EU's total exports.[61] Therefore, the loss of access to the UK would be a problem for the EU, but it would be a much bigger one, maybe a catastrophic one, for the UK to lose access to the EU.[62] This asymmetry also would lead to the "Brussels Effect," of large UK-based firms wanting to retain access to European markets, creating a constituency within the UK in favor of retaining close equivalence.[63] US banks based in the UK in particular pushed hard for a deal that would preserve access even if it diminished British regulatory autonomy.[64]

The overall sense, especially among EU policymakers, was captured in a Bundesbank simulation which concluded that "even a hard, disorderly Brexit would be manageable from Germany's viewpoint. To sum up: the costs of

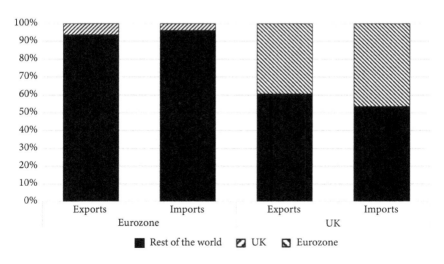

**Figure 5.3** Eurozone–UK Import and Export Composition, Percentage of Total, 2015

*Source:* International Monetary Fund Direction of Trade Statistics (DOTS) Database
*Note:* The Eurozone is used rather than the EU to avoid double-counting of UK exports and imports.

Brexit will most likely be much higher for the UK than for the remaining EU."[65] Some analysts even concluded that "for the EU-27, therefore, a no-deal Brexit could prove little more than a relatively minor irritation, if not a blessing in disguise," given the opportunities to profit from the departure of the UK.[66]

Moreover, the EU saw risks in too-soft terms of Brexit as well as in a hard Brexit. Beyond questions of the immediate economic impact, the EU had a clear interest in ensuring that the terms of Brexit discouraged other states from also leaving the union. Pierre Gramegna, the Minister of Finance for Luxembourg, warned that if a country could "just walk out and everything stays the same, there would no point to being a member."[67] Therefore, a senior European diplomat cautioned that "Any deal cannot be made too attractive for the British. That's not being punitive as such; the EU will want to demonstrate to others who are not the British that there are severe downside risks to leaving."[68] To that end, the EU negotiators were willing to draw a hard line that gave the UK no special treatment even despite the close links between the two economies. The priority became to ensure that "a state outside the European Union will not have better conditions than a state inside the European Union," in the words of Manfred Weber of the European People's Party.[69]

Within the financial sector, this meant that concerns over the loss of access to London markets were weighed against the desire to avoid granting something as valuable as continued passporting without, as French Finance Minister Michel Sapin put it, being "negotiated against a lot of reciprocal concessions."[70] This hard line was repeated across a range of actors. Bank of France President François Villeroy de Galhau argued that "There can be no cherry-picking and no free-riding," while MEP Markus Ferber maintained that "the UK will be a third-party state like any other" and would have to seek equivalence status.[71]

Valdis Dombrovskis, the European Commissioner for Financial Services, and thus a key decision-maker on the post-Brexit financial access terms between the UK and the EU, allowed that "we cannot fully mitigate the negative economic effects of Brexit, especially in the case of a no-deal scenario." At the same time, he noted that the long timeline has allowed actors on both sides of the Channel to "have already acted to minimize financial stability risks," and therefore insisted on a hard line in financial access negotiations. In his words, "leaving the EU, the Customs Union and the Single Market would mean no automatic market access for UK firms *and no passporting rights* [emphasis mine]."[72] In short, Brexit threatened the stability of European finance, but it was a risk which was generally seen as manageable due to a combination of predictability in timing of decisions if not their substance and the favorable negotiating position of the EU over the terms of access.

The final reason EU financial actors had to not be overly panicked over Brexit was that it presented substantial opportunities in addition to the dangers. British Leave advocates of course emphasized Brexit as an opportunity to enhance the British economy by replacing EU regulations with more light-touch rules and making London a "Singapore on the Thames."[73] However, European financial actors also saw both small- and large-scale opportunities to them out of Brexit.

On the smaller scale, European agencies currently based in the UK, most prominently the European Banking Authority and the European Medicines Agency (EMA), would almost inevitably need to relocate to a new location in the EU-27, with each bringing a few hundred jobs and spillover economic activity such as conference hosting.[74] In addition, euro clearing would likely be moved out of London, bringing a modest direct increase in financial activity to some new EU hub.[75] These moves were seen as almost inevitable regardless of any other negotiated terms of the future UK–EU relationship.

The potential raising of barriers between the UK's capital markets and the EU offered the potential for substantially larger gains by encouraging a relocation of financial activity out of London. London had long dominated European financial markets by combining a long-established liberal regulatory tradition with easy access to the rest of the European Union. Brexit cost it the latter, meaning that financial firms now had an incentive to move their headquarters for European operations within the rump EU.[76] Thus, it was widely expected that Brexit would cause "upside consequence of further strengthening the various financial centres of Europe."[77] The question quickly centered less on *whether* Brexit would cause a repatriation of financial activity to the EU-27, but more on *where* that activity would land.

France and Germany in particular saw opportunities out of Brexit. Both had long strived to make Paris and Frankfurt respectively capital markets hubs to rival London. While the UK was in the EU, they met with little success, given the first-mover advantages of London and the greater comfort of the British government with a light-touch regulatory approach. The raising of barriers post-Brexit, however, presented new opportunities to make either or both a new capital markets hub for Europe. Immediately following the vote, Valerie Pecresse, the president of the regional council for Île-de-France, including Paris, made this explicit, arguing that "we are not in a war with London . . . but there is competition and we want to make Paris Europe's top financial centre."[78] Heads of the French banks unanimously claimed they were unconcerned with the potential for destabilization out of Brexit, despite

France having the third largest exposure to the UK after Germany and Spain. Rather, they described Brexit as an opportunity to steal a mark on their London-based rivals.[79] Meanwhile, by a year after the vote, Volker Bouffier, the Minister-President for Hesse (including Frankfurt), anticipated at least "some 40 financial institutions and banks that are going to move over here partly or entirely as a result of this Brexit discussion."[80]

Beyond this potential relocation of financial activity, Brexit shifted the political balance within the European Union. France and Germany had been acknowledged as the dominant EU players from the creation of the European project, and that when the two powers united around a common position, they could generally overcome objections from other members.[81] However, since it joined in 1973, the United Kingdom had constituted a third major power center. The UK on its own was not necessarily able to push its own agenda the way France and Germany could, but was powerful enough to block reforms it opposed. This had been demonstrated in the financial sector through the UK's securing of opt-outs on joining the euro and banking union, and on insisting on key concessions on European Banking Authority to conform to UK positions. Prior to Britain's departure, Capital Markets Union was also looking to take a shape that largely reflected UK preferences.

The absence of the UK also altered the balance between opposing blocs in debates over EU regulation generally. The presence of the UK meant that regulatory debates in the EU often broke down between a "market-making" coalition including the UK and many small northern states favoring a liberal approach and a "market-shaping coalition" including France and many southern states favoring stricter regulation, with Germany often the crucial "swing" state in deciding outcomes.[82] With the departure of the UK, the core liberal bloc dwindled to Austria, the Netherlands, Finland, and sometimes Germany. Even including Germany, this bloc no longer commanded the 35 percent of the population necessary to form a blocking minority in qualified majority voting in the European Council. On the other hand, the UK's departure meant that the core market-shaping bloc of France, Italy, and Spain could reach that threshold with the addition of only one additional state.[83] Especially since Germany also generally sided with the market-shaping bloc in favoring stricter rules on financial matters, this looked to remove a major barrier to deeper financial integration.

As a report from think tank Bruegel argued, Brexit "create[d] an opportunity for the remaining EU-27 to accelerate the development of its financial markets and to increase its resilience against shocks."[84] Bundesbank board member Joachim Wuermeling would celebrate the opening of a "window of opportunity," while one pro-Remain Tory MP would ruefully acknowledge that "Brussels can do these things more easily now we aren't there to make the sensible case and work with those countries who also don't want the EU to move in this direction."[85] The EU's ambassador to the World Trade Organization, Marc Vanheukelen, stated the new priorities bluntly, saying that "we are now only thinking about the EU-27. Like any divorce, you no longer care about the well-being of the other."[86]

## The Window of Opportunity in an Exogenous Moderate Crisis

For the reasons outlined in the Classification section, Brexit should be considered an exogenous moderate crisis for the EU financial sector. The threat from Brexit was seen as real, and in the worst-case scenarios extremely devastating, but one that could be managed and to a degree predicted, making it possible for banks and regulators to avoid those worst-case scenarios with sufficient foresight. Advocates of deeper reform, especially European Capital Markets Union, would attempt to link those catastrophe-avoidance steps with broader regulatory architecture reforms, as had been done in the Debt Crisis, and to a lesser degree in the Banking Crisis, as per Monnet's dictum of integration out of solutions to European crises. However, unlike in those earlier crises, Brexit presented a crisis exogenous to the financial system. Some Leave advocates made arguments about the tightening grip of EU financial regulation through the EBA and banking union driving Brexit sentiments. Similar arguments carried some plausibility in immigration debates, as control over immigration was repeatedly cited as a prime consideration for many Leave voters.[87] However, the polling and voting evidence shows that such arguments were unpersuasive on financial issues, as the most affected actors in the financial sector remained overwhelmingly pro-Remain.

The combination of the moderate and exogenous dimensions of the Brexit crisis would undercut efforts at more substantial reform of the European financial architecture. Brexit's origins lay outside of the financial sector, so while reforms may help to position EU finance to better profit from the departure of the EU, tightening integration would not prevent another member state departure. Indeed, some feared increasing centralization might even have the opposite effect, driving more euroskeptics to favor Exit. Moreover, while the subsequent Coronavirus Pandemic crisis presented such a severe threat that inaction would have led to catastrophe, Brexit's threat was

## Minor Enacted Changes Out of Brexit

Despite the more ambitious goals of advocates of deeper integration, the most noteworthy changes in the European financial regulatory architecture to follow from Brexit would be relatively minor: the relocation of the European Banking Authority to Paris and the repatriation of euro clearing to EU financial markets. The former consisted of little other than a geographic relocation of an agency, and the latter would be considered relatively minor even if implementation had not ended up being indefinitely delayed.

## The Relocation of the European Banking Authority

As discussed in Chapter 3, the EU's chief institutional innovation out of the 2007–09 Banking Crisis had been the creation of the European Banking Authority, which had been headquartered in London in part to help get the United Kingdom to support its creation. Even before the UK's vote to leave the EU, there had been some discontent that the EBA was based in a non-eurozone city.[88] Once the UK voted to leave the EU, it immediately became clear that the EBA would need to be relocated, along with the European Medicines Agency, also based in London, as it would be unthinkable to leave major EU institutions headquartered in a non-EU state. The question thus immediately became not *if* the EBA or EMA would be relocated, but *where*.

Both the EBA and EMA were attractive prizes. The EMA offered more direct gain, as it employed 890 staff with a €300 million budget, while the EBA employed 189 staff and carried a €36 million budget.[89] Both offered additional spillover benefits, including attracting conferences and other related activity. The EBA carried further indirect benefits as well, as hosting a key financial regulator would send a signal that the host city should be considered a major financial hub.[90] Frankfurt already hosted the ECB and the European Insurance and Occupational Pensions Authority (EIOPA), and Paris was home to the European Securities and Markets Authority (ESMA). Advocates of each city would play up these existing connections in an attempt to attract financial firms to relocate.[91] Hosting the EBA would similarly enhance the appeal of whichever city ended up its new home.

Given these advantages, a large number of member states put forth proposals for one of their cities to become the new home for the EBA and the EMA. Eight countries bid to host the EBA and nineteen bid to host the EMA, with six submitting bids for both agencies despite a decision early on that both would not be relocated to the same country.[92] Politicking around which city should host the EBA generally centered on a combination of the existing importance of a given city as a financial hub and the ease of the transition out of London.[93] Advocates of Frankfurt, for instance, made the case that it already hosted the European Central Bank in addition to being one of the major financial hubs.[94] Dublin made the case that it offered an established financial services sector in an English-speaking city, which would "[minimize] disruption to staff."[95] Several cities made similar appeals to quality of life, emphasizing such things as the "imperial majesty" and quality of water of Vienna, the "rich cultural scene" of Frankfurt, and the "best kept secret" of the cuisine in Warsaw.[96] More practically, a number of cities offered "sweeteners" to attract the EBA, such as offers of free or reduced rent in cities including Frankfurt, Prague, Paris, Dublin, and Luxembourg.[97] Despite efforts to induce the EU institutions to take a position on the question, the European Commission remained neutral on which city should host.[98] The European Parliament similarly did not take a position, though it did argue unsuccessfully that the UK should "fully cover" the costs of relocating both the EBA and EMA.[99] Successive rounds of voting in the Council of Ministers revealed substantial divisions, with the Council turning to a drawing of lots to break a tie between Paris and Dublin.[100] Ultimately, the Council of Ministers settled on Paris to host the EBA and Amsterdam to host the EMA on 20 November 2017.[101]

The relocation of the EBA, despite attracting significant lobbying and campaigning from the candidate cities, ultimately constitutes a minor change to the European financial architecture. Some observers took the relocation of the EBA out of London to a eurozone city as a symbol that "the multicurrency narrative is over," and that EU financial regulatory policy would now be dominated by the concerns of eurozone states.[102] It is true that the departure of the UK, by far the largest EU member without an explicit opt-out from the euro, changed the balance of power within the EU in a way that pointed toward the dominance of France, Germany, and eurozone member concerns, and as such the relocation of the EBA carried some symbolic resonance. However, this was not reflected in the actual policies of the EBA. At no point in the discussions was a substantive change to the EBA's role or policies discussed. The relocation mattered a lot for the employees of the institution, and a bit for the broader Parisian economy, but ultimately this change should not be accounted as even a modest change to the EU financial architecture. The relocation was not presented as necessary to manage or prevent future crises, and while it was made necessary by the Brexit crisis, it was also not presented as a crucial step to manage the actual strains on the EU financial sector out of the current crisis. Rather, it was simply a minor but necessary adjustment to reflect the change in the UK's status from member state to nonmember.

## The Relocation of Euro Clearing

A somewhat more significant reform than the relocation of the EBA, if still relatively minor, was a revision of the EU's rules on central counterparty clearing houses (CCPs) to compel the majority of euro-denominated clearing activity into EU financial markets.[103] At the time of the Brexit vote, approximately three quarters of all euro-denominated clearing took place in London, reflecting the centrality of London as Europe's financial hub at the time of the euro's creation and since.[104] Eurozone states had long desired to bring euro clearing into the eurozone, and had debated attempting to do so during the Banking Crisis.[105] However, the presence of London made that challenging without violating the principle of free movement of capital. So long as the UK remained within the EU, the gravitational pull of London as an existing financial hub made it difficult to relocate eurozone clearing without introducing capital controls. Such an effort would both violate EU rules about nondiscrimination between member states and free movement of capital and generate substantial pushback from the UK itself.

### The Argument for Relocation

Brexit presented an opportunity to revisit the issue of euro clearing. That the EU would make such a move had been anticipated even before the vote. Lord Hill had warned on the eve of the Brexit vote that this would happen, cautioning that "if we left, absolutely I do think they would try again. Because, again, if people are thinking more about the interests of the eurozone, why would they not increase the pressure for all the euro-clearing to be done within the eurozone?"[106] With the UK now out of the EU, internal nondiscrimination rules no longer applied, making it much easier to disincentivize use of

London clearing. Immediately after the vote, French President François Hollande made clear his view that leaving the Single Market should mean loss of euro clearing as well. In his words, "London's hard-fought right to clear trades was an exorbitant situation. As soon as the UK is not part of the EU, there is no reason that this continues . . . The UK has said it doesn't want any more freedom of movement. Now it won't have access to the single market anymore."[107]

In addition to making tools to block London-based euro clearing easier to use, Britain's exit allowed the introduction of a new argument for bringing euro clearing to the eurozone. While euro clearing had previously happened within the EU but outside of the eurozone, now euro clearing would be happening outside of the EU altogether, and thus entirely outside the supervisory remit of European authorities. The Bundesbank's Andreas Dombret described this as "a level of tolerance I can neither imagine nor support," while François Villeroy de Galhau of the Bank of France argued that "a location policy is the only viable mechanism to guarantee that European authorities, and the Eurosystem in particular, can control and manage the risks that [central counterparties] are likely to pose to the financial stability of the European Union."[108]

## The Argument against Relocation

Countering these points were arguments that moving euro clearing would be potentially destabilizing. London at the time of the referendum handled over two-thirds of all euro-denominated trades, and cutting off London-based CCPs risked creating considerable financial chaos.[109] Additionally, because a significant volume of euro clearing took place in New York, any effort to exclude the UK would almost inevitably exclude the United States as well. This, therefore, threatened to have political fallout beyond just the UK–EU relationship. Moreover, it was not at all clear that the benefits would be worth the risks. Although London financial actors obviously had self-interested reasons to make these arguments, they argued that extraterritorial clearing was unproblematic and that relocation would be destabilizing. LCH, a significant London clearing house, noted that the US has allowed for almost all dollar interest rate swaps to be cleared in London, so that the EU should have no great qualms about euro clearing.[110] Xavier Rolet, the chief executive of the London Stock Exchange, further cautioned that forcing relocation would be "rump, illiquid, and systematically more dangerous."[111] Similarly, a report from the British House of Lords cautioned that the move would raise costs for the eurozone, potentially undermining efforts to create a post-Britain CMU.[112]

## Outcome

The question of euro clearing remains somewhat unsettled. In late 2019, the European Council adopted revisions to the European Market Infrastructure Regulation (EMIR) pertaining to the status of third country clearing houses, including those in the UK. Under the EMIR, only CCPs recognized by the EU are authorized to operate euro clearing. At the time of the revision, the EU recognized thirty-two third-country CCPs, including three British CCPs.[113] However, such recognition was contingent on UK regulation remaining close enough to EU standards under the EMIR's equivalence provisions. Such access therefore became contingent and subject to revision. Either a change in EU regulation not mirrored by the UK or a change in UK regulation not mirrored by the EU could lead to the revocation of equivalence, and with it the ability to engage in euro clearing. This move was designed to minimize disruption while also creating incentives for euro clearing to repatriate to the EU. However, it was undercut in practice because the EU proved unwilling to risk a withdrawal of equivalence status and the subsequent shock to capital markets. Although the initial granting of equivalence was due to expire in 2022, in January of that year it was extended at least June 2025.

The relocation of euro clearing constitutes a more substantial change than the relocation of the EBA, in that it presented a real change to the European financial architecture and a broader economic impact. However, even before the indefinite extension of equivalence, the impact looked to be relatively minor, more a geographical change than a structural one. That the EU has balked at withdrawing equivalence and compelling the repatriation of euro clearing underlines this point. It also points to an underlying tension within the debates over Brexit crisis management. A larger crisis would compel a more significant reform in response, but because the EU had so much control over the terms of exit, it could also control the size of the crisis to a large degree. A loss of access to UK markets could make a strong case for a relocation of euro clearing. However, the dynamic of financial access negotiations became that the UK would take as generous terms of access as the EU was willing to grant. Therefore, the EU could simply preserve access to UK clearing operations and sidestep the crisis, so long as UK regulation did not diverge an unacceptable amount. More crucially, these debates almost immediately fell into the realm of normal rather than emergency politics, as the EU could stop the emergency by granting access at its own discretion. Therefore, there was no cause for a shift into the more streamlined and rapid emergency mode, and the actors favoring the UK-based euro clearing status quo could assert their position to caution against excessive risk and keep London euro clearing intact.

## The Big Attempted Reform: Capital Markets Union

While the relocation of the EBA and of euro clearing rise only to the level of minor or even cosmetic changes, reformers did attempt to use the Brexit crisis as a moment to push more expansive changes. Most prominently, advocates of Capital Markets Union attempted to use Brexit as an opportunity to finally push a breakthrough in the long-debated centralization of European capital markets reform, in line with Monnet's dictum that Europe will integrate through crises. In particular, they attempted to make the case that CMU would be essential to manage both the short- and long-term challenges of the UK's departure. However, these efforts would ultimately meet with failure. The threat from Brexit was nether severe enough nor internal enough to the financial sector to successfully move CMU negotiations into emergency politics, with the attendant narrowing of veto players and imperative for rapid action. Instead, CMU negotiations remained in the realm of normal politics, where the lack of urgency and plethora of voices meant at best minor progress. CMU negotiations remained locked in a stalemate between a largely French vision of European capital markets governed by high levels of regulation and a more deregulated vision propagated chiefly by the "new Hanseatic league" of small northern member states. CMU attracted a great deal of attention in the wake of Brexit, but ultimately only minor progress on the relatively small number of issues both sides could agree on.

## Capital Markets Union before Brexit

European Capital Markets Union had been on the European issue agenda for many years, often framed as a counterpart to European banking union. While banking union aimed to make European banks themselves safer through centralized supervision and resolution, at least within the eurozone, CMU would enhance the overall stability of the financial system, even in the event of bank failure by increasing the viability of nonbank channels. The European Commission warned in a 2015 Green Paper of the risks of an overreliance on bank-based financing, explicitly citing the US as an example of a financial system made more stable through deep capital markets.[114] The IMF's 2016 Global Financial Stability report echoed these concerns, warning that "another legacy [of the banking crisis] is excess banking capacity, namely too many banks, which will have to be addressed over time. Europe must also complete the banking union and establish a common deposit guarantee scheme (DGS), *in addition to further advancing the development of a true capital markets union* [emphasis mine]."

Prior to Brexit, CMU had chiefly been thought of as a project to facilitate easier access across the EU to London capital markets. The UK was seen as likely to be the chief beneficiary of the project, and also its chief advocate. Lord Hill, the British European Commissioner for Financial Stability, had in particular often been seen as the chief individual advocate for the project.[115] As such, the potential value of CMU to British financial firms had been cited by many in the run-up to the Brexit vote as a reason to vote Remain. Mark Boleat of the City of London Corporation captured this sentiment well, arguing that "the European Capital Markets Union is the perfect illustration of an initiative that London, and the UK in general, have helped shape and will benefit from."[116]

At the time of the Brexit vote, Capital Markets Union remained more an aspirational goal than a concrete reality. Much like the European Deposit Insurance Scheme, CMU had become a proposal widely agreed-upon in principle, even as substantial details remained disputed. However, while EDIS stalemated over fundamental questions of how to deal with legacy debt and sovereign debt, debates over CMU were considerably more technical and less accessible to the public at large. The debates were also markedly less urgent. While advocates of EDIS argued that its absence presented a "ticking time bomb" for European financial stability, CMU was more modestly pitched as a potentially valuable reform, but not a necessary one to prevent a future crisis. As such, although it remained on the Commission agenda, it failed to attract a great deal of attention, especially outside of the United Kingdom, and Commissioner Hill in particular.

## Reshaping the Case for Capital Markets Union as Crisis Response

The departure of the UK raised substantial questions about the future of CMU, as its primary advocate and presumed beneficiary had left. Nicholas Véron of Bruegel captured the feeling succinctly, explaining that "the capital markets union was launched as a slogan for what was really a UK feel-good project. That motivation is no longer there. The spin has now disappeared."[117] However, CMU did not disappear from the agenda. Instead, advocates of CMU attempted to use the Brexit moment to make a new case for the reform as an essential part of the EU's short- and long-term response to the shock of losing its largest capital market. In this attempted new narrative, CMU was no longer a way for Europeans to take advantage of Britain's deep capital markets, but now an essential component of the EU's post-Brexit path to stability.

## CMU as a Response to the Immediate Brexit Shock

The first subset of arguments in the broader post-Brexit case for CMU focused on the dangers of the ripple effects of the loss of Britain. One of the chief fears in the aftermath of the Brexit vote was that it would spur greater mobilization of "Exiteers" in other member states, leading to further departures from the EU. This led some in the EU to call for the Union to rein in its ambitions, for fear that centralizing projects would only further increase the mobilization of Exiteers in the EU-27. However, others saw it as a moment precisely to demonstrate the continued value and viability of the European project by embarking on ambitious integration projects. In particular, Valdis Dombrovskis, Lord Hill's successor as Commissioner for Financial Services, made this case on CMU, arguing that "In this complicated situation, when Europe is facing multiple challenges, it's important to come up with initiatives where we can show European value-added."[118] Jeroen Dijsselbloem, the President of the Eurogroup, even pitched completing banking union and CMU as a middle ground between acquiescing to disintegration and ambitious but potentially backlash-generating reforms, calling "completing the EU's banking union, establishing a capital markets union and deepening the bloc's single market . . . desirable and within reach."[119]

Beyond the general case for CMU as way to demonstrate the continued vitality of the rump EU, it also presented a way to insulate European financial markets from the shock of a hard Brexit, both by strengthening the resilience of Continental financial systems and by preventing regulatory chaos from the repatriation of European financial activity out of London. The loss of London created two interrelated dangers. The first was that European capital markets were too shallow and underdeveloped to substitute for London's deep and well-developed markets. The second was that the competition to become the "new London" for European capital markets, rival jurisdictions would engage in a regulatory competition that would at best increase market fragmentation and at worst create a destabilizing "race to the bottom" as they competed against each other to attract business.

CMU offered a solution to both problems, and advocates explicitly therefore linked completing CMU to mitigating the dangers of Brexit. Soon after the Brexit vote, Philip Lane, the Governor of the Bank of Ireland, warned that "the new longer-term UK-EU relationship will make it more difficult to rely on London as a location for euro-denominated capital markets activity"

**204 Crises and Integration in European Banking Union**

and that "fostering scale economies and harmonisation in the EU financial system [was] essential."[120] Dombrovskis at the European Commission argued that "Britain leaving the single market makes our work to build deeper capital markets in the rest of the EU more important than ever . . . There is no doubt that the EU needs deeper capital markets more than ever."[121] Luis de Guindos, Vice President of the ECB, made a call for CMU a key component of his 2018 speech at the start of Frankfurt's Finance Week in a bid to keep momentum going for CMU, arguing that "Brexit accentuates the need to develop and integrate the EUs capital markets to prepare for the likelihood that the City of London will play a reduced role in the future."[122]

In addition to a general need to establish a replacement for London's capital markets in Europe, a range of actors raised the specific fear of fragmentation out of regulatory competition. Fears were first prominently raised by Steven Maijoor, chair of ESMA, in a March 2017 speech, where he cautioned that:

> We're all aware that some London-based market participants are looking for a new location in the EU, and when making that decision, it's key that the EU-27 do not compete on supervisory or regulatory treatment. I fully understand that financial centres across the EU try to make themselves attractive to UK market participants, that they try to be efficient and fast. But what we cannot have is a situation where we embark on regulatory competition, supervisory competition, and where we undermine the robust standards of supervising.[123]

He would continue in a subsequent address to argue that completing CMU was "aimed at avoiding competition on regulatory and supervisory practices between member states, and a possible race to the bottom."[124]

These concerns were echoed by other institutions. The Commission warned that "the expected impact on the market of [the UK's decision to leave] underline the need to reflect carefully about supervisory arrangements" and proposed substantially increasing ESMA's role to engage in more direct regulation to prevent fragmentation.[125] Luis de Guindos of the ECB warned that "on the new post-Brexit reality, we could see one or more financial centres emerge in continental Europe, possibly in competition with each other" and that this new challenge "will require policies that foster the integration of EU capital markets by addressing barriers to integration and encouraging supervisory convergence."[126] Morgan Stanley's Vice Chairman for sovereigns and official institutions, Reza Moghadam, also recognized the problem, noting that "a regulatory splintering is also on the cards—with adverse implications for consistency and efficiency" and that "a unified European capital market requires a unifier," in the form of a strengthened

ESMA.[127] Uniting all of these institutional calls for a strengthened ESMA and CMU was the sense that these were essential tools to contain the short- to medium-term fallout from Brexit.

### CMU as an Opportunity for Longer-Term Stability and Performance-Boosting Reforms Post-Brexit

In addition to arguments about the utility of CMU as a response to the imme- diate shocks of Brexit, advocates also made arguments that the reform would be necessary to secure the EU's financial position in the long term without access to London. In the words of Verena Ross, the executive director of ESMA, "The arguments supporting the acceleration of the CMU have only become stronger, also in light of Brexit."[128] In general, these were arguments that already existed prior to Britain's departure, though Brexit presented an opportunity to recast them as more crucial with the loss of London.

The loss of London's capital markets deepened the EU's dependence on bank-based financing, and CMU was pitched as a way to both insulate against future banking crises and avoid dependence on capital markets outside of the Union.[129] Philip Lane of the Bank of Ireland made this argument explicitly, arguing that

> Brexit reinforces the urgency of making progress in relation to the Capital Mar- kets Union agenda. To the extent that the new longer-term UK-EU relationship will make it more difficult to rely on London as a location for euro-denominated capital markets activity, fostering scale economies and harmonization in the EU finan- cial system is essential in order to develop the deep and liquid euro-denominated markets that are required if the EU is to reap the benefits from a more balanced financial system.[130]

Vítor Constâncio, Vice President of the ECB also connected CMU with post- Brexit financial stability, arguing that "Brexit makes it more crucial that the CMU is effectively implemented and that European growth can avail itself of the services of an integrated financial system" and that "the departure of the largest nonbanking union member state is an opportunity to explore the interlinkages between capital markets union and banking union."[131]

## The Politics of Capital Markets Union

The departure of the UK changed the political dynamics around Capital Mar- kets Union. CMU before Brexit had been seen as a project chiefly driven by Britain, and that Britain would be its chief beneficiary. It therefore became unclear whether sufficient will still existed to press for CMU. As a representative of the German alternative fund managers put it, "the approach and momentum [behind the CMU] was to a large extent coming from the UK. If this is stopped, who will bring the momentum?"[132] This was not just a problem of a lack of will, but also of a lack of technical acumen. One KPMG partner cautioned that "if you want to have large capital markets, the expertise for that at the moment is in London. [Whether] you are able to replicate that in the remaining European Union with sufficient efficiency remains to be seen."[133] Axel Weber similarly opined in September 2016 that "a European capital markets union without Britain would be difficult."[134] Therefore very real questions arose in the immediate aftermath of the 2016 vote over both the will and capacity of the EU-27 to complete CMU.

Advocates of CMU quickly deployed a new set of narratives explaining how Brexit made CMU more essential, not less, though not without a shift in its focus. As German MEP Markus Ferber put it immediately after the vote, "the Capital Markets Union project should obviously go on nonetheless as it is pivotal to strengthening the internal market and has its merits independent of whether Britain is part of it or not."[135] The original vision of CMU had been of reforms to facilitate Continental Europeans' access to London financial markets and reflected a convergence to British preferences. In the wake of the UK's departure, the new purpose of the CMU became to provide reforms to buffer the EU-27 against the shock of the loss of London and to promote the development of a European alternative, or alternatives, to London's capital markets. This shift reflected not just a different functional need, but also the shifting political balance of power as Germany and especially France emerged as the key players shaping Capital Markets Union. Lord Hill warned of just such a development in the immediate aftermath of the Brexit vote, cautioning that "the City of London should brace itself for a new era where its rule book reflects Franco-German interests unchecked by 'the British voice.'"[136]

### The Member States

France in particular looked to be the main winner, and thus the key driver, of a post-Britain CMU. A report by British think tank New Financial identified France as likely to be the home of 24 percent of post-Brexit EU financial activity, with Germany the second key player at 19 percent.[137] As such, the assumption from early after the Brexit vote would be that the future of the CMU would be a more rules-intensive dirigiste approach in line with French preferences.[138] A key architect of the new vision of CMU would be Bank of France Governor François Villeroy de Galhau, who called for reconceptualizing Capital Markets Union as a more ambitious "Financing and Investment

Union."[139] Villeroy de Galhau's vision reflected French interests in several ways. Most directly, while it rejected the idea of a single city replacing London as the lone European financial center in favor of "an integrated polycentric network of financial centres, with specializations based on areas of expertise," the plan still maintained that "Paris is well qualified to become the 'market hub' of this new European constellation."[140] It also linked CMU more explicitly with banking union, a project which, as noted in Chapter 4, also helped French finance by diminishing the ability of other Europeans to raise regulatory barriers against France's massive banks.[141] Finally, the plan reflected French preferences for a centralized regulatory body, as it called for strengthening the ESMA to promote regulatory convergence around a higher common level of regulation than the original, UK-favored, deregulated CMU vision.[142]

Initially, German goals on CMU appeared congruent with this French vision. Sven Giegold, a German MEP, celebrated in the aftermath of the Brexit vote that "without the potential threat of British reluctance towards deep integration, [Valdis Dombrovskis] can now be more ambitious."[143] German priorities were seen to be more focused on protecting the Sparkassen and Landesbanken, a goal which was not fundamentally at odds with the French vision.[144] However, as time progressed and Brexit receded as an immediate threat, Franco-German conflict would come more to the fore. By early 2019, although both sides still called for progress on CMU, German desire to protect its "national champions" began to clash with France's vision of Paris, and French finance, as the hub of a post-Britain EU financial system.[145]

Outside of the Franco-German axis, a significant cluster of states still preferring the older British vision of a liberal CMU remained. By summer 2018, Denmark, Estonia, Finland, Ireland, Latvia, Lithuania, Sweden, and the Netherlands would join in what would be called "the New Hanseatic League" to promote that older liberal vision of CMU.[146] In a joint statement, the "Hansa" finance ministers argued that "the United Kingdom's decision to leave the European Union, while regrettable, must act as a catalyst to redouble our efforts in further developing and integrating EU capital markets."[147] In practice, that would mean resisting French-style integration in favor of a lighter touch approach to capital market regulation, converging around a common low standard rather than a common high standard.

### Private Actors

Private actors also made arguments linking Brexit and the need for Capital Markets Union. They also, like the member states, divided over how to proceed with Capital Markets Union, with the banks generally favoring a French-style rules-based capital markets union and nonbank financial actors pushing for a more liberal one. Given that the French vision of CMU generally defended the interests of French banks, it comes as no surprise that French banks embraced it. Frédéric Oudéa, CEO of Société Générale, urged Europeans that "in light of Brexit" they needed to "think strategically on capital markets," and use CMU to and urged the Europeans to structure reforms to play to the strengths of Europe's existing bank-dominated financial sector.[148] The Bundesverband deutscher Banken (BdB), the association of German commercial banks, similarly argued that "a strong and profitable banking sector is an absolute prerequisite," and that "it is therefore crucial to the success of capital markets union that we regulate the financial markets in a way that avoids inconsistencies and does not obstruct banks in their task of funding businesses."[149]

Other financial actors still wanted a liberal CMU that did more to shift activity away from banks and toward nonbank financial actors. Representatives of the Association for Financial Markets in Europe (AFME) expressed fear on the eve of the Brexit vote that "the lowering of financial barriers to kick start the twenty-eight-nation European Union could be tossed overboard if Britain leaves the bloc."[150] Other actors would join in emphasizing the goal of a CMU which promoted openness to global markets rather than a high-regulation protectionist vision. Axel Weber, the chairman of UBS, implored "please, please, please! Focus on making capital markets 'open' capital markets and integrating Europe into the global system," while representatives of asset management firm Prytania Group lamented that "one of the unfortunate consequences of Brexit was to remove one of these most powerful advocates for more sensible regulation from the policy equation in Europe, especially Lord Hill and the Capital Markets Union initiative."[151]

## Proposals and Outcomes

Both member states and private actors agreed on the continued need for a Capital Markets Union post-Brexit, but were divided on the overall vision for that union. In more specific terms, it is valuable to look at the specific proposals launched and what was actually accomplished. The most ambitious proposals for a post-Brexit CMU would have transformed ESMA from a watchdog over national regulators comparable to its sister organization the EBA into a direct supervisor enforcing a common rulebook comparable to the Single Supervisory Mechanism (SSM). Benoît Cœuré of the ECB

Executive Board made this comparison explicit, arguing that "truly integrated European capital markets will ultimately require a single capital markets supervisor, much in the same spirit as we have a single bank supervisor today."[152] This newly empowered ESMA would then use its authority to create common regulations and eliminate frictions that would prevent the movement of capital across borders.[153] Specifically, three sets of proposals received the lion's share of attention: proposals to harmonize listing requirements, proposals to standardize bankruptcy rules, and proposals to create a common private pensions framework.[154] Harmonizing listing requirements and standardizing bankruptcy rules would achieve two goals: removing friction for the movement of capital across the EU and blocking regulatory fragmentation from states shaping regulation with an eye toward attracting foreign business or insulating their national champions with favorable bankruptcy protections. Creating a common private pensions framework, meanwhile, was presented as a way to spur the development of deep capital pools and establish the credibility of the new EU capital markets. Efforts were also made to connect Brexit with a case for completing banking union by creating a European Deposit Insurance Scheme and a backstop to the Single Resolution Fund. Most prominently, Luis de Guindos of the ECB made the case at the Joint Conference of the European Commission and the European Central Bank on European Financial Integration and Stability that these reforms would be a key element of developing a response to Brexit and completing CMU.[155]

The actual outcomes fell short of these lofty ambitions. Some progress was made on both simples, transparent, and standardized (STS) securitization and the Pan-European Personal Pension Product.[156] However, in both cases, their ultimate reach was substantially limited in the negotiation process. The new options were layered on top of existing structures rather than actually standardizing or unifying national rules.[157] The new STS rules did not compel a standardization of existing rules for current or new assets, but rather created a new class of assets with standardized capital requirements to compete with assets still governed by national rules. Similarly, the new Pan-European Personal Pension Product rules essentially only provided provisions for more favorable taxation standards for the new reforms, as France and Germany in particular balked at deeper harmonization. Touching national discretion on bankruptcy rules, meanwhile, proved to be a line that member states were unwilling to cross. Progress on EDIS meanwhile stalled out for the same reasons it had since 2014: no consensus existed on how to treat legacy problems and sovereign debt in a unified framework.[158]

Despite the insistence that CMU was necessary to secure the EU's post-UK future, therefore, the actual outcomes were modest at best. A representative of ICI Global, the international association of regulated funds, captured the general reception among fund managers, that "many asset managers are disappointed with the final outcome of CMU, as it falls far short of creating a more open EU market for funds and their investors." AFME examined the impact of the changes, and found that, rather than developing a capital market alternative, the EU's dependence on bank lending increased in the post-Brexit period.[159]

## Explaining the Failure of CMU Reforms

The essential reason why CMU reforms failed to progress out of the Brexit Crisis is that, despite the rhetoric used by advocates of reform, the politics of CMU never truly left the realm of normal politics and entered the accelerated and streamlined policymaking of emergency politics. The threat from Brexit was real, but like the 2007–09 Crisis, not one that demanded an immediate European response to avoid the collapse of EU financial integration. The Brexit vote itself did not immediately sever the EU from London capital markets, but left the status quo intact until the outcome of negotiations which proceeded both slowly and transparently. Even a "hard Brexit" outcome from those negotiations, although challenging to European finance, would be an outcome which would be known in advance and therefore possible to prepare form.

Despite presenting a comparable threat level, Brexit produced much less reform than the Banking Crisis, a difference traceable to the endogeneity of the threat from the Banking Crisis. The European System of Financial Supervision (ESFS), most prominently the EBA, offered a way to prevent, or at least reduce the risk of, another European banking crisis by patching the flaws in the existing system which contributed to the 2007–09 crisis. Introducing an expansive Capital Markets Union could offer no such advantages, as Brexit had manifestly not been a problem of the existing capital markets architecture, and in fact capital markets had been one of the aspects of EU membership cited as a case to vote Remain. The case for completing banking union as a Brexit response was even weaker in this regard, as the dangers from Brexit were centered on capital market access, not on banking.

Without either a crisis of sufficient scale to warrant immediate action or a clear reason to think the reform would be necessary to prevent another crisis from materializing, calls for CMU simply lacked the urgency to substantially reshape the political balance of power over the reform. Instead, CMU debates remained active but not fundamentally altered. No major actors changed their minds, and no actors were excluded by being cut out by emergency decision-making processes. If anything, the project stalemated rather than attracting greater urgency, as the departure of the most powerful actor favoring a liberal CMU led to the rise of an alternative, more rules-based CMU promoted chiefly by France, with limited German support and the sharp opposition of the remaining liberal CMU advocates in the Hansa group.

What reforms did occur therefore represented the "low hanging fruit" of reforms that were broadly popular and needed no crisis to spur their enactment. Minka Lintilä, the Finnish finance minister, admitted as much, attributing the failure of further progress to the fact that "the so-called easy work has already been done."[160] Further steps to create deeper reforms would require harder compromises on issues that that divided not just the liberal and rules-based CMU advocates, but even split the coalitions themselves. Perhaps most significantly, any effort to level the playing field by standardizing rules ran up against regulatory efforts to make a specific location the "new London" of European capital markets. Those efforts relied heavily on the ability of national regulators to draft regulations which made their national markets more appealing to European and external finance than not just London, but also other EU cities. This therefore was directly incompatible with desires to promote a single common European standard. In fact, Brexit made it harder to compromise on common standards insofar as pre-Brexit the first-mover advantage of London in depth of markets and expertise meant that efforts to build a London alternative were muted by the low likelihood of success. London's departure suddenly raised the possibility that a city such as Paris, Frankfurt, or Amsterdam might really become a "new London," and none of the major contending nation-states were keen to abandon that chance. They were especially loathe to abandon that chance given that CMU was neither necessary to contain the current crisis or nor likely affect the likelihood of another "exit" crisis.

Beyond the challenge of inducing member states to abandon efforts to become the "new London," deeper progress on CMU required harder choices on matters of great domestic importance such as bankruptcy rules with each country having its own national preferences. As one analyst put, "these obstacles have their origins in national law (insolvency, collateral, securities law, etc.) as well as in market infrastructure and tax barriers."[161] Actors in other member states quickly came to see the revamped CMU proposals as a "power grab" by France, an attempt to impose French-style rules on the EU as a whole.[162] Such a play would be to the advantage of France, as it would give

**212**   Crises and Integration in European Banking Union

Paris a distinct advantage in the quest to be the "new London" by making it the major capital market which would need to adapt the least to a putative new CMU. Other member states would be less pleased with such an outcome, however, as it both would undercut their own ambitions to host financial services post-Brexit and would potentially burden them with higher adjustment costs.

In short, the challenge for reformers became that Brexit simply failed to provide a large enough threat nor an internal-enough threat to compel the hard compromises necessary to develop a true European Capital Markets Union, at least as of 2019. By 2020, Brexit would continue to be cited as a reason to advance CMU, but its salience as a crisis had already faded and of course been overtaken by the much more proximate crisis of the COVID-19 Pandemic, as discussed in Chapter 6.[163]

## Conclusion

In final evaluation, Brexit produced a negligible impact on European financial integration. The relocation of the European Banking Authority, while consequential to its employees and producing a minor economic gain for Paris, did not produce any actual change in the regulatory architecture. Relocation of euro clearing to the EU-27 did offer a minor but real change to the architecture, but the repeated delay of its implementation meant that there has been little actual impact. Proposals to create a CMU counterpart to banking union and to complete banking union through the introduction of the long-delayed European Deposit Insurance Scheme would have been fundamental changes to the financial regulatory architecture. However, in both cases the results fell well short of that standard. Progress on EDIS remained stalemated between irreconcilable visions of how to deal with legacy problems. The changes to CMU actually introduced were, as with euro clearing, minor alterations rather than a fundamental breakthrough, and reflective more of the steady march of normal politics than the kind of crisis-induced breakthrough expected by Monnet. Given the protracted nature of the Brexit negotiations and the recurring threat of a "hard Brexit," it can be hard to definitively identify an endpoint of the crisis period, though certainly by the outbreak of the COVID-19 Pandemic in spring 2020, it had faded in the face of a newer, larger, and more dangerous threat.

Brexit, of all the crisis discussed in this book, produced the fewest and least consequential reforms, an outcome which can be traced to the moderate exogenous nature of the crisis. Unlike the later COVID-19 Pandemic

Crisis, which demanded immediate action to avoid catastrophic consequences, Brexit posed only a moderate threat to the EU as a whole, and did not obviously require an immediate European-level response to contain the fallout. The impact of the loss of London could be delayed and controlled, so there was no need for an urgent reform to prevent greater damage. Capital Markets Union and EDIS might be useful, but were not essential to prevent Brexit from triggering a deeper crisis and a further break-up of the Union. The Banking Crisis, despite its similar scale, did ultimately produce a reform of greater consequence than anything out of Brexit in form of the creation of the ESFS. Here the exogeneity of the crisis plays the determinative role. The Banking Crisis could at least partially be attributed to weaknesses in the European financial regulatory architecture, and as such created an argument for a "patch-up" reform to ensure that a similar crisis did not manifest. Brexit's causes were exogenous to the financial system, and if anything, British access to the existing financial system provided one of the stronger arguments not to leave the EU. Therefore, while reforms could be cast as helping the EU better position itself for a post-UK future, it was hard to argue that even the most ambitious form of CMU or EDIS would prevent another country from choosing Exit. In short, Brexit was neither connected enough to finance in its origins to demand a patch-up reform to prevent its reoccurrence nor large enough to demand a weatherproofing response against further external shocks.

## Notes

1. Andrew Hilton, "The City and Brexit: A CSFI Survey of the Financial Services Sector's Views on Britain and the EU" (London: Centre for the Study of Financial Innovation, April 2015), https://static1.squarespace.com/static/54d620fce4b049bf4cd5be9b/t/5536a1e8e4b0eb6a74abaf16/1429643752526/CSFI+The+City+and+Brexit.pdf.
2. "EU Referendum: The Result in Maps and Charts," *BBC News*, June 2021, sec. EU Referendum, https://www.bbc.com/news/uk-politics-36616028. The most pro-Remain voting district was Gibraltar at 95.9 percent Remain, which as a tiny British enclave much closer to Spain than the rest of Britain obviously constitutes a special case.
3. Hilton, "The City and Brexit: A CSFI Survey of the Financial Services Sector's Views on Britain and the EU."
4. "HSBC: UK Should Not Quit EU Just as Services Reforms Are Coming," *CityAM*, February 2015, https://www.cityam.com/hsbc-uk-should-not-quit-eu-just-services-reforms-are-coming/.
5. David Cameron, "Prime Minister's Speech on Europe" (November 2015), https://www.gov.uk/government/speeches/prime-ministers-speech-on-europe.

## 214 Crises and Integration in European Banking Union

6. James Titcomb, "Pensions Giant: Brexit Would Be 'disaster' for UK," *The Telegraph (UK)*, March 2015, sec. Banks and Finance, https://www.telegraph.co.uk/finance/newsbysector/banksandfinance/11491572/Pensions-giant-Brexit-would-be-disaster-for-UK.html; Huw Jones, "'Brexit' Would Be Disaster for UK Financial Sector—Industry Group," *Reuters*, June 2015, sec. Business News, https://www.reuters.com/article/uk-britain-eu-referendum-idUKKCN0P92X720150629.

7. "HSBC"; Harriet Agnew, "Hedge Funds Boost Campaign to Keep Britain in the EU," *Financial Times*, November 2015, https://www.ft.com/content/d682c838-8953-11e5-90de-f44762bf9896; Fiona Reddan, "Britain's Difficulty May Once More Prove to Be Ireland's Opportunity," *The Irish Times*, accessed September 27, 2022, https://www.irishtimes.com/business/financial-services/britain-s-difficulty-may-once-more-prove-to-be-ireland-s-opportunity-1.2305649.

8. Reddan, "Britain's Difficulty May Once More Prove to Be Ireland's Opportunity."

9. Patrick Jenkins and Harriet Agnew, "What Would Brexit Mean for the City of London?," *Financial Times*, February 2016, https://www.ft.com/content/e90885d8-d3db-11e5-829b-8564e7528e54.

10. Huw van Steenis and Bruce Hamilton, "Brexit Risk a Chance for Industry to Engage in Eurozone Recovery," *Financial Times*, December 2015, https://www.ft.com/content/5ec6cb26-9daf-11e5-8ce1-f6219b685d74.

11. Jason Douglas, "Mark Carney Says Brexit Is Biggest Domestic Risk to U.K. Financial Stability," *Wall Street Journal*, March 2016, sec. Economy, http://www.wsj.com/articles/mark-carney-says-u-k-s-eu-settlement-helps-boe-achieve-its-objectives-1457433148.

12. Jonathan Lord Hill, "Lord Hill: Brexit Risks Ruling Us out of Our Best Market," *Evening Standard*, March 2016, sec. Business, https://www.standard.co.uk/business/lord-hill-brexit-risks-ruling-us-out-of-our-best-market-a3203831.html.

13. Patrick Jenkins and Caroline Binham, "Brexit Would Make UK a 'Supplicant', Says Lord Hill," *Financial Times*, November 2015, https://www.ft.com/content/bda4e522-9519-11e5-ac15-0f7f7945adba.

14. Peter Foster, "EU Referendum: Eurozone Will Make City Pay Dearly for Brexit, Warns Lord Hill," *The Telegraph*, June 2016, https://www.telegraph.co.uk/business/2016/06/15/eu-referendum-eurozone-will-make-city-pay-dearly-for-brexit-warn/.

15. Jones, "'Brexit' Would Be Disaster for UK Financial Sector—Industry Group."

16. Hilton, "The City and Brexit: A CSFI Survey of the Financial Services Sector's Views on Britain and the EU."

17. Jenkins and Agnew, "What Would Brexit Mean for the City of London?"

18. Kalaitzake, "Brexit for Finance?"

19. "Explaining the Brexit Vote; The Immigration Paradox," *The Economist* 420, no. 8998 (July 2016): 48(US)-48(US); Eric Kaufmann, "It's NOT the Economy, Stupid: Brexit as a Story of Personal Values," *British Politics and Policy at LSE* (blog), July 2016, https://blogs.lse.ac.uk/politicsandpolicy/personal-values-brexit-vote/; Agust Arnorsson and Gylfi Zoega, "On the Causes of Brexit," *European Journal of Political Economy* 55 (December 2018): 301–323, doi:10.1016/j.ejpoleco.2018.02.001.

20. Schimmelfennig, "Brexit"; Paul Taggart and Aleks Szczerbiak, "Putting Brexit into Perspective: The Effect of the Eurozone and Migration Crises and Brexit on Euroscepticism in European States," *Journal of European Public Policy* 25, no. 8 (August 2018): 1194–1214, doi:10.1080/13501763.2018.1467955; Andrew Gamble, "Taking Back Control: The

Political Implications of Brexit," *Journal of European Public Policy* 25, no. 8 (August 2018): 1215–1232, doi:10.1080/13501763.2018.1467952.

21. James Dennison and Andrew Geddes, "Brexit and the Perils of 'Europeanised' Migration," *Journal of European Public Policy* 25, no. 8 (August 2018): 1137–1153, doi:10.1080/13501763.2018.1467953.

22. Ian Bremmer, "Brexit Is the Most Significant Political Risk the World Has Experienced since the Cuban Missile Crisis.," Tweet, *Twitter*, June 2016, https://twitter.com/ianbremmer/status/746309494267875328.

23. Directorate-General for Communication (European Commission) and Jean-Claude Juncker, *State of the Union 2016* (LU: Publications Office of the European Union, 2016), https://data.europa.eu/doi/10.2775/968989.

24. Valdis Dombrovskis, "Keynote Speech of Vice-President Valdis Dombrovskis to the Economic Club of New York" (Text, April 2019), https://ec.europa.eu/commission/presscorner/detail/en/SPEECH_19_2116.

25. Krotz and Schild, "Back to the Future?"

26. Yanis Varoufakis, "A New Deal to Save Europe | by Yanis Varoufakis," *Project Syndicate*, January 2017, sec. Opinion, https://www.project-syndicate.org/commentary/new-deal-for-europe-by-yanis-varoufakis-2017-01; John Iannis Mourmouras, "Post-Brexit Effects on Global Monetary Policy and Capital Markets" (December 2016), https://www.bis.org/review/r161216g.htm.

27. Mourmouras, "John Iannis Mourmouras."

28. Isabel Schnabel, "Brexit Would Hurt Europe and Britain," *Financial Times*, June 2016, sec. Opinion, https://www.ft.com/content/d90db55a-3933-11e6-a780-b48ed7b6126f.

29. Faye Olivier, "Marine Le Pen exulte et réclame un « Frexit »," www.lemonde.fr, June 2016, https://www.proquest.com/news/docview/2673059785/abstract/678F5EEE86A141A6PQ/14. Le Pen would in fact become one of the two final candidates in 2017, capturing 33.9 percent of the vote and losing to Emmanuel Macron.

30. Directorate-General for Communication (European Commission) and Juncker, *State of the Union 2016*.

31. Ebrahim Rahbari, Tina M. Fordham, and Willem Buiter, "Who's Next? EU Political Risks After The Brexit Vote," Global Economics View (Citi Research, July 2013); Elena Holodny, "BREMMER: Brexit Is the World's Most Significant Political Risk since the Cuban Missile Crisis," *Business Insider*, accessed September 27, 2022, https://www.businessinsider.com/ian-bremmer-on-brexit-2016-6.

32. Tony Barber, "Brexit: Haunted Europe," *Financial Times*, June 2016, https://www.ft.com/content/7cf0fd82-3b80-11e6-9f2c-36b487ebd80a.

33. Joachim Wuermeling, "Joachim Wuermeling: Prospects for European Monetary Union" (October 2017), https://www.bis.org/review/r171017e.htm.

34. Varoufakis, "A New Deal to Save Europe | by Yanis Varoufakis."

35. European Central Bank, "Annual Report 2016," Annual Report (Frankfurt am Main: European Central Bank, 2017), https://www.ecb.europa.eu/pub/annual/html/ar2016.en.html.

36. Resiliency Authors, "Making the Eurozone More Resilient: What Is Needed Now and What Can Wait?" (VoxEU/CEPR, June 2016), https://cepr.org/voxeu/columns/making-eurozone-more-resilient-what-needed-now-and-what-can-wait.

## 216 Crises and Integration in European Banking Union

37. Ciaran McGrath, "'Like Cracked Nuclear Reactor!' Brussels MUST Accept UK Rules," *Express (Online)*, March 2020, sec. World, https://www.express.co.uk/news/world/1254054/eurozone-eu-news-brexit-financial-rules-free-trade.

38. Culpepper and Tesche, "Death in Veneto?"; Reuters Staff, "Italian Bank Problems Not an 'Acute Crisis'—Dijsselbloem," *Reuters*, July 2016, sec. Regulatory News—EU, https://www.reuters.com/article/eurozone-italy-banks-dijsselbloem-idUKB5N18F003.

39. Dominic O'Neill, "Western Europe: European Banking's behind-the-Scenes Activist," *Euromoney*, November 2017, sec. BANKING, https://www.euromoney.com/article/b15gbkfp0gplgb/western-europe-european-bankings-behind-the-scenes-activist.

40. Reuters Staff, "NordLB to Take Full Control of Bremer Landesbank Unit," *Reuters*, September 2016, sec. Financials, https://www.reuters.com/article/bremer-landes-ma-nord-lb-giro-idUSL8N1BD0I1.

41. Mitchell, *Saving the Market from Itself*; "Leading Banks in Europe in 2016, by Total Assets," *Bank and Credit Union Marketing Executives* (blog), accessed September 9, 2022, https://www.volksbank.hr/leading-banks-europe-2016-total-assets/; Patrick Jenkins, "No One Should Get Excited about Buying Commerzbank," *Financial Times*, October 2017, https://www.ft.com/content/ad42faa2-acdc-11e7-beba-5521c713abf4.

42. "Leading Banks in Europe in 2016, by Total Assets"; The Editorial Board, "Deutsche Bank's Retreat Was Late but Necessary," *Financial Times*, July 2019, https://www.ft.com/content/da36554a-a16d-11e9-a282-2df48f366f7d.

43. Brooks et al., "EU Health Policy in the Aftermath of COVID-19."

44. Rebecca Hansford, "AFME Welcomes European Commission's CMU Mid-Term Review | AFME," Press Release (Brussels: Association for Financial Markets in Europe, June 2017), https://www.afme.eu/News/Press-Releases/Details/afme-welcomes-european-commissions-cmu-mid-term-review.

45. Kalaitzake, "Brexit for Finance?"

46. Mario Draghi, "Introductory Statement to the Press Conference (with Q&A)," (Introductory Statement, April 2019), https://www.ecb.europa.eu/press/pressconf/2019/html/ecb.is190410~c27197866f.en.html.

47. Heike Jahberg and Carla Neuhaus, "Bafin-Chef Felix Hufeld: 'Bei den Banken liegt noch einiges im Argen,'" *Der Tagesspiegel Online*, accessed September 30, 2022, https://www.tagesspiegel.de/wirtschaft/bei-den-banken-liegt-noch-einiges-im-argen-7394413.html.

48. Mitchell, *Saving the Market from Itself*.

49. "IMF World Economic Outlook (WEO) Update, July 2016: Uncertainty in the Aftermath of the U.K. Referendum," World Economc Outlook (Washington, D.C.: International Monetary Fund, June 2016), https://www.imf.org/en/Publications/WEO/Issues/2016/12/31/Uncertainty-in-the-Aftermath-of-the-U-K.

50. Ambrose Evans-Pritchard, "Was Brexit Fear a Giant Hoax or Is This the Calm before the next Storm?," *The Telegraph*, June 2016, https://www.telegraph.co.uk/business/2016/06/29/was-brexit-fear-a-giant-hoax-or-is-this-the-calm-before-the-next/.

51. Jahberg and Neuhaus, "Bafin-Chef Felix Hufeld"; Reuters Staff, "Interview with Irish Deputy Central Bank Governor Ed Sibley," *Reuters*, September 2019, sec. Business News, https://www.reuters.com/article/us-britain-eu-ireland-banking-highlights-idUKKCN1VN202.

52. Nell Mackenzie, "MiFID Data Deluge Opens Markets to Cyber Threats," *GlobalCapital*, September 2017, sec. Regulation, https://www.globalcapital.com/article/28mtaqi51avfxp7c0yl8g/regulation/mifid-data-deluge-opens-markets-to-cyber-threats.

53. Laura Noonan, "Former Morgan Stanley President Slams Europe's Capital Markets," *Financial Times*, February 2020, https://www.ft.com/content/fff3fa58-4e65-11ea-95a0-43d18ec715f5.

54. Valdis Dombrovskis, "Speech for ESMA Conference 2017—Paris" (Speech, October 2017), https://www.esma.europa.eu/sites/default/files/library/speech_valdis_dombrovskis_esma_conference_2017_0.pdf.

55. Kalaitzake, "Brexit for Finance?"

56. Jens Weidmann, "Jens Weidmann: Hans Möller Medal Acceptance Speech" (Speech, July 2016), https://www.bis.org/review/r160707b.htm.

57. Mario Draghi, "Introductory Statement to the Press Conference (with Q&A)" (Press Conference, October 2018), https://www.ecb.europa.eu/press/pressconf/2018/html/ecb.is181025.en.html.

58. "Interview with Sabine Lautenschläger" (Deutschlandfunk, December 2018), https://www.ecb.europa.eu/press/inter/date/2018/html/ecb.in181230.en.html; Kalaitzake, "Brexit for Finance?"

59. Evans-Pritchard, "Was Brexit Fear a Giant Hoax or Is This the Calm before the next Storm?"

60. Schimmelfennig, "Brexit."

61. International Monetary Fund, *Direction of Trade Statistics (DOTS)* (Washington, D.C.: International Monetary Fund), accessed February 20, 2023, https://data.imf.org/?sk=9D6028D4-F14A-464C-A2F2-59B2CD424B85.

62. "Interview with Christine Lagarde, President of the ECB," *NOS Nieuwsuur* (NOS, December 2019), https://www.ecb.europa.eu//press/inter/date/2019/html/ecb.in191216~8014b1bae6.en.html.

63. Kenneth A. Armstrong, "Regulatory Alignment and Divergence after Brexit," *Journal of European Public Policy* 25, no. 8 (August 2018): 1099–1117, doi:10.1080/13501763.2018.1467956.

64. David Howarth and Lucia Quaglia, "Brexit and the Battle for Financial Services," *Journal of European Public Policy* 25, no. 8 (August 2018): 1118–1136, doi:10.1080/13501763.2018.1467950; Kalaitzake, "Brexit for Finance?"

65. Andreas Dombret, "We Can Work It out—or Can We? Current Challenges in Brexit Talks" (Speech, November 2017), https://www.bundesbank.de/en/press/speeches/we-can-work-it-out-or-can-we-current-challenges-in-brexit-talks-711568.

66. Panicos O. Demetriades, "There's No Point Planning for a No Deal Brexit—If We Crash out of the EU, It Would Be No Less than Absolute Chaos," *The Independent*, October 2017, sec. Voices, https://www.independent.co.uk/voices/no-deal-brexit-theresa-may-preparations-exports-eu27-germany-financial-services-a7994716.html.

67. Pierre Gramegna, "Opening Keynote Address" (Speech, May 2017).

68. Bruno Waterfield and Sam Coates, "Leave EU and We'll Make Your Lives a Misery: Juncker's Warning to Britain," *The Times (London)*, May 2016, sec. news, https://www.thetimes.co.uk/article/leave-eu-and-well-make-your-lives-a-misery-junckers-warning-to-britain-7h2k90t8g.

## 218 Crises and Integration in European Banking Union

69. "MEPs Agree Brexit Negotiation Plan," *BBC News*, April 2017, sec. UK Politics, https://www.bbc.com/news/uk-politics-39501876.
70. Reuters Staff, "Europeans Warn of Brexit Threat to UK's Crucial Bank 'Passports,'" *Reuters*, June 2016, sec. European Currency News, https://www.reuters.com/article/britain-eu-banks-passport-idUSL8N19726G.
71. François Villeroy de Galhau, "François Villeroy de Galhau: The Future of Europe—a Central Banker's View" (Speech, October 2016), https://www.bis.org/review/r161005j.htm; Lizzie Meager, "German MEP: UK Equivalence Will Be 'Poor and Burdensome,'" *International Financial Law Review*, June 2016, https://www.proquest.com/docview/1807835511/abstract/12DADDE861584450PQ/1.
72. Dombrovskis, "Keynote Speech of Vice-President Valdis Dombrovskis to the Economic Club of New York."
73. Martin Westlake, ed., *Outside the EU: Options for Britain* (Newcastle upon Tyne: Agenda Publishing, 2020); Anastasia Nesvetailova et al., "A Singapore on the Thames? Post-Brexit Deregulation in the UK" (CITYPERC Working Paper, 2017).
74. "The Art of Attracting EU Agencies," *Plus Media Solutions*, June 2017.
75. Foster, "EU Referendum."
76. Jonathan Braude, "London's Big Bang Could Go Bust," *The Deal*, March 2017, https://www.dechert.com/knowledge/onpoint/2017/3/london-s-big-bang-could-go-bust.html.
77. Olwyn Alexander, "Brexit and beyond: Assessing the Impact on Europe's Asset and Wealth Managers" (PricewaterhouseCoopers), accessed September 30, 2022, https://www.pwc.com/gx/en/industries/financial-services/publications/brexit-and-beyond.html; Luxembourg for Finance and PriceWaterhouseCoopers, "Amazonisation Is the Future of European Financial Services" (Luxembourg for Finance & PriceWaterhouse-Coopers), accessed September 30, 2022, https://www.luxembourgforfinance.com/en/news/amazonisation-is-the-future-of-european-financial-services/.
78. France 24, "France Pitches Paris as Europe's Main Financial Hub Post-Brexit," *France 24*, July 2016, sec. europe, 24, https://www.france24.com/en/20160706-valls-paris-london-europe-finance-hub-post-brexit-eu-london-banks.
79. Howarth and Quaglia, "Brexit and the Battle for Financial Services."
80. Reinold Rehberger, "Die Stärken Stärken," *Starkes Land Hessen*, October 2017.
81. Alexander Reichwein, "Classical Realism," in *The Palgrave Handbook of EU Crises*, ed. Marianne Riddervold, Jarle Trondal, and Akasemi Newsome, Palgrave Studies in European Union Politics (Cham: Springer International Publishing, 2021), 79–97, doi:10.1007/978-3-030-51791-5_4.
82. Krotz and Schild, "Back to the Future?"; Pagliari, "A Wall around Europe?"; Quaglia, "The 'Old' and 'New' Politics of Financial Services Regulation in the European Union."
83. Krotz and Schild, "Back to the Future?"
84. André Sapir, Dirk Schoenmaker, and Nicolas Véron, "Making the Best of Brexit for the EU27 Financial System," Policy Briefs (Bruegel, February 2017), https://ideas.repec.org/p/bre/polbrf/18927.html.
85. Wuermeling, "Joachim Wuermeling"; Glen Owen, "EU Chief Juncker Plots for Chancellor for Whole of Europe | Daily Mail Online," *The Daily Mail (London)*, October 2017, https://www.dailymail.co.uk/news/article-5027823/EU-chief-Juncker-plots-Chancellor-Europe.html.

86. Bryce Baschuk, Albertina Torsoli, and Hugo Miller, "EU Won't Back Trade Deal If Britain Chooses 'Singapore-on-Thames,'" *Bloomberg.com*, April 2017, https://www.bloomberg.com/news/articles/2017-04-12/eu-won-t-back-trade-deal-if-u-k-chooses-singapore-on-thames.

87. YouGov, "YouGov / Times Survey Results 20th—22nd June 2016" (YouGov, June 2016), https://d25d2506sfb94s.cloudfront.net/cumulus_uploads/document/atmwrgevvj/TimesResults_160622_EVEOFPOLL.pdf.

88. Reuters Staff, "Euro Clearing, Bank Watchdog to Leave London after Brexit—EU Official | Reuters," *Reuters*, June 2016, https://www.reuters.com/article/uk-britain-eu-banking-idUKKCN0ZE1YL.

89. "The Art of Attracting EU Agencies."

90. David Cox and Jennifer Laidlaw, "Frankfurt and Paris Favorites to Host EBA, but Smaller City May Win," *SNL Bank & Thrift Daily*, December 2016, sec. Exclusive; Geopolitics, https://www.proquest.com/docview/1853216908/citation/CCF068B6A8474C28PQ/1.

91. Scott Lavery, Sean McDaniel, and Davide Schmid, "Finance Fragmented? Frankfurt and Paris as European Financial Centres after Brexit," *Journal of European Public Policy* 26, no. 10 (2019): 1502–1520.

92. Daniel Boffey and Lisa O'Carroll, "From Slick to Risible: The Bids for London's EU Agencies Are Unveiled," *The Guardian*, August 2017, sec. World news, https://www.theguardian.com/world/2017/aug/01/slick-risible-bids-london-eu-agencies-european-council.

93. Sheryl Obejera, "EBA to Further Analyze Fintech, Shadow Banks," *S&P Global*, sec. Market Intelligence, accessed October 3, 2022, https://www.spglobal.com/marketintelligence/en/news-insights/trending/9IdDpA02VYteVr3KBWVz3w2.

94. Ruth Berschens and Andreas Kröner, "EBA Move; Bank Watchdog Waltzes Towards Vienna," *Handelsblatt Global*, September 2017, sec. Finance.

95. Peter O'Dwyer, "Ireland Hopes to Host EU Bank Stress Tester," *The Times (London)*, August 2017, sec. Ireland, https://www.thetimes.co.uk/article/ireland-hopes-to-host-eu-bank-stress-tester-rst7tdr8l; Joe Brennan, "Ireland to Contest Luxembourg's Right to Host Banking Authority," *The Irish Times*, March 2017, sec. Financial Services, https://www.irishtimes.com/business/financial-services/ireland-to-contest-luxembourg-s-right-to-host-banking-authority-1.3031163.

96. Berschens and Kröner, "EBA Move; Bank Watchdog Waltzes Towards Vienna"; Boffey and O'Carroll, "From Slick to Risible."

97. Raf Casert, "Spoils of Brexit: EU Cities Race to Get EU Agencies from UK," *The Seattle Times*, October 2017, sec. Business, https://www.seattletimes.com/business/spoils-of-brexit-eu-cities-race-to-get-eu-agencies-from-uk/; Boffey and O'Carroll, "From Slick to Risible."

98. Reuters Staff, "EU Declines to Rank Rival Bids for Agencies Leaving Britain over Brexit," *Reuters*, September 2017, sec. UK Top News, https://www.reuters.com/article/uk-britain-eu-ema-idUKKCN1C50D1.

99. Reuters Staff, "UK Should Pay for EU Bank Agency Move after Brexit- EU Lawmakers," *Reuters*, September 2017, sec. Financials, https://www.reuters.com/article/britain-eu-agencies-idUSL8N1LM3MF.

100. Jim Brunsden and Mehreen Khan, "Paris Wins Battle to Host European Banking Regulator," *Financial Times*, November 2017, https://www.ft.com/content/f9f954b4-ce19-11e7-b781-794ce08b24dc.

101. European Council, "Offers to Host the European Banking Authority (EBA)," accessed August 23, 2022, https://www.consilium.europa.eu/en/policies/relocation-london-agencies-brexit/eba/; Council of the European Union, "Offers to Host the European Medicines Agency (EMA)," accessed September 12, 2022, https://www.consilium.europa.eu/en/policies/relocation-london-agencies-brexit/ema/.

102. Reuters Staff, "Euro Clearing, Bank Watchdog to Leave London after Brexit—EU Official | Reuters."

103. "Clearing" is the process by which a third-party clearing house (a CCP) serves as a middleman between buyers and sellers for financial transactions. Using a centralized clearing house creates a more streamlined process and minimizes the risk that one party to the transaction defaults on the exchange.

104. Katie Hope, "What on Earth Is Euro Clearing—and Why Should You Care?," *BBC News*, June 2017, sec. Business, https://www.bbc.com/news/business–40258449.

105. Pagliari, "A Wall around Europe?"

106. Foster, "EU Referendum."

107. Jim Brunsden and Alex Barker, "City to Be Sidelined by Capital Markets Union Plan," *Financial Times*, June 2016, https://www.ft.com/content/d8e0de94-3e11-11e6-8716-a4a71e8140b0; France 24, "No Access to Single Market without Freedom of Movement, EU Tells Britain," *France 24*, June 2016, sec. europe, https://www.france24.com/en/20160629-no-access-single-market-without-freedom-movement-eu-tells-britain.

108. Andreas Dombret, "What Does Brexit Mean for European Banks?" (July 2016), https://www.bis.org/review/r160715b.htm; François Villeroy de Galhau, "Closing Remarks" (Speech, June 2017), https://www.banque-france.fr/en/intervention/fese-convention-europes-future-global-capital-markets-paris-thursday-22nd-june–2017.

109. Kalaitzake, "Brexit for Finance?"

110. Victoria Marklew, "Will Brexit Lead to a Financial Big Bang for the EU-27?—Foreign Policy Research Institute" (Foreign Policy Research Institute, June 2017), https://www.fpri.org/article/2017/06/will-brexit-lead-financial-big-bang-eu–27/.

111. Huw Jones, "LSE Says Splitting Euro Clearing Would Create Rump EU Market," *Reuters*, June 2017, sec. Business News, https://www.reuters.com/article/uk-eu-derivatives-clearing-idUKKBN1931NY.

112. European Union Committee, "House of Lords—Brexit: Financial Services—European Union Committee" (UK House of Lords European Union Select Committee, December 2016), https://publications.parliament.uk/pa/ld201617/ldselect/ldeucom/81/8102.htm.

113. Katharina Pausch-Homblé, "Capital Markets Union: Presidency and Parliament Reach Provisional Deal on Clearing House Rules," Press Release (Brussels: Council of the European Union, March 2019), https://www.consilium.europa.eu/en/press/press-releases/2019/03/13/capital-markets-union-presidency-and-parliament-reach-provisional-deal-on-clearing-house-rules/.

114. European Commission, "GREEN PAPER Building a Capital Markets Union," Green Paper (Brussels: European Commission, 2015), https://eur-lex.europa.eu/legal-content/EN/TXT/?uri=celex%3A52015DC0063.

Brexit and the Failure to Reform **221**

115. Ben Wright, "Vast Majority of City Would Vote for UK to Stay in EU," *The Telegraph (UK)*, April 2015, https://www.telegraph.co.uk/finance/newsbysector/banksandfinance/11550872/Vast-majority-of-City-would-vote-for-UK-to-stay-in-EU.html.

116. Mark Boleat, "Capital Markets Union Speech by Mark Boleat" (Speech, April 2016), https://news.cityoflondon.gov.uk/speech-by-mark-boleat-policy-chairman-city-of-london-corporation-at-european-capital-markets-union-conference-city-and-financial-global-london-7-april–2016/.

117. EuroWeek, "Going Gets Tough for Europe's Capital Markets Union," *GlobalCapital Securitization*, October 2019, sec. EuroWeek, https://www.globalcapital.com/securitization/article/28mtzhuukcqzvowzr3ncw/derivatives/going-gets-tough-for-europes-capital-markets-union.

118. Jim Brunsden, "Brexit Makes EU Capital Markets Union More Urgent, Says Commissioner," *Financial Times*, September 2016, https://www.ft.com/content/54944cf2-7a4d-11e6-ae24-f193b105145e.

119. Barber, "Brexit."

120. Philip R. Lane, "The Eurozone after Brexit" (Speech, October 2016), https://www.bis.org/review/r161014h.htm.

121. Louise Bowman, "Capital Markets: Has Brexit Killed CMU?," *Euromoney*, November 2016, sec. CAPITAL MARKETS, https://www.euromoney.com/article/b12kqj3tts1bg6/capital-markets-has-brexit-killed-cmu.

122. Luis de Guindos, "Promoting the Stability and Efficiency of EU Financial Markets beyond Brexit" (Speech, November 2018), https://www.bis.org/review/r181114c.htm.

123. "European Asset Management Conference 2017—Post Conference Report," Post-Conference Report (Luxembourg: Association of the Luxembourg Fund Industry (ALFI), August 2017), https://events.alfi.lu/european-asset-management-conference-2017-post-conference-report/.

124. Steven Maijoor, "Closing Keynote CMU Mid Term Review Public Hearing—Steven Maijoor" (Speech, April 2017), https://www.esma.europa.eu/document/closing-keynote-cmu-mid-term-review-public-hearing-steven-maijoor.

125. Reuters Staff, "Brexit to Shape Rethink of EU Financial Supervision," *Reuters*, March 2017, sec. Financials, https://www.reuters.com/article/eu-markets-regulations-idUSL5N1GY3ZJ.

126. Luis de Guindos, "Building the EU's Capital Markets—What Remains to Be Done" (Speech, May 2019), https://www.bis.org/review/r190523d.htm.

127. Reza Moghadam, "How a Post-Brexit Redesign Can Save the Capital Markets Union," *Financial Times*, February 2017, https://www.ft.com/content/6682da18-efb0-11e6-ba01-119a44939bb6.

128. Verena Ross, "Keynote Address: 'European Capital Markets Union—Update and Future'" (Speech, November 2018), https://www.dsw-info.de/fileadmin/Redaktion/Dokumente/PDF/International_Investors__Conference/esma35-43-1376_verena_ross_keynote_speech_international_investors_conference_2018_11_27.pdf.

129. Marklew, "Will Brexit Lead to a Financial Big Bang for the EU-27?"

130. Lane, "Philip R Lane."

131. Vítor Constâncio, "Effectiveness of Monetary Union and the Capital Markets Union" (SPeech, April 2017), https://www.bis.org/review/r170410b.htm.

132. Attracta Mooney, "Fears Grow Brexit Will Slow Capital Markets Union," *Financial Times*, July 2016, https://www.ft.com/content/bf7c5b5a-4833-11e6-8d68-72e9211e86ab.
133. Matei Rosca, "Capital Markets Union to Limp on, but London's Role One of Many Brexit Question Marks," *SNL Financial*, June 2016, sec. European Financials.
134. "Axel Weber; Markets Flying Blind, Ex-Central Banker Warns," *Handelsblatt Global*, n.d., sec. Finance.
135. Graham Bippart, "Capital Markets Upheaval: CMU Loses Leadership," *Global Capital Euroweek*, June 2016, sec. Brexit.
136. Alex Barker, "City of London Has Lost Its Voice with Brexit, Says Lord Hill," *Financial Times*, June 2016, https://www.ft.com/content/2b84027e-3b93-11e6-9f2c-36b487ebd80a.
137. Panagiotis Asimakopoulos, "Report: What Do EU Capital Markets Look like on the Other Side of Brexit?," September 2019, https://newfinancial.org/report-what-do-eu-capital-markets-look-like-on-the-other-side-of-brexit/.
138. Jeremy Warner, "Europe's Capital Markets Union Is Lost without Britain's Liberal Voice," *Daily Telegraph (London)*, May 2016, National edition, sec. Business.
139. Villeroy de Galhau, "François Villeroy de Galhau," October 2016.
140. François Villeroy de Galhau, "How to Develop a 'Financial Eurosystem' Post-Brexit" (Speech, April 2019), https://www.bis.org/review/r190405e.htm.
141. François Villeroy de Galhau, "The Challenge of Brexit: Banks' Resilience Is No Excuse for Complacency," *The Banker*, October 3016, sec. World, https://www.thebanker.com/World/Western-Europe/France/The-challenge-of-Brexit-banks-resilience-is-no-excuse-for-complacency.
142. François Villeroy de Galhau and Jens Weidmann, "Towards a Genuine Capital Markets Union: Article by F. Villeroy de Galhau et J. Weidmann," Banque de France, April 2019, https://www.banque-france.fr/en/intervention/towards-genuine-capital-markets-union-article-f-villeroy-de-galhau-et-j-weidmann.
143. Brunsden and Barker, "City to Be Sidelined by Capital Markets Union Plan."
144. Warner, "Europe's Capital Markets Union Is Lost without Britain's Liberal Voice."
145. Jeremy Weltman, "France, Germany Risk Spike Shows Core Europe Wobbling," *Euromoney*, sec. Country Risk, accessed October 18, 2022, https://www.euromoneycountryrisk.com/article/b1dn39w4zfzm37/france-germany-risk-spike-shows-core-europe-wobbling; Shawn Donnelly, "Post-Brexit Financial Services in the EU," *Journal of European Public Policy* (April 2022), doi:10.1080/13501763.2022.2061579.
146. Joe Brennan, "Ireland and Nordic-Baltic States Press Urgency of Capital Markets Plan," *The Irish Times*, July 2018, https://www.irishtimes.com/business/personal-finance/ireland-and-nordic-baltic-states-press-urgency-of-capital-markets-plan-1.3568243.
147. Finance Ministers from Denmark, Estonia, Finland, Ireland, Latvia, Lithuania, Sweden, and The Netherlands, "Shared Views of the Finance Ministers from Denmark, Estonia, Finland, Ireland, Latvia, Lithuania, Sweden, and The Netherlands about Capital Markets Union," Text (New Hanseatic League, July 2018), https://www.government.se/statements/2018/07/shared-views-of-the-finance-ministers-from-denmark-estonia-finland-ireland-latvia-lithuania-sweden-and-the-netherlands-about-capital-markets-union/.

148. Frédéric Oudéa, "Societe Generale SA at Goldman Sachs European Financials Conference," (Presentation, June 2018), https://www.societegenerale.com/sites/default/files/documents/Investisseurs/europeanfinancialsconferencesg-07062018.pdf.

149. Kerstin Altendorf, "Association of German Banks welcomes progress on capital markets union," Press Release (Berlin: Bundesverband deutscher Banken, June 2018), https://en.bankenverband.de/newsroom/press-release/association-german-banks-welcomes-progress-capital-markets-union/.

150. "Handelsblatt Exclusive; Brexit Threatens E.U. Financial Union," *Handelsblatt Global*, June 2016, sec. Finance.

151. Nell Mackenzie, "Europe Risks Losing Its Way over Brexit, Say Bank CEOs," *GlobalCapital*, May 2018, sec. Market News, https://www.globalcapital.com/article/28mtje7cf15detc44md4w/market-news/europe-risks-losing-its-way-over-brexit-say-bank-ceos; Sam Kerr, "The EU's Simple and Standard ABS Framework Is Anything But," *GlobalCapital*, May 2017, sec. Euroweek.

152. Benoît Cœuré, "European Capital Markets: Priorities and Challenges" (Dinner remarks, June 2019), https://www.ecb.europa.eu/press/key/date/2019/html/ecb.sp190625_1~49befd1908.en.html.

153. Jean Comte, "CMU's End-of-Term Report: Could Have Done Better," *GlobalCapital*, March 2019, sec. Euroweek.

154. Jorge Valero, "Leak: These Are the Five Priorities for the next Finance Commissioner," *Euractiv*, June 2019, sec. Energy & Environment, https://www.euractiv.com/section/energy-environment/news/leak-these-are-the-five-priorities-for-the-next-finance-commissioner/; Brunsden, "Brexit Makes EU Capital Markets Union More Urgent, Says Commissioner"; Cœuré, "European Capital Markets"; Directorate-General for Financial Stability, Financial Services and Capital Markets Union, "Commission Proposal for a Regulation on a Pan-European Personal Pension Product (PEPP)," Proposal for a Decision (European Commission), accessed October 18, 2022, https://finance.ec.europa.eu/publications/commission-proposal-regulation-pan-european-personal-pension-product-pepp_en.

155. Luis de Guindos, "Deepening EMU and the Implications for the International Role of the Euro" (Speech, May 2019), https://www.bis.org/review/r190517b.htm.

156. The Pan-European Personal Pension Product should not be confused with the Pandemic Emergency Purchase Programme, an entirely separate initiative used in the COVID-19 Pandemic which is also frequently abbreviated PEPP. To avoid confusion, in this text the PEPP abbreviation is only used in reference to the Pandemic Emergency Purchase Programme.

157. Comte, "CMU's End-of-Term Report: Could Have Done Better."

158. Jens Weidmann, "No Time for Complacency—Current Economic Challenges in the Euro Area" (Speech, November 2016), http://www.bis.org/review/r161109a.pdf; Andreas Dombret, "What's the State of Play in Germany's Banking Sector?" (Statement, November 2016), https://www.bis.org/review/r161116c.htm.

159. Comte, "CMU's End-of-Term Report: Could Have Done Better."

160. EuroWeek, "Going Gets Tough for Europe's Capital Markets Union."

161. Gabriel Wang, "Capital Markets Union: Blue-Sky Thinking in a Gray-Sky World | Aite-Novarica" (London: Aite Novarica, June 2017), https://aite-novarica.com/report/

capital-markets-union-blue-sky-thinking-gray-sky-world; Andrew Neil, "Europe's CMU Plan Facing Major Hurdles," *Global Investor*, June 2017.

162. Hannah Brenton, "New Powers for Europe's Watchdogs 'bad News' for Luxembourg," *Luxembourg Times*, December 2017, sec. Luxembourg, https://www.luxtimes.lu/en/luxembourg/new-powers-for-europe-s-watchdogs-bad-news-for-luxembourg-602d0d86de135b9236c3391a.

163. Stephen Morris and Owen Walker, "UBS Chairman Backs London to Remain Europe's Top Financial Centre," *Financial Times*, December 2020, https://www.ft.com/content/bdbe701d-53fa-41e6-9de3-2a49f06d31a7; Martin Sandbu, "Brexit and Covid Harden the Case for a Proper EU Financial Market," *Financial Times*, December 2020, Europe Edition edition, sec. News.

# 6
# The 2020–21 COVID Pandemic

Weatherproofing Integration and the Single Resolution
Fund Backstop

## Introduction

The COVID-19 Pandemic had a massive impact on virtually every facet of life
in the European Union, and the financial system was no exception. Although
the primary focus of the impact of the virus obviously centered on the public health infrastructure, it would have substantial impacts on the financial
system as well. In an effort to prevent massive loss of human life, especially
from cases overwhelming the public health infrastructure, countries across
Europe and the rest of the world issued stay-at-home lockdown measures to
slow transmission of the virus. The massive economic contraction from lockdown measures produced a shock comparable to the Great Depression, and
threatened a wave of loan defaults that risked bringing down an already weak
banking and financial system. Making this threat especially acute was that the
countries hardest hit in the early phase of the Pandemic, Spain and Italy, were
also among the most vulnerable to a potential sovereign default. Because of
these factors, the COVID crisis presented a threat comparable in scale to the
Debt Crisis earlier in the decade.

Because of the scale of the threat, advocates of financial sector reform saw
the potential for another "Monnet Crisis," and an opportunity to complete
banking union and push forward capital markets union.[1] This, however,
was not to be. Reforms to introduce a common European Deposit Insurance
Scheme (EDIS) or a full Capital Markets Union (CMU) failed to gain traction. Instead of fundamental reforms, the EU adopted a series of temporary
relief measures, most prominently the NextGenerationEU (NGEU) spending package. The only significant reform to the regulatory architecture would
be an acceleration of the schedule for using the European Stability Mechanism as an emergency backstop for the Single Resolution Fund (SRF). This
reform would more accurately be described as "weatherproofing" against

*Crises and Integration in European Banking Union.* Christopher Mitchell, Oxford University Press.
© Christopher Mitchell (2023). DOI: 10.1093/oso/9780198889069.003.0006

future shocks rather than a fundamental shift, as it accelerated already agreed upon actions rather than introducing a fundamental change.

The Pandemic differed from the Debt Crisis because, while it presented a severe threat, that threat was exogenous to the financial system. Efforts to use the Pandemic as a justification for longer-term reforms fell short because the crisis had not been caused by a deficiency in the regulatory architecture and no amount of financial reform would prevent another pandemic-driven crisis from emerging. The Pandemic could be used to justify one-time buffers such as NextGenerationEU and to justify reforms to insulate banks against another external shock such as the Single Resolution Fund backstop, but not more fundamental changes such as completing banking union or capital markets union. It was a crisis that happened *to* the financial system, not a crisis *of* the financial system, and as such produced only modest reforms.

# A Brief Summary of the Crisis

## The Pre-Pandemic Situation

As outlined in the previous chapters, fundamental flaws in the financial architecture of the European Union remained when COVID-19 hit Europe in earnest in March of 2020. Despite efforts to address these flaws in the wake of the Brexit Crisis, significant gaps remained in the partial banking union among the eurozone members, in particular the lack of a European Deposit Insurance Scheme and the lack of a backstop for the Single Resolution Fund. In addition, little progress had been made on the Capital Markets Union.[2] Moreover, the partial banking union itself only covered the member states in the eurozone, and not the EU members retaining their national currencies.

The two largest functional gaps in the banking union, the lack of EDIS and of a sufficient SRF backstop, had been well documented since the end of the Debt Crisis, but remained unaddressed. Debates over EDIS remained essentially as deadlocked as they had been since 2014. Northern creditor states feared that common deposit insurance would increase moral hazard by insulating southern debtor states and banks from the consequences of their actions, and would result in a "transfer union" where the creditor states would be subsidizing southern losses. As such, they continued to block movement on EDIS until southern legacy debts were dealt with first. Increasingly southern states, in particular Italy, also came to resist progress on EDIS. As the Debt Crisis faded, and after Brexit failed to trigger a substantial new shock, Italian officials increased their resistance to existing proposals for European deposit insurance, fearing that further centralization would restrict their national discretion.

The lack of an SRF backstop presented a second vulnerability, as the existing Single Resolution Fund resources of €52 billion were judged by most observers as insufficient to manage the resolution of more than a single significant institution and definitely insufficient to manage a broader wave of bank failures. As with EDIS, this vulnerability was well known. Long-term plans called for the SRF to gain the ability to automatically tap the European Stability Mechanism as a backstop if its own funds were to be depleted, but those provisions would only take effect at the beginning of 2024. Until that time, the Single Resolution Mechanism (SRM) ran the risk of being overwhelmed by even a relatively moderate wave of bank failures.

Finally, the Capital Markets Union remained largely unachieved. States expressed robust support for its creation, but attempts to translate that into specific policies quickly stalemated over reluctance to compromise on the specifics of common bankruptcy laws, common securities standards, and whether to promote a single financial hub or a more decentralized approach. As such, attempts to take concrete steps toward creating the CMU failed to take hold, despite the promise of European capital markets union to both drive economic growth and insulate the Union from banking crises by providing an alternative mechanism to provide capital and liquidity to the broader economy.

In addition to these structural weaknesses, the core vulnerability of European finance, the Doom Loop between banks and their sovereigns, which had been a primary driver of the Debt Crisis, had worsened rather than improved in recent years.[3] Rather than the expected surge in cross-border mergers and acquisitions with the introduction of banking union, crisis-stung banks largely retreated to operations in their home countries in both the north and south. This reflected in no small part the limits of the existing banking union. The Single Supervisory Mechanism (SSM) covered only some banks, meaning that banks focused on a single country, especially below a certain threshold, could still enjoy regulatory protection from their home regulators. Moreover, bank failures in Italy and Germany since the creation of the Single Resolution Mechanism demonstrated that the new mechanism failed to consistently discourage regulatory favoritism for banks in resolution. This, in turn, further encouraged banks to position themselves to be indispensable to their home states in hope of securing more favorable assistance if they ran into distress. Therefore, in the years between the creation of the banking union and the outbreak of the Pandemic, the Doom Loop had increased rather than decreased in importance.

## Phases of the Pandemic

Broadly speaking, the debates over the impact of the Pandemic on European finance may be divided into two broad periods: an early period of emergency regulatory relief in the initial weeks, followed by a debate over what reforms would be necessary for a return to normal operation. The first confirmed COVID-19 cases in Europe appeared in Italy on January 31, 2020, and the disease spread rapidly from that point. Italy would initially see the most cases, but by early March, case counts surged in Spain as well. By mid-March, cases spread rapidly across most member states.[4] At that point, confronting a rapidly spreading disease with significant fatalities, no vaccine, and no effective treatments yet developed, states around the world began turning toward lockdown measures designed to slow the disease's spread and prevent new infections from overwhelming overtaxed medical facilities. While several states had introduced quarantines for international travel or restrictions on mass gatherings in January and February, Italy became the first state to introduce severe social distancing restrictions on March 4. Other countries would soon follow. Germany introduced a general stay-at-home recommendation on March 9, and by the end of March most member states adopted requiring or at least strongly encouraging the population to remain in self-quarantine.[5]

One of the immediate consequences of this, of course, was a rapid drop in economic activity, as shops closed and consumers were actively discouraged from engaging in any but the most necessary in-person commerce. In addition to the immediate impact on retail firms, especially among small and medium-sized businesses, this posed a clear threat to banks and other lenders. The sudden contraction of profits for firms and wages for furloughed workers threatened to create a surge of nonperforming loans (NPLs) that in turn would threaten the stability of the banks. This first phase, in the early weeks of the Pandemic as lockdowns spread over Europe and the scale of the immediate contraction became clear, saw an initial surge of emergency measures primarily focused on public health, and on economic measures designed to discourage as much as possible social interaction. Within the realm of financial regulation, this period was dominated by emergency loan moratoria and other measures designed to prevent or contain the immediate economic damage of lockdowns without a focus beyond riding out the immediate surge of infections and social distancing.

As Europe entered the summer of 2020, the tenor of the debate began to shift away from immediate measures focused on establishing a lockdown and toward measures to manage the rising economic crisis. This is the period where substantial reforms of the European financial architecture received the most attention, as advocates of various reforms pitched them as necessary to withstand the current wave of the Pandemic, prepare European finance for the removal of the emergency supports, and reinforce the system against potential new waves of COVID-19 or other pandemics. Specifically, reform advocates focused on the need to complete European banking union by introducing a European Deposit Insurance Scheme and measures to strengthen the Single Supervisory Mechanism and Single Resolution Mechanism, as well as the need to create a European Capital Markets Union to enhance the resilience of finance beyond commercial banking. Some advocates, especially in the European Central Bank (ECB) and European Commission, also called for the creation of a European "bad bank" or other supports to centrally manage the anticipated surge of NPLs. Beyond finance, this period saw the creation of the NextGenerationEU mechanism to fund recovery efforts in the broader economy. However, despite the presence of a crisis striking the financial system hard, the reforms within financial regulation itself were modest. The most significant of these, an agreement to backstop the Single Resolution Fund with access to the European Stability Mechanism, would fall well short of the ambitious proposals to complete banking union and CMU.

The end of the crisis period for European banks in the Pandemic can be fairly clearly dated to July 2021, when the European Central Bank unveiled the results of its latest stress tests. These tests had been explicitly designed to evaluate the ability of banks to withstand a strain comparable to the impact of spring 2020. The results demonstrated broad resilience among the banks to do so, and were generally regarded as signifying that European finance had passed the crisis point.[6] This, therefore, can be regarded as the end of the financial crisis out of the Pandemic. While the Pandemic has persisted, and new mutations have created new surges of cases, the sense within the financial sectors has become that the crisis moment has passed. From this point on, debates on reform to the European financial architecture could be more fairly described as back in the realm of normal politics rather than the emergency moment of March 2020–June 2021. Should a resurgence of COVID-19 prompt a new financial emergency, it would more properly be considered a second crisis out of the Pandemic rather than a continuation of the initial crisis moment.

## Classification of the Crisis

### Severe

The severity of the COVID-19 Pandemic to the world in public health terms is obvious. While several other outbreaks in the twenty-first century, including SARS, MERS, and various flu outbreaks, suggested the potential for a global pandemic, COVID-19's combination of fatality, rapid spread, and global reach is truly comparable only to the 1918 Influenza Pandemic. Beyond the threat to public health, COVID-19 also presented a threat to the stability of European financial integration comparable only to the heights of the European Debt Crisis.[7]

As can be seen in Figure 6.1, the initial outbreak of COVID-19 hit France, Germany, Italy, and Spain disproportionately hard.[8] These four countries each had initial case counts comparable to the rest of the European Union combined for the first two months of the Pandemic. France, Italy, and Spain each had death totals greater than the rest of the EU combined as well, with Germany's mortality totals lower, but still substantial. From a financial stability standpoint, these were especially unfortunate cases to be hit so hard so early. Spain and Italy both were still recovering from the strain on their sovereign debt and banking systems in the Debt Crisis, while significant questions lingered over the health of both the largest German commercial banks and the broad Sparkassen sector.

Most directly, the lockdowns that quickly followed from the outbreak of the Pandemic produced a sharp reduction of economic activity virtually everywhere in the world. These restrictions impacted the global economy through both a contraction of consumer activity and a massive disruption of the global supply chain. Europe, especially Italy, as among the first regions to be hit hard and among the first to respond with lockdowns, therefore faced what ECB Vice President Luis de Guindos described as "the most severe economic downturn in recent history,"[9] and that Valdis Dombrovskis of the European Commission called "unprecedented."[10] Absent some manner of support, the lockdowns and contraction of economic activity couldn't help but impact European banks as a wave of personal and firm defaults would become all but inevitable. As with the earlier Brexit crisis, the complexity of European supply chains made the scale of the contraction difficult to predict.[11] Even the most optimistic predictions, however, envisioned substantial issues. At the most modest estimate of the impact, the European Banking Authority (EBA) warned in May 2020 that "there could be weaker banks, including those that entered the crisis with existing idiosyncratic problems or those heavily exposed to the sectors more affected by the crisis, and whose capital ratios might not suffice to weather the upcoming challenges."[12] Other observers took a much more pessimistic view. A Brookings Institute report warned that "the devastating impact of COVID-19 now threatens to reawaken the unfinished business of euro crisis."[13] By October, José Manuel Campa, the President of the EBA, took a grimmer tone than the EBA's earlier assessment,

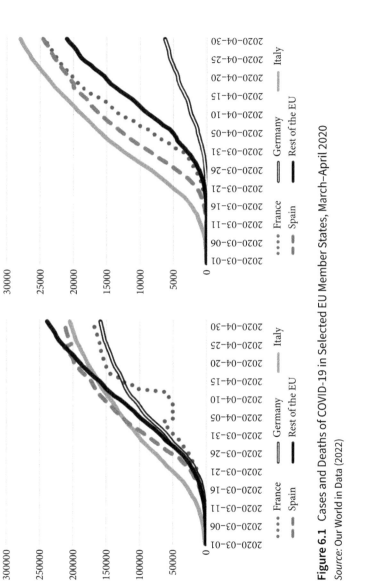

**Figure 6.1** Cases and Deaths of COVID-19 in Selected EU Member States, March–April 2020
*Source:* Our World in Data (2022)

warning that the economic and financial crisis would be on the scale of the Great Depression.[14]

Specifically within finance, the Crisis threatened to exacerbate the existing weaknesses of the European financial architecture and the legacy problems of the Banking Crisis and Debt Crisis. The waves of previous crises had left European banks in an already vulnerable position, especially the large banks with significant investment banking operations. The financial weekly GlobalCapital cautioned that BNP-Paribas appeared to be the only European investment bank not already facing significant pressures.[15] Spanish and German banks, in particular, appeared particularly vulnerable. The four largest Spanish banks were grouped by Standards & Poor as the four weakest of the top forty banks in Europe by strength of capital position at the end of 2019, with the largest, Santander, the worst of all of them.[16] Fitch, meanwhile, warned that "persistent structural weaknesses in the German banking sector [would] make it challenging for bank to maintain acceptable earnings as the disruptions from the coronavirus outbreak unfold."[17]

European banks already struggled with significant volumes of NPLs as a legacy of the Banking Crisis and Debt Crisis.[18] They were therefore ill-suited to absorb a new wave of NPLs as the economic shock of COVID deepened. Such a surge of NPLs could easily trigger a return to the wave of failures in those earlier crises.[19] The European Parliament's Directorate for Economic and Scientific Policies warned that "the dire economic consequences of the corona crisis will unavoidably bring about another wave of non-performing loans."[20] Deutsche Bank analysists similarly warned that this coming surge could "expose the cracks of an imperfect union," creating the same risks to European financial integration of those earlier crises.[21]

The crisis threatened not just the banks themselves, but the stability of European sovereigns as well through a reactivation of the same Doom Loop fears of the 2010–14 Debt Crisis. As can be seen in Figure 6.2, nonperforming loans remained a persistent problem in the European Union, especially in those countries which had been hardest hit by the Debt Crisis, and therefore had the most vulnerable public finances as well. The problem was even greater in Cyprus and Greece, which are omitted from Figure 6.2. Cyprus's 17.1 percent NPL-to-Gross Loans ratio and Greece's 36.4 percent ratio were considerably larger than even Italy and Portugal's respective 6.7 percent and 6.2 percent ratios.[22] Moreover, as illustrated in Figure 6.3, despite substantial improvement in the member states hardest hit in the Debt Crisis, member states continued to face Doom Loop concerns from banking sectors comparable in size to the entire GDP of their countries. As spelled out by Alessandro Missale, a Professor of Economics at the University of Milan, "If firms can't

The 2020–21 COVID Pandemic   233

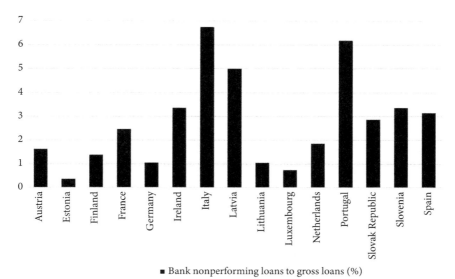

**Figure 6.2** Bank Nonperforming Loans as a Percentage of Gross Loans, Selected Eurozone States, 2019

*Source:* Mare, Bertay, and Zhou, *World Bank Global Financial Development Database*

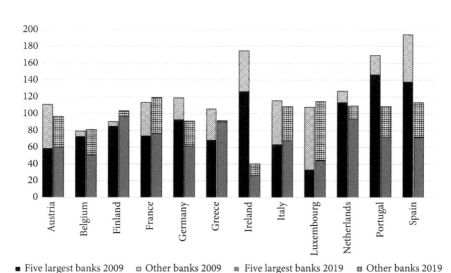

**Figure 6.3** Deposit Money Banks' Assets to GDP (%), Select Eurozone States, 2009 and 2019

*Source:* Mare, Bertay, and Zhou, *World Bank Global Financial Development Database*

repay these loans to the banks, then that debt will become government debt. That's a concern because Italian public finances are not all that sound to begin with. This raises concerns about the Doom Loop, as Italian banks already hold a lot of government debt."[23] Other large economies such as Spain and Germany faced similar concerns. This, in turn, would create a negative feedback loop. Although the Single Resolution Mechanism and the bail-in provisions of the Bank Recovery and Resolution Mechanism (BRRD) were intended to insulate states from the costs of bank failure, these were widely regarded as insufficient. In part, this reflected the small size of the Single Resolution Fund. At €52 billion, it was regarded as potentially too small to manage the failure of even one large systemically important institution.[24] In part, this also reflected concern over the operation of these mechanisms in practice. The injection of €2.5 billion of Italian state funds into Veneto Banca in 2017 and €3.6 billion of German state funds into Norddeutsche Landesbank (NordLB) in 2019 both demonstrated that states could still be on the hook for considerable sums from bank failures.[25] Therefore, the COVID-related failure of one or more significant institutions could easily balloon the deficit of even a large European economy to unsustainable levels. States that recently recovered from the Debt Crisis raised particular concerns, especially Spain and Italy, the two states first to be hit hard by the Pandemic.[26] The vulnerability of sovereign debt in turn increased the vulnerability of the banks themselves. Investors aware that sovereigns may have insufficient resources to support ailing banks would be that much readier to withdraw from potential problem banks, and in doing so increase pressure on both bank and sovereign.

Compounding these problems from within the financial sector itself was the pressure from the broader economic downturn. In addition to potentially needing to fund the resolution of failing financial institutions, states faced a more general fiscal crunch. The need to manage the sharp and deep economic downturn strained state resources, both through the activation of automatic stabilizers such as unemployment insurance and the broader social safety net, and through the introduction of new spending designed specifically to address the costs of a rapid and substantial quarantine, such as paycheck protection programs and emergency support to SMEs. At the same time, revenues declined substantially with the contraction of the real economy. Therefore, European states faced the Doom Loop pressures of the sovereign–bank nexus precisely at a period when they were least equipped to do so. By making national default a serious possibility, the Pandemic thus threatened to raise the same threats to European integration as the Debt Crisis did, pushing members into default, and thus potentially into exit from the eurozone and even the European Union itself. As that threat had been described as one of the most serious ever to strike European integration, it follows that the COVID-19 Pandemic should be accounted a problem of similar magnitude, both within the financial sector and more generally.

## Exogenous

While the scale of the threat from COVID to European financial integration was as great as that of the Debt Crisis, it differed from that earlier crisis in at least one crucial way. While the Debt Crisis clearly originated within the European financial system, the Pandemic just as clearly originated outside of the financial system. As outlined in the previous section, it did threaten to exacerbate existing vulnerabilities, but unlike with either the Banking Crisis or the Debt Crisis, this was a crisis that *happened to* the financial system, rather than one *caused by* it. At most, one could come up with some strained argument about finance-driven globalization leading to greater interconnectedness which made pandemics more likely, but such arguments found little traction and at any rate could not be laid at the feet of flaws in the European financial architecture specifically.

The consensus across private actors, think tanks, public officials, and academics was essentially uniform that this was a pure exogenous shock. A Brookings Institute analysis described it as "a classic 'exogenous shock,' for which no European country could be legitimately blamed,"[27] while banking sector analysts similarly cautioned that banks were being "hit by the virus, not their own poor practice."[28] Representatives of the European Central Bank in particular took the position that "the banks are not to be blame in the crisis, and they should be part of the solution," a sentiment expressed directly by Isabel Schnabel, and echoed by Andres Enria, Luis de Guindos, and Bundesbank President Jens Weidmann.[29] Academics would similarly agree that the exogenous origin made this crisis different from earlier ones, changing the terms of debate over how to respond.[30]

## The Perceived Window for Action

Obviously, the Pandemic was first and foremost a public health crisis, and as such, it would be expected to generate substantial discussion of reform in the public health sector. However, because of the sharp economic contraction out of lockdown and the fall in economic activity, the Pandemic also created severe strains on the European financial sector. It therefore became a crisis *in* the financial sector, even if it was not a crisis *of* the financial sector.

Because of the severe impact on European finance, in the early days of the Pandemic, the crisis was seen as an opportunity to deepen reform, one actually enhanced rather than hurt by the exogenous nature of the shock. In the eyes of the reformers, the crisis presented a moment to adopt more fundamental reforms for three key reasons: the scale of the crisis creating a need for action, the nature of the crisis highlighting structural weaknesses, and the freedom of action because moral hazard was less of an issue than in earlier crises. However, ultimately the exogenous nature of the crisis meant that the appetite for structural reform instead of short-term relief would be limited.

The scale of the crisis, especially in the early days of the Pandemic, was seen as massive and likely to grown. Multiple observers anticipated an economic shock comparable to the Great Depression.[31] Correspondingly, it followed in the eyes of many reform advocates that a response of a scale commensurate to the New Deal programs launched in response to the Depression would also be needed. Maria Joao Rodrigues and Paul Magnette at the Foundation for European Progressive Studies captured this sentiment, arguing that "Only a very bold and ambitious plan, combining urgent measures and a long-term vision as did President Roosevelt's New Deal in the US in the aftermath of the 1929 Great Crash, can rescue the European project."[32] This view was by no means confined to figures of the left. Deutsche Bank CEO Christian Sewing argued that if the banks were to "support immediate recovery and deliver the investment required to put Europe onto a sustainable growth path," it would be necessary to complete the unfinished banking union. Doing so, he argued, would free up bank capital that could fund the recovery.[33]

Sewing was far from alone in linking the recovery to the need to complete banking union. Representatives of the European Central Bank, from President Lagarde down, described the importance of addressing structural weaknesses in the European financial architecture. Lagarde herself agreed with Sewing, arguing that reform was necessary to maximize the ability of banks to contribute to the recovery.[34] Executive Board member Philip R. Lane focused on the downside risk instead, arguing that without reforms in place, banks risked becoming a problem rather than part of the solution.[35] Schnabel emphasized not only the need for fundamental regulatory change, but the fact that the crisis presented "an opportunity, in that it underlines the need to push forward banking union and capital markets union to improve the resilience of the European financial system."[36] Such attitudes were widespread outside of the ECB as well. Olaf Scholz, at the time the German Finance Minister, similarly saw it as a chance to complete the "long-awaited" European banking union.[37]

This was seen as a moment where progress would be possible precisely because of the exogeneity of the crisis. Virtually no one saw the banks or their sovereigns as to blame for the pressures of the Pandemic. Schnabel at the ECB captured the tone, arguing that the "the shock has hit all countries, out of the blue, through no fault of their own."[38] In the words of one banking sector analyst, "they [were] getting hit by the virus, not their own poor practice."[39] As Buti and Fabbrini put it, the crisis's combination of exogenous origin and asymmetrical effects created ideal conditions to build a response around European solidarity.[40] That these asymmetrical effects threatened the single currency, a common goal of all the eurozone states, only increased the potential for a solidarity-based response.[41]

This blamelessness was seen as a way to circumvent the debates that had previously paralyzed progress on EDIS in particular. Essentially, debates over EDIS had split over how to handle the moral hazard issues surrounding legacy debts. The French-led coalition of mostly southern member states, prioritizing stability over moral hazard questions, saw EDIS as a potential tool to finally move past the banking sector weaknesses of the Banking Crisis and Debt Crisis, by creating a backup mechanism to handle banks still struggling under high volumes of NPLs and Doom Loop pressures. On the other side of the debate, a German-led coalition of mostly northern states generally agreed to the need for EDIS in principle, but were reluctant to sign on to a pan-European deposit guarantee scheme (DGS) that would potentially cause their own banks to bear the costs of helping resolve southern banks' legacy problems. Doing so, it was feared, would not just put a fiscal burden on northern states and banks, but also spare the southern states and banks the responsibility of cleaning up their own mess, introducing moral hazard by allowing them to escape the costs of their earlier actions. However, action to address the Pandemic's impact on banking would create virtually no moral hazard problems. The banks were not at fault for the costs imposed by the Pandemic, and therefore a pan-European scheme to support them did not incentivize future bad behavior. A Brookings report crystalized this sentiment, arguing that because the Pandemic was a "classic exogenous shock, . . . no European country could be legitimately blamed," and thus the crisis created "a perfect opportunity" to resurrect ideas such as a Eurobond or EDIS.[42]

The advocates of action explicitly framed the window of opportunity in terms of the classic Monnet framework of crises as a spur for integration. Several of them would explicitly cite Monnet's dictum that "Europe will be forged in crises and will be the sum of the solutions adopted for those crises," including Christine Lagarde and Governor of the Bank of Spain Pablo Hernández de Cos. Both would use this as a prelude to urging their fellow Europeans not to waste the opportunity provided by the crisis.[43] Eurogroup President Pascal Donohoe would also cite Monnet, specifically his call that "people only accept change when they are faced with necessity, and only recognize necessity when a crisis is upon them."[44] In a separate speech, Lagarde would also cite Schuman's similar sentiment that Europe "will be built through concrete achievements which first create a de facto solidarity," arguing "we have been passed the baton of European integration."[45] The European Commission would follow up this rhetoric with action, proposing a series of collective responses as both superior to individual member state actions and reflective of the European need to integrate through crises.[46] All of these advocates both echoed the conventional wisdom that Europe integrates through crises, both identifying the Pandemic as a moment where change would be potentially most possible and hoping to use it to craft a narrative designed to tie crisis management to those specific, long-advocated reform items.

## Major Crisis Response Proposals

The major crisis response proposals impacting the financial sector coming out of the COVID-19 Pandemic may be broadly grouped into three categories. The first are temporary emergency measures that made no long-term impact on the financial regulatory architecture. Most prominent among these are the emergency regulatory relief in the initial weeks of the crisis and in the longer term the NextGenerationEU funding. Neither of these altered the regulatory architecture of European finance in any enduring way, but both would impact the costs faced by banks and states, and thus the debates over the necessity of regulatory architecture reforms. The second major category of proposals were the ambitious but ultimately unsuccessful calls to make fundamental changes to the regulatory architecture. These proposals, including "completing the banking union" through EDIS and an expansion of the existing SSM and SRM, the creation of CMU, and the introduction of a European Bad Bank, would have been changes comparable to the introduction of the SSM and SRM in the Debt Crisis. If only the scale of the crisis were to be considered, it would be reasonable to expect reforms of this magnitude out of the Pandemic, as indeed was reflected in the comments of reformers at the time. However, all of these reforms would in the end be passed over in favor of the third major category of reforms, the modest "weatherproofing" responses actually enacted. The most prominent of these would be an acceleration of the establishment of the ESM as the formal backstop for the SRF by several years. This was by no means an insignificant accomplishment, and not uncontroversial, as the introduction of the ESM as a backstop had been debated since the SRM's creation in 2014 without action. Like debates over CMU, promises to establish the backstop had taken on an "Augustine" quality, with states perpetually promising action, but not yet, making its completion noteworthy. However, it did not reflect a truly fundamental change in the regulatory architecture, as it merely accelerated and formalizing existing commitments, as in the absence of a formal mechanism, the ESM would likely have been tapped on an emergency basis anyway. The success of this more modest weatherproofing fix rather than the more fundamental changes can be traced to the exogenous nature of the crisis. Rather than providing a means to circumvent the moral hazard question, this exogeneity instead provided an argument for actors to resist truly fundamental reforms.

## Temporary Emergency Measures

### Emergency Regulatory Relief

The first moves deployed in the initial weeks of the Pandemic were a series of emergency relief measures adopted by private, state, and European actors. They chiefly focused on freeing up capital by tapping capital reserve "rainy day" buffers, and in doing so aimed to accomplish two goals. The first was to protect banks from the anticipated surge of nonperforming loans. The second was to encourage banks to continue to lend, and even increase lending, in order to preserve the overall health of the economy and discourage banks from a "retreat to safety," pulling back from new lending in a way that maximized the bank's own health but increased that collapse of the real economy. These measures generally consisted of actions that could be taken rapidly, with minimal input from outside actors.

The banks themselves, at the recommendation of the ECB and EBA, took direct steps to preserve their position by suspending payments of dividends. By the start of April 2020, prominent European Union institutions including BNP Paribas, Crédit Agricole, Commerzbank and Nordea Bank all suspended dividends until at least October, along with British banks HSBC, Barclays, Royal Bank of Scotland (RBS), and Standard Chartered.[47] The joint action here is significant. A single bank may be reluctant to suspend dividends, as investors and creditors may take it as a signal of distress and concern that capital buffers are insufficient. However, the joint action of a host of significant institutions provides cover for each individual, and means that market actors are more likely to read the suspension as good practice in face of an exogenous challenge rather than a signal as to an individual bank's health.

Several states also responded with individual measures in response to the Pandemic. The measure which attracted the most attention was Italy's state guarantees of its banks, both because it was one of the first such measures and because of the pressure such guarantees threatened to potentially put on Italy's sovereign debt.[48] In that, it echoed the decision of Ireland to guarantee bank debt in the Banking Crisis, a move which stabilized Irish banking but had a devastating effect on Ireland's sovereign debt-to-GDP ratio. Nevertheless, these state measure in Italy and elsewhere in March were met with support from the European Banking Authority as helping to contain the economic fallout of the Pandemic.[49]

Perhaps the most significant emergency responses came from the various European institutions. In addition to the recommendations and endorsements of private and state actions, the relevant supranational institutions adopted a range of measures designed to increase bank flexibility with a lightening of the regulatory requirements. The EBA, without a direct regulatory role, could not relax regulations directly, but did announce that the 2020 Supervisory Review and Evaluation Process, a monitoring exercise, would use modified standards to account for the Pandemic's impact.[50] The European Securities and Markets Authority (ESMA) similarly announced that it would factor in loan repayment moratoria into its expected credit losses. The ECB announced that it would postpone bank stress tests.[51] It also issued a memorandum in the early days of March 2020 urging firms to adopt remote working, flexibility, and contingency planning, and would urge banks to dip into their capital buffers to confront the crisis.[52] The European Commission in April amended bank capital rules to free up lending capacity.[53]

The initial statements from the European Central Bank suggested that they did not see the Pandemic as a substantial threat to either financial markets or sovereign debt. ECB President Christine Lagarde in particular in February 2020 expressed skepticism that the Pandemic would impact inflation, and therefore indicated that the ECB had no imminent plans to change policy in response to the threat. This contrasted sharply with her predecessor Mario Draghi's statement in the Debt Crisis that the ECB would do "whatever it takes" to preserve the currency union. Lagarde's initial statements produced a sharp reaction from market actors, who *did* see the Pandemic as a major financial crisis comparable to the Debt Crisis. Italy in particular was seen as teetering on the edge of a major sovereign debt crisis in early 2022. One analyst described it as "the perfect storm," noting that "liquidity has essentially evaporated [and], the BTP [Italian government bond] market has essentially broken today. There are basically no bids and a lot of sellers."[54] As the crisis grew, Spain quickly also came under pressure, and concerns were even raised about Germany.[55] Not only were Italy and potentially other states seen as being at risk, but the existing ECB programs, especially through the ESM, were regarded as inadequate. The Outright Monetary Transaction (OMT) bond-purchase facility, which proved crucial in the Debt Crisis, was seen as carrying too many onerous preconditions, while the ESM more generally was too unpopular politically for any leader to tap except in the most extreme situation.[56]

Given that circumstance, Lagarde and the ECB had little choice but to pivot to a much more aggressive stance.[57] This chiefly took the form of two programs: Targeted Longer-Term Refinancing Operation (TLTRO) III and the Pandemic Emergency Purchase Program (PEPP). TLTRO III was a program to increase bank lending to the economy by providing long-term credit to banks conditional on those banks passing it on to customers through loans. TLTRO III had been initially introduced in September 2019, as an extension of TLTRO I and II, which had been introduced in 2014 and 2016 as part of the ECB's Debt Crisis response. However, TLTRO III was quickly repositioned as part of the ECB's pandemic response.[58] PEPP was a temporary asset purchase program aimed at increasing liquidity in the eurozone. It was initially authorized to spend €750 billion in March 2020 on securities to prevent a collapse in asset prices. It would be expanded multiple times over 2020, reaching a total size of €1850 billion by December.[59]

These programs were directly linked to a need to save European integration by ECB officials. In contrast to her earlier ambivalence, and in a clear echo of Mario Draghi, Lagarde would assert that "Extraordinary times require extraordinary action. There are no limits to our commitment to the euro."[60] She would more broadly cast the ECB's programs as a necessary weatherproofing against further disruptions to the European economy, arguing that "we need to make sure that there is ample liquidity around in order to respond to any kind of shocks."[61] In this she was supported even by figures otherwise skeptical of deeper integration. For instance, the Wall Street Journal editorial board had generally expressed hostility toward further integration. However, they reluctantly concluded in an editorial that "The price northerners pay for refusing to make tough choices earlier is that they have little choice now but to let Ms. Lagarde try to save the euro single-handedly.

**242  Crises and Integration in European Banking Union**

They had better hope it works."[62] Market actors generally reacted positively to the developments, with the chief economist of Deutsche Bank Securities saying that "it sends a very, very strong signal to markets" and that "this is the bazooka."[63]

However, the programs soon came under criticism from both actors arguing that the ECB had exceeded its mandate, and actors arguing that it did not go far enough. Critics in the first camp focused both on the massive size of PEPP in particular and on fears that it would disproportionately favor southern economies, deviating from the principle that aid from ECB programs should be scaled to member states' contributions to ECB capital, in line with the "capital key."[64] Some of these critics pursued a challenge in the German Constitutional Court in Karlsruhe, winning an early ruling in March 2020 that the program must adhere strictly to proportionality and giving the ECB three months to rectify the issue.[65] The ECB would respond both by noting that the program's implementations were proportionate and that the European Court of Justice, which had earlier ruled that the program was acceptable, was the binding authority.[66] In this they were supported both by the Court of Justice itself, which noted that "the Court of Justice alone— which was created for that purpose by the member states—has jurisdiction to rule that an act of an EU institution is contrary to EU law," and by European Commission President Ursula von der Leyen, who agreed that "EU law has primacy over national law and that rulings of the European Court of Justice are binding on all national courts" and that "the final word on EU law is always spoken in Luxembourg. Nowhere else."[67]

The second camp of critics took the opposite tact, and argued that the problem with the ECB's bond-buying responses was that they were insufficient to the challenge. François Villeroy de Galhau, the governor of the Bank of France, celebrated the creation of the program, but also warned that "we will very probably need to go even further," given the scale of the crisis.[68] Irish financial journalist David Chance lamented that the program was insufficient to the challenges facing southern Europe, and that "Europe has a sticking plaster, but Italy is going to need a transfusion."[69] Public intellectual Marshall Auerback would similarly conclude that the program was insufficient, and that "the EU can ill afford any more baby steps if it wants the European Union to survive as a workable political construct, or the euro to survive as a viable currency."[70]

In the long run, the second camp's criticisms proved more trenchant than the first camp's. The German Constitutional Court would ultimately accept the ECB's response to its May 2020 ruling, and in May of 2021 would dismiss further challenges.[71] In part, this reflected the fact that in actual application, these programs deviated far less from the capital key than critics had feared. While initially Italy received disproportional support, in the long run, as the ECB had expected, support equalized among the member states.[72] On the other hand, ECB bond-buying alone failed to contain the pressures on the European financial system, and, as will be discussed in the rest of the chapter, further reforms were necessary out of the crisis. Lagarde herself would argue the same, maintaining that in the long run, European stability still required completing banking and capital markets union, and an increased joint fiscal capacity.[73]

## Evaluation

The ECB's emergency liquidity support programs ultimately present only a minor advance in European integration. As the European Court of Justice and ultimately even the German Constitutional Court agreed, both PEPP and TLTRO III were within the existing mandate of the European Central Bank. Although the scale of these programs, especially of PEPP, was significant, neither ultimately was a qualitative innovation. Rather, they were an extension of the ECB's existing policy toolkit, increasing the scale but not the range of activities of the central bank.[74] In Lagarde's own words, the EBC's "crisis-related measures [were] temporary, targeted, and proportionate."[75] These programs nevertheless warrant some discussion, as they helped stave off the worst economic and financial impacts of the Pandemic in the initial months.[76] As such, they both bought policymakers time to construct more long-term solutions and potentially dampened some of the appetite for those solutions by sparing Europe from the worst-case scenario of an immediate banking and sovereign debt crisis in the spring of 2020.

In evaluating the initial wave of relief, perhaps the most significant thing to note is that these were measure that essentially imposed no direct costs on either banks or states. Capital buffer reductions and other relaxing of regulatory capital reserve requirements might increase the long-term likelihood of a bank's failure, but in the short run offer a way to essentially increase the ability of banks to lend without a direct expenditure. Similarly, suspending dividend payments may hurt market confidence in the long run, but enhance a bank's available capital without a new injection of funds. The state-level guarantees offered in places like Italy presented a significant *potential* cost to the state, but not a direct one. Indeed, the offering of such guarantees can often be enough to stave off bank failure by reassuring investors, and in doing so may ultimately be less costly than not extending them depending on whether they succeed in preventing bank failures that might otherwise happen. The only genuine direct cost in this wave of assistance was the ECB's PEPP. However, since that focused on the purchase of safe assets, it was not a significant long-term risk to the Bank. Moreover, it was deployed within the existing authority of the ECB, and therefore was not an expansion of the ECB's authority or a reform of the regulatory architecture of the financial system.

It is not a coincidence that these measures had little to no direct cost, as that is precisely what made them the sort of actions that could be taken rapidly and minimal controversy, without the input of a wide range of actors. Actions that would have imposed a potential cost were considered in this initial wave, but ran into trouble and failed to come to fruition. Most prominent among these was a proposal to freeze financial contributions made by banks to the Single Resolution Fund.[77] Like relaxing capital buffers or suspending dividend payments, such a move would increase the available capital for banks without a new capital injection. As such, Bundesbank executive board member Joachim Wuermeling argued that there were "good grounds" for suspending payment into the SRF.[78] It unsurprisingly proved popular among bankers as well. Christian Ossig, the head of the Bundesverband deutscher Banken (BdB), the association of German commercial banks, argued that "it is better to let banks use the money to bulk up their capital."[79] However, such a move would also directly reduce the amount of money available to the SRF to manage any potential bank failures, at a time when critics were already concerned that the Fund was insufficient to manage a bank failure that involved a large institution or more than one medium-sized one. As such, the proposal found no support at the ECB or the SRM. Emergency relief measures would remain restricted to the "low-hanging fruit" of costless and easy-to-implement measures.

At the same time, the measures were generally taken as a qualified success, and held up as a testament to the efficacy of existing reforms. Luis de Guindos, the Vice-President of the European Central Bank, argued that "recent efforts to build a stronger banking union allowed the banks to enter this crisis with healthier starting capital and liquidity positions than they had in 2008," despite "the most severe economic downturn in recent history."[80] For some, this would be taken as evidence that existing reforms were sufficient, feeding into a crisis framing that cast the status quo in finance as sustainable and additional changes as unnecessary.[81] Therefore, the effectiveness of the structures set up after the Banking Crisis and Debt Crisis, especially the EBA and the SSM, inadvertently undercut the argument for completing those reforms.

Even the responses that did happen were not without their problems, problems which could be linked to the case for completing European banking union. The state guarantees of Italy in particular highlighted the potential restarting of Doom Loop concerns from the sovereign–bank nexus.[82]

Schnabel of the ECB here was especially critical, arguing that the move mean Europe was "once again creating a direct link between the solvency of banks and of sovereigns, when one of the aims of banking union was to decouple them." She further argued that "in that sense, this crisis represents a backward step for the banking union," one that should instead be met with a deepening of banking union and CMU.[83] With a more robust banking union, including EDIS, the Doom Loop could finally be broken, by disconnecting the solvency of banks from the solvency of their sovereigns. De Guindos concurred, arguing that an expansion of the EU's and in particular the ECB's toolkit would have enabled a better and faster response.[84]

The banks also proved reluctant to use their capital buffers. Andrea Enria, chair of the supervisory board of the ECB, noted that banks were extremely reluctant to be the first to use the buffers, for fear of sending a negative signal to markets.[85] This may also be seen in the reluctance of the American bank JP Morgan to suspend dividends for the first time in its history, as the refusal to do so would signal that it was in a superior position than its rivals.[86] In addition, the "mindboggling complexity" of European bank capital requirement rules discouraged banks from taking advantage of their buffers, for fear that they might inadvertently exceed them and tip into insolvency.[87] This, therefore, became an argument for a greater centralization of banking regulation, to produce a simpler and clearer European standard instead of the patchwork of national and supranational standards.

## NextGenerationEU

The most significant policy innovation to come out of the Pandemic was almost certainly the NextGenerationEU package. Agreed to in July 2020 and implemented the following December, NGEU created a massive €750 billion pool of money to be raised by issuing common EU debt distributed to member states in a mixture of grants and loans. Because of its mixture of common European debt and hundreds of billions of euros being transferred to member states as grants, it became popularly dubbed Europe's "Hamiltonian moment," drawing parallels to a crucial moment in the early history of the United States when the federal government established itself as a fiscal union by taking on state debts. This rhetoric was to some degree overblown, especially insofar as NGEU was an explicitly temporary program. In that sense, it was more akin to the European Financial Stability Fund (EFSF) and European Financial Stabilization Mechanism (EFSM) from the early days of the Debt Crisis, explicitly temporary programs, than the permanent European

Stability Mechanism that would succeed them. Conceivably such a program could similarly succeed NEGU, and some prominent politicians did call for such an action, including the German Green Party.[88] However, that reform did not happen before the end of the crisis period, and thus will most likely only happen in response to a future crisis.

NextGenerationEU also shared similarities with the EFSF and EFSM insofar as both essentially addressed the financial crisis in Europe by essentially throwing money at the problem, rather than driving deeper regulatory architecture reforms. NGEU arguably failed to even go as far as those earlier programs, as it lacked the rigid focus on austerity or the specific focus on finance. As such, NGEU helped provide resources to states to manage the financial crisis within the Pandemic, but did not have a significant impact on the regulatory architecture. This was highlighted by advocates of deeper financial reform, who essentially cast NGEU as an important step toward European solidarity, but one that should be cast as proof that deeper solidarity specifically within finance is both needed and possible, and not as a substitute for those reforms. Ursula von der Leyen, President of the European Commission, argued that "the historic agreement on NextGenerationEU shows the political backing that it has. We must now use this opportunity to make structural reforms in our economies and complete the Capital Markets Union and the Banking Union."[89] Paschal Donohoe, Irish Finance Minister and President of the Eurogroup, similarly argued that "Next Generation EU is providing a real boost to investment and reforms, but we have much work to do individually and collectively to move forward but Banking Union and Capital Markets Union."[90] For both, NGEU was not a substitute for deeper financial integration, but proof that more should be done to achieve that integration.

Many observers, especially in the media, saw the creation of NextGenerationEU as a major reform, and a notable step toward common European debt and even fiscal union. Buti and Fabbrini described it as potentially heralding a paradigm shift from member state-dominated "unconstrained intergovernmentalism," which dominated in earlier crises, to "constrained supranationalism," where the Commission in particular plays a key role in crisis management.[91] De la Porte and Jensen similarly saw a potential normative shift in European decision-making, especially in Germany's shift to embracing grants as an instrument and the other northern member states accepting the move.[92] Both sets of scholars, however, cautioned that the temporary nature of the program meant that it was premature to evaluate the actual long-term impact.

Regardless of the long-term influence on future policies, NGEU itself was only modest reform, both due to its temporary nature and because of its indirect impact on the European financial regulatory architecture. On the first point, NGEU was explicitly designed as an emergency program in response to extraordinary circumstances, not a standing program. Howarth and Quaglia would describe it as a "sticking plaster," rather than a fundamental reform.[93] Advocates for considering it a significant reform would focus on parallels to the EFSF and EFSM, temporary programs that proved clear precursors to the permanent ESM. Were NGEU to be similarly replaced by a permanent mechanism of common European borrowing, it undeniably would represent a major move toward fiscal union. However, as a temporary program, it presents a more modest reform, a one-off emergency program explicitly linked to an exogenous shock of a type and magnitude not seen in a century. If it remains a "one-off" emergency program, it may point the way toward greater reforms in future crises, but in itself did not transform European fiscal policies in a long-term fashion. In that sense, the more apt analogy may be to the creation of the EBA, a reform that on its own was relatively insignificant, but pointed in the direction of the creation of the more significant SSM in the next crisis. Even Buti and Fabbrini, who see the potential for a paradigm shift out of NGEU, caution that it is too early to tell for certain.[94] Tellingly, policymakers more deeply invested in the program's creation, especially in institutions such as the European Commission and the European Central Bank, expressed considerably greater skepticism on the long-term impact of NGEU than outside observers.[95] Bundesbank representatives in particular argued that pressing for a permanent common borrowing facility at the peak of the crisis was a political impossibility, and that doing so might risk a substantial surge in euroskeptic sentiment, and even potentially lead to a resurgence in movements toward member state exit from the Union.[96] These divisions led one critic to argue that describing NGEU as a "Hamiltonian moment," was "about as accurate a characterization as comparing the dabbling of a five-year-old finger painter with the works of Claude Monet."[97] By early 2023, well after the end of the crisis period in summer 2021, NGEU has yet to be replaced by a permanent facility, in sharp contrast to the implementation of ESM in the midst of the Debt Crisis. Even should a permanent facility emerge, it would not be linked to the emergency politics of the Pandemic, and would be either the product of post-pandemic normal politics or more likely a response to a future crisis shock.

The second reason to consider NGEU a modest reform in the context of the European financial sector is that it had little direct impact on the regulation of European finance. NGEU funds in some cases certainly helped shore up the banking sector, either by funding direct state support of banks or more generally easing Doom Loop concerns by increasing market confidence in the solvency of member states. However, NGEU funding was not directly connected to bank regulation or resolution, at least in its final form. As discussed in the subsequent section, initial proposals did include a direct bank support element, the Solvency Support Instrument (SSI). However, that element would be stripped out prior to passage of the package. The ESM similarly lacked a direct connection to bank supervision and resolution, though unlike NGEU, as a permanent program, the ESM's impact was at least enduring beyond the crisis period. By contract, any impact of NGEU on the financial regulatory architecture of the EU was not only indirect but temporary. NGEU may therefore eventually ultimately prove to be a precursor to more significant reforms, and did play a role in resolving the crisis, but in itself only presents a modest step toward deeper integration, especially in financial regulation.

## Common Themes

Both the emergency regulatory relief and NextGenerationEU essentially dealt with the financial crisis within the Pandemic by throwing money at it. The emergency regulatory relief did so by unlocking existing capital reserves through a relaxation of capital buffer rules. NextGenerationEU did so by issuing new debt and releasing it to member states, enabling them to support banks both directly via loan guarantees or other supports and indirectly by propping up the broader economy and reducing the supply of new non-performing loans. Neither the regulatory relief nor NGEU imposed any enduring regulatory reform on finance, either by requiring a restructuring of bank operations or by altering the regulatory architecture of the European Union or its member states. The emergency regulatory relief may be taken as proof of the efficacy of the reforms that happened previously, and NGEU may have great significance to the broader development of fiscal union. However, neither increased the regulatory harmonization or centralization of European banking, and neither created mutualization of financial risk management. Both left the structural issues contributing to the Doom Loop in place. NGEU offered temporary relief by increasing the solvency of states without addressing the underlying issues, and the emergency regulatory relief may even have increased the strain on the sovereign–bank nexus.

Both responses also proved to be effective in the short run, helping prevent the financial crisis from reaching the peaks of 2007–09 or 2010–14. As such, both may be judged a qualified success. However, the efforts of reformers to take those successes as evidence of the benefits of deepening integration

The 2020–21 COVID Pandemic **249**

would fail, and the very success of the existing measures may have undercut the case for additional reforms that would address the remaining gaps in the European regulatory architecture.

## Ambitious but Unsuccessful Proposals to Confront Nonperforming Loans: The European Bad Bank and the Solvency Support Instrument

Among the most ambitious emergency programs proposed in the Pandemic was to create a European "bad bank" to deal with the nonperforming loan problem. Essentially, this proposal called for the European Central Bank to buy NPLs from the distressed banks, allowing banks to replace assets of uncertain or dubious value with an infusion of cash, and in doing so prevent bank failure. Doing so would address head-on the core problem facing banks, by removing NLPs from their balance sheets. In the words of Yannis Stournaras, the Governor of the Bank of Greece, "The lesson from the crisis is that only with a bad bank can you quickly get rid of the NPLs."[98] Bad banks are frequently raised as a potential solution to the problem of "toxic assets," assets that are not necessarily worthless, but due to investor skittishness, lack of liquidity, or other factors hard to accurately price. While banks cannot afford to hold such assets until their true value becomes clear, the state is in a better position to do so.

In the Pandemic, European banks confronted two significant batches of such "toxic" NPLs, and a bad bank could help address both. The first batch were legacy NPLs out of the Banking Crisis and the Debt Crisis. The subprime mortgage-backed securities and complex credit derivatives at the heart of the Banking Crisis were such complex financial instruments that their true value was often only clear by the time the underlying mortgages all either defaulted or fully repaid, a process that might take years. Moreover, these assets acquired such a negative stigma in 2007–09 that any would-be buyers would favor the lowest end of any potential attempt to estimate the assets' long-term value. This was a problem for both northern and southern banks, but more acute in the south, because of the greater overall weakness of the banking systems in those states. This batch of NPLs were not directly connected to the Pandemic, and indeed proposals for a bad bank to confront these legacy problems had been floated as a solution as far back as 2017.[99] However, the Pandemic, by increasing the strain on banks, threatened to make such legacy NPLs an increasingly important problem.

**250    Crises and Integration in European Banking Union**

In addition to existing legacy NPLs, market actors and regulators anticipated a new surge of NPLs from new pandemic-related defaults. The massive economic contraction from the Pandemic would put immense pressure on firms in the real economy, especially among the SMEs. This, in turn, would result in a wave of missed payments and loan defaults, with additional uncertainly because it would be unclear which firms faced merely a gap in ability to pay but could anticipate a post-pandemic return to health and which firms were likely to not survive at all. This especially was complicated as speculation ran rampant that entire industries might be reshaped by the Pandemic, such as speculation that the movie theater business would be radically shrunken.[100]

A bad bank could solve the problem of both of these batches of NPLs. In particular, Andrea Enria, chairman of the ECB Supervisory Board, warned that suspension of dividends and emergency regulatory relief may prove insufficient, and the Pandemic would "require more forceful action such as the creation of a bad bank."[101] Enria had been advocating for a bad bank since 2017, and therefore clearly saw the Pandemic as the kind of crisis that could be used as a window of opportunity to advance a favored policy. In this he found several allies, including in the Bank of Greece and among some bankers and analysts. Moody's opined that "The option of a bad bank would be positive for European banks as it could involve some degree of government support if necessary, which would help banks protect their solvency and possibly avoid bankruptcies," while Deutsche Bank analysists saw a potential for the crisis to "be the catalyst for more European financial solidarity."[102]

However, even within the European Central Bank, Enria's proposal found an ambivalent reception. Luis de Guindos, the ECB's Vice President, argued that discussion of a bad bank was "premature" until banking union was completed with the introduction of EDIS.[103] Other actors were more emphatic in shutting down discussion. A European Commission spokesman argued that debates over a bad bank were limited to press reports, and that the Commission would not consider such a proposal.[104] Joachim Wuermling at the Bundesbank more emphatically argued that "the essence of this proposal is three years old, and there were good reasons for not pursuing it at the time."[105] Economists argued that a bad bank would be inefficient at best and ineffective at worst, and inferior to direct capital injections.[106]

While elements within the ECB focused on a bad bank as a way to manage an impending wave of NPLs, the European Commission launched its own ultimately unsuccessful proposals to deal with the problem, the Solvency Support Instrument (SSI). While the bad bank aimed to contain the damage done by NPLs by creating a mechanism to get them off bank balance sheets once the borrowers defaulted, the SSI aimed to limit the creation of NPLs in the first place, though generous capital infusions into firms that would otherwise fail in the Pandemic. Introduced as part of the initial NGEU proposal, the SSI was designed to incentivize private equity support to firms impacted by the Pandemic through between €26 billion and €75 billion in loan guarantees administered through the European Investment Bank (EIB).[107] By doing so, the Commission hoped to produce €300 billion in private support to firms, which would stave off default and a surge of NPLs.[108] Such support would in particular be targeted at firms in the member states hardest hit by the Pandemic, and also include requirements that firms receiving support produce green transition plans to reduce their carbon footprint.[109]

The proposal soon came under criticism, both because of its centralization of funding and cost. Opponents questioned why such state aid should be centralized through the EIB rather than leaving the decisions up to individual member states.[110] The "frugal four" countries, Denmark, Sweden, Austria, and the Netherlands, also raised concerns about the overall cost of NGEU.[111] Faced with these twin arguments against, and hoping for a rapid passage of the broader NGEU package, the Commission opted to drop the SSI proposal, as a way to both reduce centralization and the overall price tag in one move.

Following the failure of the SSI initiative, Enria attempted to renew interest in the idea of a European bad bank in November 2020, amid discussions around the removal of the emergency relief measures.[112] This time, he attracted a more sympathetic audience in the European Commission, its own attempt to deal with NPLs through the SSI having fallen short. The Commission agreed that "it [was] imperative to address any renewed buildup of NPLs on banks' balance sheets as early as possible," though it fell short of fully endorsing a bad bank proposal.[113] Nevertheless, the bad bank proposal still failed to gain significant traction, and a formal proposal was never developed.

## Discussion

Despite proposals to deal with NPLs through a centralized European mechanism failing to gain much traction as policy proposals, they remain worthy of examination. On the surface, the bad bank appears to be the kind of proposal that would attract significant support in a crisis, as it offered a solution to a serious threat that both could be rapidly implemented and would clearly contain the NPL problem. While bad banks frequently raise moral hazard issues, this arguably would be less of an issue in a pandemic context, when especially the new surge of NPLs created a challenge that few observers thought

## 252   Crises and Integration in European Banking Union

the banks should have anticipated. Nevertheless, there was little support for such a reform, especially one that would focus as much on cleaning up legacy problems as dealing with the new surge.

The SSI sidestepped the legacy problems issue by focusing instead on containing the creation of new NPLs, but ran into opposition for going further toward centralization than needed to address the crisis by introducing the EIB, rather than member states, as the actor determining the allocation of loan guarantees and support. In the Debt Crisis, the Troika had justified its intrusion into the fiscal policies of member states through a narrative that cast the southern states as victims of their own profligacy and mismanagement. The exogenous nature of the Pandemic meant that, while some member states were harder hit than others, that was essentially due to unfortunate chance rather than policy failures. As such, the argument in favor of centralizing disbursement of support through the EIB rather than simply giving money to states to distribute could not be connected to the crisis at hand. As such, opponents of centralization and those worried about the size of NGEU could both unite against the SSI as an expensive and unnecessary concentration of power at the EU level.

Once the anticipated surge of new NPLs failed to materialize, the already limited support for the bad bank and the SSI faded. Emergency regulatory measures such as loan moratoria blunted the initial surge of NPLs, and NGEU transfers to the member states provided sufficient measures to supports SMEs and banks without a transfer of authority or funding to the EIB or ECB. Such measures better suited the nature of the crisis as one that required weatherproofing measures rather than deeper structural fixes. As such, both proposals to deal with NPLs directly failed to win support and were dropped.

## Completing Banking Union: The European Deposit Insurance Scheme and Capital Markets Union

While proposals for a European bad bank and a Solvency Support Instrument would have created more immediate up-front fiscal transfers, the most ambitious proposals for regulatory architecture reform out of the Pandemic came in a renewed push to "complete the banking union" by finally creating a European Deposit Insurance Scheme and a Capital Markets Union. Per the classic Monnet logic of integration through crises, this would appear to be a prime moment to advance this reform agenda. An existing and long-desired integration reform existed, along with a broad coalition of supranational, national, and subnational actors to promote it, fulfilling Kingdon's "policy" stream.[114] The COVID-19 Pandemic posed a great threat to Europe as a whole, and specifically to the European financial system, providing a "problem" stream. Finally, the crisis created a moment of enhanced European solidarity and a heightened sense of urgency, seemingly creating the "political" stream creating a space for deeper integration. This was certainly the expectation of a large range of actors.[115] However, the crisis produced no significant movement on either EDIS or CMU despite these seemingly ideal conditions for reform. The exogenous nature of the crisis, while cast by some actors as a positive, proved instead to be a barrier to reform, as the pro-reform narrative could not convince recalcitrant opponents that the Pandemic truly demonstrated a need for either EDIS or CMU.

Certainly, few actors would argue that banking union was "complete." The system at the dawn of the Pandemic presented significant gaps, even within the existing institutions. The SSM's direct reach still only extended to the largest banks, while the complicated politics around bank failures in a number of countries demonstrated persisting issues in bank resolution despite the SRM.[116] However, neither of these gaps were the chief focus of reformers in the crisis. Rather, most of their efforts focused on promoting the missing "third pillar" of banking union, the European Deposit Insurance Scheme, and on creating a European Capital Markets Union.

On the eve of the Pandemic in early 2020, debates on both reforms had stalled out. EDIS negotiations remained essentially where they had been since the end of the Debt Crisis, stuck on the question of whether EDIS should be seen as a tool for fixing current problems or limited to only potential future issues. Southern member states and their banks favored an expansive EDIS that would supersede national deposit guarantee schemes and become active imminently, meaning it could serve as a tool to help remedy the legacy problems of the Banking Crisis and Debt Crisis, including persisting NPLs and high volumes of sovereign debt on bank balance sheets. Northern member states, on the other hand, generally conceded the value of EDIS in principle, while focusing on the potential moral hazard of guaranteeing deposits at banks with persisting legacy problems. They therefore argued that any European deposit insurance scheme could only become active after those legacy issues were cleaned up, and moreover even then favored a reinsurance scheme, where EDIS would only come into play after national deposit guarantee schemes were exhausted. Northern banks, especially smaller banks, generally opposed EDIS altogether. They generally already had national and private DGS that faced little danger and therefore saw EDIS primarily as a mechanism to lead to them potentially paying to insure banks in other countries.

254    Crises and Integration in European Banking Union

Debates on CMU, as discussed in Chapter 5, focused less on conceptual questions over its purpose or design than on the specific terms. Most significant actors agreed that larger and better developed capital markets would offer an extra layer of protection for European finance, by providing an alternative nonbank channel of access to equity and liquidity to firms, and that the surest route to do so would be through reforms that made cross-border capital markets easier to develop. Some division existed over which cities would be best as the center of European capital markets following the loss of the City of London in Brexit. However, the chief barrier to action was more a combination of debates over whose standards to move to and a lack of urgency that encouraged all parties to resist movement and wait the other side out. Most major actors conceded the desirability of CMU in practice, but few put it at the top of their agenda, and instead focused much more energy on other potential reforms, including EDIS.

## The Coalition for Action

A wide range of actors saw the Pandemic as a moment to complete banking union. Most of the supranational actors at the EU level endorsed a move to banking union. Luis de Guindos of the ECB argued as early as April 2020 that completing banking union was a necessary part of making the euro area "more resilient" in response to the Pandemic.[117] Creating CMU and EDIS would, he argued, help contain the damage of the Pandemic because it would "help ensure access to funding for a wide range of firms, support a level playing field, and counter fragmentation along the path to recovery."[118] This call would be echoed by other ECB representatives throughout the summer of 2020. ECB Executive Board member Isabel Schnabel would argue in August that "completion of the European Banking Union, as well as the advancement of the capital markets union . . . have become ever more important in response to the coronavirus (COVID-19) pandemic."[119] The linking of pandemic responses to completing banking union by the ECB would reach all the way to Christine Lagarde, President of the ECB, who would explicitly cite Monnet's quote on Europe being forged in crisis in a September 2020 speech at the Franco-German Parliamentary Assembly. In that speech, she argued that COVID-19 was "a crisis of unprecedented magnitude," which Europe must respond to by "[removing] all obstacles to the development of a cross-border market for sustainable financial products. In other words, we need to finally complete the banking union and create a genuine capital markets union."[120]

While the ECB took the initial lead in promoting EDIS and CMU in response to the Pandemic, the message was soon echoed by the other major European Union institutions. The same month that Lagarde explicitly argued for treating the Pandemic as a "Monnet Crisis," Ursula von der Leyen, President of the European Commission, would make a similar argument. In her 2020 State of the Union address, von der Leyen argued for "using this opportunity to make structural reforms," especially in completing banking union and CMU.[121] By November, the European Council, would join these public calls for reform. At the annual EU Ambassadors' conference, Charles Michel, the President of the Council, would argue that "the priority is to complete the banking union and then create a fully fledged capital markets union."[122] Two weeks later, the Managing Director of the International Monetary Fund (IMF), Kristalina Georgieva, would also urge the EU to use the crisis to spur action, arguing that "now is a good moment to advance financial sector architecture reforms, close gaps in the crisis management framework, especially important to make progress in completing the banking union."[123]

National actors would also take up the call for completing banking union in response to the Pandemic, especially among the national central banks. Hernandez de Cos of the Bank of Spain, embraced using the moment of international cooperation in the Pandemic to improve the financial architecture of the eurozone through completion of banking union.[124] Representatives of the Bank of Portugal and Central Bank of Ireland would make similar calls in late 2020.[125] Banque de France Governor François Villeroy de Galhau would make perhaps the most forceful embrace of reform among the national central bankers, arguing that "We must never give up on the goal of a genuine Banking Union, despite protectionist resistance from 'host' countries."[126] Calls among elected officials were somewhat rarer, though Irish Finance Minister and President of the Eurogroup Paschal Donohoe would argue in January 2021 that "I have the firm intention to capitalise on the cooperative spirit that prevailed throughout 2020 to make good progress on the completion of the banking union. And that includes the pursuit of the European Deposit Insurance Scheme."[127]

Finally, proposals for completing banking union received considerable support among private actors. From early in the crisis, the European Banking Federation (EBF) argued that Capital Markets Union in particular should be a cornerstone of the response to the Pandemic. In May of 2020, just two months into the Pandemic hitting Europe in force, the EBF "[called] on the European Commission to continue its push for a Capital Markets Union which will be crucial in the recovery phase for relaunching the European economy."[128] The Association for Financial Markets in Europe (AFME) also

**256  Crises and Integration in European Banking Union**

strongly argued that CMU in particular should be an essential part of the part of the response, seeing it as essential to break the sovereign/bank nexus and to ensure long-term stability out of the Pandemic.[129] Multiple European banks also called for action on completing banking union, especially among the southern member states. Of these, the most prominent was Santander, whose chairwoman, Ana Botín, argued that European deposit insurance in particular would be necessary to resolve the issues raised by the Pandemic.[130]

## Arguments for Action Now

The arguments for reform now by this coalition of actors fell broadly into three overlapping categories. The first were arguments that completing banking union would address the immediate strains on the European financial system, either independent of or in concert with the Next Generation EU reforms. The second set of arguments cast the reforms as a necessary part of the recovery process, while the third set cast the reforms as part of the "weatherproofing" efforts in preparation for the next crisis to batter European finance. What all of these arguments had in common was an attempt to cast completing banking union as not just desirable, but an essential way to respond to the specific challenges and failings highlighted by the Pandemic. Broadly speaking, the three arguments were deployed chronologically, as each spoke to a different moment of the crisis, and each took a somewhat different approach in making the argument that completing banking union was an essential part of the reform process.

The first of these arguments, regulatory architecture reform as an essential part of the immediate crisis response, echoed how the reforms of the SSM and SRM were cast as an essential part of crisis management in the Debt Crisis. Isabel Schnabel captured the tenor of these arguments in arguing that crisis response required new policies beyond the existing toolkit, arguing that "solutions to the underlying structural causes go beyond the remit of monetary policy." Specifically, this more effective response "would require the completion of the European Banking Union, as well as the advancement of the capital markets union, which have become ever more important in response to the coronavirus (COVID-19) pandemic."[131] In particular, reformers raised concern that the fiscal response to the Pandemic by the member states, largely funded through borrowing, would increase pressure on the sovereign–bank nexus, and in doing so would raise questions as to the sustainability of national DGS. Introducing EDIS would separate questions of DGS sustainability from sovereign debt, and thus avoid a scenario where state spending in response to the real economy crisis inadvertently created a banking panic. S&P Global analysts warned of this tightening of the sovereign–bank nexus as early as summer 2020.[132] Bank of Portugal Director Anna Paula Serra similarly questioned in November 2020 "whether the existing crisis framework is sufficient to properly deal with bank failures in a systemic scenario" in the absence of EDIS.[133]

Schnabel attempted to directly link the pressures from the Pandemic to the need for immediate regulatory architecture reform in January 2021, warning that "the pandemic has once again exposed old vulnerabilities," and that "the policy response to the pandemic has visibly intensified the interdependencies between sovereigns, banks and firms." She continued that these "interlinkages between banks, sovereigns and corporates, which were crucial for stabilising the economic and financial situation during the pandemic, could turn into a vicious circle, giving rise to destabilising feedback loops and that "these vulnerabilities are a reminder of the urgent need to make further progress on reforming the euro area's institutional architecture, in particular by completing the Banking Union, advancing the Capital Markets Union and reviewing the European fiscal framework."[134]

Luis de Guindos echoed both this diagnosis and cure, arguing that "so long as deposit insurance remains at the national level, the link between a bank and its home sovereign persists," and that only EDIS with full risk-sharing could break that link.[135] Eurogroup President Paschal Donohoe similarly made the case that EDIS was necessary to "to break the link between banks and sovereigns."[136] Bruno Le Maire, the French Minister of the Economy and Finance, would also connect reforms to the development of biomedical technologies to address COVID, arguing that "the development of coronavirus vaccines requiring billions of euros of investment, shows us the extent to which innovation needs deep capital markets," which could best be provided by introducing CMU.[137]

From the beginning of the Pandemic, reform advocates also emphasized the second argument, that EDIS and CMU would play an essential role in driving the economic recovery, and that failing to implement them would potentially fatally undercut that recovery. However, as the initial shock of lockdowns in spring 2020 passed, this increasingly became the primary argument reformers deployed. A weaker version of this argument cast the crisis as a chance to implement useful reforms, as when Financial Times columnist Martin Sandbu argued the crisis was "an opportunity to force business activity to shift from credit to equity financing," or when Jonás Fernandez, the spokesman for the Socialists & Democrats in the European Parliament argued that CMU "can play an important role in relaunching the

**258 Crises and Integration in European Banking Union**

weakened post-COVID-19 economy."[138] Most advocates went further, however, attempting to make the case that the recovery would not just benefit from reforms, but that reforms were vital to making sure there was a recovery. European Banking Federation (EBF) President Jean Pierre Mustier argued as early as May 2020 that CMU "will be crucial in the recovery phase for relaunching the European economy."[139] By fall 2020, the Eurogroup would argue that completing banking union would be "key to financing the recovery," and the ECB would assert that "at this point a single EU capital market is no longer something that is 'nice to have' but that we 'need to have.'"[140]

Advocates of the essential role of completing banking union and CMU specifically focused on the danger of an uneven recovery without reform. The Central Bank of Ireland foresaw the European Union trapped in a "halfway house" of "uncertainty, disruption and differing sectoral effects" without a completed banking union.[141] ECB representatives focused on the danger of a "two-speed recovery" across countries, not just sectors, without reform.[142] COVID-19 presented two interrelated risks that could fuel divergence among the European economies. The first was that the impact of the Pandemic, especially in the early months, was unevenly felt across the member states. The second was that states had varying fiscal resources to pay for their response. In some cases, these two factors were felt in tandem, as Spain and Italy were both among the hardest hit and the least able to mount a large-scale response funded through sovereign borrowing. Central bankers were acutely aware of the danger posed by both risks.[143] ECB Vice President Luis de Guindos therefore argued that banking union and CMU were essential, as they would "help limit the risk of growing asymmetries among euro area countries in the recovery from the COVID-19 shock."[144]

By late 2020, advocates of reform started to rely on the third argument, calling for the reforms not just to survive and recover from the current pandemic, but to ensure that the system would be capable of surviving future comparable shocks. As with the earlier arguments, these attempts to link completing banking union to the need to weatherproof against future crisis were made by a range of actors. The ECB was the first to deploy them, with Christine Lagarde asserting in September 2020 that the reforms would "ensure that Europe is better protected in the world of tomorrow," and Luis de Guindos in November similarly maintaining that "we need to . . . secure an even better and more resilient future" and that the Pandemic revealed "vulnerabilities [which] remind us that we cannot afford to be complacent."[145] Eurogroup actors would also take up this thread, with Pascal Donohoe asserting that the long-advocated reforms were "critical," while private actors in the Association for Financial Markets in Europe would similarly argue that "it is necessary to promote a highly integrated, resilient, competitive and profitable European banking sector to support growth and ensure long-term stability."[146]

## The Failure to Link Regulatory Architecture Reforms to Crisis Recovery

The strategies deployed by reformers echoed those used successfully in the Debt Crisis. As in that earlier crisis, reformers saw in the Pandemic a crisis of sufficient scale to produce a disruption of the status quo and create a window of opportunity to advance desired reforms. To that end, they crafted a narrative casting those reforms as directly addressing the issues raised by the crisis, and therefore essential to surviving the crisis, ensuring a post-crisis recovery, and "future-proofing" against future crises. However, this time the strategy failed to work. While the Pandemic presented a crisis of similar scale, the exogenous nature of it made it harder for reform advocates to link crisis management and reform, and easier for status quo advocates to reject that putative link. As such, the reformers failed to win over enough support to change the balance of power which left reform efforts deadlocked for most of the preceding decade. The reform coalition was broad, but essentially the same one which had failed to advance EDIS or CMU out of the Debt Crisis or the Brexit Crisis. While arguments for the SSM and SRM won over new supporters in the Debt Crisis, this time the arguments failed to convince new supporters.

The key difference this time in contrast to the Debt Crisis was that the exogenous nature of the crisis meant that opponents of reform could more easily reject the causal link between crisis and lack of reform. The refrain adopted by the ECB and European Commission that "this time the banks are part of the solution, not the problem" explicitly rejected moral hazard as a concern in the face of a shock that no bank or regulator could reasonably be held accountable for or expected to have anticipated. This framing justified emergency regulatory relief and the open-ended fiscal support of NGEU. It also existed in tension with the narrative deployed by banking union reform advocates, which cast banks as vulnerable, burdened with legacy problems, and a prime source of instability. Efforts to argue that EDIS and CMU were also essential reform efforts therefore fell flat, given that the general narrative coming out of the exogenous shock had already established the blamelessness of banks and the regulatory architecture in the crisis. A prime example here may be the position of Nicolas Véron, a senior fellow at the think tank Bruegel. Véron had been one of the key advocates of banking union as a

**260** Crises and Integration in European Banking Union

necessary response to regulatory architecture failings in the Debt Crisis, and his early advocacy had played a crucial role in shaping a broader understanding of supervisory and resolution integration as essential to resolving the Debt Crisis.[147] This time, however, Véron took a more skeptical view of the need for further integration, arguing that he "[did] not see a direct mechanical link between [NGEU] and banking union."[148]

Some actors went even further, arguing that reform of the European financial architecture was not only unnecessary, but potentially actively harmful to crisis management. Even some advocates of completing banking union in the long run argued that it should not be considered until the immediate crisis management phase passed. Mario Ceneto, Governor of the Bank of Portugal, noted that efforts on banking union were "halted by the immediate response to the COVID-19 crisis," implicitly conceding that deepening banking union was not itself a crucial part of the crisis response, but rather a less immediately essential longer-term objective.[149] Spain's Economics Minister, Nadia Calviño, similarly conceded that EDIS had been regarded as a less essential reform, with "all energy" focused on other crisis mitigation policies.[150]

Groups already opposed to the reforms before the Pandemic even cast EDIS in particular as potentially harmful to crisis management and recovery. Finance Finland, the trade association of Finnish banks, warned that deepening banking union would add an "additional burden" on Finnish banks, and that "if risk-sharing and regulatory burden are further increased, it will slow down economic recovery in Finland." Instead, the managing director of Finance Finland, Pilia-Noora Kauppi reiterated the pre-Pandemic argument that EDIS couldn't proceed until legacy issues were resolved, and that "risk-sharing must have clearly defined boundaries, or else we risk spreading moral hazard."[151] The German savings banks, another bloc hostile to EDIS prior to the crisis, similarly cautioned that introducing EDIS could create more problems than it would solve. Karl-Peter Schackmann-Fallis, a member of the German Savings Bank Association (DSGV) Executive Board argued that "the trust of depositors must not be compromised by challenging the entire legal framework that is currently in place."[152] This call was echoed by the German Banking Industry Committee (GBIC), the umbrella organization for all the German banking pillars, which argued that "it makes no sense for the EU Commission to link the discussion on strengthening crisis management with its unchanged proposal of 2015 for establishing a European Deposit Insurance Scheme."[153]

The key difference between the initial introduction of banking union in the Debt Crisis and the attempts to "complete" it in the Pandemic therefore hinged on whether the causes of the crisis could be traced to an existing flaw in European banking. That the European regulatory architecture remained flawed was not disputed, but while the Pandemic strained European finance, those strains were external in origin and not linked to those regulatory flaws. This external threat therefore made moral hazard concerns moot, enabling the deployment of policies which essentially "threw money at the problem," including regulatory relief and NGEU's generous fiscal support. The "throw money at the problem" solution was viable here but not in the Debt Crisis for both backward-looking and forward-looking reasons. The lack of moral hazard meant that such support ran no risk of rewarding past behavior, a concern of the northern member states in particular. Perhaps even more importantly, the external nature of the crisis meant that regulatory architecture reform, while potentially advantageous in managing future exogenous shocks, not only was not necessary to prevent future crises, but could not prevent them from occurring. This made EDIS and CMU potentially nice to have, but not necessary in the manner of the SSM and SRM, and left the European status quo broadly stable. Therefore, the crisis was not enough to swing opponents of the reforms to grudging support the way that the northern Europeans conceded the urgent need for some form of supervisory and resolution integration in the Debt Crisis. Instead, all member states could support regulatory relief and NGEU, which contained the crisis without requiring any side to make hard compromises on EDIS or CMU. Once those reforms contained the crisis, the urgency of calls for reform similarly diminished. In the words of one analyst, "the deposit insurance scheme is not that necessary, as a bank in distress will never get to the terminal stage of needing such a scheme's funds. National governments will intervene well before in such an unlikely scenario."[154]

## Backstopping the Single Resolution Fund

Although no progress occurred on either EDIS or CMU, there was at least one noteworthy change to the European financial regulatory architecture, as the eurozone states agreed to accelerate the formal adoption of the European Stability Mechanism as a backstop for the Single Resolution Fund. This was by no means a change on the scale of the creation of the SSM and SRM, or the potential introduction of EDIS or CMU, but did present a nontrivial increase in mutualization and reinforcement of the changes introduced in the earlier Debt Crisis. In the terminology of this argument, it should be considered a "weatherproofing" reform, designed to reinforce the status quo against external threats rather changing the underlying structure of the

# 262 Crises and Integration in European Banking Union

regulatory architecture in a minor "patch-up" or major "Monnet" reform. That this kind of reform succeeded where other efforts failed may be traced to the exogenous severe nature of the Pandemic, a crisis which severely threatened the status quo, but not originating with internal flaws in the current arrangements.

## Why Was a Backstop Needed?

Although the introduction of the Single Resolution Mechanism in 2014 provided a major step forward in European financial integration by mutualizing the cost of bank resolution, even at the time many observers were acutely aware of its flaws and limitations. Two in particular attracted considerable attention both at the time and in the years to follow: a cumbersome and complex decision-making process and an insufficiently large Single Resolution Fund to pay for bank resolutions. In both cases, these limitations emerged out of the compromises necessary to implement the SRM in a timely fashion, but observers would worry that both would impede its functioning in the future.

The decision-making process was considerably more complex than that of the SSM, which simply was housed in the ECB. SRM decisions on bank resolution would have to be reviewed and potentially amended by both the European Commission and the European Council, ensuring European actors outside of the ECB and member states would have input. Such a mechanism was a necessary concession to national interests concerned about surrendering control over resolution entirely to a supranational body, and insisting on an intergovernmental check on its operations. However, this complexity also raised fears that the SRM would be unable to make the sort of rapid decisions that may be crucial in a bank panic. Other critics feared that the complexity would also provide a channel for struggling banks to avoid the "bail-in" provisions of the new reforms and secure more generous state bailouts, and suggested that it was precisely this channel that led states such as Italy to accept the compromise.

In the half-decade since the SRM's implementation, the fear that it would not operate fast enough has not manifested, but predictions that it would be unable to enforce stringent terms of "bail-in" and prevent taxpayer bailouts proved accurate in several cases. In particular, NordLB in Germany and several banks in Italy all managed to escape the full implementation of "bail-in" provisions, and instead secure the sort of taxpayer-funded bailouts that the BRRD and SRM had been designed to eliminate.[155]

The second significant weakness of the SRM was that the Single Resolution Fund, the standby fund to pay for bank resolutions, was by almost every account too small for its purpose. At €52 billion, it would struggle to fund the resolution of even a single large systemically important financial institution or more than a handful of medium-sized banks. Certainly, it would be woefully insufficient in the face of a 2007–09-scale crisis, which saw Germany alone commit €500 billion in bank support.[156] However, as with the compromises over decision-making, the relatively small size was seen as a necessary concession to get some manner of SRM up and running at the time. Concerns over insufficient size were generally mollified by two hopes: that the SRF would gradually increase in size over time, ideally getting large enough before another major banking crisis hit, and that in extremis member states would likely agree to tap the European Stability Mechanism to supplement the SRF.[157] In essence, the process would be that, after the SRF funds were exhausted, member states would use their own resources, and if those should be exhausted, turn then to the ESM.[158] Both hopes would fall short in the Pandemic.

The first hope, that the Fund would be increased through the process of normal politics, failed to manifest in time. By spring 2020, the Single Resolution Fund was still only €52 billion, insufficient to manage a wave of bank failures comparable to the Banking or Debt Crises should one appear. The second hope, that states would authorize emergency transfer of funds from the ESM to the SRF if necessary, was complicated by the politics of tapping the ESM in both the northern and southern states. The northern states had long held to the position that the ESM existed to support nation-states, not supranational funds or resources for private institutions. Wolfgang Schäuble spelled out the German position that "the only way to the ESM is through the nation state," a process that required the member state in need to affirmatively request assistance and gave the other members leverage to insist on conditions in exchange for that assistance.[159] These conditions, and the need to publicly admit need, meant that such a move would be so politically unpopular that member states would only do so at the absolute last moment, even though earlier action would result in fewer funds being needed to contain a crisis.[160] This therefore created a significant vulnerability, as the SRM lacked the authority and the member states lacked the will save in extremis to tap the ESM, a scenario that would be extremely likely in a financial crisis of any significant size. The clear solution, to automatically establish the ESM as an automatic backstop to the SRF, had been broadly agreed to by the Eurogroup in late 2018, but only on condition that it not actually come into force until the start of 2024 and with lingering questions about details that

## 264    Crises and Integration in European Banking Union

made even that date somewhat speculative.[161] Much like the CMU, the ESM backstop appear to risk remaining more a distant "Augustine" promise than a concrete reality.

## The Backstop and the Pandemic

The Pandemic striking Europe in earnest in spring 2020 highlighted the flaws of the SRM, and in particular the unbackstopped and insufficient SRF. Hopes that the SRF would gradually be increased through normal noncrisis policy-making before a crisis clearly had fallen short, and the reluctance of states to tap the ESM meant that emergency access was also problematic. Per a Brookings report in April 2020, "recourse to the ESM in response to COVID-19 [carried] the stigma of being forced to come hat-in-hand to the ESM," and as such would be insufficient to contain the crisis in a timely and relatively low-cost fashion.[162] Given that a wave of bank failures were anticipated out of the early days of the Pandemic, this exposed a serious flaw in the banking union resolution regime.

By May of 2020, representatives of the Single Resolution Board (SRB) began highlighting the problem and advocating an accelerated ESM backstop as a viable solution. Timo Löyttyniemi, the Vice Chair of the SRB in charge of the SRF, argued that "market confidence in a time of crisis is key. For credibility, the existence of a Backstop to the SRF is crucial, in particular for situations where the SRF might not be able to provide sufficient funds or those financial means are not readily available."[163] These calls were soon taken up by others at the ECB, promoting the importance of the backstop as part of a broader strategy of crisis management alongside EDIS and other crisis-response measures.[164] Luis de Guindos would describe the backstop as "crucial" to "credibility and confidence in the resolution framework."[165]

Establishing an ESM backstop offered advantages over other alternatives. Member states had broadly agreed in principle to the use of the ESM as a backstop, although they envisioned a longer timeline and continued to feud over details. Even given that, accelerating the timeline and smoothing over the details presented an easier lift than establishing a new mechanism. Moreover, as a Brookings analysis put it, "the ESM has one principal advantage. It already exists and has access to funding backed by all eurozone governments."[166] As an existing pool of money, it did not require additional immediate expenditures from member states, at least until and unless the ESM itself were to become depleted, a scenario meaning the crisis would have grown substantially in magnitude. By contrast, a more direct expansion of the SRF itself would have required states, and potentially their banks, to provide additional funds immediately. This would have imposed a new cost burden on states and banks precisely at a moment when their ability to shoulder existing burdens was in question. Even in noncrisis times, the speed with which member states and banks filled the SRF had been almost as contentious a topic as the ultimate size of the fund.[167] Other proposals, such as the issuing of common "Eurobonds" specifically to fund the SRF, were even more controversial. Although they attracted the support of some central bankers early on, they also attracted significant opposition from northern member states, especially the Netherlands.[168]

In contrast to the prolonged and ultimately unresolved debates over the bad band, EDIS, and CMU, debate over establishing the backstop was resolved relatively quickly. The Eurogroup announced at the end of November 2020 that it had agreed to the establishment of the ESM as a formal backstop to the SRF, effective January 1, 2022.[169] This was a significant acceleration of the timeline, as member states previously opposed to rapid adoption waived their concerns over legacy issues from the earlier crises. Despite the fact that NPL levels were expected to continue to rise out of the Pandemic economic strain, the Eurogroup report argued that "member states participating in the Banking Union consider that sufficient progress has been made in risk reduction to proceed with the early introduction of the backstop to the SRF."[170]

The decision met widespread acclaim, both from advocates of deeper integration and those skeptical of EDIS, CMU, and integration in other areas. European Economy Commissioner Paolo Gentiloni called it "good news for the stability of the euro zone and for European businesses and citizens."[171] Although Germany remained opposed to movement on EDIS at the time, German Finance Minister Olaf Scholz argued that the backstop "strengthen[ed] the euro and the European banking sector as a whole."[172] BdB representatives, similarly reluctant to move forward on EDIS, described the backstop as "very helpful."[173] Others saw it as an important step toward broader integration. A *Financial Times* editorial held that it as a sign that "bit by bit, Europe is fixing the holes in monetary union."[174] Klaus Regling, Managing Director of the ESM, similarly argued that "this reform of the ESM Treaty will move us towards completing banking union," praise echoed by the Socialists & Democrats group in the European Parliament.[175]

## Why Does the Backstop Pass Where EDIS Failed?

The success in securing the backstop stands in sharp contrast to the failure to secure EDIS. Both policies were designed to plug a widely acknowledged gap in the existing European resolution regime and in doing so increase the overall stability of the system. Neither threatened to impose substantial costs up front, as both would only impose costs on member states in the event of a crisis that spread beyond the capacity of existing resources. Both were the sort of relatively technical issues that generally do not attract widespread public attention, but instead remain in the technocratic realm of "quiet politics."[176]

However, the two reforms differed crucially in the scale of innovation and the ways in which narratives around the need for reform could or could not fit the facts of the crisis at hand. EDIS ultimately was a more fundamental regulatory architecture reform, "completing" banking union by adding a third pillar and establishing a pan-eurozone mutualization of depositor protections. Whatever the functional merits of the reform, its implementation would be a shift from the current status quo. On the other hand, the backstop ultimately served to reinforce the existing status quo, where bank resolution was mutualized but deposit insurance remained a national obligation. Had the Pandemic produced a shock sufficient to deplete the SRF, member states would still have been obligated to fund resolution costs, but in a less orderly, less timely, and ultimately more costly way than if a formal backstop existed. A shock that depleted national DGS, however, would not compel states to honor any preestablished pan-European obligation.

This distinction is crucial because it establishes why the framing of the crisis as exogenous in nature, and thus banks and banking system as the blamelessness, reinforced the arguments for a backstop while undercutting those for EDIS. Implementing EDIS would potentially impose significant new costs on member states, as well as potentially introducing moral hazard by taking on additional obligation to manage legacy problems. This could be justified if the crisis had been caused by a lack of EDIS, as in that case at least EDIS would prevent future crises from emerging. However, that was not the case. On the other hand, establishing the backstop did not impose new costs, but rather just established a superior channel to manage existing obligations. Therefore, it served as a "weatherproofing" reform; no one pitched it as preventing a future crisis, but instead it was presented as a way to ensure that existing pan-European obligations future exogenous shocks would be manageable.

## Conclusion

The crisis period of the Pandemic, at least within finance, reached its close in July 2021. That month, the ECB released the results of its latest stress tests, which specifically examined the ability of eurozone banks to withstand a shock comparable to that of the early period of the Pandemic, with a focus in particular on their ability to withstand a new surge in NPLs. The results were overwhelmingly positive, with virtually all major European institutions passing. With those results, fears of a wave of bank closures out of the COVID-19 Pandemic passed. While debates on further reforms continued, those ongoing debates moved into the realm of normal politics, without the urgent drive for action of the emergency period. This has caused some observers to see a closing of a window of opportunity.[177] As Nicolas Véron noted by late 2021, "It is not clear what catalyst could unlock [the banking union], short of a new crisis."[178]

With the close of the window of emergency politics, it becomes possible to evaluate the overall impact of the Pandemic crisis on European financial integration. The crisis should ultimately be judged a severe one, especially insofar as it was treated as such by European policymakers at the time. The expected surge of nonperforming loans, and with it a surge of bank failures and potential sovereign defaults, never materialized, but this ultimately speaks more to the urgency with which European actors acted rather than an overstatement of the danger in the moment. Without the emergency regulatory relief measures and billions of euros of financial assistance, the economic and financial crisis surely would have risen to the levels feared at the time, and of course the human cost of the public health crisis should not be understated.

With hindsight, it is clear that the actual actions taken on financial integration in the Pandemic were either minor, temporary, or not directly related to finance. Both the emergency regulatory relief and the Next Generation EU funding were explicitly temporary measures designed to be one-off responses, and neither made long-term changes to the European financial regulatory architecture. The regulatory relief was generally lifted by the end of July 2021, while NGEU helped insulate banks from losses without any actual change to regulation. The backstopping of the SRF with the ESM did present a change to the regulatory architecture, but ultimately a relatively minor one, accelerating the timeframe for existing commitments and ensuring they would be managed properly rather than creating new obligations. The common thread of these actions was a focus on "polity maintenance" rather than deeper reforms.[179] As described by Ferrera et al., they reflected "a deliberate strategy driven by the primary objective of safeguarding the polity as such," rather than a more fundamental reform.[180] These were programs designed to preserve the status quo rather than advance a change in the design of the European Union and its financial system.

More substantial proposed changes, including the creation of a European bad bank, EDIS, and CMU, all failed to win sufficient support to be implemented in the crisis. They failed despite reformers' efforts to follow the traditional narrative of a Monnet Crisis, using a crisis to make the case for a long-desired reform by taking advantage of an emergency politics moment and framing the reforms as an opportunity to patch a known regulatory architecture weakness. However, unlike in the Debt Crisis, these efforts ultimately fell short. The bad bank failed to win substantial support even within the European Central Bank. EDIS and CMU already enjoyed a wide coalition supporting the reforms, albeit one not large enough to secure their passage. However, their advocates failed to grow that coalition in the crisis, and thus both reform efforts failed.

The failure of more substantial reforms may be attributed to a number of factors. To some degree, it reflects the success of earlier reforms. The existing partial banking union, in particular the Single Supervisory Mechanism, enabled a rapid deployment of pan-European forbearance measures, which helped prevent a surge of nonperforming loans.[181] The pan-European nature of this action should not be underemphasized, as it avoided creating a circumstance where individual states resisted deploying measures first for fear of signaling that they were distinctly hard hit or vulnerable. Some respondents would maintain that this success, while a testimony to the success of previous integration, limited the case for more reform.[182] On the other hand, the success of these measures could also have been cited as evidence for the potential value of further reforms, by demonstrating the utility of integration in the face of a crisis. Luis de Guindos made this case at the time, arguing that "the ECB acted quickly and effectively. But other EU tools, including fiscal instruments, would ensure that we are never taken by surprise again."[183] However, such pro-integration arguments failed to win over enough converts to successfully push deeper reform.

The failure of more substantial reforms may also be partially attributed to the success of action elsewhere, in particular the Next Generation EU spending. Commentators at the time cast NGEU as Europe's "Hamiltonian Moment," a bold step forward toward fiscal solidarity, despite it being an explicitly temporary measure. It also undeniably had an impact on the immediate crisis in finance, by providing member states with deep fiscal resources enabling them to prop up both their real economy firms and their financial institutions. However, its long-term important remains unclear, as it made no permanent change to the European regulatory or fiscal architecture.[184] This also leaves open the question of why the Europeans chose to rely on temporary measures rather a permanent deepening of integration. The success

The 2020–21 COVID Pandemic    **269**

of NGEU helps explain why deeper integration didn't follow *after* the decision in favor of NGEU, but cannot explain why the Europeans chose to adopt NGEU *instead of* or *before* attempting deeper reforms.

Ultimately, the key to answering these questions lies in the exogeneity of the crisis. The exogeneity of the crisis made the politics of temporary measures substantially easier, while at the same time weakening the case for more fundamental changes. Virtually all actors agreed early on that the banks and European regulatory architecture were blameless in this crisis, unlike in the Banking Crisis or the Debt Crisis. Because the banks and member states weren't vulnerable because their own past missteps, generous aid would not generate negative incentives and moral hazard. This made generous temporary aid easier to organize.[185] Solidarity measures could limit spillover damage to other member states, though this had been true in the Debt Crisis as well. More importantly, such solidarity measures didn't run the risk of generating future crises by incentivizing "bad" behavior. They thus had a great deal of upside, but little in way of downside.

On the other hand, this same exogeneity actually hurt the case for more fundamental reforms. Weaknesses in the banks and in the regulatory architecture didn't cause the crisis. Therefore, no amount of financial reform would prevent a similar crisis from striking Europe. Such reforms may still be arguably necessary for existing reasons, but the reforms wouldn't prevent another crisis. Therefore, the focus needed to be on ensuring the resilience of a system that was broadly functional before the crisis hit, not on fixing internal problems that generated a crisis. This made it hard to expand the coalition in favor of deeper reforms. The bad bank and EDIS would have helped clean up legacy issues of the previous crises, but the exogenous crisis narrative logic implied the problem was an impending surge of *new* NPLs and other issues, *not* legacy issues. Legacy issues made the problem harder to manage, but didn't create it, and as such, efforts to clean up those problems were helpful, but not essential. This left those reforms in essentially the same place they had been before the crisis, where advocates argued that cleaning up the legacy issues was helpful, but opponents argued it was inessential, and focused more on the negatives in terms of moral hazard. Since the exogeneity narrative didn't change that core "helpful but inessential" logic, the crisis did not in that sense threaten the status quo enough to expand the pro-reform coalition. Similarly, CMU was a "nice to have," but wouldn't have prevented a substantial challenge, as could be seen in countries with deep capital markets that still faced a threat of a surge of NPLs, such as the US and UK.

The reform that did happen, the backstopping of the SRF, succeeded because it addressed a structural flaw that *was* highlighted by the crisis.

Although the exogenous crisis narrative didn't put blame on the banks, it did raise the possibility of bank failures and thus the very real possibility that a crisis could follow from the weaknesses of the existing resolution regime. Specifically, it highlighted that the existing resources of the SRF were insufficient to handle bank failures beyond a relatively low threshold of size. This, then, did create the space for a weatherproofing reform, a fix that didn't fundamentally change the regulatory architecture, but did address a weakness. Left unaddressed, issues of EDIS and lack of CMU would not in themselves cause an escalating crisis, because the real threat was from a surge of new NPLs, not widespread lack of faith in national DGS or a lack of capital market alternatives. On the other hand, failing to secure deep enough reserves for the SRF could very clearly reactivate the Doom Loop, even if banks and states would be blameless for failing to anticipate a global pandemic. Therefore, backstopping the SRF was the one long-term regulatory architecture reform where an argument could be made successfully that reform was essential to both containing the existing crisis and preventing future financial crises from future pandemics or comparable exogenous shocks.

The Pandemic provides a clear example of a severe exogenous shock. The European responses to it—generous temporary relief measures and a deepening of the resources for existing funds without significant regulatory architecture reform—should be considered a moderate weatherproofing reform. The severity enabled such generous but temporary reform through NGEU and modest stability-enhancing reinforcement of existing arrangements. However, the exogeneity precluded deeper structural reforms, despite the explicit attempts of would-be reformers to use the Monnet narrative of crises as drivers of integration.

## Notes

1. Lucia Quaglia and Amy Verdun, "The COVID-19 Pandemic and the European Union: Politics, Policies and Institutions," *Journal of European Public Policy* 30, no. 4 (April 2023): 599–611, doi:10.1080/13501763.2022.2141305; Marco Buti and Sergio Fabbrini, "Next Generation EU and the Future of Economic Governance: Towards a Paradigm Change or Just a Big One-Off?," *Journal of European Public Policy* 30, no. 4 (April 2023): 676–695, doi:10.1080/13501763.2022.2141303.

2. Luis de Guindos, "Remarks at the European Economics and Financial Centre" (March 2020), https://www.ecb.europa.eu/press/key/date/2020/html/ecb.sp200302~0aa9fbaddd.en.html.

3. Economist Intelligence Unit, "Contagion: The Coronavirus Risk to European Banks," *Economist Intelligence Unit*, April 2020, NA-NA.

4. "Data on COVID-19 (Coronavirus)," Our World in Data, July 2022, https://github.com/owid/covid-19-data.
5. European Centre for Disease Prevention and Control, "Data on Country Response Measures to COVID-19," European Centre for Disease Prevention and Control, June 2022, https://www.ecdc.europa.eu/en/publications-data/download-data-response-measures-covid–19.
6. In this regard, they differed from the 2010 and 2011 tests, which were regarded as insufficiently rigorous and failed to calm markets. See Chapter 3 for more.
7. Luis de Guindos, "Presentation of the ECB Annual Report 2019 to the Committee on Economic and Monetary Affairs of the European Parliament (by Videoconference)" (May 2020), https://www.ecb.europa.eu/press/key/date/2020/html/ecb.sp200507~576464bc66.en.html.
8. Boin and Rhinard, "Crisis Management Performance and the European Union."
9. "Guindos Says the ECB Has Not Decided Whether to Buy 'Fallen Angels,'" *CE Noticias Financieras English*, May 2020.
10. Valdis Dombrovskis, "Remarks by Executive Vice-President Dombrovskis" (Text, April 2020), https://ec.europa.eu/commission/presscorner/detail/en/speech_20_769.
11. Brooks et al., "EU Health Policy in the Aftermath of COVID-19."
12. European Banking Authority, "The EU Banking Sector: First Insights into the COVID-19 Impacts," Thematic Note (Paris, France: European Banking Authority, May 2020), https://www.eba.europa.eu/sites/default/documents/files/document_library/Risk%20Analysis%20and%20Data/Risk%20Assessment%20Reports/2020/Thematic%20notes/883986/Thematic%20note%20-%20Preliminary%20analysis%20of%20impact%20of%20COVID-19%20on%20EU%20banks%20%E2%80%93%20May%202020.pdf.
13. Douglas A. Rediker and Giovanna De Maio, "Europe and the Existential Challenge of Post-COVID Recovery," *Brookings* (blog), April 2020, https://www.brookings.edu/blog/order-from-chaos/2020/04/20/europe-and-the-existential-challenge-of-post-covid-recovery/.
14. "IMF Points to Spain as the Economy Hit Hardest by Coronavirus," *CE Noticias Financieras English*, October 2020.
15. David Rothnie, "Crisis Sparks Endgame Fears for Europe's Investment Banks," *GlobalCapital Euroweek*, April 2020, sec. Southpaw, https://www.globalcapital.com/article/28mu5f4ik9vw9d2rmpz40/southpaw/crisis-sparks-endgame-fears-for-europes-investment-banks.
16. Standards & Poor, "Spanish Banks Have Little Room to Maneuver in Case of Coronavirus Capital Crunch," *S&P Global Market Intelligence* (blog), April 2020, https://www.spglobal.com/marketintelligence/en/news-insights/latest-news-headlines/spanish-banks-have-little-room-to-maneuver-in-case-of-coronavirus-capital-crunch-57900235.
17. Fitch Ratings, "German Banks' Weaknesses Exposed as Economic Outlook Worsens," Non-Rating Action Commentary (Fitch Ratings, April 2020), https://www.fitchratings.com/research/banks/german-banks-weaknesses-exposed-as-economic-outlook-worsens-08-04–2020.
18. Arnaboldi, *Risk and Regulation in Euro Area Banks*; Tolo and Viren, "How Much Do Non-Performing Loans Hinder Loan Growth in Europe?"

19. Marcel Magnus, Cristina Sofia Pacheco Dias, and Kristina Grigaitė, "Exchange of Views with Andrea Enria, Chair of the Supervisory Board of the ECB," Briefing, Think Tank (European Parliament, May 2020), https://www.europarl.europa.eu/thinktank/en/document/IPOL_BRI(2020)645742.
20. Magnus, Pacheco Dias, and Grigaitė.
21. Jasper Cox and Tom Brown, "Eurozone Bad Bank Would Be 'Incredibly Complex', Say Experts," *GlobalCapital Securitization*, April 2020, sec. Regulation, https://www.globalcapital.com/securitization/article/28mu5vj3skqqfyax3ywhs/regulation/eurozone-bad-bank-would-be-incredibly-complex-say-experts.
22. Mare, Bertay, and Zhou.
23. Sophia Furber and Mohammad Abbas Taqi, "Italy's €750B COVID-19 Guarantee Poses Operational, 'doom Loop' Risk for Banks | S&P Global Market Intelligence," *S&P Global*, April 2020, sec. Market Intelligence, https://www.spglobal.com/marketintelligence/en/news-insights/latest-news-headlines/italy-s-8364-750b-covid-19-guarantee-poses-operational-doom-loop-risk-for-banks-58041297.
24. Asimakopoulos, "International Law as a Negotiation Tool in Banking Union; the Case of the Single Resolution Fund."
25. Economist Intelligence Unit, "Contagion."
26. Moritz Schularick, Sascha Steffen, and Tobias H. Troeger, "Bank Capital and the European Recovery from the COVID-19 Crisis," 2020.
27. Rediker and De Maio, "Europe and the Existential Challenge of Post-COVID Recovery."
28. Tyler Davies, "Banks Call for Regulatory Forbearance over Covid-19 Stress," *GlobalCapital Euroweek*, March 2020, sec. Regulatory Capital, https://www.globalcapital.com/article/28mu4cuh0wjxtzhjwmbk0/regulatory-capital/banks-call-for-regulatory-forbearance-over-covid-19-stress.
29. Isabel Schnabel, Interview with Perspektiven der Wirtschaftspolitik, interview by Karen Horn, May 2020, https://www.ecb.europa.eu/press/inter/date/2020/html/ecb.in200527_1~cda9c3f6f9.en.html; Andrea Enria, "Flexibility in Supervision: How ECB Banking Supervision Is Contributing to Fighting the Economic Fallout from the Coronavirus," European Central Bank, *The Supervision Blog* (blog), March 2020, https://www.bankingsupervision.europa.eu/press/blog/2020/html/ssm.blog200327~abd2a8244b.en.html; Marco Zatterin, "Interview with La Stampa" (European Central Bank, July 2020), https://www.ecb.europa.eu/press/inter/date/2020/html/ecb.in200701~601bc1b5ff.en.html; Gerald Von Braunberger, "Bundesbank-Präsident zu Corona: Wie schlimm wird es, Herr Weidmann?," *Frankfurter Allgemeine Zeitung*, March 2020, https://www.faz.net/aktuell/wirtschaft/bundesbank-praesident-jens-weidmann-zum-coronavirus-16676519.html.
30. David Howarth and Lucia Quaglia, "Failing Forward in Economic and Monetary Union: Explaining Weak Eurozone Financial Support Mechanisms," *Journal of European Public Policy* 28, no. 10 (2021): 1555–1572; Quaglia and Verdun, "The COVID-19 Pandemic and the European Union"; Buti and Fabbrini, "Next Generation EU and the Future of Economic Governance"; Anghel and Jones, "Is Europe Really Forged through Crisis?"
31. "IMF Points to Spain as the Economy Hit Hardest by Coronavirus."
32. Maria João Rodrigues and Paul Magnette, "Only a 'New Deal' Can Rescue the European Project," *Social Europe* (blog), April 2020, https://socialeurope.eu/only-a-new-deal-can-rescue-the-european-project.

33. Christian Sewing, "A Partnership for Growth: Financing Recovery and Growth in Europe," *Views: The EUROFI Magazine*, September 2020.
34. Christine Lagarde, "Opening Remarks at the EUI's State of the Union Event" (Opening Remarks, May 2020), https://www.ecb.europa.eu/press/key/date/2020/html/ecb.sp200508~81cd924af6.en.html.
35. Philip R. Lane, Interview with El País, interview by Luis Doncel, May 2020, https://www.ecb.europa.eu/press/inter/date/2020/html/ecb.in200518~fc93497956.en.html.
36. Schnabel, Interview with Perspektiven der Wirtschaftspolitik.
37. Reuters Staff, "Germany's Scholz: EU Needs to Make More Progress on European Banking Union," *Reuters*, September 2020, sec. Banks, https://www.reuters.com/article/us-eu-economy-scholz-banks-idUSKBN25U1RM.
38. Schnabel, Interview with Perspektiven der Wirtschaftspolitik.
39. Davies, "Banks Call for Regulatory Forbearance over Covid-19 Stress."
40. Buti and Fabbrini, "Next Generation EU and the Future of Economic Governance."
41. Howarth and Quaglia, "Failing Forward in Economic and Monetary Union."
42. Rediker and De Maio, "Europe and the Existential Challenge of Post-COVID Recovery."
43. Christine Lagarde, "Jointly Shaping Europe's Tomorrow" (September 2020), https://www.ecb.europa.eu/press/key/date/2020/html/ecb.sp200921~5a30d9013b.en.html; Pablo Hernández de Cos, "Pablo Hernández de Cos: The Value of the European Project in Today's Global Landscape" (July 2021), https://www.bis.org/review/r210714b.htm.
44. Paschal Donohoe, "Speech by the Eurogroup President, Paschal Donohoe, at the IMF Governor Talk on 'Euro Area Recovery from Covid-19—Economic Policy Reflections and Challenges Ahead', 12 October 2021," (October 2021), https://www.consilium.europa.eu/en/press/press-releases/2021/10/13/speech-by-the-eurogroup-president-paschal-donohoe-at-imf-annual-meetings-conference-on-euro-area-recovery-from-covid-19-economic-policy-reflections-and-challenges-ahead-12-october–2021/.
45. Lagarde, "Opening Remarks at the EUI's State of the Union Event."
46. Hussein Kassim, "The European Commission and the COVID-19 Pandemic: A Pluri-Institutional Approach," *Journal of European Public Policy* 30, no. 4 (April 2023): 612–634, doi:10.1080/13501763.2022.2140821.
47. Sarah Cottle, "COVID-19 Hits Bank Dividends; Piraeus Q4'19 Result; Barclays' New Climate Policy," *S&P Global*, April 2020, https://www.spglobal.com/marketintelligence/en/news-insights/latest-news-headlines/covid-19-hits-bank-dividends-piraeus-q4-19-result-barclays-new-climate-policy–57897096.
48. Furber and Taqi, "Italy's €750B COVID-19 Guarantee Poses Operational, 'doom Loop' Risk for Banks | S&P Global Market Intelligence."
49. European Securities and Markets Authority, "Accounting Implications of the COVID-19 Outbreak on the Calculation of Expected Credit Losses in Accordance with IFRS 9" (European Securities and Markets Authority, March 2020), https://www.esma.europa.eu/file/55097/download?token=Zo8hB9kn.
50. European Banking Authority, "Guidelines on the Pragmatic 2020 Supervisory Review Nd Evaluation Process in Light of the COVID-19 Crisis" (European Banking Authority, July 2020), https://www.eba.europa.eu/sites/default/documents/files/document_library/Publications/Guidelines/2020/Guidelines%20on%20the%20pragmatic%202020%20SREP/897419/EBA-GL-2020-10%20Guidelines%20on%20the%20pragmatic%202020%20SREP.pdf.

51. European Central Bank, "ECB Banking Supervision Provides Temporary Capital and Operational Relief in Reaction to Coronavirus" (European Central Bank, March 2020), https://www.bankingsupervision.europa.eu/press/pr/date/2020/html/ssm.pr200312~43351ac3ac.en.html; European Securities and Markets Authority, "Accounting Implications of the COVID-19 Outbreak on the Calculation of Expected Credit Losses in Accordance with IFRS 9."

52. Andrea Enria, "Contingency Preparedness in the Context of COVID-19" (European Central Bank, March 2020), https://www.bankingsupervision.europa.eu/press/letterstobanks/shared/pdf/2020/ssm.2020_letter_on_Contingency_preparedness_in_the_context_of_COVID-19.en.pdf; Cyril Couaillier et al., "Bank Capital Buffers and Lending in the Euro Area during the Pandemic," Financial Stability Review, November 2021 (European Central Bank, November 2021), https://www.ecb.europa.eu/pub/financial-stability/fsr/special/html/ecb.fsrart202111_01~111d31fca7.en.html.

53. Tyler Davies, "EC Adopts Covid-19 Banking Package with 'Quick Fix' for CRR," GlobalCapital, April 2020, sec. Regulatory Capital, https://www.globalcapital.com/article/28mu66gty3zakc8qyrc3k/regulatory-capital/ec-adopts-covid-19-banking-package-with-quick-fix-for-crr.

54. Tom Fairless, Anna Hirtenstein, and Giovanni Legorano, "The Coronavirus Pandemic: ECB Unveils Surprise Bond-Buying Plan," Wall Street Journal, Eastern Edition, March 2020.

55. Tom Fairless, "European Central Bank Ramps Up Stimulus Program Beyond $1.5 Trillion; Stimulus Efforts Are Now in Line with the Fed's, Reflecting a Policy Turnaround in Europe to Counter Sharp Downturn," Wall Street Journal (Online), June 2020, sec. Economy, https://www.proquest.com/docview/2409176329/citation/38A02BF4FA57413FPQ/2.

56. Bundesbank Official, Interview by author.

57. Bundesbank Official.

58. European Central Bank, "What Are Targeted Longer-Term Refinancing Operations (TLTROs)?," March 2021, https://www.ecb.europa.eu/ecb/educational/explainers/tell-me/html/tltro.en.html.

59. European Central Bank, "Pandemic Emergency Purchase Programme," European Central Bank, July 2022, https://www.ecb.europa.eu/mopo/implement/pepp/html/index.en.html.

60. Christine Lagarde, "Extraordinary Times Require Extraordinary Action. There Are No Limits to Our Commitment to the Euro. We Are Determined to Use the Full Potential of Our Tools, within Our Mandate.," Tweet, Twitter, March 2020, https://twitter.com/Lagarde/status/1240414918966480896.

61. Christine Lagarde and Luis de Guindos, "Monetary Policy Statement (with Q&A)," Press Conference (Frankfurt am Main: European Central Bank, October 2020), https://www.ecb.europa.eu/press/pressconf/2023/html/ecb.is230202~4313651089.en.html.

62. "Can Lagarde Save the Euro? The European Central Bank Buys the Eurozone as Much Time as It Can," Wall Street Journal (Online), March 2020, sec. Opinion, https://www.proquest.com/docview/2379034479/citation/38A02BF4FA57413FPQ/10.

63. Fairless, Hirtenstein, and Legorano, "The Coronavirus Pandemic."

64. Tom Fairless, "The Coronavirus Pandemic: ECB Chief, Germany Clash on Aid," Wall Street Journal, Eastern Edition, March 2020; "Lagarde Does Whatever She Can;

The 2020–21 COVID Pandemic **275**

And Who Can Fault Her When No Other EU Leader Has a Better Idea?," *Wall Street Journal (Online)*, December 2020, sec. Opinion, https://www.proquest.com/docview/2468365756/citation/4A51032E75154595PQ/19; Bundesbank Official, Interview by author.

65. "Roundup: German Court's ECB Ruling Draws Divisive Response," *Xinhua News Agency—CEIS*, May 2020, sec. cMilitary700Politics & Law, https://www.proquest.com/docview/2400607972/citation/4A51032E75154595PQ/38; Jean Garcia, "Top German Court Says European Central Bank Bond Buying Scheme Partially Contravenes the Law," *University Wire*, May 2020, sec. markets, https://www.proquest.com/docview/2436114359/citation/4A51032E75154595PQ/29.

66. Tim Bartz and Stefan Kaiser, "Interview with ECB Vice President 'Faced With This Big Drop in GDP and Inflation, We Had to Act,'" *Yerepouni Daily News*, June 2020, https://www.proquest.com/docview/2415715076/citation/4A51032E75154595PQ/28; "Roundup."

67. Garcia, "Top German Court Says European Central Bank Bond Buying Scheme Partially Contravenes the Law."

68. William Horobin, "ECB Indicates More Stimulus Is on the Way, Says Bank of France Chief," *Irish Independent*, May 2020, sec. News.

69. David Chance, "Europe Has a Sticking Plaster, but Italy Is Going to Need a Transfusion: ANALYSIS," *Irish Independent*, April 2020, sec. News.

70. Marshall Auerback, "The European Union Still Hasn't Considered An Economic Proposal That Can Save It—OpEd," *Eurasia Review* (blog), June 2020, https://www.eurasiareview.com/16062020-the-european-union-still-hasnt-considered-an-economic-proposal-that-can-save-it-oped/.

71. "Top German Court Dismisses Challenge to ECB's Bond-Buying Program," *Xinhua News Agency—CEIS*, May 2021, https://www.proquest.com/docview/2528466378/citation/4A51032E75154595PQ/5; Francesco Canepa, "Germany's Top Court Rejects Complaint against ECB's Bond Buying Scheme," National Post (Online) (Toronto, Canada: Postmedia Network Inc., May 2021), https://www.proquest.com/docview/2528733540/citation/4A51032E75154595PQ/6.

72. Bartz and Kaiser, "Interview with ECB Vice President 'Faced with This Big Drop in GDP and Inflation, We Had to Act'"; Lagarde and de Guindos, "Monetary Policy Statement (with Q&A)."

73. Christine Lagarde and Luis de Guindos, "Introductory Statement to the Press Conference (with Q&A)," Press Conference (Frankfurt am Main: European Central Bank, September 2020), https://www.ecb.europa.eu/press/pressconf/2020/html/ecb.is200910~5c43e3a591.en.html.

74. Lucia Quaglia and Amy Verdun, "Explaining the Response of the ECB to the COVID-19 Related Economic Crisis: Inter-Crisis and Intra-Crisis Learning," *Journal of European Public Policy* 30, no. 4 (April 2023): 635–654, doi:10.1080/13501763.2022.2141300.

75. Christine Lagarde, "Hearing at the Committee on Economic and Monetary Affairs of the European Parliament" (Introductory Statement, June 2020), https://www.ecb.europa.eu/press/key/date/2020/html/ecb.sp200608~4225ba8a1b.en.html.

76. "Lagarde Does Whatever She Can; And Who Can Fault Her When No Other EU Leader Has a Better Idea?"

77. Jean Comte, "Member States to Call for Full Regulatory Flexibility for EU Banks," *GlobalCapital*, April 2020, sec. FIG People and Markets, https://www.globalcapital. com/article/28mu546seqnc4ypxwary8/fig-people-and-markets/member-states-to-call-for-full-regulatory-flexibility-for-eu-banks.

78. Vanya Damyanova, "German Regulator Sees 'good Grounds' to Pause Payments to EU Bank Failure Fund," *SNL European Financials Daily*, February 2021, sec. CONFERENCE CHATTER; Extra.

79. Damyanova.

80. de Guindos, "Presentation of the ECB Annual Report 2019 to the Committee on Economic and Monetary Affairs of the European Parliament (by Videoconference)"; "Guindos Says the ECB Has Not Decided Whether to Buy 'Fallen Angels.'"

81. Valentina Pop, "Leaders Agree to Disagree on EU Role in the World," *Financial Times*, October 2021.

82. Furber and Taqi, "Italy's €750B COVID-19 Guarantee Poses Operational, 'doom Loop' Risk for Banks | S&P Global Market Intelligence."

83. Schnabel, Interview with Perspektiven der Wirtschaftspolitik.

84. Zatterin, "Interview with La Stampa."

85. Andrea Enria, "Introductory Statement" (June 2020), https://www.bankingsupervision. europa.eu/press/speeches/date/2020/html/ssm.sp200612~eae5123290.en.html.

86. Jamie Dimon, "Letter to Shareholders from Jamie Dimon, Annual Report 2019," Annual Report (JPMorgan-Chase, April 2020), https://reports.jpmorganchase.com/investor-relations/2019/ar-ceo-letters.htm.

87. Andrea Enria, "Transcript of the Media Briefing on June 9, 2020 (with Q&A)" (Media Briefing, June 2020), https://www.bankingsupervision.europa.eu/press/speeches/date/2020/html/ssm.sp200610~27b3ba0a0d.en.html.

88. Fitch Solutions, "German Social Democrats Now Likely To Win Election, Swing Policy Leftwards," *Fitch Solutions*, September 2021, sec. Country Risk, http://www. fitchsolutions.com/country-risk/german-social-democrats-now-likely-win-election-swing-policy-leftwards-14-09-2021.

89. Ursula von der Leyen, "State of the Union Address by President von Der Leyen" (Text, September 2020), https://ec.europa.eu/commission/presscorner/detail/en/SPEECH_20_1655.

90. Paschal Donohoe, "Remarks by Paschal Donohoe Following the Eurogroup Meeting of 4 October 2021," accessed August 31, 2022, https://www.consilium.europa.eu/en/press/press-releases/2021/10/04/remarks-by-paschal-donohoe-following-the-eurogroup-meeting-of-4-october-2021/.

91. Buti and Fabbrini, "Next Generation EU and the Future of Economic Governance."

92. Caroline De la Porte and Mads Dagnis Jensen, "The next Generation EU: An Analysis of the Dimensions of Conflict behind the Deal," *Social Policy & Administration* 55, no. 2 (2021): 388–402.

93. Howarth and Quaglia, "Failing Forward in Economic and Monetary Union."

94. Buti and Fabbrini, "Next Generation EU and the Future of Economic Governance."

95. European Commission official, Interview by author; Bundesverband deutscher Banken official, Interview by author; European Central Bank official, Interview by author, 2022.

96. Bundesbank Official, Interview by author.

The 2020–21 COVID Pandemic **277**

97. Auerback, "The European Union Still Hasn't Considered An Economic Proposal That Can Save It—OpEd."
98. Martin Arnold, "ECB Pushes for Eurozone Bad Bank to Clean up Soured Loans," *Financial Times*, April 2020.
99. Magnus, Pacheco Dias, and Grigaitė, "Exchange of Views with Andrea Enria, Chair of the Supervisory Board of the ECB."
100. Anna Nicolaou and Alice Hancock, "Lockdowns Force Cinemas into Intermission: Operators Fear Power Will Permanently Tilt Further towards Streaming as Customers Spend Enforced Time at Home," *Financial Times*, March 2020, sec. Companies and Markets.
101. Andrea Enria, "Letter from Andrea Enria, Chair of the Supervisory Board, to Mr Schäfler, Member of the German Bundestag, on Possible Policy Responses to the Crisis—25 May 2020," May 2020, https://service.betterregulation.com/document/442179.
102. Cox and Brown, "Eurozone Bad Bank Would Be 'Incredibly Complex', Say Experts"; "Moody's Says ECB Paves the Way for the Creation of a Bad Bank," *CE Noticias Financieras English*, June 2020.
103. Zatterin, "Interview with La Stampa."
104. Cox and Brown, "Eurozone Bad Bank Would Be 'Incredibly Complex', Say Experts."
105. Andreas Kroner and Yasmine Osman, "Interview: Bundesbank-Vorstand Wuermeling: Die Kreditrisiken Bereiten Uns Die Größten Sorgen," *Handelsblatt*, accessed August 31, 2022, https://www.handelsblatt.com/finanzen/banken-versicherungen/banken/interview-bundesbank-vorstand-wuermeling-die-kreditrisiken-bereiten-uns-die-groessten-sorgen/25768132.html.
106. Schularick, Steffen, and Troeger, "Bank Capital and the European Recovery from the COVID-19 Crisis."
107. Marta Wieczorek and Siobhán Millbright, "Questions and Answers: Solvency Support Instrument," Questions and Answers (Brussels: European Commission, May 2020), https://ec.europa.eu/commission/presscorner/detail/en/qanda_20_946; Jim Brunsden, "Macron Relaunches Presidency in Bastille Day Pitch," *Financial Times*, July 2020, https://www.proquest.com/docview/2476170186/citation/9D06D640C49D4875PQ/20.
108. Balazs Ujvari, Susanne Conze, and Claire Joawn, "Europe's Moment: Repair and Prepare for the next Generation," Press Release (Brussels: European Commission, May 2020), https://ec.europa.eu/commission/presscorner/detail/en/ip_20_940.
109. Frans Timmermans, "Opening Remarks by Executive Vice-President Frans Timmermans," Opening Remarks (Brussels: European Commission, May 2020), https://ec.europa.eu/commission/presscorner/detail/hr/SPEECH_20_964; Wieczorek and Millbright, "Questions and Answers."
110. Ben Hall, "State-Funded Equity Injections Will Be Fraught with Moral Hazard: INSIDE BUSINESS EUROPE," *Financial Times*, July 2020, sec. News.
111. Mehreen Khan, "Frugal States Push to Cut Recovery Package: European Capitals at Loggerheads over Size of Covid-19 Support Funds," *Financial Times*, July 2020, sec. News.
112. Andrea Enria, "Hearing at the European Parliament's Economic and Monetary Affairs Committee" (October 2020), https://www.bankingsupervision.europa.eu/press/speeches/date/2020/html/ssm.sp201027~d284d6d6c8.en.html.

113. Jon Hay and Owen Sanderson, "ECB Supervisor's Bad Bank Dream Faces Huge Obstacles," *GlobalCapital Securitization*, November 2020, sec. FIG People and Markets, https://www.globalcapital.com/securitization/article/28mudmf4ppazk1uicf5z4/fig-people-and-markets/ecb-supervisors-bad-bank-dream-faces-huge-obstacles.

114. Kingdon, *Agendas, Alternatives, and Public Policies.*

115. Fitch Solutions, "German Social Democrats Now Likely To Win Election, Swing Policy Leftwards"; Pablo Hernández de Cos, "Europe Should Commit to Global Financial Cooperation for Its Own Recovery," *Views: The EUROFI Magazine*, September 2020; Jean Garcia, "European Union Proposes 750 Billion-Euro Coronavirus Recovery Fund," *University Wire*, May 2020, sec. markets, https://www.proquest.com/docview/2436119122/citation/A884EB5D33384F20PQ/21; Frank Elderson, "Hearing at the Committee on Economic and Monetary Affairs of the European Parliament" (Speech, January 2021), https://www.ecb.europa.eu/press/key/date/2021/html/ecb.sp210125_2~5d8b84dc5a.en.html; Paschal Donohoe, "Opening Remarks by Paschal Donohoe at the European Parliament's ECON Committee, 25 January 2021," (January 2021), https://www.consilium.europa.eu/en/press/press-releases/2021/01/25/opening-remarks-by-paschal-donohoe-at-the-european-parliament-s-econ-committee-25-january-2021/.

116. Culpepper and Tesche, "Death in Veneto?"; Javier Espinoza and Olaf Storbeck, "EU's Green Light for NordLB Rescue Provokes Backlash," *Financial Times*, December 2019, https://www.ft.com/content/18bff16e-1990-11ea-97df-cc63de1d73f4; James Shotter, "EU and HSH Nordbank Reach Provisional Restructuring Deal," *Financial Times*, October 2015, https://www.ft.com/content/09f3379a-767e-11e5-933d-efcdc3c11c89; Asimakopoulos and Howarth, "Stillborn Banking Union."

117. Luis de Guindos, "Interview with La Vanguardia." Interview by Manel Pérez, April 2020, https://www.ecb.europa.eu/press/inter/date/2020/html/ecb.in200412~b773e66772.en.html.

118. Luis de Guindos, "Financial Stability and the Pandemic Crisis" (June 2020), https://www.ecb.europa.eu/press/key/date/2020/html/ecb.sp200622~422531a969.en.html.

119. Isabel Schnabel, "Isabel Schnabel: Going Negative—the ECB's Experience" (August 2020), https://www.bis.org/review/r200827b.htm.

120. Lagarde, "Jointly Shaping Europe's Tomorrow."

121. von der Leyen, "State of the Union Address by President von Der Leyen."

122. Charles Michel, "Address by President Charles Michel at the Annual EU Ambassadors' Conference" (November 2020), https://www.consilium.europa.eu/en/press/press-releases/2020/11/10/discours-du-president-charles-michel-lors-de-la-conference-annuelle-des-ambassadeurs-de-l-ue/.

123. Kristalina Georgieva, Alfred Kammer, and Gerry Rice, "Transcript: Euro Area Press Conference" (Press Conference, November 2020), https://www.imf.org/en/News/Articles/2020/12/01/tr113020-transcript-euro-area-press-conference.

124. Hernández de Cos, "Europe Should Commit to Global Financial Cooperation for Its Own Recovery."

125. Sharon Donnery, "Ireland's Engagement in Europe and Deeper Integration of Europe," (January 2020), https://www.bis.org/review/r201002b.pdf; Anna Paula Serra, "Keynote Speech by Director Ana Paula Serra in the 'CIRSF Annual International Conference 2020': 'Economic Recovery and Financial Stability' | Banco de Portugal," (November

The 2020–21 COVID Pandemic    **279**

2020), https://www.bportugal.pt/en/intervencoes/keynote-speech-director-ana-paula-serra-cirsf-annual-international-conference-2020.

126. François Villeroy de Galhau, "Presentation of the 2020 Annual Report of the Autorité de Contrôle Prudentiel et de Résolution (ACPR)," (Press conference, May 2021), https://www.bis.org/review/r210531a.pdf.

127. Donohoe, "Opening Remarks by Paschal Donohoe at the European Parliament's ECON Committee, 25 January 2021."

128. Francesco Indaco, "Banks Commit to Supporting Communities, Businesses in Covid-19 Era—EBF Board Communiqué May 2020," Press Release, EBF Board Communiqué (Brussels: European Banking Federation, May 2020), https://www.ebf.eu/ebf-media-centre/ebf-board-communique-may-2020/.

129. Rebecca Hansford, "AFME Calls for Renewed Efforts towards Banking Union and Capital Markets Union to Deepen Europe's Financial Integration," Press Release (Brussels: Association for Financial Markets in Europe), accessed September 1, 2022, https://www.afme.eu/News/Press-Releases/Details/AFME-calls-for-renewed-efforts-towards-Banking-Union-and-Capital-Markets-Union-to-deepen-Europes-financial-integration-.

130. Jesús Aguado and Emma Pinedo, "European Banks Need Regulation Reset to Catch U.S. Rivals, Botin Says," *Reuters*, September 2021, sec. Finance, https://www.reuters.com/business/finance/european-banks-need-regulation-reset-catch-us-rivals-botin-says-2021-09-30/.

131. Schnabel, "Isabel Schnabel."

132. Cihan Duran, "European Banks Pile on Home Country Sovereign Debt amid Pandemic, S&P Says | S&P Global Market Intelligence," *S&P Global Market Intelligence*, September 2020, https://www.spglobal.com/marketintelligence/en/news-insights/latest-news-headlines/european-banks-pile-on-home-country-sovereign-debt-amid-pandemic-s-p-says-60418632.

133. Serra, "Keynote Speech by Director Ana Paula Serra in the 'CIRSF Annual International Conference 2020.'"

134. Isabel Schnabel, "The Sovereign-Bank-Corporate Nexus—Virtuous or Vicious?" (Speech, January 2021), https://www.ecb.europa.eu/press/key/date/2021/html/ecb.sp210128~8f5dc86601.en.html.

135. Luis de Guindos, "Banking Union: Achievements and Challenges," (Speech, March 2021), https://www.ecb.europa.eu/press/key/date/2021/html/ecb.sp210318_1~e2126b2dec.en.html.

136. Paschal Donohoe, "Keynote Speech by the Eurogroup President, Paschal Donohoe, at the Single Resolution Board's Annual Conference on 'Bank Resolution: Delivering for Financial Stability,'" (Speech, October 2021), https://www.consilium.europa.eu/en/press/press-releases/2021/10/14/keynote-speech-by-the-eurogroup-president-paschal-donohoe-at-the-single-resolution-board-s-annual-conference-on-bank-resolution-delivering-for-financial-stability/.

137. Ninon Renaud, "Bruno Le Maire: «Plus de coopération franco-allemande veut dire plus de croissance pour toute l'Europe," *Les Echos*, December 2020, sec. Monde, https://www.lesechos.fr/monde/europe/bruno-le-maire-plus-de-cooperation-franco-allemande-veut-dire-plus-de-croissance-pour-toute-leurope-1272615.

138. Sandbu, "Brexit and Covid Harden the Case for a Proper EU Financial Market"; Jonás Fernández, "The Capital Market Union Must Make Financing More Stable, Sustainable and Cheaper for Citizens and SMEs | Socialists & Democrats," Press Release (Brussels: Socialists & Democrats, September 2020), https://www.socialistsanddemocrats.eu/newsroom/capital-market-union-must-make-financing-more-stable-sustainable-and-cheaper-citizens-and.

139. Indaco, "Banks Commit to Supporting Communities, Businesses in Covid-19 Era—EBF Board Communiqué May 2020."

140. "Eurogroup Work Programme until June 2021," Press Release (Brussels: Eurogroup, October 2020), https://www.consilium.europa.eu/en/press/press-releases/2020/10/05/eurogroup-work-programme-until-june-2021/; Luis de Guindos, "Banking Union and Capital Markets Union after COVID-19" (November 2020), https://www.ecb.europa.eu/press/key/date/2020/html/ecb.sp201112~0913fc32f3.en.html.

141. Donnery, "Ireland's Engagement in Europe and Deeper Integration of Europe."

142. Zatterin, "Interview with La Stampa."

143. Bundesbank Official, Interview by author.

144. de Guindos, "Banking Union and Capital Markets Union after COVID-19."

145. Lagarde, "Jointly Shaping Europe's Tomorrow"; de Guindos, "Banking Union and Capital Markets Union after COVID-19."

146. Donohoe, "Remarks by Paschal Donohoe Following the Eurogroup Meeting of 4 October 2021"; Hansford, "AFME Calls for Renewed Efforts towards Banking Union and Capital Markets Union to Deepen Europe's Financial Integration."

147. Nicolas Véron, "EU Financial Services Policy since 2007: Crisis, Responses, and Prospects," *Global Policy* 9 (June 2018): 54–64, doi:10.1111/1758-5899.12564.

148. S&P Global, "As €750B Package Creates Safe Asset, EU Banking Union Inches Closer | S&P Global Market Intelligence," *S&P Global*, sec. Market Intelligence, accessed September 1, 2022, https://www.spglobal.com/marketintelligence/en/news-insights/latest-news-headlines/as-8364-750b-package-creates-safe-asset-eu-banking-union-inches-closer-59580305.

149. Mário Centeno, "Remarks by Mário Centeno Following the Eurogroup Videoconference of 11 June 2020" (Statements and Remarks, June 2020), https://www.consilium.europa.eu/en/press/press-releases/2020/06/11/remarks-by-mario-centeno-following-the-eurogroup-videoconference-of-11-june-2020/.

150. "Eurogroup Agrees on EESM Reform to Make It More Effective," *CE Noticias Financieras English*, November 2020.

151. Piia-Noora Kauppi, "Finnish Financial Sector Supports the Banking Union—but Rushing Risk Sharing Could Slow down Economic Recovery" (Finance Finland, December 2020), https://www.finanssiala.fi/en/news/finnish-financial-sector-supports-the-banking-union-but-rushing-risk-sharing-could-slow-down-economic-recovery/.

152. Bundesverband der Deutschen Volksbanken und Raiffeisenbanken, "German Banking Industry Committee Urges 'Prudent' Discussion When Revising the EU Rules on Crisis Management for Banks," Press Release (Berlin: Bundesverband der Deutschen Volksbanken und Raiffeisenbanken, January 2021), https://www.bvr.de/Press/Press_releases/German_Banking_Industry_Committee_urges_prudent"_discussion_when_revising_the_EU_rules_on_crisis_management_for_banks.

153. Bundesverband der Deutschen Volksbanken und Raiffeisenbanken.

The 2020–21 COVID Pandemic **281**

154. S&P Global, "As €750B Package Creates Safe Asset, EU Banking Union Inches Closer | S&P Global Market Intelligence."
155. Culpepper and Tesche, "Death in Veneto?"; Shotter, "EU and HSH Nordbank Reach Provisional Restructuring Deal"; Espinoza and Storbeck, "EU's Green Light for NordLB Rescue Provokes Backlash"; Asimakopoulos and Howarth, "Stillborn Banking Union."
156. Mitchell, *Saving the Market from Itself.*
157. Ida-Maria Weirsøe Fallesen, "The Challenges of the EU Banking Union—Will It Succeed in Dealing with the next Financial Crisis?," *Bruges European Economic Policy Briefings*, Bruges European Economic Policy Briefings (European Economic Studies Department, College of Europe, October 2015), https://ideas.repec.org/p/coe/wpbeep/36.html; Asimakopoulos and Howarth, "Stillborn Banking Union"; Ignazio Angeloni, "Time to Address the Shortcomings of the Banking Union" (SAFE, 2019), http://publikationen.ub.uni-frankfurt.de/frontdoor/index/index/docId/53057.
158. Kristina Grigaitė, Cristina Dias, and Marcel Magnus, "Public Hearing with Elke König, Chair of the Single Resolution Board," Public Hearing, Register of Commission Documents (European Commission, May 2020).
159. Skuodis, "Playing the Creation of the European Banking Union."
160. Bundesbank Official, Interview by author; European Commission official, Interview by author.
161. Grigaitė, Dias, and Magnus, "Public Hearing with Elke König, Chair of the Single Resolution Board."
162. Rediker and De Maio, "Europe and the Existential Challenge of Post-COVID Recovery."
163. Grigaitė, Dias, and Magnus, "Public Hearing with Elke König, Chair of the Single Resolution Board."
164. Centeno, "Remarks by Mário Centeno Following the Eurogroup Videoconference of 11 June 2020."
165. de Guindos, "Banking Union and Capital Markets Union after COVID-19."
166. Rediker and De Maio, "Europe and the Existential Challenge of Post-COVID Recovery."
167. Council of the European Union, "Member States Sign Agreement On Bank Resolution Fund," Press Release (Brussels: Council of the European Union, May 2014), https://www.proquest.com/news/docview/1526576034/citation/22F74C2A8BD84E6FPQ/15; Rebecca Christie and Rainer Buergin, "Schaeuble in Clash with the ECB on Pooling of Bank Levies [Edition 3]," *Irish Independent*, January 2014, sec. News; Alex Barker, "Project on Survival of Banks Nears Fruition: Eurozone Controls," *Financial Times*, December 2013, sec. WORLD NEWS; Tom Fairless and Stephen Fidler, "European Commission Seeks Authority to Wind Down Banks," *Wall Street Journal (Online)*, July 2013, sec. Markets.
168. Pablo Hernández de Cos, "EDIS: Is a Political Agreement Nearer?," *Views: The EUROFI Magazine*, April 2020; Rediker and De Maio, "Europe and the Existential Challenge of Post-COVID Recovery."
169. Mehreen Khan, "Eurozone Finance Ministers Strike Deal over Bailout Fund Reform," *Financial Times*, November 2020, https://www.ft.com/content/827f3d0c-ff1d-417e-bdc9-afd55be003b0.
170. Eurogroup, "Statement of the Eurogroup in Inclusive Format on the ESM Reform and the Early Introduction of the Backstop to the Single Resolution Fund," Press Release (Brussels: Eurogroup, November 2020), https://www.consilium.europa.eu/en/

press/press-releases/2020/11/30/statement-of-the-eurogroup-in-inclusive-format-on-the-esm-reform-and-the-early-introduction-of-the-backstop-to-the-single-resolution-fund/.

171. "Eurogroup Agrees on ESM Reform and 'backstop' for Single Resolution Fund," *CE Noticias Financieras English*, November 2020.

172. "Eurogroup Agrees on ESM Reform and 'backstop' for Single Resolution Fund."

173. Bundesverband deutscher Banken official, Interview by author.

174. The Editorial Board, "A Chance to Press on with EU Banking Union," *Financial Times*, December 2020, https://www.ft.com/content/8f91f48f-ce5d-48d5-998d-b8d714dbdab7.

175. Klaus Regling, "Klaus Regling at Eurogroup Video Press Conference," Press Conference (virtual meeting: Eurpoean Stability Mechanism, November 2020), https://www.esm.europa.eu/press-releases/klaus-regling-eurogroup-video-press-conference-2020-11-30; Jonás Fernández, "S&Ds Welcome Eurogroup Breakthrough on ESM Reform to Reduce Risks for the Banking Sector," Press Release (Brussels: Socialists & Democrats, December 2020), https://www.socialistsanddemocrats.eu/newsroom/sds-welcome-eurogroup-breakthrough-esm-reform-reduce-risks-banking-sector.

176. Pepper D. Culpepper, *Quiet Politics and Business Power: Corporate Control in Europe and Japan* (Cambridge: Cambridge University Press, 2010); Cassell and Hutcheson, "Explaining Germany's Position on European Banking Union"; Bundesbank Official, Interview by author.

177. European Commission official, Interview by author.

178. Valentina Pop, "EU Policies Await German Election Outcome," *Financial Times*, September 2021, https://www.ft.com/content/d510d968-eabb-4d98-b759-1d65af2d2384.

179. Quaglia and Verdun, "Explaining the Response of the ECB to the COVID-19 Related Economic Crisis"; Quaglia and Verdun, "The COVID-19 Pandemic and the European Union."

180. Maurizio Ferrera, Joan Miró, and Stefano Ronchi, "Walking the Road Together? EU Polity Maintenance during the COVID-19 Crisis," *West European Politics* 44, no. 5–6 (2021): 1329–1352.

181. European Commission official, Interview by author.

182. European Commission official.

183. Zatterin, "Interview with La Stampa."

184. Bundesbank Official, Interview by author.

185. Bundesbank Official; European Commission official, Interview by author.

# 7
# Conclusion

## Introduction

As demonstrated in the previous chapters, the twin factors of crisis threat and crisis origin explain much of the variance in reform outcomes out of crises in European finance. This conclusion will examine those crises in comparison with each other, illuminating how those dynamics become even clearer when the crises are contrasted and the implications for the future of European financial integration. Moreover, this project focused on finance as a test case for the theory of crisis response and European integration, but has broader implications. Therefore, the second part of this will sketch how this approach may be applied to crises and integration in a range of other sectors, including immigration policy, energy policy, and foreign and security policy, as well as its implications for integration in contexts beyond the European Union.

## Comparing the Crises

Having examined each of the crises individually, it is now possible to examine them in comparative perspective, which demonstrates the importance of both severity and origin in shaping patterns of crisis response, especially in terms of how actors perceive the nature and degree of threat to the status quo. Both paired comparisons across the crises and more general discussion can provide valuable insights.

### The Impact of Severity

As noted in Chapter 2, severity is likely the most obvious dimension in shaping crisis responses, as has been well reflected in the existing literature on crises. As can be seen in comparing crises that share endogenous or exogenous origin, its importance should not be discounted. The greater the severity, in terms of the threat to integration, the easier a time reformers will have in convincing reluctant actors that they must act, and act with urgency,

*Crises and Integration in European Banking Union.* Christopher Mitchell, Oxford University Press.
© Christopher Mitchell (2023). DOI: 10.1093/oso/9780198889069.003.0007

## 284 Crises and Integration in European Banking Union

to choose between deeper integration and the deterioration of the status quo. The greater the threat, therefore, the easier it will be to expand a coalition and advance a reform agenda.

### Comparing the Endogenous Crises: The Banking Crisis and the Debt Crisis

Of the crises considered here, no two share more in common than the 2007–09 Banking Crisis and 2010–14 Debt Crisis. The underlying issues and dynamics involved overlap to the point where some scholars consider them one continuous crisis. However, important elements differentiate the two crises, especially in terms of the severity of the threat, which was far greater in the Debt Crisis; the key actors, as the Debt Crisis focused much more on the southern member states and their banks; and the breadth, as the Debt Crisis centered on the eurozone states, while the Banking Crisis drew in the rest of the EU as well as the United States.

Differences notwithstanding, reformers took both crises as a moment to push for centralization of European financial regulation, identifying essentially the same flaws and advocating for essentially the same solution. Specifically, reformers identified the twin problems of the inadequacy of national regulation of a dense network of cross-national banking and the threat to both national solvency and financial stability from banks so large that their sovereigns would struggle to afford their resolution. Moreover, the maximal reform agenda proposed in response was essentially the same in both crises: a shift of supervision and resolution, including deposit guarantee schemes (DGS), from national governments to a European body. They differed some in detail, as the proposals in the Banking Crisis were for the creation of a new body while those in the Debt Crisis called for vesting the new authority in the European Central Bank (ECB), but otherwise had essentially the same functional goals.

Despite these similarities, the outcomes were substantially different, a difference best explained by focusing on the difference in severity of threat to European integration. The Banking Crisis imposed high costs on individual member states, but presented little threat of a collapse of European integration. A status quo of recurring banking crisis would be undesirable, but, as long as they only hit the wealthier member states, that would not be fundamentally unsustainable. The Debt Crisis, on the other hand, posed a severe and proximate threat to European integration. A sovereign default of a member state would almost certainly mean their exit from the eurozone. Such an exit in turn would put pressure on the remaining states under pressure, and thus possibly lead to a further breakup. Moreover, this threat was seen as imminent, not merely theoretical, with several states seen as only weeks or months away from a default at the peak of the crisis. This meant that reform in the Debt Crisis needed to be both more urgent and more fundamental than in the Banking Crisis, where the status quo was undesirable but not unsustainable. This, in turn, created conditions for the reform coalition to both expand and compromise more readily in the Debt Crisis. Actors who would have opted to preserve the status quo rather than either deepen or reduce integration in the Banking Crisis could no longer remain on the fence. A deteriorating status quo in the Debt Crisis meant that they must now choose between deeper integration and disintegration.

The role of the UK in the two cases here is especially instructive. As a non-eurozone member, the UK was more insulated from the Debt Crisis than the other major players. The collapse of the eurozone would certainly affect the British, but not to the degree of those states that had adopted the euro as their currency. Especially given the already-present euroskeptic elements in British politics that would manifest a few years later in Brexit, the UK had little appetite for substantial increases in integration. It thus primarily played a blocking role in discussions of reforms in both crises. However, the reaction of reformers in the member states to British intransigence in the two cases differed substantially. It became clear early on in the Banking Crisis that the British would not compromise on key elements of the proposed European Banking Authority (EBA), including any mechanism that would allow the new body to compel fiscal actions by member states, including demanding the resolution of a failing bank. If even this more modest proposal could not win UK support, the maximalist calls from the European Parliament for a complete banking union thus clearly had no chance of passage. European reformers chose to accede to all but the most minor British demands rather than contemplate an end-run around British opposition by enacting eurozone-only reforms. The British similarly opposed any involvement in joint European supervision and resolution in the Debt Crisis. However, in this latter crisis, European reformers almost immediately pivoted from an EU-wide approach to a eurozone-only one, opting for deeper reforms without the UK rather than engaging in any sustained effort to bring the UK on board. Moreover, while British intransigence was met with negotiation in the Banking Crisis, it was met with real anger in the Debt Crisis, especially around the creation of the European Stability Mechanism (ESM).

This different response, both in content and tone, can be traced to the severity of the crisis facing the eurozone member states. Creation of joint supervision and regulation was a "nice to have" reform out of the Banking Crisis, which would have helped avoid future crises, but it was enough in the

## 286    Crises and Integration in European Banking Union

short run to settle the more immediate issue of regulatory confusion through creation of the EBA. However, by the Debt Crisis, failure to act presented an existential threat to the eurozone, which pushed actors reluctant to reform to choose between reform and disintegration. This helped push member states previously skeptical of deeper integration, including France and Germany, into embrace of the more ambitious reform agenda, if still with some reluctance around ECB supervision of smaller banks and concerns over the scale and control of the Single Resolution Fund (SRF). It also meant that British intransigence could be accommodated in the earlier crisis, but needed to either be shut down or circumvented in the latter.

### Comparing the Exogenous Crises: Brexit and the COVID-19 Pandemic

The two exogenous crises, Brexit and the COVID-19 Pandemic, shared less in common than the two endogenous crises, which is to be expected insofar as endogenous crises originate from the specific nature of the existing sectoral integration, while exogenous crises may originate from a myriad of possible sources. Nevertheless, they do share some similarities in both the response of actors and the reform agenda proposed. In both crises, reformers attempted to build a case for the reform agenda by focusing on the worst-case scenarios possible out of the crises. In Brexit, this meant the danger that the UK's departure would trigger a broader panic in financial markets, either originating in the rump EU itself or originating in the UK and spreading to the EU. In the Pandemic, this meant a surge in nonperforming loans (NPLs) imposing substantial costs on banks just as emergency health and economic spending limited states' ability to afford spending to support their ailing banks. In a worst-case scenario in either case, therefore, a new wave of banking crises could trigger sovereign default and eurozone collapse, just as they had threatened to do in the earlier Debt Crisis. However, in both cases, that worst-case scenario failed to develop. In Brexit, a long and transparent negotiation process reduced the danger of a panic, while in the Pandemic, massive emergency spending, especially through the Pandemic Emergency Purchase Programme (PEPP) and NextGenerationEU (NGEU) programs meant that the feared NPL surge never hit.

Reformers attempted to use both crises to advance a broadly similar reform agenda, especially centered on advancing Capital Markets Union (CMU) to guarantee continued access to financial resources and adding a European Deposit Insurance Scheme (EDIS) to the existing elements of banking union. In both cases, those debates quickly became ensnarled in questions of how to balance addressing legacy issues around the previous crises versus addressing new challenges, as well as a reluctance of member states to make the big concessions on surrendering control of bankruptcy law and other key elements necessary to truly unlock CMU. In both cases, reformers fell short of their more ambitious goals, with CMU remaining mostly incomplete and progress on creating EDIS still stalemated.

The Pandemic did produce more reforms than Brexit. In addition to the temporary PEPP and NGEU spending, member states in the Pandemic agreed to backstop the SRF with the ESM, ensuring that the Single Resolution Mechanism (SRM) would have sufficient resources to accomplish its purposes. Brexit saw only the relocation of the EBA, a move with no regulatory implications, and an indefinitely delayed plan to repatriate euro-clearing activity out of London. As with the two endogenous crises, severity provides a clear driver of the difference in outcome between the two crises here. A sense of urgency over Brexit's threat to financial integration failed to develop, with reformers working hard to even convince others that the UK's departure posed enough of a threat to shift conversations out of normal and into emergency politics. On the other hand, even as most attention entirely reasonably focused on the public health crisis in COVID, the threat to financial integration was clear enough that actors shifted very quickly into emergency policymaking. Even with that shift, financial integration reforms out of the Pandemic fell well short of the maximal goals advocated, but the real sense of a threat to the status quo present in the Pandemic and not in Brexit proved sufficient to win at least enough support to advance the relatively modest permanent reforms that did emerge out of the Pandemic.

## The Impact of Origin

Even as severity's importance should not be discounted, it clearly cannot alone explain the range of reform outcomes out of a crisis. Contrasting crises that share a level of severity but differ in origin is in turn also instructive. A crisis which can be traced to flaws in integration is one that will reoccur without a fix to those flaws, while fixing flaws in integration can only help manage future exogenous crises, not prevent them from happening. As such, even when crises provide comparably severe threats, origin crucially shapes the willingness of actors to embrace a deeper reform agenda.

### Comparing the Moderate Crises: The Banking Crisis and Brexit
Although they differ substantially in their origins, the Banking Crisis and Brexit posed roughly comparable threats to European integration. In both cases, the status quo was not in imminent threat of collapse, and would be

broadly sustainable if vulnerable even in the absence of reforms. The more ambitious reform agenda in both cases also broke down over the same essential issue of states refusing to surrender national control in the name of reinforcing the stability of the European financial system. In the Banking Crisis, states, especially the UK, balked at granting the EBA the authority to overrule national regulators, especially on questions of resolution, limiting the new institution to a reliance on moral authority over national bodies. In Brexit, the fear of losing national discretion over bankruptcy rules in particular proved an insurmountable barrier to the creation of a CMU and the question of how to manage legacy issues continued to bedevil debates over EDIS.

The Banking Crisis undeniably produced more meaningful reform than Brexit. The major reform out of the Banking Crisis, the creation of the European System of Financial Supervision (ESFS), replaced the old Lamfalussy Committees with new authorities with stronger mechanisms for communication and coordination between national regulators, including the creation of the EBA. On the other hand, while the Banking Crisis led to the creation of the EBA, Brexit merely drove the EBA's relocation to a new city. The difference between the two crisis outcomes can be traced to their origin, and the implication of that origin to the continued status quo. The Banking Crisis's origin could be traced at least in part to flaws in the Lamfalussy process method of regulating cross-border banking in the EU. This meant that failure to reform that process would leave in place a mechanism for generating the seeds of the next crisis. The status quo was therefore sustainable but unsatisfactory, as it meant locking in a manageable but expensive perpetual internal instability. By contrast, the question over post-Brexit reforms was whether to reinforce the system against external shocks. The immediate danger out of Brexit, market actors panicking from losing easy contact between the UK and the EU, was real, but also, barring the decision of another member state to leave, not one likely to reoccur, and at any rate the reforms would be unlikely to block another member state from exiting. Creating a CMU and EDIS would help reinforce against new external shocks, but not prevent them from happening.

The difference in origins, and thus in the capacity of reforms to prevent further crises, shaped the differences in negotiating dynamics. The reform debates in the Banking Crisis were marked by a willingness of reformers to satisfice, to accept an imperfect solution as preferable to the status quo. The European Parliament's maximal demands were quickly blocked, despite the fact that the subsequent Debt Crisis would vividly demonstrate that concerns over the sovereign-bank Doom Loop and continued gaps in the cross-border regulatory architecture could and would create future problems. Even the reformers in Parliament themselves conceded that partial reform was preferable to no reform. British unwillingness to accept any European control over national regulators was met with accommodation per the same logic, that even the minimal reforms the UK would accept represented an improvement that could potentially block another crisis. By contrast, opponents in the post-Brexit reform debates repeatedly chose stalemate over compromise, on the CMU and on EDIS. If the reforms would only help manage the next crisis, rather than actually prevent it, key actors would repeatedly choose to block limited progress in the short run in the hopes that their intransigence would produce a more favorable outcome in the long term. Post-Brexit debates centered on ways to make a stable system better, rather than a threat of further instability from flaws in the system itself as in the Banking Crisis, meaning that the need to accept partial reforms was felt less urgently.

## Comparing the Severe Crises: The Debt Crisis and the COVID-19 Pandemic

The Debt Crisis and the COVID-19 Pandemic shared a good deal in common despite differing in their origins. Both presented essentially the same worst-case scenario: that of a wave of bank failure would lead to sovereign debt crises from member states unable to afford the costs of rescuing them, which in turn would lead to those states collapsing out of the eurozone. Italy and Spain in particular soon emerged as points of concern in both crises. Reformers in both crises explicitly cited Monnet's dictum on integration through crisis, in service of broadly the same maximal reform goals. Reformers in both called for establishing a complete banking union including an expansive Single Supervisory Mechanism (SSM), a Single Resolution Mechanism with a large Single Resolution Fund, and the introduction of a common European Deposit Insurance Scheme. Moreover, in both crises, the Europeans responded initially with large but temporary programs, including the European Financial Stability Facility (EFSF) and European Financial Stability Mechanism (EFSM) in the Debt Crisis and PEPP and NGEU in the Pandemic.

However, in the Debt Crisis, the Europeans went beyond temporary programs to introduce a true pan-European supervisor in the SSM and a mutualization of bank resolution in the SRM. Their limits on reach, size, and continued influence of member states notwithstanding, these presented substantial reforms to the European financial regulatory architecture, arguably the most substantial reforms since the Maastricht Treaty itself. By contrast, in the Pandemic, the only permanent reform to the regulatory architecture was the backstopping of the SRF with the ESM, a real but relatively minor change.

**290  Crises and Integration in European Banking Union**

This difference in outcomes can be linked to the origins of the crises. The Pandemic posed a clear exogenous threat, and given that the previous pandemic of comparable scale, the Spanish Influenza, hit approximately a century earlier, it also posed a threat unlikely to reoccur soon. As such, the threat, while severe, was also temporary. The Pandemic might wreak substantial damage, but would pass in time. As such, temporary responses would be sufficient. Even if another such crisis should hit, that crisis could also be met with temporary responses, and at any rate no reform of the financial sector could prevent another pandemic. By contrast, the Debt Crisis could be clearly traced to fundamental flaws in the European financial regulatory architecture. Failure to address those flaws would not only ensure that another crisis would hit soon, but also would hamper efforts to resolve the current crisis. This can be seen clearly in the transition from a reliance on the temporary EFSF and EFSM to the permanent ESM and later to the creation of banking union once it became clear that the flaws were more in bank supervision and resolution than in sovereign debt as such. The EFSF and EFSM fell short not simply because of their size, but because of their transience; eventually they would expire but the flaws would still remain, giving market actors no reason to stop panicking because the reason for their panic remained. The ESM and banking union both therefore were necessarily permanent, because enduring problems require enduring fixes.

Understood from that perspective, the key question becomes not why the Pandemic failed to produce more permanent reforms but rather why it produced even the relatively minor permanent reform of backstopping the SRF with the ESM. Here the context of the pre-backstop status quo becomes important, specifically the existing plan if the SRF should be exhausted. In such an event, a member state needing to resolve its banks would need to draw on its own resources, and when those were exhausted turn to the ESM. Especially given the political unpopularity of tapping the ESM, states could be reasonably certain to only turn to the ESM at the very last resort, increasing both market panic and the direct cost of resolution. The multiple waves of crises hitting European finance in the previous decade and a half, both of endogenous and exogenous origin, made it clear that the threat of SRF exhaustion was real and enduring. Given that the existing process already foresaw tapping the ESM, albeit in a messier and costlier fashion, and given that the member states had already agreed to adopt an ESM backstop in the more distant future, the decision to accelerate that timeline to weatherproof against further shocks to the European financial system offered a relatively low-cost fix to an enduring problem. However, this also meant that the introduction of the ESM backstop presented only a minor reform in comparison to the introduction of the SSM and SRM. On the other hand, introducing the SSM and SRM promised to block future crises, while backstopping the SRF with the ESM only promised to make it easier to endure them.

## Comparing the Most-Different Cases

### The Debt Crisis and Brexit

Comparing the endogenous severe Debt Crisis and the exogenous moderate Brexit Crisis clearly illustrates the importance of the shift to emergency politics. Although the Debt Crisis lasted for years, the negotiations at virtually every point in that period carried a great deal of urgency, given the perception of an imminent threat of the catastrophic failure of the common currency. This produced a willingness for states to compromise on previously firmly held positions, including Germany's shift to tolerate mutualized bank resolution and a general willingness of the eurozone members to deepen the differences between eurozone and non-eurozone states by introducing banking union only in the former. It also produced a series of compromises that may be described as "quick and dirty," focused on ensuring immediate action with crucial details and limitations left to be addressed at a later point. This dynamic is most obvious in the Single Resolution Mechanism. The Single Resolution Fund was even at the time broadly agreed to be too small, and would lack a clear backstop should it be exhausted until the Pandemic reforms half a decade later. Similarly, the decision-making process for bank resolution, involving the new Single Resolution Board (SRB), the European Council, and the European Commission, was slow, cumbersome, and, as became clear in the subsequent years, permeable to member state influence to protect their ailing banks. These compromises fully satisfied no one, but could be implemented quickly, which at the peak of the crisis became the priority. In contrast, the reform debates following Brexit had no such urgency. Actors frequently held fast to their positions and debates got bogged down in minutia because moderate exogenous Brexit crisis simply failed to produce the drive for immediate action that followed from the severe and exogenous Debt Crisis.

### The Banking Crisis and the COVID-19 Pandemic

Comparing the Banking Crisis and the Pandemic is in some ways more instructive than comparing the Debt Crisis and Brexit, as both the Banking Crisis and the Pandemic produced modest reforms, but of different types and with different priorities in the debates around their creation. The Banking

Crisis's chief reform, the creation of the ESFS, provides an example of a "patch-up" reform, insofar as it made real but modest changes to the core functioning of the European financial system. The debates around the ESFS focused primarily on identifying the origin of the crisis and addressing existing weaknesses in the financial regulatory architecture. At the same time, member states, especially but not exclusively the UK, demonstrated great hostility to any reforms that might impose fiscal obligations on them. The conversation thus became about how to make permanent changes to the regulatory architecture which would avoid future crises at minimal cost. Debates around financial reforms in the Pandemic showed the opposite dynamic. From early in the crisis, virtually all actors dismissed out of hand any conversation about origin or blame, with a nearly universal agreement that the Pandemic presented a purely exogenous shock. This meant that the concerns about moral hazard central to Banking Crisis debates about fiscal obligations were explicitly dismissed in the Pandemic, and the member states showed a willingness to make large, albeit temporary, spending commitments in sharp contrast to the hostility toward fiscal obligations in the Banking Crisis. It also meant that the conversations around financial reform in the Pandemic paid relatively little attention to questions of origin, and to questions of regulatory tweaks that might make future crises less likely. Thus the two crises provide a study in contrasts. The Banking Crisis's endogenous origins prompted a focus on fixing regulatory gaps, while its moderate severity meant a reluctance among member states to commit their own fiscal resources, leading to "patch-up" reform. On the other hand, the Pandemic's exogenous origin meant that no one paid much attention to persistent flaws in the system, while its severity meant a willingness to commit substantial but temporary fiscal resources to endure it and similar future crises, and "weatherproofing" reform.

## Overall Lessons from Comparing the Crises

Comparing all four crises demonstrates the importance of attention to both crisis origin and crisis severity to build an effective model of what kinds of reforms a given crisis will produce. The Brexit Crisis, exogenous in origin and moderate in threat, failed to generate sufficient urgency to produce notable reform. This did not stop reformers from attempting to use the crisis moment as a window of opportunity to drive their favored reforms. However, the combination of only moderate severity and an exogenous origin meant that they simply failed to convince a critical mass of actors to join their reform efforts.

The Banking Crisis and the Pandemic each met one of the two necessary dimensions for reform, but each in their own way demonstrate how without the other dimension, reforms will likely only be moderate. In the Banking Crisis, the endogeneity of the crisis produced a clear drive for reforms to prevent a future crisis from emerging out of the same flaw that produced that crisis. However, the threat posed by the Banking Crisis proved insufficient to move actors broadly content with the status quo toward more radical reforms, especially reforms that would impose fiscal costs on member states. The status quo could be maintained, but the Crisis revealed the undesirability of maintaining a status quo of perpetually recurring crises due to regulatory gaps.

The Pandemic provided a more severe threat than the Banking Crisis, but its origins were clearly exogenous to the financial system. Contrary to the expectations of reformers, this in fact undercut the case for reform of the financial architecture; moral hazard was not an issue in the crisis, but if the regulatory architecture's flaws hadn't caused the crisis, fixing those flaws was not a priority in confronting the crisis. The Pandemic posed a real threat to the integration status quo, but one that could be handled with temporary spending rather than fundamental reforms.

Of the four crises under examination, only the Debt Crisis therefore fit the classic Monnet narrative of a crisis prompting Europeans to move past their previous disagreements to embrace a fundamental reform and deeper integration. It, like the Pandemic, provided such a clear threat to European integration that it could not be left unaddressed. However, the Pandemic was exogenous. No amount of financial system reform would prevent another crisis from hitting, dampening the appetite for more fundamental changes. By contrast, the Debt Crisis, like the Banking Crisis, originated with flaws in the regulatory architecture itself. As such, failure to act would mean perpetually recurring crises. In the Banking Crisis, this produced an appetite for reform, but a limited one, as the alternative of a status quo of perpetual manageable instability was endurable enough to prompt member states to dig in on blocking certain reforms. On the other hand, the Debt Crisis was not only endogenous but severe, meaning that the status quo could not endure at any cost, and urgent expansive action was the only way to move out of the emergency period. As such, member states proved willing to compromise and accept unsatisfactory but effective solutions, as the only alternative to deeper integration had become disintegration. Only both severity and endogeneity, therefore, produced the conditions for a true Monnet Crisis, one that would lead to fundamental reforms toward deeper integration.

## Implications for the Future of EU Finance

Given the unresolved questions and entrenched interests on either side of key issues, significant reform of the EU financial regulatory architecture appears unlikely without a crisis shock to the status quo. There may be some slow progress on Capital Markets Union, as has been the case for the last decade. However, as has been the pattern in this time, it seems unlikely that these reforms will tackle the hard questions about harmonization of bankruptcy rules or centralization of actual authority that have proven to be the enduring stumbling blocks. Progress on banking union will most likely also be chiefly at the margins. The Single Resolution Fund will gradually fill to its designated capacity, and may even grow through the course of normal politics. However, motion toward a dramatic increase in size is unlikely. Movement on European Deposit Insurance could conceivably become possible in normal politics, if only because of the wide acknowledgment of the desirability of the reform. However, that reform is only really possible with a significant reduction in NPLs and sovereign debt to levels acceptable to Germany and the other northern member states. That level of reduction is not likely to arrive anytime soon, even in the absence of shocks that might increase sovereign debt levels. There also remains the risk that acceptable levels may be a moving target, enabling northern policymakers to retain support for EDIS in principle while also never actually needing to persuade their reticent publics that the time is finally upon them to enact the reform.

Deeper progress absent a crisis is unlikely. The current status quo reflects a balance between factions with fundamentally different answers to key questions around European integration. On banking union, the core question remains the degree to which European resolutions should be considered an emergency last resort only after national reserves are exhausted or a first-choice option. The former preserves more national discretion, but the latter increases overall stability, and different factions calculate that trade-off in incompatible ways. Similarly, a core division over EDIS remains on whether the reform is exclusively forward-looking and future-proofing, or also a potential tool to help clean up legacy problems. Broad agreement already exists over the need for the former, but the latter splits member states, with the northerners unwilling to take on the legacy costs and the southerners unwilling to accept an EDIS without a role for legacy debt which would increase their regulatory burdens but not help resolve their existing problems.

Finally, CMU remains stalemated because key questions about the future of European finance remain unanswered. While the departure of the UK made deeper integration in some fields easier, it complicated CMU by opening the door to a new conversation about the future shape of European finance. So long as the UK was a member, EU nonbank finance would clearly be centered in the City of London, with other cities having more peripheral roles. With the departure of Britain, the EU now faced essentially three alternatives: it could negotiate terms of access with the UK that would preserve London's role in EU finance, it could attempt to build a distributed financial system with activity spread across multiple roughly balanced centers, or it could create a "new London" by centering financial activity in a new central hub. That hub would most likely be Paris or Frankfurt, but could be any of a number of other potential sites.

Each of these models would, in turn, require the construction of a different kind of CMU. The first option, keeping London's central role, would require little in way of internal reforms and mostly involve keeping barriers to movement of capital to the UK low. The second, a distributed system, would require a fairly well calibrated CMU to overcome the network effects that frequently drives financial market activity to concentrate in a single hub. Finally, building a new hub could be done either simply by creating common rules and letting market actors go where they will, actively promoting a common solution at the European level, or letting individual nation-states adopt policies to make their own sites attractive hosts. In practice, while a consensus exists that preserving London's central role is unacceptable, none of the major contenders to host the "new London" proved willing to give up on their ambitions. This produced the least efficient outcome from a financial market perspective, as the EU raised some barriers to keeping London, but also failed to block states from engaging in their own activity to attract financial markets, creating or preserving national divergence within the EU. This stalemate does not appear to be breaking any time soon, absent a crisis or the emergence of a clear new center. As of the end of 2022, Paris appeared to be the leading contender, and if Paris's lead continues to grow, it is conceivable that the EU could adapt accordingly, building a CMU that allowed or encouraged Paris's central role. However, doing so would require Germany to step back from its own efforts to promote Frankfurt as a rival center, which to date appears unlikely to happen.

## Crises and the Future of European Financial Integration

If the status quo of European financial integration is stalemate on fundamental questions, the most likely driver of change is then probably a crisis that makes the status quo unsustainable and forces a decision. As outlined in this book, the more endogenous and the more severe a crisis, the more likely reform becomes. Especially given the depth of the existing divisions, a moderate exogenous crisis remains unlikely to prompt much more than cosmetic reforms. A moderate endogenous crisis driven by or exacerbated by flaws in the existing system could potentially produce a patch-up reform, though the specific form would depend on the nature of the challenge. For instance, a failure of a national deposit guarantee scheme to pay out to cross-border customers would likely prompt some movement toward cross-border reinsurance of DGS, though on its own would probably not be enough to bring full EDIS, and would be extremely unlikely to prompt action on at best tangentially related issues such as CMU. Similarly, weatherproofing reforms out of a severe exogenous crisis would depend on the nature of the shock and how it produced the threat.

A severe endogenous crisis is the most likely to prompt the European Union and its members to settle the bigger questions around banking union and capital market integration. Here, though, it is important to caution that just because the previous answers to challenges have been deeper integration, forcing the question could also plausibly prompt a disintegrative reform that enhances stability by increasing separation and barriers to capital movement.

### The Post-COVID Inflationary Moment

Although it has not generally been described in crisis terms, the EU has faced in 2022 and into 2023 strain on its financial system through increases in inflation. This could at least partially be classified as an endogenous problem, given that it is in large part a product of the loose monetary policy of the ECB in the years since the 2007–09 Banking Crisis and especially the 2010–14 European Debt Crisis. It also has some exogenous causes, born out of both the continuing supply chain disruption of the COVID-19 Pandemic and the energy shock from the Russian invasion of Ukraine and subsequent retaliatory sanctions. However, as of the end of 2022, it is at most a moderate crisis for Europe. The euro has declined and member state bond spreads have grown, but neither precipitously, especially in comparison to what happened in the Debt Crisis. The crisis in the now non-EU United Kingdom, especially in the brief time Liz Truss served as Prime Minister, provides a clearer example of a more severe crisis, with a sharp fall in the pound and a sharp rise in yield on gilts, but as it is no longer an EU member, this does not constitute a crisis for the EU itself.

Given these parameters, inflation presents most plausibly a moderate endogenous crisis, and therefore the most likely outcome would be some manner of patch-up reform. This would most likely look something like a harmonization of bankruptcy rules or an increase in size of the SRF. However, to the degree the cause is seen as the Russian war in Ukraine or lingering

COVID effects, this would be a moderate exogenous crisis, and little to no reform should be expected. All of this could, of course, change if something happened to shift the severity of the crisis, such as a sovereign debt crisis in Italy or one of the other more vulnerable member states.

## The Disintegrative Alternative

One point which is important to emphasize in considering this model is that it focuses on the intensity of change in integration based on the origin and severity of a crisis. Because the master narrative of European politics continues to be one of "ever closer union" that regards moves toward disintegration as deeply undesirable, the assumption has been that the direction of that change will be toward deeper integration. Certainly, all of the cases considered here either produced deeper integration to some degree or, in the case of managing the fallout from Brexit, little change in either direction for the rump EU. However, this is by no means inevitable, and disintegrative crises have occurred in the past. The Empty Chair Crisis, for instance, presented an endogenous moderate crisis. Its origins lay in the mechanisms of decision-making in the European Economic Community (EEC), making it endogenous, but it also occurred at a time of low enough integration that the paralysis of decision-making in the EEC presented less of a threat than it would after the establishment of the Single Market. The outcome of that crisis, a veto for member states, could best be described as "patch-up disintegration," reducing integration as a way out of the crisis. The decision of the UK to leave the EU in 2016 presented a more fundamental shift toward disintegration, arguably driven by endogenous crises in European immigration policies and the broader metacrisis of EU legitimacy.

Much of the earlier literature on European integration, especially out of the neo-functionalist approach, assumes that integration may accelerate or slow, but almost never reverse. For much of European history, it is true that the preponderance of power has been held by actors who either favored greater integration or a preservation of the status quo. Moreover, the status quo actors have generally chosen deeper integration over disintegration if they have been forced to choose by a collapsing status quo. However, as the post-functionalists rightly highlight, that state of affairs should not be assumed to persist indefinitely into the future. The COVID-19 Pandemic and to a lesser degree the Russian invasion of Ukraine have generated evidence of the value of European solidarity, and the UK's post-Brexit struggles have been cited as evidence of the danger of forgoing that solidarity. This may ensure that the pro-integration bias dominates for the near-term future. However, the undercurrent of euroskepticism that swelled in the 2010s remains present, and it is entirely conceivable therefore that a future European crisis may prompt a move toward disintegration instead of integration.

In the event that such a swell of euroskepticism occurs, and the master narrative of "ever closer union" should lose its hold, this would not in itself invalidate the model. Greater severity and greater endogeneity should both be associated with more fundamental change, with the deepest change coming out of crises with severe threats and endogenous origin. Absent the dominance of a pro-integration master narrative, the model would simply be neutral as to the direction of that change. It would predict a similar magnitude of disintegration based on the origin and severity of the crisis, with the direction of change being determined by whether forcing actors to abandon an unsustainable or undesirable status quo shifts them to favoring disintegration or integration. A moderate exogenous crisis should produce little change in either direction, while a moderate endogenous crisis or severe exogenous crisis will likely produce modest disintegration if it does not produce modest integration. Only in the case of a severe endogenous crisis, therefore, should we expect to see substantial disintegration, just as that is the only case in which we should expect to see a crisis produce substantial integration.

## Other Crises and the Model

The cases examined in the prior chapters are all within the European financial system, in part to control for the nature of the crises and the problems they exposed. However, the model itself is not confined to the financial system, and could work in other sectors as well. The following section will briefly sketch out the implications of the model in several additional sectors with a focus on the kinds of crises most likely to prompt a reform.

## Immigration Policy

Perhaps the most obvious sector where the model can provide insight is immigration, where a clear divide can be made between endogenous and exogenous crises. An endogenous crisis can be taken to be one caused by internal migration policies related to the design of the EU, especially the freedom of movement of EU citizens. Reform in this area could plausibly take the form of smoother incorporation of intra-EU migrants or alternatively imposing restrictions on freedom of movement. Conversely, an exogenous immigration crisis would be one focused on the influx of non-EU migrants into the EU. Such crises could be classified as exogenous because the core of the problem is not EU migration policies as such, but events in third countries creating an impetus for migration. For instance, EU border and refugee policies may make the EU a more or less attractive destination, but would not solve the root causes of the waves of immigration into the EU in recent years, the civil wars in Syria and Libya.

Historically, immigration has not been a source of significant threats to integration, outside of moments of peak concern such as the height of the Syrian conflict. That has changed in recent years both with the massive and sustained flows of migrants out of Africa and the Middle East in the past decade and with the rise of nationalist populist parties hostile to the influx of immigrants both from within and outside of the EU. The scale of the threat to EU integration from that populist backlash may be seen in the decision of the UK to leave the EU, a decision driven in large part by nativists concerned that the UK was barred from blocking immigration by EU membership.[1] Although no other state has to date followed the UK's lead, anti-immigration sentiment continues to motivate political candidates in a range of countries, including core member states such as France and Italy.

Immigration thus provides a clear way to classify endogeneity or exogeneity, and a means to classify the severity of the threat to integration. As such, it becomes possible to examine how various kinds of immigration-related crises might be expected to shape future integration.

### Moderate Exogenous Crisis

This sort of crisis would involve an influx of non-EU migrants, but not in a volume sufficient to trigger substantial threats to integration. The steady but moderate influx of immigrants since the late 2010s arguably fits this category. It has strained social services in the receiving countries, leading to calls for solidarity either in terms of financial support from other members or through interior member states accepting a portion of the refugee populations. The reluctance of nonborder member states other than Germany to take up this burden has in turn created internal strains on integration. The late 2022 clash between Italy and France over where to dock the *Ocean Viking*, a ship filled with 234 mostly African refugees provides an example of this strain.[2] This influx has also empowered anti-immigrant and euroskeptic leaders, most prominently in Hungary, which has created spillover clashes between Hungary and the EU on a host of other issues. However, the core problem is not EU policies but rather economic and political instability in

**300** Crises and Integration in European Banking Union

neighboring countries, and therefore can only be mitigated, not resolved, by changes in EU immigration policy. Moreover, the scale of the challenge is not at present enough to warrant substantial change. Therefore, the model predicts little change in the absence of a substantial increase in the influx of migrants or some other cascading consequence.

### Severe Exogenous Crisis

The massive influx of refugees in the early 2010s, especially that resulting from Syrians and Libyans fleeing the civil wars in the respective countries, provides an example of a severe exogenous crisis. As with the ongoing moderate exogenous crisis post-2015, this influx strained social services in receiving countries, but to a much greater degree. It therefore also created much greater strain between member states, as Greece, Italy, and Spain bore substantial costs for hosting refugees at the very moment they were struggling to emerge from their sovereign debt crises out of the European Debt Crisis. As such, the early 2010s refugee crisis prompted calls to radically revamp the Dublin Regulation, the agreement governing member state responsibility for refugees and other immigrants. A significant modification to the Dublin Regulation, such as applying freedom of movement to refugees or mandating solidarity payments from interior to refugee-hosting member states, would have constituted a significant reform. However, as predicted by the model, the exogeneity of the crisis led instead to weatherproofing reforms. In particular, while some minor tweaks were made to asylum rules for member states, the most significant response to the refugee crisis was the deal struck with Turkey wherein Turkey would agree to host refugees in exchange for financial support from the EU and a handful of other concessions. This was a much less ambitious proposal than the more fundamental reforms proposed. It did involve cross-border fiscal transfers, but by virtue of being transfers to a nonmember rather than a member state were less likely to be seen as a movement toward full fiscal union. However, it sufficed to get the EU through the crisis, especially as migrant numbers declined to a more manageable level in the second half of the decade.

### Moderate Endogenous Crisis

A moderate endogenous crisis would be one where a substantial increase in internal migration within the EU leads to an increased burden on the fiscal resources of the host states and/or a strain on the domestic politics of the hosts. Obviously, internal migration has been an ever-present feature of European integration since the introduction of freedom of movement in the 1957 Treaty of Rome creating the European Economic Community, so it can be here especially difficult to specify when the level of internal migration rises to the level of moderate or severe crisis. A most likely period to examine would be the significant east-to-west migration following the Great Enlargement of the 2000s, the expansion of EU membership into the post-communist states of central and eastern Europe. In most of continental Europe, this produced what would broadly be considered a moderate crisis, one that did not require substantial changes to the structure of the EU's freedom of movement policies, but one that motivated patch-up reforms to clarify the rights and obligations of member states toward their immigrant and emigrant populations.

### Severe Endogenous Crisis

A severe endogenous crisis would be one where the internal migration of EU citizens reached an unacceptable crisis point. The closest example of this would be the UK's response to the increase in internal migration out of the Great Enlargement. For reasons that are beyond the scope of this work, this influx spurred a far greater anti-EU mobilization in the UK than in other EU member states. Here, as predicted, we also see the most significant modification to European integration in form of the UK decision to exit the EU. While the other examples discussed are crises that produced deeper integration, this obviously provides an example going in the opposite direction. Immigration was not the only factor contributing to the Brexit decision, but it did form both a centerpiece of the Leave campaign and was a core focus of Prime Minister David Cameron's attempt to renegotiate the UK's terms of membership in the run-up to the referendum. When the rest of the EU proved unwilling to grant significant concessions on freedom of movement, the UK chose the undeniably significant reform of leaving the European Union.

## Energy Policy

Another sector that can be examined in this framework would be energy policy. Here the fungibility of fossil fuels in particular blur the barriers between endogenous and exogenous somewhat in a manner akin to that of global finance. However, broadly speaking, endogenous crises can be taken to mean those related to internal EU energy generation or transfer, and exogenous crises can be taken to be those involving a cutoff of external supply. Once again, the model can make predictions as to the most likely outcome of various kinds of energy shocks.

## Moderate Exogenous Crisis

A moderate exogenous crisis would be something like the Iraq War in the early 2000s that affected the global supply of oil, leading to substantial but not critical increases in energy costs in Europe. The origins and resolution of the problems in such a crisis would be outside of the remit of European energy policy, at least on an emergency basis. At the same time, the moderate nature of the impact means that it may introduce some shifts in consumer spending and energy consumption, and perhaps an increase in welfare support at the national level, but not the sort of fundamental shift in European energy integration or energy policy that would more fully insulate the EU from such price shocks. Any shift for greater European energy generation or a shift to green energy out of such a crisis would thus likely amount to only that which could be accomplished through noncrisis normal politics, as the size of the crisis would be too modest to move states toward more dramatic emergency action.

## Moderate Endogenous Crisis

A moderate endogenous crisis is most likely to occur because something causes a decrease in European energy production. The most appropriate example here may be the post-Fukushima popular turn against nuclear energy in several European countries. Although the indirect cause was a nuclear accident in Japan, this did not directly make European nuclear energy more expensive or less safe than it had been prior to the accident. Because the proximate cause and key intervening factor was European public opinion, the European, and especially German, turn against nuclear energy may be classified as endogenous, and a crisis that could be resolved by changes in both national and European energy policy. At the same time, however, it did not precipitate a massive loss of access to energy for the Europeans, but rather a moderate crisis which could be dealt with through relatively modest patch-up reforms. Most of the activity was at the national level, with states phasing out nuclear energy and increasing reliance on both green energy and especially Russian fossil fuel imports. At the EU level, the most prominent action was the introduction of an extra round of nuclear safety stress tests beyond the normal safety inspections.[3] However, these tests were one-off voluntary tests and reliant on national self-assessments, so did not represent a significant move toward deeper integration.

## Severe Exogenous Crisis

The European Union is currently in the midst of a severe exogenous crisis, as the Russian invasion of Ukraine, an exogenous shock, prompted the Europeans to back away as quickly as they could from their dependence on

Russian energy imports.[4] The sudden spike in energy costs prompted a wave of weatherproofing solutions across Europe. The most prominent integrative solution was an increase in energy transfers across borders from states more independent of Russian energy such as Spain, with its reliance on North African energy sources, and France, with its more robust nuclear energy base. As some states, especially in Eastern Europe, are less able to cope with the rising energy costs, it is plausible that emergency fiscal support to cover the rising costs may also be forthcoming. This is made especially plausible because the other, disintegrative, solution to the crisis would be a breakdown in European solidarity on Russian sanctions as individual members grant Russia concessions in exchange for cheaper Russian energy. Hungary has already sent signals that it is considering such an option, and hard-hit countries such as Romania may be tempted to follow suit as well. Such a break in solidarity would be a significant breakdown in integration, but not a severe one, as it would only be a break from an emergency policy, and not a rupture on a more fundamental question of integration.

### Severe Endogenous Crisis

The European Union has yet to confront a severe endogenous crisis on energy. It would likely entail something on the scale of a Fukushima-type nuclear accident in Europe itself, that would cause a much more rapid and intense shift against nuclear energy. Such a crisis would almost inevitably involve a substantial remaking of European energy markets, as France in particular could ill-afford a rapid shift away from nuclear energy. Here is where an energy crisis is most likely to produce real centralization of European energy generation and regulation in face of major crisis originating in Europe itself.

## Foreign and Security Policy

The model could also be plausibly applied to crises in foreign and security policy, with discussion here focusing on foreign policy crises over security issues, rather than trade disputes or other nonsecurity foreign policy. In examining foreign and security policy, it is worth noting that virtually every foreign policy clash that might rise to the level of a crisis involving EU member states has been exogenous. Indeed, one of the core purposes of the European project has been to ensure that there are no foreign or especially security policy crises between member states. As such, any discussion of endogenous foreign policy crises, meaning crises between member states, are almost entirely hypothetical.

### Moderate Endogenous Crisis

A moderate endogenous security policy crisis might be something like a border dispute between member states. Such outcomes are perhaps most likely with expansion to include member states with unsettled border disputes, such as if Turkey were admitted without a permanent resolution of its disputes with Greece or Cyprus, or if both Serbia and Kosovo were to be admitted without a permanent settlement of their conflicts. Such a crisis would likely draw the EU in as an interlocutor for the dispute, but because any solution would only be stable with the agreement of the involved parties themselves, the EU would primarily be in the role of facilitator of a settlement rather than adjudicator of the dispute.

### Severe Endogenous Crisis

A severe endogenous crisis would be one that escalated to actual armed conflict between members. The closest the EU has come to such a dispute is perhaps the Troubles in Northern Ireland, an armed separatist conflict where the insurgent group explicitly sought to leave one member state (the United Kingdom) and join another (the Republic of Ireland). Crucially, however, the Republic of Ireland itself did not provide material support to the Northern Irish insurgents. This meant that the Troubles remained a domestic conflict within the United Kingdom rather than a true interstate conflict. An actual armed conflict between member states would almost inevitably force a choice between a real centralization of authority in the EU, giving it the capacity to forcibly settle conflicts, or disintegration in face of conflict, either through the expulsion of one or more of the involved parties or the collapse of the EU itself. A historical analogy may be to the United States in the run-up to its Civil War, where individual states grew increasingly assertive and the balance of power between the federal government and states which has existed since independence became increasingly precarious. The US Civil War thus proved to be a decisive moment in the evolution of the US federation, establishing definitively that the federal government had both authority over the states and the capacity to enforce its decisions with military force. An armed conflict involving member states would similarly likely force the EU to either move toward true federation or assume a permanently diminished role.

### Moderate Exogenous Crisis

Much more likely, and common historically, are foreign and security crises involving third countries. A moderate exogenous security crisis would be something like the Iraq War, a conflict that internally divided the member states between those, mostly in the West, that opposed the US-led invasion of Iraq, and those mostly eastern member states which supported the US in the run-up to the War. This led to some sniping back and forth between the two camps, such as when French President Jacques Chirac chided the pro-War members that "they missed a good opportunity to keep quiet."[5] At the same time, however, those internal divisions never rose to the level of actually threatening permanent divisions in the European Union. As such, while the European experience in the run-up to the Iraq War led to a lot of talk on the need to increase the Common Foreign and Security Policy, and ensured that those items were part of the conversation around the rejected European Constitution and the later Treaty of Lisbon, those conversations took place in a broader conversation under normal politics. The crisis over the war itself failed to produce any significant reform to European integration.

### Severe Exogenous Crisis

The Russian invasion of Ukraine in 2022 rose to the level of a severe foreign and security crisis for the European Union. Russia's goals included not just the annexation of Ukrainian territory, but also the fracturing of the key institutions of the Western alliance, especially the North Atlantic Treaty Organization (NATO) and the European Union. In addition, the ex-communist member states bordering Russia saw in the Ukraine invasion a direct threat to their own territorial integrity and independence. As such, this posed a major threat to European integration, albeit one originating outside of the EU itself. It therefore produced moderate but significant moves toward deeper integration in security policy, most notably in a sanctions regime against Russia that has held together much more than many observers had expected. It has not, however, produced a truly fundamental shift on European security policy, such as a real move toward a common European armed forces. Here it is worth noting that in security policy more than other sectors, there is likely greater potential for an exogenous crisis to generate truly substantial reforms with a severe enough threat. A direct Russian invasion of an EU member state, for instance, much like an armed conflict between member states, would very likely force the EU to either assume a more central role in rallying a collective response as a true federation or step back into irrelevance in the face of an existential threat.

## Implications Outside of Europe

The European Union, as has been noted by many observers, is largely *sui generis* in the modern world. No other institution exists in a similar liminal space, involving such deep integration while also not truly constituting a state in its own right. Although the model of integration outlined in this work was developed specifically around the argument that crises are essential to *European* integration, it could plausibly also carry implications for the integration of other political bodies made up of independent or partially independent subunits. Broadly speaking, such entities would occupy one of two categories: federal states and strong regional associations.

## Crises in Federal States

Federal states almost by definition involve greater integration than exists in the European Union. They possess much greater ability to manage internal tensions and external threats, through the use of greater ease in passing binding legislation and regulation on their constituent elements, greater ability to facilitate fiscal transfers around the federations, and other established mechanisms the EU lacks. They therefore encounter fewer crises that genuinely threaten integration. The 2007–09 Banking Crisis and 2020–21 COVID-19 Pandemic, for instance, presented substantial economic and, in the latter case, public health threats to the United States and Canada, but in neither federation was disintegration of the union seriously considered, nor was there need for substantial further centralization of existing authority to confront either crisis. Hence, the model is most useful in an American or Canadian context as a lens through which to view the earlier development of a strong federation. In the United States, for instance, the model is most useful to explain the early nineteenth century, where a series of moderate endogenous conflicts, such as the Nullification Crisis or Bloody Kansas, produced only patch-up reforms. Only the declaration of secession of South Carolina, a severe endogenous crisis, prompted the major steps toward integration through the Civil War. This model thus recasts early nineteenth-century US history not as a story of rising and inevitable conflict, but rather a contingent struggle over integration resolved only when a crisis of sufficient severity emerged to force the issue.

Where the model may contain the most contemporary relevance is in newer and less settled federations. In Europe, the model could conceivably have implications for struggles between the Spanish government in Madrid and regional separatists in Catalonia and the Basque Country. Similarly, although the UK is a long-established polity, and moreover not a true federation, its experiments with devolution in recent decades has left it facing a wave of crises of various degrees of endogeneity and severity that can impact the future of British centralization, devolution, or even integrity, given the nontrivial movements in favor of Scottish secession and Northern Irish unification with the Republic of Ireland.

## Crises in Strong Regional Associations

The second category of institutions where the model may be applicable are strong regional associations, especially those which have explicitly cited the EU as a model, such as the African Union or the Association of Southeast Asian Nations (ASEAN). A long-standing question around international integration is why the EU has produced so much greater integration than these other bodies. This model suggests an answer in the severity and endogeneity of the crises faced by Europe in the decades prior to the start of European integration and in the early decades of the European project. The three major wars between France and Germany from the Franco-Prussian War to the Second World War hit Europe with a series of severe endogenous security crises without parallel in those other regions. By contrast, when Southeast Asia or Africa faced severe security threats, they were largely exogenous, and thus less likely to serve as a spur for integration. In the Cold War period, the EU again faced more endogenous crises than the other regional associations. In part, this was due to greater early steps toward integration producing greater scope for crises. An endogenous crisis such as the Empty Chair Crisis or the European Debt Crisis could only occur if substantial integration already existed. The greater European integration in this period also reflects the greater strength of the European states in this period, as many of the major problems confronting Africa and Southeast Asia were traceable to exogenous sources and foreign interference that the Europeans were able to resist to a greater degree. The model thus suggests an explanation for why Europe achieved greater integration rooted in historical contingencies rather than structural or cultural stories.

## Concluding Remarks

The theory outlined here provides several avenues for future research, some of which are sketched out in the sections on "Other Crises and the Model" and "Implications Outside of Europe." The surveys provided here are necessarily brief, but offer valuable lines for future research. It would also be valuable to apply the theoretical framework to a historical analysis of

European integration in the twentieth century. Perhaps among the most valuable avenues of future research would be to analyze how to modify this framework to address two related challenges confronting European integration in the future: the "polycrisis" of simultaneous strains on multiple sectors and of multiple origins and the "metacrisis" of European legitimacy. A single source of strain may create what can be termed a "wicked" crisis, where action to address the crisis in one sector deepens the problems in another. For instance, the social distancing measures introduced to contain the public health crisis in the COVID-19 Pandemic deepened the economic and financial crisis by restricting economic activity and driving a surge in nonperforming loans. Similarly, the efforts to confront the security threat of Russia's invasion of Ukraine triggered an energy crisis by restricting access to Russian fossil fuels. These problems may be even more complicated when multiple crises of differing origins are confronted simultaneously. As briefly discussed in the list of strains on the EU in the Other Crises and the Model section, the EU has spent much of the twenty-first century in such a position. For instance, a massive wave of refugees arrived in southern Europe just as those southern European states wrestled with the Debt Crisis. In the interest of foundational theory-building, the exploration of the theoretical framework in this project has focused on crises in European finance in isolation. Future research that explored the interactions between sectors in a single crisis, or of the interactions across multiple simultaneous crises, could be extremely valuable.

More broadly, as the postfunctionalist literature highlights, the European Union's efforts to manage these simultaneous crises connects to a broader "metacrisis" of legitimacy as public attitudes shift from a "permissive consensus" generally in favor of deeper integration toward a "constraining dissensus" with increasing skepticism of further integration. This has helped fuel the severity of these crises, by increasing the possibility of a disintegrative outcome, while also making it harder for the EU and member states to manage the crises. This affects the operation of the theory outline here as well. By undermining the consensus around a master narrative of ever closer union, it weakens the default assumption that the reforms out of a crisis will be integrative. As discussed in the Disintegrative Alternative section, this does not in itself undermine the theory, as the magnitude of change should still be shaped by the interaction of severity and origin, but now increases the possibility that the direction of that change will be disintegrative. Regardless, the metacrisis remains one of the most important challenges facing the European Union, and well worthy of additional examination, including in this framework.

One common understanding across virtually all approaches to the study of the European Union is the central role that crises play in driving the process of integration. The theory described in this book demonstrates how it is possible to move beyond ex post analysis of crises by building an ex ante set of expectations based on the interaction of the origin and severity of a threat. While the cases here are necessarily limited to crises of finance in the twenty-first century, this theory more broadly provides clear expectations of the likelihood of deeper integration and reform out of crises in the European Union. Given that crises will all but certainly continue to batter the European Union and its member states, the continued exploration of what factors are most likely to generate substantial change remains a topic of great importance.

## Notes

1. Matthew Goodwin and Caitlin Milazzo, "Taking Back Control? Investigating the Role of Immigration in the 2016 Vote for Brexit," *The British Journal of Politics and International Relations* 19, no. 3 (2017): 450–464.
2. Angelique Chrisafis, "France to Let Migrant Rescue Ship Dock as It Criticises Italy's Refusal to Help," *The Guardian*, November 2022, sec. World news, https://www.theguardian.com/world/2022/nov/10/france-let-migrant-rescue-ship-dock-criticises-italy-refusal-help.
3. European Commission, "What Has the EU Done after the Fukushima Accident?," Press Release (Brussels: European Commission, March 2012), https://ec.europa.eu/commission/presscorner/detail/en/MEMO_12_157.
4. In a somewhat ironic twist, that dependence had increased in recent years because increasing Russian energy imports had been one of the patch-up solutions to the post-Fukushima turn against nuclear energy.
5. Ian Black, "Furious Chirac Hits out at 'infantile' Easterners," *The Guardian*, February 2003, sec. World news, https://www.theguardian.com/world/2003/feb/18/france.iraq.

# Bibliography

Acharya, Viral V. "Is the International Convergence of Capital Adequacy Regulation Desirable?" *The Journal of Finance* 58, no. 6 (2003): 2745–2782.

Acharya, Viral V., and Tanju Yorulmazer. "Too Many to Fail—An Analysis of Time-Inconsistency in Bank Closure Policies." *Journal of Financial Intermediation* 16, no. 1 (2007): 1–31.

Agnew, Harriet. "Hedge Funds Boost Campaign to Keep Britain in the EU." *Financial Times*, November 2015. https://www.ft.com/content/d682c838-8953-11e5-90de-f44762bf9896.

Aguado, Jesús, and Emma Pinedo. "European Banks Need Regulation Reset to Catch U.S. Rivals, Botin Says." *Reuters*, September 2021, sec. Finance. https://www.reuters.com/business/finance/european-banks-need-regulation-reset-catch-us-rivals-botin-says-2021-09-30/.

Akman, Pinar, and Hussein Kassim. "Myths and Myth-Making in the European Union: The Institutionalization and Interpretation of EU Competition Policy\*." *JCMS: Journal of Common Market Studies* 48, no. 1 (2010): 111–132. https://doi.org/10.1111/j.1468-5965.2009.02044.x.

Alcidi, Cinzia, Daniel Gros, Jorge Núñez Ferrer, and David Rinaldi. "The Instruments Providing Macro-Financial Support to EU Member States." *CEPS Research Reports* 6 (2017).

Alexander, Harriet. "Britain Treated Us like Al-Qaeda, Says Iceland's Former PM as He Avoids Jail." *The Sunday Telegraph* (April 2012), sec. News.

Alexander, Olwyn. "Brexit and beyond: Assessing the Impact on Europe's Asset and Wealth Managers" (PricewaterhouseCoopers). Accessed September 30, 2022. https://www.pwc.com/gx/en/industries/financial-services/publications/brexit-and-beyond.html.

Allen, Franklin, Elena Carletti, and Andrew Gimber. "The Financial Implications of a Banking Union," In *Banking Union for Europe: Risks and Challenges* edited by Thorsten Beck. (London: Centre for Economic Policy Research, 2012): 113–118.

Alloway, Tracy. "Bafin Bashes the EBA over Stress Tests." *Financial Times*, June 2011.

Altendorf, Kerstin. "Association of German Banks welcomes progress on capital markets union." Press Release (Berlin: Bundesverband deutscher Banken, June 2018). https://en.bankenverband.de/newsroom/press-release/association-german-banks-welcomes-progress-capital-markets-union/.

Anderson, Jeffrey J. "A Series of Unfortunate Events: Crisis Response and the European Union After 2008." In *The Palgrave Handbook of EU Crises*, edited by Marianne Riddervold, Jarle Trondal, and Akasemi Newsome. Palgrave Studies in European Union Politics (Cham: Springer International Publishing, 2021), 765–789. https://doi.org/10.1007/978-3-030-51791-5_45.

Andrews, Philip. "Is the EU Breaking Up?" *Business & Finance Magazine*, n.d.

Angeloni, Ignazio. "Time to Address the Shortcomings of the Banking Union" (SAFE, 2019). http://publikationen.ub.uni-frankfurt.de/frontdoor/index/index/docId/53057.

Anghel, Veronica, and Erik Jones. "Is Europe Really Forged through Crisis? Pandemic EU and the Russia—Ukraine War." *Journal of European Public Policy* 30, no. 4 (April 2023): 766–786. https://doi.org/10.1080/13501763.2022.2140820.

Archard, David. "Myths, Lies and Historical Truth: A Defence of Nationalism." *Political Studies* 43, no. 3 (1995): 472–481.

Armstrong, Kenneth A. "Regulatory Alignment and Divergence after Brexit." *Journal of European Public Policy* 25, no. 8 (August 2018): 1099–1117. https://doi.org/10.1080/13501763.2018.1467956.

Arnaboldi, Francesca. *Risk and Regulation in Euro Area Banks: Completing the Banking Union* Palgrave Macmillan Studies in Banking and Financial Institutions (New York: Palgrave Macmillan, 2019). https://doi.org/10.1007/978-3-030-23429-4.

Arnold, Martin. "ECB Pushes for Eurozone Bad Bank to Clean up Soured Loans." *Financial Times*, April 2020.

Arnorsson, Agust, and Gylfi Zoega. "On the Causes of Brexit." *European Journal of Political Economy* 55 (December 2018): 301–323. https://doi.org/10.1016/j.ejpoleco.2018.02.001.

Asimakopoulos, Ioannis G. "International Law as a Negotiation Tool in Banking Union; the Case of the Single Resolution Fund." *Journal of Economic Policy Reform* 21, no. 2 (June 2018): 118–131. https://doi.org/10.1080/17487870.2018.1424631.

Asimakopoulos, Ioannis, and David Howarth. "Stillborn Banking Union: Explaining Ineffective European Union Bank Resolution Rules." *JCMS: Journal of Common Market Studies* 60, no. 2 (2022): 264–282. https://doi.org/10.1111/jcms.13212.

Asimakopoulos, Panagiotis. "Report: What Do EU Capital Markets Look like on the Other Side of Brexit?," September 2019. https://newfinancial.org/report-what-do-eu-capital-markets-look-like-on-the-other-side-of-brexit/.

Atkins, Ralph. "EU Warned on Risk of Financial Market Problems." *Financial Times*, January 2009, sec. WORLD NEWS.

Atkins, Ralph, and Nikki Tait. "Crisis Mismanagement Casts ECB as Saviour." *Financial Times*, January 2009, sec. WORLD IN RECESSION.

Atkins, Ralph, and James Wilson. "Transcript of FT Interview with Axel Weber, President of the Bundesbank." *Financial Times*, April 2009. https://www.ft.com/content/085d83b4-2e9f-11de-b7d3-00144feabdc0.

Auerback, Marshall. "The European Union Still Hasn't Considered an Economic Proposal That Can Save It—OpEd." *Eurasia Review* (blog), June 2020. https://www.eurasiareview.com/16062020-the-european-union-still-hasnt-considered-an-economic-proposal-that-can-save-it-oped/.

"Axel Weber; Markets Flying Blind, Ex-Central Banker Warns." *Handelsblatt Global*, n.d., sec. Finance.

Baglioni, Angelo. *The European Banking Union: A Critical Assessment* Palgrave Macmillan Studies in Banking and Institutions Financial (London: Palgrave Macmillan UK, 2016). https://doi.org/10.1057/978-1-137-56314-9.

Baldwin, Richard E., and Francesco Giavazzi. *The Eurozone Crisis: A Consensus View of the Causes and a Few Possible Remedies* (CEPR Press Londres, 2015).

Bankscope. "Germany Banking System Concentration—Data, Chart." TheGlobalEconomy.com. Accessed July 13, 2022. https://www.theglobaleconomy.com/Germany/banking_system_concentration/.

Barber, Tony. "Brexit: Haunted Europe." *Financial Times*, June 2016. https://www.ft.com/content/7cf0fd82-3b80-11e6-9f2c-36b487ebd80a.

Barber, Tony. "London Mayor Back to Do Battle with Brussels." *Financial Times*, September 2009. https://www.proquest.com/news/docview/229291127/citation/16F6F87D8AA84B5BPQ/1.

Barber, Tony, and Ralph Atkins. "Extracts from FT Interview with Joaquín Almunia." *Financial Times*, February 2009. https://www.ft.com/content/0f8fe744-0357-11de-b405-000077b07658.

## 312   Bibliography

Barber, Tony, Benoit Bertrand, Guy Dinmore, Ben Hall, George Parker, and Michael Steen. "Sarkozy Recoils from EU-Wide EUR300bn Bail-Out." *Financial Times*, October 2008, sec. GLOBAL FINANCIAL CRISIS.

Barber, Tony, Benoit Bertrand, Guy Dinmore, Ben Hall, Nikki Tait, and James Wilson. "European States Seek Financial Fraternity." *Financial Times*, October 2008, sec. GLOBAL FINANCIAL CRISIS.

Barker, Alex. "City of London Has Lost Its Voice with Brexit, Says Lord Hill." *Financial Times*, June 2016. https://www.ft.com/content/2b84027e-3b93-11e6-9f2c-36b487ebd80a.

Barker, Alex. "Project on Survival of Banks Nears Fruition: Eurozone Controls." *Financial Times*, December 2013, sec. WORLD NEWS.

Barker, Alex, Alice Ross, and Peter Spiegel. "France to Pay Most for Bank Rescue Fund: Brussels Proposal." *Financial Times*, October 2014, sec. WORLD NEWS.

Barker, Alex, and Nikki Tait. "EU Set for Regulatory Reform." *Financial Times*, March 2009, sec. FRONT PAGE—COMPANIES & MARKETS.

Barroso, José Manuel. "Financial Reform Is Necessary and Urgent" (Speech, Brussels, February 2009). http://www.efmlg.org/Docs/Meeting%2030/Item%208%20-%20JMD%20Barroso%20speech.pdf.

Barroso, José Manuel. "Fostering Economic Recovery: The EU Moves from Crisis Management to Reform" (Speech presented at the Council on Foreign Relations Presents, Washington, D.C., September 2010). https://www.cfr.org/event/fostering-economic-recovery-eu-moves-crisis-management-reform-0.

Barroso, José Manuel. "Opening Remarks by President Barroso at the Friends of Europe Working Dinner" (Opening Remarks presented at the Friends of Europe Working Dinner, Brussel, October 2010).

Bartz, Tim, and Stefan Kaiser. "Interview with ECB Vice President 'Faced with This Big Drop in GDP and Inflation, We Had to Act.'" *Yerepouni Daily News* (June 2020). https://www.proquest.com/docview/2415715076/citation/4A51032E75154595PQ/28.

Baschuk, Bryce, Albertina Torsoli, and Hugo Miller. "EU Won't Back Trade Deal if Britain Chooses 'Singapore-on-Thames.'" *Bloomberg.Com*, April 2017. https://www.bloomberg.com/news/articles/2017-04-12/eu-won-t-back-trade-deal-if-u-k-chooses-singapore-on-thames.

Bases, Daniel. "EU's Barroso Urges Shift to Reforms from Crisis." *Reuters*, September 2010, sec. Business News. https://www.reuters.com/article/uk-eu-recovery-barroso-idUKTRE68N07Y20100924.

Beck, Thorsten. *Banking Union for Europe: Risks and Challenges*. Vol. 16 (London: Centre for Economic Policy Research, 2012).

Beck, Thorsten, and Daniel Gros. "Monetary Policy and Banking Supervision: Coordination Instead of Separation. CEPS Policy Brief No. 286, 12 December 2012," 2012.

Beck, Thorsten, Radomir Todorov, and Wolf Wagner. "Supervising Cross-Border Banks: Theory, Evidence and Policy." *Economic Policy* 28, no. 73 (2013): 5–44.

Beesley, Arthur. "Currency Crisis Cannot Be Solved by Institutional Debates." *Irish Times*, December 2011.

Begg, David KH. *The ECB: Safe at Any Speed?* Vol. 1 (London: Centre for Economic Policy Research, 1998).

Belka, Marek, and Wim Fonteyne. "A Banking Framework to Secure Single Market." *Financial Times*, June 2009. https://www.ft.com/content/01193d96-5082-11de-9530-00144feabdc0.

Belke, Ansgar, Anna Dobrzańska, Daniel Gros, and PawełSmaga. "(When) Should a Non-Euro Country Join the Banking Union?" *The Journal of Economic Asymmetries* 14 (2016): 4–19.

Belke, Ansgar, and Daniel Gros. "On the Shock-Absorbing Properties of a Banking Union: Europe Compared with the United States." *Comparative Economic Studies* 58, no. 3 (2016): 359–386.

Bénassy-Quéré, Agnès. "Maastricht Flaws and Remedies." In *The Eurozone Crisis: A Consensus View of the Causes and a Few Possible Solutions*, edited by Richard Baldwin and Francesco Giavazzi (London: CEPR Press, 2016): 72-84.

Bénassy-Quéré, Agnès. "The Euro as an International Currency." In *Routledge Handbook of the Economics of European Integration* edited by Harald Badlinger and Volker Nitsch (New York: Routledge, 2015), 82–99.

Bennhold, Katrin, Carter Dougherty, Mark Landler, Edmund L. Andrews, and Landon Jr. Thomas. "European Leaders Agree to Inject Cash into Banks." *New York Times, Online*, October 2008, sec. business. https://www.proquest.com/news/docview/2221377680/abstract/20483DF84EFC44AFPQ/376.

Berschens, Ruth, and Andreas Kröner. "EBA Move; Bank Watchdog Waltzes Towards Vienna." *Handelsblatt Global*, September 2017, sec. Finance.

Bieling, Hans-Jürgen. "Shattered Expectations: The Defeat of European Ambitions of Global Financial Reform." In *Europe's Place in Global Financial Governance after the Crisis* edited by Daniel Mügge (New York: Routledge, 2014), 31–51.

Bini Smaghi, Lorenzo. "Regulation and Supervisory Architecture: Is the EU on the Right Path?" Speech presented at the 2009 ECON meeting with national parliaments. (European Central Bank: :Brussels, February 2009). https://www.ecb.europa.eu/press/key/date/2009/html/sp090212.en.html.

Bippart, Graham. "Capital Markets Upheaval: CMU Loses Leadership." *Global Capital Euroweek*, June 2016, sec. Brexit.

Black, Ian. "Furious Chirac Hits out at 'infantile' Easterners." *The Guardian*, February 2003, sec. World news. https://www.theguardian.com/world/2003/feb/18/france.iraq.

Blumenberg, Hans. *The Legitimacy of the Modern Age* (Cambridge, MA: MIT Press, 1985).

Boffey, Daniel, and Lisa O'Carroll. "From Slick to Risible: The Bids for London's EU Agencies Are Unveiled." *The Guardian*, August 2017, sec. World news. https://www.theguardian.com/world/2017/aug/01/slick-risible-bids-london-eu-agencies-european-council.

Boin, Arjen, Magnus Ekengren, Mark Rhinard, and (Firm) ProQuest. *The European Union as Crisis Manager: Patterns and Prospects*. Electronic resource (Cambridge, England; New York: Cambridge University Press, 2013). https://ebookcentral.proquest.com/lib/uma/detail.action?docID=1303716.

Boin, Arjen, and Mark Rhinard. "Crisis Management Performance and the European Union: The Case of COVID-19." *Journal of European Public Policy* 30, no. 4 (April 2023): 655–675. https://doi.org/10.1080/13501763.2022.2141304.

Boissieu, Christian de. "The Banking Union Revisited." In *Financial Regulation in the EU* edited by Raphaël Douady, Clément Goulet, and Pierre-Charles Pradier (New York: Springer, 2017), 85–103.

Boleat, Mark. "Capital Markets Union Speech by Mark Boleat" (Speech presented at the European Capital Markets Union Conference, London, April 2016). https://news.cityoflondon.gov.uk/speech-by-mark-boleat-policy-chairman-city-of-london-corporation-at-european-capital-markets-union-conference-city-and-financial-global-london-7-april-2016/.

Börzel, Tanja A., and Thomas Risse. "From the Euro to the Schengen Crises: European Integration Theories, Politicization, and Identity Politics." *Journal of European Public Policy* 25, no. 1 (January 2018): 83–108. https://doi.org/10.1080/13501763.2017.1310281.

Boschat, Nathalie, and Gabriele Parussini. "Lagarde Isn't Sure the ECB Can Easily Oversee EU Banks." *Wall Street Journal, Europe*, February 2009, sec. Economy & Politics.

## 314 Bibliography

Boston, William, Susann Kreutzmann, and Gabriele Parussini. "Summit Reveals Wider Franco-German Discord." *Wall Street Journal (Online)*, October 2012, sec. Europe.

Botin, Emilio. "Europe Needs Banking Union to Avert Irrelevance." *Financial Times*, November 2012, sec. COMMENT.

Bowman, Louise. "Capital Markets: Has Brexit Killed CMU?" *Euromoney*, November 2016, sec. CAPITAL MARKETS. https://www.euromoney.com/article/b12kqj3tts1bg6/capital-markets-has-brexit-killed-cmu.

Boyd, Tony. "Brexit Suits Germany's Merkel." *Australian Financial Review* (June 2016).

Brack, Nathalie, and Seda Gürkan. "Introduction: European Integration (Theories) in Crisis?" In *Theorising the Crises of the European Union* edited by Nathalie Brack and Seda Gürkan (London: Routledge, 2020). https://doi.org/10.4324/9781003001423.

Brack, Nathalie, and Seda Gürkan, eds. *Theorising the Crises of the European Union* (London: Routledge, 2020). https://doi.org/10.4324/9781003001423.

Brandt, Florian, and Matthias Wohlfahrt. "A Common Backstop to the Single Resolution Fund." *Journal of Economic Policy Reform* 22, no. 3 (September 2019): 291–306. https://doi.org/10.1080/17487870.2018.1482745.

Braude, Jonathan. "London's Big Bang Could Go Bust." *The Deal*, March 2017. https://www.dechert.com/knowledge/onpoint/2017/3/london-s-big-bang-could-go-bust.html.

Braude, Jonathan. "U.K. Wins Only Limited EC Concessions." *Daily Deal/The Deal* (June 2009).

Braun, Benjamin. "Preparedness, Crisis Management and Policy Change: The Euro Area at the Critical Juncture of 2008–2013." *The British Journal of Politics and International Relations* 17, no. 3 (2015): 419–441.

Braun-Munzinger, Karen, Jacopo Carmassi, Wieger Kastelein, Claudia Lambert, and Fatima Pires. "From Deadlocks to Breakthroughs: How We Can Complete the Banking Union and Why It Matters to All of Us." In *New Challenges for the Eurozone Governance: Joint Solutions for Common Threats?*, edited by José Caetano, Isabel Vieira, and António Caleiro (Cham: Springer International Publishing, 2021), 69–90. https://doi.org/10.1007/978-3-030-62372-2_4.

Bremer, Catherine. "French Socialists Dig in Heels on EU Austerity." *Cyprus Mail* (February 2012). https://www.proquest.com/news/docview/922568811/citation/71934BF811CA4ABFPQ/63.

Bremmer, Ian. "Brexit Is the Most Significant Political Risk the World Has Experienced since the Cuban Missile Crisis." Tweet. *Twitter*, June 2016. https://twitter.com/ianbremmer/status/746309494267875328.

Brennan, Joe. "Ireland and Nordic-Baltic States Press Urgency of Capital Markets Plan." *The Irish Times*, July 2018. https://www.irishtimes.com/business/personal-finance/ireland-and-nordic-baltic-states-press-urgency-of-capital-markets-plan-1.3568243.

Brennan, Joe. "Ireland to Contest Luxembourg's Right to Host Banking Authority." *The Irish Times*, March 2017, sec. Financial Services. https://www.irishtimes.com/business/financial-services/ireland-to-contest-luxembourg-s-right-to-host-banking-authority-1.3031163.

Brenton, Hannah. "New Powers for Europe's Watchdogs 'Bad News' for Luxembourg." *Luxembourg Times*, December 2017, sec. Luxembourg. https://www.luxtimes.lu/en/luxembourg/new-powers-for-europe-s-watchdogs-bad-news-for-luxembourg-602d0d86de135b9236c3391a.

Bronk, Richard, and Wade Jacoby. "Avoiding Monocultures in the European Union: The Case for the Mutual Recognition of Difference in Conditions of Uncertainty." *LEQS Paper*, no. 67 (2013).

Brooks, Eleanor, Anniek de Ruijter, Scott L. Greer, and Sarah Rozenblum. "EU Health Policy in the Aftermath of COVID-19: Neofunctionalism and Crisis-Driven Integration." *Journal of European Public Policy* 30, no. 4 (April 2023): 721–739. https://doi.org/10.1080/13501763.2022.2141301.

Brown, Gordon. "Spring European Council—Hansard—UK Parliament" (Speech presented at the UK House of Commons Debate, London, March 2009). https://hansard.parliament.uk//Commons/2009-03-23/debates/0903235000002/details.

"Brown to Defend City of London against EU Financial Supervision." *Irish Examiner*, June 2009, sec. IE-Business/BUSINESS.

Brunnermeier, Markus Konrad, Harold James, and Jean-Pierre Landau. *The Euro and the Battle of Ideas* (Princeton: Princeton University Press, 2016).

Brunsden, Jim. "Brexit Makes EU Capital Markets Union More Urgent, Says Commissioner." *Financial Times*, September 2016. https://www.ft.com/content/54944cf2-7a4d-11e6-ae24-f193b105145e.

Brunsden, Jim. "Macron Relaunches Presidency in Bastille Day Pitch." *Financial Times*, July 2020. https://www.proquest.com/docview/2476170186/citation/9D06D640C49D4875PQ/20.

Brunsden, Jim. "Showdown over Supervision." *Politico*, March 2010. https://www.politico.eu/article/showdown-over-supervision/.

Brunsden, Jim, and Alex Barker. "City to Be Sidelined by Capital Markets Union Plan." *Financial Times*, June 2016. https://www.ft.com/content/d8e0de94-3e11-11e6-8716-a4a71e8140b0.

Brunsden, Jim, and Mehreen Khan. "Paris Wins Battle to Host European Banking Regulator." *Financial Times*, November 2017. https://www.ft.com/content/f9f954b4-ce19-11e7-b781-794ce08b24dc.

Brunsden, Jim, and James Politi. "Italy Pledges to Block Limit on Sovereign Debt Holdings: Eurozone." *Financial Times*, February 2016, sec. WORLD NEWS.

Brunsden, Jim, and James Shotter. "Brussels' Plan for Deposits Likely to Set up Berlin Clash: Mutualised System." *Financial Times*, November 2015, sec. WORLD NEWS.

"Brussels Pushes for Pan-European Financial Regulators." *Deutsche Presse-Agentur* (May 2009), sec. Finance.

Bulmer, Simon, and William E. Paterson. "Germany as the EU's Reluctant Hegemon? Of Economic Strength and Political Constraints." *Journal of European Public Policy* 20, no. 10 (2013): 1387–1405.

Bundesbank Official. Interview by author, 2022.

Bundesverband der Deutschen Volksbanken und Raiffeisenbanken. "German Banking Industry Committee Urges 'Prudent' Discussion When Revising the EU Rules on Crisis Management for Banks." Press Release (Berlin: Bundesverband der Deutschen Volksbanken und Raiffeisenbanken, January 2021). https://www.bvr.de/Press/Press_releases/German_Banking_Industry_Committee_urges_prudent"_discussion_when_revising_the_EU_rules_on_crisis_management_for_banks.

Bundesverband deutscher Banken official. Interview by author, 2022.

Burns, Charlotte, Judith Clifton, and Lucia Quaglia. "Explaining Policy Change in the EU: Financial Reform after the Crisis." *Journal of European Public Policy* 25, no. 5 (2018): 728–746.

Buti, Marco, and Sergio Fabbrini. "Next Generation EU and the Future of Economic Governance: Towards a Paradigm Change or Just a Big One-Off?" *Journal of European Public Policy* 30, no. 4 (April 2023): 676–695. https://doi.org/10.1080/13501763.2022.2141303.

Calomiris, Charles W., and Stephen H. Haber. *Fragile by Design* (Princeton, NJ: Princeton University Press, 2014).

## 316 Bibliography

Cameron, David. "Prime Minister's Speech on Europe" (Prime Minister's Office, 10 Downing Street, London, November 2015). https://www.gov.uk/government/speeches/prime-ministers-speech-on-europe.

"Can Lagarde Save the Euro? The European Central Bank Buys the Eurozone as Much Time as It Can." *Wall Street Journal (Online)* (March 2020), sec. Opinion. https://www.proquest.com/docview/2379034479/citation/38A02BF4FA57413FPQ/10.

Canepa, Francesco. "Germany's Top Court Rejects Complaint against ECB's Bond Buying Scheme." National Post (Online) (Toronto, Canada: Postmedia Network Inc., May 2021). https://www.proquest.com/docview/2528733540/citation/4A51032E75154595PQ/6.

Capoccia, Giovanni, and R. Daniel Kelemen. "The Study of Critical Junctures: Theory, Narrative, and Counterfactuals in Historical Institutionalism." *World Politics* 59, no. 3 (2007): 341–369.

Caporaso, James A., and Martin Rhodes. *Political and Economic Dynamics of the Eurozone Crisis* (Oxford: Oxford University Press, 2016).

Carletti, Elena, Hendrik Hakenes, and Isabel Schnabel. "The Privatization of Italian Savings Banks: A Role Model for Germany?" *Vierteljahrshefte Zur Wirtschaftsforschung* 74, no. 4 (2005): 32–50.

Carswell, Simon. "A Failure to Tackle Cross-Border Banking." *Irish* Times, February 2009.

Casert, Raf. "Spoils of Brexit: EU Cities Race to Get EU Agencies from UK." *The Seattle Times*, October 2017, sec. Business. https://www.seattletimes.com/business/spoils-of-brexit-eu-cities-race-to-get-eu-agencies-from-uk/.

Casert, Raf, and Geir Moulson. "Greece Readies for Bailout Talks as Plan B Details Revealed." *University Wire* (July 2015), sec. From Ap. https://www.proquest.com/news/docview/1699089233/abstract/BDD06560B64C4502PQ/35.

Cash, Bill. "EU Supervisory Scheme That Will Be against UK's Interests." *Financial Times*, February 2009, sec. Letters to the Editor.

Cassell, Mark K. "A Tale of Two Crises: Germany's Landesbanken and the United States' Savings and Loans." *Journal of Banking Regulation* 17, no. 1 (2016): 73–89.

Cassell, Mark K., and Anna Hutcheson. "Explaining Germany's Position on European Banking Union." *German Politics* 28, no. 4 (2019): 562–582.

Castle, Stephen, and Katrin Bennhold. "European Officials Debate Need for a Bailout Package." *The New York Times*, October 2008, sec. Business. https://www.nytimes.com/2008/10/02/business/worldbusiness/02regulate.html.

Centeno, Mário. "Remarks by Mário Centeno Following the Eurogroup Videoconference of 11 June 2020" (Statements and Remarks presented at the Eurogroup videoconference of 11 June 2020, virtual meeting, June 2020). https://www.consilium.europa.eu/en/press/press-releases/2020/06/11/remarks-by-mario-centeno-following-the-eurogroup-videoconference-of-11-june-2020/.

Cerrone, Rosaria. "Deposit Guarantee Reform in Europe: Does European Deposit Insurance Scheme Increase Banking Stability?" *Journal of Economic Policy Reform* 21, no. 3 (September 2018): 224–239. https://doi.org/10.1080/17487870.2017.1400434.

Chance, David. "Europe Has a Sticking Plaster, but Italy Is Going to Need a Transfusion: ANALYSIS." *Irish Independent* (April 2020), sec. News.

Chapman, James, and Hugo Duncan. "Euro in a Tailspin [Edition 3]." *Daily Mail* (December 2011), sec. News.

Charter, David. "Brussels Regulators Could Order Britain to Bail out Banks under New Rules." *The Times, London*, September 2009, sec. News.

Charter, David. "Jubilant Sarkozy Sees EU Take Powers over the City." *The Times, London*, June 2009. https://www.thetimes.co.uk/article/jubilant-sarkozy-sees-eu-take-powers-over-the-city-nrrkcfdm87h.

Chrisafis, Angelique. "France to Let Migrant Rescue Ship Dock as It Criticises Italy's Refusal to Help." *The Guardian*, November 2022, sec. World news. https://www.theguardian.com/world/2022/nov/10/france-let-migrant-rescue-ship-dock-criticises-italy-refusal-help.

Christie, Rebecca, and Rainer Buergin. "Schaeuble in Clash with the ECB on Pooling of Bank Levies [Edition 3]." *Irish Independent* (January 2014), sec. News.

"City Resists European Reform 'Straitjacket.'" *Investment Adviser*, March 2009.

Clift, Ben, and Magnus Ryner. "Joined at the Hip, but Pulling Apart? Franco-German Relations, the Eurozone Crisis and the Politics of Austerity." *French Politics* 12, no. 2 (2014): 136–163.

Cody, Edward, and Kevin Sullivan-Washington Post Foreign Service. "European Leaders Split on Rescue Strategy." *The Washington Post* (October 2008), sec. A SECTION.

Cœuré, Benoît. "European Capital Markets: Priorities and Challenges" (Dinner remarks presented at the International Swaps and Derivatives Association, Frankfurt am Main, June 2019). https://www.ecb.europa.eu/press/key/date/2019/html/ecb.sp190625_1~49befd1908.en.html.

Cohen, Adam, and Charles Forelle. "Leading the News: EU Proposes New Bloc-Wide Regulators—They Would Monitor Risk and Companies; U.K. Likely to Object." *Wall Street Journal* (September 2009), Europe edition.

Comte, Jean. "CMU's End-of-Term Report: Could Have Done Better." *GlobalCapital*, March 2019, sec. Euroweek.

Comte, Jean. "Member States to Call for Full Regulatory Flexibility for EU Banks." *GlobalCapital*, April 2020, sec. FIG People and Markets. https://www.globalcapital.com/article/28mu546seqnc4ypxwary8/fig-people-and-markets/member-states-to-call-for-full-regulatory-flexibility-for-eu-banks.

Constâncio, Vítor. "Effectiveness of Monetary Union and the Capital Markets Union" (Speech presented at the EUROFI Conference, Malta, April 2017). https://www.bis.org/review/r170410b.htm.

Copelovitch, Mark, and David A. Singer. "Tipping the (Im)Balance: Capital Inflows, Financial Market Structure, and Banking Crises." *Economics & Politics* 29, no. 3 (2017): 179–208. https://doi.org/10.1111/ecpo.12097.

Corrigan, Tracy. "The Most Sensible Solution Is to Police the Banks from the Bottom Up." *The Daily Telegraph* (February 2009), sec. City.

Cottle, Sarah. "COVID-19 Hits Bank Dividends; Piraeus Q4'19 Result; Barclays' New Climate Policy." *S&P Global*, April 2020. https://www.spglobal.com/marketintelligence/en/news-insights/latest-news-headlines/covid-19-hits-bank-dividends-piraeus-q4-19-result-barclays-new-climate-policy-57897096.

Couaillier, Cyril, Marco Lo Duca, Alessio Reghezza, Costanza Rodriguez d'Acri, and Alessandro Scopelliti. "Bank Capital Buffers and Lending in the Euro Area during the Pandemic." Financial Stability Review, November 2021 (European Central Bank, November 2021). https://www.ecb.europa.eu/pub/financial-stability/fsr/special/html/ecb.fsrart202111_01~111d31fca7.en.html.

Council of the European Union. "Member States Sign Agreement on Bank Resolution Fund." Press Release (Brussels: Council of the European Union, May 2014). https://www.proquest.com/news/docview/1526576034/citation/22F74C2A8BD84E6FPQ/15.

Council of the European Union. "Offers to Host the European Medicines Agency (EMA)." Accessed September 12, 2022. https://www.consilium.europa.eu/en/policies/relocation-london-agencies-brexit/ema/.

## 318    Bibliography

Cox, David, and Jennifer Laidlaw. "Frankfurt and Paris Favorites to Host EBA, but Smaller City May Win." *SNL Bank & Thrift Daily* (December 2016), sec. Exclusive; Geopolitics. https://www.proquest.com/docview/1853216908/citation/CCF068B6A8474C28PQ/1.

Cox, Jasper, and Tom Brown. "Eurozone Bad Bank Would Be 'Incredibly Complex,' Say Experts." *GlobalCapital Securitization*, April 2020, sec. Regulation. https://www.globalcapital.com/securitization/article/28mu5vj3skqqfyax3ywhs/regulation/eurozone-bad-bank-would-be-incredibly-complex-say-experts.

Crawford, David, and Marcus Walker. "Germany Ignored Regulator's Hypo Warning; Documents Show Market Watchdog Bafin Raised Alarm Bells Six Months before Massive Government Bailout." *The Globe and Mail (Canada)*, May 2009, sec. REPORT ON BUSINESS: INTERNATIONAL; CREDIT CRISIS.

Cross, Mai'a K. Davis. "Social Constructivism." In *The Palgrave Handbook of EU Crises*, edited by Marianne Riddervold, Jarle Trondal, and Akasemi Newsome. Palgrave Studies in European Union Politics (Cham: Springer International Publishing, 2021), 195–211. https://doi.org/10.1007/978-3-030-51791-5_10.

Cross, Mai'a K. Davis. *The Politics of Crisis in Europe* (Cambridge, United Kingdom; New York, NY, USA: Cambridge University Press, 2017).

Cross, Mai'a K. Davis, and Xinru Ma. "A Media Perspective on European Crises." In *Europe's Prolonged Crisis: The Making or the Unmaking of a Political Union*, edited by Hans-Jörg Trenz, Carlo Ruzza, and Virginie Guiraudon. Palgrave Studies in European Political Sociology (London: Palgrave Macmillan UK, 2015), 210–231. https://doi.org/10.1057/9781137493675_11.

Culpepper, Pepper D. *Quiet Politics and Business Power: Corporate Control in Europe and Japan* (Cambridge: Cambridge University Press, 2010).

Culpepper, Pepper D., and Tobias Tesche. "Death in Veneto? European Banking Union and the Structural Power of Large Banks." *Journal of Economic Policy Reform* 24, no. 2 (June 2021): 134–150. https://doi.org/10.1080/17487870.2020.1722125.

Dammann, Jens. "The Banking Union: Flawed by Design." *Georgetown Journal of International Law* 45 (2013): 1057.

Damyanova, Vanya. "German Regulator Sees 'good Grounds' to Pause Payments to EU Bank Failure Fund." *SNL European Financials Daily*, February 2021, sec. CONFERENCE CHATTER; Extra.

"Data on COVID-19 (Coronavirus)." Our World in Data, July 2022. https://github.com/owid/covid-19-data.

Davies, Howard. "Europe's Banks Need a Federal Fix." *Financial Times*, January 2009, sec. COMMENT.

Davies, Tyler. "Banks Call for Regulatory Forbearance over Covid-19 Stress." *GlobalCapital Euroweek*, March 2020, sec. Regulatory Capital. https://www.globalcapital.com/article/28mu4cuh0wjxtzhjwmbk0/regulatory-capital/banks-call-for-regulatory-forbearance-over-covid-19-stress.

Davies, Tyler. "EC Adopts Covid-19 Banking Package with 'Quick Fix' for CRR." *GlobalCapital*, April 2020, sec. Regulatory Capital. https://www.globalcapital.com/article/28mu66gty3zakc8qyrc3k/regulatory-capital/ec-adopts-covid-19-banking-package-with-quick-fix-for-crr.

Daynamora, Vanya. "German Bank Warns of 'Irrational Exuberance' around Eurozone Deposit Insurance." *SNL European Financials Daily*, March 2018. https://www.spglobal.com/marketintelligence/en/news-insights/trending/qohre4uRaJSAkOwhJvzomw2.

De la Porte, Caroline, and Mads Dagnis Jensen. "The next Generation EU: An Analysis of the Dimensions of Conflict behind the Deal." *Social Policy & Administration* 55, no. 2 (2021): 388–402.

De Rynck, Stefaan. "Banking on a Union: The Politics of Changing Eurozone Banking Supervision." *Journal of European Public Policy* 23, no. 1 (2016): 119–135.

Della Sala, Vincent. "Political Myth, Mythology and the European Union*." *JCMS: Journal of Common Market Studies* 48, no. 1 (2010): 1–19. https://doi.org/10.1111/j.1468-5965.2009.02039.x.

Demetriades, Panicos O. "There's No Point Planning for a No Deal Brexit—If We Crash Out of the EU, It Would Be No Less than Absolute Chaos." *The Independent*, October 2017, sec. Voices. https://www.independent.co.uk/voices/no-deal-brexit-theresa-may-preparations-exports-eu27-germany-financial-services-a7994716.html.

Demirgüç-Kunt, Asli, and Enrica Detragiache. "Does Deposit Insurance Increase Banking System Stability? An Empirical Investigation." *Journal of Monetary Economics* 49, no. 7 (2002): 1373–1406.

Dennison, James, and Andrew Geddes. "Brexit and the Perils of 'Europeanised' Migration." *Journal of European Public Policy* 25, no. 8 (August 2018): 1137–1153. https://doi.org/10.1080/13501763.2018.1467953.

Diamond, Douglas W., and Philip H. Dybvig. "Bank Runs, Deposit Insurance, and Liquidity." *Journal of Political Economy* 91, no. 3 (1983): 401–419.

Dimon, Jamie. "Letter to Shareholders from Jamie Dimon, Annual Report 2019." Annual Report (JPMorgan-Chase, April 2020). https://reports.jpmorganchase.com/investor-relations/2019/ar-ceo-letters.htm.

Dinan, Desmond, Neill Nugent, and William E. Paterson. *The European Union in Crisis* (New York: Macmillan International Higher Education, 2017).

Directorate-General for Communication (European Commission), and Jean-Claude Juncker. *State of the Union 2016* (LU: Publications Office of the European Union, 2016). https://data.europa.eu/doi/10.2775/968989.

Directorate-General for Financial Stability, Financial Services and Capital Markets Union. "Commission Proposal for a Regulation on a Pan-European Personal Pension Product (PEPP)." Proposal for a Decision (European Commission). Accessed October 18, 2022. https://finance.ec.europa.eu/publications/commission-proposal-regulation-pan-european-personal-pension-product-pepp_en.

Dixon, Hugo. "Diplomacy Dilutes Europe's Crisis-Prevention Plan." *Breakingviews.Com*, May 2009. https://www.breakingviews.com/considered-view/diplomacy-dilutes-europes-crisis-prevention-plan/.

Dombret, Andreas. "Six Months of European Banking Supervision—What Does This Mean for 'Less Significant Institutions'?" (Bank of International Settlements, May 2015).

Dombret, Andreas. "We Can Work It out—or Can We? Current Challenges in Brexit Talks"; (Speech presented at the Atlantik-Brücke at the Travellers Club, London, November 2017). https://www.bundesbank.de/en/press/speeches/we-can-work-it-out-or-can-we-current-challenges-in-brexit-talks-711568.

Dombret, Andreas. "What Does Brexit Mean for European Banks?" (presented at the Conference of the Association of German Banks and the Center for Financial Studies, Goethe University Frankfurt, Frankfurt am Main, July 2016). https://www.bis.org/review/r160715b.htm.

Dombret, Andreas. "What Is 'Good' Regulation?" (presented at the 16th Euro Finance Week, November 2013).

Dombret, Andreas. "What's the State of Play in Germany's Banking Sector?" (Statement presented at the Press conference to unveil the Deutsche Bundesbank's Financial Stability Review, Frankfurt am Main, November 2016). https://www.bis.org/review/r161116c.htm.

## 320 Bibliography

Dombrovskis, Valdis. "European Union: College Orientation Debate: Vice-President Dombrovskis Remarks on Steps towards Completing Banking Union." *Asia News Monitor* (November 2015), sec. General News. https://www.proquest.com/news/docview/1732351364/abstract/759EBB74A9D64639PQ/4.

Dombrovskis, Valdis. "Keynote Speech of Vice-President Valdis Dombrovskis to the Economic Club of New York" (Text, New York City, April 2019). https://ec.europa.eu/commission/presscorner/detail/en/SPEECH_19_2116.

Dombrovskis, Valdis. "Remarks by Executive Vice-President Dombrovskis" (Text presented at the Press conference on the Commission banking package to facilitate lending to households and businesses in the EU, Brussels, April 2020). https://ec.europa.eu/commission/presscorner/detail/en/speech_20_769.

Dombrovskis, Valdis. "Speech for ESMA Conference 2017—Paris" (Speech presented at the ESMA Conference 2017, Paris, October 2017). https://www.esma.europa.eu/sites/default/files/library/speech_valdis_dombrovskis_esma_conference_2017_0.pdf.

Donnelly, Shawn. "Advocacy Coalitions and the Lack of Deposit Insurance in Banking Union." *Journal of Economic Policy Reform* 21, no. 3 (September 2018): 210–223. https://doi.org/10.1080/17487870.2017.1400437.

Donnelly, Shawn. "Expert Advice and Political Choice in Constructing European Banking Union." *Journal of Banking Regulation* 17, no. 1 (2016): 104–118.

Donnelly, Shawn. "Post-Brexit Financial Services in the EU." *Journal of European Public Policy* (April 2022). https://doi.org/10.1080/13501763.2022.2061579.

Donnelly, Shawn, and Gaia Pometto. "Banking Nationalism and Resolution in Italy and Spain." *Government and Opposition* (August 2022). https://doi.org/10.1017/gov.2022.27.

Donnery, Sharon. "Ireland's Engagement in Europe and Deeper Integration of Europe" (presented at the European Movement Ireland., January 2020). https://www.bis.org/review/r201002b.pdf.

Donohoe, Paschal. "Keynote Speech by the Eurogroup President, Paschal Donohoe, at the Single Resolution Board's Annual Conference on 'Bank Resolution: Delivering for Financial Stability'" (Speech presented at the Single Resolution Board's annual conference on "Bank resolution: delivering for financial stability," October 2021). https://www.consilium.europa.eu/en/press/press-releases/2021/10/14/keynote-speech-by-the-eurogroup-president-paschal-donohoe-at-the-single-resolution-board-s-annual-conference-on-bank-resolution-delivering-for-financial-stability/.

Donohoe, Paschal. "Opening Remarks by Paschal Donohoe at the European Parliament's ECON Committee, 25 January 2021" (presented at the European Parliament's ECON Committee, 25 January 2021, January 2021). https://www.consilium.europa.eu/en/press/press-releases/2021/01/25/opening-remarks-by-paschal-donohoe-at-the-european-parliament-s-econ-committee-25-january-2021/.

Donohoe, Paschal. "Remarks by Paschal Donohoe Following the Eurogroup Meeting of 4 October 2021" (presented at the Eurogroup Meeting of 4 October 2021). Accessed August 31, 2022. https://www.consilium.europa.eu/en/press/press-releases/2021/10/04/remarks-by-paschal-donohoe-following-the-eurogroup-meeting-of-4-october-2021/.

Donohoe, Paschal. "Speech by the Eurogroup President, Paschal Donohoe, at the IMF Governor Talk on 'Euro Area Recovery from Covid-19—Economic Policy Reflections and Challenges Ahead', 12 October 2021" (presented at the IMF Governor Talk, October 2021). https://www.consilium.europa.eu/en/press/press-releases/2021/10/13/speech-by-the-eurogroup-president-paschal-donohoe-at-imf-annual-meetings-conference-on-euro-area-recovery-from-covid-19-economic-policy-reflections-and-challenges-ahead-12-october-2021/.

Douglas, Jason. "Mark Carney Says Brexit Is Biggest Domestic Risk to U.K. Financial Stability." *Wall Street Journal*, March 2016, sec. Economy. http://www.wsj.com/articles/mark-carney-says-u-k-s-eu-settlement-helps-boe-achieve-its-objectives-1457433148.

Draghi, Mario. "Introductory Statement to the Press Conference (with Q&A)" (Introductory Statement, April 2019). https://www.ecb.europa.eu/press/pressconf/2019/html/ecb.is190410~c27197866f.en.html.

Draghi, Mario. "Introductory Statement to the Press Conference (with Q&A)" (Press Conference, Frankfurt am Main, October 2018). https://www.ecb.europa.eu/press/pressconf/2018/html/ecb.is181025.en.html.

Duff, Andrew. "Why Britain Needs the Euro." *Financial Times*, March 2009. https://www.ft.com/content/aa181ad4-19e1-11de-9f91-0000779fd2ac.

Duran, Cihan. "European Banks Pile on Home Country Sovereign Debt amid Pandemic, S&P Says | S&P Global Market Intelligence." *S&P Global Market Intelligence*, September 2020. https://www.spglobal.com/marketintelligence/en/news-insights/latest-news-headlines/european-banks-pile-on-home-country-sovereign-debt-amid-pandemic-s-p-says-60418632.

Dyson, Kenneth. "Playing for High Stakes: The Eurozone Crisis." *The European Union in Crisis*, 2017, 54–76.

"ECON Hearing on Financial Supervisory Package—de Larosière Stresses Progress Has Been Satisfactory." Press Release (Brussels: European Parliament Economic and Monetary Affairs Committee, January 2010).

Economist. "A Weary Lender; Deutsche Bank." *The Economist* 413, no. 8911 (November 2014): 68.

Economist. "Explaining the Brexit Vote; The Immigration Paradox." *The Economist* 420, no. 8998 (July 2016): 48.

Economist Intelligence Unit. "Contagion: The Coronavirus Risk to European Banks." *Economist Intelligence Unit*, April 2020, NA-NA.

Elderson, Frank. "Hearing at the Committee on Economic and Monetary Affairs of the European Parliament" (Speech presented at the ECON Committee of the European Parliament, Brussels, January 2021). https://www.ecb.europa.eu/press/key/date/2021/html/ecb.sp210125_2~5d8b84dc5a.en.html.

Enria, Andrea. "Contingency Preparedness in the Context of COVID-19" (European Central Bank, March 2020). https://www.bankingsupervision.europa.eu/press/letterstobanks/shared/pdf/2020/ssm.2020_letter_on_Contingency_preparedness_in_the_context_of_COVID-19.en.pdf.

Enria, Andrea. "Flexibility in Supervision: How ECB Banking Supervision Is Contributing to Fighting the Economic Fallout from the Coronavirus." European Central Bank. *The Supervision Blog* (blog), March 2020. https://www.bankingsupervision.europa.eu/press/blog/2020/html/ssm.blog200327~abd2a8244b.en.html.

Enria, Andrea. "Hearing at the European Parliament's Economic and Monetary Affairs Committee" (presented at the Hearing at the European Parliament's Economic and Monetary Affairs Committee, Frankfurt am Main, October 2020). https://www.bankingsupervision.europa.eu/press/speeches/date/2020/html/ssm.sp201027~d284d6d6c8.en.html.

Enria, Andrea. "Introductory Statement" (presented at the virtual meeting of the European CFO Network organized by UniCredit Group, virtual meeting, June 2020). https://www.bankingsupervision.europa.eu/press/speeches/date/2020/html/ssm.sp200612~eae5123290.en.html.

Enria, Andrea. "Letter from Andrea Enria, Chair of the Supervisory Board, to Mr Schäffler, Member of the German Bundestag, on Possible Policy Responses to the Crisis—25 May 2020," May 2020. https://service.betterregulation.com/document/442179.

## 322 Bibliography

Enria, Andrea. "Transcript of the Media Briefing on June 9, 2020 (with Q&A)" (Media Briefing, Frankfurt am Main, June 2020). https://www.bankingsupervision.europa.eu/press/speeches/date/2020/html/ssm.sp200610~27b3ba0a0d.en.html.

Epstein, Rachel A., and Martin Rhodes. "International in Life, National in Death? Banking Nationalism on the Road to Banking Union," In *The Political and Economic Dynamics of the Eurozone Crisis* edited by James A. Caporaso and Martin Rhodes (New York: Oxford University Press, 2016a): 200–232. https://doi.org/10.1093/acprof:oso/9780198755739.001.0001

Epstein, Rachel A., and Martin Rhodes. "States Ceding Control: Explaining the Shift to Centralized Bank Supervision in the Eurozone." *Journal of Banking Regulation* 17, no. 1 (2016b): 90–103.

Epstein, Rachel A., and Martin Rhodes. "The Political Dynamics behind Europe's New Banking Union." *West European Politics* 39, no. 3 (2016c): 415–437.

Epstein, Rachel, and Martin Rhodes. "From Governance to Government: Banking Union, Capital Markets Union and the New EU." *Competition & Change* 22, no. 2 (2018): 205–224.

Erlanger, Steven, and Liz Alderman. "Euro Saved, for Now, but Danger Is Far from Over: E.U. Deal Doesn't Resolve Several Major Issues and Still Needs to Be Ratified." *International Herald Tribune* (December 2011).

Espinoza, Javier, and Olaf Storbeck. "EU's Green Light for NordLB Rescue Provokes Backlash." *Financial Times*, December 2019. https://www.ft.com/content/18bff16e-1990-11ea-97df-cc63de1d73f4.

Estes, Carroll L. "Social Security: The Social Construction of a Crisis." *The Milbank Memorial Fund Quarterly. Health and Society* 61, no. 3 (1983): 445–461.

"EU Pushes Ahead with Finance Oversight Shake-Up." *Agence France Presse* (June 2009).

"EU Referendum: The Result in Maps and Charts." *BBC News*, June 2021, sec. EU Referendum. https://www.bbc.com/news/uk-politics-36616028.

"EU Regulators' Role Sparks Debate." *Global Investor*, September 2010.

"EU to Fund Supervisory Bodies for Accounting, Auditing." *Xinhua General News Service* (January 2009). https://www.theglobaltreasurer.com/2009/01/27/commission-looks-to-strengthen-standard-setting-bodies-for-accounting-and-auditing/.

Eurogroup. "Statement of the Eurogroup in Inclusive Format on the ESM Reform and the Early Introduction of the Backstop to the Single Resolution Fund." Press Release (Brussels: Eurogroup, November 2020). https://www.consilium.europa.eu/en/press/press-releases/2020/11/30/statement-of-the-eurogroup-in-inclusive-format-on-the-esm-reform-and-the-early-introduction-of-the-backstop-to-the-single-resolution-fund/.

"Eurogroup Agrees on EESM Reform to Make It More Effective." *CE Noticias Financieras English*, November 2020.

"Eurogroup Agrees on ESM Reform and 'backstop' for Single Resolution Fund." *CE Noticias Financieras English*, November 2020.

"Eurogroup Work Programme until June 2021." Press Release (Brussels: Eurogroup, October 2020). https://www.consilium.europa.eu/en/press/press-releases/2020/10/05/eurogroup-work-programme-until-june-2021/.

"Europe Agrees New Agencies to Supervise Financial Firms." *BBC News*, September 2010, sec. Business. https://www.bbc.com/news/business-11171800.

"European Asset Management Conference 2017—Post Conference Report." Post-Conference Report (Luxembourg: Association of the Luxembourg Fund Industry (ALFI), August 2017). https://events.alfi.lu/european-asset-management-conference-2017-post-conference-report/.

European Banking Authority. "Guidelines on the Pragmatic 2020 Supervisory Review Nd Evaluation Process in Light of the COVID-19 Crisis"

(European Banking Authority, July 2020). https://www.eba.europa.eu/sites/default/documents/files/document_library/Publications/Guidelines/2020/Guidelines%20on%20the%20pragmatic%202020%20SREP/897419/EBA-GL-2020-10%20Guidelines%20on%20the%20pragmatic%202020%20SREP.pdf.

European Banking Authority. "The EU Banking Sector: First Insights into the COVID-19 Impacts." Thematic Note (Paris, France: European Banking Authority, May 2020). https://www.eba.europa.eu/sites/default/documents/files/document_library/Risk%20Analysis%20and%20Data/Risk%20Assessment%20Reports/2020/Thematic%20notes/883986/Thematic%20note%20-%20Preliminary%20analysis%20of%20impact%20of%20COVID-19%20on%20EU%20banks%20%E2%80%93%20May%202020.pdf.

European Central Bank. "Annual Report 2016." Annual Report (Frankfurt am Main: European Central Bank, 2017). https://www.ecb.europa.eu/pub/annual/html/ar2016.en.html.

European Central Bank. "ECB Banking Supervision Provides Temporary Capital and Operational Relief in Reaction to Coronavirus" (European Central Bank, March 2020). https://www.bankingsupervision.europa.eu/press/pr/date/2020/html/ssm.pr200312~43351ac3ac.en.html.

European Central Bank. "Pandemic Emergency Purchase Programme." European Central Bank, July 2022. https://www.ecb.europa.eu/mopo/implement/pepp/html/index.en.html.

European Central Bank. "The ECB's Response to the Financial Crisis." *ECB Monthly Bulletin*, October 2010. https://www.ecb.europa.eu/pub/pdf/other/art1_mb201010en_pp59-74en.pdf.

European Central Bank. "What Are Targeted Longer-Term Refinancing Operations (TLTROs)?," March 2021. https://www.ecb.europa.eu/ecb/educational/explainers/tell-me/html/tltro.en.html.

European Central Bank official. Interview by author, 2022.

European Centre for Disease Prevention and Control. "Data on Country Response Measures to COVID-19." European Centre for Disease Prevention and Control, June 2022. https://www.ecdc.europa.eu/en/publications-data/download-data-response-measures-covid-19.

European Commission. Communication from the Commission to the European Parliament, the Council, the European Central Bank, the European Economic and Social Committee and the Committee of the Regions "Towards the completion of the Banking Union" (2015). https://eur-lex.europa.eu/legal-content/EN/TXT/?uri=CELEX:52015DC0587.

European Commission. "GREEN PAPER Building a Capital Markets Union." Green Paper (Brussels: European Commission, 2015). https://eur-lex.europa.eu/legal-content/EN/TXT/?uri=celex%3A52015DC0063.

European Commission. "What Has the EU Done after the Fukushima Accident?" Press Release (Brussels: European Commission, March 2012). https://ec.europa.eu/commission/presscorner/detail/en/MEMO_12_157.

European Commission official. Interview by author, 2022.

European Council. "Offers to Host the European Banking Authority (EBA)." Accessed August 23, 2022. https://www.consilium.europa.eu/en/policies/relocation-london-agencies-brexit/eba/.

"European Parliament Plans Super-Regulator." *Investment Adviser*, May 2010.

European Securities and Markets Authority. "Accounting Implications of the COVID-19 Outbreak on the Calculation of Expected Credit Losses in Accordance with IFRS 9" (European Securities and Markets Authority, March 2020). https://www.esma.europa.eu/file/55097/download?token=Zo8hB9kn.

European Union Committee. "House of Lords—Brexit: Financial Services—European Union Committee" (UK House of Lords European Union Select Committee, December 2016). https://publications.parliament.uk/pa/ld201617/ldselect/ldeucom/81/8102.htm.

## 324 Bibliography

EuroWeek. "Going Gets Tough for Europe's Capital Markets Union." *GlobalCapital Securitization*, October 2019, sec. EuroWeek. https://www.globalcapital.com/securitization/article/28mtzhuukcqzvowzr3ncw/derivatives/going-gets-tough-for-europes-capital-markets-union.

Evans-Pritchard, Ambrose. "Germany Wants to Rein in EU Plans." *The Daily Telegraph* (September 2009), sec. City.

Evans-Pritchard, Ambrose. "Was Brexit Fear a Giant Hoax or Is This the Calm before the next Storm?" *The Telegraph*, June 2016. https://www.telegraph.co.uk/business/2016/06/29/was-brexit-fear-a-giant-hoax-or-is-this-the-calm-before-the-next/.

Everson, Michelle, and Ellen Vos. "European Union Agencies." In *The Palgrave Handbook of EU Crises*, edited by Marianne Riddervold, Jarle Trondal, and Akasemi Newsome. Palgrave Studies in European Union Politics (Cham: Springer International Publishing, 2021), 315–337. https://doi.org/10.1007/978-3-030-51791-5_17.

Fairless, Tom. "European Central Bank Ramps Up Stimulus Program Beyond $1.5 Trillion; Stimulus Efforts Are Now in Line with the Fed's, Reflecting a Policy Turnaround in Europe to Counter Sharp Downturn." *Wall Street Journal (Online)* (June 2020), sec. Economy. https://www.proquest.com/docview/2409176329/citation/38A02BF4FA57413FPQ/2.

Fairless, Tom. "The Coronavirus Pandemic: ECB Chief, Germany Clash on Aid." *Wall Street Journal*, Eastern Edition (March 2020).

Fairless, Tom, and Stephen Fidler. "European Commission Seeks Authority to Wind Down Banks." *Wall Street Journal (Online)* (July 2013), sec. Markets.

Fairless, Tom, Anna Hirtenstein, and Giovanni Legorano. "The Coronavirus Pandemic: ECB Unveils Surprise Bond-Buying Plan." *Wall Street Journal, Eastern Edition* (March 2020).

Fallesen, Ida-Maria Weirsøe. "The Challenges of the EU Banking Union—Will It Succeed in Dealing with the next Financial Crisis?" *Bruges European Economic Policy Briefings* Bruges European Economic Policy Briefings (European Economic Studies Department, College of Europe, October 2015). https://ideas.repec.org/p/coe/wpbeep/36.html.

Farrand, Benjamin, and Marco Rizzi. "There Is No (Legal) Alternative: Codifying Economic Ideology into Law." In *The Crisis behind the Eurocrisis: The Eurocrisis as a Multidimensional Systemic Crisis of the EU*, edited by Eva Nanopoulos and Fotis Vergis (Cambridge: Cambridge University Press, 2019), 23–48. https://doi.org/10.1017/9781108598859.002.

Farrell, Henry. "The Shared Challenges of Institutional Theories: Rational Choice, Historical Institutionalism, and Sociological Institutionalism." In *Knowledge and Institutions*, edited by Johannes Glückler, Roy Suddaby, and Regina Lenz Knowledge and Space (Cham: Springer International Publishing, 2018), 23–44. https://doi.org/10.1007/978-3-319-75328-7_2.

Federal Reserve Board. "FRB: Large Commercial Banks—December 31, 2021." Accessed July 11, 2022. https://www.federalreserve.gov/releases/lbr/20211231/default.htm.

Federal Reserve Board. "FRB: Large Commercial Banks—March 23, 2010." Accessed July 11, 2022. https://www.federalreserve.gov/releases/lbr/20091231/default.htm.

Fell, Charlie. "Only Resolution of Solvency Crisis Can Repair Euro Zone." *Irish Times*, December 2010.

Fernández, Jonás. "S&Ds Welcome Eurogroup Breakthrough on ESM Reform to Reduce Risks for the Banking Sector." Press Release (Brussels: Socialists & Democrats, December 2020). https://www.socialistsanddemocrats.eu/newsroom/sds-welcome-eurogroup-breakthrough-esm-reform-reduce-risks-banking-sector.

Fernández, Jonás. "The Capital Market Union Must Make Financing More Stable, Sustainable and Cheaper for Citizens and SMEs | Socialists & Democrats." Press Release

(Brussels: Socialists & Democrats, September 2020). https://www.socialistsanddemocrats.eu/newsroom/capital-market-union-must-make-financing-more-stable-sustainable-and-cheaper-citizens-and.

Ferrera, Maurizio, Joan Miró, and Stefano Ronchi. "Walking the Road Together? EU Polity Maintenance during the COVID-19 Crisis." *West European Politics* 44, no. 5–6 (2021): 1329–1352.

Finance Ministers from Denmark, Estonia, Finland, Ireland, Latvia, Lithuania, Sweden, and The Netherlands. "Shared Views of the Finance Ministers from Denmark, Estonia, Finland, Ireland, Latvia, Lithuania, Sweden, and The Netherlands about Capital Markets Union." Text (New Hanseatic League, July 2018). https://www.government.se/statements/2018/07/shared-views-of-the-finance-ministers-from-denmark-estonia-finland-ireland-latvia-lithuania-sweden-and-the-netherlands-about-capital-markets-union/.

"Financial Services: Commission Proposes Stronger Financial Supervision in Europe." Press Release (Brussels: European Commission, May 2009). https://ec.europa.eu/commission/presscorner/detail/en/IP_09_836.

"Financial Supervision for EU." *Polish News Bulletin*, April 2009, sec. Law News.

Fitch Ratings. "German Banks' Weaknesses Exposed as Economic Outlook Worsens" Non-Rating Action Commentary (Fitch Ratings, April 2020). https://www.fitchratings.com/research/banks/german-banks-weaknesses-exposed-as-economic-outlook-worsens-08-04-2020.

Fitch Solutions. "German Social Democrats Now Likely to Win Election, Swing Policy Leftwards." *Fitch Solutions*, September 2021, sec. Country Risk. http://www.fitchsolutions.com/country-risk/german-social-democrats-now-likely-win-election-swing-policy-leftwards-14-09-2021.

Foster, Peter. "EU Referendum: Eurozone Will Make City Pay Dearly for Brexit, Warns Lord Hill." *The Telegraph*, June 2016. https://www.telegraph.co.uk/business/2016/06/15/eu-referendum-eurozone-will-make-city-pay-dearly-for-brexit-warn/.

Fox, Benjamin. "Franco-German Rift Derails Banking Union Deal." *EUobserver* (December 2012). https://euobserver.com/green-economy/118415.

France 24. "France Pitches Paris as Europe's Main Financial Hub Post-Brexit." *France 24*, July 2016, sec. Europe. https://www.france24.com/en/20160706-valls-paris-london-europe-finance-hub-post-brexit-eu-london-banks.

France 24. "No Access to Single Market without Freedom of Movement, EU Tells Britain." *France 24*, June 2016, sec. Europe. https://www.france24.com/en/20160629-no-access-single-market-without-freedom-movement-eu-tells-britain.

Frankel, Jeffrey. "The Euro Crisis: Where to from Here." *Journal of Policy Modeling* 37, no. 3 (2015): 428–444.

Fromage, Diane. "La protection des citoyens de l'Union face aux risques dans le domaine bancaire." *Revue de l'Union Européenne*, no. 654 (January 2022): 17.

Furber, Sophia, and Mohammad Abbas Taqi. "Italy's €750B COVID-19 Guarantee Poses Operational, 'doom Loop' Risk for Banks | S&P Global Market Intelligence." *S&P Global*, April 2020, sec. Market Intelligence. https://www.spglobal.com/marketintelligence/en/news-insights/latest-news-headlines/italy-s-8364-750b-covid-19-guarantee-poses-operational-doom-loop-risk-for-banks-58041297.

Gamble, Andrew. "Taking Back Control: The Political Implications of Brexit." *Journal of European Public Policy* 25, no. 8 (August 2018): 1215–1232. https://doi.org/10.1080/13501763.2018.1467952.

## 326 Bibliography

Garcia, Jean. "European Union Proposes 750-Billion Euro Coronavirus Recovery Fund." *University Wire* (May 2020), sec. markets. https://www.proquest.com/docview/2436119122/citation/A884EB5D33384F20PQ/21.

Garcia, Jean. "Top German Court Says European Central Bank Bond Buying Scheme Partially Contravenes the Law." *University Wire* (May 2020), sec. markets. https://www.proquest.com/docview/2436114359/citation/4A51032E75154595PQ/29.

Garicano, Luis. *Five Lessons from the Spanish Cajas Debacle for a New Euro-Wide Supervisor*, (VoxEU/CEPR, October 2012). https://cepr.org/voxeu/columns/five-lessons-spanish-cajas-debacle-new-euro-wide-supervisor

Gelpern, Anna, and Nicolas Veron. "Europe's Banking Union Should Learn the Right Lessons from the US." *Bruegel-Blogs*, October 2020. http://proxy.mtholyoke.edu:2048/login?url=https://search.ebscohost.com/login.aspx?direct=true&db=edsgao&AN=edsgcl.640581704&site=eds-live&scope=site.

Georgieva, Kristalina, Alfred Kammer, and Gerry Rice. "Transcript: Euro Area Press Conference" (Press Conference presented at the Euro Area Press Conference, virtual meeting, November 2020). https://www.imf.org/en/News/Articles/2020/12/01/tr113020-transcript-euro-area-press-conference.

Gergely, Andreas, and Kevin Smith. "Ireland Guarantees All Bank Deposits." *Reuters*, September 2008, sec. Business News. https://www.reuters.com/article/uk-ireland-banks-guarantee-idUKTRE48T2EA20080930.

"German Commercial Banks Call for Single Supervisor." *GlobalCapital*, August 2012, sec. FIG. https://www.globalcapital.com/article/28mv7umx0dglp46zrwmbl/fig/german-commercial-banks-call-for-single-supervisor.

"German Website Sees EU Summit Paving Way for 'Split Continent.'" *BBC Monitoring European* (November 2011). https://www.proquest.com/news/docview/901176193/abstract/71934BF811CA4ABFPQ/15.

"Germany's Merkel Facing Increasing Domestic Opposition to Euro Policy." *BBC Monitoring European* (July 2012). https://www.proquest.com/news/docview/1023319884/abstract/71934BF811CA4ABFPQ/40.

"Germany's Possibilities to Rescue Eurozone 'Not Endless'—Chancellor." *BBC Monitoring European* (January 2012). https://www.proquest.com/news/docview/917917025/abstract/71934BF811CA4ABFPQ/61.

Giles, Chris. "Grand Ideas Fail to Mop up the Mess." *Financial Times*, February 2009, sec. FINANCIAL REGULATION.

Giugliano, Ferdinando. "Athens Faces Uphill Struggle despite Eurozone Deal." *FT.com*, March 2015. https://www.proquest.com/news/docview/2461177393/citation/BDD06560B64C4502PQ/2.

Giuseppe Pennisi. "The Impervious Road to the Single Resolution Mechanism (SRM) of the European Banking Union (EBU)." *Rivista Di Studi Politici Internazionali* 82, no. 2 (326) (April 2015): 229–238.

Glöckler, Gabriel, Johannes Lindner, and Marion Salines. "Explaining the Sudden Creation of a Banking Supervisor for the Euro Area." *Journal of European Public Policy* 24, no. 8 (2017): 1135–1153.

Goodwin, Matthew, and Caitlin Milazzo. "Taking Back Control? Investigating the Role of Immigration in the 2016 Vote for Brexit." *The British Journal of Politics and International Relations* 19, no. 3 (2017): 450–464.

Gordon, Sarah, Robin Harding, Victor Mallet, Megan Murphy, and James Wilson. "Leaning Lenders." *Financial Times*, June 2010, sec. ANALYSIS.

Gow, David. "Berès Leads the Charge for Tougher European Regulation." *The Guardian*, October 2008, sec. Business. https://www.theguardian.com/business/2008/oct/21/europe-regulators.

Gow, David. "Britain Is Favour of Europe Again—at Least for a While." *The Guardian*, March 2009, sec. World news. https://www.theguardian.com/business/2009/mar/26/britain-in-favour-of-europe.

Gow, David. "Brussels Looks at Europe-Wide Bank Regulation." *The Guardian*, February 2009, sec. Business. https://www.theguardian.com/business/2009/feb/26/brussels-europe-bank-regulation.

Goyal, Rishi, Petya Koeva Brooks, Mahmood Pradhan, Thierry Tressel, Giovanni Dell'Ariccia, and Ceyla Pazarbasioglu. "A Banking Union for the Euro Area." *Staff Discussion Notes* 2013, no. 001 (February 2013). https://doi.org/10.5089/9781475521160.006.A001.

Gramegna, Pierre. "Opening Keynote Address" (Speech presented at the ICMA Annual General Meeting & Conference, Luxembourg, May 2017).

Gren, Jakub, David Howarth, and Lucia Quaglia. "Supranational Banking Supervision in Europe: The Construction of a Credible Watchdog." *JCMS: Journal of Common Market Studies* 53 (2015): 181.

Grigaitė, Kristina, Cristina Dias, and Marcel Magnus. "Public Hearing with Elke König, Chair of the Single Resolution Board." Public Hearing Register of Commission Documents (European Commission, May 2020).

Gros, Daniel. "Completing the Banking Union: Deposit Insurance." *CEPS Policy Brief*, 2015. https://www.ceps.eu/ceps-publications/completing-banking-union-deposit-insurance/

Gros, Daniel, and Dirk Schoenmaker. "European Deposit Insurance and Resolution in the Banking Union." *JCMS: Journal of Common Market Studies* 52, no. 3 (2014): 529–546.

Guindos, Luis de. "Banking Union: Achievements and Challenges" (Speech presented at the The High-level conference on "Strengthening the EU's bank crisis management and deposit insurance framework: for a more resilient and efficient banking union" organized by the European Commission, March 2021). https://www.ecb.europa.eu/press/key/date/2021/html/ecb.sp210318_1~e2126b2dec.en.html.

Guindos, Luis de. "Banking Union and Capital Markets Union after COVID-19" (presented at the CIRSF (Research Centre on Regulation and Supervision of the Financial Sector, Portugal) online Annual International Conference 2020 on Major Trends in Financial Regulation, Frankfurt am Main, November 2020). https://www.ecb.europa.eu/press/key/date/2020/html/ecb.sp201112~0913fc32f3.en.html.

Guindos, Luis de. "Building the EU's Capital Markets—What Remains to Be Done" (Speech presented at the Association for Financial Markets in Europe Conference, Supervision and Integration Opportunities for European Banking and Capital Markets, Frankfurt am Main, May 2019). https://www.bis.org/review/r190523d.htm.

Guindos, Luis de. "Deepening EMU and the Implications for the International Role of the Euro" (Speech presented at the Joint Conference of the European Commission and the European Central Bank on European Financial Integration and Stability, Brussels, May 2019). https://www.bis.org/review/r190517b.htm.

Guindos, Luis de. "Financial Stability and the Pandemic Crisis" (presented at the Frankfurt Finance Summit, Frankfurt am Main, June 2020). https://www.ecb.europa.eu/press/key/date/2020/html/ecb.sp200622~422531a969.en.html.

Guindos, Luis de. "Interview with La Vanguardia." Interview by Manel Pérez, April 2020. https://www.ecb.europa.eu/press/inter/date/2020/html/ecb.in200412~b773e66772.en.html.

## 328 Bibliography

Guindos, Luis de. "Presentation of the ECB Annual Report 2019 to the Committee on Economic and Monetary Affairs of the European Parliament (by Videoconference)" (Frankfurt am Main, May 2020). https://www.ecb.europa.eu/press/key/date/2020/html/ecb.sp200507~576464bc66.en.html.

Guindos, Luis de. "Promoting the Stability and Efficiency of EU Financial Markets beyond Brexit" (Speech presented at the Deutsche Bundesbank reception on the occasion of the Euro Finance Week, Frankfurt am Main, November 2018). https://www.bis.org/review/r181114c.htm.

Guindos, Luis de. "Remarks at the European Economics and Financial Centre" (London, United Kingdom, March 2020). https://www.ecb.europa.eu/press/key/date/2020/html/ecb.sp200302~0aa9fbaddd.en.html.

"Guindos Says the ECB Has Not Decided Whether to Buy 'Fallen Angels.'" *CE Noticias Financieras English* (May 2020).

Győrffy, Dóra. *Trust and Crisis Management in the European Union. [Electronic Resource]: An Institutionalist Account of Success and Failure in Program Countries* Springer EBooks (New York: Springer International Publishing, 2018). http://proxy.mtholyoke.edu:2048/login?url=https://search.ebscohost.com/login.aspx?direct=true&db=cat06626a&AN=mhc.016289225&site=eds-live&scope=site.

Habermas, Juergen. *Legitimation Crisis.* Translated by Thomas McCarthy. First edition (Boston, Mass: Beacon Press, 1975).

Hakenes, Hendrik, and Isabel Schnabel. "Bank Size and Risk-Taking under Basel II." *Journal of Banking & Finance* 35, no. 6 (2011): 1436–1449.

Hakenes, Hendrik, and Isabel Schnabel. "Banks without Parachutes: Competitive Effects of Government Bail-out Policies." *Journal of Financial Stability* 6, no. 3 (2010): 156–168.

Hakenes, Hendrik, and Isabel Schnabel. "The Threat of Capital Drain: A Rationale for Regional Public Banks?" *Journal of Institutional and Theoretical Economics (JITE)/Zeitschrift Für Die Gesamte Staatswissenschaft* 116, no. 4 (2010): 662–689.

Hall, Allan. "Germany Hits out at Britain over 'blocks' on Strict Rules." *London Evening Standard* (September 2009), West End final ed. edition, sec. News.

Hall, Ben. "State-Funded Equity Injections Will Be Fraught with Moral Hazard: INSIDE BUSINESS EUROPE." *Financial Times*, July 2020, sec. News.

Hall, Ben. "Transcript: Christine Lagarde." *Financial Times*, February 2009.

Hall, Ben, George Parker, and Nikki Tait. "Britain Heads for EU Rift over Regulation." *Financial Times*, March 2009, sec. NATIONAL NEWS.

Hall, Peter A. "Policy Paradigms, Social Learning, and the State: The Case of Economic Policymaking in Britain." *Comparative Politics* 25, no. 3 (1993), 275–296.

"Handelsblatt Exclusive; Brexit Threatens E.U. Financial Union." *Handelsblatt Global*, June 2016, sec. Finance.

Hansford, Rebecca. "AFME Calls for Renewed Efforts towards Banking Union and Capital Markets Union to Deepen Europe's Financial Integration." Press Release (Brussels: Association for Financial Markets in Europe). Accessed September 1, 2022. https://www.afme.eu/News/Press-Releases/Details/AFME-calls-for-renewed-efforts-towards-Banking-Union-and-Capital-Markets-Union-to-deepen-Europes-financial-integration-.

Hansford, Rebecca. "AFME Welcomes European Commission's CMU Mid-Term Review | AFME." Press Release (Brussels: Association for Financial Markets in Europe, June 2017). https://www.afme.eu/News/Press-Releases/Details/afme-welcomes-european-commissions-cmu-mid-term-review.

Hardie, Iain, and Huw Macartney. "EU Ring-Fencing and the Defence of Too-Big-to-Fail Banks." *West European Politics* 39, no. 3 (2016): 503–525.

Hay, Colin. "Crisis and the Structural Transformation of the State: Interrogating the Process of Change." *The British Journal of Politics & International Relations* 1, no. 3 (1999): 317–344.

Hay, Jon, and Owen Sanderson. "ECB Supervisor's Bad Bank Dream Faces Huge Obstacles." *GlobalCapital Securitization*, November 2020, sec. FIG People and Markets. https://www.globalcapital.com/securitization/article/28mudmf4ppazk1uicf5z4/fig-people-and-markets/ecb-supervisors-bad-bank-dream-faces-huge-obstacles.

Heath, Allister. "EU Not City Dictates Capital's Future." *CityAM* (November 2010). https://www.cityam.com/eu-not-city-dictates-capitals-future/.

Heinrich, Mathis, and Amelie Kutter. "A Critical Juncture in EU Integration? The Eurozone Crisis and Its Management 2010-2012." In *Moments of Truth: The Politics of Financial Crises in Comparative Perspective*, edited by Francisco Panizza and George Philip (New York: Routledge, 2014): 120–140.

Heller, Gernot, and Kevin Krolicki. "Key German Bank Rescued; Italy Presses for EU-Wide Bailout Fund." *The Windsor Star* (October 2008), sec. Business.

Hernández de Cos, Pablo. "EDIS: Is a Political Agreement Nearer?" *Views: The EUROFI Magazine*, April 2020.

Hernández de Cos, Pablo. "Europe Should Commit to Global Financial Cooperation for Its Own Recovery." *Views: The EUROFI Magazine*, September 2020.

Hernández de Cos, Pablo. "Pablo Hernández de Cos: The Value of the European Project in Today's Global Landscape" (presented at the Graduation ceremony, Barcelona Graduate School of Economics, Barcelona, July 2021). https://www.bis.org/review/r210714b.htm.

Hilton, Andrew. "The City and Brexit: A CSFI Survey of the Financial Services Sector's Views on Britain and the EU" (London: Centre for the Study of Financial Innovation, April 2015). https://static1.squarespace.com/static/54d620fce4b049bf4cd5be9b/t/5536a1e8e4b0eb6a74abaf16/1429643752526/CSFI+The+City+and+Brexit.pdf.

Hodson, Dermot, and Uwe Puetter. "The European Union in Disequilibrium: New Intergovernmentalism, Postfunctionalism and Integration Theory in the Post-Maastricht Period." *Journal of European Public Policy* 26, no. 8 (August 2019): 1153–1171. https://doi.org/10.1080/13501763.2019.1569712.

Holodny, Elena. "BREMMER: Brexit Is the World's Most Significant Political Risk since the Cuban Missile Crisis." *Business Insider*. Accessed September 27, 2022. https://www.businessinsider.com/ian-bremmer-on-brexit-2016-6.

Hooghe, Liesbet, Brigid Laffan, and Gary Marks. "Introduction to Theory Meets Crisis Collection." *Journal of European Public Policy* 25, no. 1 (January 2018): 1–6. https://doi.org/10.1080/13501763.2017.1310282.

Hooghe, Liesbet, and Gary Marks. "A Postfunctionalist Theory of European Integration: From Permissive Consensus to Constraining Dissensus." *British Journal of Political Science* 39, no. 1 (January 2009): 1–23. https://doi.org/10.1017/S0007123408000409.

Hooghe, Liesbet, and Gary Marks. "Grand Theories of European Integration in the Twenty-First Century." *Journal of European Public Policy* 26, no. 8 (August 2019): 1113–1133. https://doi.org/10.1080/13501763.2019.1569711.

Hope, Katie. "What on Earth Is Euro Clearing—and Why Should You Care?" *BBC News*, June 2017, sec. Business. https://www.bbc.com/news/business-40258449.

Horobin, William. "ECB Indicates More Stimulus Is on the Way, Says Bank of France Chief." *Irish Independent* (May 2020), sec. News.

Hougaard Jensen, Svend E, and Dirk Schoenmaker. "Should Denmark and Sweden Join the Banking Union?" *Journal of Financial Regulation* 6, no. 2 (September 2020): 317–326. https://doi.org/10.1093/jfr/fjaa005.

## 330 Bibliography

House of Lords—European Union Committee. "The Future of EU Financial Regulation and Supervision." Minutes of Evidence (London: House of Lords, January 2009). https://publications.parliament.uk/pa/ld200809/ldselect/ldeucom/106/9012702.htm.

Hovakimian, Armen, and Edward J. Kane. "Effectiveness of Capital Regulation at US Commercial Banks, 1985 to 1994." *The Journal of Finance* 55, no. 1 (2000): 451–468.

Howarth, David, and Lucia Quaglia. "Banking on Stability: The Political Economy of New Capital Requirements in the European Union." *Journal of European Integration* 35, no. 3 (2013): 333–346.

Howarth, David, and Lucia Quaglia. "Brexit and the Battle for Financial Services." *Journal of European Public Policy* 25, no. 8 (August 2018): 1118–1136. https://doi.org/10.1080/13501763.2018.1467950.

Howarth, David, and Lucia Quaglia. "Failing Forward in Economic and Monetary Union: Explaining Weak Eurozone Financial Support Mechanisms." *Journal of European Public Policy* 28, no. 10 (2021): 1555–1572.

Howarth, David, and Lucia Quaglia. "The Difficult Construction of a European Deposit Insurance Scheme: A Step Too Far in Banking Union?" *Journal of Economic Policy Reform* 21, no. 3 (September 2018): 190–209. https://doi.org/10.1080/17487870.2017.1402682.

Howarth, David, and Lucia Quaglia. *The Political Economy of European Banking Union* (New York: Oxford University Press, 2016).

Howarth, David, and Lucia Quaglia. "The Steep Road to European Banking Union: Constructing the Single Resolution Mechanism." *JCMS: Journal of Common Market Studies* 52 (2014): 125.

Howarth, David, and Joachim Schild. "Reinforcing Supranational Bank Regulation, Supervision, Support and Resolution in Europe: Introduction." *Journal of Economic Policy Reform* 22, no. 3 (September 2019): 203–207. https://doi.org/10.1080/17487870.2018.1424519.

"HSBC: UK Should Not Quit EU Just as Services Reforms Are Coming." *CityAM*, February 2015. https://www.cityam.com/hsbc-uk-should-not-quit-eu-just-services-reforms-are-coming/.

Hughes, Jennifer. "London's Nervous Wait for Tougher Regulation." *Financial Times*, March 2009. https://www.ft.com/content/2b16a9b8-1e1d-11de-830b-00144feabdc0.

Hughes, Jennifer. "UK Makes Its Presence Felt on Financial Reform." *Financial Times*, January 2009, sec. WORLD NEWS.

Ikenberry, G. John. "The Rise of China and the Future of the West-Can the Liberal System Survive." *Foreign Affairs* 87 (2008): 23.

"IMF Points to Spain as the Economy Hit Hardest by Coronavirus." *CE Noticias Financieras English*, October 2020.

"IMF World Economic Outlook (WEO) Update, July 2016: Uncertainty in the Aftermath of the U.K. Referendum" World Economic Outlook (Washington, D.C.: International Monetary Fund, June 2016). https://www.imf.org/en/Publications/WEO/Issues/2016/12/31/Uncertainty-in-the-Aftermath-of-the-U-K.

Indaco, Francesco. "Banks Commit to Supporting Communities, Businesses in Covid-19 Era—EBF Board Communiqué May 2020." Press Release EBF Board Communiqué (Brussels: European Banking Federation, May 2020). https://www.ebf.eu/ebf-media-centre/ebf-board-communique-may-2020/.

International Monetary Fund. *Direction of Trade Statistics (DOTS)* (Washington, D.C.: International Monetary Fund). Accessed February 20, 2023. https://data.imf.org/?sk=9D6028D4-F14A-464C-A2F2-59B2CD424B85.

"Interview with Christine Lagarde, President of the ECB." *NOS Nieuwsuur* (NOS, December 2019). https://www.ecb.europa.eu//press/inter/date/2019/html/ecb.in191216~8014b1bae6.en.html.

"Interview with Sabine Lautenschläger" (Deutschlandfunk, December 2018). https://www. ecb.europa.eu/press/inter/date/2018/html/ecb.in181230.en.html.

Ioannidou, Vasso. "A First Step towards a Banking Union." In *Banking Union for Europe: Risks and Challenges*, edited by Thorsten Beck (London, United Kingdom: VoxEU, 2012): 85–94.

Ioannou, Demosthenes, Patrick Leblond, and Arne Niemann. "European Integration and the Crisis: Practice and Theory." *Journal of European Public Policy* 22, no. 2 (2015): 155–176.

Jabko, Nicolas. *Playing the Market: A Political Strategy for Uniting Europe, 1985–2005* (Ithaca, UNITED STATES: Cornell University Press, 2012). http://ebookcentral.proquest.com/lib/mtholyoke/detail.action?docID=3138289.

Jabko, Nicolas. "The Elusive Economic Government and the Forgotten Fiscal Union." In *The Future of the Euro*, edited by Mattias Matthijs and Mark Blyth (New York: Oxford University Press, 2015). https://doi.org/10.1093/acprof:oso/9780190233235.003.0004.

Jabko, Nicolas. "The Hidden Face of the Euro." *Journal of European Public Policy* 17, no. 3 (2010): 318–334.

"Jacques de Larosière, the Reformer." *Institutional Investor*, April 2009. https://www. institutionalinvestor.com/article/b150qb2kyg5t0x/jacques-de-larosire-the-reformer.

Jahberg, Heike, and Carla Neuhaus. "Bafin-Chef Felix Hufeld: 'Bei den Banken liegt noch einiges im Argen.'" *Der Tagesspiegel Online*. Accessed September 30, 2022. https://www. tagesspiegel.de/wirtschaft/bei-den-banken-liegt-noch-einiges-im-argen-7394413.html.

Jamieson, Bill. "The Future of Regulation Is up in the Air." *Scotland on Sunday*, June 2009.

Jenkins, Patrick. "No One Should Get Excited about Buying Commerzbank." *Financial Times*, October 2017. https://www.ft.com/content/ad42faa2-acdc-11e7-beba-5521c713abf4.

Jenkins, Patrick, and Harriet Agnew. "What Would Brexit Mean for the City of London?" *Financial Times*, February 2016. https://www.ft.com/content/e90885d8-d3db-11e5-829b-8564e7528e54.

Jenkins, Patrick, and Caroline Binham. "Brexit Would Make UK a 'Supplicant,' Says Lord Hill." *Financial Times*, November 2015. https://www.ft.com/content/bda4e522-9519-11e5-ac15-0f7f7945adba.

Jo, Sam-Sang. *European Myths: Resolving the Crises in the European Community/European Union* (University Press of America, 2007).

Jolly, David, and James Kanter. "Germany Once More on Defensive in Euro Zone." *International Herald Tribune* (June 2012).

Jonathan Adair, Turner. "The Turner Review: A Regulatory Response to the Global Banking Crisis" (London (UK), United Kingdom: Financial Servcies Authority, n.d.).

Jones, Erik. "The Economic Mythology of European Integration." *JCMS: Journal of Common Market Studies* 48, no. 1 (2010): 89–109. https://doi.org/10.1111/j.1468-5965.2009.02043.x.

Jones, Erik, R. Daniel Kelemen, and Sophie Meunier. "Failing Forward? Crises and Patterns of European Integration." *Journal of European Public Policy* 28, no. 10 (Taylor & Francis, 2021): 1519–1536.

Jones, Erik, R. Daniel Kelemen, and Sophie Meunier. "Failing Forward? The Euro Crisis and the Incomplete Nature of European Integration." *Comparative Political Studies* 49, no. 7 (June 2016): 1010–1034. https://doi.org/10.1177/0010414015617966.

Jones, Huw. "'Brexit' Would Be Disaster for UK Financial Sector—Industry Group." *Reuters*, June 2015, sec. Business News. https://www.reuters.com/article/uk-britain-eu-referendum-idUKKCN0P92X720150629.

Jones, Huw. "ECB and France Spar over Future Bank Supervision." *Reuters*, February 2009, sec. Financial Services and Real Estate. https://www.reuters.com/article/eu-financial-supervision-idUKLK24496720090220.

## 332 Bibliography

Jones, Huw. "EU Sets up Crisis Unit to Boost Financial Oversight." *Reuters*, October 2008, sec. Banks. https://www.reuters.com/article/eu-financial-supervision-idUSLG70246420081016.

Jones, Huw. "LSE Says Splitting Euro Clearing Would Create Rump EU Market." *Reuters*, June 2017, sec. Business News. https://www.reuters.com/article/uk-eu-derivatives-clearing-idUKKBN1931NY.

Jones, Huw. "Report Urges Phased Reform of EU Financial Oversight." *Reuters*, February 2009, sec. Business News. https://www.reuters.com/article/uk-financial-eu-sb-idUKTRE51O3TT20090225.

Jones, Huw, and Paul Taylor. "France, Germany Clash on Financial Rescue; Paris Floating Plan for EU Bailout Fund for Banks." *The Ottawa Citizen*, October 2008, sec. Business & Technology.

Jones, Sam. "UK Slams EU Hedge Fund Rules." *Financial Times*, July 2009. https://www.proquest.com/news/docview/229220082/citation/F002DE44158A4712PQ/1.

Juncker, Jean-Claude, and Jean-Claude Trichet. "Trichet en Juncker voorzichtig optimistisch over economish herstel in 2010 (en)" (Reparks to the European Parliament presented at the European Parliament, Brussels, March 2009). https://www.parlement.com/id/vi3tivff3lwt/nieuws/trichet_en_juncker_voorzichtig.

Kalaitzake, Manolis. "Brexit for Finance? Structural Interdependence as a Source of Financial Political Power within UK-EU Withdrawal Negotiations." *Review of International Political Economy* 28, no. 3 (2021): 479–504.

Kaltenthaler, Karl. "German Interests in European Monetary Integration." *JCMS: Journal of Common Market Studies* 40, no. 1 (2002): 69–87.

Kassim, Hussein. "The European Commission and the COVID-19 Pandemic: A Pluri-Institutional Approach." *Journal of European Public Policy* 30, no. 4 (April 2023): 612–634. https://doi.org/10.1080/13501763.2022.2140821.

Kaufmann, Eric. "It's NOT the Economy, Stupid: Brexit as a Story of Personal Values." *British Politics and Policy at LSE* (blog), July 2016. https://blogs.lse.ac.uk/politicsandpolicy/personal-values-brexit-vote/.

Kauppi, Piia-Noora. "Finnish Financial Sector Supports the Banking Union—but Rushing Risk Sharing Could Slow Down Economic Recovery" (Finance Finland, December 2020). https://www.finanssiala.fi/en/news/finnish-financial-sector-supports-the-banking-union-but-rushing-risk-sharing-could-slow-down-economic-recovery/.

Keene, Tom, and Francine Lacqua. "Paul De Grauwe and Hans-Guenter Redeker Are on BB TV." *CEO Wire* (May 2018). https://www.proquest.com/news/docview/2036784500/citation/6CEBCBE6AD274D6DPQ/2.

Kerr, Sam. "The EU's Simple and Standard ABS Framework Is Anything But." *GlobalCapital*, May 2017, sec. Euroweek.

Khan, Mehreen. "Eurozone Finance Ministers Strike Deal over Bailout Fund Reform." *Financial Times*, November 2020. https://www.ft.com/content/827f3d0c-ff1d-417e-bdc9-afd55be003b0.

Khan, Mehreen. "Frugal States Push to Cut Recovery Package: European Capitals at Loggerheads over Size of Covid-19 Support Funds." *Financial Times*, July 2020, sec. News.

Killick, Marcus. "Time for an EU Banking Regulator?" *Gibraltar Magazine*, March 2009. https://issuu.com/thegibraltarmagazine/docs/march2009.

Kingdon, John W. *Agendas, Alternatives, and Public Policies*. Updated second edition. Longman Classics in Political Science (Boston: Longman, 2011).

Kirkup, James, and Bruno Waterfield. "Tories Could Wreck EU Talks, Says PM: France 'trying to Poison EU Summit' [Scot Region]." *The Daily Telegraph* (December 2011), sec. News; Front Page.

Klein, Naomi. *The Shock Doctrine: The Rise of Disaster Capitalism* (New York: Macmillan, 2007).

Krampf, Arie. "From the Maastricht Treaty to Post-Crisis EMU: The ECB and Germany as Drivers of Change." *Journal of Contemporary European Studies* 22, no. 3 (2014): 303–317.

Kroner, Andreas, and Yasmine Osman. "Interview: Bundesbank-Vorstand Wuermeling: Die Kreditrisiken Bereiten Uns Die Größten Sorgen"." *Handelsblatt*. Accessed August 31, 2022. https://www.handelsblatt.com/finanzen/banken-versicherungen/banken/interview-bundesbank-vorstand-wuermeling-die-kreditrisiken-bereiten-uns-die-groessten-sorgen/25768132.html.

Krotz, Ulrich, and Joachim Schild. "Back to the Future? Franco-German Bilateralism in Europe's Post-Brexit Union." *Journal of European Public Policy* 25, no. 8 (August 2018): 1174–1193. https://doi.org/10.1080/13501763.2018.1467951.

Kudrna, Zdenek. "Financial Market Regulation: Crisis-Induced Supranationalization." *Journal of European Integration* 38, no. 3 (2016): 251–264.

Kudrna, Zdenek. "Governing the Ins and Outs of the EU's Banking Union." *Journal of Banking Regulation* 17, no. 1 (2016): 119–132.

Kuhn, Theresa. "Grand Theories of European Integration Revisited: Does Identity Politics Shape the Course of European Integration?" *Journal of European Public Policy* 26, no. 8 (August 2019): 1213–1230. https://doi.org/10.1080/13501763.2019.1622588.

Laeven, Luc, and Fabian Valencia. "Resolution of Banking Crises: The Good, the Bad, and the Ugly." *IMF Working Papers* 2010, no. 146 (June 2010). https://doi.org/10.5089/9781455201297.001.A001.

Lagarde, Christine. "Extraordinary Times Require Extraordinary Action. There Are No Limits to Our Commitment to the Euro. We Are Determined to Use the Full Potential of Our Tools, within Our Mandate." Tweet. *Twitter*, March 2020. https://twitter.com/Lagarde/status/1240414918966480896.

Lagarde, Christine. "Hearing at the Committee on Economic and Monetary Affairs of the European Parliament" (Introductory Statement presented at the Hearing at the Committee on Economic and Monetary Affairs of the European Parliament, videoconference, June 2020). https://www.ecb.europa.eu/press/key/date/2020/html/ecb.sp200608~4225ba8a1b.en.html.

Lagarde, Christine. "Jointly Shaping Europe's Tomorrow" (presented at the Franco-German Parliamentary Assembly, Frankfurt am Main, September 2020). https://www.ecb.europa.eu/press/key/date/2020/html/ecb.sp200921~5a30d9013b.en.html.

Lagarde, Christine. "Opening Remarks at the EUI's State of the Union Event" (Opening Remarks presented at the Online Edition of The State of the Union conference organized by the European University Institute, online, May 2020). https://www.ecb.europa.eu/press/key/date/2020/html/ecb.sp200508~81cd924af6.en.html.

Lagarde, Christine, and Luis de Guindos. "Introductory Statement to the Press Conference (with Q&A)." Press Conference (Frankfurt am Main: European Central Bank, September 2020). https://www.ecb.europa.eu/press/pressconf/2020/html/ecb.is200910~5c43e3a591.en.html.

Lagarde, Christine, and Luis de Guindos. "Monetary Policy Statement (with Q&A)." Press Conference (Frankfurt am Main: European Central Bank, October 2020). https://www.ecb.europa.eu/press/pressconf/2023/html/ecb.is230202~4313651089.en.html.

"Lagarde Does Whatever She Can; And Who Can Fault Her When No Other EU Leader Has a Better Idea?" *Wall Street Journal (Online)* (December 2020), sec. Opinion. https://www.proquest.com/docview/2468365756/citation/4A51032E75154595PQ/19.

## 334 Bibliography

Lamfalussy, Alexandre, Luis Angel Rojo, Bengt Ryden, Luigi Spaventa, Norbert Walter, and Nigel Wicks. "Final Report of the Committee of Wise Men on the Regulation of European Securities Markets." ESMA document (Brussels: European Council, February 2001).

Lane, Philip R. Interview with El País. Interview by Luis Doncel, May 2020. https://www.ecb. europa.eu/press/inter/date/2020/html/ecb.in200518~fc93497956.en.html.

Lane, Philip R. "The Eurozone after Brexit" (Speech presented at the Euro50 Group & CIGI Breakfast Meeting, Washington, D.C., October 2016). https://www.bis.org/review/r161014h.htm.

Larsson, Per, Eva Hagström Frisell, and Stefan Olsson. "Understanding the Crisis Management System of the European Union." In *Crisis Management in the European Union: Cooperation in the Face of Emergencies*, edited by Stefan Olsson (New York: Springer Berlin Heidelberg, 2009), 1–16.

Lavery, Scott, Sean McDaniel, and Davide Schmid. "Finance Fragmented? Frankfurt and Paris as European Financial Centres after Brexit." *Journal of European Public Policy* 26, no. 10 (2019): 1502–1520.

"Leading Banks in Europe in 2016, by Total Assets." *Bank and Credit Union Marketing Executives* (blog). Accessed September 9, 2022. https://www.volksbank.hr/leading-banks-europe-2016-total-assets/.

Lex. "EU Bank Stress Tests." *Financial Times*, July 2011. https://www.ft.com/content/dc85d1fc-b131-11e0-a43e-00144feab49a.

Leyen, Ursula von der. "State of the Union Address by President von Der Leyen" (Text presented at the European Parliament Plenary, Brussels, September 2020). https://ec.europa.eu/commission/presscorner/detail/en/SPEECH_20_1655.

Lord Hill, Jonathan. "Lord Hill: Brexit Risks Ruling Us out of Our Best Market." *Evening Standard*, March 2016, sec. Business. https://www.standard.co.uk/business/lord-hill-brexit-risks-ruling-us-out-of-our-best-market-a3203831.html.

Luxembourg for Finance, and PriceWaterhouseCoopers. "Amazonisation Is the Future of European Financial Services" (Luxembourg for Finance & PriceWaterhouseCoopers). Accessed September 30, 2022. https://www.luxembourgforfinance.com/en/news/amazonisation-is-the-future-of-european-financial-services/.

Mackenzie, Nell. "Europe Risks Losing Its Way over Brexit, Say Bank CEOs." *GlobalCapital*, May 2018, sec. Market News. https://www.globalcapital.com/article/28mtje7cf15detc44md4w/market-news/europe-risks-losing-its-way-over-brexit-say-bank-ceos.

Magnus, Marcel, Cristina Sofia Pacheco Dias, and Kristina Grigaitė. "Exchange of Views with Andrea Enria, Chair of the Supervisory Board of the ECB." Briefing Think Tank (European Parliament, May 2020). https://www.europarl.europa.eu/thinktank/en/document/IPOL_BRI(2020)645742.

Maijoor, Steven. "Closing Keynote CMU Mid Term Review Public Hearing—Steven Maijoor" (Speech presented at the CMU Mid-Term Review Public Hearing, Brussels, April 2017). https://www.esma.europa.eu/document/closing-keynote-cmu-mid-term-review-public-hearing-steven-maijoor.

Mare, Davide S., Ata Can Bertay, and Nan Zhou. *Global Financial Development Database* (Washington, DC: The World Bank). Accessed January 23, 2023. https://www.worldbank.org/en/publication/gfdr/data/global-financial-development-database.

Marklew, Victoria. "Will Brexit Lead to a Financial Big Bang for the EU-27?—Foreign Policy Research Institute" (Foreign Policy Research Institute, June 2017). https://www.fpri.org/article/2017/06/will-brexit-lead-financial-big-bang-eu-27/.

Masters, Brooke, and George Parker. "Darling Pressed to Hold Back on EU Regulation." *Financial Times*, November 2009, sec. NATIONAL NEWS.

Masters, Brooke, Nikki Tait, and James Wilson. "Common Rules Likely to Be Enforced." *Financial Times*, September 2009, sec. WORLD NEWS.

Maurice, Eric. "Berlin Risks Being 'culprit' for Stalling EU, Warns Green MEP." *EUobserver*, November 2017. https://euobserver.com/eu-political/140001.

Mayes, David G. "Banking Union: The Problem of Untried Systems." *Journal of Economic Policy Reform* 21, no. 3 (September 2018): 178–189. https://doi.org/10.1080/17487870.2017.1396901.

McGrath, Ciaran. "'Like Cracked Nuclear Reactor!' Brussels MUST Accept UK Rules." *Express (Online)*, March 2020, sec. World. https://www.express.co.uk/news/world/1254054/eurozone-eu-news-brexit-financial-rules-free-trade.

McNamara, Kathleen R. *The Currency of Ideas: Monetary Politics in the European Union* Cornell Studies in Political Economy (Ithaca, NY: Cornell University Press, 2019).

Meade, Geoff. "'Early Warning System' Plan for Banks." *Press Association Mediapoint* (February 2009), sec. Home News.

Meager, Lizzie. "German MEP: UK Equivalence Will Be 'Poor and Burdensome.'" *International Financial Law Review*, June 2016. https://www.proquest.com/docview/1807835511/abstract/12DADDE861584450PQ/1.

"MEPs Agree Brexit Negotiation Plan." *BBC News*, April 2017, sec. UK Politics. https://www.bbc.com/news/uk-politics-39501876.

Mérő, Katalin, and Dora Piroska. "Banking Union and Banking Nationalism—Explaining Opt-out Choices of Hungary, Poland and the Czech Republic." *Policy and Society* 35, no. 3 (2016): 215–226.

Meyer, John W., and Brian Rowan. "Institutionalized Organizations: Formal Structure as Myth and Ceremony." *American Journal of Sociology* 83, no. 2 (1977): 340–363.

Michailidou, Asimina, and Hans-Jörg Trenz. "The European Crisis and the Media: Media Autonomy, Public Perceptions and New Forms of Political Engagement." In *Europe's Prolonged Crisis: The Making or the Unmaking of a Political Union*, edited by Hans-Jörg Trenz, Carlo Ruzza, and Virginie Guiraudon. Palgrave Studies in European Political Sociology (London: Palgrave Macmillan UK, 2015), 232–250. https://doi.org/10.1057/9781137493675_12.

Michel, Charles. "Address by President Charles Michel at the Annual EU Ambassadors' Conference" Press Release (Brussels: European Council, November 2020). https://www.consilium.europa.eu/en/press/press-releases/2020/11/10/discours-du-president-charles-michel-lors-de-la-conference-annuelle-des-ambassadeurs-de-l-ue/.

Miliband (Chair), David, and Paul Myners. "'European Affairs' on Tuesday 16 June 2009." (Debate presented at the UK House of Commons Debate, London, June 2009). https://hansard.parliament.uk//Commons/2009-06-16/debates/09061634000001/EuropeanAffairs.

Mitchell, Christopher. *Saving the Market from Itself: The Politics of Financial Intervention* (Cambridge: Cambridge University Press, 2016).

Moghadam, Reza. "How a Post-Brexit Redesign Can Save the Capital Markets Union." *Financial Times*, February 2017. https://www.ft.com/content/6682da18-efb0-11e6-ba01-119a44939bb6.

Monnet, Jean. *Memoirs*. First edition (Garden City, NY: Doubleday, 1978).

"Moody's Says ECB Paves the Way for the Creation of a Bad Bank." *CE Noticias Financieras English*, June 2020.

Mooney, Attracta. "Fears Grow Brexit Will Slow Capital Markets Union." *Financial Times*, July 2016. https://www.ft.com/content/bf7c5b5a-4833-11e6-8d68-72e9211e86ab.

Moreno Badia, Marialuz, Samba Mbaye, and Kyungla Chae. *Global Debt Database: Methodology and Sources* (Washington, DC: International Monetary Fund, 2018).

## 336   Bibliography

Morlino, Leonardo, and Cecilia Emma Sottilotta, eds. *The Politics of the Eurozone Crisis in Southern Europe: A Comparative Reappraisal*. First edition. (Cham, Switzerland: Palgrave Macmillan, 2020).

Morris, Stephen, and Owen Walker. "UBS Chairman Backs London to Remain Europe's Top Financial Centre." *Financial Times*, December 2020. https://www.ft.com/content/bdbe701d-53fa-41e6-9de3-2a49f06d31a7.

Mourmouras, John Iannis. "Post-Brexit Effects on Global Monetary Policy and Capital Markets" (presented at the Hellenic American Association for Professionals in Finance (HABA), New York City, December 2016). https://www.bis.org/review/r161216g.htm.

Mulholland, Hélène. "Boris Johnson Warns of Threat from EU Regulation Plans." *The Guardian*, September 2009, sec. Politics. https://www.theguardian.com/politics/2009/sep/02/boris-johnson-eu-regulation.

Munchau, Wolfgang. "Default Now or Default Later, That Is the Question." *Financial Times*, May 2012, sec. COMMENT.

Munchau, Wolfgang. "Plan D Stands for Default . . . and the Death of the Euro." *Financial Times*, July 2011, sec. COMMENT.

Muñoz, Sara Schaefer, and Neil Shah. "Europe Reels Amid Investor Fears; Bank Stocks and the Euro Take the Hit; Vulnerability Seen in Exposure to Sovereign Debt of Greece, Portugal, Others." *Wall Street Journal (Online)*, February 2010, sec. Markets.

Neil, Andrew. "Europe's CMU Plan Facing Major Hurdles." *Global Investor*, June 2017.

Nell Mackenzie. "MiFID Data Deluge Opens Markets to Cyber Threats." *GlobalCapital*, September 2017, sec. Regulation. https://www.globalcapital.com/article/28mtaqi51avfxp7c0yl8g/regulation/mifid-data-deluge-opens-markets-to-cyber-threats.

Nesvetailova, Anastasia, Ronen Palan, Stefano Pagliari, John Grahl, Richard Murphy, Izabella Kaminska, and John Christiansen. "A Singapore on the Thames? Post-Brexit Deregulation in the UK" (CITYPERC Working Paper, 2017).

Nicolaou, Anna, and Alice Hancock. "Lockdowns Force Cinemas into Intermission: Operators Fear Power Will Permanently Tilt Further towards Streaming as Customers Spend Enforced Time at Home." *Financial Times*, March 2020, sec. Companies and Markets.

Niemann, Arne. *Explaining Decisions in the European Union* (New York: Cambridge University Press, 2006).

Niemann, Arne. "Neofunctionalism." In *The Palgrave Handbook of EU Crises*, edited by Marianne Riddervold, Jarle Trondal, and Akasemi Newsome. Palgrave Studies in European Union Politics (Cham: Springer International Publishing, 2021), 115–133. https://doi.org/10.1007/978-3-030-51791-5_6.

Nixon, Simon. "Much Euro Ado About Nothing." *Wall Street Journal (Online)* (May 2012), sec. Markets. https://www.wsj.com/articles/SB1000142405270230406570457742406391234458

Noonan, Laura. "Former Morgan Stanley President Slams Europe's Capital Markets." *Financial Times*, February 2020. https://www.ft.com/content/fff3fa58-4e65-11ea-95a0-43d18ec715f5.

Oberndorfer, Lukas. "Between the Normal State and an Exceptional State Form: Authoritarian Competitive Statism and the Crisis of Democracy in Europe." In *The State of the European Union: Fault Lines in European Integration*, edited by Stefanie Wöhl, Elisabeth Springler, Martin Pachel, and Bernhard Zeilinger. Staat—Souveränität—Nation (Wiesbaden: Springer Fachmedien, 2020), 23–44. https://doi.org/10.1007/978-3-658-25419-3_2.

Obstfeld, Maurice. "Crises and the International System." *International Economic Journal* 27, no. 2 (June 2013): 143–155. https://doi.org/10.1080/10168737.2013.793901.

O'Dwyer, Peter. "Ireland Hopes to Host EU Bank Stress Tester." *The Times, London*, August 2017, sec. Ireland. https://www.thetimes.co.uk/article/ireland-hopes-to-host-eu-bank-stress-tester-rst7tdr8l.

OECD. "GDP and Spending—Gross Domestic Product (GDP)—OECD Data." Organisation for Economic Co-operation and Development. Accessed July 11, 2022. http://data.oecd.org/gdp/gross-domestic-product-gdp.htm.

Office of the Bundespräsident, Germany, 2011.

O'Grady, Sean. "Sarkozy's Plan to Muscle in on the City?" *The Independent* (June 2009), sec. Business.

Olivier, Faye. "Marine Le Pen exulte et réclame un 'Frexit.'" *www.lemonde.fr* (June 2016). https://www.proquest.com/news/docview/2673059785/abstract/678F5EEE86 A141A6PQ/14.

Olsson, Stefan. *Crisis Management in the European Union. [Electronic Resource]: Cooperation in the Face of Emergencies* Springer EBooks (Berlin: Springer, 2009). http://proxy.mtholyoke.edu:2048/login?url=https://search.ebscohost.com/login.aspx?direct=true&db=cat06626a&AN=mhc.015053998&site=eds-live&scope=site.

O'Neill, Dominic. "Western Europe: European Banking's behind-the-Scenes Activist." *Euromoney*, November 2017, sec. BANKING. https://www.euromoney.com/article/b15gbkfp0gplgb/western-europe-european-bankings-behind-the-scenes-activist.

Organisation for Economic Co-operation and Development. "Long-Term Government Bond Yields: 10-Year: Main (Including Benchmark) for Greece." FRED, Federal Reserve Bank of St. Louis (FRED, Federal Reserve Bank of St. Louis, June 1997). https://fred.stlouisfed.org/series/IRLTLT01GRM156N.

Oudéa, Frédéric. "Societe Generale SA at Goldman Sachs European Financials Conference" (Presentation presented at the Goldman Sachs European Financials Conference, June 2018). https://www.societegenerale.com/sites/default/files/documents/Investisseurs/europeanfinancialsconferencesg-07062018.pdf.

Owen, Glen. "EU Chief Juncker Plots for Chancellor for Whole of Europe | Daily Mail Online." *The Daily Mail (London)* (October 2017). https://www.dailymail.co.uk/news/article-5027823/EU-chief-Juncker-plots-Chancellor-Europe.html.

Pagliari, Stefano. "A Wall around Europe? The European Regulatory Response to the Global Financial Crisis and the Turn in Transatlantic Relations." *Journal of European Integration* 35, no. 4 (2013): 391–408.

Papademos, Lucas. "Presentation of the ECB's Annual Report 2008 to the European Parliament" (Introductory Statement presented at the European Parliament's Committee on Economic and Monetary Affairs, Strasbourg, April 2009). https://www.bis.org/review/r090423e.pdf.

Parsons, Craig. *A Certain Idea of Europe* (Cornell University Press, 2003).

Paterson, William E. "The Reluctant Hegemon: Germany Moves Centre Stage in the European Union." *JCMS: Journal of Common Market Studies* 49 (2011): 57.

Patrona, Marianna, and Joanna Thornborrow. "Mediated Constructions of Crisis." In *The Mediated Politics of Europe: A Comparative Study of the Discourse*, edited by Mats Ekström and Julie Firmstone (New York: Springer, 2017), 59–88.

Pausch-Homblé, Katharina. "Capital Markets Union: Presidency and Parliament Reach Provisional Deal on Clearing House Rules." Press Release (Brussels: Council of the European Union, March 2019). https://www.consilium.europa.eu/en/press/press-releases/2019/03/13/capital-markets-union-presidency-and-parliament-reach-provisional-deal-on-clearing-house-rules/.

## 338 Bibliography

Pedersen, Thomas. "Cooperative Hegemony: Power, Ideas and Institutions in Regional Integration." *Review of International Studies* 28, no. 4 (October 2002): 677–696. https://doi.org/10.1017/S0260210502006770.

Peel, Quentin. "Backlash Threat Grows as German Patience Wears Thin." *Financial Times*, January 2012, sec. WORLD NEWS.

Peel, Quentin. "Constitutional Court Refuses to Block Creation of Rescue Fund." *Financial Times*, September 2012, sec. EUROZONE WOES.

Peel, Quentin. "German Court Backs ESM Bailout Fund." *FT.com*, September 2012. https://www.proquest.com/news/docview/1039230077/citation/71934BF811CA4ABFPQ/94.

Peel, Quentin. "German Opposition Makes Fiscal Treaty Demands." *FT.com*, March 2012. https://www.proquest.com/news/docview/959788101/citation/71934BF811CA4ABFPQ/98.

Peel, Quentin. "Merkel Coalition Partner Survives Rebellion." *FT.com*, December 2011. https://www.proquest.com/news/docview/911717253/citation/71934BF811CA4ABFPQ/27.

Peel, Quentin, and Gerrit Wiesmann. "Berlin Denies Pressing Court on Euro Fund." *FT.com*, July 2012. https://www.proquest.com/news/docview/1024371178/citation/71934BF811CA4ABFPQ/100.

Pepe, Anthony. "Banking Union: Long March Towards Unity." *Europolitics*, September 2013.

Pierson, Paul. *The Path to European Integration: A Historical Institutionalist Analysis* (London: Palgrave Macmillan, 1998).

Pisani-Ferry, Jean. "A Growing Crisis Puts the Euro in Danger." *Financial Times*, December 2010, sec. COMMENT.

"Plan for EU Financial Sector Supervision Has Faults-CNB's Tomsik." *CTK Business News Wire*, March 2009, sec. Business News.

"Polish Finance Minister Comments on Banking Sector, Euro Adoption Plan." *BBC Worldwide Monitoring*, November 2008, sec. BBC Monitoring Europe—Political.

Pop, Valentina. "EU Policies Await German Election Outcome." *Financial Times*, September 2021. https://www.ft.com/content/d510d968-eabb-4d98-b759-1d65af2d2384.

Pop, Valentina. "Leaders Agree to Disagree on EU Role in the World." *Financial Times*, October 2021.

Posner, Elliot, and Nicolas Véron. "The EU and Financial Regulation: Power without Purpose?" *Journal of European Public Policy* 17, no. 3 (2010): 400–415.

Press Association. "Brown Blueprint Rejected as 'European Ideas Wrapped in a British Flag.'" *The Guardian*, March 2009, sec. Politics. https://www.theguardian.com/politics/2009/mar/19/gordon-brown-economic-blueprint-brussels.

Princen, Sebastiaan. *Agenda-Setting in the European Union.* Palgrave Studies in European Union Politics (New York: Palgrave Macmillan, 2009). http://proxy.mtholyoke.edu:2048/login?url=https://search.ebscohost.com/login.aspx?direct=true&db=cat06626a&AN=mhc.010916262&site=eds-live&scope=site.

Quaglia, Lucia. "The 'Old' and 'New' Politics of Financial Services Regulation in the European Union." *New Political Economy* 17, no. 4 (2012): 515–535.

Quaglia, Lucia, and David Howarth. "The Policy Narratives of European Capital Markets Union." *Journal of European Public Policy* 25, no. 7 (2018): 990–1009.

Quaglia, Lucia, David Howarth, and Moritz Liebe. "The Political Economy of European Capital Markets Union." *JCMS: Journal of Common Market Studies* 54 (2016): 185.

Quaglia, Lucia, and Aneta Spendzharova. "The Conundrum of Solving 'Too Big to Fail' in the European Union: Supranationalization at Different Speeds." *JCMS: Journal of Common Market Studies* 55, no. 5 (2017): 1110–1126.

Quaglia, Lucia, and Amy Verdun. "Explaining the Response of the ECB to the COVID-19 Related Economic Crisis: Inter-Crisis and Intra-Crisis Learning." *Journal of European Public Policy* 30, no. 4 (April 2023): 635–654. https://doi.org/10.1080/13501763.2022.2141300.

Quaglia, Lucia, and Amy Verdun. "The COVID-19 Pandemic and the European Union: Politics, Policies and Institutions." *Journal of European Public Policy* 30, no. 4 (April 2023): 599–611. https://doi.org/10.1080/13501763.2022.2141305.

Rahbari, Ebrahim, Tina M. Fordham, and Willem Buiter. "Who's Next? EU Political Risks After the Brexit Vote" Global Economics View (Citi Research, July 2013).

Rangan, MC Govardhana, and BODHISATVA GANGULI. "I Think Most Would Rather Have India's Problems than the West's: Anshu Jain, Co-CEO, Deutsche Bank [Interviews]." *The Economic Times*, January 2013. https://www.proquest.com/news/docview/1272354088/citation/5CE02F3B15854BF9PQ/1.

"Reams of Reform." *Financial Times*, March 2009, sec. Financial Advisor.

Reddan, Fiona. "Britain's Difficulty May Once More Prove to Be Ireland's Opportunity." *The Irish Times*, August 2015. Accessed September 27, 2022. https://www.irishtimes.com/business/financial-services/britain-s-difficulty-may-once-more-prove-to-be-ireland-s-opportunity-1.2305649.

Rediker, Douglas A., and Giovanna De Maio. "Europe and the Existential Challenge of Post-COVID Recovery." *Brookings* (blog), April 2020. https://www.brookings.edu/blog/order-from-chaos/2020/04/20/europe-and-the-existential-challenge-of-post-covid-recovery/.

Regling, Klaus. "Klaus Regling at Eurogroup Video Press Conference." Press Conference (virtual meeting: Eurpoean Stability Mechanism, November 2020). https://www.esm.europa.eu/press-releases/klaus-regling-eurogroup-video-press-conference-2020-11-30.

Rehberger, Reinold. "Die Stärken Stärken." *Starkes Land Hessen* (October 2017).

Rehm, Moritz. "Tug of War over Financial Assistance: Which Way Forward for Eurozone Stability Mechanisms?" *Politics and Governance* 9, no. 2 (2021): 173–184.

Rehn, Olli. "The Euro Is Back, But There Is No Room for Complacency" (Introductory Statement presented at the The Economist Conferences Inaugural Eurozone Dialogue, Berlin, September 2010). https://www.parlement.com/id/viiulz17dkyj/nieuws/toespraak_eurcommissaris_olli_rehn_over.

Reichwein, Alexander. "Classical Realism." In *The Palgrave Handbook of EU Crises*, edited by Marianne Riddervold, Jarle Trondal, and Akasemi Newsome. Palgrave Studies in European Union Politics (Cham: Springer International Publishing, 2021), 79–97. https://doi.org/10.1007/978-3-030-51791-5_4.

Renaud, Ninon. "Bruno Le Maire: 'Plus de coopération franco-allemande veut dire plus de croissance pour toute l'Europe.'" *Les Echos* (December 2020), sec. Monde. https://www.lesechos.fr/monde/europe/bruno-le-maire-plus-de-cooperation-franco-allemande-veut-dire-plus-de-croissance-pour-toute-leurope-1272615.

REPORTER, CITY AM. "ECB's Coeure Demands Power to Inject Capital into Banks." *City A.M.* (June 2012), sec. News.

Resiliency Authors. "Making the Eurozone More Resilient: What Is Needed Now and What Can Wait?" (VoxEU/CEPR, June 2016). https://cepr.org/voxeu/columns/making-eurozone-more-resilient-what-needed-now-and-what-can-wait.

Reuters Staff. "Brexit to Shape Rethink of EU Financial Supervision." *Reuters*, March 2017, sec. Financials. https://www.reuters.com/article/eu-markets-regulations-idUSL5N1GY3ZJ.

Reuters Staff. "EU Declines to Rank Rival Bids for Agencies Leaving Britain over Brexit." *Reuters*, September 2017, sec. UK Top News. https://www.reuters.com/article/uk-britain-eu-ema-idUKKCN1C50D1.

Reuters Staff. "Euro Clearing, Bank Watchdog to Leave London after Brexit—EU Official | Reuters." *Reuters*, June 2016. https://www.reuters.com/article/uk-britain-eu-banking-idUKKCN0ZE1YL.

Reuters Staff. "Europeans Warn of Brexit Threat to UK's Crucial Bank 'Passports.'" *Reuters*, June 2016, sec. European Currency News. https://www.reuters.com/article/britain-eu-banks-passport-idUSL8N19726G.

Reuters Staff. "Germany's Scholz: EU Needs to Make More Progress on European Banking Union." *Reuters*, September 2020, sec. Banks. https://www.reuters.com/article/us-eu-economy-scholz-banks-idUSKBN25U1RM.

Reuters Staff. "HIGHLIGHTS-ECB's Weber Says Bailout Talk Not Productive." *Reuters*, March 2010, sec. Hot Stocks. https://www.reuters.com/article/ecb-weber-idUSLDE6280WB20100309.

Reuters Staff. "Interview with Irish Deputy Central Bank Governor Ed Sibley." *Reuters*, September 2019, sec. Business News. https://www.reuters.com/article/us-britain-eu-ireland-banking-highlights-idUKKCN1VN202.

Reuters Staff. "Italian Bank Problems Not an 'Acute Crisis'—Dijsselbloem." *Reuters*, July 2016, sec. Regulatory News—EU. https://www.reuters.com/article/eurozone-italy-banks-dijsselbloem-idUKB5N18F003.

Reuters Staff. "NordLB to Take Full Control of Bremer Landesbank Unit." *Reuters*, September 2016, sec. Financials. https://www.reuters.com/article/bremer-landes-ma-nord-lb-giro-idUSL8N1BD0I1.

Reuters Staff. "UK Should Pay for EU Bank Agency Move after Brexit- EU Lawmakers." *Reuters*, September 2017, sec. Financials. https://www.reuters.com/article/britain-eu-agencies-idUSL8N1LM3MF.

Riddervold, Marianne, Jarle Trondal, and Akasemi Newsome. "Theoretical Approaches to Crisis: An Introduction." In *The Palgrave Handbook of EU Crises*, edited by Marianne Riddervold, Jarle Trondal, and Akasemi Newsome. Palgrave Studies in European Union Politics (Cham: Springer International Publishing, 2021), 51–60. https://doi.org/10.1007/978-3-030-51791-5_2.

Rodrigues, Maria João, and Paul Magnette. "Only a 'New Deal' Can Rescue the European Project." *Social Europe* (blog), April 2020. https://socialeurope.eu/only-a-new-deal-can-rescue-the-european-project.

Rodrigues, Nuno Cunha, and José Renato Gonçalves. "The European Banking Union and the Economic and Monetary Union: The Puzzle Is Yet to Be Completed." In *The Euro and the Crisis: Perspectives for the Eurozone as a Monetary and Budgetary Union*, edited by Nazaré da Costa Cabral, José Renato Gonçalves, and Nuno Cunha Rodrigues. Financial and Monetary Policy Studies (Cham: Springer International Publishing, 2017), 271–288. https://doi.org/10.1007/978-3-319-45710-9_16.

Roos, Christof, and Natascha Zaun. "The Global Economic Crisis as a Critical Juncture? The Crisis's Impact on Migration Movements and Policies in Europe and the US." *Journal of Ethnic and Migration Studies* 42, no. 10 (2016): 1579–1589.

Rosca, Matei. "Capital Markets Union to Limp on, but London's Role One of Many Brexit Question Marks." *SNL Financial*, June 2016, sec. European Financials.

Rosenthal, Uriel, Arjen Boin, and Louise K. Comfort. *Managing Crises: Threats, Dilemmas, Opportunities* (Springfield, IL: Charles C Thomas Publisher, 2001).

Ross, George. *The European Union and Its Crises: Through the Eyes of the Brussels' Elite* (New York: Palgrave Macmillan, 2011). http://proxy.mtholyoke.edu:2048/login?url=https://search.ebscohost.com/login.aspx?direct=true&db=cat06626a&AN=mhc.012139324&site=eds-live&scope=site.

Ross, Verena. "Keynote Address: 'European Capital Markets Union—Update and Future'" (Speech presented at the DSW-Better Finance International Investors' Conference, Weisbaden, Germany, November 2018). https://www.dsw-info.de/fileadmin/Redaktion/Dokumente/PDF/International_Investors__Conference/esma35-43-1376_verena_ross_keynote_speech_international_investors_conference_2018_11_27.pdf.

Rothnie, David. "Crisis Sparks Endgame Fears for Europe's Investment Banks." *GlobalCapital Euroweek*, April 2020, sec. Southpaw. https://www.globalcapital.com/article/28mu5f4ik9vw9d2rmpz40/southpaw/crisis-sparks-endgame-fears-for-europes-investment-banks.

"Roundup: German Court's ECB Ruling Draws Divisive Response." *Xinhua News Agency—CEIS* (May 2020), sec. cMilitary700Politics & Law. https://www.proquest.com/docview/2400607972/citation/4A51032E75154595PQ/38.

Salzborn, Samuel. "Extreme Right-Wing Parties in and Against Europe. A Systematizing Comparison." In *The State of the European Union: Fault Lines in European Integration*, edited by Stefanie Wöhl, Elisabeth Springler, Martin Pachel, and Bernhard Zeilinger. Staat—Souveränität—Nation (Wiesbaden: Springer Fachmedien, 2020), 103–130. https://doi.org/10.1007/978-3-658-25419-3_5.

Samuel, Juliet. "German Election Leaves Macron's Big Idea in Tatters." *The Telegraph*, September 2017. https://www.telegraph.co.uk/business/2017/09/26/german-election-leaves-macrons-big-idea-tatters/.

Sandbu, Martin. "Brexit and Covid Harden the Case for a Proper EU Financial Market." *Financial Times*, December 2020, Europe edition, sec. News.

Sapir, André, Dirk Schoenmaker, and Nicolas Véron. "Making the Best of Brexit for the EU27 Financial System." *Policy Briefs* Policy Briefs (Bruegel, February 2017). https://ideas.repec.org/p/bre/polbrf/18927.html.

"Sarkozy Floats Idea of EU-Wide Plan." *Irish Times*, October 2008.

Scally, Derek. "German Banks Resist EU Plan for Regulator." *The Irish Times*, September 2012. https://www.irishtimes.com/news/german-banks-resist-eu-plan-for-regulator-1.540712.

Scally, Derek. "German Greens on Campaign Trail Criticise Irish Corporate Tax Regime: Coalition Option with Merkel Not Ruled out after Shift on Nuclear Issue." *Irish Times*, August 2013.

Schäfer, David. "A Banking Union of Ideas? The Impact of Ordoliberalism and the Vicious Circle on the EU Banking Union." *JCMS: Journal of Common Market Studies* 54, no. 4 (2016): 961–980.

Schäuble, Wolfgang. "How to Protect EU Taxpayers against Bank Failures." *Financial Times*, August 2012, sec. COMMENT.

Schild, Joachim. "Germany and France at Cross Purposes: The Case of Banking Union." *Journal of Economic Policy Reform* 21, no. 2 (June 2018): 102–117. https://doi.org/10.1080/17487870.2017.1396900.

Schimmelfennig, Frank. "Brexit: Differentiated Disintegration in the European Union." *Journal of European Public Policy* 25, no. 8 (August 2018): 1154–1173. https://doi.org/10.1080/13501763.2018.1467954.

Schimmelfennig, Frank. "European Integration (Theory) in Times of Crisis. A Comparison of the Euro and Schengen Crises." *Journal of European Public Policy* 25, no. 7 (2018): 969–989.

Schimmelfennig, Frank. "Liberal Intergovernmentalism." In *The Palgrave Handbook of EU Crises*, edited by Marianne Riddervold, Jarle Trondal, and Akasemi Newsome. Palgrave Studies in European Union Politics (Cham: Springer International Publishing, 2021), 61–78. https://doi.org/10.1007/978-3-030-51791-5_3.

Schimmelfennig, Frank. "Liberal Intergovernmentalism and the Euro Area Crisis." *Journal of European Public Policy* 22, no. 2 (2015): 177–195.

## 342  Bibliography

Schimmelfennig, Frank, and Thomas Winzen. "Grand Theories, Differentiated Integration." *Journal of European Public Policy* 26, no. 8 (August 2019): 1172–1192. https://doi.org/10.1080/13501763.2019.1576761.

Schmidt, Vivien Ann. *Europe's Crisis of Legitimacy: Governing by Rules and Ruling by Numbers in the Eurozone*. First edition (Oxford, UK: Oxford University Press, 2020). http://proxy.mtholyoke.edu:2048/login?url=https://search.ebscohost.com/login.aspx?direct=true&db=cat06626a&AN=mhc.017482341&site=eds-live&scope=site.

Schnabel, Isabel. "Brexit Would Hurt Europe and Britain." *Financial Times*, June 2016, sec. Opinion. https://www.ft.com/content/d90db55a-3933-11e6-a780-b48ed7b6126f.

Schnabel, Isabel. "Interview with Perspektiven der Wirtschaftspolitik." Interview by Karen Horn, May 2020. https://www.ecb.europa.eu/press/inter/date/2020/html/ecb.in200527_1~cda9c3f6f9.en.html.

Schnabel, Isabel. "Isabel Schnabel: Going Negative—the ECB's Experience" (presented at the 35th Congress of the European Economic Association, Frankfurt am Main, August 2020). https://www.bis.org/review/r200827b.htm.

Schnabel, Isabel. "The Sovereign-Bank-Corporate Nexus—Virtuous or Vicious?" Speech Speech presented at the LSE conference on "Financial Cycles, Risk, Macroeconomic Causes and Consequences," (London: European Central Bank, January 2021). https://www.ecb.europa.eu/press/key/date/2021/html/ecb.sp210128~8f5dc86601.en.html.

Schoenmaker, Dirk. "Banking Union: Where We're Going Wrong." In *Banking Union for Europe: Risks and Challenges* edited by Thorsten Beck. (London: Centre for Economic Policy Research, 2012): 95–102.

Schoenmaker, Dirk. *Governance of International Banking: The Financial Trilemma* (Oxford: Oxford University Press, 2013).

Schoenmaker, Dirk. "The Financial Trilemma." *Economics Letters* 111, no. 1 (2011): 57–59.

Schoenmaker, Dirk, and Daniel Gros. "A European Deposit Insurance and Resolution Fund-An Update." *CEPS Policy Brief*, no. 283 (2012).

Schoenmaker, Dirk, and Arjen Siegmann. "Efficiency Gains of a European Banking Union." SSRN Scholarly Paper (Rochester, NY, February 2013). https://doi.org/10.2139/ssrn.2214919.

Schranz, John. "MEPs Vote to Beef up Financial Supervisory Package." Press Release (Brussels: European Parliament Economic and Monetary Affairs Committee, May 2010). https://www.europarl.europa.eu/pdfs/news/expert/infopress/20100510IPR74360/20100510IPR74360_en.pdf.

Schranz, John. "The European Parliament and Financial Supervision Reform." Press Release (Brussels: European Parliament, September 2010). https://www.europarl.europa.eu/news/en/press-room/20100506BKG74226/the-european-parliament-and-financial-supervision-reform.

Schularick, Moritz, Sascha Steffen, and Tobias H. Troeger. "Bank Capital and the European Recovery from the COVID-19 Crisis," 2020.

Schweiger, Christian. "The Legitimacy Challenge." In *The European Union in Crisis* (New York: Macmillan International Higher Education, 2017), 188–211.

Schweiger, Christian. "The 'Reluctant Hegemon': Germany in the EU's Post-Crisis Constellation." In *The European Union in Crisis: Explorations in Representation and Democratic Legitimacy*, edited by Kyriakos N. Demetriou (Cham: Springer International Publishing, 2015), 15–32. https://doi.org/10.1007/978-3-319-08774-0_2.

Searle, John R. *The Construction of Social Reality* (New York: Simon and Schuster, 1995).

Serra, Anna Paula. "Keynote Speech by Director Ana Paula Serra in the 'CIRSF Annual International Conference 2020': 'Economic Recovery and Financial Stability' | Banco de Portugal" (presented at the CIRSF Annual International Conference 2020, November 2020). https://www.bportugal.pt/en/intervencoes/keynote-speech-director-ana-paula-serra-cirsf-annual-international-conference-2020.

Sewing, Christian. "A Partnership for Growth: Financing Recovery and Growth in Europe." *Views: The EUROFI Magazine*, September 2020.

Sheryl Obejera. "EBA to Further Analyze Fintech, Shadow Banks." *S&P Global*, sec. Market Intelligence. Accessed October 3, 2022. https://www.spglobal.com/marketintelligence/en/news-insights/trending/9IdDpA02VYteVr3KBWVz3w2.

Shipman, Tim. "Hands off the City Chancellor Warns Sarkozy's EU Man [Edition 3]." *Daily Mail* (December 2009), sec. News.

Shotter, James. "EU and HSH Nordbank Reach Provisional Restructuring Deal." *Financial Times*, October 2015. https://www.ft.com/content/09f3379a-767e-11e5-933d-efcdc3c11c89.

Sillavan, James. "No End of Trouble." *The Economist*, November 2008. https://www.economist.com/news/2008/11/19/no-end-of-trouble.

Skuodis, Marius. "Playing the Creation of the European Banking Union: What Union for Which Member States?" *Journal of European Integration* 40, no. 1 (January 2018): 99–114. https://doi.org/10.1080/07036337.2017.1404056.

Smith, Dennis. "Not Just Singing the Blues: Dynamics of the EU Crisis." In *Europe's Prolonged Crisis: The Making or the Unmaking of a Political Union*, edited by Hans-Jörg Trenz, Carlo Ruzza, and Virginie Guiraudon. Palgrave Studies in European Political Sociology (London: Palgrave Macmillan UK, 2015), 23–43. https://doi.org/10.1057/9781137493675_2.

Smyth, Jamie. "Barroso Calls for Consensus on Financial Supervision." *Irish Times*, May 2009.

Smyth, Jamie. "German Finance Minister Dismisses Proposed Pan-European Rescue Fund." *Irish Times*, October 2008.

Somerville, Glenn, and David Milliken. "G7 Partners Cool to U.S.-Style Bailout Plans; Guarded Promises to Co-Operate. European Union Makes It Clear It Will Not Join Any Sort of Rescue Package." *The Gazette*, September 2008, sec. Business.

S&P Global. "As €750B Package Creates Safe Asset, EU Banking Union Inches Closer | S&P Global Market Intelligence." *S&P Global*, sec. Market Intelligence. Accessed September 1, 2022. https://www.spglobal.com/marketintelligence/en/news-insights/latest-news-headlines/as-8364-750b-package-creates-safe-asset-eu-banking-union-inches-closer-59580305.

Standards & Poor. "Spanish Banks Have Little Room to Maneuver in Case of Coronavirus Capital Crunch." *S&P Global Market Intelligence* (blog), April 2020. https://www.spglobal.com/marketintelligence/en/news-insights/latest-news-headlines/spanish-banks-have-little-room-to-maneuver-in-case-of-coronavirus-capital-crunch-57900235.

Stark, Alastair. "New Institutionalism, Critical Junctures and Post-Crisis Policy Reform." *Australian Journal of Political Science* 53, no. 1 (2018): 24–39.

Steenis, Huw van, and Bruce Hamilton. "Brexit Risk a Chance for Industry to Engage in Eurozone Recovery." *Financial Times*, December 2015. https://www.ft.com/content/5ec6cb26-9daf-11e5-8ce1-f6219b685d74.

Steinhauser, Gabriele. "Tougher EU Bank Tests Could Ease Crisis." The Globe and Mail (Online) (Toronto, Canada: The Globe and Mail, December 2010). https://www.proquest.com/news/docview/2385154779/citation/438E37CE41144168PQ/6.

Stenstad, Eirik Tegle, and Bent Sofus Tranøy. "Failing Forward in Financial Stability Regulation." In *The Palgrave Handbook of EU Crises*, edited by Marianne Riddervold, Jarle Trondal, and Akasemi Newsome. Palgrave Studies in European Union Politics (Cham: Springer International Publishing, 2021), 401–419. https://doi.org/10.1007/978-3-030-51791-5_22.

## 344 Bibliography

Stewart, Heather. "Darling Wins Brussels Battle Over Financial Super-Regulator." *The Guardian*, June 2009, sec. Business. https://www.theguardian.com/business/2009/jun/10/alistair-darling-european-finance-regulator.

Straatman, Jan. "Eurozone Needs Clarity from Its Policymakers." *Financial Times*, December 2010, sec. INSIGHT—JAN STRAATMAN.

Tabellini, Guido. "The Main Lessons to Be Drawn from the European Financial Crisis." In *The Eurozone Crisis: A Consensus View of the Causes and a Few Possible Solutions*, edited by Richard Baldwin and Francesco Giavazzi (London: CEPR Press, 2015): 170–175. https://voxeu.org/article/main-lessons-be-drawn-european-financial-crisis.

Taggart, Paul, and Aleks Szczerbiak. "Putting Brexit into Perspective: The Effect of the Eurozone and Migration Crises and Brexit on Euroscepticism in European States." *Journal of European Public Policy* 25, no. 8 (August 2018): 1194–1214. https://doi.org/10.1080/13501763.2018.1467955.

Tait, Nikki. "Brussels Left to Finish 'Mission Impossible.'" *Financial Times*, February 2009, sec. Financial Regulation.

Tait, Nikki. "EU Oversight Reform given Backing." *Financial Times*, July 2010. https://www.proquest.com/news/docview/594872539/citation/8098126AFCA34809PQ/1.

Tait, Nikki. "European Plan for Financial Regulation Faces UK Obstacles." *Financial Times*, May 2009), sec. World News.

Tait, Nikki. "Taskforce Calls for New Risk Bodies." *Financial Times*, February 2009, sec. Financial Regulation.

Tait, Nikki. "UK Insurers Back Idea of EU Regulator." *Financial Times*, February 2009. https://www.ft.com/content/860fa482-f84d-11dd-aae8-000077b07658.

Tait, Nikki, and Jennifer Hughes. "Trichet Urges More Oversight." *Irish Times*, February 2009.

Taylor, Paul. "Sarkozy and Merkel Diverge Over Euro Strategy." *New York Times* (Online), October 2011. https://www.proquest.com/news/docview/2216513006/abstract/71934BF811CA4ABFPQ/14.

Thal Larsen, Peter. "Bank Regulation Needs Straightening Out." *Financial Times*, March 2009. https://www.ft.com/content/723612ce-1d42-11de-9eb3-00144feabdc0.

"The Art of Attracting EU Agencies." *Plus Media Solutions* (June 2017).

The Editorial Board. "A Chance to Press on with EU Banking Union." *Financial Times*, December 2020. https://www.ft.com/content/8f91f48f-ce5d-48d5-998d-b8d714dbdab7.

The Editorial Board. "Deutsche Bank's Retreat Was Late but Necessary." *Financial Times*, July 2019. https://www.ft.com/content/da36554a-a16d-11e9-a282-2df48f366f7d.

Thomas, Leigh. "Britain Fights EU Pressure on Financial Supervision." *Agence France Presse* (June 2009).

Thomas, Nathalie, and Rosemary Gallagher. "The Lehman's Legacy: Has Banking's Dragon Finally Been Tamed?" *Scotland on Sunday*, September 2009.

Timmermans, Frans. "Opening Remarks by Executive Vice-President Frans Timmermans." Opening Remarks (Brussels: European Commission, May 2020). https://ec.europa.eu/commission/presscorner/detail/hr/SPEECH_20_964.

Tinning, William, and Torquil Crichton. "Pressure on Darling as Germany Guarantees All Savings." *HeraldScotland*, October 2008. https://www.heraldscotland.com/default_content/12368486.pressure-darling-germany-guarantees-savings/.

Titcomb, James. "Pensions Giant: Brexit Would Be 'disaster' for UK." *The Telegraph (UK)* (March 2015), sec. Banks and Finance. https://www.telegraph.co.uk/finance/newsbysector/banksandfinance/11491572/Pensions-giant-Brexit-would-be-disaster-for-UK.html.

Tolo, Eero, and Matti Viren. "How Much Do Non-Performing Loans Hinder Loan Growth in Europe?" *European Economic Review* 136 (July 2021). http://proxy.mtholyoke.

edu:2048/login?url=https://search.ebscohost.com/login.aspx?direct=true&db=ecn&AN=1911048&site=eds-live&scope=site.

Tomann, Horst. *Monetary Integration in Europe* (New York: Springer, 2017).

"Top German Court Dismisses Challenge to ECB's Bond-Buying Program." *Xinhua News Agency—CEIS* (May 2021). https://www.proquest.com/docview/2528466378/citation/4A51032E75154595PQ/5.

Traynor, Ian. "Brown Wins Independence from European Banking Regulator." *The Guardian*, June 2009, sec. Business. https://www.theguardian.com/business/2009/jun/18/brown-independence-europe-banking-watchdog.

Traynor, Ian. "Europe in Crisis: A Show of Unity, but Euro Wrangling Continues: Germans May Soften Stance on Bailout Fund: Cameron 'isolated' as He Tries to Get Loophole Closed." *The Guardian* (December 2010), sec. Guardian Financial Pages.

Traynor, Ian. "European Commission Keen for More Market Co-Operation." *The Guardian*, October 2008, sec. Business. https://www.theguardian.com/business/2008/oct/09/europe.eu.

Traynor, Ian. "Eurozone Crisis: Brussels Summit: 24-Hour Strike Expected to Paralyse City as EU Leaders Arrive for Talks." *The Guardian* (January 2012), sec. Guardian Home Pages.

Traynor, Ian. "George Osborne Rules out Taking Part in European Bank Bailout Fund." *The Guardian*, September 2010, sec. Business. https://www.theguardian.com/business/2010/sep/07/osborne-rules-out-euro-bailout-fund.

Traynor, Ian, and David Gow. "Brown Backs New Franco-German Plan to Curb City Excesses." *The Guardian*, March 2009, sec. World news. https://www.theguardian.com/world/2009/mar/21/gordon-brown-european-central-bank.

Trichet, Jean-Claude. "Remarks on the Future of European Financial Regulation and Supervision" (Speech presented at the Committee of European Securities Regulators (CESR) Conference, Paris, February 2009). https://www.ecb.europa.eu/press/key/date/2009/html/sp090223.en.html.

Ujvari, Balazs, Susanne Conze, and Claire Joawn. "Europe's Moment: Repair and Prepare for the next Generation." Press Release (Brussels: European Commission, May 2020). https://ec.europa.eu/commission/presscorner/detail/en/ip_20_940.

Valero, Jorge. "Leak: These Are the Five Priorities for the next Finance Commissioner." *Euractiv*, June 2019, sec. Energy & Environment. https://www.euractiv.com/section/energy-environment/news/leak-these-are-the-five-priorities-for-the-next-finance-commissioner/.

Varoufakis, Yanis. "A New Deal to Save Europe | by Yanis Varoufakis." *Project Syndicate*, January 2017, sec. Opinion. https://www.project-syndicate.org/commentary/new-deal-for-europe-by-yanis-varoufakis-2017-01.

Véron, Nicolas. "EU Financial Services Policy since 2007: Crisis, Responses, and Prospects." *Global Policy* 9 (June 2018): 54–64. https://doi.org/10.1111/1758-5899.12564.

Véron, Nicolas. "The European Union Has Not Yet Solved Its Banking Problem | PIIE" (Peterson Institute for International Economics, October 2010). https://www.piie.com/blogs/realtime-economic-issues-watch/european-union-has-not-yet-solved-its-banking-problem.

Villeroy de Galhau, François. "Closing Remarks" (Speech presented at the FESE Convention—"Europe's future in global capital markets," Paris, June 2017). https://www.banque-france.fr/en/intervention/fese-convention-europes-future-global-capital-markets-paris-thursday-22nd-june-2017.

Villeroy de Galhau, François. "François Villeroy de Galhau: The Future of Europe—a Central Banker's View" (Speech presented at the Hearing of the Committee on Economic and Monetary Affairs of the European Parliament, Brussels, October 2016). https://www.bis.org/review/r161005j.htm.

## 346 Bibliography

Villeroy de Galhau, François. "How to Develop a 'Financial Eurosystem' Post-Brexit" (Speech presented at the Eurofi High Level Seminar 2019, Bucharest, April 2019). https://www.bis.org/review/r190405e.htm.

Villeroy de Galhau, François. "Presentation of the 2020 Annual Report of the Autorité de Contrôle Prudentiel et de Résolution (ACPR)" (Press conference, May 2021). https://www.bis.org/review/r210531a.pdf.

Villeroy de Galhau, François. "The Challenge of Brexit: Banks' Resilience Is No Excuse for Complacency." *The Banker*, October 3016, sec. World. https://www.thebanker.com/World/Western-Europe/France/The-challenge-of-Brexit-banks-resilience-is-no-excuse-for-complacency.

Villeroy de Galhau, François, and Jens Weidmann. "Towards a Genuine Capital Markets Union: Article by F. Villeroy de Galhau et J. Weidmann." Banque de France, April 2019. https://www.banque-france.fr/en/intervention/towards-genuine-capital-markets-union-article-f-villeroy-de-galhau-et-j-weidmann.

Violle, Alexandre. "Banking Supervision and the Politics of Verification: The 2014 Stress Test in the European Banking Union." *Economy and Society* 46, no. 3–4 (January 2017): 432–451. https://doi.org/10.1080/03085147.2017.1408216.

Vollaard, Hans. *European Disintegration: A Search for Explanations* (New York: Springer, 2018).

Von Braunberger, Gerald. "Bundesbank-Präsident zu Corona: Wie schlimm wird es, Herr Weidmann?" *Frankfurter Allgemeine Zeitung* (March 2020). https://www.faz.net/aktuell/wirtschaft/bundesbank-praesident-jens-weidmann-zum-coronavirus-16676519.html.

Vries, Catherine E. de. *Euroscepticism and the Future of European Integration* (Oxford; New York, NY: Oxford University Press, 2018).

Walker, Marcus, Joellen Perry, and David Gauthier-Villars. "Germany, France Disagree on Bailout Strategy." *The Globe and Mail* (October 2008), sec. Report on Business: International.

Wallace, Tim. "Euro Leaders Reach Late Night Bank Union Deal." *City A.M.* (December 2012), sec. News.

Wallace, Tim. "UK Left out of Pocket as Iceland Draws a Line under Bank Collapse." *Telegraph.co.uk* (September 2015), sec. Finance. https://www.proquest.com/news/docview/1713697090/abstract/D81532257B704339PQ/1.

Wang, Gabriel. "Capital Markets Union: Blue-Sky Thinking in a Gray-Sky World | Aite-Novarica" (London: Aite Novarica, June 2017). https://aite-novarica.com/report/capital-markets-union-blue-sky-thinking-gray-sky-world.

Warner, Jeremy. "Clamour Grows for More Regulation." *The Independent* (February 2009), sec. Business.

Warner, Jeremy. "Europe's Capital Markets Union Is Lost without Britain's Liberal Voice." *Daily Telegraph (London)* (May 2016), National edition, sec. Business.

Waterfield, Bruno. "German Memo Shows Secret Slide towards a Super-State." *The Daily Telegraph* (November 2011), sec. News.

Waterfield, Bruno, and Sam Coates. "Leave EU and We'll Make Your Lives a Misery: Juncker's Warning to Britain." *The Times, London*, May 2016, sec. news. https://www.thetimes.co.uk/article/leave-eu-and-well-make-your-lives-a-misery-junckers-warning-to-britain-7h2k90t8g.

Webber, Douglas. *European Disintegration?: The Politics of Crisis in the European Union* (New York: Macmillan International Higher Education, 2018).

Webber, Douglas. *New Europe, New Germany, Old Foreign Policy?: German Foreign Policy since Unification* (New York: Routledge, 2014).

Webber, Douglas. "Trends in European Political (Dis)Integration. An Analysis of Postfunctionalist and Other Explanations." *Journal of European Public Policy* 26, no. 8 (August 2019): 1134–1152. https://doi.org/10.1080/13501763.2019.1576760.

Weidmann, Jens. "Jens Weidmann: Hans Möller Medal Acceptance Speech" (Speech presented at the Annual Meeting of the Munich Volkswirte Alumni-Club, Munich, July 2016). https://www.bis.org/review/r160707b.htm.

Weidmann, Jens. "No Time for Complacency—Current Economic Challenges in the Euro Area" (Speech presented at the Annual General Meeting for the Members of the Foreign Bankers' Association, Amsterdam, November 2016). http://www.bis.org/review/r161109a.pdf.

Weltman, Jeremy. "France, Germany Risk Spike Shows Core Europe Wobbling." *Euromoney*, sec. Country Risk. Accessed October 18, 2022. https://www.euromoneycountryrisk.com/article/b1dn39w4zfzm37/france-germany-risk-spike-shows-core-europe-wobbling.

Westlake, Martin, ed. *Outside the EU: Options for Britain* (Newcastle upon Tyne: Agenda Publishing, 2020).

White, Aoife. "Amid Divisions, EU Agrees New Financial Regulation." *Associated Press Internatioanl* (December 2009), sec. Business News.

White, Aoife. "EU: Central Banks to Pick New Regulator Chief." *Associated Press Internatioanl* (June 2009), sec. Business News.

White, Jonathan. *Politics of Last Resort: Governing by Emergency in the European Union*. First edition (Oxford: Oxford University Press, 2020).

Wieczorek, Marta, and Siobhán Millbright. "Questions and Answers: Solvency Support Instrument." Questions and Answers (Brussels: European Commission, May 2020). https://ec.europa.eu/commission/presscorner/detail/en/qanda_20_946.

Wilde, Pieter de. "Media Logic and Grand Theories of European Integration." *Journal of European Public Policy* 26, no. 8 (August 2019): 1193–1212. https://doi.org/10.1080/13501763.2019.1622590.

Wilde, Pieter de. "Rebound? The Short- and Long-Term Effects of Crises on Public Support and Trust in European Governance." In *The Palgrave Handbook of EU Crises*, edited by Marianne Riddervold, Jarle Trondal, and Akasemi Newsome. Palgrave Studies in European Union Politics (Cham: Springer International Publishing, 2021), 667–683. https://doi.org/10.1007/978-3-030-51791-5_39.

Wöhl, Stefanie, Elisabeth Springler, Martin Pachel, and Bernhard Zeilinger, eds. "The State of the European Union: Fault Lines in European Integration." *Springer EBooks*. (New York: Springer, 2020).

Wolf, Martin. "Europe's Lonely and Reluctant Hegemon." *Financial Times* 9 (2014).

World Bank. and World Bank Group. "Financial Structure Database," 2000. https://www.worldbank.org/en/publication/gfdr/data/financial-structure-database.

Wright, Ben. "Vast Majority of City Would Vote for UK to Stay in EU." *The Telegraph (UK)* (April 2015). https://www.telegraph.co.uk/finance/newsbysector/banksandfinance/11550872/Vast-majority-of-City-would-vote-for-UK-to-stay-in-EU.html.

Wuermeling, Joachim. "Joachim Wuermeling: Prospects for European Monetary Union" (presented at the Finanzwelt Europa, Brussels, October 2017). https://www.bis.org/review/r171017e.htm.

Wunderlich, Uwe, and Stefan Gänzle. "Asean and the EU in Times of Crises: Critical Junctures from the Perspective of Comparative Regionalism." In *Theorising the Crises of the European Union* (New York: Routledge, 2020).

Wymeersch, Eddy. "Giving Europe a Single Voice." *Professional Wealth Management*, sec. Market Monitor. Accessed January 20, 2023. https://www.pwmnet.com/Archive/Giving-Europe-a-single-voice.

## 348 Bibliography

Wyplosz, Charles. "The Eurozone Crisis: Too Few Lessons Learned." In *The Eurozone Crisis: A Consensus View of the Causes and a Few Possible Solutions*, edited by Richard Baldwin and Francesco Giavazzi (London: CEPR Press, 2015): 198–207. https://voxeu.org/article/eurozone-crisis-too-few-lessons-learned.

Yeandle, Mark. "The Global Financial Centres Index 19" Global Financial Centres Index (London: Z/Yen, March 2016). https://www.longfinance.net/programmes/financial-centre-futures/global-financial-centres-index/gfci-publications/the-global-financial-centres-index-19/.

YouGov. "YouGov / Times Survey Results 20th—22nd June 2016" (YouGov, June 2016). https://d25d2506sfb94s.cloudfront.net/cumulus_uploads/document/atmwrgevvj/TimesResults_160622_EVEOFPOLL.pdf.

Zatterin, Marco. "Interview with La Stampa" (European Central Bank, July 2020). https://www.ecb.europa.eu/press/inter/date/2020/html/ecb.in200701~601bc1b5ff.en.html.

Zysman, John. *Governments, Markets, and Growth: Financial Systems and the Politics of Industrial Change* (Ithaca: Cornell University Press, 1983).

# Index

*For the benefit of digital users, indexed terms that span two pages (e.g., 52–53) may, on occasion, appear on only one of those pages.*

*Figures are indicated by an italic f following the page number*

ABN AMRO, 66–67, 186–187
Acharya, Viral V., 127–128
African Union, 14–15, 307
Allied Irish Bank, 134
Almunia, Joaquin, 74, 77–78, 81
Amsterdam, 188f, 197, 211
Anghel, Veronica, 32, 52–53
Argentina, 116
Association for Financial Markets in Europe (AFME), 208, 210, 255–256
Association of British Insurers (ABI), 78–79, 81
Association of German Banks, *see* Bundesverband deutscher Banken
Association of Southeast Asian Nations (ASEAN), 307
Atlante, 185–186
Aubry, Martine, 121
Auerback, Marshall, 242
Augustine Promises, 162, 238–239, 263–264
Austria, 69f, 110f, 113f, 120–121, 130–131, 143, 146–147, 156, 185f, 194, 233f, 233f, 251
Avian Flu, 24

backstop, 11, 13–14, 123–124, 152, 154–155, 161–164, 184–185, 208–209, 225–229, 238–239, 261–265, 267, 269–270, 287, 289–291
bad bank, 13–14, 228–229, 238–239, 249–251, 268, 269
BaFin, 134, 186–187
bail in, 107–108, 143–144, 185–187, 262
bailout, 11–12, 65, 68–70, 69f, 72–73, 76–77, 88–92, 94–95, 166 n.2, 107–111, 115, 123–129, 140, 142–150, 152–153, 164–165, 262

European bailout mechanism, 72–73, 76–77, 90, 94–95, *see also* Single Resolution Mechanism
Balkanization, 46–47f, 48–49, 55, 70–71, 111–112, 128
Baltic states, 161–163, *see also* Estonia, Latvia, and Lithuania
Banca Monte dei Paschi di Siena (MPS), 107–108, 134, 185–186
Banca Popolare di Vicenza, 108, 163, 185–186
Banco Popular, 108, 163, 185–186
Bank of England, 88–89, 180–181, 205, *see also* Carney, Mark
Bank of France, 5, 80, 192, 199, 206–207, *see also* Villeroy de Galhau, François
Bank of Greece, 249–250, *see also* Stournaras, Yannis
Bank of International Settlements (BIS), 183–184
Bank of Ireland, 203–204, 255, 258, *see also* Lane, Philip R.
Bank of Italy, 5
Bank of Portugal, 255–257, 260, *see also* Ceneto, Mario and Serra, Anna Paula
Bank of Spain, 237–238, 255, *see also* Hernández de Cos, Pablo
Bank Recovery and Resolution Mechanism (BRRD), 107–108, 142, 145, 148–151, 232–234, 262
bank run, 50–51, 65, 116, 123–125, 153–155, 157–158, *see also* sovereign debt run
Barclays PLC, 239–240
Barnier, Michel, 96
Barroso, José Manuel, 80–81, 85, 93
Basel III Accords, 143
Basque Country, 306–307
Bavaria, 122
Bear Stearns, 65, 123–124

## 350  Index

Belgium, *69f*, 74–75, 91–92, *110f*, *113f*, *185f*, *233f*, *see also* Benelux
Bénassy-Quéré, Agnès, 113–114
Benelux, 63–64, 66–67, 74, 76, 82, 130–131, 136, *see also* Belgium, Luxembourg, and Netherlands
Berès, Pervenche, 78–79
Berlusconi, Silvio, 75
Bild, 120
Black Wednesday, 6
BNP Paribas, 38, 48–49, 65, 148, 232, 239–240
Boin, Arjen, 31
Boleat, Mark, 202
Borg, Anders, 90
Bos, Wouter, 75
Botín, Ana, 255–256
Botín, Emilio, 137–138
branch-subsidiary issues, 67–68, 78, 111, 123, *see also* home-host issues
Bremmer, Ian, 183
Britain, *see* United Kingdom
British Bankers' Association, 79
British Venture Capital Association, 82–83
Brookings Institution, 230–232, 235, 237, 264–265
Brooks, Eleanor, 32
Brown, Gordon, 70, 74–75, 86–88, 90
Bruegel, 194–195, 202–203, 259–260
Brunnermeier, Markus Konrad, 27
Brussels Effect, 191
Bundesbank, 5–6, 70–71, 105–106, 122, 125–126, 131, 148, 184, 189–192, 194–195, 199, 235, 244, 246–247, 250
Bundestag (Germany), 120, 159
Bundesverband deutscher Banken (BdB), 35–36, 90, 137–138, 157, 207–208, 244, 265
Buti, Marco, 237, 246–247

Cable, Vince, 65
Caja de Ahorros Mediterráneo, 134
Caja Sur, 134
Cajas (Spain), 65–66, 107–108, 113–114, 127, 128, 130, 131–132, 135, 137–140, 142, 143–144, 146, 147, 152, 161–163, 165, *see also* Caja de Ahorros Mediterráneo and Caja Sur
Calviño, Nadia, 260
Cameron, David, 118–119, 180, 301

Campa, José Manuel, 230–232
Canada, 14–15, 47–48, 306
capital buffers, 109, 239–240, 243–245, 248
capital key, 242–243
Capital Markets Union (CMU), 1, 12–14, 42, 50, 54, 55–56, 124, 125, 162–164, 178–181, 187–189, 194, 195, 199, 201–210, 212–213, 225–229, 236–239, 242–246, 252–259, 265, 268–270, 286–289, 294–296
capital requirements, 67, 209, 245
Carney, Mark, 180–181
Cash, Bill, 82–83
Catalonia, 306–307
catastrophic equilibrium, 22–23, 25, 32, 46–47
Ceneto, Mario, 260
Central and Eastern Europe, 65, 114–115, 300–301, *see also* Czech Republic, Hungary, Poland, Romania, Slovakia, and Slovenia
central counterparty clearing houses (CCPs), 198–200, 220 n.103
Centre for European Policy Studies, 78, 82
Centre for the Study of Financial Innovation (CSFI), 179–180, 182
Chance, David, 242
Chatham House Speech, 180
Chirac, Jacques, 304–305
Christian Democratic Union (Germany), 157, *see also* Christian Social Union (CSU)
Christian Democrats, 26, *see also* Christian Democratic Union (Germany) and Christian Social Union (CSU)
Christian Social Union (CSU), 122
Citigroup, 169 n.55
Civil War (US), 36, 304, 306
clearing, *see* euro clearing
Clegg, Nick, 119
CMS, 82–83
Cœuré, Benoît, 122, 145–146, 208–209
Cohen, Lady Shirley, 79
Cold War, 4–5, 307
Commerzbank, 72–73, 131–132, 138–139, 147–148, 185–186, 239–240
Committee of European Banking Supervisors (CEBS), 77, 80, 123

Committee of European Insurance and Occupational Pensions Supervisors (CEIOPS), 77, 80
Committee of European Securities Regulators (CESR), 77–78, 80, 92
Common Foreign and Security Policy, 5, 304–305
Conservative Party (UK), 118–119, 194–195
Constâncio, Vítor, 205
constraining dissensus, 8–9, 33, 308
Council of Ministers, *see* Council of the European Union
Council of the European Union, 141, 197
Crédit Agricole, 239–240
Creuzfeld-Jakobsen vCJD, *see* Mad Cow Disease
critical juncture, 17–18, 20–22, 25, 29, 39
Cross, Maïa, 18
Customs Union, 192–193
Cyprus, 107–108, 113*f*, 185*f*, 232–234, 304
Czech National Bank, 82–83
Czech Republic, 185*f*

Daily Telegraph, 82–83, 118–119, 190
Darling, Alistair, 87–88
Daul, Joseph, 119
Davies, Sir Howard, 78–79
De Gaulle, Charles, 20–21
de Guindos, Luis, 203–205, 208–209, 230–232, 235, 244–245, 250, 254, 257, 258–259, 264, 268
De la Porte, Caroline, 246
de Larosière Report, 80–81, 84–86, 88, 95
de Larosière, Jacques, 71, 80–81
Denmark, 69*f*, 130–131, 161, 162–163, 185*f*, 207, 251
Depfa, 63–64, 67–68, 82, *see also* Hypo RE
deposit guarantee scheme (DGS), 42, 49, 50–51, 54, 66–67, 82, 88–89, 123–126, 128, 132, 143, 153, 201–202, 237, 253, 256–257, 266, 269–270, 284, 295–296, *see also* European Deposit Insurance Scheme, ex ante funding schemes, and ex post funding schemes
Deutsche Bank, 48–49, 54, 131–132, 137–138, 147–148, 157, 185–186, 232, 236, 241–242, 250
Dijsselbloem, Jeroen, 203
Dimon, Jamie, 180–181

Directorate-General for Competition (DG Comp), 72–73, 145
Dixon, Hugo, 82
Dombret, Andreas, 148, 199
Dombrovskis, Valdis, 159, 183, 187–189, 192–193, 203–204, 207, 230–232
Donohoe, Paschal, 237–238, 246, 255, 257, 258–259
Doom Loop, 12–13, 43, 44, 68–70, 76, 91, 96, 108–109, 112, 113–115, 123, 124, 127–133, 136–141, 144–146, 148, 153–154, 157–158, 160, 164–165, 227, 232–235, 237, 244–245, 247–248, 255–257, 269–270, 288–289
Dot Com Crisis, 6, 11–12, 65
Draghi, Mario, 107, 125, 133, 139–140, 158–159, 186–187, 189–190, 240–242
Dublin, 188*f*, 197
Dublin Regulation, 300
Duff, Andrew, 70
DZ Bank, 147–148

East Asian Financial Crisis, 6, 65, 106
Economic and Financial Affairs Council (ECOFIN), 70, 139–140
emergency politics, 5, 18–20, 22–23, 28, 29–30, 36, 45–46, 54–55, 71–72, 87–88, 93, 108, 121, 140, 160, 200–201, 210–211, 229, 246–247, 266–268, 287, 291, 293, 302–303
Empty Chair Crisis, 20–21, 38, 297, 307
enlargement, 300–301.
Enria, Andres, 235, 245, 250–251
equivalence, regulatory, 181, 191, 192, 200
Estonia, 162–163, 185*f*, 207, 233*f*
euro clearing, 13, 147–148, 178, 181, 189–190, 193, 196, 198–200, 220 n.103, 212, 287
Eurobond, 20, 119–120, 237, 245–247, 264–265
Eurogroup, 68–70, 77–78, 203, 237–238, 246, 255, 257–259, 263–265
European Bank for Reconstruction and Development, 80
European Banking Authority (EBA), 13, 22–23, 50, 63–64, 72, 76, 80, 91–96, 111, 112–113, 123, 134–136, 142, 150–151, 160, 163–165, 178, 181, 193, 194–196, 198, 200–201, 208–210, 212, 230–232, 239–240, 244, 246–247, 285–288

**352  Index**

European Banking Federation (EBF), 74, 137–138, 255–258

European Central Bank (ECB), 2, 52–53, 74–75, 85, 86–89, 105–108, 115, 119–120, 122, 125, 133, 139–140, 146, 150, 158–159, 183–184, 186–187, 189–190, 196–197, 203–205, 208–209, 228–232, 235, 236–237, 240–242, 244–247, 249, 250–252, 254, 255, 257–260, 264, 268, 284, 285–286
  as supervisor, 12–13, 50, 54, 77, 78–81, 84, 85, 107–108, 134, 141–142, 150–151, 161, 184–185, 229, 239–240, 245, 262, 266–268
  liquidity support, 63–64, 70, 73, 240–244
  monetary policy, 73, 296

European Coal and Steel Community (ECSC), 1, 5–6

European Commission, 2, 20, 52–53, 72–73, 93, 95, 108, 112–113, 164–165, 183, 230–232, 240, 242, 259–260, *see also* Barnier, Michel, Barroso, José Manuel, and Directorate-General for Competition (DG Comp)
  and bad bank proposals, 228–229, 250, 251
  and Brexit implementation, 189–193, 197, 208–209
  and CMU, 201–204, 208–209, 255
  and EDIS, 125, 155, 158–159, 237–238, 255
  and NGEU, 246–247, 250–251
  and the de Larosière Report and the ESFS, 84–85, 96, 111–112, 197
  and the SRM, 139, 146–147, 150–151, 158–159, 262, 291
  and the SSM, 133, 139, 158–159

European Conservatives and Reformists, 90

European Council, 92–93, 150, 151, 194, 200, 255, 262, 291

European Court of Justice, 242–243

European Deposit Insurance Scheme (EDIS), 12–14, 42, 49–51, 54–56, 63–64, 90, 104–105, 117, 124–125, 128, 132,153, 162–164, 184–185, 201–202, 208–209, 212–213, 225–229, 237, 238–239, 244–245, 250, 252–259, 261–262, 264, 265, 268, 269–270, 284, 286–289, 294, 295–296, *see also* deposit guarantee scheme (DGS)

European Economic Area (EEA), 66–67, 97 n.10, 190–191

European Economic Community (EEC), 5, 20–21, 297, 300–301

European Financial Stability Facility (EFSF), 106–107, 143–144, 245–247, 289, 290

European Financial Stabilization Mechanism (EFSM), 106–107, 117–118, 245–247, 289, 290

European Insurance and Occupational Pensions Authority (EIOPA), 80, 196–197

European Insurance Federation, 81

European Investment Bank (EIB), 250–252

European Market Infrastructure Regulation (EMIR), 200

European Medicines Agency (EMA), 193, 196–197

European Monetary System, 5

European Parliament, 5–6, 78–79, 190–191
  and banking union, 125, 133
  and EBA, 84, 90, 94–95, 197, 285, 288–289
  Directorate for Economic and Scientific Policies, 232
  Economic and Monetary Affairs Committee (European Parliament), 78–79, 90, 91

European Peoples Party, 90, 119, 192

European Securities and Markets Authority (ESMA), 63–64, 80, 196–197, 204–209, 240

European Supervisory Authorities (ESAs), 89, 91, 92–93, 163–164, *see also* European Banking Authority (EBA), European Securities and Markets Authority (ESMA), and European Insurance and Occupational Pensions Authority (EIOPA)

European System of Financial Supervision (ESFS), 11–12, 50, 52f, 63–64, 76–77, 80–81, 84–85, 88, 93, 111, 112–113, 210, 212–213, 288, 291–292, *see also* European Banking Authority (EBA), European Securities and Markets Authority (ESMA), European Insurance and Occupational Pensions Authority (EIOPA), European Supervisory Authorities (ESA), and

European Systemic Risk Council (ESRC)

European Systemic Risk Council (ESRC), 80–81, 84, 85–89

Evans-Pritchard, Ambrose, 190

ex ante funding schemes, 128–129, 154–158, 160, *see also* deposit guarantee scheme (DGS) and European Deposit Insurance Scheme (EDIS)

ex post funding schemes, 128–129, 156–158, 160, *see also* deposit guarantee scheme (DGS) and European Deposit Insurance Scheme (EDIS)

Fabbrini, Sergio, 237, 246–247

failing forward, 32

false negative, 22–24

false positive, 24

Federal Deposit Insurance Corporation (FDIC), 123–124, 169 n.55, 151, 154–155

Federal Reserve (US), 65, 73, 124, 134–135, 169 n.54

Ferber, Markus, 192, 206

Fernandez, Jonás, 257–258

Ferrera, Maurizio, 267

Fidelity Worldwide, 180–181

Financial Services Authority (UK), 78–79, 86

Financial Times, 82, 257–258, 265

Finland, 88, 110*f*, 113*f*, 130–131, 143, 146–147, 161, 162–163, 185*f*, 194, 207, 233*f*, 233*f*, 260

First World War, 26, 167 n.20, 307

Fitch Ratings, 232

Fitschen, Jürgen, 157

Fortis, 63–64, 66–67, 74, 76, 80–82, 88

Foundation for European Progressive Studies, 236

France, 4–5, 12–13, 69f, 70, 74, 75, 110f, 113f, 121, 167 n.16, 299–300, 302–305, *see also* Bank of France
and banking union, 110, 129–130, 132–133, 137, 139, 255, 285–286
and Brexit negotiations, 181, 192, 193–194, 198–199
and CMU, 178–179, 201, 206–208, 209–212, 254
and COVID-19, 230, 231*f*, 242

and economic approach, 26–27, 41–42, 91–92, 94, 95, 147, 194
and EDIS, 54–55, 156–158, 237, 254, 257
and exit from the European Union, 12–13, 183–184
and the SSM, 134, 137
and the de Larosière Report and the ESFS, 78–84, 86, 90, 95, 285–286
and the Doom Loop, 76, 112–113, 123–124, 137, 142, 144–145
and the ESM, 119–122
and the European rescue fund, 74–75, 82
and the SRM, 123–124, 127–128, 136–137, 142, 145–148, 150, 152–153, 161–162

Franco-German relations, 4–5, 86, 129, 139, 141, 194, 197–198, 207, 210–211, 307

French banks, 38, 48–49, 54, 65, 76, 110, 129, 130–132, 137, 138–141, 144–145, 147–148, 150, 179–180, 185f, 233f, 233f

Franco-Prussian War, 307

Frankfurt, 90, 92–93, 188*f*, 193–194, 196–197, 203–204, 211, 294–295

Frankfurter Allgemeine Zeitung, 120

Franz Ferdinand moment, 65, 167 n.20

Frasier, Stuart, 91–92

Free Democratic Party (Germany), 120

free movement, 179–180, 190–191, 198

French Banking Federation, 81

Fromage, Diane, 163

Fukushima Accident, 302–303, 309 n.4

Gänzle, Stefan, 20–21

García-Margallo, José Manuel, 91

Gentiloni, Paolo, 265

Georgieva, Kristalina, 255

German Banking Industry Committee (GBIC), 260

German Constitutional Court, 120, 242–243

German Savings Bank Association (DSGV), 260

Germany, 4, 11–12, 110, 112–113, 129, 183–184, 299–300, 302, *see also* Bundesbank, Bundesverband deutscher Banken, Commerzbank, Deutsche Bank, and HypoRE
and banking union, 129–130, 143, 285–286

**354  Index**

Germany, (*Continued*)
  and Brexit, 181, 186–189, 191–194
  and COVID-19, 228, 230, 231*f*, 240–243
  and EDIS, 155–159, 236–237, 254, 260, 265, 294
  and European rescue fund and ESM, 41–42, 73–75, 118–122, 149, 159, 161–162
  and NGEU, 245–246
  and ordoliberalism, 26–27, 94, 140, 194, 210–211
  and the CMU, 205–206, 209, 210–211, 254, 295
  and the de Larosière Report and the ESFS, 82–84, 86, 88, 91–92, 95, 134
  and the ESM backstop of the SRM, 152, 161–162232–234, 263
  and the SRM, 143–144, 146–148, 150, 152–153, 158, 159, 161–162, 291
  and the SSM, 133, 135–139, 141, 227
  bank bailouts and the Doom Loop, 65, 67–68, 69*f*, 72–73, 76, 82, 91–92, 123–124, 127–128, 138–139, 144–145, 227, 232–234, 262
  Franco-German relations, 4–5, 194, 197–198, 206, 307
  German banks, 5, 48–49, 54, 65–67, 110*f*, 110, 113*f*, 113–114, 127, 128–129, 131–132, 135–138, 140–141, 147–148, 157–158, 179–180, 185–186, 185*f*, 232, 233*f*, 233*f*, 260
Gibraltar, 213 n.2
Giegold, Sven, 207
Giles, Chris, 82
Goldman Sachs, 78
Gramegna, Pierre, 192
Grand Theories of European Integration, 2–3, 6–9, 17, 21, 31–33, *see also* intergovernmentalism, neofunctionalism, and postfunctionalism
Great Depression, 36, 225, 230–232, 236
Great Enlargement, *see* enlargement
Greece, 12–13, 26–27, 69*f*, 105–106, 108–110, 113*f*, 116–117, 138–139, 147, 185*f*, 232–234, 233*f*, 249–250, 300, 304
Green Party (European Parliament), 90
Green Party (Germany), 120, 122, 148, 157, 245–246
Greenspan Put, 65

Greenwich Market Pulse, 91–92
Grexit, 12–13, 27, 116–117, 138–139, 147
Grimstone, Sir Gerry, 180–181
Gysi, Gregor, 120

Haddrill, Stephen, 81
Hall, Peter A., 37–38, 40–41
Hamiltonian moment, 245–247, 268–269
Handelsblatt, 74
hard Brexit, 186, 189–192, 203, 210, 212
Hay, Colin, 18–19, 22–23, 25, 32, 46–47
Heath, Allister, 94
Hernández de Cos, Pablo, 237–238, 255
Herstatt, 5
Hill, Lord Jonathan, 181, 198–199, 202, 203, 206, 208
Hilton, Andrew, 182
Hoban, Mark, 89
Hollande, François, 121, 198–199
home-host issues, *see* branch-subsidiary issues, national champion, and Doom Loop, 12–13, 53–54, 67–68, 111, 255, 257
House of Lords (UK), 79, 181, 199
HSBC, 180, 239–240
Hufled, Felix, 186–187
Hungary, 69*f*, 185*f*, 299–300, 302–303
HypoRE, 63–64, 67–68, 82

Iceland, 66–67, 69*f*, 78–79, 88–89, 97 n.10, 153–155
ICI Global, 210
IKB, 65
immigration, 14–15, 22–23, 26, 41–42, 283, 297–301
  and Brexit, 179, 182, 195
inflation, 14–15, 115, 116, 240–241, 296
ING, 68–70
intergovernmental policymaking, 20–21, 142, 150–151, 163, 246, 262
intergovernmentalism (Grand Theory), 2, 4, 6–9, 29–30, 32–33, 49, 53
International Monetary Fund, 80, 82, 108, 120–121, 187–189, 255
Iraq, 23–24, 302, 304–305
Ireland, 63–64, 67–68, 88, 187–189, 203–204, 207, 233*f*, 233*f*, 246, 255, 258, 304, 306–307

Irish banking crisis, 11–12, 65–67, 69f, 70, 76, 82, 88–90, 109–110f, 113f, 144–146, 185f, 240
Italy, 5, 41–42, 75, 184, 299–300, *see also* Bank of Italy
and banking union, 129, 141, 146–149, 163, 227, 262
and COVID-19, 13–14, 43, 225, 228, 230–232, 231f, 240, 242–244, 258, 289
and EDIS, 54, 156–159, 226–227
and the de Larosière Report and the ESFS, 86, 91
and the ESM, 120–121, 149–150
and the ESM backstop of the SRF, 161–162, 262
debt crisis, 12–13, 44, 76, 106, 108–109, 116–117, 138–139, 147, 149–150, 232–234, 240–245, 289, 296–297
Italian banks, 54, 107–110f, 113f, 134, 148–149, 163, 179–180, 185–186, 185f, 187–189, 194, 227, 232–234, 233f, 233f

Jabko, Nicolas, 29
Jain, Anshu, 137–138
James, Harold, 27
Jensen, Mads Dagnis, 246
Johnson, Boris, 87–88
Jones, Erik, 26, 32, 52–53
Jouyet, Pierre, 82
JP Morgan-Chase, 144–145, 180–181, 245
Juncker, Jean-Claude, 68–70, 74, 77–79, 183, 184

Kalaitzake, Manolis, 189
Karlsruhe, *see* German Constitutional Court
Kauppi, Pilia-Noora, 260
Kelleher, Colm, 187–189
Keynesianism, 26, 140, 147
Kingdon, John W., 20, 26–27, 31, 252–253, *see also* multiple streams
Klein, Naomi, 23–24
Kosovo, 304
KPMG, 205–206

L3 holdings, 109–110, *see also* toxic assets
Labour Party (UK), 94, *see also* Brown, Gordon and Darling, Alistair
Lagarde, Christine
as French Finance Minister, 70, 74, 75, 78–79, 134

as President of the European Central Bank, 236–238, 240–243, 254, 255, 258–259
Lamfalussy Committees, 63–64, 77, 78, 80–81, 84–85, 87–88, 288, *see also* Committee of European Banking Supervisors (CEBS), Committee of European Insurance and Occupational Pensions Supervisors (CEIOPS), and Committee of European Securities Regulators (CESR)
Lamfalussy Process, 49, 288
Lamfalussy Report, 47–49, 93–94, 111–112, 133
Landau, Jean-Pierre, 27
Länder, 131–132, 135–136, 140–141, 148
Landesbanken, 65–67, 131–132, 135–138, 140–141, 148, 185–186, 207, *see also* Norddeutsche Landesbank (NordLB)
Landsbanki, 66–67, 88–89, 153–154
Lane, Philip R., 203–205, 236–237
Lannoo, Karel, 82
Latin American Debt Crisis, 6
Latvia, 69f, 162–163, 185f, 207, 233f, 233f
LCH, 199
Le Maire, Bruno, 257
Le Pen, Marine, 183–184, 215 n.29
Leave, 33, 179, 182, 189–190, 193, 195, 301
Lehman Brothers, 65, 71–72, 115, 123–124, 167 n.20
Lenihan, Brian, 90
Liberal Democratic Party (UK), 65, 119
Liberal group (European Parliament), 119
Liberation (newspaper), 121
Libya, 298–300
Linke Party (Germany), 120–121
Lintilä, Minka, 211
liquidity support, 63–64, 70, 73, 117–118, 122, 241, 243, 249
Lithuania, 162–163, 185f, 207, 233f
loan guarantees, 248, 250–252
loan moratoria, 228, 240, 252
London, 43, 87–88, 91–92, 179183, 193, 202
as Europe's financial services hub, 41–43, 51, 65–66, 79, 81–83, 162–163, 178, 179–181, 185–189, 188f, 192–194, 202, 203–206, 210, 211–213, 294–295
as the site of euro clearing, 13, 178, 193, 198–200, 203–204, 287

**356** Index

London, (*Continued*)
as the site of the EBA, 13, 92–93, 178, 196–198
London Club, 6
London School of Economics, 78–79
London Stock Exchange, 199
Long Term Refinancing Operations (LTROs), 73, *see also* Targeted Long Term Refinancing Operation (TLRO) III
Löyttyniemi, Timo, 264
Luxembourg Compromise, 20–21
Luxembourg, 69*f*, 74, 88, 113*f*, 188*f*, 192, 197, 233*f*, 233*f*, 242, *see also* Benelux

Maastricht Treaty, 3, 5, 105–106, 132–133, 150–151, 163–164, 166 n.2, 289
Macron, Emmanuel, 215 n.29
Mad Cow Disease, 6
Magnette, Paul, 236
Maijoor, Steven, 204
master narrative, 4, 18, 25–27, 34, 35–36, 45
crises as driving integration narrative, 12–13, 270, 293
neofunctional 'ever closer union' narrative, 8–9, 26, 32–33, 38, 79, 116–117, 134, 297–298, 308
postfunctional narrative, 8–9, 28–29, 33, 134
McCreevy, Charlie, 77–78, 85, 89
McFall, John, 87–88
McKenna, Cameron, 82–83
McNamara, Kathleen R., 27
Merkel, Angela, 74–75, 86, 120, 122
Merrill Lynch, 123–124
MERS, 6, 24, 229–230
metacrisis, 9, 33, 297, 307–308
Michel, Charles, 255
Missale, Alessandro, 232–234
Mittelstand, 66–67
Moghadam, Reza, 204–205
Monnet Crisis, 1–3, 10*f*, 12–13, 24–25, 32–34, 37–38, 41, 52*f*, 195, 289, 293
Brexit as a Monnet Crisis, 201, 212
COVID-19 as a Monnet Crisis, 225–226, 237–238, 252–255, 261–262, 268, 270, 289
Debt Crisis as a Monnet Crisis, 104–105, 117, 159–160, 164–165, 289, 293
Monnet, Jean, 1, 5–8, 237–238, 254

moral hazard, 55, 111, 116–117, 125–126, 131, 145, 152–153
and EDIS, 158–160, 226–227, 237, 253, 260, 266
as not relevant in the Pandemic, 236–239, 251–252, 259–261, 269, 291–293
Morgan Stanley, 180–181, 187–189, 204–205
Moscovici, Pierre, 146
multiple streams, 20, 26–27, 252–253, *see also* Kingdon, John W.
Myners, Lord Paul, 79, 87–88

narrative framework, 1–4, 9, 25–26, 37, 134–135, 197–198, *see also* There Is No Alternative (TINA)
CMU narratives, 202–203, 206, 237–238, 252–253
Crises and narratives, 23–28, 35–36, 45
pandemic narratives, 252, 259–260, 266, 268–270
national champion, 53–54, 65–67, 111, 127, 137–138, 145, 155, 165, 207–209
National Front (France), 183–184
neofunctionalism, 2, 4, 6–9, 22–23, 30, 32–33, 35–36, 297–298
Netherlands, 75, 110*f*, 112–113*f*, 120, 137, 143, 146–147, 185*f*, 186–187, 194, 207, 233*f*, 251, 264–265, *see also* Benelux and new Hanseatic League
in the banking crisis, 11–12, 66–70, 69*f*, 7074, 88–89, 153–154
New Financial, 206–207
New Hanseatic League, 207, 210–211
new London, 193–194, 203, 204, 206–207, 211–212, 254, 294–295
New York, 183, 199
NextGenerationEU (NGEU), 225–226, 228–229, 238–239, 245, 248, 259–261, 267, 268–270, 286, 287, 289, *see also* Solvency Support Instrument (SSI)
and the SSI, 250–252
no bailouts clause, 105–107, 166 n.2, 115, 131, 136–137
non-performing loans (NPLs), 109, 110*f*, 110, 125–126, 185*f*, 237, 249, 251–252, *see also* L3 assets and toxic assets
anticipated COVID surge, 13–14, 43, 228–229, 232, 239, 248, 249–251, 266–270, 286, 307–308

legacy issues, 157–158, 184–185, 232–234, 233*f*, 249–253, 294
Norddeutsche Landesbank (NordLB), 185–186, 232–234, 262
Nordea Bank, 161–163, 239–240
NordLB, *see* Norddeutsche Landesbank (NordLB)
normal politics, 5, 7–8, 18, 22–24, 28, 29–30, 32–33, 36, 45–46, 54–55, 263–264
  and Brexit, 200, 210, 212, 287
  and COVID-19, 229, 246–247, 263–264
  and non-crisis European integration, 264, 266–267, 294, 302, 304–305
  and the Banking Crisis, 71–72, 87–88, 93
  and the Debt Crisis, 108, 121–122, 159–161
North Atlantic Treaty Organization (NATO), 305
Northern Ireland, 304, 306–307
Northern Rock, 38, 65, 88–89, 153–154
Norway, 161–163

Oberndofer, Lukas, 19
Ocean Viking, 299–300
Office of the Comptroller of the Currency (OCC), 124, 126, 169 n.54
Office of Thrift Supervision (OTS), 126, 169 n.54
Ordoliberalism, 26, 131, 139, 150
Organisation for Economic Co-operation and Development (OECD), 78
Osborne, George, 91–92
Ossig, Christian, 244
Oudéa, Frédéric, 207–208
Outright Monetary Transaction (OMT), 240–241

Pandemic Emergency Purchase Program (PEPP), 223 n.156, 241–244, 286, 287, 289
Pan-European Personal Pension Product, 209, 223 n.156
Papandreou, George, 105–106
Papoademos, Lucas, 85–86
Paris
  as a financial hub, 188*f*, 193–194, 206–207, 211–212, 294–295
  EBA relocation, 13, 196–198, 212
Paris Club, 6
passporting, 179–181, 192–193

patch-up reform, 2–3, 10*f*, 11, 30, 35, 37–38, 40–41, 52*f*, 72, 81, 85, 96, 111, 134–136, 142, 150–151, 163–165, 178–179, 195–196, 210, 212–213, 261–262, 291–292, 295–297, 302, 306, 309 n.4
Paulson, Henry, 74
Pecresse, Valerie, 193–194
permissive consensus, 8–9, 308
Poland, 78, 86, 185*f*
polycrisis, 183, 307–308
Portugal, 110*f*, 113*f*, 185*f*, 187–189, 232–234, 233*f*, 233*f*, 255–257, 260
  threat of exit from the EU, 26–27, 106, 108–109, 116–117, 138–139, 147
postfunctionalism, 2, 6–8, 20–21, 30, 32–33, 55, 297–298, 308
Prague, 188*f*, 197
PricewaterhouseCoopers, 79

Ravoet, Giodo, 74
Regling, Klaus, 265
Rehn, Olli, 93
re-insurance, 253, 295–296
Remain, 43, 178–179, 213 n.2, 180–182, 194–195, 202, 210
Renzi, Mario, 159
Report on the Regulation of European Securities Markets, *see* Lamfalussy Report
Republican Party (France), 121
Reynders, Didier, 75
Rhinard, Mark, 31
Riddervold, Marianne, 25
Rodrigues, Maria Joao, 236
Rolet, Xavier, 199
Romania, 88, 185*f*, 302–303
Rosenthal, Uriel, 17–18
Ross, George, 23–24
Ross, Verena, 205
Rostowski, Jacek, 78
Royal Bank of Scotland (RBS), 66–67, 88, 186–187, 239–240
Russia, 55–56, 296–298, 302–303, 309 n.4, 305, 307–308

Saar Crisis, 5
Sandbu, Martin, 257–258
Sanio, Jochen, 134
Santander, 66–67, 137–138, 232, 255–256
Sapin, Michel, 192

## 358  Index

Sarkozy, Nicolas, 75, 81, 86, 90, 119, 121
SARS, 6, 24, 229–230
Satanic Panic, 24
Schackmann-Fallis, Karl-Peter, 260
Schäuble, Wolfgang, 134, 139–140, 146–147, 152, 263–264
Schimmelfennig, Frank, 18, 36–37, 114–115
Schnabel, Isabel, 183–184, 235, 236–237, 244–245, 254, 256–257
Schoenmaker, Dirk, *see* Schoenmaker's Trilemma
Schoenmaker's Trilemma, 46–47*f*, 49, 66, 70–71, 94–95, 123, 133
Scholz, Olaf, 236–237, 265
Schuman, Robert, 5–6, 41, 237–238
Scotland, 179, 306–307
Second World War, 4–5, 26, 36, 307
Seehofer, Horst, 122
Serbia, 304
Serra, Anna Paula, 256–257
Sewing, Christian, 236–237
simple, transparent, and standardized (STS) securitization, 209
Single European Act, 5, 20–21
Single Market, 27, 51, 70, 114–115, 137–138, 180–181, 192–193, 198–199, 203–204, 297
Single Resolution Board (SRB), 107–108, 145, 150–151, 163–164, 264, 291, *see also* Single Resolution Fund (SRF) and Single Resolution Mechanism (SRM)
Single Resolution Fund (SRF), 50–51, 52*f*, 151, 163–164, 184–185, 244, *see also* Single Resolution Board (SRB) and Single Resolution Mechanism (SRM)
  backstopping with the ESM, 13–14, 50, 152, 162, 184–185, 208–209, 225–229, 238–239, 261–265, 267, 269–270, 287, 289–291
  creation, 11, 107–108, 144–146, 150, 285–286, 289
  size, 50, 150–152, 154, 161–164, 184–185, 232–234, 263, 264, 269–270, 291, 294, 296–297
Single Resolution Mechanism (SRM), 50–51, 54–55, 107–108, 122, 155–156, 158, 163–164, 238–239, 244, 256–257, 259, 260–262, 289, 290–291, *see also* Single Resolution Board (SRB) and Single Resolution Fund (SRF)

creation, 11, 52*f*, 53–54, 90, 104–105, 117, 124–126, 128–130, 139, 142–150, 154–155, 157, 158–161, 262
gaps, 12–13, 50, 61 n.76, 125, 153–154, 161–164, 227, 228–229, 232–234, 238–239, 253, 262, 264, 287, 291
in operation, 163, 227
Single Supervisory Mechanism (SSM), 12–13, 104–105, 107–108, 124–125, 142, 148–149, 151, 152–153, 163–164, 208–209, 244, 259–262, 268, 289
creation, 11, 52*f*, 53–54, 90, 117, 122, 126, 128–130, 133–141, 146, 157–161, 246–247, 256–257, 290–291
gaps, 12–13, 46–47, 50, 54–55, 61 n.76, 145–146, 153–156, 161, 162, 227, 228–229, 238–239, 253
six pack, 107
Slovakia, 74, 88, 110*f*, 113*f*, 185*f*, 233*f*
Slovenia, 69*f*, 88, 110*f*, 113*f*, 185*f*, 233*f*
snake in the tunnel, 5
Social Democratic Party (Germany), 120, 122, 139–140, 157, 159
Socialist Party (France), 121
Socialists & Democrats, 90, 257–258, 265
Société de Financement de l'Economie Française (SFEF), 76
Société de Prise de Participation de l'Etat (SPPE), 76
Société Générale, 207–208
soft Brexit, 192
soft touch regulation, 86, 111, 137–138
Solvency Support Instrument (SSI), 247–253
Soros, George, 120–121
sovereign debt run, 106, 147
sovereign-bank nexus, *see* Doom Loop
Spain, 41–42, 54, 66–67, 69*f*, 86, 108, 110*f*, 113*f*, 127, 129, 130, 134, 137–138, 140, 141, 148–150, 163, 179–180, 185–186, 185*f*, 193–194, 213 n.2, 233*f*, 233*f*, 237–238, 255, 260, 300, 302–303, 306–307, *see also* Bank of Spain
and COVID-19, 13–14, 43, 228, 230, 231*f*, 232–234, 240–241, 258, 289
and risk of default, 26–27, 44, 65–66, 91, 106–110, 116–117, 138–139, 147, 149, 225, 289, 300

and the cajas crisis, 107–108, 113–114, 128, 131–132, 135, 140, 142, 143–144, 146, 147, 149, 152, 162–163, 165
Spanish Influenza, 290
Sparkassen, 113–114, 131–132, 135–136, 140–141, 148, 207, 230
Stability and Growth Pact, 107
Standard Chartered PLC, 239–240
Standard Life, 180–181
Standards & Poor, 232, 256–257
Stark, Alastair, 18, 39
Steinbrück, Peer, 74–75, 88, 139–140
Stournaras, Yannis, 249
strategic constructivism, 29
stress test (bank), 134–135, 229, 240, 266–267, 271 n.6
stress test (nuclear), 302
subprime mortgage assets, 38, 49, 65, 109, 249
Suez Crisis, 6
Supervisory Review and Evaluation Process, 240
Sweden, 69f, 90, 185f, 207, 251
Syria, 298–300
Syriza, 108

Targeted Longer-Term Refinancing Operation (TLTRO) III, 241, 243
Tattersall, John, 79
TheCityUK, 180–182
There Is No Alternative (TINA), 30–31, 34, 38, 133
Tietmeyer, Hans, 125–126
Tomsik, Vladimir, 82–83
Too Big to Fail, 143, 161
toxic assets, 109, 125–126, 157–158, 249, see also L3 assets and non-performing loans
Treaty of Lisbon, 304–305
Treaty of Rome, 300–301
Trichet, Jean-Claude, 74–75, 78
Trittin, Jürgen, 148
Troika, 108, 252, see also European Central Bank, European Commission, and International Monetary Fund
Troubled Asset Relief Program (TARP), 74
Trump, Donald, 36
Truss, Liz, 296
Turkey, 300, 304
Turner Review, 86–87

two pack, 107

UBS, 208
Ukraine, 55–56, 296–298, 302–303, 305, 307–308
United Kingdom (UK), 6, 113f, 162, 167 n.16, 239–240, 269, 287, 296, 304, 306–307, see also Bank of England
and banking union, 129–130, 161, 285, 288–289
and Brexit, 9, 11, 13, 20–21, 27, 33, 43, 51, 55–56, 178–189, 286, 288, 297–299, 301
and CMU, 194, 201, 202–208, 210, 212–213, 288–289, 294–295
and euro clearing, 198–200, 203–204
and leadership of the EU's liberal bloc, 26, 41–42, 65–66, 71–72, 84, 94, 181, 194, 294–295
and the Banking Crisis, 11–12, 38, 65–67, 69f, 70–73, 88, 97 n.10, 108–110, 113f, 114–115, 130, 153–154, 185f
and the de Larosière Report and the ESFS, 73–76, 78–79, 81–93, 95–96, 182, 285–289, 291–292
and the ESM, 118–121, 285–286, 288–289
post-Brexit relocation of financial activity, 187–189, 193–194, 196, 204–205, 294–295
post-Brexit UK-EU relations, 13, 44, 178, 180–181, 183, 189–194, 191f, 204–205, 212–213, 295
relocation of the EBA, 193, 196
United States, 14–15, 24, 36–37, 120–121, 179–181, 183, 191, 199, 236, 245–246, 269, 304–306
and financial regulation, 19, 46–47, 61 n.73, 71–72, 86, 108–109, 112–113f, 123–128, 134–135, 144–145, 151, 154–155, 162, 169 n.55, 201–202
and the Banking Crisis, 38, 43, 63–66, 68, 69f, 71, 73, 74, 86, 115, 134, 135, 284, 306

Vanheukelen, Marc, 194–195
variant Creuzfeld-Jakobsen vCJD, see Mad Cow Disease
Varoufakis, Yanis, 184
Veneto Banca, 108, 163, 185–186, 232–234
Venice, 185–186

**360** Index

Verhofstadt, Guy, 119

Véron, Nicholas, 93, 135–136, 202–203, 259–260, 266–267

Vienna, 188*f*, 197

Villeroy de Galhau, François, 192, 199, 206–207, 242, 255

von der Leyen, Ursula, 242, 246, 255

VoxEU, 184–185

Wachovia, 123–124

Walker, Simon, 82–83

Warner, Jeremy, 82

Warsaw, 197

Washington Mutual, 123–124

weatherproofing reform, 2–3, 10*f*, 37–38, 40, 295–296, 300, 302–303

and Brexit, 178–179, 195–196, 212–213

and COVID-19, 11, 13–14, 52*f*, 225–226, 238–239, 241–242, 252, 256, 258–259, 261–262, 266, 269–270, 290–292

and the Debt Crisis, 165

Weber, Axel, 70–71, 105–106, 205–206, 208

Weber, Manfred, 90, 192

Weidmann, Jens, 189–190, 235

WestLB, 72–73

White, Jonathan, 26, 29–30

wicked crisis, 39, 307–308

World Bank, 120–121

World Trade Organization, 190, 194–195

Wuermeling, Joachim, 184, 194–195, 244, 250

Wunderlich, Uwe, 20–21

Wymeersch, Eddy, 77–78, 92

Yorulmazer, Tanju, 127–128

Zöllmer, Manfred, 159